Web Service Composition and New Frameworks in Designing Semantics:

Innovations

Patrick C. K. Hung
University of Ontario Institute of Technology, Canada

Information Science
REFERENCE

Managing Director:	Lindsay Johnston
Senior Editorial Director:	Heather A. Probst
Book Production Manager:	Sean Woznicki
Development Manager:	Joel Gamon
Acquisitions Editor:	Erika Gallagher
Typesetter:	Russell A. Spangler
Cover Design:	Nick Newcomer, Lisandro Gonzalez

Published in the United States of America by
Information Science Reference (an imprint of IGI Global)
701 E. Chocolate Avenue
Hershey PA 17033
Tel: 717-533-8845
Fax: 717-533-8661
E-mail: cust@igi-global.com
Web site: http://www.igi-global.com

Library of Congress Cataloging-in-Publication Data

Web service composition and new frameworks in designing semantics: innovations / Patrick Hung, editor.
    p. cm.
  Includes bibliographical references and index.
  Summary: "Detailing the functions, issues and trends of service composition, this book offers the most relevant research and models pertaining to the design and maturity of semantic use"--Provided by publisher.
  ISBN 978-1-4666-1942-5 (hardcover) -- ISBN 978-1-4666-1943-2 (ebook) -- ISBN 978-1-4666-1944-9 (print & perpetual access) 1. Web services--Research. 2. Semantic computing--Research. I. Hung, Patrick C. K.
  TK5105.88813.W3385 2012
  006.7'8--dc23
                                            2012005467

British Cataloguing in Publication Data
A Cataloguing in Publication record for this book is available from the British Library.

The views expressed in this book are those of the authors, but not necessarily of the publisher.

Table of Contents

Section 2
Matchmaking and Substitution

Section 3
Quality of Services (QoS)

Section 4
Security and Privacy

Detailed Table of Contents

Section 1
Services Composition

Chapter 1

Mohsen Rouached, Laboratoire d'InfoRmatique en Image et Systèmes d'information (LIRIS), France
Walid Fdhila, Université Henri Poincaré, France
Claude Godart, Université Henri Poincaré, France

In Rouached et al. (2006) and Rouached and Godart (2007) the authors described the semantics of WSBPEL by way of mapping each of the WSBPEL (Arkin et al., 2004) constructs to the EC algebra and building a model of the process behaviour. With these mapping rules, the authors describe a modelling approach of a process defined for a single Web service composition. However, this modelling is limited to a local view and can only be used to model the behaviour of a single process. The authors further the semantic mapping to include Web service composition interactions through modelling Web service conversations and their choreography. This paper elaborates the models to support a view of interacting Web service compositions extending the mapping from WSBPEL to EC, and including Web service interfaces (WSDL) for use in modelling between services. The verification and validation techniques are also exposed while automated induction-based theorem prover is used as verification back-end.

Chapter 2

Eduardo Adilio Pelinson Alchieri, Federal University of Santa Catarina, Brazil
Alysson Neves Bessani, University of Lisbon, Portugal
Joni da Silva Fraga, Federal University of Santa Catarina, Brazil

A current trend in the web services community is to define coordination mechanisms to execute collaborative tasks involving multiple organizations. Following this tendency, in this paper the authors present a dependable (i.e., intrusion-tolerant) infrastructure for cooperative web services coordination that is based on the tuple space coordination model. This infrastructure provides decoupled communication and implements several security mechanisms that allow dependable coordination even in presence of malicious components. This work also investigates the costs related to the use of this infrastructure and possible web service applications that can benefit from it.

Chapter 3

PengCheng Xiong, Georgia Institute of Technology, USA

Calton Pu, Georgia Institute of Technology, USA

MengChu Zhou, Tongji University, China

Protocol-level mismatch is one of the most important problems in service composition. The state-of-the-art method to deal with protocol mismatch is to generate adaptors to check deadlock-freeness based on a reachability graph. When this property is violated, the generation process will repeat itself until no deadlock state is found; however, the main drawback of this method is that it does not take into account the future deadlock state and requires many interactions with a developer. In this regard, it suffers from low efficiency. In this paper, the authors model multiple web service interaction with a Petri net called Composition net (C-net). The protocol-level mismatch problem is transformed into the empty siphon problem of a C-net. The authors take future deadlock states into consideration through this model, while finding the optimal solution that involves fewest interactions with a developer. The proposed method is proved to achieve higher efficiency for resolving protocol-level mismatch issues than traditional ones.

Chapter 4

Mehmet S. Aktas, TUBITAK-Marmara Research Center, Turkey

Geoffrey C. Fox, Indiana University, USA

Marlon Pierce, Indiana University, USA

We propose a novel approach to managing information in grids. The proposed approach is an add-on information system that provides unification and federation of grid information services. The system interacts with local information services and assembles their metadata instances under one hybrid architecture to provide a common query/publish interface to different kinds of metadata. The system also supports interoperability of major grid information services by providing federated information management. We present the semantics and architectural design for this system. We introduce a prototype implementation and present its evaluation. As the results indicate, the proposed system achieves unification and federation of custom implementations of grid information services with negligible processing overheads.

Section 2
Matchmaking and Substitution

Chapter 5

Puwei Wang, Renmin University of China, China

Zhi Jin, Peking University and Chinese Academy of Sciences, China

Lin Liu, Tsinghua University, China

Budan Wu, Beijing University of Posts and Telecommunications, China

Precise capability specification is the key for identifying and composing the right Web services. This paper specifies service capabilities in terms of the environment entities from the application domain and the effects imposed by the Web service on these entities. An environment ontology for Web services is adopted to provide formal sharable representations of the domain-specific environment entities. A hierarchical state machine is constructed for each environment entity to describe its behaviors, and the effects imposed by a Web service are described as the state transitions traces of environment entities, which define the capability of the Web service. Web service composition that satisfies a set of requested effects is then conducted by reasoning on the effects of services. The proposed approach emphasizes the external manifestation of Web services and service composition based on the effect reasoning. An example of online travel service illustrates the proposed approach.

Chapter 6

Dunlu Peng, University of Shanghai for Science and Technology, Shanghai, China
Xiaoling Wang, East China Normal University, Shanghai, China
Aoying Zhou, East China Normal University, Shanghai, China

In the context of web services, service replaceability refers to the ability of substituting one service for another. With the bloom of service-oriented computing, the effective management of service replaceability is important to make the applications unaffected once the requested service cannot work. This work studies the quantitative aspect of the replaceability of web services. FCA (Formal Concept Analysis) method is applied to reveal the pairwise replaceable relationship among web services. A novel structure, called RSLattice, is proposed to index web services on the basis of the underlying semantics, and the replaceability among services at the operation level is represented accurately. It ensures that the services having mutual replaceability are organized in the same path of RSLattice. Based on this property, we can greatly reduce the search space when retrieving the replaceable services in RSLattice. Experimental evaluation shows that RSLattice is an efficient and flexible structure for service replaceability management.

Chapter 7

Maricela Bravo, Centro de Investigación y de Estudios Avanzados, Mexico
Matias Alvarado, Centro de Investigación y de Estudios Avanzados, Mexico

Web service substitution is one of the most advanced tasks that a composite Web service developer must achieve. Substitution occurs when, in a composite scenario, a service operation is replaced to improve the composition performance or fix a disruption caused by a failing service. To move the automation of substitution forward, a set of measures, considering structure and functionality of Web services, are provided. Most of current proposals for the discovery and matchmaking of Web services are based on the semantic perspective, which lacks the precise information that is needed toward Web service substitution. This paper describes a set of similarity measures to support this substitution. Similarity measurement accounts the differences or similarities by the syntax comparison of names and data types, followed by the comparison of input and output parameters values of Web service operations. Calculation of these measures was implemented using a filtering process. To evaluate this approach, a software architecture was implemented, and experimental tests were carried on both private and public available Web services. Additionally, as is discussed, the application of these measures can be extended to other Web services tasks, such as classification, clustering and composition.

Chapter 8

Harshavardhan Jegadeesan, SAP Labs, India
Sundar Balasubramaniam, BITS, India

In a services marketplace where a particular service is provided by multiple service providers, service offerings have to be differentiated against competitor services in order to gain market share. Differentiation of services is also needed for different markets and for different consumer segments. Strategies to differentiate service offerings have to be unintrusive—without requiring major changes to the existing service realization mechanisms. In this article, the authors present Service Flavors, a strategy for service providers to differentiate services. By using this strategy, it is possible to analyze and adapt various aspects of a service that help differentiate it from that of the competitors. The authors model differentiating aspects as policies and also provide a mechanism for enforcing these policies in the middleware.

Section 3
Quality of Services (QoS)

Chapter 9

Sidney Rosario, INRIA Centre Rennes Bretagne Atlantique, France
Albert Benveniste, INRIA Centre Rennes Bretagne Atlantique, France
Claude Jard, ENS Cachan Bretagne, IRISA, Bruz, France

In this paper, the authors develop a comprehensive framework for QoS management based on soft probabilistic contracts. The authors approach also encompasses general QoS parameters, with "response time" as a particular case. In addition, the authors support composite QoS parameters, for example, combining timing aspects with "quality of data" or security level. They also study contract composition (how to derive QoS contracts for an orchestration from the QoS contracts with its called services), and contract monitoring.

Chapter 10

Zibin Zheng, The Chinese University of Hong Kong, China
Michael R. Lyu, The Chinese University of Hong Kong, China

Service-oriented systems are usually composed by heterogeneous Web services, which are distributed across the Internet and provided by organizations. Building highly reliable service-oriented systems is a challenge due to the highly dynamic nature of Web services. In this paper, the authors apply software fault tolerance techniques for Web services, where the component failures are handled by fault tolerance strategies. In this paper, a distributed fault tolerance strategy evaluation and selection framework is proposed based on versatile fault tolerance techniques. The authors provide a systematic comparison of various fault tolerance strategies by theoretical formulas, as well as real-world experiments. This paper also presents the optimal fault tolerance strategy selection algorithm, which employs both the QoS performance of Web services and the requirements of service users for selecting optimal fault tolerance strategy. A prototype is implemented and real-world experiments are conducted to illustrate the advantages of the evaluation framework. In these experiments, users from six different locations perform evaluation of Web services distributed in six countries, where over 1,000,000 test cases are executed in a collaborative manner to demonstrate the effectiveness of this approach.

Chapter 11

Freddy Lecue, The University of Manchester, UK
Nikolay Mehandjiev, The University of Manchester, UK

Semantic web service compositions must be aligned with requirements from the target users in terms of quality requirements. Given a set of quality requirements, one can choose to either find the optimal composition or a "good enough" composition, which satisfies these requirements. Since optimizing compositions of semantic services under quality constraints is known to be NP-hard, it is unsuitable for realistic problems within large search spaces. The authors address the issue by using the "good enough" approach, selecting the first composition that passes their quality threshold. Firstly, this paper defines quality constraints within an innovative and extensible model designed to balance semantic fit (or functional quality) with quality of service (QoS) metrics. The semantic fit criterion evaluates the quality of semantic links between the semantic descriptions of Web services parameters, while QoS focuses on non-functional criteria of services. User quality requirements are met by selecting a valid composition. To allow the use of this model with a large number of candidate services as foreseen by the strategic EC-funded project SOA4All the authors formulate the selection problem as a Constraint Satisfaction Problem and test the use of a stochastic search method.

Chapter 12

Osama Al-Haj Hassan, University of Georgia, USA
Lakshmish Ramaswamy, University of Georgia, USA
John A. Miller, University of Georgia, USA

In recent years, Web 2.0 applications have experienced tremendous growth in popularity. Mashups are a key category of Web 2.0 applications, which empower end-users with a highly personalized mechanism to aggregate and manipulate data from multiple sources distributed across the Web. Surprisingly, there are few studies on the performance and scalability aspects of mashups. In this paper, the authors study caching-based approaches to improve efficiency and scalability of mashups platforms. This paper presents MACE, a caching framework specifically designed for mashups. MACE embodies three major technical contributions. First, the authors propose a mashup structure-aware indexing scheme that is used for locating cached data efficiently. Second, taxonomy awareness into the system is built and provides support for range queries to further improve caching effectiveness. Third, the authors design a dynamic cache placement technique that takes into consideration the benefits and costs of caching at various points within mashups workflows. This paper presents a set of experiments studying the effectiveness of the proposed mechanisms.

Section 4
Security and Privacy

Chapter 13

Wei She, University of Texas at Dallas, USA
I-Ling Yen, University of Texas at Dallas, USA
Bhavani Thuraisingham, University of Texas at Dallas, USA

In recent years, security issues in web service environments have been widely studied and various security standards and models have been proposed. However, most of these standards and models focus on individual web services and do not consider the security issues in composite services. In this article, the authors propose an enhanced security model to control the information flow in service chains. It extends the basic web service security models by introducing the concepts of delegation and pass-on. Based on these concepts, new certificates, certificate chains, delegation and pass-on policies, and how they are used to control the information flow are discussed. The authors also introduce a case study from a healthcare information system to illustrate the protocols.

Chapter 14

Masoom Alam, Institute of Management Sciences, Pakistan
Mohammad Nauman, Institute of Management Sciences, Pakistan
Xinwen Zhang, Samsung Information Systems America, USA
Tamleek Ali, Institute of Management Sciences, Pakistan
Patrick C. K. Hung, University of Ontario Institute of Technology, Canada
Quratulain Alam, Institute of Management Sciences, Pakistan

Service Oriented Architecture (SOA) is an architectural paradigm that enables dynamic composition of heterogeneous, independent, multi-vendor business services. A prerequisite for such inter-organizational workflows is the establishment of trustworthiness, which is mostly achieved through non-technical measures, such as legislation, and/or social consent that businesses or organizations pledge themselves to adhere. A business process can only be trustworthy if the behavior of all services in it is trustworthy. Trusted Computing Group (TCG) has defined an open set of specifications for the establishment of trustworthiness through a hardware root-of-trust. This paper has three objectives: firstly, the behavior of individual services in a business process is formally specified. Secondly, to overcome the inherent weaknesses of trust management through software alone, a hardware root of-trust devised by the TCG, is used for the measurement of the behavior of individual services in a business process. Finally, a verification mechanism is detailed through which the trustworthiness of a business process can be verified.

Chapter 15

Babak Khosravifar, Concordia University, Canada
Jamal Bentahar, Concordia University, Canada
Ahmad Moazin, Concordia University, Canada
Philippe Thiran, University of Namur, Belgium

This paper proposes an effective mechanism dealing with reputation assessment of communities of web services (CWSs) known as societies composed of a number of functionally identical web services. The objective is to provide a general incentive for CWSs to act truthfully. The considered entities are designed as software autonomous agents equipped with advanced communication and reasoning capabilities. User agents request CWSs for services and accordingly rate their satisfactions about the received quality and community responsiveness. The strategies taken by different parties are private to individual agents, and the logging file that collects feedback is investigated by a controller agent. Furthermore, the accurate reputation assessment is achieved by maintaining a sound logging mechanism. To this end, the incentives for CWSs to act truthfully are investigated and analyzed, while the proposed framework defines the evaluation metrics involved in the reputation assessment of a community. In this paper, the proposed framework is described, a theoretical analysis of its assessment and its implementation along with discussion of empirical results are provided. Finally, the authors show how their model is efficient, particularly in very dynamic environments.

Service-oriented systems facilitate business workflows to span multiple organizations (e.g., by means of Web services). As a side effect, data may be more easily transferred over organizational boundaries. Thus, privacy issues arise. At the same time, there are personal, business and legal requirements for protecting privacy and IPR and allowing customers to request information about how and by whom their data was handled. Managing these requirements constitutes an unsolved technical and organizational problem. The authors propose to solve the information request problem by attaching meta-knowledge about how data was handled to the data itself. The authors present their solution, in form of an architecture, a formalization and an implemented prototype for logging and collecting logs in service-oriented and cross-organizational systems.

Chapter 17

In general, provenance describes the origin and well-documented history of a given object. This notion has been applied in information systems, mainly to provide data provenance of scientific workflows. Similar to this, provenance in Service-oriented Computing has also focused on data provenance. However, the authors argue that in service-centric systems the origin and history of services is equally important. This paper presents an approach that addresses service provenance. The authors show how service provenance information can be collected and retrieved, and how security mechanisms guarantee integrity and access to this information, while also providing user-specific views on provenance. Finally, the paper gives a performance evaluation of the authors' approach, which has been integrated into the VRESCo Web service runtime environment.

Preface

In the past few years, many companies have been forced to reorganize their business processes by using heterogeneous technologies in order to remain competitive in a global business environment. Companies increasingly like to focus on their core expertise area and use Information Technology (IT) services to address all their peripheral needs in their business processes. In 2003, a new scientific discipline called "Services Computing," which covers the science and technology of leveraging computing and IT to model, create, operate, and manage business processes from both theoretical and technical perspectives. In addition, Services Computing shapes the thinking of business modeling, business consulting, solution creation, service delivery, and software architecture design, development and deployment. The global nature of Services Computing leads to many opportunities and challenges and creates a new networked economic structure for supporting different business processes in these days. One of the key technological components in Services Computing is called Web services.

Current trends in Information and Communication Technology (ICT) such as Software as a Service (SaaS) and Cloud Computing have further accelerated the widespread use of Web services in business processes. In this book, a Web service is defined as an autonomous unit of application logic that provides either some business functionality or information to other applications through an Internet connection. Web services let individuals and organizations do business over the Internet using standardized protocols to facilitate application-to-application interaction. Web services offer many benefits, including platform and vendor independence, faster time to production, and convergence of disparate business functionalities. In general, there are three major entities in the Web services model: (1) A provider is the person or organization that provides an appropriate Web service for a particular business purpose; (2) A requestor is a person or organization that seeks to use a provider's Web service to meet business requirements; and (3) A broker, or discovery agency, acts as a matchmaker between the Web services provider and requestor.

Web services are fundamentally based on a set of eXtensible Markup Language (XML) standards, such as Web Services Description Language (WSDL), Simple Object Access Protocol (SOAP), and Universal Description, Discovery and Integration (UDDI). Each service makes its functionality available through well-defined or standardized XML-format Application Programming Interface (API) on the Internet. The result of this approach is called Services Oriented Architecture (SOA). The life cycle of SOA is called a publish-find-bind model. In the publish phase, the Web services provider uses the WSDL to describe its service's technical details. A WSDL document describes the Web service's interface, such as which operations the Web service supports, which protocols to use, and how to pack the exchanged data. Eventually, this WSDL document will serve as a sort of contract between the Web service provider and requestor. The provider publishes the WSDL document to a Web services broker via universal description, discovery, and integration registries. UDDI is like a "yellow pages" of WSDL documents. In the find phase, UDDI provides a standard means for organizations to describe their businesses and services and publish them so requestors can discover them online. In this scenario, the Web services broker serves as a discovery agency to help requestors find Web services that match their specific requirements. Once requestors find a Web service at the UDDI registries, they enter the bind phase, requesting the service's corresponding WSDL document so that they can attempt to bind with the service via a SOAP message. SOAP, an XML-based messaging protocol, is independent of the underlying transport protocol (HTTP, SMTP, FTP, and so on). Service requestors use SOAP messages to invoke Web services, and Web services use SOAP messages to answer the requests. The Web service thus receives the input SOAP message from the requestor and generates an output SOAP message to the requestor.

From the architectural perspective, Web services each have a unique Uniform Resource Identifier (URI) located at a Web server on the Internet. Web services can be defined, described, and discovered using SOAP messages, which are typically on HTTP binding. On the other side, the Web services clients can be any device: a computer, tablet PC, or even a smart phone. Different systems interact with the Web service using SOAP messages, in a manner prescribed by the service description. Today, nearly all major computing companies, including Microsoft, IBM, SAP, Amazon, Sun, Oracle, and Hewlett-Packard, provide Web services tools. There are seven key properties in Web services: (1) *Loosely coupled*: Web services can run independently of each other on entirely different implementation platforms and runtime environments; (2) *Encapsulated*: The only visible part of a Web service is the public interface, such as WSDL and SOAP; (3) *Standard protocols and data formats*: Interfaces are based on a set of standards, such as XML, UDDI, WSDL, and SOAP; (4) *Invoked over an intranet or the Internet*: Web services can be executed within or outside a firewall; (5) *Components*: Web services composition can enable business-to-business transactions or connect separate enterprise systems, such as those related to workflow; (6) *Ontology*: All interacting entities must understand the functionality behind the data value computations; and (7) *Business-oriented technology*: Web services are not end-user software.

To stay competitive, companies must be agile in adapting their business processes to the ever-changing market dynamics. The adaptive business process based enterprises should look beyond the traditional enterprises and marketplaces through collaborative interactions and dynamic e-business solution bindings. The enterprise infrastructure has to provide the capability for dynamic discovery of trading partners and service providers as well as enabling federated security mechanisms, solution monitoring, and management. Thus business processes have played an important role in enabling business application integration and collaboration across multiple organisations. The integration can be categorised into two types: internal integration and external integration. Internal integration includes all the integration aspects within one enterprise. Enterprise application integration (EAI) is a typical example of internal integration. External integration covers all the possible integration patterns across multiple enterprises. The typical business process based external application integration includes business process to application integration as well as business process to business process integration.

For the external integration, traditional business-to-business applications connect trading partners through a centralised architecture. A major drawback is that setting up an additional connection with another trading partner is costly and time consuming. In contrast, the benefits of adopting Web services include faster time to production, convergence of disparate business functionalities, a significant reduction in total cost of development, and easy to deploy business applications for trading partners. In particular, Grid and Cloud infrastructures increase the need for sharing and coordinating the use of Web services for different business processes in a loosely coupled execution environment. In this context, a business process contains a set of activities which represent both business tasks and interactions between Web services. It is believed that the major adopters of Web services include several industries that involve a set of diverse trading partners working closely together in a highly competitive market such as insurance, financial services and high technology industries. Another difference between traditional business-to-business applications and Web Services is a secure environment versus an exposed environment.

This book aims to cover major components of the lifecycle of innovation research and enabling technologies in Web services composition between the business level and IT implementation level, which includes enterprise modeling, business consulting, solution creation, services delivery, services orchestration, services optimization, services management, services marketing, services delivery and cloud computing, business process integration and management, and Web services technologies and standards. This book also aims to promote and coordinate developments in the field of business process integration and management with Web services. The chapters in this book crystallize the emerging technologies, evolution, challenges, and trends into positive efforts to focus on the most promising and innovative solutions with related issues in Web service composition. The chapters are categorized into four sections: (1) Services Composition; (2) Matchmaking and Substitution; (3) Quality of Services (QoS); and (4) Security and Privacy. It is expected that the covered topics in the chapters would further research new best practices and directions in this challenging research area. In summary, the chapters provide clear proof that Web service technologies are playing a more and more important and critical role in supporting business processes and applications.

SECTION 1 - SERVICES COMPOSITION

There is a growing need for an integrated view of Web services from different sources with the blooming of information sources and services over the Web. Automation for the assembly a coherent view of distributed heterogeneous Web services and information processing resources is a challenging and important process for inter- or intra-organizational collaboration and service provision. One of the major goals of Web services is to make easier their composition to form more complex services. In particular, a current trend in the research community is to define coordination mechanisms to execute collaborative tasks involving multiple organizations. To this purpose, many emerging languages, such as Web Service Business Process Execution Language (WS-BPEL) and Business Process Model Language (BPML) have been proposed to coordinate Web services into a workflow.

Nowadays a business process is supported by a Workflow Management System (WFMS). A workflow is a computer supported business process. WFMS is the software to support the specification, decomposition, execution, coordination, and monitoring of workflow. In general, a workflow includes many different entities, such as, activities, humans, agents, events, and flows. An event is an atomic occurrence of something interesting to the system itself or user applications. Events arise during the execution of an activity. Usually events are classified into four types: control, data, exception, and security. A flow is a directed relationship that transmits events from a source activity to a sink activity. Thus, events partition activity relationships into control-flows, data-flows, security-flows, and exception-flows. There may be constraints among flows. A workflow is a set of activities connected by flows. One can imagine that every activity starts when one or more relevant events arrive, and when the activity finishes it also generates one or more events to other dependent activity/activities. The combination of workflow technologies and Web services as a model of services composition has become more and more important in both the research community and the industry.

Despite great interests in services composition, complicated technical issues and organizational challenges remain to be solved. Thus, the management of Web services composition poses a very challenging problem. The integration of Web services into business processes is imminent. Interoperability with Web services is also an important issue in services integration. This section contains four chapters related to modelling, technical architecture, and theoretical choreographies analysis with illustrative examples in services composition shown as follows.

In chapter one, Rouached et al. present a semantic modelling approach of a process defined for a multiple Web service compositions extended from the mapping from WS-BPEL to event Calculus, and including Web service interfaces in WSDL for use in modelling between services process behaviour and choreography. For verification and validation techniques, this chapter also describes an algorithm as part of the analysis to semantically check and link partner process interactions based on automated induction-based theorem. In conclusion, this chapter gives the readers a conceptual overview of services composition modelling and analysis.

In chapter 2, Alchieri et al. present a dependable infrastructure, called WS-DependableSpace (WSDS), for cooperative stateless Web services coordination with an implementation prototype. WSDS is based on the tuple space coordination model to share data and synchronize their actions. This infrastructure shows several decoupled communication and implements several security mechanisms that allow dependable coordination even in presence of malicious components. The WSDS architecture integrates several dependability and security properties such as reliability, integrity, confidentiality, and availability in a modular way. In conclusion, this chapter gives the readers an illustrative technical architecture for supporting services composition.

In chapter 3, Xiong et al. present a model of multiple Web service interaction based on a Petri net called Composition net (C-net). In service composition, mismatches at the interface and protocol levels may render the composite service unusable. The protocol-level mismatch problem is transformed into the empty siphon problem of a C-net in this model. Further this chapter takes future deadlock states into consideration through this model, while finding the optimal solution that involves fewest interactions with a developer. In conclusion, this chapter gives the readers a mathematical model to find out the mismatch patterns at the interface and protocol level in services composition.

In the final chapter in section 1, Aktas et al. present a Grid information service architecture called Hybrid Grid Information Service (Hybrid Service) that provides unification, interaction and federation of metadata instances of grid information services with a prototype implementation and its evaluation. This chapter discusses unification, federation, interoperability, and performance aspects of the system. Based on the fundamental knowledge in services composition discussed in Chapter 1-3, this chapter concludes this topic with an illustrative example based on Grid infrastructure in services composition.

SECTION 2 - MATCHMAKING AND SUBSTITUTION

Due to the nature of SOA, the service oriented applications present a different characteristic on the issue of "availability" than traditional network applications. The application logic, defined by the SOA, requires that the applications are designed and architected in a way that makes them naturally decomposed into the components of large granules with well-circumscribed functional responsibilities. These components are delivered by loosely-coupled, autonomous and dynamically bound network-accessible software. Unlike traditional distributed applications, an application by the SOA can no longer assume a direct control over its components. This is due to the facts that the components may belong to the different owners, that they may be built and designed to run on the different platforms, and that they can conform to the agreements of different service levels on the quality and performance. The unique characteristic of service-oriented applications posts new requirement from service oriented applications on handling availability of Web services, which forms a challenge that has not been studied in traditional fault-tolerant computing. When an application author is no longer allowed to manipulate the component services, the best way is to arrange substitute Web service to function as a replacement.

On the other side, one of the major processes in a loosely coupled Web services execution environment is matchmaking, that is, an appropriate Web service is assigned to satisfy a requestor's requirements with or without the assistance of a service locator. Alternatively, matchmaking can also provide a ranked list of the n best candidates with respect to the requestor's requirements. This section contains of four chapters which are related to semantic model, data structure, functional and non-functional requirements, with illustrative examples in matchmaking and substitution shown as follows.

In chapter 5, Wang et al. present environment ontology of service capabilities in terms of the domain-specific environment entities from the application scenario and the effects imposed by Web service on the entities. A hierarchical state machine is constructed for each environment entity to describe its behaviors, and the effects imposed by Web services are described as the state transitions traces of environment entities, which define the capability specification of the Web service. In conclusion, this chapter gives the readers an overview of ontology to model Web services` capabilities.

In chapter 6, Peng et al. present a theoretical model called RSLattice based on Formal Concept Analysis (FCA) method which is applied to reveal the pairwise replaceable relationship among Web services at the operation level with an experimental evaluation of the model. Web service replaceability refers to the ability of substituting one service for another. Once RSLattice has been built for a specific service collection, searching replaceable services in the collection should be very efficient. In conclusion, this chapter gives the readers a formal model of supporting Web service replacement in a systematic approach.

In chapter 7, Bravo and Alvarado present a set of structural and functional measures to support Web service substitution with experimental tests. The process for calculating these measures is implemented using a structural-syntactical and functional filtering approach. Web service substitution occurs when, in a composite scenario, a service operation is replaced to improve the composition performance or fix a disruption caused by a failing service. In conclusion, this chapter describes a sample measure methodology to support Web service substitution in a probability approach.

In chapter 8, the final chapter of section 2, Jegadeesan and Balasubramaniam present service flavors which are a strategy for service providers to differentiate services by the non-functional aspects in a marketplace. This chapter models differentiating aspects as policies and also provides a mechanism for enforcing these policies in the middleware by a flavoring SOAP intermediary acting as a policy enforcement point. The strategy could also be used to provide services to business partners or consumers based on custom Service Level Agreements (SLAs). Based on the fundamental knowledge shown in Chapter 5-7, this chapter concludes this topic with an illustrative example of marketplace to conduct Web service`s matchmaking and substitutions and result in SLAs. A SLA is a formal contract between a Web services requestor and provider guaranteeing quantifiable issues at defined levels only through mutual concessions.

SECTION 3 – QUALITY OF SERVICES (QOS)

Quality of Services (QoS) management is critical for service-oriented enterprise architectures because services have different QoS characteristics and their interactions are dynamic and decoupled. For the publish/subscribe style of SOA, different publishers and subscribers may have different QoS requirements in terms of performance, response time, availability, throughput, reliability, timeliness, and security. Usually, there is more than one Web services claim that they have the same or very similar capabilities to accomplish a requestor's requirements. In many cases, the QoS may vary from Web service to Web service. In many cases, the majority of Web services providers may not concern about the level of QoS provided to their requestors. However, there exist an increasing number of concerns to maintain their popularity and reputation about the QoS. It is obvious that the QoS perceived by the requestors is thus becoming a dominant factor for the success of a Web service. In general, the principal QoS attributes of a Web service include a diverse set of service requirements such as the service availability, performance, time, efficiency, reliability, scalability, dependability and security. Matchmaking can also be based on binding support, historical performance, and QoS classifications. As Web services become more popular and complex, the need for locating Web services with specific capabilities at the service locator become more important. This section contains of four chapters which are related to mathematical model, cache data structure, and Web 2.0 with illustrative examples in QoS management shown as follows.

In chapter 9, Rosario et al. present a comprehensive framework for single or composite QoS management in business processes based on soft probabilistic contracts. This chapter also discusses contract composition on how to derive QoS contracts for an orchestration from the QoS contracts, and contract monitoring. QoS relates to performance that a Web service outperforming its contract should do well for the orchestration with SLA. In conclusion, this chapter describes a technical contract framework in an orchestration approach.

In chapter 10, Zheng and Lyu present a distributed fault tolerance strategic framework for Web services failures with a prototype. This chapter also present the optimal fault selection algorithm, which employs both the QoS performance of Web services and the requirements of service users for selecting optimal fault tolerance strategy. In conclusion, this chapter gives the reader an overview of fault tolerance methodology with an implementation.

In chapter 11, Lecue and Mehandjiev present an optimal approach to select semantic Web service compositions within a stochastic model designed to balance semantic links with QoS metrics and search method, which is formalized as a Constraint Satisfaction Problem (CSP) with multiple constraints. The overall architecture has also been tested in three realistic scenarios in use. In conclusion, this chapter gives the reader an overview of semantic methodology to support service compositions with real examples.

In chapter 12, the final chapter of section 3, Hassan et al. present a caching framework called MACE, which is specifically designed for the performance and scalability aspects of mashups. MACE is based upon a formal mashup model wherein an individual mashup is represented as a tree of operators. MACE's design includes a dynamic mashup cache point selection scheme which maximizes the benefit of mashup caching. In conclusion, this chapter presents a set of experiments studying the effectiveness of the proposed framework in mashups.

SECTION 4 – SECURITY AND PRIVACY

Web services architectures are built on an insecure, unmonitored, and shared environment, which is open to events such as security threats. This may result in conflicts since the open architecture of Web services makes it available to many parties, who may have competing interests and goals. For example, a party's commercial secrets may be released to another competing company via the Web services execution. As is the case in many other applications, the information processed in Web services might be commercially sensitive so it is important to protect it from security threats such as disclosure to unauthorized parties. Since security is an essential and integral part of many business processes, Web services have to manage and execute the activities in a secure way. However, the research area of Web services security is challenging as it involves many disciplines, from authentication/encryption to access management/security policies. Security concerns and the lack of security conventions are the major barriers that prevent many business organizations from implementing or employing Web services composition.

On the other hand, privacy policies describe an organization's data practices, what information they collect from individuals (e.g., consumers), and what (e.g., purposes) they do with it. One can imagine that information privacy is usually concerned with the confidentiality of the sensitive information. One of the most significant objectives of enforcing privacy policies is to protect Personal Identifiable Information (PII). Privacy control is usually not concerned with individual subjects. A subject releases his/her data to the custody of an enterprise while consenting to the set of purposes for which the data may be used. In business-to-business activities, information privacy is usually concerned with the confidentiality of the business information. Thus, it is required to have a privacy policy for Web services composition. The privacy policy expresses clearly and concisely what the data protection mechanisms are to achieve. The policy states also the privacy the services requestor expects the services to enforce. As a result, each information security system should enforce the privacy policy stated by the organization. In this circumstance, the information security mechanism should also be embedded with privacy-enhancing technologies.

All this evidence shows the importance of integrating privacy concepts into security mechanisms for resolving the business-to-business security and privacy concerns. However, no comprehensive solutions to the various security and privacy issues have been so far defined in a business-to-business services computing application. It is because the composite services bring a new set of security and privacy challenges to be taken into account during service composition, deployment, and execution, such as confidentiality, integrity, anonymity, authentication, authorization, and availability of composite services. As security and privacy have become an essential component for all software, several security and privacy solutions for XML data have been proposed, which may be the basis to the development of security and privacy solutions for service composition. Additionally, it is important that security and privacy solutions for service compositions are not developed on a "stand-alone" basis; rather they must be integrated into the SOA life cycle, as well as with the solutions developed to fulfill the other main requirements of service compositions. This section contains five chapters related to security and privacy in Web services composition shown as follows.

In chapter 13, She et al. present an enhanced security model to control the information flow in composite services with the concepts of delegation and pass-on with a case study from a healthcare information system. Based on these concepts, new certificates, certificate chains, delegation and pass-on policies, and how they are used to control the information flow are also discussed in this chapter. In conclusion, this chapter gives the readers an overview of the fundamental properties of a security model for Web services composition.

In chapter 14, Alam et al. present a technical framework called BA4BP which enables finer-granular attestation at the Web services level for bringing trust into business processes. This chapter also discusses the behavior of individual services in a business process to overcome the inherent weaknesses of trust management through Trust Computing Group (TCG) for the measurement of the behavior of individual services in a business process. For illustration, the framework incorporates eXtensible Access Control

Markup Language (XACML) on top of business processes. In conclusion, this chapter gives an overview of a design of security architecture in supporting trust computing.

In chapter 15, Khosravifar et al. present an incentive-based reputation model for a theoretical analysis of reputation assessment of Communities of Web services (CWSs) with an implementation. The model represents a logging and auditing mechanism in order to maintain effective reputation assessment for the communities. User agents request CWSs for services and accordingly rate their satisfactions about the received quality and community responsiveness. The strategies taken by different parties are private to individual agents, and the logging file that collects feedback is investigated by a controller agent. In conclusion, this chapter shows the importance of logging and auditing mechanism to support the security framework for services compositions.

In chapter 16, Ringelstein and Staab present a technical architecture called DIALOG for protecting information privacy with a prototype for logging and collecting logs in service-oriented and cross-organizational systems. DIALOG is based on a semantic formalism and ontology to express sticky logs. There are personal, business and legal requirements for protecting privacy and Intellectual Property Rights (IPR) and allowing customers to request information about how and by whom their data was handled. In addition to Chapter 15, this chapter further elaborates the role of logging and auditing mechanisms to protect information privacy in Web services composition.

In the final chapter of the book, chapter 17, Michlmayr et al. present an integrative technical approach into a Web service runtime environment called VRESCo that addresses service provenance. In general, provenance describes the origin and well-documented history of a given object. Several security mechanisms have been implemented to guarantee access control and integrity of service provenance information. This chapter also show the performance and applicability of the integrative technical approach for both service consumers and service providers based on some illustrative examples. Based on Chapter 13 to 16, this chapter concludes this section with an integrative technical approach to support service provenance in Web services composition.

Patrick C. K. Hung
University of Ontario Institute of Technology, Canada

Section 1
Services Composition

Chapter 1
Web Services Compositions Modelling and Choreographies Analysis

Mohsen Rouached
Laboratoire d'InfoRmatique en Image et Systèmes d'information (LIRIS), France

Walid Fdhila
Université Henri Poincaré, France

Claude Godart
Université Henri Poincaré, France

ABSTRACT

In Rouached et al. (2006) and Rouached and Godart (2007) the authors described the semantics of WSBPEL by way of mapping each of the WSBPEL (Arkin et al., 2004) constructs to the EC algebra and building a model of the process behaviour. With these mapping rules, the authors describe a modelling approach of a process defined for a single Web service composition. However, this modelling is limited to a local view and can only be used to model the behaviour of a single process. The authors further the semantic mapping to include Web service composition interactions through modelling Web service conversations and their choreography. This paper elaborates the models to support a view of interacting Web service compositions extending the mapping from WSBPEL to EC, and including Web service interfaces (WSDL) for use in modelling between services. The verification and validation techniques are also exposed while automated induction-based theorem prover is used as verification back-end.

INTRODUCTION

The ability to compose complex Web services from a multitude of available component services is one of the most important problems in service-oriented computing paradigm. Web service composition is the ability to aggregate multiple services into a single composite service that would provide a certain functionality, which otherwise cannot be provided by a single service.

While the technology for developing basic services and interconnecting them on a point-to-point basis has attained a certain level of maturity, there remain open challenges when it comes to

DOI: 10.4018/978-1-4666-1942-5.ch001

engineering services that engage in complex interactions that go beyond simple sequences of requests and responses or involve large numbers of participants.

In practice, there are two different (and competing) notions of modeling Web service compositions: orchestration and choreography. Orchestration describes how multiple services can interact by exchanging messages including the business logic and execution order of the interactions from the perspective of a single endpoint (i.e., the orchestrator). It refers to an executable process that may result in a persistent, multi step interaction model where the interactions are always controlled from the point of view of a single entity involved in the process. Choreography, on the other hand, provides a global view of message exchanges and interactions that occur between multiple process endpoints, rather than a single process that is executed by a party. Thus, choreography is more akin to a peer-to-peer (P2P) architecture and offers a means by which the rules of participation for collaboration are clearly defined and agreed upon. Even though there exists competing standards for both the models of composition, WSBPEL for orchestration and WS-CDL (Barros et al., 2005) for choreography, it is widely accepted that both orchestration and choreography can (and should) co-exist within one single environment.

Concerning WS-CDL, as discussed in (Barros et al., 2005), there are several places where its specification is not yet fully developed and a number of known issues remain open. Some issues of a more fundamental or practical nature are difficult to address and are likely to require a significant review of the language's underlying meta-model and implied techniques. These issues primarily stem from three factors: (i) lack of separation between meta-model and syntax, (ii) lack of direct support for certain categories of use cases and, (iii) lack of comprehensive formal grounding (see Barros et al., 2005).

On the contrary, WSBPEL is quickly emerging as the language of choice for Web service composition. It opens up the possibility of applying a range of formal techniques to the verification of Web services behaviour (see, e.g., Foster et al., 2003; Fu et al., 2004; Pistore et al., 2004). For instance, it is possible to check the internal business process of a participant against the external business protocol that the participant is committed to provide; or, it is possible to verify whether the composition of two or more processes satisfies general properties (such as deadlock freedom) or application-specific constraints (e.g., temporal sequences, limitations on resources). These kinds of verifications are particularly relevant in the distributed and highly dynamic world of Web services, where each partner can autonomously redefine business processes and interaction protocols.

However, one common problem of the different techniques adopted is related to the model used for representing the communications among the Web services. Indeed, the actual mechanism implemented in the existing WSBPEL execution engines is both very complex and implementation dependent. More precisely, WSBPEL processes exchange messages in an asynchronous way; incoming messages go through different layers of software, and hence through multiple queues, before they are actually consumed in the WSBPEL activity; and overpasses are possible among the exchanged messages. On the other hand, the semantics for how to translate the connectivity and communication between activities of the partner processes rather than from a single process focus are not taken into account.

To address these shortcomings, we propose in this paper a semantic framework that provides a foundation for addressing the above limitations by supporting models of service choreography with multiple interacting Web services compositions, from the perspective of a collaborative distributed composition development environment. The process of behaviour analysis moves from a single local process to that of modelling and analyzing the behavior of multiple processes across composition domains. We show also how to translate the connectivity and communication between activities of the partner processes rather than from a single process focus. These may also contain communication actions or dependencies between communication actions that do not appear in any of the service's behavioral interface(s). This is because behavioral interfaces may be made available to external parties, and thus, they should only show the information that actually needs to be visible to these parties.

The remainder of this paper is structured as follows. In Section 2, we discuss the Web services composition modelling aspects. Three viewpoints and the relationships between them are presented. Section 3 details our approach of modelling services choreographies and explains the different steps for getting our communication model. A running example is used to illustrate the main ideas. The verfication and validation aspects are discussed in Section 4. More precisely, this section introduces the verfication techniques that we have used, the ingredients of our encoding, and the implementation of the model. Section 5 describes the related work, and outlines where our work is positioned alongside these. Finally, Section 6 summarizes the ideas explained in the paper and outlines some future directions.

WEB SERVICE COMPOSITIONS MODELLING

Standards for service composition cover three different, although overlapping, viewpoints: Choreography, Behavioral interface (also called abstract process in WSBPEL), and Orchestration (also called executable process in WSBPEL). While a choreography model describes a collaboration between a collection of services in order to achieve a common goal, an orchestration model describes both the communication actions and

the internal actions in which a service engages. Internal actions include data transformations and invocations to internal software modules (e.g., legacy applications that are not exposed as services). An orchestration may also contain communication actions or dependencies between communication actions that do not appear in any of the service's behavioral interface(s). This is because behavioral interfaces may be made available to external parties, and thus, they should only show the information that actually needs to be visible to these parties.

Choreography is typically initiated by an external source (a client or service) and ends with a target service or a reply to the source. Such interactions during this choreography pose questions such as; *can messages be sent and received in any order? What are the rules governing the sequencing of messages?* And can a global view of the overall exchange of messages be drawn? *Can we verify, modify and monitor the behaviour?*

The viewpoints presented above have some overlap (Dijkman & Dumas, 2004). This overlap can be exploited within service composition methodologies to perform consistency checks between viewpoints or to generate code. For example, a choreography model can be used to generate the behavioral interface that each participating service must provide in order to participate in collaboration. This interface can then be used during the development of the service in question. The choreography model can be used also to check (at design time) whether the behavioral interface of an existing service conforms to a choreography and thus, whether the service in question would be able to play a given role in that choreography.

Similarly, a behavioral interface can be used as a starting point to generate an *orchestration* skeleton that can then be filled up with details, regarding internal tasks, and refined into a full orchestration. On the other hand, an existing orchestration could be checked for consistency against an existing behavioral interface. In this way, it would be possible, for example, to detect situations where a given orchestration does not send messages in the order in which these are expected by other services.

A more subtle dependency is semantic consistency of a global choreography and local process orchestrations. A choreography definition introduces message ordering constraints over the interface views of local process orchestration definitions. These need to be supported at the orchestration level in which they are mapped. The expressive power of orchestration semantics, at the same time, should not be limited by the choreography layer. Interactions supported by WS-CDL specifications occur between a pair of roles; in other words, only binary interactions are supported. Missing in WS-CDL is the explicit support for multi-party interactions and more complicated messaging constraints which these bring.

However, if we compare the development of WS-CDL with that of WSBPEL, we observe that WSBPEL stemmed from two sources, WSFL and XLang, which derived themselves from languages supported by existing tools (namely MQSeries Workflow and BizTalk). Furthermore, together with the first draft of WSBPEL, a prototype implementation was released. In contrast, WS-CDL has been developed without any prior implementation and does not derive (directly) from any language supported by an implementation (Dijkman & Dumas, 2004). For this, we propose in this work to extend WSBPEL compositions with communications semantics and therefore both orchestration and choreography co-exist within one single environment.

COMMUNICATION SEMANTICS FOR BPEL PROCESSES

In our previous work (Rouached et al., 2006; Rouached & Godart, 2007), the design and implementation of Web service composition interactions was discussed and models were

produced to provide a formal representation of the behaviour specified. These models are useful to describe individual compositions; however, an elaboration of modelling is required to represent the behaviour of interacting compositions across partnered processes. A series of compositions in Web service choreography needs specific modelling activities that are not explicitly derived from an implementation. In what follows, we describe this elaboration of models to support a view of interacting Web service compositions extending the mapping from WSBPEL to EC discussed in our previous work, and including Web service interfaces (WSDL) for use in modelling between services.

Motivating Example

We present a brief overview of the problem along with our solution mechanism using the following running example implemented as a composition with several WSBPEL processes (see Figure 1). The collaboration represents a *loan approval* and includes three partners namely *credit approval, Risk Assesment and Decision*. Each of these components is implemented as a bpel process since it needs some other processes to ensure its role in the collaboration. A customer makes a new credit request to the *Credit Approval* composite service. The latter invokes the *CollectInfo* service to know more about the customer. Once the data are available, *Credit Approval* sends them to *Risk Assesment* composite service which considers whether the risk of the credit is low or high. The risk evaluation is then sent to the *Decide* composite service which decides even to approve the credit or not. If the assessment is low then the lowest rate is calculated and a reply is sent to the costumer following approval. If the assessment is high risk then the customer is asked to apply through an alternative process. Customer notification is achieved through the *Notify* service.

Figure 1. Credit approval process example

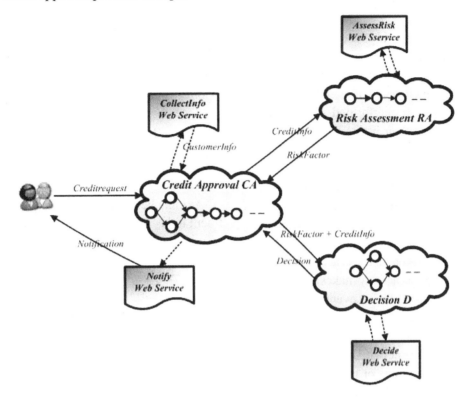

WSBPEL Language

WSBPEL introduces a stateful model of Web services interacting by exchanging sequences of messages between business partners. The major parts of a WSBPEL process definition consist of (1) the business process partners (Web services that the process interacts with), (2) a set of variables that keep the state of the process, and (3) an activity defining the logic behind the interactions between the process and its partners. Activities that can be performed are categorized into basic, structured, and scope-related activities. Basic activities perform simple operations like receive, reply, invoke and others. Structured activities impose an execution order on a collection of activities and can be nested. Then, scope-related activities enable defining logical units of work and delineating the reversible behavior of each unit. Below, we describe the main activities (basic and structured).

Basic Activities

Basic activities in a WSBPEL process support primitive functions (e.g., invocation of operations and assignments of variable values): (i) the invoke activity calls an operation in one of the partner services of the composition process, (ii) the receive activity makes the composition process to wait for the receipt of an invocation of its operations by some of its partner services, (iii) the reply activity makes the composition process to respond to a request for the execution of an operation previously accepted through a receive activity, (iv) the assign activity is used to copy the value from a variable to another one, (v) the throw activity is used to signal an internal fault, (vi) the wait activity is used to specify a delay in the process that must last for a certain period of time.

Structured Activities

Structured activities provide the control and data flow structures that enable the composition of basic activities into a business process: (i) the sequence activity includes an ordered list of other activities that must be performed sequentially in the exact order of their listing, (ii) the switch activity includes an ordered list of one or more conditional branches that include other activities and may be executed subject to the satisfiability of the conditions associated with them, (iii) the flow activity includes a set of two or more activities that should be executed concurrently. A flow activity completes when all these activities have completed, (iv) the pick activity makes a composition process to wait for different events (expressed by onMessage elements) and perform activities associated with each of these events as soon as it occurs, (v) the while activity is used to specify iterative occurrence of one or more activities as long some condition holds true.

Event Calculus

Event calculus (Kowalski & Sergot, 1986) is a general logic programming treatment of time and change. The formulation of the event calculus is defined in first order predicate logic like the situation calculus. Likewise, there are actions and effected fluents. Fluents are changing their valuations according to effect axioms defined in the theory of the problem domain. However there are also big differences between both formalisms. The most important one is that in the event calculus, narratives and fluent valuations are relative to time points instead of successive situations. The most appearing advantage of this approach is the inherent support for concurrent events. Events occurring in overlapping time intervals can be deduced. Inertia is an assumption, which accounts a solution to the frame problem together with other techniques and it is saying that a fluent preserves its valuation unless an event specified to affect (directly or indirectly) the fluent occurs.

Each event calculus theory is composed of axioms. A fluent that holds since the time of the initial state can be described by the following axioms (Shanahan, 1999):

$$holdsAt(f, t) \leftarrow initially(f) \wedge \neg clipped(t0, f, t)$$

$$holdsAt(\neg f, t) \leftarrow initially(\neg f) \wedge \neg declipped(t0, f, t)$$

Axioms below are used to deduce whether a fluent holds or not at a specific time.

$$holdsAt(f, t) \leftarrow happens(e, t1, t2) \wedge initiates(e, f, t1) \wedge \neg clipped(t1, f, t) \wedge t2 < t$$

$$holdsAt(\neg f, t) \leftarrow happens(e, t1, t2) \wedge terminates(e, f, t1) \wedge \neg declipped(t1, f, t) \wedge t2 < t$$

The predicate *clipped* defines a time frame for a fluent that is overlapping with the time frame of an event which terminates this fluent. Similarly *declipped* defines a time frame for a fluent which overlaps with the time frame of an event that initiates this fluent. The formula *initiates* (e, f, t) means that fluent f holds after event e at time t. The formula *terminates* (e, f, t) denotes that fluent f does not hold after event e at time t. The formula *happens* (e, t1, t2) indicates that event e starts at time t1 and ends at time t2. The instantaneous events are described as *happens* (e, t).

```
clipped(t1, f, t4) ↔ (∃ E,t2, t3) [
happens(e, t2, t3) ∧

terminates(e, f, t2) ∧ t1 < t3 ∧ t2
< t4]
declipped(t1, f, t4) ↔ (∃ e,t2, t3) [
happens(f, t2, t3) ∧

initiates(e, f, t2) ∧ t1 < t3 ∧ t2 <
t4]
```

Given the fact that we consider communications actions where ordering and timing are relevant and we adopt event driven reasoning, the event calculus seems to be a solid basis to start from. Another key element of this choice is that orchestration and choreography should co-exist within one single environment, and in our case the orchestration verification framework is based on EC logic.

Event Driven Specification

To formally specify and reason about the interactions between a set of BPEL processes, we use four different types of events resumed in Table 1.

1. **invoke_input:** The invocation of an operation by the composition process of the system in one of its partner services. The term *invoke_ic(PartnerService,Op(oId,in Var))* represents the invocation event. In this term, *Op* is the name of the invoked operation, *PartnerService* is the name of the service that provides *Op*, *oId* is a variable whose value determines the exact instance of the invocation of *Op* within a specific instance of the execution of the composition process, and *inVar* is a variable whose value is the value of the input parameter of *Op* at the time of its invocation.

2. **invoke_output:** The return from the execution of an operation invoked by the composition process in a partner service. The term *invoke_ir(PartnerService,Op(oId))* in this predicate represents the return event. *PartnerService, Op* and *oId* in this term are as defined in (1). In cases where *Op* has an output variable *outVar*, the value of this variable at the return of the operation is represented by the predicate: *initiates(invoke_ir(PartnerService,Op(oId)), equalTo(outVar1, outVar), t)*. This predicate expresses the initialization of a fluent variable (*outVar1*) with the value of *outVar*. The

fluent *equalTo(VarName,val)* signifies that value of *VarName* is equal to *val*.

3. **receive:** The invocation of an operation in the composition process by a partner service. The term *invoke_rc(PartnerService,Op(oId))* in this predicate represents the invocation event. *Op* and *oId* are as defined in (1) and *PartnerService* is the name of the service that invokes the operation. In cases where *Op* has an input variable *inVar*, the value of this variable at the time of its invocation is represented by the predicate *initiates(invoke_rc(PartnerService,Op(oId)), equalTo(inVar1, inVar), t)*. This predicate expresses the initialization of a fluent variable in *Var1* with the value of *inVar*.

4. **reply:** The reply following the execution of an operation that was invoked by a partner service in the composition process. The term *reply(PartnerService,Op(oId,outVar))* in this predicate represents the reply event. In this term, *Op* and *oId* are as defined in (1), *PartnerService* is the name of the service that invoked *Op*, and *outVar* is a variable whose value is the value of the output parameter of the operation at the time of the reply.

Compositions Interactions

Here we seek to further our modelling of Web service interactions through two viewpoints. Firstly, we examine the *interactions* within the choreography layer of Web service compositions collaborating in a global goal. Secondly, through further behaviour analysis, we model the interaction sequences built to support multiple-partner conversations across enterprise domains and with a view of wider goals.

As mentioned so far, our objective is to provide a model of service choreography with multiple interacting Web services compositions, from the perspective of a collaborative distributed composition development environment. The process of behaviour analysis moves from a single local process to that of modelling and analyzing the behaviour of multiple processes across composition domains. We look also for translating the connectivity and communication between activities of the partner processes rather than from a single process focus (see Figure 2). These may also contain communication actions or dependencies between communication actions that do not appear in any of the service's behavioral interface(s). In this section, we discuss how to realize this objective.

To start, we require a process to analyze which activities are partnered in the composition. For example, *invoke* from the *Credit Aproval* process *CA* (a risk assessment request) will be received by the Risk Assessment process *RA* (*receive* a risk assessment request). Equally, the *CA invoke* activity, to check the decision for the credit request by contacting *Decision* process, will be aligned with *receive* in the *CA* process. In WSBPEL, the communication is based upon a protocol of behavior for a local service. However, the partner communication can concisely be modeled using the synchronous event passing model, described in (Magee & Kramer, 1999). The Sender-Receiver example discussed uses *Channels* to facilitate message/event passing between such a sender and

receiver model. The representation of a channel in WSBPEL is known as a *port*. The significant element of this discussion used in our process is that of synchronization of the invoking and receiving events within compositions between ports and whether this has been constructed concurrently (*flow* construct in WSBPEL) or as a sequence (*sequence* construct in WSBPEL) of activities.

In the following, we seek to further our modelling of WSBPEL interactions through two viewpoints. First, we examine the interactions within the choreography layer of Web service compositions collaborating in a global goal. Secondly, through further behaviour analysis, we model the interaction sequences built to support multiple-partner conversations across enterprise domains and with a view of wider goals.

Our approach relies on four steps: (1) identifying services conversations, (2) identifying partners involved in the composition and their respective roles, (3) linking composition interactions by revealing the invocation style, points at which interaction occurs and linking between partners using port connectors, and (4) building interaction models using our formalism. We detail also, the interaction modelling algorithm we proposed.

Figure 2. Web service compositions interactions

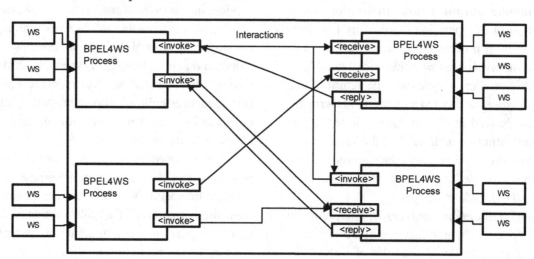

Service Conversations Identification

Events exchange is a basic concept of Web service composition interactions. In this sense, Web service modelling involves interactions and their interdependencies description from structural and behavioral point of view. In this step, we mainly identify conversations between two or more participants. It should be noted that a service may be engaged simultaneously in several conversations with different partners. A conversation defines how interactions can start and end depending on the goal of conversation. It specifies also the order in which several scenarios could occur.

To model these conversations in the context of several Web service compositions, we perform an analysis process on all the implementation processes and use an algorithm as part of this analysis to semantically check and link partner process interactions. The algorithm takes as inputs the partner service interfaces (WSDL documents) and the implementation models (WSBPEL documents). The output of this phase is a list of interaction activities.

Service Partners and Roles Identification

An important requirement for realistic modelling of business processes is the ability to model the required relationship with a partner process. WSDL already describes the functionality of a service provided by a partner, at both the abstract and concrete levels. The relationship between a business process and a partner is typically peer-to-peer, requiring a two-way dependency at the service level. In other words, a partner represents both a consumer of a service provided by the business process and a provider of a service to the business process. In this sense, a partner may be considered to have one or many roles depending on what behaviour the partner's service provides. The role indicator is used primarily to distinguish

what the business process is referencing as part of the collaborative business process.

Linking Compositions Interactions

To model interacting Web service compositions there is clearly a need to elaborate our analysis of implementations by linking compositional interactions based upon: (i) activities within the process (identifying invocation style (rendez vous or request only), identifying and recording the points at which interaction occurs), (ii) the abstract interface (linking between the private process activities and the public communication interface declared in the abstract WSDL service description).

To model the semantics of linking interactions between processes requires a mapping between activities in each of the processes translated and building an event port connector for each of the interaction activities linking invoke (input) with receives, and replies (output) with the returned message to an *invoke*. The choreography modelling algorithm is shown in Algorithm 1 Where:

1. O is the set of all operations provided by a Web service in the choreography.

2. C_w is the WSBPEL process of the partner W.

3. A BPEL process C_{wi} is a quadruple *(In, P, A, W)* where

   ○ *In* $\subset O$ represents the WSDL process interface: $In = \{w_i o_n \mid O \leq n \leq n_{wi}\}$.

   ○ W_i the set of partners defined in the process C_{wi}

   ○ P $\subset$ O the set of the operations of partner w_j of w_i *(j $\in$ I)*, such as $P = \{w_j o \mid w_j \leq wi$ *and* $\exists j \in I, w_j o \in In_j\}$

   ○ *A* is the set of the invocation activities such as $\forall a \in A$:

     ▪ *a.o* represents the invoked operation.

     ▪ *a.p* represents the invoked partner

The physical linking of *partnerlinks*, partners and process models is undertaken as follows. For each invocation in a process, a messaging port is created. WSBPEL defines communication in a synchronous messaging model. WSBPEL process instance support in the specification specifies that in order to keep consistency between process activities, a synchronous request mechanism must be governed. The synchronous model can be formed by the following process.

For every composition process selected for modelling we extract all the interaction activities in this process. Interaction activities are service operation invocations (requests), receiving operation requests and replying to operation requests. In addition to an invocation request, we also add an invocation reply to synchronize the reply from a partner process with that of the requesting client process. The list is then analyzed for invocation requests, and for each one found a partner/port lookup is undertaken to gather the actual partner that is specified in a partnerlink declaration. To achieve this, a partner list is used and the partner referenced in the invocation request is linked back to a partnerlink reference. The partnerlink specifies the porttype to link operation and partner with an actual interface definition. To complete the partner match, all interface definitions used in composition analysis are searched and matched on porttype and operation of requesting client process. This concludes the partner match. A port connector bridge is then built to support either a simple request invocation (with no reply expected) or in "rendez-vous" style, building both invoke-receive and *reply-invoke_output* models. This supports the model mapping. The sequence is then repeated for all other invocations in the selected composition process, and then looped again for any other composition processes to analyze. We therefore specify an algorithm that will enable mechanical linking between activities, partners and process compositions. The algorithm supports a mechanical implementation of linking composition processes together based upon their interaction behaviour. Two build phases are required as part of the algorithm, being that of building a *reply-invoke_output* port and *invoke-receive* connector between partnered processes

In summary, the algorithm described provides a port connector based implementation of the communication between two partner processes. Where multiple partners, communication is undertaken in

Algorithm 1. Choreography modelling algorithm

```
begin
    For each composition C_wi do
        For each a ∈ A_wi do
            P_local ← a.p
            P_link ← P_link.partnerLink
            PLT ← P_link.partnerLinkType
            Port_type ← PLT.portType
            For each In_wj (w_j ∈ W) do
                if In_wj.porttype = Port_typethen
                    actual_partner ← w_j
                        Lookup w_j.o ∈ A_wj such as w_j.o = a.o

            ifa.o.out is in (rendez-vous style) then
                add invokeOutput action to activity model
                Build reply-invokeOutput connector

        Build invoke-receive connector

end
```

a composition, a port connector is built between each instance of a message (and optionally a reply if used in rendez-vous interaction style). In the following, we explain how to construct our port connector model.

Building Interaction Models

The activity of building port connectors for our integration mapping is based on the basic concept of event passing in the formation of Web service composition communication. The essence of this work is that events are passed through channels. A channel connects two and only two processes, in which a single process can receive from a channel. The term channel is used to symbolize that a one-to-one channel is used in process synchronization. A connector is the implementation between port and channel, in that a sender port is connected to a sender-receiver channel.

Event Invocations Connectors

To build connected composition interactions, port connector channels are used for each of the invocation styles between two or more partnered compositions. The algorithm is used from the viewpoint of a process composition at the "center of focus", that is, the one in which initial process analysis is being considered. The interface of subsequent partner interactions is used in the algorithm to obtain a link between two partners and an actual operation. For example in Figure 3, two WSBPEL processes interact using both a request only invocation (Channel A) and a Rendez-vous style (Channel A and B).

Our model of interactions using channels takes into consideration both synchronous and asynchronous interactions between partners. The model produced from analysis of the compositions is from the viewpoint of the composition performing as part of a role in choreography. This makes the model providing an abstract view of interactions for the purpose of linking invocations and not on the actual order of messages received by the process host architecture (synchronous and asynchronous messaging models for Web services can be referred in (Fu et al., 2004)).

Request Only Invocation Modelling (Channel A)

Web service compositions specified with the *invoke* construct and only an *input* container at-

Figure 3. Channels and Interaction activities of Web service compositions

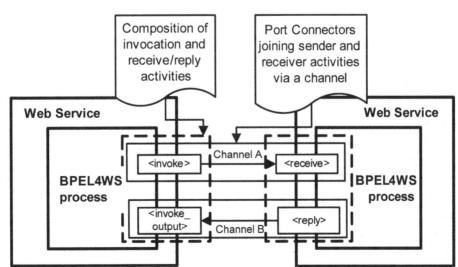

Exhibit 1. Channel A

```
∀ (t1: time) happens (invoke-ic (PartnerService, Operation (old, inVar)), t1)
=> (∃ t2) happens (invoke-rc (PartnerService, Operation (old)), t2) ∧
initiates (invoke-rc (PartnerService, Operation (old)), equalTo (inVar1, inVar), t2)) ∧ (t1 < t2).

∀ (t2: time) happens (invoke-rc (PartnerService, Operation (old)), t2)) ∧
initiates (invoke-rc (PartnerService, Operation (old)), equalTo (inVar1, inVar), t2)
=> (∃ t1) happens (invoke-ic (PartnerService, Operation (old, inVar)), t1) ∧ (t1 < t2).
```

Exhibit 2. Channels A and B.

```
∀ (t1: time) happens (invoke-ic (PartnerService, Operation (old, inVar)), t1)
=> (∃ t2) happens (invoke-rc (PartnerService, Operation (old)), t2) ∧
initiates (invoke-rc (PartnerService, Operation (old)), equalTo (inVar1, inVar), t2)) ∧ (t1 < t2).

∀ (t2: time) happens (invoke-rc (PartnerService, Operation (old)), t2)) ∧
initiates (invoke-rc (PartnerService, Operation (old)), equalTo (inVar1, inVar), t2)
=> (∃ t1) happens (invoke-ic (PartnerService, Operation (old, inVar)), t1) ∧ (t1 < t2).

∀ (t3: time) happens (reply (PartnerService, Operation (old2, outVar)), t3)
=> (∃ t4) happens (invoke-ir (PartnerService, Operation (old2)), t4) ∧ initiates (invoke-ir (PartnerService, Operation (old2)), equalTo
(outVar1, outVar), t4)) ∧ (t3 < t4).

∀ (t4: time) happens (invoke-ir (PartnerService, Operation (old2)), t4)) ∧
initiates (invoke-ir (PartnerService, Operation (old2)), equalTo (outVar1, outVar), t4)
=> (∃ t3) happens (reply (PartnerService, Operation (old2, outVar)), t3) ∧ (t3 < t4).
```

tribute declare an interaction on a request only basis (there is no immediate reply expected). More generally this requirement is for a reliable message invocation without any output response from the service host (other than status of receiving the request). The model for this is illustrated in Exhibit 1.

Rendezvous Style Invocation Modelling (Channels A and B)

"Rendezvous" (Request and Reply) invocations are specified in WSBPEL with the $invoke$ construct, with both *input* and *output* container attributes. To model these types of interactions, we use a generic port model for each process port. A synchronous event model in Web services compositions (such as WSBPEL) requires an additional activity of an "input_output" to link a reply in a partnered process to that of the caller receiving the output of the invoke, however, this

is necessary only if the invocation style is that of rendez-vous. The event synchronization for this port model is represented in Exhibit 2.

Considering the loan approval example introduced so far (Figure 1), Figure 4 shows the corresponding model to an interaction scenario between the *Credit Approval CA* and *Risk Assessment RA* processes. The resulting model is interpreted as follows: The invocation event of the *CA* operation (*AssessRisk*) at time *t1* should be received by *RA* at time *t2* such as *t1<t2*. The response to this request should happen at time *t3* such as *t3>t2*, and be received by *CA* at time *t4>t3*.

Mapping Process Activities to Port Connectors

The next step in the port connector modelling process is to map the activities of the WSBPEL process to the port connector activities. This is achieved using the semantics of WSBPEL for the

Figure 4. Event invocation connectors

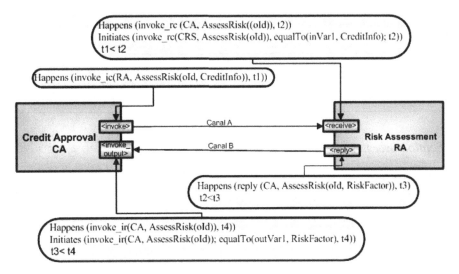

Table 1. Events expressed in EC

Type	Event
invoke_input	*happens(invoke_ic(PartnerService,Op(oId,inVar)),t)*
invoke_output	*happens(invoke_ir(PartnerService,Op(oId)),t)*
receive	*happens(invoke_rc(PartnerService,Op(oId)),t)*
reply	*happens(reply(PartnerService,Op(oId,outVar)),t)*

interaction activities discussed earlier and replacing the port connector activities appropriately.

The *invoke* activity in WSBPEL is mapped from the client process to the *invoke_input* action of the port connector - this represents the initial step of a request between Web service partners.

The associated receiving action of the WSBPEL partner process is mapped to the receive activity in the port connector. The reply from the partner process to the client process is mapped to the reply in the partnered process. Both *receive* and *reply* activities in the WSBPEL are discovered as part of the interface analysis described before. Table 2 lists the mapping explained here

VERIFICATION AND VALIDATION

In the previous section we have described our approach to model Web service compositions with respect to their specification processes and interactions. These models provide a representation that can be used to perform verification and validation analysis using formal techniques. In this section we discuss this analysis (Figure 5).

Recorded Events

There are two main sources of data for Web log collecting, corresponding to the interacting two software systems: data on the Web server side and data on the client side. The existing techniques are commonly achieved by enabling the respective Web server's logging facilities. There already exist

Table 2. Mapping process activities to port connectors

WS interactions	Port action	BPEL actions (example)
Invoke (client)	Invoke-input	Invoke-CA-RA-AssessRisk
Receive (Partner)	Receive	Receive-CA-RA-AssessRisk
Reply (Partner to client)	Reply	Reply-RA-CA-AssessRisk
	Invoke-output	Output-RA-CA-AssessRisk

Figure 5. Verification overview

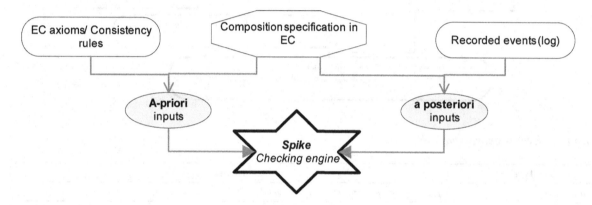

many investigations and proposals on Web server log and associated analysis techniques. Actually, papers on Web Usage Mining WUM (Punin et al., 2001) describe the most well-known means of Web log collection. Basically, server logs are either stored in the *Common Log Format[1]* or the more recent *Combined Log Format[2]*. They consist primarily of various types of logs generated by the Web server. Most of the Web servers support as a default option the *Common Log Format*, which is a fairly basic form of Web server logging.

However, the emerging paradigm of Web services requires richer information in order to fully capture business interactions and customer electronic behavior in this new Web environment. Since the Web server log is derived from requests resulting from users accessing pages, it is not tailored to capture service composition or orchestration. That is why, we propose in the following a set of advanced logging techniques that allows to record the additional information to mine more advanced behavior.

Successful logging facilities for advanced architectures in Web Services models require composition (choreography/orchestration) information in the log record. Such information is not available in conventional Web server logs. Therefore, the advanced logging solutions must provide for both choreography or orchestration identifier and a case identifier in each interaction that is logged.

To adress this shortcoming, basically, we modify SOAP headers to include and gather the additional needed information capturing **choreography** details. Those data are stored in the special *<WSHeaders>*. This tag encapsulates headers attributes like: *choreographyprotocol, choreographyname, choreographycase* and any other tag inserted by the service to record optional information; for example, the *<soapenv: choreographyprotocol>* tag, may be used to register that the service was called by WS-CDL choreography protocol. The SOAP message header may look as shown in Figure 6.

Figure 6. The SOAP message header

```
< soapenv : Header >
    < soapenv : choreographyprotocol
            soapenv : mustUnderstand = "0"
            xsi : type = "xsd : string" >WS−CDL
    < /soapenv : choreographyprotocol >
    < soapenv : choreographyname
            soapenv : mustUnderstand = "0"
            xsi : type = "xsd : string" > OTA
    < /soapenv : choreographyname >
    < soapenv : choreographycase
            soapenv : mustUnderstand = "0"
            xsi : type = "xsd : int" > 123
    < /soapenv : choreographycase >
< /soapenv : Header >
```

Concerning **orchestration** log collecting, since the most Web services orchestration are using a WSBPEL engine, which coordinates the various orchestration's Web services, interprets and executes the grammar describing the control logic, we can extend this engine with a sniffer that captures orchestration information, i.e., the orchestration-ID and its instance-ID. This solution is centralized, but less constrained than the previous one which collects choreography information.

Finally, the focus is on collecting and analyzing **single** Web service composition instance. The exact structure of the Web logs or the event collector depends on the Web service execution engine that is used. In our experiments, we have used the engine bpws4j[3] that uses log4j[4] to generate logging events. Log4j is an Open Source logging API developed under the Jakarta Apache project. It provides a robust, reliable, fully configurable, easily extendible, and easy to implement framework for logging Java applications for debugging and monitoring purposes. The event collector (which is implemented as a remote log4j server) sets some log4j properties of the bpws4j engine to specify level of event reporting (INFO, DEBUG etc.), and the destination details of the logged events.

At runtime bpws4j generates events according to the log4j properties set by the event collector. Figure 7 shows some example of log4j 'logging event' generated by bpws4j engine. The event extractor captures logging event and converts it to a unique TCS log format. These expressions are described in next section.

Our previous work (Rouached et al., 2006) has contained more details and examples about the previous logging facilities.

Verification Engine

As shown in Figure 5, the verification of the composition requirements can be done either *a-priori*, i.e., at design time, or *a-posteriori*, i.e., after runtime to test and repair design errors, and formally verify whether the process design does have certain desired properties.

The need for a-priori verification is important for compositions because they can be very complex processes, and therefore we need to check if the specified behavior is consistent, which is not a trivial task as soon as a composition process manages complex service dependencies. Indeed, these processes expect to enforce some

Figure 7. Example of log4j 'logging event'

```
2008-03-13 10:40:39,634        [Thread-35]     INFO    bpws.runtime – Outgoing response:
[WSIFResponse:serviceID = ' {http://tempuri.org/services/CRS}CustomerRegServicefb0b0-
fbc5965758--8000'operationName = 'completed'
        isFault = 'false' outgoingMessage = 'org.apache.wsif.base.WSIFDefaultMessage@
        1df3d59 name:null parts[0]:[JROMBoolean: : true]'
        faultMessage = 'null' contextMessage = 'null']
2008-03-13 10:40:39,634        [Thread-35]     DEBUG         bpws.runtime.bus -Response
        for external invoke is[WSIFResponse:serviceID=' {http://tempuri.org/services
        /CCRS}CustomerRegServicefb0b0-fbc5965758--8000'
        operationName = 'authenticate' isFault = 'false'        outgoingMessage =
        org.apache.wsif.base.WSIFDefaultMessage@1df3d59 name:null parts[0]:
        [JROMBoolean: : true]'faultMessage = 'null'      contextMessage = 'null']
2008-03-13 10:40:39,634        [Thread-35]     DEBUG         bpws.runtime.bus -Waiting
for request
```

high-level policies which we have defined in a set of consistency rules. Our interest is to use these rules specified formally in EC to check process consistency.

The a-posteriori verification is important to provide knowledge about the context of and the reasons of discrepancies between process models and related instances. This kind of verification is necessary since some interactions between Web services that constitute a process may be dynamically specified at runtime, causing unpredictable interactions with other services, and making the a-priori verification method insufficient as it only takes into account static aspects.

Overview of SPIKE

Theorem provers have been applied to the formal development of software. They are based on logic-based specification languages and they provide support to the proof of correctness properties, expressed as logical formulas. In our work, we use the SPIKE induction prover (Stratulat, 2001). SPIKE was chosen for the following reasons: (i) its high automation degree (to help a Web service designer), (ii) its ability on case analysis, (iii) its refutational completeness (to find counter-

examples), and (iv) its incorporation of decision procedures (to automatically eliminate arithmetic tautologies produced during the proof attempt[5].

SPIKE proof method is based on cover set induction. Given a theory, SPIKE computes in a first step induction variable where to apply induction and induction terms which basically represent all possibles values that can be taken by the induction variables. Typically for a non-negative integer variable, the induction terms are 0 and $x+1$, where x is a variable.

Given a conjecture to be checked, the prover selects induction variables according to the previous computation step, and substitute them in all possible way by induction terms. This operation generates several instances of the conjecture which are then simplified by rules, lemmas, and induction hypotheses.

Encoding EC in SPIKE

Here we describe a method for representing EC in SPIKE language. In the sequel, we assume that all formulas are universally quantified. Then the ingredients of this encoding are:

- **Data:** All data information manipulated by the system is ranged over a set of sorts. This data concerns generally the argument types of events and fluents. For instance, the sets of customers, Credits and Risks are defined respectively by the sorts *Customer*, *Credit* and *Risk*. The sort *Bool* represents the Boolean values, where *true* and *false* are its constant constructors.

- **Events:** We consider that all events of the system are of sort *Event*, where the event symbols are the constructors of this sort. These constructors are free as all event symbols are assumed distincts. For instance, the event symbol *Credit_order(x, y, z)* is a constructor of *Event* such that *x, y, z* and *t* are variables of sorts *Customer*, *Credit* and *Risk* respectively. We define also an idle event which when occuring it lets the system unchanged. We represent it by the constant constructor *Noact*.

- **Fluents:** The sort *Fluent* respresents the set of fluents. All fluent symbols of the systems are the constructors of sort *Fluent*, which are also free. The fluent symbol *EqualItem(x, y)*, for example, means that the variables *x* and *y*, of sort *Item*, are equal.

- **Time:** The sort of natural numbers, *Nat*, which is reflected by constructors *0* and successor *succ(x)* (meaning *x+1*).

- **Axioms:** We express all predicates used in EC as Boolean function symbols. For instance *happens: Event * Nat -> Bool, initiates: Event *Fluent * Nat -> Bool, terminates: Event *Fluent * Nat ->Bool*, and *holdsAt: Fluent *Nat *Nat -> Bool* are the signatures of predicates *happens*, *initiates*, *terminates* and *holdsAt* respectively. Then, the EC axioms are expressed in conditional equations.

- **Log:** Recorded logs are also expressed in equational form: *ListEvent= (e1, e2... en)*.

- **Requirements:** In the same way, we express the composition requirements in

equational form. For instance, a requirement that concerns a purchase order can be represented by *happens(Credit_ request(x,y,i),t1)=true ∧ happens(Asses sRisk(y,w,i),t2)=true => (t1 < t2)=true*, where t1, *t2, x, y, w* and *i* are variables.

Finally, we build an algebraic specification from EC specification. Once building this specification, we can check all behavioural properties by means the powerful deductive techniques (rewriting and induction) provided by SPIKE.

Checking Composition Requirements

All the generated axioms can be directly given to the prover SPIKE, which automatically transforms these axioms into conditional rewrite rules. When SPIKE is called, either the requirement proof succeeds, or the SPIKE's proof-trace is used for extracting all scenarios which may lead to potential deviations. There are two possible scenarios. The first scenario is meaningless because conjectures are valid but it comes from a failed proof attempt by SPIKE. Such cases can be overcome by simply introducing new lemmas. The second one concerns cases corresponding to real deviations. The trace of SPIKE gives all necessary informations (events, fluents and timepoints) to understand the inconsistency origin. Consequently, these informations help designer to detect behavioural problems in the composite Web service.

Below, we present a fragment of the SPIKE trace showing a deviation detection when checking a requirement (Figure 8).

Implementation

The validation tool that we have developed is shown in Figure 9. At run-time, a process execution engine executes the WSBPEL composition process and delivers the functionality of the process. This process execution engine is referred

Figure 8. A fragment of SPIKE trace example

Uncaught exception: Failure("fail induction on [10973] CreditInfo (u2, u1, u3, u5) <> Credit_request (e1, e2, e3, e4) /\\ CreditInfo (u2, u1, u3, u5) <> AssessRisk (e2, e5, e3) /\\ u2 = e5 /\\ u1 = e2 /\\ u3 = e3 /\\ u5 = 3 /\\ u6 = 10 /\\ AssessRisk (u1, u2, u3) <> Credit_request (e1, e2, e3, e4) /\\ u1 = e2 /\\ u2 = e5 /\\ u3 = e3 /\\ u4 = 3 => u6 < (u4 + (6)) = true ;")while proving the following initial conjectures
[6584] Happens (p (AssessRisk (u1, u2, u3), u4)) = true /\ Happens (p (CreditInfo (u2, u1, u3, u5), u6)) = true => u6 < (u4 + (6)) = true ;
Elapsed time: 0.186 s
We failed

Figure 9. Validation tool

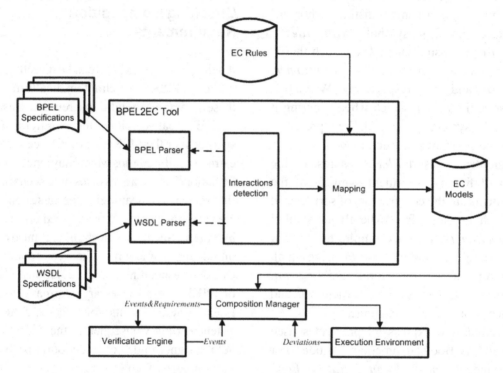

to as *composition execution environment. The composition manager* has responsibility for overseeing the monitoring of requirements regarding the composition process. *The BPEL2EC tool,* is built as a parser that can automatically transform a given WSBPEL process into EC formulas according to the transformation scheme (Rouached, Godart 2007). It takes as input the specification of the Web service composition as a set of coordinated Web services in WSBPEL and produces

as output the behavioural specification of this composition in Event Calculus. The description of this implementation is beyond the scope of this paper and may be found in (Rouached & Godart, 2007). Then, to support the choreography aspects introduced in this paper, we have extended the BPEL2EC tool with two xml parsers developed using the application programming interface JDOM (Java Document Object Model).

Figure 10. A screenshot of the validation tool

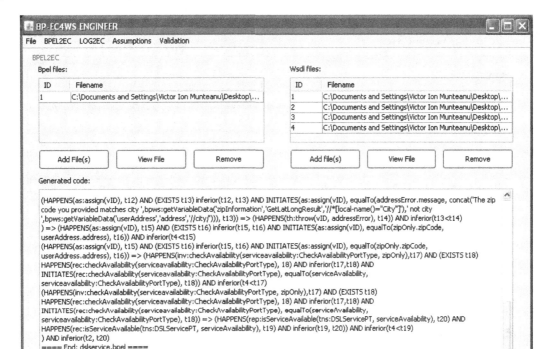

The starting point is a set of Web service compositions specifications in BPEL and all interfaces of the Web services participating in the collaboration. Interactions detection module serves to reveal all inter-compositions interactions using BPEL and WSDL parsers. The output of this step is a set of all peer-to-peer relationships between the actual partners. The mapping step uses the EC translation rules defined so far in the paper to model interactions previously identified and build port connectors between every two interacting partners. Those models are saved into log files which will be useful for both verification and validation by measuring the actual run time deviation with respect to the models. Figure 10 shows a snapshot of the validation tool in action. It shows how global models (choreography aspects) and local models (orchestration aspects) are generated in the same way. It gives also the

possibility to save the resulting EC models to be used in the verification process.

The verification engine, shown in Figure 11 is responsible for checking requirements of the composition processes and their services at runtime. It consists of an EC checker that processes the events recorded in the event log and checks if they are compliant with the requirements of the composition. The check carried out determines whether the set of the recorded events generated by the composition process execution entails the negation of a requirement or not [6].

RELATED WORK

Creating new services by combining a number of existing ones is becoming an attractive way of developing value added Web services. This pattern

Figure 11. A screenshot of the verification engine

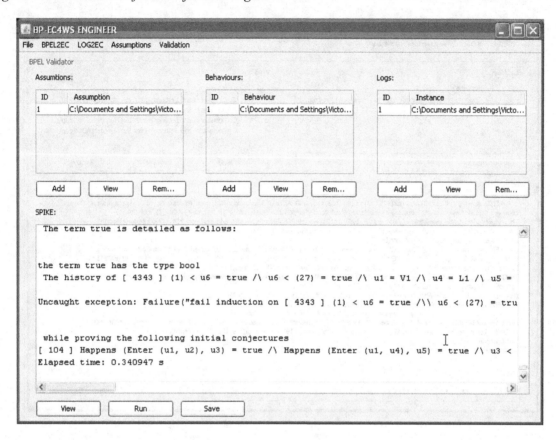

is not new but it does pose some new challenges which have yet to be addressed by current technologies and tools for Web service composition. WSBPEL (Arkin et al., 2004) opens up the possibility of applying a range of formal techniques to the verification of Web service behaviors from two points of view: constraints between activities within the same process and dependencies between activities of different processes. To that end, several methods for this purpose have been proposed. In particular, most researches conducted fall in the realm of AI planning. Despite all these efforts, the modelling and analysis of Web service composition still is a highly complex task. The complexity, in general, comes from the following sources. First, the number of services available over the Web increases dramatically during the recent years, and one can expect to have a huge

Web service repository to be searched. Second, Web services can be created and updated on the fly, thus the composition system needs to detect the updating at runtime and the decision should be made based on the up to date information. Third, Web services can be developed by different organizations, which use different concept models to describe the services, however, there does not exist a unique language to define and evaluate the Web services in an identical means. Below, we present an overview of recent methods related to our work.

With respect to Web service analysis approaches, in particular BPEL processes, several works were described to capture the behavior of BPEL (Andrews et al., 2003) in some formal way. Some advocate the use of finite state machines (Fisteus et al., 2004), others process algebras (Ferrara 2004), and yet others abstract state machines (Fahland & Reisig, 2005) or Petri nets (Ouyang et al., 2005; Martens, 2005; Stahl, 2004). But they mainly focus on introducing a semantic discovery service and facilitating semantic translations. Other attempts to formalize BPEL specification and a detailed comparison between them can be found in (Yang et al., 2005; Van Breugel & Koshkina, 2006). Van Breugel and Koshkina (2006) is a tutorial that provides an overview of the different models of BPEL that have been proposed. Furthermore, the authors discuss the verification techniques for BPEL that have been put forward and the verification tools for BPEL that have been developed. Spanoudakis and Mahbub (2006) presents a framework for monitoring the compliance of systems composed of Web services with requirements set for them at run-time. This framework assumes systems composed of Web services which are co-coordinated by a service composition process expressed in BPEL and uses event calculus to specify the requirements to be monitored.

There have been some works on providing formal semantics for Web service composition languages. In (Ankolekar et al., 2002), the mark-up and semantics for DAML-S is described. They describe the notion of a "semantic Web" as a series of Web resources that provide services, which effect some action or change in the world, such as the sale of a product or the control of a physical device. The semantic Web should enable users to locate, select, employ, compose, and monitor Web-based services automatically. Whilst in Duan et al. (2004), WSBPEL abstract processes are analyzed and semantics given on the construction of WSBPEL implementations behind this. WSBPEL and DAML-S are similar attempts at a standard for workflow of services. However, WSBPEL focuses more on business Web service orchestration whilst DAML-S is more generic in terms of any Web based service or object (Seeley, 2003). In Woodman et al. (2004), the authors

present an extension to the WSDL specification to describe the interactions between Web services. This, in turn, is mapped to π-calculus processes and sequencing formed using its operators. Tasks are represented as processes and dependencies linking the tasks, represented by channels (representing data dependencies in conditional linking). As WSBPEL extends WSDL with an abstract process this mapping is aimed more at the choreography level (where the inner process of a service is not directly observed).

In terms of choreography and Web service conversations, work on asynchronous Web service communication has been described in Fu et al. (2004) and Fu (2004), with an example focus on the WSBPEL specification reported in Fu et al. (2004). A formal specification framework is described to analyze the conversations proposed by the asynchronous communication channels utilized on the Internet. The technique proposed appears more useful for modelling general Web service communications, rather than that of compositional specifics. Both the work on asynchronous and WSBPEL interaction modelling is achieved through the use of Guarded Finite State Automata (GFSA) which enables data dependencies to be modeled alongside process transitions. In Brogi et al. (2004) the authors describe an approach to formalizing conversations, by way of mapping the WSCI standard to CCS for Web service choreography descriptions. The technique is similar to that of formalizing compositions by way of mapping each of the actions and data parameters between two or more partnered services in choreography. The conversation is traced by modelling the Web service invocations with that of the receive and reply actions of the partnered service. The authors call for a common view of representing both composition and choreography models, such that fluid design and maintenance of individual specifications are not detrimental to the development effort.

Kazhamiakin et al. (2006) describes an approach for the verification of Web service compositions defined by a set of WSBPEL processes. The key aspect of such a verification task is the model adopted for representing the communications among the services participating to the composition. Indeed, these communications are asynchronous and buffered in the existing execution frameworks, while most verification approaches adopt a synchronous communication model for efficiency reasons. Berardi et al. (2005a) and Berardi et al. (2005b) also provide a formal framework where services are represented using transition systems. The approach assumes that the services exchange messages according to a predefined communication topology (referred to as the linkage structure), which is expressed as a set of channels. Manolescu et al. (2005) presents a high-level language and methodology for designing and deploying Web applications using Web services. In particular, the authors extend WebML (Ceri et al., 2000) to support message-exchange patterns present in WSDL and use the WebML hypertext model for describing Web interactions and defining specific concepts in the model to represent Web service calls. Consequently, the Web service invocation is captured by a visual language representing the relationships between the invocations and the input/output messages.

In Foster et al. (2004a), Foster et al. (2005a) and Foster et al. (2005b) the authors have described the semantics of WSBPEL by way of mapping each of the WSBPEL constructs to the FSP algebra and building a model of the process behaviour. Then, they have described an elaboration of composition models to support a view of interacting Web service composition processes extending this mapping, and introducing Web service interfaces for use in modelling between services. The ability to model these conversations is important to discovering how Web service interactions fulfil a choreography scenario and if the conversation protocol implement (by way of interaction sequences) is compatible with that of partnered services.

Amongst the assumptions in their semantic mappings of WSBPEL to FSP, they have considered that a process lifecycle begins at the first receive activity specified in the process document. The possibility of multiple start points as parts of a series of receive activities would affect the order in which activities are executed. Related to this is also a limitation on modelling the correlation attribute of activities, which are used to match returning or known clients to interact in long-running processes (in a message to correlation linking). They have not implemented a synchronisation of such events, but they anticipate these mappings would be evolved to consider this in our future work. The mapping does not consider translating event handling, as part of an activity scope. Such a mapping would however, take a form similar to the fault and compensation handling although the semantics behind event handling are much more towards a time based simulation basis.

Compared to our work, in contrast to FSP models, the EC ontology includes an explicit time structure that is independent of any (sequence of) events under consideration. This helps for managing cases where a number of input messages may occur simultaneously (risk of non-deterministic behavior). Second, the EC ontology is close enough to the WSBPEL specification to allow it to be mapped automatically into the logical representation. Thus, we use the same logical foundation for verification at both design time (static analysis) and runtime (dynamic analysis). Third, the semantics of non-functional requirements can be represented in EC, so that verification is once again straightforward. One other advantage of our work is that we provide a mechanism to check the models produced in our approach against trace runs output from WSBPEL process engine instances. This is one way to evaluate how accurate the translation is, although consequently, there is always the question of whether the engine itself has been built to standards. We can therefore only compare expected with actual results based upon an assumption that the implementation engine and execution of a process are on best endeavours.

Except the previous work, a common pattern of the above attempts is that the orchestration and the choreography are not usually expressed within one single environment and therefore the verification techniques must be modified before using them. Instead, in our research work, we aim to provide a uniform framework that is capable of addressing this shortcoming by providing a guide on how to translate the semantics of the BPEL specification to EC and map implementation abstractions which preserve the interaction behaviour between services, yet also disposing of process characteristics which are not required in the analysis. Then, we elaborated these models to analyze the conversations of compositions across choreography scenarios, providing both interface and behavioral compatibility verification processes.

Another common pattern of the above attempts is that they adapt static verification techniques and therefore violations of requirements may not be detectable. This is because Web services that constitute a composition process may not be specified at a level of completeness that would allow the application of static verification, and some of these services may change dynamically at run-time causing unpredictable interactions with other services.

CONCLUSION AND FUTURE WORK

In this paper, we have described a modelling approach of a process defined for a multiple Web service compositions. We detailed an elaboration of models to support a view of interacting Web service compositions extending the mapping from WSBPEL to EC, and including Web service interfaces (WSDL) for use in modelling between services. To model conversations in the context of Web service compositions we perform an analysis process on all the implementation processes and use an algorithm as part of this analysis to semantically check and link partner process interactions. The algorithm uses as input partner service interfaces (in the form of a WSDL document) and the implementation of models created in the initial implementation synthesis. The output of the composition modelling is a list of composition mapping requirements and information on non-interaction activities encountered and unmatched partner process references. The ability to model these conversations is important to discovering how Web service interactions fulfill a choreography scenario and if the conversation protocol implement is compatible with that of partnered services. In essence, our view of modelling has moved from analyzing a local process or in other word a single composition, with that of other services and their interactions. We have also extended the BPEL2EC tool to support multiple process conversations as an implementation of our approach. The extension provides a representation that enables us to perform analysis of service interaction for behaviour properties. The approach to verifying and validating these properties has been also discussed.

The future opportunities from undertaking this work are as follows. The types of property used in verification are open to a much broader range than suggested in this work. Within this future work, we wish to continue describing behaviour by elaborating on the wider choreography aspects of partnered service compositions. This includes considering fault, compensation and transactional, security, privacy, and integrity within and between distributed processes. As part of this we are working on privacy and confidentiality policies in Web services compositions models.

REFERENCES

Andrews, T., Curbera, F., Dholakia, H., Goland, Y., Klein, J., & Leymann, F. (2003). *Business Process Execution Language for Web Services, Version 1.1. Standards proposal by BEA Systems.* International Business Machines Corporation, and Microsoft Corporation.

Ankolekar, A., Burstein, M., et al. (2002). DAML-S: Web Service Description for the Semantic Web. In *Proceedings of the 1st International Semantic Web Conference (ISWC), Sardinia, Italy.*

Arkin, A., Askary, S., Bloch, B., & Curbera, F. (2004, December). *Web services business process execution language version 2.0* (Tech. Rep. OASIS).

Barros, A., Dumas, M., & Oaks, P. (2005, March). *Critical overview of the Web services choreography description language (ws-cdl).* Retrieved from http://www.bptrends.com

Berardi, D., Calvanese, D., Giacomo, G. D., Hull, R., Lenzerini, M., & Mecella, M. (2005a). Modeling data processes for service specifications in colombo. In M. Missiko & A. D. Nicola (Eds.), *Proceedings of EMOI-INTEROP, volume 160 of CEUR Workshop.* Retrieved from CEUR-WS.org

Berardi, D., Calvanese, D., Giacomo, G. D., Hull, R., & Mecella, M. (2005b). Automatic composition of Web services in colombo. In A. Cal, D. Calvanese, E. Franconi, M. Lenzerini, & L. Tanca (Eds.), *Proceedings of SEBD* (pp. 815).

Brogi, A., Canal, C., Pimentel, E., & Vallecillo, A. (2004). Formalizing Web service choreographies. *Electronic Notes in Theoretical Computer Science, 105,* 73–94. doi:10.1016/j.entcs.2004.05.007

Ceri, S., Fraternali, P., & Bongio, A. (2000). Web modeling language (Webml): a modeling language for designing Web sites. *Computer Networks, 33*(1-6), 137-157.

Duan, Z., Bernstein, A., et al. (2004). Semantics Based Verification and Synthesis of WSBPEL Abstract Processes. In *Proceedings of the 3rd IEEE International Conference on Web Services,* San Diego, CA.

Fahland, D., & Reisig, W. (2005, March). ASM-based semantics for BPEL: The negative control flow. In D. Beauquier, E. B¨orger, & A. Slissenko (Eds.), *Proceedings of the 12th International Workshop on Abstract State Machines,* Paris (pp. 131-151).

Ferrara, A. (2004). Web services: A process algebra approach. In *Proceedings of the 2nd international conference on Service oriented computing* (pp. 242-251). New York: ACM Press.

Fisteus, J., Fernandez, L., & Kloos, C. (2004, August). Formal verification of WSBPEL business collaborations. In K. Bauknecht, M. Bichler, & B. Proll (Eds.), *Proceedings of the 5th International Conference on Electronic Commerce and Web Technologies (EC-Web '04),* Zaragoza, Spain (LNCS 3182, pp. 7994). Berlin: Springer Verlag.

Foster, H., Sebastian, U., Jeff, M., & Jeff, K. (2003). Model-based Verification of Web Service Compositions. In *Proceedings of the 18th IEEE International Conference on Automated Software Engineering (ASE'03)* (p. 152).

Foster, H., Uchitel, S., et al. (2004a). Compatibility for Web Service Choreography. In *Proceedings of the 3rd IEEE International Conference on Web Services (ICWS),* San Diego, CA. Washington, DC: IEEE.

Foster, H., Uchitel, S., et al. (2005a). Tool Support for Model-Based Engineering of Web Service Compositions. In *Proceedings of the 3rd IEEE International Conference on Web Services (ICWS2005),* Orlando, FL. Washington, DC: IEEE.

Foster, H., Uchitel, S., et al. (2005b). Using a Rigorous Approach for Engineering Web Service Compositions: A Case Study. In *Proceedings of the 2nd IEEE International Conference on Services Computing (SCC2005)*, Orlando, FL. Washington, DC: IEEE.

Fu, X. (2004). Formal Specification and Verification of Asynchronously Communicating Web Services. Unpublished doctoral thesis, University of California, Santa Barbara, CA.

Fu, X., Bultan, T., & Su, J. (2004). Analysis of interacting bpel Web services. In *Proceedings of the 13th international conference on World Wide Web (WWW '04)* (pp. 621-630). New York: ACM Press.

Kazhamiakin, R., Pistore, M., & Santuari, L. (2006). Analysis of communication models in Web service compositions. In *Proceedings of the 15th international conference on World Wide Web (WWW '06)* (pp. 267-276). New York: ACM.

Kowalski, R., & Sergot, M. J. (1986). A logic-based calculus of events. *New generation. Computing, 4*(1), 67–95.

Magee, J., & Kramer, J. (1999). *Concurrency: state models & Java programs*. New York: John Wiley & Sons, Inc.

Manolescu, I., Brambilla, M., Ceri, S., Comai, S., & Fraternali, P. (2005). Model-driven design and deployment of service-enabled Web applications. *ACM Transactions on Internet Technology, 5*(3), 439–479. doi:10.1145/1084772.1084773

Martens, A. (2005). Analyzing Web Service Based Business Processes. In M. Cerioli (Ed.), *Proceedings of the 8th International Conference on Fundamental Approaches to Software Engineering (FASE 2005)* (LNCS 3442, pp. 19-33). Berlin: Springer Verlag.

Ouyang, C., Aalst, W., Breutel, S., Dumas, M., & Verbeek, H. (2005). *Formal Semantics and Analysis of Control Flow in WS-BPEL* (BPM Center Report BPM-05-15). Retrieved from BPMcenter.org

Pistore, M., Roveri, M., & Busetta, P. (2004). Requirements-driven verification of Web services. *Electronic Notes in Theoretical Computer Science, 105*, 95–108. doi:10.1016/j.entcs.2004.05.005

Rouached, M., Gaaloul, G., van der Aalst, W., Bhiri, S., & Godart, C. (2006, November). Web service mining and verification of properties: An approach based on event calculus. In *Proceedings 14th International Conference on Cooperative Information Systems (CoopIS 2006)*.

Rouached, M., & Godart, C. (2007, July 9-13). Requirements-driven verification of wsbpel processes. In *Proceedings of the IEEE International Conference on Web Services (ICWS'07)*, Salt Lake City, Utah.

Seeley, R. (2003). *Berners-Lee: Integrate Web services and Semantic Web*. Retrieved from http://www.adtmag.com/article.asp?id=7662

Shanahan, M. P. (1999). The Event Calculus Explained. In *Artificial Intelligence Today* (LNCS 1600, pp. 409-430). New York: Springer Verlag.

Spanoudakis, G., & Mahbub, K. (2006). Non Intrusive Monitoring of Service Based Systems. *International Journal of Cooperative Information Systems, 15*(3), 325–358. doi:10.1142/S0218843006001384

Stahl, C. (2004). *Transformation von WSBPEL in Petrinetze*. Unpublished master's thesis, Humboldt University, Berlin.

Stratulat, S. (2001). A general framework to build contextual cover set induction provers. *Journal of Symbolic Computation, 32*(4), 403–445. doi:10.1006/jsco.2000.0469

Van Breugel, F., & Koshkina, M. (2006). *Models and verification of bpel*. Retrieved from http://www.cse.yorku.ca/ franck/research/drafts/tutorial.pdf

Woodman, S., Palmer, D., et al. (2004). Notations for the Specification and Verification of Composite Web Services. In *Proceedings of the 8th IEEE International Enterprise Distributed Object Computing (EDOC) Conference*, Monterey, CA.

Yang, Y., Tan, Q., & Xiao, Y. (2005). Verifying Web services composition based on hierarchical colored petri nets. In *Proceedings of the first international workshop on Interoperability of heterogeneous information systems (IHIS '05)* (pp. 47-54). New York: ACM Press.

ENDNOTES

[1] http://httpd.apache.org/docs/logs.html
[2] http://www.w3.org/TR/WD-logfile.html
[3] http://alphaworks.ibm.com/tech/bpws4j
[4] http://logging.apache.org/log4j
[5] $x + z > y = \text{false} \wedge z + x < y = \text{false} \Rightarrow x + z = y$.
[6] $\neg (\forall s.Spec(s) \Rightarrow \neg R(s))$ where *Spec(s)* is the specification of *s* and *R(s)* is the requirement about *s*.

This work was previously published in the International Journal of Web Services Research, Volume 7, Issue 2, edited by Liang-Jie (LJ) Zhang, pp. 87-110, copyright 2010 by IGI Publishing (an imprint of IGI Global).

Chapter 2
A Dependable Infrastructure for Cooperative Web Services Coordination

Eduardo Adilio Pelinson Alchieri
Federal University of Santa Catarina, Brazil

Alysson Neves Bessani
University of Lisbon, Portugal

Joni da Silva Fraga
Federal University of Santa Catarina, Brazil

ABSTRACT

A current trend in the web services community is to define coordination mechanisms to execute collaborative tasks involving multiple organizations. Following this tendency, in this paper the authors present a dependable (i.e., intrusion-tolerant) infrastructure for cooperative web services coordination that is based on the tuple space coordination model. This infrastructure provides decoupled communication and implements several security mechanisms that allow dependable coordination even in presence of malicious components. This work also investigates the costs related to the use of this infrastructure and possible web service applications that can benefit from it.

INTRODUCTION

The Web Services technology, an instantiation of the service oriented computing paradigm (Bichier & Lin, 2006), is becoming a *de facto* standard for the development of distributed systems on the Internet. The attractiveness of web services are its interoperability and simplicity, based on technolo-

gies widely used in the web, like HTTP and XML. Its attributes have been the motivation for many industrial and academic efforts for developing concepts and models for distributed applications based on the service-oriented paradigm.

The service oriented computing - and more specifically Web Services - is a natural evolution of classical concepts such as RPC and technologies like CORBA (Object Management Group, 2002). In the same way of these, web services provided by

DOI: 10.4018/978-1-4666-1942-5.ch002

an organization must be described in an interface that can be understood and invoked by other parts of a distributed system. The main standards for web services, all based on XML, are: SOAP (*Simple Object Access Protocol*) - protocol for exchange messages among clients and services, which can operate over several communication protocols; the WSDL (*Web Service Description Language*) - language used to describe web services; and the UDDI (*Universal Description, Discovery and Integration*) - the repository where the web services are registered in order to be discovered by clients.

The main goal of web services is the interoperability. Thus, many efforts have appeared to define adequate forms of services composition in order to execute complex tasks. These compositions aim the cooperation in the execution of tasks involving multiple organizations (Bichier & Lin, 2006; Peltz, 2003). Specifications like *WS-Orchestration* (Alves, 2006) and *WS-Choreography* (Burdett & Kavantzas, 2004) address exactly this problem, specifying mechanisms for definition and execution of tasks that involve several web services.

Current approaches, as the cited above, aim the web services integration through the specification of message flows among the services (control-driven coordination (Papadopolous & Arbab, 1998)). Another approach, which complements the first one, is the web services coordination through the use of a shared data repository (data-driven coordination (Papadopolous & Arbab, 1998)). In this approach, the cooperating services communication is done through a shared data repository, which can be used as data storage or as a coordination mediator, providing decoupled communication. *Tuple spaces* (Gelernter, 1985) are a popular data-driven coordination model.

In the tuple space model, processes interact through a shared memory abstraction, the tuple space, where generic data structures called tuples are stored and retrieved. The basic operations supported by the tuple space are insertion, reading and removal of tuples. The main attractiveness of this model is its support for communication that is decoupled both in time (communicating processes do not need to be active at the same time) and space (communicating processes do not need to know each others locations or addresses) (Cabri et al., 2000).

There has been some research about the integration of web services using the tuple space model (Bright & Quirchmayr, 2004; Lucchi & Zavattaro, 2004; Maamar et al., 2005; Bellur & Bondre, 2006). The main advantage of this approach is the decoupling among the cooperating services: not even the services interfaces needs to be completely known. This work follows in the same line and proposes a cooperation infrastructure for web services that provides the inherent benefits of the tuple spaces model but that is also dependable.

The infrastructure proposed in this paper, called **WS-DependableSpace** (WSDS), extends previous works of the authors on tuple space dependability (Bessani et al., 2008; Bessani et al., 2009), incorporating new components that provide the integration of a dependable tuple space on the web services world. The WSDS architecture relies on stateless gateways that execute operations on a dependable tuple space, forwarding client requests from web service clients to it and vice-versa. Several mechanisms have been introduced in this architecture in order to tolerate accidental faults (like crashes and software bugs) as well as malicious attempts to disable the operation of system components (like attacks and intrusions) (Verissimo et al., 2003). Moreover, WSDS maintains all the dependability properties of a dependable tuple space (Bessani et al., 2008) *without further extensions to the web services core specifications.*

Why use WSDS to Coordinate Web Services?

Since or objective with WSDS is to provide a coordination infrastructure for web services, the attentive reader can ask: Why someone would use a service like WSDS to coordinate web services, instead of using some tool that implements web services coordination specifications? Here we list several reasons to use a service like WSDS to coordinate web services.

In usual web services coordination, the communication is often coupled in at least two levels: *(1)* cooperative services must be active and running at the same time in order to complete some interaction; and *(2)* the interactions are based on the services interfaces, if any interface change it is necessary reprogram these iterations.

These limitations can be overcome through the use of a coordination service based on tuple spaces (WSDS), since in this model any service (client of some other service) is allowed to send a request and terminate. After some time, this service can be reactivated to get the response of its request, which was produced while such service was disabled.

Other advantage of WSDS is related with services interfaces evolution. In this model, all interactions are mediated by a mediator (the tuple space - WSDS). Thus, services (and also clients of these services) do not need know their interfaces. This means that if some service interface changes it is not necessary to reprogram any interaction involving the service that had its interface modified. For example, services interfaces can change due to the evolution of these services, where new operations will become available to clients and other services.

Other point to highlight is that this type of coordination can be used as a mechanism for synchronization among multiple web services (e.g., to concurrency control). WSDS implements a coordination infrastructure that provides all of the advantages discussed here in a dependable way.

Summary of the Contributions

The main contributions of this paper can be summarized as follows:

1. The design and implementation of the WSDS infrastructure, which is the first dependable web services data-centered coordination service;
2. The evaluation of the cost to access this type of infrastructure through an analysis of the operations latency and its causes;
3. An analysis of some real applications that can be built over WSDS;
4. A study about WSDS relationship with the main standards for cooperating web services.

Paper Organization

This paper is organized as follows. First, the basic concepts about tuple spaces are discussed and a dependable tuple space, the DepSpace, is briefly reviewed. The WSDS, our proposal for a dependable infrastructure for coordinate web services, is then presented. An analysis, both analytical and experimental, about WSDS performance is then discussed. Some applications built over WSDS are then described. Interesting relations between the architecture proposed in this paper and some web services specifications are then presented. Finally, related work and conclusions are given.

TUPLE SPACES

A *tuple space* (Gelernter, 1985) can be seen as a shared memory object that provides operations for storing and retrieving ordered data sets called *tuples*. A tuple t in which all fields have a defined value is called an *entry*. A tuple with one or more undefined fields is called a *template* (denoted by t'). An undefined field is represented by a *wildcard* ('*'). Templates are used to allow content-addressable access to tuples in the tuple space. An entry t and a template t' *match* if they have the same number of fields and all defined field values of t' are equal to the corresponding field values of t. For example, template ⟨*1, 2, ** ⟩ matches any tuple with three fields in which *1* and *2* are the values of the first and second fields, respectively. A tuple *t* can be inserted in the tuple space using the *out(t)* operation. The operation *rd(t')* is used to read tuples from the space, and returns any tuple of the space that *matches* the template *t'*. A tuple can be read *and* removed from the space using the *in(t')* operation. The *in* and *rd* operations are blocking. Non-blocking versions, *inp* and *rdp*, are also usually provided (Gelernter, 1985).

To increase the synchronization power of the tuple space, we consider also the *cas(t',t)* operation (conditional atomic swap) (Segall, 1995), that works like an indivisible execution of the code: **if** ¬ *rdp(t')* **then** *out(t)* (*t'* is a template and *t* an entry). The *cas* operation is important mainly because a tuple space that supports it is capable of solving the consensus problem (Segall, 1995; Bessani et al., 2009), which is a building block for solving many important distributed synchronization problems like atomic commit, total order multicast and leader election.

Table 1 presents a summary of the tuple space operations supported by WSDS.

DEPSPACE: A DEPENDABLE TUPLE SPACE

A tuple space is dependable if it satisfies the *dependability attributes* (Avizienis et al., 2004). The relevant attributes in this case are:

- **Reliability:** operations on the tuple space have to behave according to their specification;
- **Availability:** the tuple space has to be ready to execute the requested operations;
- **Integrity:** no improper alteration of the tuple space can occurs;
- **Confidentiality:** the content of tuple fields can not be disclosed to unauthorized parties.

DepSpace (Bessani et al., 2008) is an implementation of a dependable tuple space that satisfies these properties using a combination of some mechanisms, which are described below. The DepSpace architecture consists in a series of integrated layers that enforce each one of the dependability attributes listed above. Figure 1 presents the DepSpace architecture with all its layers.

On the top of the client-side stack is the proxy layer, which provides access to the replicated tuple space, while on the top of the server-side stack is the tuple space implementation (a local tuple space). The communication follows a scheme similar to remote procedure calls. The application interacts with the system by calling functions with the usual signatures of tuple spaces operations: *out(t), rd(t'),* ... These functions are called on the proxy. The layer below handles tuple level access control. After, there is a layer that takes care of confidentiality and then one that handles replication. The server-side is similar, except that there

Table 1. Operations supported by WSDS

Operation	Description
out(t)	Inserts the tuple *t* in the space.
rdp(t')	Reads a tuple that matches *t'* from the space (returning *true*). Returns *false* if no tuple is found.
inp(t')	Reads and removes a tuple that matches *t'* from the space (returning *true*). Returns *false* if no tuple is found.
rd(t')	Reads a tuple that matches *t'* from the space. Stays blocked until some matching tuple is found.
in(t')	Reads and removes a tuple that matches *t'* from the space. Stays blocked until some matching tuple is found.
cas(t',t)	If there is no tuple that matches *t'* on the space, inserts *t* and returns *true*. Otherwise returns *false*.

Figure 1. DepSpace architecture

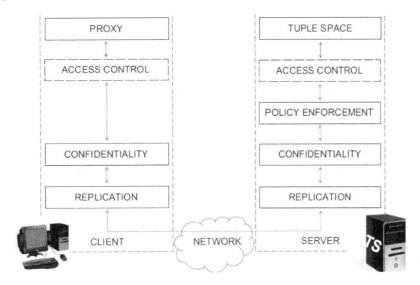

is a new layer to check the access policy for each operation requested.

Other important feature of DepSpace is its support for multiple logical tuple spaces: the system has administrative interfaces that allow (logical) tuple space creation and destruction. Two different logical tuple spaces have no relationship between themselves. We must remark that not all layers must be used in every logical tuple space configuration (only the replication layer is essential). The idea is that layers are added or removed according to the quality of service desired for the logical tuple space.

Intrusion-Tolerant Replication

The most basic technique used in DepSpace is *replication*, i.e., the tuple space is maintained by a set of n servers in such a way that failure of up to f of them does not impair the reliability, availability and integrity of the system. The idea is that if some servers fail, the tuple space is still ready (availability) and operations work correctly (reliability and integrity) because correct replicas manage to overcome the misbehavior of the faulty ones. A simple approach for replication

is *state machine replication* (SMR) (Schneider, 1990). SMR guarantees *linearizability* (Herlihy and Wing 1990), which is a strong form of consistency in which all replicas appear to take the same sequence of states. SMR delivery properties are guaranteed by the Byzantine Paxos protocol (Castro & Liskov, 2002).

Cryptography

DepSpace uses cryptographic processing to ensure confidentiality of tuples. The enforcement of confidentiality in a replicated tuple space is not trivial, since we can not trust a single server that can be compromised. Then, replication is often seen not as a helper but as an impediment for confidentiality. The reason is easy to understand: if secret information is stored not in one but in several servers, it probably becomes easier for an attacker to get it, not harder.

The solution for confidentiality adopted in DepSpace relies on a set of servers, where no server individually can have access to the tuples (Bessani et al., 2008). The basic tool it uses to implement confidentiality is a special kind of *secret sharing scheme* (Shamir, 1979).

To insert a confidential tuple in the space, the client encrypts the tuple with some secret s that it generates randomly. The client generates different secrets for each tuple that it inserts in the space. After this, client uses the secret sharing scheme to generate shares of s. Each server receives the encrypted tuple and one share of the secret s used to encrypt it. It is necessary a set of shares to obtain the secret s (to reconstruct s), the size of this set can be configured in the scheme (Shamir, 1979), usually this size is configured to $f+1$ in order to tolerate up to f failures of servers, i.e., it is necessary at least one correct server to disclosure the secret. Thus, a single server is not able to obtain s and decrypt the tuple.

Since DepSpace clients use total order multicast to insert tuples on the system, it is impossible to send different versions of a request to each server, containing only its secret share. Then, the client must encrypt each share with a secret key exchanged with the server that will hold this share. In this way, the request contains all encrypted shares, but each server is able to obtain only its share.

The confidentiality scheme has also to handle the problem of matching encrypted tuples with templates. When a client inserts a tuple in the space, it chooses one of three types of protection for each tuple field: *Public* - the field is not encrypted so it can be compared arbitrarily but its content may be disclosed if a server is faulty; *Comparable* - the field is encrypted but its cryptographic *hash* obtained with a *collision-resistant hash function* is also stored and can be compared; *Private* - the field is encrypted and no hash is stored so no comparisons are possible.

To access some tuple (read or remove operations), the client must wait for a set of responses from the servers. Each response contains the encrypted tuple and the share hold by the server that is replying (to avoid eavesdropping of responses, the share must be encrypted with the secret key exchanged by client and each server). Then, the

client obtains the secret by combining a set of shares and decrypts the tuple. Further discussion about this mechanism, including all confidentiality protocols, is presented in (Bessani et al., 2008).

Access Control

This mechanism allows only authorized clients to perform operations in the tuple space. Access control is fundamental to preserve integrity and confidentiality properties of a dependable tuple space. DepSpace provides two types of access control:

- **Credential-based:** For each tuple inserted in DepSpace, it is possible to define the credentials required for having access to this tuple (i.e., read or remove). These credentials are provided by the process that inserts the tuple in the space. There is also another level of access control: it is possible to define what are the credentials required to insert tuples in the space.
- **Fine-grained security policies:** DepSpace supports the enforcement of fine-grained security policies for access control (Bessani et al., 2009). These kind of policies takes into account three types of parameters to decide if an operation can be executed or not: the invoker *id*; the operation and its arguments; and the tuples currently in the space. An example is the policy: *"an operation out(⟨CLIENT,id,x⟩) can only be executed if there is no tuple on the space that matches (⟨CLIENT,id,*⟩)"*. This policy does not allow the insertion of two tuples representing clients, with the same value on the second field (client identifier).

Credentials required for tuple insertion and security policies are always defined during the tuple space creation.

WS-DEPENDABLESPACE

This section describes the **WS-DependableSpace** (**WSDS**) infrastructure. First, our system model is presented. Then, the WSDS architecture and some details of the gateway operation are discussed. How our architecture ensures the security properties of the system despite the possibility of having malicious components is then described. Finally, some system implementation details are given.

System Model

The processes of the system are divided in three sets: n DepSpace servers $U = \{s_1,...,s_n\}$, g access gateways $G = \{g_1,...,g_g\}$ and an unknown set of clients $\Pi = \{c_1,c_2,...\}$. The gateways are the only processes of the system that export WSDL interfaces, i.e., they are web services. The communication among clients and gateways is done using SOAP messages, and among gateways and servers (and among servers) using authenticated reliable point-to-point channels, that can be implemented using standard technologies such as SSL/TLS.

We assume an eventually synchronous system model (Dwork et al., 1988): in all executions of the system, there is a bound Δ and an instant *GST* (Global Stabilization Time), so that every message sent by a correct process to another correct process at instant $u > GST$ is received before u + Δ. Δ and *GST* are unknown. The intuition behind this model is that the system can work asynchronously (respecting no delay bounds) most of the time but there are stable periods in which the communication delay is bounded. Notice that this model reflects the behavior of the Internet: the communication latency is stable most of the time; however a limit for this value does not exist. We also assume that all local computations require negligible time. This assumption is based on the fact that, even if the time required for some local operations is considerable, these computations are not susceptible to the external interferences,

and therefore its asynchronous behavior is not observed in practice.

System processes are subject to Byzantine failures (Lamport et al., 1982), i.e., they can deviate arbitrarily from the algorithm they are specified to execute and work in collusion to corrupt the system behavior. Processes that do not follow their algorithm are said to be faulty. A process that is not faulty is said to be correct. We assume fault independence for servers, i.e., the probability of a server being faulty is independent of another server being faulty. This assumption can be substantiated in practice through the use of diversity (Obelheiro et al., 2006). WSDS works correctly while a bound of up $f_n \leq (n+1)/3$ DepSpace servers (the optimal resilience for this type of replication (Castro & Liskov 2002)), $f_g \leq g - 1$ *gateways* (at least one correct) and an arbitrary number of client fails. In the same way as in DepSpace, the secret sharing scheme used for confidentiality (Schoenmakers, 1999) requires at least $f_n + 1$ out of n shares of a secret to recover its secret.

Our last assumption is that each process handles a pair of keys (called public and private keys) from an asymmetric cryptosystem, used for generation and verification of digital signatures. Private keys are known only by each owner, however all processes know all public keys (through certificates).

WSDS Architecture

Figure 2 presents the WSDS architecture. The idea in this architecture is to have gateways connecting web service clients and the DepSpace servers. To do this, the gateways publish their WSDL interface in an UDDI repository. Thus, clients are able to access them.

The main component introduced in this architecture is the *gateway* web service that works as a bridge among clients (of the coordination service) and the dependable tuple space, the DepSpace. The gateway receives SOAP messages sent by clients and transforms them in DepSpace requests.

Figure 2. WSDS architecture

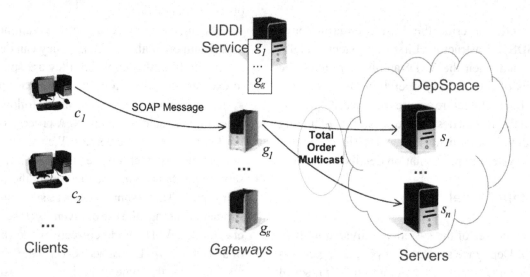

The system works as follows: first of all, each gateway registers itself in one UDDI service. To improve the system availability, gateways can be registered in more than one UDDI service. Before accessing the tuple space, a client must find one or more gateway address on a UDDI service. Thereafter, the client sends its requests to one of the gateways, which, in turn, forwards it to the DepSpace using a total order multicast protocol. DepSpace servers process the request and send the response to the gateway, which collects $n - f_n$ responses from different servers and forward this set of responses to the client. The client determines the response of its request by verifying which response was replied by at least $f_n + 1$ servers (at least one correct server).

The gateway does not execute any processing on the content of requests or responses, only the transformations between the two "worlds" (SOAP and DepSpace), previously described. Moreover, this service is stateless, i.e., it does not have state and thus there is no need of any synchronization among the g gateways of the system.

Gateway Operation

This section details the operation of the WSDS gateways, which provides the WSDS service to web service clients and act as clients of DepSpace.

Gateway State Machine

To better understand, Figure 3 presents the automaton that represents the processing at the gateway to execute some request. First, the gateway is idle and waiting some request (state 1). When some client sends a request to the gateway (transition a), it goes into state 2 where it has received the client request. Then, the gateway forwards the request to DepSpace servers (transition b) and goes to wait for replies (state 3). At this point, each correct DepSpace server executes the request and sends the reply to the gateway (transition c) that moves to state 4. In this stage, the gateway computes the reply received and takes one of two actions:

- If it has received enough replies (i.e., $n - f_n$): then it sends the collected replies to the client (transition e) and becomes idle again (goes to state 1).

Figure 3. Request execution flow at the gateway

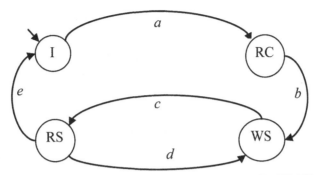

States	Transitions
I: idle.	*a*: Client sends a request to the gateway.
RC: received client.	*b*: Gateway forwards the request to DepSpace servers.
WS: waiting server.	*c:* Some DepSpace server sends a reply to the gateway.
RS: received server.	*d*: Gateway come back to wait more replies.
	e: Gateway sends collected replies to the client.

- If more replies are necessary: then it comes back to state 3 (transition *d*) and waits for more replies before send them to the client.

This automaton represents the processing flow to execute some request. If the gateway receives a new request while it is processing some other request, it starts a new flow (in parallel) to attend this new request. All executions flows are independent.

Gateway to Client and Client to Gateway Messages

This section presents the structure of requests that are sent by clients to the gateways, as well as responses for these requests, that clients receive from gateways. The structures presented here correspond to operations executed in a logical tuple space where all layers are turned on. However, these messages present some variations depending of the layers used (e.g., if confidentiality layer is not active on DepSpace, no tuples are encrypted and no shares are necessary).

Figure 4 presents the structure of a request message that clients send to gateways. The structure is divided into two parts: context (CONTEXT) and contents (CONTENTS). The context contains information about the operation context, which comprises: *(1)* the request unique identifier (REQ_ID) that is formed by the concatenation of the client identifier (CLIENT_ID) and a timestamp (TIMESTAMP) that works like an incremental counter; *(2)* the operation identifier (OP_ID) that informs if the operation is an *out, rd, rdp, in, inp* or *cas*; *(3)* the logical tuple space name to be accessed (TS_NAME); and *(4)* the client signature (SIGNATURE) that ensures the authenticity of this request.

The contents side of requests contains the tuple (TUPLE) and/or template (TEMPLATE). Notice that, in write operations (*out*) this structure contains only the tuple, while that in read/remove operations (*rd, rdp, in, inp*) only the template is part of the message. However, in conditional atomic swap operations (*cas*) both, tuple and template are present in the message structure.

The tuple contains the following data: *(1)* credentials required to read (C_RD) ant to remove (C_IN) it from the space (to tuple access control); *(2)* tuple fields' data (FIELDS) that is composed by the encrypted fields (ENCRYPTED_FIELDS) and

Figure 4. Client to gateway request structure

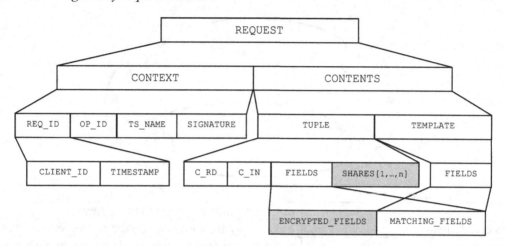

by the matching fields (MATCHING_FIELDS) that are constructed according with the protection chosen for each field and are used to compare tuples and templates; and *(3)* the set of *n* shares (SHARES[*1,...,n*]) of the secret used by the client to encrypt the fields of the tuple, each share is encrypted with the secret key exchanged by client and the server that will hold this share. The template contains only the fields used to compare it with tuples (MATCHING_FIELDS).

The confidential contents of requests are presented in gray color in Figure 4. Thus, as tuple fields are encrypted with some secret and also shares of this secret are encrypted, no gateway is able to access confidential contents of requests.

Figure 5 presents the structure of a response message that clients receive from some gateway. As already mentioned, this message contains a set of $n - f_n$ responses of DepSpace servers. Each response is formed by: *(1)* the server identifier (SERVER_ID); *(2)* the request identifier (REQ_ID) that is the concatenation of the client identifier (CLIENT_ID) and a timestamp (TIMESTAMP), which works like an incremental counter; *(3)* the server signature (SIGNATURE) that ensures the authenticity of this response; and *(4)* the tuple read/removed from the space in read/remove operations (*rd, rdp, in, inp*), in write operations (*out*) this

tuple contains only one special field indicating if the operation has successfully completed or not.

The tuple contains the following data: *(1)* tuple fields' data (FIELDS) that is composed by the encrypted fields (ENCRYPTED_FIELDS) and by the matching fields (MATCHING_FIELDS) that are constructed according whit the protection chosen for each field and are used to compare tuples and templates; and *(2)* the share (SHARES(i)) of the secret used by the client to encrypt the fields of the tuple that is held by this server, the share is encrypted with the secret key exchanged by this server and the client that is executing the operation.

As done with requests, the confidential contents of responses are presented in gray color in Figure 5. Thus, as tuple fields are encrypted with some secret and also the share of this secret held by the server that is replying are encrypted, no gateway is able to access confidential contents of responses.

Dealing with Faulty Gateways

Although the apparent simplicity of the architecture depicted in Figure 2, the use of access gateways to make DepSpace accessible from the web services world makes the coordination system susceptible to several security problems.

Figure 5. Gateway to client response structure

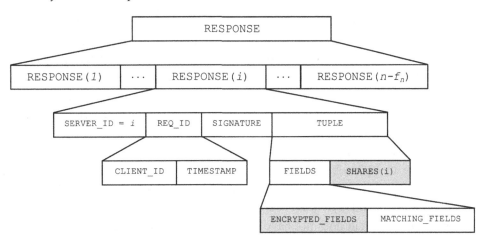

These problems, together with the solutions used in WSDS, are described in this section.

Authenticity and Integrity of Messages

The first problem to be solved in WSDS is that a faulty gateway can request the execution of invalid requests that were not issued by a valid client. Moreover, it would be able to corrupt requests, modifying some of their data (ex., parameters or operation types). In the same way, it would be able to forge or modify replies of servers. The main point here is to guarantee that only non-corrupted requests issued by clients and valid responses produced by DepSpace servers are processed, avoiding all kinds of *man in the middle* behaviors that a faulty gateway can have.

Moreover, the client needs to send its credentials together with the requests, then the servers will be able to verify the client access permission, i.e., if the client can access the space and/or the tuple. These credentials are sent to the servers through a digital certificate, which is also used to prove the request authenticity (i.e., the client's digital signature). Thus, each client signs its requests before sending them. Servers only execute an operation if the signature is valid, in accordance with the corresponding certificate.

To prove the authenticity of the replies, the same approach is used. Each reply must be signed by a server with its private key. Thus, clients will be able to verify the authenticity of the replies, using the public keys of the servers, also contained in certificates (sent together with the replies). These signatures ensure the authenticity and integrity of the end-to-end communications between WSDS clients and DepSpace servers, i.e., messages can not be modified by faulty gateways without being detected by DepSpace servers or WSDS clients. The certificates sent together with requests and responses are verified using some public key infrastructures such as X.509.

Incomplete Execution of Requests

Notice that nothing guarantees that a client will obtain the response of its request if it is accessing a faulty gateway. In fact, if the gateway accessed does not send the responses to the client, it will stay blocked indefinitely (waiting for the responses). Also, in the execution of removal operations, a malicious gateway can remove tuples from DepSpace and not send them to the client. Thus, these tuples will "disappear" from the space without being returned by a requesting client.

To solve this problem, a timer is associated with each request sent by the client. If a timeout occurs before the response is obtained, the client sends the request to other f_g gateways (one at time), ensuring that eventually it has accessed at least one correct gateway. In this way, the execution of the request ends when the client receives the first set of valid responses (from some gateway) and determines the response of the request. This mechanism is activated whenever a client can not determine a response, which is caused either by timeout occurrence or by problems in the responses signatures.

In blocking operations (*in* and *rd*) it is not possible to determine why the client does not have received the replies, i.e., if the gateway accessed is faulty or if there is no tuple in the space that matches the template. Thus, it is not possible to use timeouts in these operations. For solving this problem, the client needs to send these requests to f_g + *1* different gateways and determine the response as previously described (when a timeout occurs).

Duplicated Requests

If some gateway is correct but very slow, the mechanism introduced in previous section can result in the same request being sent to more than one gateway. Consequently, it is possible that this request is sent more than once to the DepSpace servers. Moreover, a malicious gateway can request the execution of an operation already executed by the DepSpace (*replay attacks*). In these cases, duplicated requests need to be discarded in order to maintain the consistency of the tuple space. To make this in a safe way, two mechanisms were introduced in WSDS:

1. Each request has a unique identifier, composed by the client identity plus a sequence number. This number is inspected by DepSpace servers before the request execution, to verify if the request was already executed;
2. Each server has a buffer that stores replies to the previous request of each client. Thus,

for each client, a request is executed by a server only if its sequence number is one unit greater than the last request executed (the reply is stored in the buffer). If the request has the same identification of the last executed, only the previously stored reply is sent to the gateway. In all other cases, the request is discarded.

Using these two mechanisms, a client can not send a request without completing the previous one. This limitation can be relaxed for at most k requests if the servers store the last k replies to each client. Besides preventing that a request is executed more than once, this strategy also solves the tuple disappearance problem (caused by incomplete execution of requests). In fact, when the client requests the re-execution of an operation through another gateway, the same reply (with the same tuple) is in the servers buffers ready to be sent to the client.

Ensuring Confidentiality

Confidentiality is an important property of dependable systems. To ensure confidentiality, we must avoid that some components of the system (especially gateways and unauthorized clients) have access to the shares of the secrets used to encrypt tuples.

To insert a tuple in the space, client sends the tuple encrypted with a secret that is used to obtain a set of shares. The generated shares are also sent encrypted with secret keys exchanged by client and each server. In this way, each server will have the encrypted tuple and its share of the key needed to decrypt it. The gateways, by the other hand, can have access to the encrypted tuple and all encrypted shares, but they can not decrypt shares (and combine them in order to get the secret and decrypt also the tuple) without help from each server that will hold each share. Recall that at least f_n + *1* shares are required to rebuild the secret. Then, gateways only can access confidential tuples with help from at least one correct DepSpace server. Consequently, gateways will not be able to access any confidential tuple.

In read operations each server replies with both, the encrypted tuple and the share of the secret used to encrypt it. The share must be encrypted with the secret key established between the client and the server that is replying. Then, only the client is able to: *(1)* access the shares, *(2)* combine a set of them to get the secret, and *(3)* decrypt the tuple with this secret.

Implementation

The prototype was developed in Java and uses the DepSpace implementation described in (Alchieri et al., 2008). Signatures were implemented by the algorithms *SHA-1* and *RSA*, for hashes and asymmetric cryptography, respectively. Reliable authenticated point-to-point channels were implemented by TCP sockets and session keys based on *HmacSHA-1* algorithm. All cryptographic primitives were provided by the default provider of JCE (Java Cryptography Extensions) - version 1.5. The only exception was the secret sharing scheme used for confidentiality, which we implemented following the specification in (Schoenmakers, 1999), using algebraic groups of 192 bits (more than the 160 bits recommended). This implementation makes extensive use of the *BigInteger* class, provided by the Java API, which provides several utility methods for implementing cryptography.

The gateways were implemented using *Axis 1.3* (http://ws.apache.org/axis/), an open-source SOAP protocol implementation that provides a set of APIs for the development of client applications and web servers, and deployed on *Tomcat 5.5.20* J2EE container (http://tomcat.apache.org/) that is a robust and open-source application server.

All additional mechanisms required in our architecture (e.g., signature verifications and message identifiers) were integrated in DepSpace through *interceptors*. Interceptors allow change the behavior of the servers without alterations on their structure. The implementation of interceptors on DepSpace was inspired by CORBA portable interceptors (Object Management Group, 2002), and was integrated to the system architecture (Figure 1) as an additional layer between replication and access control layers. Additional data, necessary to execute a request (e.g., signatures), is sent through an abstraction (context) that is part of the messages, as we can see in Figure 6 that presents the gateways interface. In this interface, the abstraction *WSResponse* encapsulates the set of DepSpace server responses and is sent to the client as a reply to the request previously made by that client. The abstraction *WSDepTuple* represents tuples or templates, while the abstraction *WSMessageContext* represents the context of the operation, containing essential data for the execution of operations as already discussed.

The first two methods of gateways interface are to create and to delete "logical" spaces, respectively. In order to create a logical space, the client must supply information about the configuration desired to the space (e.g., what layers should be turned on). These informations are encapsulated in the Properties parameter of the createSpace operation. On the other hand, to delete a logical space, the client only should inform the space name (deleteSpace method).

The others methods represent each one of the operations defined to tuple spaces (Table 1). We must recall that the prototype implementation hides all aspects related to the access of these methods, i.e., the prototype contains administration interfaces that are used to create and delete spaces and accessor interfaces that are used to access the operations defined for tuple spaces.

EVALUATION

In this section we present both, an analytical analysis and an experimental analysis about the

Figure 6. Gateway interface (without throws clauses)

```
public interface WSDepSpace extends java.rmi.Remote{

        WSReponse createSpace(Properties prop, WSMessageContext ctx);
        WSReponse deleteSpace(String name, WSMessageContext ctx);

        WSReponse out(WSDepTuple tuple, WSMessageContext ctx);
        WSReponse rd(WSDepTuple template, WSMessageContext ctx);
        WSReponse rdp(WSDepTuple template, WSMessageContext ctx);
        WSReponse in(WSDepTuple template, WSMessageContext ctx);
        WSReponse inp(WSDepTuple template, WSMessageContext ctx);
        WSReponse cas(WSDepTuple template, WSDepTuple tuple,
                                WSMessageContext ctx);

    }
```

WSDS performance, considering the latency to access this service.

Analytical Evaluation

The latency of each operation is determined by the following equation:

$$L_{wsds} = L^c_{sign} + L^{c \to g}_{comm} + L^{g \to s}_{tom} + L^s_{ver} + L^s_{op}$$

$$+ L^s_{sign} + L^{s \to g}_{comm} + L^{g \to c}_{comm} + (f_n + 1)L^c_{ver}$$

The sources of latency represented in this equation are: L^c_{sign} - time to request signature; $L^{c \to g}_{comm}$ - latency for sending the request to the gateway; $L^{g \to s}_{tom}$ - time for forwarding the request to servers and its ordination; L^s_{ver} - time for verifying request signature; L^s_{op} – operation execution; L^s_{sign} - time to sign the reply; $L^{s \to g}_{comm}$ - time to send the reply to the gateway; $L^{g \to c}_{comm}$ - latency for forwarding replies to the client; and finally, L^c_{ver} - time to verify the reply integrity. In fact, the client needs verify $f_n + 1$ replies from correct servers in order to get a response for some operation, then this equation represents the latency in failure-free scenarios. All equations presented here are for failure-free scenarios. When there are failures, more responses have to be verified and, also, more shares must be decrypted (see below).

The following two equations give the additional latency overheads on tuple insertions and reads (read or remove operations) when the confidentiality layer is enabled:

$$L(insert)_{conf} = L^c_{tencrypt} + L^c_{share} + n\, L^c_{sencrypt}$$

$$+ L^s_{sdecrypt}$$

$$L(read)_{conf} = L^s_{sencrypt} + (f_n + 1)L^c_{sdecrypt} + L^c_{combine}$$

$$+ L^c_{tdecrypt}$$

The additional sources of latency represented in these equation are: $L^c_{tencrypt}$ (resp. $L^c_{tdecrypt}$) - time spent on the client to encrypt (resp. decrypt) the tuple with some symmetric key; L^c_{share} - latency for generating n shares from a given secret; $L^c_{sencrypt}$ (resp. $L^c_{sdecrypt}$) - time for the client to encrypt (resp. decrypt) the share using some symmetric key; $L^c_{combine}$ - time spent to combine $f_n + 1$ correct shares and recover the secret. L^s components of the equation are exactly like their L^c counterparts, but the processing occurs at server side.

Latency with Confidentiality Disabled

Considering that clients and servers spend similar amount of time in cryptographic operations, that the cost of local operations in tuple space is negligible (i.e., $L^s_{op} = 0$), and knowing that $L^{c \leftrightarrow g}_{comm} = L^{c \to g}_{comm} + L^{g \to c}_{comm}$ represents the communication between client and gateway, the latency of WSDS can be expressed as:

$$L_{wsds} = 2L_{sign} + L^{c \leftrightarrow g}_{comm} + L_{tom} + L^{s \to g}_{comm}$$

$$+ (f_n + 2)L_{ver}.$$

Following this, the latency in DepSpace access is $L_{ds} = L_{tom} + L^{s \to g}_{comm}$. Thus, the additional cost related to WSDS consists in: request and responses signatures; extra communication step to access the gateway; verification of the request and $f+1$ responses authenticity.

Latency with Confidentiality Enabled

Using the same consideration of previous section and also assuming that the cost of symmetric encryption is similar to the cost of decryption – called L_{sym_crypto} - we can rewrite the confidentiality overhead equations as:

$$L(insert)_{conf} = L^c_{share} + (n + 2)L_{sym\_crypto}$$

$$L(read)_{conf} = (f_n + 3)L_{sym\_crypto} + L^c_{combine}$$

There are two interesting observations that we can make based on previous equations. First, most of the cryptographic work is performed on clients, which does not have impact on the service latency but improves the overall throughput of the system (servers can handle operations fast). Second, the scheme is heavily based on symmetric cryptography, which is usually considered fast. For more details about the cost of this kind of confidentiality scheme, see (Bessani et al., 2008).

Experimental Evaluation

In order to quantify this latency, some experiments were conducted in a local area network. The execution environment was composed by a set of four *Athlon 2.4GHz* PCs with 512M of memory and running Linux (*kernel 2.6.12*). They were connected by a *1Gbps* switched Ethernet network. The Java runtime environment used was *Sun's JDK 1.5.0_06* and the just-in-time compiler was always turned on.

The system was configured with four DepSpace servers (one server per machine, *n = 4*), one gateway (*g = 1*) and one client, executed in different machines (together with one DepSpace server). We executed each operation *1000* times and obtained the mean time discarding the *5%* values with greater variance.

Figure 7 presents the latency observed in the execution of the three main operations defined to tuple spaces and supported by WSDS (varying the tuple size). We present results for the system configured with confidentiality layer activated and with this layer disabled. The figure shows that, even with large tuples, the decrease is reasonably small in the WSDS performance for both configurations, e.g., increasing the tuple size *64* times (*64* to *4096* bytes) causes a decrease of about *7%* in the system performance. Moreover, the variance presented (*2 - 6 ms*) is appropriate for this class of system (web services).

Read operations (*rdp*) are faster due to an optimization incorporated in the read protocol of DepSpace, which execute these operations without use the agreement protocol (see Bessani et al., 2008). Also, Figure 7 shows that confidentiality impact only about *15%* in the system performance and that even for large tuples, the decrease in the performance is reasonable small. This happens due to one implementation feature: the secret shared in the secret sharing scheme is not the tuple, but a symmetric key used to encrypt it. Then, all cryptography required by this scheme can be executed in the same, which means that the tuple size has no effect in these computations and confidentiality implies almost the same overhead regardless of the tuple size.

To better understand the sources of latency, Table 2 presents the costs of each phase of the protocol to insert (*out*) and to remove (*inp*) a tuple of *64* bytes (recall that *n = 4*). The table

Figure 7. WSDS latency with confidentiality layer disabled (left) and WSDS latency with confidentiality layer enabled (right)

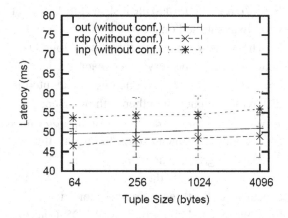
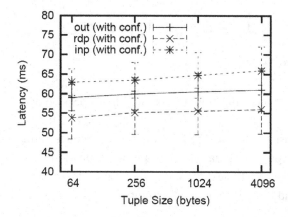

shows also the percentage of the cost of each phase in the total latency observed by clients, in accordance with the latency equations presented. Cryptographic processing represents the bigger contribution (*~55%*) to the total latency of the operation execution. If we exploit these results considering a large scale network like the Internet, where the communication latencies are at least *100* times higher, the communication latency is expected to be much greater than *~40%* of the total access time observed in our experiments (communication between client and gateway plus gateway and DepSpace servers). In these scenarios, cryptographic costs tend to dilute.

APPLICATIONS

In this section we present some examples of services that can be built over WSDS. The objective is not only to show that WSDS is useful for solving some different problems, but also to show that the WSDS is sufficiently generic to be used by many applications.

Secure Biddings

An application to manage biddings can be easily implemented over WSDS. Using WSDS, a consumer interested in some service (or product) inserts a tuple describing the service to be contracted (or the product to be bought) in the space. Then, service providers (that can have been previously registered in WSDS) also insert a tuple describing its proposal for service execution. Finally, after the proposal period, the consumer reads all proposal tuples and does one of the following: *(i.)* chooses the provider with best proposal, ending the bidding; *(ii.)* does not choose some proposal, because it decides that all proposals are inadequate in terms of quality of service or price (specified in the bidding description); *(iii.)* makes a summary of proposals and publishes it in the space, initializing another round of biddings (as an auction, where service providers could do new proposals lowering the price and/or offering better services). Figure 8 illustrates this application and shows tuples that can be inserted in WSDS.

To properly work on an untrusted environment, this application needs to enforce the following prohibitions: *(i.)* a service provider can not be allowed to access the proposals of others providers; *(ii.)* a provider can not be allowed to do more

Table 2. Latency costs for insert (out) and for remove (inp) a tuple of 64 bytes (n = 4)

Operation	out (without conf.)		out (with conf.)		inp (without conf.)		inp (with conf.)	
Latency	Cost (ms)	%L_{wsds}	Cost (ms)	%L_{wsds}	Cost (ms)	%L_{wsds}	Cost (ms)	%L_{wsds}
$L^{s \to g}_{comm}$	00.63	01.27	00.65	01.10	01.31	02.44	02.25	03.58
$L^{c \leftrightarrow g}_{comm}$	13.53	27.27	16.23	27.50	17.39	32.42	19.95	31.71
L_{sign}	13.51	54.45	13.51	45.79	13.51	50.38	13.51	42.94
L_{ver}	00.85	05.13	00.85	04.32	00.85	04.75	00.85	04.05
L_{tom}	05.90	11.88	06.61	11.20	05.37	10.01	05.98	09.50
$L(insert)_{conf}$	---	---	05.95	10.09	---	---	---	---
$L(read)_{conf}$	---	---	---	---	---	---	05.17	08.22
L_{wsds}	49.63	100.00	59.01	100.00	53.64	100.00	62.92	100.00
L_{ds}	06.53	13.15	13.21	22.39	06.68	12.45	13.40	21.30

than one proposal; *(iii.)* if a previous registration is necessary, an unregistered provider can not be able to make proposals; and other requirements specific to each bidding.

Using WSDS features, more specifically the access control mechanisms, it is possible to guarantee that: requirement *(i.)* can be implemented under the presentation of credentials for reading the proposals tuples; and requirements *(ii.)* and *(iii.)* can be implemented through fine-grained security policies containing rules like *"if exists a proposal of the provider A for the bidding X in the space, the inclusion of a new proposal of this provider for X is not allowed"* and *"the provider*

Figure 8. Secure biddings

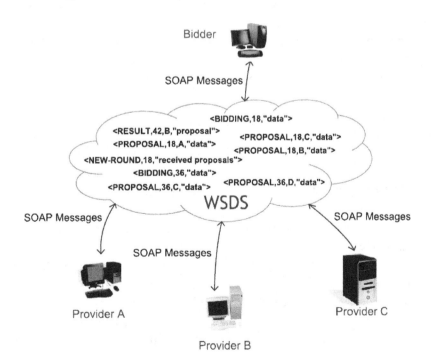

A can only insert a proposal if there is a tuple ‹*PROVIDER,A*› *in the space"* (this rule must be complemented with another one which specifies that only an administrator will be allowed to insert this type of tuple), respectively. As already mentioned, WSDS also supports confidentiality of tuples. Thus, providers are able to insert proposals tuples in a way that no other provider can see its proposal even if some servers are compromised or messages are captured in the network (eavesdropping).

Other examples of distributed applications in which a tuple space is used as a decoupled communication mechanism are: the I3 system (Stoica et al., 2004) offers multicast, anycast and support to mobile communication on the Internet through an abstraction similar to a tuple space; the master-worker pattern, a classical parallel programming design pattern used to distribute tasks in cluster, can be easily implemented over a tuple space (Carriero & Gelernter, 1989). If this space is deployed on the Internet, the same programming model can be used to distribute tasks in a computational grid (Favarim et al., 2007). The high availability and the fine-grained access control provided by WSDS make it able to ensure dependability properties even in the presence of faults and intrusions. Moreover, the decoupled coordination provided by the tuple space model allows distributed processes to interact without knowing their addresses and without be active at the same time (supporting temporary disconnections).

Data Sharing Among Services

The applications that invoke several web services to execute complex tasks often need to share information among these services. These applications may use a *shared database* (accessed by several services) or need the *session information* of each task to be included in all messages exchanged during the task execution.

Since web services are usually not deployed in the same administrative domain, the existence of a database, accessed from the Internet, can incur into serious security problems. Moreover, the cooperating services become dependent of a single point of failure (the database). On the other hand, the session information exchange can demand that a high amount of extra data has to be sent together with all messages and, in this way, affecting the system performance.

If a service like WSDS is available, cooperatives services can store the session information in a shared and dependable tuple space. WSDS ensure *(i.)* reliability and availability of this repository (due to intrusion-tolerant replication); *(ii.)* space- and tuple-level access control; and *(iii.)* universal accessibility (through the gateways, that are web services).

A travel agency is an example of this type of system (Figure 9), where a set of web services are used by the agency to allocate the resources required in a vacation trip (e.g., air transport, accommodation, car renting, tours planning). To execute this automatically, information about the traveller, its preferences and its schedule must be available to those services. The agency can contract each service through secure bidding protocols (like the one presented in previous section) to find the best service at a lower price. Moreover, when a service executes its part of the travel planning it can modify that data (e.g., the traveller schedule).

This example is interesting because it explores the WSDS synchronization capabilities: the SCHEDULE tuples and the tuple space operations with synchronization power (*cas* and *inp*) can be used to solve concurrency problems (i.e., different services specifying simultaneous activities in the space).

The security policies can define what information (tuple) each service is allowed to access. Also, policies can specify that only the travel agency is allowed to remove a commitment or cancel a resource allocation (accommodation, car, and so

Figure 9. Travel agency

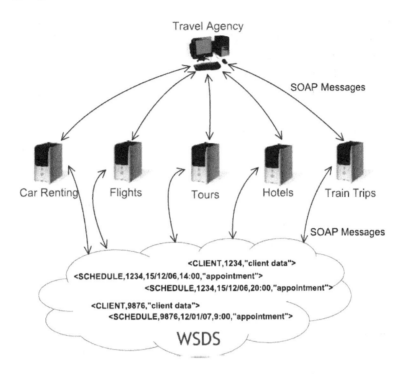

on). Moreover, tuples with client data must be confidential, in order to maintain information privacy.

In this example, the agency can contract each service through the mechanism of secure biddings presented in the previous section. These applications can use the same tuple space or different logical spaces for each bidding and for the client schedule.

Other examples of this class of services are: integration of intrusion detection systems (Yegneswaran et al., 2004), where the summary of events observed by different intrusion detection systems are shared (in the tuple space) to allow the correlation of suspect activities; and the support to virtual enterprises (Bright & Quirchmayr, 2004; Ricci et al., 2001), where a space is used by partners that compose the virtual enterprise to share information.

RELATIONSHIP WITH WS SPECIFICATIONS

There are many specifications that aim the integration of web services. This section presents possible relationships between WSDS and some of these specifications.

- **WS-Coordination:** This specification defines a generic model that can be used by several web services in order to coordinate the execution of some distributed task (Cabrera, 2005). The main component of this model is the *coordination context*, an abstraction responsible for managing information about the coordination of participants. At present, this model was already used to implement distributed transactions involving web services. The tuple space abstraction, provided by WSDS, can be implemented as an instance of WS-Coordination, where the coordination context is the logical tuple space and services registered in the context can be understood as the clients able to interact with the space.

- **WS-Orchestration:** Orchestration of web services consists in the coordination of these services by using an orchestration engine. The basic idea is to define the invocations flow (i.e., the sequence that services will be invoked), using a coordination language such as WSBPEL (*Web Services Business Process Execution Language*) (Alves, 2006). The travel agency presented in this paper is an example of task that can be implemented using orchestration. Currently, there is no standard based on shared data repositories to be used by cooperating web services being orchestrated. In this way, all information required by services must be maintained by the orchestration engine and sent to each service as a parameter of invoked operations. If the amount of shared data is large, this approach can be very inefficient. Thus, a dependable data repository is useful and its integration with WSBPEL language is easy, i.e., all orchestrated services access shared data on WSDS.

- **WS-Choreography:** Choreography is a composition of web services that allows: a formal definition of the interactions among the web services; the verification of the correctness (e.g., if it is deadlock-free); and code generation for the interactions (Burdett & Kavantzas 2004). The choreography differs from the orchestration in at least two aspects: it is distributed (while the orchestration has a coordinator - the orchestration engine); and the choreography languages (as the WSCL - *Web Services Choreography Language*) are used to specify the interactions required during the tasks execution, and not to execute the coordination (differing from the orchestration languages, such as WSBPEL) (Peltz,

2003). The choreography aims to make these interactions less susceptible to errors, through a more rigorous specification of the relations among the services. However, this technology does not guarantee that the interactions will occur (in execution time) as specified. The use of a mediator as WSDS fills this gap. The interactions can be controlled through tuples inserted and retried from the tuple space. Policies can be generated from the specified choreography (described in WSCL) and deployed in the tuple space to ensure that only legal interactions can be carried on, even in the presence of faults and intrusions. Moreover, the use of WSDS allows the implementation of multi-part interactions and the recording of all interactions executed by the services, ensuring the auditability of the system.

RELATED WORK

Currently, there is a large effort in the development of standardized mechanisms that allow the cooperation and integration of web services. Some examples are WS-Coordination (Cabrera, 2005), WS-Orchestration (Alves, 2006) and WS-Choreography (Burdett & Kavantzas, 2004). These approaches aim the web services integration through message exchanges, and do not define an abstraction to support shared data storage. This type of abstraction is crucial in applications where a large amount of data is shared or where decoupled communication is needed. WSDS implements this abstraction in a dependable way, i.e., the coordination service provided by WSDS is fault and intrusion-tolerant.

The integration of the tuple space coordination model in the web service environment has become an active research topic in the last years (Bellur & Bondre, 2006; Bright & Quirchmayr, 2004; Lucchi & Zavattaro, 2004; Maamar et al., 2005).

These works highlight the advantages that a shared data repository with a well defined interface and some synchronization power can provide in web services coordination (Maamar et al., 2005) and in workflows execution (Bellur & Bondre, 2006; Bright & Quirchmayr, 2004).

An important aspect that is not addressed by most of these works is the dependability attributes required for this service (Avizienis et al., 2004). The dependability must be provided at two levels: *(1)* security mechanisms for access control and *(2)* availability of the coordination service. The majority of the works in this area does not implement any of these levels, emphasizing the integration of the tuple space coordination model and web services standards (Bellur & Bondre, 2006; Bright & Quirchmayr, 2004; Maamar et al., 2005). *WS-SecSpaces* (Lucchi & Zavattaro, 2004) is an exception, that contemplates the level *(1)*, providing a model with space (and tuple) access control. WSDS supports a model of access control similar to the one provided by *WS-SecSpaces* and also supports the definition of fine-grained security policies that enable coordination even in the presence of malicious processes (Bessani et al., 2009). Moreover, WSDS implements mechanisms to supply the level *(2)* of dependability, through a simple and efficient architecture that uses gateways to access a dependable coordination service - *DepSpace* (Bessani et al., 2008). The resulting system tolerates accidental and malicious failures in all of its components. These characteristics are provided in accordance with web services standards.

The type of policy enforcement offered by WSDS to protect distributed interactions between web services is similar to the one offered by Moses, a Law-Governed Interaction middleware (Minsky & Ungureanu, 2000). Moreover, Moses is not dependable in the sense that it is not fault- and intrusion-tolerant and does not directly provides any means for implementing data-driven coordination.

CONCLUSION

This paper described WSDS, a dependable coordination service that can be used by web services to share data and synchronize their actions. The proposed architecture is based on a dependable tuple space and stateless web services (gateways) that provide access to it. An important feature of this system is that it is completely fault- and intrusion-tolerant. This architecture integrates several dependability and security mechanisms in order to enforce dependability properties like reliability, integrity, confidentiality, and availability in a modular way.

The system was implemented using open source tools and a performance analysis done on a local area network shows that the main latency cost comes from the use of digital signatures. These relative costs are expected to be much small if the system runs on the Internet, where the communication latency is orders of magnitude greater than local area networks.

WSDS can be used to facilitate web services coordination in applications where this is required. For example, it can be used to implement secure interactions following the semantics defined by WS-Choreography specification (Burdett & Kavantzas, 2004).

ACKNOWLEDGMENT

Eduardo Adilio Pelinson Alchieri and Joni da Silva Fraga are supported by CNPq (Brazilian National Research Council). Alysson Neves Bessani is supported by FCT through Multi-annual and CMU-Portugal programs.

REFERENCES

Alves, A., et al. (2006). Web Services Business Process Execution Language, version 2.0. *OASIS Public Draft*. Retrieved November 16, 2006, from http://docs.oasis-open.org/wsbpel/2.0/

Avizienis, A., Laprie, J.-C., Randell, B., & Landwehr, C. (2004). Basic Concepts and Taxonomy of Dependable and Secure Computing. *IEEE Transactions on Dependable and Secure Computing, 1*(1), 11–33. doi:10.1109/TDSC.2004.2

Bellur, U., & Bondre, S. (2006, April 23-27). xSpace: a Tuple Space for XML and its Application in Orchestration of Web Services. In *Proceedings of the 21st ACM symposium on Applied computing (SAC'06)*, Dijon, France (pp. 766-772).

Bessani, A. N., Alchieri, E. A. P., Correia, M., & Fraga, J. S. (2008, March 31-April 4). DepSpace: A Byzantine Fault-Tolerant Coordination Service. In *Proceedings of the 3rd ACM SIGOPS/EuroSys European Systems Conference (EuroSys'08)*, Glasgow, Scotland (pp. 163-176).

Bessani, A. N., Correia, M., Fraga, J. S., & Lung, L. C. (2009). Sharing Memory between Byzantine Processes using Policy-enforced Tuple Spaces. *IEEE Transactions on Parallel and Distributed Systems, 20*(3), 419–432. doi:10.1109/TPDS.2008.96

Bichier, M., & Lin, K.-J. (2006). Service-Oriented Computing. *IEEE Computer, 39*(3), 99–101.

Bright, D., & Quirchmayr, G. (2004, August 30-September 3). Supporting Web-Based Collaboration between Virtual Enterprise Partners. In *Proceedings of the 15th International Workshop on Database and Expert Systems Applications*, Zaragoza, Spain (pp. 1029-1035).

Burdett, D., & Kavantzas, N. (2004). The WS-Choreography Model Overview. *W3C Working Draft*. Retrieved March 14, 2004, from http://www.w3.org/TR/ws-chor-model/

Cabrera, L. F., et al. (2005). *Web Services Coordination Specification - version 1.0*. Retrieved August 15, 2005, from http://www-128.ibm.com/developerworks/library/specification/ws-tx/

Cabri, G., Leonardi, L., & Zambonelli, F. (2000). Mobile Agents Coordination Models for Internet Applications. *IEEE Computer, 33*(2), 82–89.

Carriero, N., & Gelernter, D. (1989). How to Write Parallel Programs: a Guide to the Perplexed. *ACM Computing Surveys, 21*(3), 323–357. doi:10.1145/72551.72553

Castro, M., & Liskov, B. (2002). Practical Byzantine Fault-Tolerance and Proactive Recovery. *ACM Transactions on Computer Systems, 20*(4), 398–461. doi:10.1145/571637.571640

Dwork, C., Lynch, N. A., & Stockmeyer, L. (1988). Consensus in the Presence of Partial Synchrony. *Journal of the ACM, 35*(2), 288–322. doi:10.1145/42282.42283

Favarim, F., Fraga, J. S., Lung, L. C., & Correia, M. (2007, July 12-14). GridTS: A New Approach for Fault Tolerant Scheduling in Grid Computing. In *Proceedings of the 6th IEEE International Symposium on Network Computing and Applications (NCA'07)*, Cambridge, MA (pp. 187-194). Washington, DC: IEEE Computer Press.

Gelernter, D. (1985). Generative Communication in Linda. *ACM Transactions on Programming Languages and Systems, 7*(1), 80–112. doi:10.1145/2363.2433

Herlihy, M., & Wing, J. M. (1990). Linearizability: A Correctness Condition for Concurrent Objects. *ACM Transactions on Programming Languages and Systems, 12*(3), 463–492. doi:10.1145/78969.78972

Lamport, L., Shostak, R., & Pease, M. (1982). The Byzantine Generals Problem. *ACM Transactions on Programming Languages and Systems, 4*(3), 382–401. doi:10.1145/357172.357176

Lucchi, R., & Zavattaro, G. (2004, March 14-17). WSSecSpaces: a Secure Data-Driven Coordination Service for Web Services Applications. In *Proceedings of the 19th ACM Symposium on Applied Computing (SAC'04)*, Nicosia, Cyprus (pp. 487-491).

Maamar, Z., Benslimane, D., Ghedira, C., Mahmoud, Q. H., & Yahyaoui, H. (2005, March 13-17). Tuple spaces for self-coordination of web services. In *Proceedings of the 20th ACM Symposium on Applied computing (SAC'05)*, Santa Fe, New Mexico (pp. 1656-1660).

Minsky, N. H., & Ungureanu, V. (2000). Law-Governed Interaction: a Coordination and Control Mechanism for Heterogeneous Distributed Systems. *ACM Transactions on Software Engineering and Methodology, 9*(3), 273–305. doi:10.1145/352591.352592

Obelheiro, R. R., Bessani, A. N., Lung, L. C., & Correia, M. (2006, September). How Practical are Intrusion-Tolerant Distributed Systems? (Tech. Rep. No. DI-FCUL TR 06-15). Lisbon, Portugal: University of Lisbon, Dep. of Informatics.

Object Management Group. (2002, December 6). The Common Object Request Broker Architecture: Core Specification v3.0. *Standart formal.*

Papadopolous, G., & Arbab, F. (1998). Coordination Models and Languages. *The Engineering of Large Systems, 46.*

Peltz, C. (2003). Web Services Orchestration and Choreography. *IEEE Computer, 36*(10), 46–52.

Ricci, A., Omicini, A., & Denti, E. (2001, June 20-22). The TuCSoN Coordination Infrastructure for Virtual Enterprises. In *Proceedings of the 10th IEEE International Workshops on Enabling Technologies: Infrastructure for Collaborative Enterprises*, Cambridge, MA (pp. 348-353).

Schneider, F. B. (1990). Implementing Fault-Tolerant Service Using the State Machine Approach: A Tutorial. *ACM Computing Surveys, 22*(4), 299–319. doi:10.1145/98163.98167

Schoenmakers, B. (1999, August 15-19). A simple publicly verifiable secret sharing scheme and its application to electronic voting. In *Proceedings of the 19th International Cryptology Conference on Advances in Cryptology (CRYPTO 1999)*, Santa Barbara, CA (pp. 148-164).

Segall, E. J. (1995, January 25-27). Resilient Distributed Objects: Basic Results and Applications to Shared Spaces. In *Proceedings of the 7th IEEE Symposium on Parallel and Distributed Processing (PDP'95)*, San Remo, Italy (pp. 320-327).

Shamir, A. (1979). How to Share a Secret. *Communications of the ACM, 22*(11), 612–613. doi:10.1145/359168.359176

Stoica, I., Adkins, D., Zhuang, S., Shenker, S., & Surana, S. (2004). Internet Indirection Infrastructure. *IEEE/ACM Transactions on Networking, 12*(2), 205-218.

Verissimo, P., Neves, N. F., & Correia, M. (2003). Intrusion-Tolerant Architectures: Concepts and Design. *Architecting Dependable Systems, 2677.*

Yegneswaran, V., Barford, P., & Jha, S. (2004, February 4-6). Global Intrusion Detection in the DOMINO Overlay System. In *Proceedings of the 11th Network and Distributed Security Symposium (NDSS 2004)*, San Diego, CA.

This work was previously published in the International Journal of Web Services Research, Volume 7, Issue 2, edited by Liang-Jie (LJ) Zhang, pp. 43-64, copyright 2010 by IGI Publishing (an imprint of IGI Global).

Chapter 3
Protocol-Level Service Composition Mismatches:
A Petri Net Siphon Based Solution

PengCheng Xiong
Georgia Institute of Technology, USA

Calton Pu
Georgia Institute of Technology, USA

MengChu Zhou
Tongji University, China

ABSTRACT

Protocol-level mismatch is one of the most important problems in service composition. The state-of-the-art method to deal with protocol mismatch is to generate adaptors to check deadlock-freeness based on a reachability graph. When this property is violated, the generation process will repeat itself until no deadlock state is found; however, the main drawback of this method is that it does not take into account the future deadlock state and requires many interactions with a developer. In this regard, it suffers from low efficiency. In this paper, the authors model multiple web service interaction with a Petri net called Composition net (C-net). The protocol-level mismatch problem is transformed into the empty siphon problem of a C-net. The authors take future deadlock states into consideration through this model, while finding the optimal solution that involves fewest interactions with a developer. The proposed method is proved to achieve higher efficiency for resolving protocol-level mismatch issues than traditional ones.

INTRODUCTION

In web service composition, when multiple web services are developed by different groups or vendors, they often fail to invoke each other because of mismatches. Service composition mismatches can be divided into interface and protocol-level ones (Nezhad, 2007). Table 1 gives a detailed taxonomy of already known service composition mismatches.

DOI: 10.4018/978-1-4666-1942-5.ch003

Table 1. Taxonomy of service composition mismatches

Service composition mismatches	Interface mismatches	message signature mismatches
		message split/merge mismatches
		message missing/extra mismatches
	Protocol level mismatches	unspecified reception
		mutual waiting mismatches
		non-local choice mismatches

Interface Mismatches

Interface mismatches include message signature mismatches, message split/merge and message missing/extra mismatches (Benatallah, 2005; Benatallah, 2006) as shown in Figure 1.

Message signature mismatches can be defined as: a service client's message has a different name and/or data type and/or data range from that of a service provider. For example, the message with the name "ClientOrder" on the service client's site may correspond to the message with the name "Order" on the provider's site. Note that, the case when the provider's message has a different data range from that of the client is also defined as parameter constraint mismatch in (Benatallah, 2005).

Message split mismatch can be defined as: a service client requires multiple messages to achieve certain functionality while a service provider can offer only a single message. For example, a provider's message mp contains n parts, i.e., $mp_1, mp_2, \ldots$, and mp_n while a client considers $mp_1, mp_2, \ldots$, and mp_n as n separate messages.

Message merge mismatch can be defined as: a service client requires a single message to achieve certain functionality while a service provider can offer multiple messages. This is the reverse case of message split mismatch. For example, a client requires message mc that is a combination of messages $mc_1, mc_2, \ldots$, and mc_n from a provider.

Missing message mismatches can be defined as: a service client expects a message that a service provider does not issue. For example, a client

Figure 1. Illustration for interface mismatches

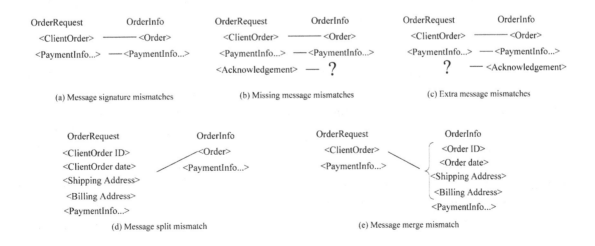

(a) Message signature mismatches   (b) Missing message mismatches   (c) Extra message mismatches

(d) Message split mismatch   (e) Message merge mismatch

expects an acknowledgement message while although a provider receives the previous message, it does not issue an acknowledgement. Note that, the missing message should not affect the semantics of the client. Extra message mismatches are defined as: a provider issues an extra message that a client does not expect. This is the opposite case of missing message mismatches. For example, a provider is sending an acknowledgement message that a client does not expect. Figure 1 shows the cases for interface mismatches.

Services can be composed if there is no interface mismatches. There are significant research results towards service interface level mismatches such as service adaptation-based method (Benatallah, 2005; Benatallah, 2006), schema matching-based method (Nezhad, 2007), information retrieval techniques (Wang, 2003) and clustering-based approach (Dong, 2004). Service adaptation generates a service (the adaptor) that mediates the interactions among two services with interface mismatches such that two services are interoperable. For example, Nezhad et al. (2007) propose a service adaptor that is based on matching of schemas of messages to solve the service interface mismatch problem. They firstly obtain the XML schemas of all the messages on a service provider and a service client. Secondly, they calculate the similarity between all the possible message pairs considering message types and message orders. Finally, they pick the pair with the largest similarity. This method is proved to be useful to solve the message signature mismatches. To solve the other kinds of interface mismatches, Benatallah et al. (2005) propose a method based on a service adaptor. To solve message split mismatch, the adaptor extracts mp_1, mp_2, ..., and mp_n from mp and then sends them to a service client. To avoid message merge mismatch, it integrates mc_1, mc_2, ..., and mc_n to generate a single message mc and sends it to a service client. To avoid missing message mismatch, it generates a new message by using the template of the expected message

and sends it to the service client. Finally, to avoid extra message mismatch, it simply intercepts the extra message and discards it.

Protocol Level Mismatches

Even if the service interface level matches perfectly, there may be protocol-level mismatches causing problems such as unspecified reception and deadlock (Yellin, 1997). Figure 2 shows the cases for unspecified reception, mutual waiting mismatches and non-local choice mismatches, respectively. Unspecified reception mismatches can be defined as: a service client's sending message order is different from a service provider's receiving message order. For example, as shown in Figure 2 (a), the client is sending message a first (denoted as a!), then message b (denoted as b!). However, the service provider is expecting to receive message b first (denoted as b?), then a (denoted as a?). Their interaction will result in an unspecified reception mismatches for the provider.

Deadlock mainly comes from mutual waiting mismatches (Nezhad, 2007) and non-local choice mismatches (Ben-Abdallah, 1997; Martens, 2003). Mutual waiting mismatches can be defined as: both of a service client and provider are expecting to receive a message from each other. For example, as shown in Figure 2 (b), after the client sends message a (denoted as a!), it is expecting to receive c (denoted as c?) from a provider. However, the provider is expecting to receive b (denoted as b?) from the client. Both of them are waiting for messages from each other.

Non-local choice mismatches can be defined as: a service client and provider make different local choices that should actually be synchronized. For example, as shown in Figure 2 (c), after the service client sends message a (denoted as a!), it makes a local choice, i.e., either to send a message b (denoted as b!) or send a message c (denoted as c!). However, the service provider also makes a local choice, i.e., after it receives message a (de-

Figure 2. Illustration for protocol mismatches

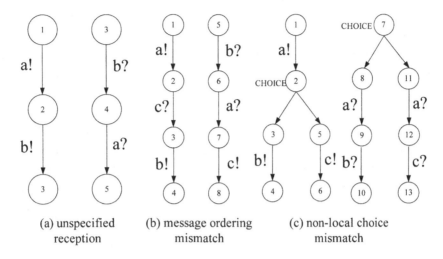

(a) unspecified reception   (b) message ordering mismatch   (c) non-local choice mismatch

noted as *a*?), it waits for message *b* (denoted as *b*?) or message *c* (denoted as *c*?). If the service client and provider happen to make the same choices, e.g., the client is sending *b* and the provider is expecting to receive *b*, then there is no problem. However, if the client is sending message *b* and the provider is expecting to receive *c*, then there is a non-local choice mismatch.

To solve unspecified reception mismatches, Nezhad et al. (2007) propose a service adaptor-based method. The adaptor first buffers the pending message, e.g., message *a* in Figure 2 (a) and then send it to the provider when it is expected. Actually, some commercial products, e.g., the Oracle BPEL engine already have the function to automatically buffer the pending messages for web service interactions. To solve deadlock mismatches, previously proposed methods (Nezhad, 2007) mainly take the following steps: (1) check the deadlock using a state-space based method; and (2) provide some message and repeat testing the state-space until there is no deadlock. In other words, they offer quite limited help in resolving deadlock mismatches. Finding deadlocks involve intense interactions with developers. When protocols become complicated, it is very hard for developers to find the best solutions. For example, it is non-trivial (Nezhad, 2007) to find the best

solution for the mutual waiting mismatches outlined in Figure 2 (b).

Contributions of This Work

The main contribution of the paper is a Petri net-based method to find protocol-level mismatches and then generate solutions to fix the mismatch problems. Our approach is based on an observation of Petri net objects called siphons. A siphon is a subset of Petri net nodes with a property analogous to program safety properties. The number of tokens in a siphon never increases and an empty siphon always remains empty. Our observation is that protocol-level mismatch happens if and only if there is an empty siphon (see Theorems 1 and 2) in Petri net models derived from BPEL composition.

Technically, our approach consists of three steps. First, we adopt Business Process Execution Language for Web Services (BPEL) as the web service composition language. In the first step, the BPEL description of a composite service is translated into a Petri net model. Second, we use a mix-integer programming formulation to detect the maximal empty siphons, which are then used to find protocol-level mismatches. Third, we describe an algorithm to find siphon-based solutions for protocol-level mismatches by adding tokens in siphons to prevent them from becoming empty. Finally, we make time complexity comparisons between our approach and existing ones and prove that the proposed method can achieve higher efficiency for resolving protocol-level mismatching issues.

The rest of the paper is organized as follows. The basic Petri net concepts and how we model web service composition with Petri nets is discussed. We then show how we detect and solve protocol-level mismatches and provide two concrete examples for mutual waiting mismatches and non-local choice mismatches respectively to show how we use the siphon-based algorithms to solve the mismatches. We then make comparisons between the existing methods and the proposed one from two perspectives, i.e., the coverage of BPEL semantics and time efficiency of solutions.

MODELING SERVICE INTERACTION WITH PETRI NETS

In this section, we give basic Petri net concepts, simple sequential workflow net (SSN), workflow module net (WMN) and Composition net (C-net) and then show how we model service interaction with a C-net.

Basic Petri Nets

Definition 1: A Petri net (Zhou, 1998; Aalst, 1998; Murata, 1989) is a 3-tuple, N=(P, T, F) where:

1. $P=\{p_1, p_2,..., p_m\}$, $m>0$, is a finite set of places pictured by circles;
2. $T=\{t_1, t_2,..., t_n\}$, $n>0$, is a finite set of transitions pictured by bars, with $P \cup T \neq \varnothing$ and $P \cap T = \varnothing$;
3. $F \subseteq (P \times T) \cup (T \times P)$ is the incidence relation. Based on F, we can derive the input and output functions that are

$m \times n$ matrices. I: $P \times T \rightarrow \{0,1\}$ is an input function. $I(p, t)=1$ if $(p,t) \in F$; and 0 otherwise. O: $P \times T \rightarrow \{0,1\}$ is an output function. $O(p, t)=1$ if $(t,p) \in F$; and 0 otherwise.

Postset of t is the set of output places of t, i.e., $t^{\bullet} =\{p|O(p, t)\neq 0\}$. Preset of t is the set of input places of t, i.e., ${}^{\bullet}t =\{p| I(p, t)\neq 0\}$. Post (Pre) set of p is the set of output (input) transitions of p, denoted by $p^{\bullet}$ and ${}^{\bullet}p$ respectively. $M : P \rightarrow Z^+$, is a marking where $M(p)$ represents the number of tokens in place p and $Z^+=\{0,1,2...\}$. An initial marking is denoted by M_0. Tokens are pictured by dots. (N, M) is called a net system or marked net. p is marked by M iff $M(p) > 0$. A place subset $S \subseteq P$ is marked by M iff at least one place in S is marked. The sum of tokens in S is denoted by $M(S) = \sum_{p \in S} M(p)$. A transition $t \in T$ is enabled under M, if and only if $\forall p \in {}^{\bullet}t$: $M(p)>0$ holds, denoted as $M[t\triangleright$. If $M[t\triangleright$ holds, t may fire, resulting in a new marking M', denoted as $M[t\triangleright M'$, with $M'(p)=M(p)-I(p,t)+O(p,t)$.

M' is reachable from M iff there exists a firing sequence $\sigma = t_{i1}t_{i2}...t_{ik}$, such that $M[t_{i1}>M_1[t_{i2}>... M_{n-1}[t_{ik}> M'$ holds. The set of markings reachable from M_0 in N is denoted as $R(N, M_0)$. Given a marked net (N, M_0) and $N=(P, T, F)$, a transition $t \in T$ is live under M_0 if $\forall M \in R(N, M_0)$, $\exists M' \in R(N, M)$, $\ni M'[t >$ holds. N is dead under M_0 if $\forall t \in T$, $M_0[t\triangleright$ cannot hold. (N, M_0) is live if $\forall t \in T$: t is live under M_0. A Petri net N is said to be deadlock-free if at least one transition is enabled at every reachable marking.

$N_X=(P_X, T_X, F_X)$ is a subnet of the Petri net $N=(P, T, F)$ iff $P_X \subseteq P$, $T_X \subseteq T$ and $F_X =F \cap ((P_X \times T_X) \cup (P_X \times T_X))$. N_X is generated by P_X iff $T_X= {}^{\bullet}P_X \cup P_X{}^{\bullet}$ (where the presets and postsets are taken w.r.t. F). Note that $\forall Q \subseteq P$, ${}^{\bullet}Q = \bigcup_{p \in Q} {}^{\bullet}p$ and $Q^{\bullet} = \bigcup_{p \in Q} p^{\bullet}$. A Petri net is called a state machine if $\forall t \in T$, $| {}^{\bullet}t |=| t^{\bullet} |= 1$. An asymmetric choice

Figure 3. Illustration of a Petri net siphon

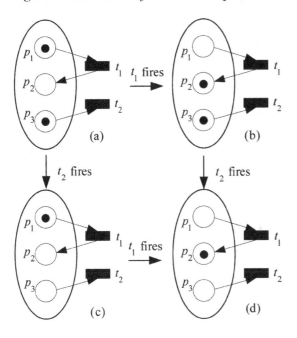

net or AC net is a Petri net such that $\forall p_1, p_2 \subseteq P \ : \ p_1^\bullet \cap p_2^\bullet \neq \varnothing \Rightarrow p_1^\bullet \subseteq p_2^\bullet$ or $p_1^\bullet \supseteq p_2^\bullet$.

A P-vector is a column vector $X : P \to Z$ indexed by P and a T-vector is a column vector $Y : T \to Z$ indexed by T, where Z is the set of integers. The incidence matrix of N is a matrix $[N] = \boldsymbol{O\text{-}I}$. X is a P-invariant (place invariant) if $X \neq 0$ and $X^T[N] = \boldsymbol{0}^T$ hold. Y is a T-invariant (transition invariant) if $Y \neq 0$ and $[N]Y = \boldsymbol{0}$ hold. $\| X \| = \{ p \in P \mid X(p) \neq 0 \}$ and $\| Y \| = \{ t \in T \mid Y(t) \neq 0 \}$ are called the support of X and Y, respectively.

A nonempty place set $S \subseteq P$ is called a siphon if $^\bullet S \subseteq S^\bullet$ holds as shown in Figure 3. A siphon is minimal if there does not exist a siphon such that $S' \subset S$. A siphon has a property: a siphon free of tokens at a marking remains token-free. Marking M is a dead marking if no transition is enabled at M. A siphon S that eventually becomes empty is called potential deadlock. A Petri net is called potential deadlock free if all the siphons are always marked.

Definition 2: A simple sequential workflow net (SSN) is a Petri net $N = \{P \cup \{\alpha, \beta\}, T, F\}$ if:

1. N has two special places: α and β where α is a source place, i.e., $^\bullet\alpha = \varnothing$, and β is a sink place, i.e., $\beta^\bullet = \varnothing$;

2. If we add a new transition t to N which connects α with β, i.e., $^\bullet t = \beta$ and $t^\bullet = \alpha$, then the resulting extended net $\overline{N} = (\overline{P}, \overline{T}, \overline{F})$ where $\overline{P} = P$, $\overline{T} = T \cup \{t\}$, and $\overline{F} = F \cup \{(\beta, t), (t, \alpha)\}$, is a strongly connected state machine;

3. Every circuit of N contains t; and

4. $M_0(\alpha) = 1$ and $M_0(p) = 0$, $\forall p \neq \alpha$

State α is defined as $M(\alpha) = 1$ and $M(p) = 0$, $\forall p \in P \setminus \{\alpha\}$ while state β is defined as $M(\beta) = 1$ and $M(p) = 0$, $\forall p \in P \setminus \{\beta\}$. Note that SSN is a special kind of workflow net (Aalst, 1998) and is close to the definition of simple sequential processes in (Ezpeleta, 1995). SSN has a sound property:

1. For every state M reachable from state α, there exists a firing sequence leading from M to β;

2. State β is the only state reachable from α with at least one token in β; and

3. There are no dead transitions in it.

Definition 3: A workflow module net (WMN) is an extended Petri net $N = \{P \cup P_I \cup P_O, T, F\}$, where:

1. The subnet generated by P is an SSN;

2. $M_0(\alpha) = 1$ and $M_0(p) = 0$, $\forall p \neq \alpha$;

3. P_I and P_O denote the input and output interfaces for the workflow module respectively, satisfying

   a. $P_I \neq \varnothing$, $P_O \neq \varnothing$, $P_I \cap P_O = \varnothing$ and $(P_I \cup P_O) \cap P = \varnothing$;

   b. $\forall p \in P_I,\ p^{\bullet\bullet} \cap P \neq \varnothing$ and $\mid p^\bullet \mid = 1$;

   c. $\forall p \in P_O,\ ^{\bullet\bullet}p \cap P \neq \varnothing$ and $\mid ^\bullet p \mid = 1$; and d.　　$\forall p \in P_I \cup P_O,\ {}^\bullet p \cap p^\bullet = \varnothing.$

We define P as the set of process places and $P_I \cup P_O$ as the set of interface ones. The initial marking of a WMN follows that of its SSN according to ii of Definition 3.

Definition 4: Two WMNs

$N_j = \{P_j \cup P_{I_j} \cup P_{O_j}, T_j, F_j\},\ j \in \{1,2\}$ *are composable, if* $P_1 \cap P_2 = \varnothing,\ T_1 \cap T_2 = \varnothing$ *and* $(P_{I_1} \cap P_{O_2}) \cup (P_{I_2} \cap P_{O_1}) = P_E \neq \varnothing.$ *For every* $p \in P_E,$ *if* $x \in {}^\bullet p$ *and* $y \in p^\bullet,$ *we call* (x, p, y) *an information channel. The 2-member Composition net (C-net) denoted as* $N = N_1 \oplus N_2$ *is defined as follows:*

1.　　$P = P_1 \cup P_2,$
2.　　$P_I = \{(P_{I_1} \cup P_{I_2}) \setminus P_E\}, P_O = \{(P_{O_1} \cup P_{O_2}) \setminus P_E\},$
3.　　$T = T_1 \cup T_2,$ and
4.　　$F = F_1 \cup F_2.$

Definition 5: Two WMN N_1 and N_2 are composable when they interact through a set of common places. For example, if $P_{I_2} \cap P_{O_1} = P' \neq \varnothing,\ N_1$ sends information through the set of interfaces P' that is received by N_2.

Definition 6: An n-member C-net denoted as $N = \oplus_{i=1}^{n} N_i$ is defined recursively following Definition 5. A C-net is a complete net iff $P_I = \varnothing$ and $P_O = \varnothing.$

For example, Figure 4 (a-c) shows an SSN, WMN and C-net respectively. In an SSN, place α (i.e., p_1) and β (i.e., p_4) denote the start and end status, respectively and $p_{2\text{-}3}$ are internal places. A WMN is formed by adding two interface places and their corresponding arcs to an SSN. In Figure 4 (b), p_5 and p_6 are output and input places respectively. A WMN can be considered as a

single-member C-net. Two or more WMNs can be composed to form a C-net. A complete C-net does not have additional input and output interfaces for external interaction. Figure 4 (c) shows a complete C-net composed of two WMNs. One of the WMN is shown in Figure 4 (b) which has an output and input place, which are denoted as p_5 and p_6 respectively. The other one has an input and output place, which are denoted as p_5 and p_6 respectively. Thus, they can be composed to form a complete C-net.

Model Web Service Interaction with C-Net

We then show how we model web service interaction with C-nets. We assume that no service interface level mismatches exist, i.e., the message signature and number of interfaces in both parties match. We divide the basic structures in BPEL, i.e., *receive, reply, invoke, assign, throw, terminate, wait, empty* and *link* into two categories. The first category is internal control logic that includes *assign, terminate, wait* and *empty*. The second category is external control logic that includes *receive, reply, invoke, throw* and *link*. Basic structures in the first category are not related to the interaction between different web services and we model them as internal places and transitions in a WMN. Basic structures in the second category are related to the interaction between different web services and we model them as transitions connected with internal and interface places as shown in Figure 5. Note that, *invoke* is a combination of *reply* and *receive*, and *link* is modeled as an information channel.

There are *sequence, flow, pick, switch* and *while* structured activities in a BPEL process. Based on basic structures, a WMN can cover the *sequence, pick* and *switch* structures. The semantics of *while* structure are similar to while-loop in programming languages like *Java*. Here we approximate the number of loops in a finite *while* structured activity and transform the activity to a

Figure 4. Illustration for Petri net siphon

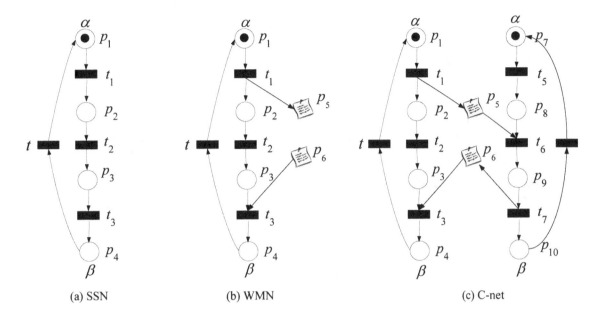

(a) SSN	(b) WMN	(c) C-net

sequence activity by expanding cycles (Ezpeleta, 1995). We can transform the processes that are executed in parallel in the *flow* structure into the same processes that are invoked simultaneously in the *invoke* structure while maintaining the business logic. For example, we can divide the processes that are executed in parallel into separate BPEL processes while maintaining the business logic as shown in Figure 5 (g).

For example, assume that we have two web services as shown in Figure 6, i.e., a customer service and an online shop service. The customer service first sends an order message, waits for delivery and then sends a payment message; while the online shop service waits for the order and payment, and then delivers the product.

We model the action of sending order information of a customer service in Figure 7 (a). Here we model the order information message as p_{11} and the customer service status before and after sending the message as p_1 and p_2, respectively. We also model the action of receiving order information of an online Shop service in Figure 7 (b). We model the order information message as

the same p_{11} and the online shop service status before and after receiving the message as p_6 and p_7, respectively.

Note that the interface places do not have tokens initially because no message is created. They can have tokens if and only if some transition wants to send a message through the information channel while they can lose a token if and only if some transition wants to receive a message through the information channel. A token in them models the situation when the required message is ready. We assume that the maximum number of tokens that an interface place can hold is one. Otherwise a BPEL process is not correct.

The firing of transitions in a C-net simulates the interaction of web services. For example, order information is ready in Figure 8 (a). After t_6 fires, the order information is received by the online shop service in Figure 8 (b). Following the modeling method, the final C-net for two web services is shown in Figure 9 (a).

Figure 5. Transforming BPEL into WMNs

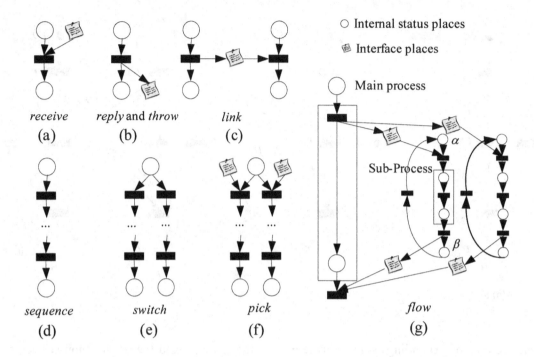

Figure 6. A customer service and an online shop service

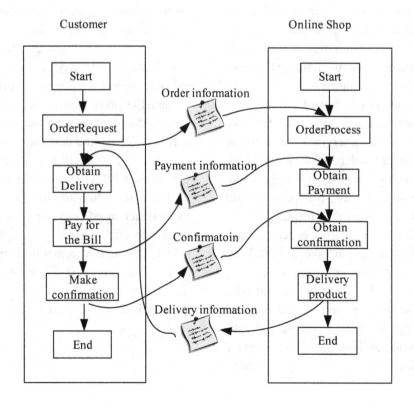

Figure 7. Modeling the case in Figure 6 as C-net

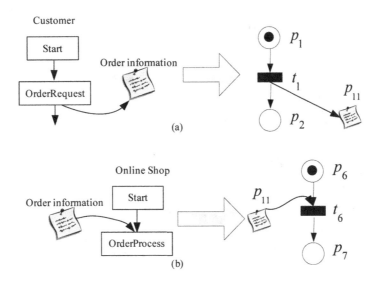

Figure 8. Modeling the interaction of web services

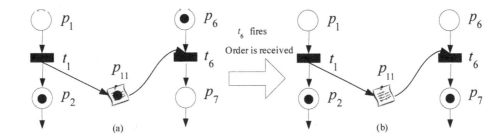

PROTOCOL-LEVEL MISMATCH ANALYSIS

As stated previously, mismatches in protocol-level mainly come from mutual waiting mismatches and non-local choice mismatches. In this section, we propose a detection method, a core algorithm, as well as a comprehensive solution method for protocol-level mismatch.

Protocol-Level Mismatch Detection

Definition 7: A C-net $N = \oplus_{i=1}^{n} N_i$ *matches at protocol-level if N is live.*

Note that, according to Theorem 4 in Murata (1989), a state machine N is live iff N is strongly connected and M_0 has least one token. Following this theorem, since an SSN is a strongly connected state machine with one token, it is live. However, this theorem is not true for C-nets.

Theorem 1: A C-net is live iff it is potential deadlock free.

Proof:

1.   A C-net is an asymmetric choice net.

Figure 9. Modeling the interaction of web services in Figure 6

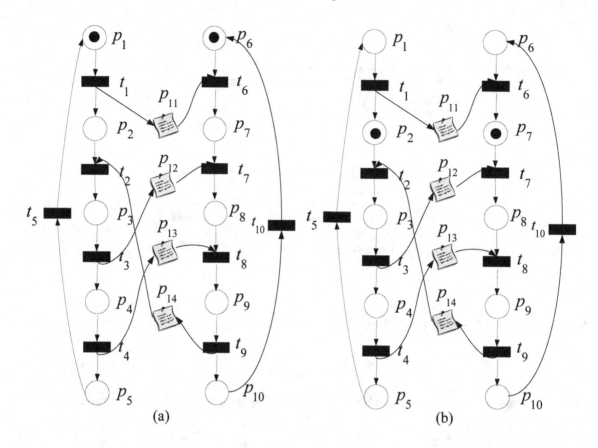

(a)   (b)

$\forall p_1, p_2 \subseteq$ C-net and $p_1^{\bullet} \cap p_2^{\bullet} \neq \varnothing$, there are four cases.

Case 1: $p_1 \in P_E$ and $p_2 \in P_E$. According to Definition 3, we have $p_1^{\bullet} \cap p_2^{\bullet} = \{t\}$.

Case 2: $p_1 \in P_E$ and $p_2 \notin P_E$. We have $p_1^{\bullet} \subseteq p_2^{\bullet}$.

Case 3: $p_2 \in P_E$ and $p_1 \notin P_E$. We have $p_1^{\bullet} \supseteq p_2^{\bullet}$.

Case 4: $p_1 \notin P_E$ and $p_2 \notin P_E$. However, since the extended SSN is a strongly connected state machine, we have $\forall t \in T$, $|{}^{\bullet}t| = |t^{\bullet}| = 1$. This case is impossible.

For all the case, we have $p_1^{\bullet} \cap p_2^{\bullet} \neq \varnothing \Rightarrow p_1^{\bullet} \subseteq p_2^{\bullet}$ or $p_1^{\bullet} \supseteq p_2^{\bullet}$. Then a C-net is an asymmetric choice net.

2. According to (Chu, 1997), an asymmetric choice net is live iff it is potential deadlock free.

Based on (1) and (2), a C-net is live iff it is potential deadlock free. □

According to the definition of potential deadlock, a siphon S eventually becomes empty when a C-net is not live and all the siphons are always marked when a C-net is live.

Theorem 2: A C-net $N = \oplus_{i=1}^{n} N_i$ matches at protocol-level iff all the siphons are always marked, i.e., $\forall M \in R(N, M_0)$, $\forall$ (minimal) siphon S, $M(S) \neq 0$.

Proof: Obvious from Definition 7 and Theorem 1. □

For instance, there are 5 minimum siphons in Figure 6 (a), i.e., $S_1=\{p_{1-5}\}$, $S_2=\{p_{6-10}\}$, $S_3=\{p_1,p_{3-5}, p_{7-9}, p_{11}, p_{14}\}$, $S_4=\{p_3, p_{8-9}, p_{12}, p_{14}\}$, $S_5=\{p_{3-4}, p_9, p_{13-14}\}$. $M_0(S_{1-3})=1$ and $M_0(S_{4-5})=0$. Since there are initial empty siphons, i.e., S_4 and S_5, there exists protocol-level mismatching. This is true because after t_1 and t_6 fire, there is a deadlock as shown in Figure 9 (b).

Thus the problem of protocol-level mismatching of web service interaction is transformed to the problem of empty minimal siphons in a C-net. We can use the mix-integer programming algorithm to detect the maximal empty siphon (Chu, 1997).

In the aspect of detecting protocol-level mismatch, neither of the reachability analysis based method and mix-integer programming has clear computational advantage over the other because both of them have exponential complexity (Li, 2004).

Suppose that we have a C-net $N = \oplus_{i=1}^{n} N_i$ where some minimal siphons can become empty. Our main goal is to introduce into the system a solution to guarantee that no empty minimal siphons are reachable during the evolution of the new C-net, i.e., the new C-net at protocol-level matches.

Core Algorithm

As stated in Theorem 2, a C-net $N = \oplus_{i=1}^{n} N_i$ matches at protocol-level iff $\forall\ M \in R(N, M_0)$, $\forall$ (minimal) siphon S, $M(S) \neq 0$. According to the property of a siphon, the number of tokens in a siphon will never increase and an empty siphon will always remain empty.

From a modeling perspective, the most intuitive way is to add tokens to the C-net in order to make one or more tokens to interface places to make all of the empty siphons marked. For example, adding one token to p_{11} in Figure 9 means that the order information is ready while adding to p_{12} means that the payment information is ready. From a service perspective, the customer is waiting for the delivery information while the online shop is waiting for the payment information. Thus, developers must be involved to provide additional information at the deadlock point, i.e., to ask the customer to provide the payment information or to ask the online shop to provide the delivery information.

In the above cases, there are at least 4 choices for a developer:

Choice 1(C1): provide nothing
Choice 2(C2): provide the payment information
Choice 3(C3): provide the delivery information
Choice 4(C4): provide the payment and delivery information

But developers may not always make a good decision. A good decision implies correctness and efficiency of the solution.

Correctness means, the solution should resolve the current protocol level mismatch. C1 is obviously not a correct solution since both the customer and online shop web services are still waiting. C2 is also not a correct solution although it can solve the current waiting status for the online shop. After choosing C2, payment information is provided and t_7 can fire. However, the system goes to another mutual waiting state, i.e., the online shop is waiting for confirmation and the customer is waiting for delivery. This is because siphon S_5 is empty.

Efficiency means, the solution should require the smallest amount of information to solve as many as future protocol-level mismatches. C4 is also not an efficient solution because it needs 2 kinds of messages. For example, payment, confirmation and delivery information is three different kinds of messages. Choices 1-4 require 0,1,1 and 2 kinds of messages respectively. Then although C3 and C4 are all correct solutions, C3 is more efficient than C4 because it requires fewer kinds of messages.

We propose an algorithm to choose the correct and also the most efficient solution by linear programming.

Core Algorithm:

INPUT: (1) *n*-member C-net N with minimum siphon set $\Omega=\Omega_N\cup\Omega_Y$. Ω_N denotes the non-empty siphon set, and $\Omega_Y =\{S_1, S_2, ...S_i\}$ denotes the empty siphon set when a protocol mismatch happens. (2) Interface place set P_E $=\{p_1, p_2, ...p_j\}$

OUTPUT: A list of messages that should be provided. We denote the list as a $j \times 1$ vector L where $L(j)=1$ if $p_j\in L$; and 0 otherwise.

BEGIN:

Step 1. /* Calculate the contribution matrix of every message to the siphon*/

Constitute an $i \times j$ matrix A, where $A(i, j)=1$ if $p_j\in S_i$; and 0 otherwise.

Step 2. /* Optimization*/

Compute the following linear programming problem:

Minimize $\mathbf{1}*L$

s.t. $A*L=\mathbf{1}^T$

Step 3. /* Return result*/

Return L

END

The time complexity for the algorithm is linear. We explain the idea underlying this algorithm as follows:

Firstly, the constraint function $A*L =\mathbf{1}^T$ can return the correct solutions. As shown in Figure 10, because we have $A(i, j)=1$ if $p_j\in S_i$; and 0 otherwise, and $L(j)=1$ if $p_j\in L$; and 0 otherwise, the solutions of the constraint function guarantee that each empty siphon is marked by exactly one token. Moreover, if the constraint function is not satisfied, there is at least one empty siphon.

Secondly, the objective function of the linear programming formulation can return the best solution. In the contribution matrix, the more siphons the message p_j is involved in, the more $\mathbf{1}$'s it has in the *j*th column. Since the objective function calculates the sum of messages, the solution has the smallest total number of messages if the proposed objective function is minimized.

Finally, we can claim that, through the algorithm, we can provide a correct and also efficient solution to protocol-level mismatch.

Comprehensive Solution to Protocol-Level Mismatch

Based on the core algorithm, we propose a comprehensive solution to protocol-level mismatch as follows. The input of the solution is web services and their interaction described in BPEL. We assume that there is no interface mismatches for these web services' interaction.

Comprehensive solution:

BEGIN:

Step 1. Transform web service interaction into Petri net models as simple sequential workflow net (SSN), workflow module net (WMN) and Composition net (C-net).

Step 2. Check if there is/will be empty siphon by using mix-integer programming according to "protocol-level mismatch detection". If none of them can become empty, go to end.

Step 3. Find the set of minimal siphons. Monitor all the minimal siphons until all the web services terminate properly, i.e., for each SSN, state β is reached from state α. During the monitoring period, if one of the

Figure 10. Illustration of linear programming

$$\begin{array}{c} \begin{array}{cccc} P_1 & P_2 & P_3 & \cdots & P_j \end{array} \\ \begin{array}{c} S_1 \\ S_2 \\ S_3 \\ \vdots \\ S_i \end{array} \begin{pmatrix} a_{11} & \cdots & a_{1j} \\ \vdots & \ddots & \vdots \\ a_{i1} & \cdots & a_{ij} \end{pmatrix} \begin{pmatrix} L_1 \\ L_2 \\ L_3 \\ \vdots \\ L_j \end{pmatrix} = \begin{pmatrix} 1 \\ 1 \\ 1 \\ \vdots \\ 1 \end{pmatrix} \end{array}$$

minimal siphons becomes empty, denote the empty siphon set as Ω_γ. Go to step 4. When monitoring period ends, go to end.

Step 4. Take Ω_γ as the input of core algorithm. Run the core algorithm. Provide the list of messages that are returned by the algorithm. Go back to step 3.

END

We explain the idea underlying the solution as follows:

Firstly, according to the taxonomy of service composition mismatches, we may have both the interface and protocol mismatches. Since interface matches are a prerequisite to achieve protocol matches, before using the solution, we have to guarantee that there is no interface mismatches.

Secondly, we model web service interaction by Petri net models so that we can identify and check the minimal siphons. If we cannot detect any empty minimal siphon, then there is no protocol mismatches and we end. Otherwise, we have to monitor those minimal siphons until all the web services terminate properly. Before they terminate, when there is an empty siphon, we can use the core algorithm to obtain the list of messages that should be provided.

Finally, we provide those messages and solve the protocol mismatches.

We make an overview of the solution. As mentioned previously, there are three kinds of protocol level mismatches, i.e., unspecified reception, mutual waiting mismatches and non-local choice mismatches. The cause for unspecified reception is a wrong sequence of sending messages and it can be solved by buffering previous messages. The cause for mutual waiting mismatches is that the web services follow a conflict "send and receive" sequence and they are waiting for each other to send messages. The cause for non-local choice mismatches is that the web services follow a conflict "send and receive" choice and wait for each other to send messages. In both of the cases, the missing messages are responsible for

the mismatch. By using our core algorithm, we are not only trying to find those missing messages but also find the smallest set of those missing ones. Thus, after we provide those messages, we are able to resolve the protocol mismatches.

We outline a complexity analysis of the solution step by step.

Step 1 is doing transformation tasks. Thus its complexity linearly depends on the size of BPEL.

Step 2 is answering a "Yes or No" question, i.e., whether or not there is an empty siphon at any reachable markings. Then its complexity depends on the time when the algorithm will find an empty siphon. In one case, if there is a mutual waiting mismatch, generally speaking, there is at least one empty siphon at the initial marking. For example, there is a mutual waiting mismatch in Figure 6 and there is an empty siphons at the initial marking, i.e., $S_4 = \{p_3, p_{8-9}, p_{12}, p_{14}\}$. Using the method to detect empty siphon at the initial marking, the maximal empty siphon that contains S_4 can be detected in polynomial time (Chu, 1997). In another case, if there is a non-local choice mismatch, generally speaking, there is no empty siphon at the initial marking but there will be an empty siphon at a future marking. This is because a non-local choice mismatch will happen only when services make conflicting choices. In other words, it may be "hidden" when services happen to make the same choices. To detect an empty siphon for a non-local choice mismatch at a future marking has exponential complexity in the worse case. Fortunately, since we already propose an approach to resolve the mismatch, the answer to whether or not there is an empty siphon at any reachable markings is not very important.

Step 3 is generating the minimal siphons. It is a prerequisite for Step 4. The generation of minimal siphons has exponential complexity in the worse case. Fortunately, since siphons are a kind of special structure of Petri nets, they are not related with the states and we can generate them offline.

Step 4 is trying to control the empty siphons. Because it is using linear programming, the complexity is polynomial.

EXAMPLES

As previously mentioned, protocol mismatch includes mutual waiting mismatch and non-local choice mismatches. In this section, we use two concrete examples to illustrate how to use the method mentioned above, especially the core algorithm.

The scenario in Figure 6 can be classified as mutual waiting mismatch. After t_1 and t_6 fire, there is a deadlock. We have $\Omega_N=\{S_{1-3}\}$, $\Omega_Y=\{S_{4-5}\}$ where $S_4=\{p_3, p_{8-9}, p_{12}, p_{14}\}$, $S_5=\{p_{3-4}, p_9, p_{13-14}\}$, and $P_E=\{p_{11-14}\}$. Because $p_{12}\in S_4$, $p_{14}\in S_4$, $p_{13}\in S_5$, $p_{14}\in S_5$, we have $A=((0\ 1\ 0\ 1)\ (0\ 0\ 1\ 1))$. The result is $L=(0\ 0\ 0\ 1)^T$. It means that a developer should ask the online shop to provide the delivery information (the token in the interface place p_{14} denotes the delivery information). Moreover, if we check the method that the developer asks the customer to provide the payment information, i.e., $L'=(0\ 1\ 0\ 0)^T$, we find that this method will fail. This is simply because L' is not a solution of the linear programming problem. Because $A*L'=(1\ 0)^T$, although S_4 is marked, S_5 is still empty.

We use a scenario mentioned in (Ben-Abdallah, 1997; Martens, 2003) as shown in Figure 11 to illustrate the non-local choice mismatches. There are three web services, denoted as WS1-WS3. We first denote their interaction through Message Sequence Charts (MSC). WS1 first sends "Dreq" to WS2, and then WS2 sends "DA" to WS3. After WS1 first sends "Dreq" to WS2, it is the first web service to decide whether to MSC2 or MSC3. For example, if it decides to proceed by following MSC3, it will send "Creq" to WS2,

WS2 sends "RC" to WS3 and then WS1 waits for WS3 to send back "Crep".

We model the messages "Dreq", "DA", "Creq", "RC", "Crep", "DC", "Dind" and "Drep" with p_{17}, p_{20}, p_{18}, p_{22}, p_{23}, p_{21}, p_{19} and p_{24} respectively. Then we build the C-net for the scenario as shown in Figure 12 (a). There will be no non-local choice mismatches if WS1 and WS3 can make the same choices, i.e., following MSC2 or MSC3. However, if they follow different MSCs, then there is a non-local choice mismatch as shown in Figure 12 (b). For example, if WS1 decides to proceed following MSC3 and WS3 decides to proceed following MSC2, then after t_1, t_3, t_7, t_8, t_{10}, t_{13}, t_{14}, t_{11}, and t_{18} fire, there will be a deadlock. The situation will be: WS1 is waiting for "Crep" to fire t_5; WS2 is waiting to fire t_9 because "DC" arrives; WS3 is waiting for "Drep" to fire t_{16}.

The three web services are waiting for each other. There are 15 minimal siphons in the C-nets. We have $\Omega_N=\{S_{1-11}\}$, $\Omega_Y=\{S_{12-15}\}$, and $P_E=\{p_{17-24}\}$. For simplicity, we only list the siphons in Ω_Y, i.e., $S_{12}=\{p_1, p_3, p_5, p_{7-9}, p_{13}, p_{15}, p_{17}, p_{19-20}, p_{23}\}$, $S_{13}=\{p_1, p_3, p_5, p_{7-9}, p_{12-13}, p_{15-17}, p_{19}, p_{23-24}\}$, $S_{14}=\{p_{1-3}, p_5, p_7, p_{13}, p_{15}, p_{17}, p_{20}, p_{23}\}$, $S_{15}=\{p_{1-3}, p_5, p_{12-13}, p_{15-16}, p_{23-24}\}$. The result is $L=(0\ 0\ 0\ 0\ 0\ 0\ 1\ 0)^T$. Here p_{23} denotes "Crep". It means that the developer should ask WS3 to provide "Crep".

RELATED WORK

Web Services Business Process Execution Language (BPEL) (Curbera, 2006; Wohed, 2003) is an OASIS standard executable language for specifying interactions with web services. It is becoming the de facto standard for implementing business processes using web service technology. However, it lacks a formal semantics, which makes the web service composition mismatches hard to analyze. In order to avoid this disadvantage, several attempts have been made to translate BPEL into formal models. By using them, it is able to detect inconsistencies in the BPEL specification

Figure 11. Non-local choice protocol mismatch

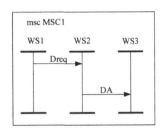

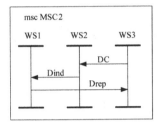

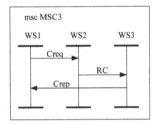

and formally analyze BPEL processes using techniques of computer aided verification.

For example, Fisteus et al. (2004) use finite state machines, Ferrara (2004) uses process algebra Fahland and Reisig (2005) use abstract state machines, and Ouyang et al. (2005), Hinz et al.

(2005) and Lohmann et al. (2007) use Petri nets. Other methods, like pi-calculus (Lucchia, 2007), message sequence charts (Foster, 2005) and conversations (Fu, 2004) are also used.

Because Petri nets are appropriate for both modeling and analyzing BPEL, in this article, we

Figure 12. The C-nets for the non-local choice protocol mismatch in Figure 11

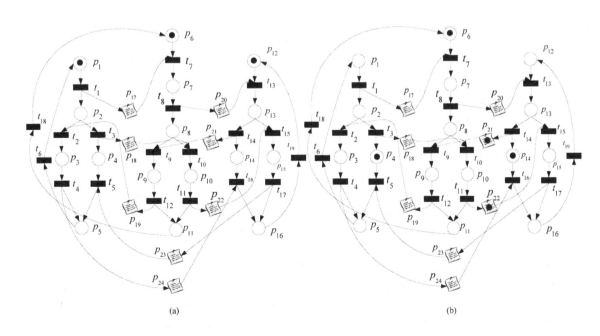

propose our own semantics for BPEL translation to Petri nets, e.g., SSN, WMN and C-net and our own analysis methods based on siphons. We focus on the other Petri net-based methods and make comparisons among them.

Coverage of Petri Net Semantics

Different researchers propose different Petri net semantics for BPEL. Ouyang et al. (2005) transform BPEL into Petri nets represented in the Petri Nets Markup Language (PNML) by BPEL2PNML. They model a BPEL process as a work flow net (WFN) (Aalst, 1998). Lohmann adopts open workflow nets (oWFNs) (Lohmann, 2006) for modeling BPEL processes and developed a compiler BPEL2oWFN. Both BPEL2PNML and BPEL2oWFN implement reduction techniques to reduce the model after their generation. Our semantics cover the main components of BPEL process, e.g., the basic structures and structured activities instead of covering all the elements in BPEL. For example, we model the control flow by undistinguishable black tokens and we provide little data information (e.g., data values and message content). In this case, C-net is a kind of low-level Petri nets and it is more like a WFN than an oWFNs. The most distinguished modeling advantage for the C-net is that it enables the useful conclusions for analyzing protocol mismatches.

Efficiency of Discovering and Solving Protocol Mismatches

After transforming BPEL into Petri nets represented in PNML, Ouyang et al. (2005) use WofBPEL to support three types of analysis, i.e., reachability analysis, competing message-consuming activities and garbage collection of queued messages by generating the full state space. Similarly, König et al. (2008) uses Fiona to automatically analyze the interactional behavior of a given oWFN. Martens (2003) proposes a BPEL annotated Petri nets (BPN) and presents a decision algorithm for

the controllability of a BPN model based on the communication graph (c-graph). The examination of interactions between the composed BPEL processes is transformed into the verification of deadlock-freeness of a BPN. Nezhad et al. (2007) generate a mismatch tree to handle deadlock situations. The basis of such tree is similar to the reachability graph in Petri nets. Although the current methods provide useful insights into the problem by adopting Petri net based analysis methods, e.g., WofBPEL, Fiona, c-graph and mismatch tree, their analysis is mainly based on a reachable state space and they do not propose an effective solution to resolve the protocol-level mismatch issues.

For example, following the mismatch tree approach that is proposed by Nezhad et al., we have choices 1-4 for the scenarios in Figure 4. For each choice, we have to search all the reachable state space and find out if it results in a future deadlock. Note that, the complexity for generating the reachable state space is exponential. Normally, assume that there are w web services and each of them is waiting for a message, the number of solutions to consider should be $O(2^w)$. Assume that there are k nodes in a Petri net. Then the complexity for generating the reachable state space is $O(Ce^k)$ for each solution. Thus the total complexity to find the best solution would be $O(C2^w e^k)$.

Compared with their work, the proposed one is more efficient. For example, to solve the same problem in Figure 4, after generating the siphons, it simply uses the linear programming to find the best solution. Assume that there are k nodes in the Petri net. Then the complexity for generating the minimal siphons is exponential, i.e., $O(Ce^k)$. Because the complexity to solve linear programming is polynomial-time, the total complexity is still $O(Ce^k)$.

Moreover, because siphons depend on only the structure of Petri nets, they can be generated off-line. Thus, the generation process can run in parallel with web services' interaction. That is to say, we can generate the minimal siphons before the protocol mismatch appears and we can run the linear programming right after the protocol mismatch appears. However, the reachable state space method is strongly based on the input status. Thus, only when the protocol mismatch really happens, we can obtain the input status and then we can test the candidate solutions in reachable state space method. A detailed comparison is shown in Figure 13.

Our previous work (Xiong, 2010) also proposes a method to solve non-local choice mismatches. There are two major differences between this work and (Xiong, 2010). (1) The protocol-mismatches that this work can solve include both mutual-waiting and non-local choice mismatches. Our previous work (Xiong, 2010) can only solve non-local choice mismatches. Compared with previous work, this work can solve more general

protocol-mismatches. (2) Although both of the works can solve non-local choice mismatches, they are using different methods. The previous work uses a method based on adding information links and needs to modify BPEL source code. It does not allow non-local choice mismatches to happen. Compared with it, this work proposes a method based on providing missing messages. It can allow non-local choice mismatches to happen and then it provides those messages to resolve protocol-mismatches.

CONCLUSION

In service composition, services interact with each other through a sequence of messages to achieve a certain business goal. However, mismatches at

Figure 13. The comparison between Petri net siphon based and reachability state space based methods

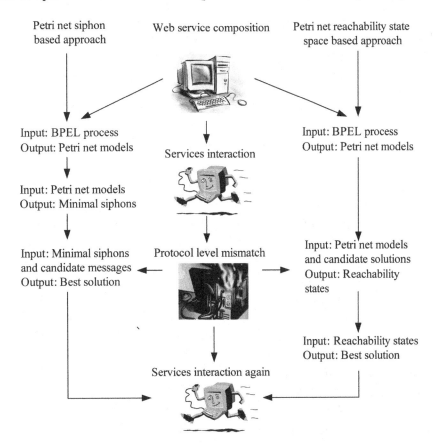

the interface and protocol levels may render the composite service unusable. There are a plethora of works on service interface level mismatches and most of the interface level mismatch can be solved by using adaptors. However, the mismatches at protocol levels are not well addressed. Existing studies based on adaptors and reachability analyses fails to provide an efficient solution.

The main contribution of this paper is to propose a Petri net siphon-based solution to protocol level mismatches. The whole approach follows the steps of modeling, analysis and solution. Firstly, the web service composition is modeled by a set of Petri nets, i.e., SSN, WMN, and C-net. Secondly, the protocol level mismatch problem is analyzed by Petri net siphons. We make a useful conclusion that, there should be a protocol level mismatch if and only if there is an empty siphon in the C-net. Finally, based on this conclusion, we use a linear programming method to find the best solution. Our approach provides an optimized and also automatic solution for correcting protocol-mismatches. This approach greatly reduces the amount of interactions with developers.

In the future, first, we would like to extend our approach to address the protocol discovery from message logs. Our current approach is based on the already known BPEL. We would like to extend our approach to deal with the situation when BPEL is unknown and conversations between two or more services should be discovered by message logs. Data mining and machine learning technique may help to accomplish this goal (Aalst, 2008). Second, we would like to extend our approach to address the dynamically evolving service protocols. As mentioned in (Ryu, 2007; Ryu, 2008), service protocols can dynamically adapt to changes in business needs and/or regulations. For example, Ryu et al. (2008) propose a comprehensive approach to dynamic protocol evolution management using a finite state machine model. In this paper, we only target at static service protocols. We plan to adapt our approach to deal with dynamic protocol evolution and find out how changes in protocol

can impact the analysis and solution. Finally, although the search for siphons can be performed offline and the computation of minimum siphons is simple, in some complex structured C-net, such computation can be expensive. Some polynomial complex algorithms to find and control siphons should be explored for C-nets by making full use of their special structural information. Some recent advance (Wang, 2009; Li, 2009; Hu, 2009; Wu, 2008) may provide good help along this direction.

ACKNOWLEDGMENT

This research has been partially funded by National Science Foundation grants ENG/EEC-0335622, CISE/CNS-0646430, CISE/CNS-0716484, AFOSR grant FA9550-06-1-0201, NIH grant U54 RR 024380-01, IBM, Hewlett-Packard, Wipro Technologies, and Georgia Tech Foundation through the John P. Imlay, Jr. Chair endowment. Any opinions, findings, and conclusions or recommendations expressed in this material are those of the authors and do not necessarily reflect the views of the National Science Foundation or other funding agencies and companies mentioned above.

REFERENCES

Aalst, W. M. P. (1998). The application of Petri Nets to workflow management. *The Journal of Circuits. Systems and Computers, 8*(1), 21–66.

Aalst, W. M. P., & Verbeek, H. (2008). Process Mining in Web Services: The WebSphere Case. *IEEE Data Eng. Bull., 31*(3), 45–48.

Ben-Abdallah, H., & Leue, S. (1997). Syntactic detection of process divergence and non-local choice in message sequence charts. In *Proceedings of the 2nd International Workshop on Tools and Algorithms for the Construction and Analysis of Systems*, Enschede, The Netherlands (pp. 259-274).

Benatallah, B., Casati, F., Grigori, D., Nezhad, H., & Toumani, F. (2005). Developing Adaptors for Web services Integration. In *Proceedings of the CAiSE*, Porto, Portugal (pp. 415-429).

Benatallah, B., Casati, F., & Toumani, F. (2006). Representing, analysing and managing web service protocols. *Data & Knowledge Engineering*, *58*(3), 327–357. doi:10.1016/j.datak.2005.07.006

Chu, F., & Xie, X. L. (1997). Deadlock analysis of Petri nets using siphons and mathematical programming. *IEEE Transactions on Robotics and Automation*, *13*(6), 793–804. doi:10.1109/70.650158

Curbera, F., Mukhi, N., Nagy, W., & Weerawarana, S. (2006). Implementing BPEL4WS: the Architecture of a BPEL4WS Implementation. *Concurrency and Computation*, *18*(10), 1219–1228. doi:10.1002/cpe.1003

Dong, X., Halevy, A., Madhavan, J., Nemes, E., & Zhang, J. (2004). Similarity Search for Web Services. In *Proceedings of the 30th Intern. Conf. on Very Large Data Bases*, Toronto, Canada (pp. 372-383).

Ezpeleta, J., Colom, J., & Martinez, J. (1995). A Petri Net based Deadlock Prevention Policy for Flexible Manufacturing Systems. *IEEE Transactions on Robotics and Automation*, *11*(2), 173–184. doi:10.1109/70.370500

Fahland, D., & Reisig, W. (2005). ASM-based semantics for BPEL: The negative control flow. In *Proceedings of the 12th International Workshop on Abstract State Machines*, Paris (pp. 131-151).

Ferrara, A. (2004). Web Services: a Process Algebra Approach. In *Proceedings of the 2nd International Conference on Service Oriented Computing*, New York (pp. 242-251).

Fisteus, J., Fernández, L., & Kloos, C. (2004). Formal verification of BPEL4WS business collaborations. In *Proceedings of the 5th International Conference on Electronic Commerce and Web Technologies*, Zaragoza, Spain (pp. 76-85).

Foster, H., Uchitel, S., Magee, J., & Kramer, J. (2005). Tool support for model-based engineering of Web service compositions. In *Proceedings of the 2005 IEEE International Conference on Web Services*, Orlando, FL (pp. 95-102).

Fu, X., Bultan, T., & Su, J. (2004). Analysis of Interacting BPEL Web Services. In *Proceedings of the 13th International World Wide Web Conference*, New York (pp. 621-630).

Hinz, S., Schmidt, K., & Stahl, C. (2005). Transforming BPEL to Petri Nets. In *Proceedings of the 3rd International Conference on Business Process Management*, Nancy, France (pp. 220-235).

Hu, H., Zhou, M. C., & Li, Z. W. (2009). Liveness Enforcing Supervision of Video Streaming Systems Using Non-sequential Petri Nets. *IEEE Transactions on Multimedia*, *11*(8), 1446–1456. doi:10.1109/TMM.2009.2032678

König, D., Lohmann, N., Moser, S., Stahl, C., & Wolf, K. (2008). Extending the Compatibility Notion for Abstract WS-BPEL Processes. In *Proceedings of the 17th International World Wide Web Conference*, Beijing, China (pp. 785-794).

Li, Z. W., & Zhou, M. C. (2004). Elementary Siphons of Petri Nets and Their Applications to Deadlock Prevention in Flexible Manufacturing Systems. *IEEE Trans. on Sys., Man and Cybern. Part A*, *34*(1), 38–51.

Li, Z. W., & Zhou, M. C. (2009). *Deadlock Resolution in Automated Manufacturing Systems: A Novel Petri Net Approach*. New York: Springer.

Lohmann, N. (2007). A feature-complete Petri net semantics for WS-BPEL 2.0. In *Proceedings of the 4th International Workshop on Web Services and Formal Methods*, Brisbane, Australia (pp. 77-91).

Lohmann, N., Massuthe, P., Stahl, C., & Weinberg, D. (2006). Analyzing Interacting BPEL Processes. In *Proceedings of the 4th International Conference on Business Process Management*, Vienna, Austria (pp. 17-32).

Lucchia, R., & Mazzara, M. (2007). A pi-calculus based semantics for WS-BPEL. *Journal of Logic and Algebraic Programming*, *70*(1), 96–118. doi:10.1016/j.jlap.2006.05.007

Martens, A. (2003). Usability of Web services. In *Proceedings of the 4th Intern. Conf. on Web Info. Systems Eng. Workshops*, Rome, Italy (pp. 182-190).

Martens, A., Hamadi, R., & Benatallah, B. (2003). A Petri Net based Model for Web Service Composition. In *Proceedings of the 14th Australian Database Conf.*, Adelaide, Australia (pp. 191-200).

Murata, T. (1989). Petri nets: Properties, analysis and applications. *Proceedings of the IEEE*, *77*(4), 541–580. doi:10.1109/5.24143

Nezhad, H., Benatallah, B., Martens, A., Curbera, F., & Casati, F. (2007). SemiAutomated Adaptation of Service Interactions. In *Proceedings of the 16th International World Wide Web Conference*, Banff, Alberta, Canada (pp. 993-1002).

Ouyang, C., Verbeek, E., Aalst, W. M. P., Breutel, S., Dumas, M., & Hofstede, A. (2005). WofBPEL: A Tool for Automated Analysis of BPEL Processes. In *Proceedings of the 3rd Intern. Conf. on Service Oriented Computing*, Amsterdam (pp. 484-489).

Ryu, S., Casati, F., Skogsrud, H., Benatallah, B., & Saint-Paul, R. (2008). Supporting the dynamic evolution of Web service protocols in service-oriented architectures. *ACM Transactions on the Web*, *2*(2).

Ryu, S., Saint-Paul, R., Benatallah, B., & Casati, F. (2007). A Framework for Managing the Evolution of Business Protocols in Web Services. In *Proceedings of the 4th Asia-Pacific Conference on Conceptual Modelling*, Ballarat, Victoria, Australia (pp. 49-59).

Wang, A. R., Li, Z. W., Jia, J. Y., & Zhou, M. C. (2009). An Effective Algorithm to Find Elementary Siphons in a Class of Petri Nets. *IEEE Trans. on Sys., Man and Cybern., Part A*, *39*(4).

Wang, Y., & Stroulia, E. (2003). Flexible interface matching for web-service discovery. In *Proceedings of the 4th Intern. Conf. on Web Info. Sys. Eng.*, Rome, Italy (pp. 147-156).

Wohed, P., Aalst, W. M. P., Dumas, M., & Hofstede, A. (2003). Analysis of Web services composition languages: The case of BPEL4WS. In *Proceedings of the 22nd International Conference on Conceptual Modeling*, Chicago (pp. 200-215).

Wu, N. Q., Zhou, M. C., & Li, Z. W. (2008). Resource-Oriented Petri Net for Deadlock Avoidance in Flexible Assembly Systems. *IEEE Trans. on Systems, Man, and Cybernetics. Part A*, *38*(1), 56–69.

Xiong, P. C., Fan, Y. S., & Zhou, M. C. (2010). A Petri Net Approach to Analysis and Composition of Web Services. *IEEE Trans. on Sys., Man and Cybern. Part A*, *40*(2), 376–387.

Yellin, D., & Strom, R. (1997). Protocol specifications and component adaptors. *ACM Trans. on Prog. Lang. and Sys.*, *19*(2), 292–333.

Zhou, M., & Venkatesh, K. (1998). *Modeling, Simulation and Control of Flexible Manufacturing Systems: A Petri Net Approach*. Singapore, Singapore: World Scientific.

This work was previously published in the International Journal of Web Services Research, Volume 7, Issue 4, edited by Liang-Jie (LJ) Zhang, pp. 1-20, copyright 2010 by IGI Publishing (an imprint of IGI Global).

Chapter 4
A Federated Approach to Information Management in Grids

Mehmet S. Aktas
TUBITAK-Marmara Research Center, Turkey

Geoffrey C. Fox
Indiana University, USA

Marlon Pierce
Indiana University, USA

ABSTRACT

We propose a novel approach to managing information in grids. The proposed approach is an add-on information system that provides unification and federation of grid information services. The system interacts with local information services and assembles their metadata instances under one hybrid architecture to provide a common query/publish interface to different kinds of metadata. The system also supports interoperability of major grid information services by providing federated information management. We present the semantics and architectural design for this system. We introduce a prototype implementation and present its evaluation. As the results indicate, the proposed system achieves unification and federation of custom implementations of grid information services with negligible processing overheads.

1. INTRODUCTION

Independent Grid projects have developed their own solutions to problems associated with Information Services. These solutions target vastly different systems and address diverse sets of re-

quirements (Zanikolas et al., 2005). For example, large-scale Grid applications require management of large amounts of relatively slow and varying metadata, while others such as e-Science Grid applications dynamically assemble modest numbers of distributed services and are designed for specific tasks, tasks that can be as diverse as forecasting earthquakes (Aktas et al., 2004) or managing

DOI: 10.4018/978-1-4666-1942-5.ch004

audiovisual collaboration sessions (Wu, 2005). These dynamic Grid/Web service collections require specific support for dynamic metadata.

Existing solutions to Grid Information Services present some challenges for metadata services: First, independent Grid applications use customized implementations of Grid Information Services, whose data model and communication language is application specific (Zanikolas et al., 2005). These information services are in need of greater interoperability to enable communication between different grid projects so that they can share and utilize each other's resources (OGF-GIN, n.d.). Second, previous solutions do not address metadata management requirements of most Grid applications that have both large-scale, static and small-scale, highly dynamic metadata associated with Grid/Web Services (Zanikolas et al., 2005). Third, existing solutions do not provide uniform interfaces for publishing and discovery of both dynamically generated and static information (Zanikolas et al., 2005). The lack of a uniform interface limits clients, who must interact with more than one metadata service. In turn, this necessity increases the complexity of clients and creates fat clients. We therefore see the existing solutions of Grid Information Services as an important area of investigation.

To address these challenges, an ideal Grid Information Service Architecture should meet the following requirements: *uniformity:* the architecture should support one-to-many information services and their communication protocols; *federation:* the architecture should present a federation capability where different information services can interoperate with each other; *interoperability:* the architecture should be compatible with widely used, existing Grid/Web Service standards; *performance:* the architecture should search/access/store metadata with negligible processing overheads; *persistency:* the architecture should back-up metadata without degradation of the system performance; and *fault tolerance:*

the architecture should achieve distribution and redundancy of information.

We have previously investigated the design, implementation, and evaluation of two specific data-systems: UDDI XML Metadata Service and WS-Context XML Metadata Service (Aktas et al., 2008a). We designed, implemented, and evaluated centralized versions of these metadata-systems and applied them to different application domains, such as geographical information systems, sensor grids (Aktas et al., 2004), and collaboration grids (Wu, 2005). However, these systems did not fully meet the aforementioned metadata management requirements of these application use domains.

We propose a Hybrid Grid Information Service called Hybrid Service that addresses the challenges of announcing and discovering resources in Grids, as seen in previous work and that improves our own previous work by addressing complete metadata management requirements of a number of application use domains.

In this study, we present the semantics and architectural design of the centralized Hybrid Service. We introduce a prototype implementation of this architecture and present its performance evaluation. As the main focus of this paper is information federation in Grid Information Services, we discuss unification, federation, interoperability, and performance aspects and leave out distribution and fault-tolerance aspects of the system. The main novelty of this study is that it describes an architecture, implementation, and evaluation of a Hybrid Grid Information Service that supports both distributed and centralized paradigms and manages both dynamic, small-scale and quasi-static, large-scale metadata. This novel approach unifies custom implementations of Grid Information Services to provide a common access interface to different kinds of metadata. It also provides federation of information among the Grid Information Services, so that they can share or exchange metadata with each other. This study should inspire the design of other information systems along with similar metadata management requirements.

The organization of the rest of this paper is as follows. Section 2 reviews work relevant to this study. Section 3 gives an overview of the proposed Hybrid Service system. Section 4 presents the semantics of the Hybrid Service. Section 5 presents the architectural design details and the prototype implementation of the system. Section 6 analyzes the performance evaluation of the Hybrid Service prototype. It presents benchmarking on performance and scalability aspects of the system. Section 7 contains the summary and the future research directions.

2. RELEVANT WORK

2.1. Information integration

Information integration is the process of unifying information that resides at multiple sources and providing a unified access interface (Lenzerini, 2002). Unifying heterogeneous data sources under a single architecture has been the target of many investigations (Ziegler, 2004). For example, information integration research is studied within distributed database systems research (Ozsu, 1999). Such research investigates how to share data at a higher conceptual level, while ignoring the implementation details of the local data systems. In turn, this effort enables transparent access to multiple, logically interrelated distributed databases. Based on this scheme, an application can pose a query to the distributed database system, which maps the query into local queries, integrates the results coming from different data systems, and returns the results to the client. Previous work on merging heterogeneous information systems can be categorized broadly as either global-as-view or local-as-view integration (Florescu, 1998). In the former category, data from several sources are transformed into a global schema and can be queried with a uniform query interface. In the latter

category, queries are transformed into specialized queries over the local databases. In this category, integration is carried out by transforming queries.

2.1.1. Limitations

The global schema approach captures expressiveness capabilities of customized local schemas. However, this approach cannot scale up to a high number of data sources. Another drawback is the need to update the global schema whenever a new schema is to be integrated and/or an existing local system changes its schema. In the local-as-view approach, because of the lack of a global schema in the data integration architecture, each local-system's schema may need to be mapped against each other. This in turn will lead to a large number of mappings that need to be created and managed.

2.1.2. Discussion

To achieve data integration, global-as-view or local-as-view approaches can be utilized. In the local-as-view approach, information integration happens through query processing. In other words, the local-as-view approach transforms the client's query into local queries and integrates the results. This methodology has performance drawbacks due to overhead of query mapping and forwarding. Furthermore, in architectures such as those of federated database systems, a high number of query mappings may be required. To achieve high performance, a higher-level add-on architecture that can assemble the information coming from different metadata systems and that can carry out queries on the heterogeneous information space is needed. This approach should be designed in such a way that the single repository should be distributed to avoid single point of failure. We think that once we achieve such higher-level architecture, the global-as-view approach can be used for integrating heterogeneous local information services. This approach encapsulates the expressiveness power of the customized schemas that are being integrated. In this research, we design and build an architecture for a Grid Information Service that would support information integration. To achieve this objective, we revisit the research ideas in distributed database systems and utilize global-as-view approach in our architecture. In sum, we take as a design requirement that the proposed system should be designed as an add-on architecture above existing Grid Information Services to provide unification and federation of information coming from different metadata systems.

2.2. Efforts toward Interoperability

Efforts toward interoperability in the Grid community have recently been promoted by the Open Grid Forum (OGF) (OGF, n.d.). The OGF has started a research activity called GIN (Grid Interoperation Now) (OGF-GIN, n.d.) to manage interoperation among major grid projects such as EGEE (EGEE, n.d.), UK National Grid Service (NGS, n.d.). This effort includes interoperation in the areas of authorization and identity management, data management and movement, job description and submission, information services and schema, and operations experience of pilot test applications. Among these interoperation efforts, interoperability of information services is also addressed. The OGF suggests guidelines for interoperability in such a way that each grid's internal information system will act as a translator for accessing information from other information services. As the information service schema, the Open Grid Forum GIN workgroup utilizes a subset of the Glue schema as the common description schema for information services. The Grid Laboratory Uniform Environment (Glue) Schema (GLUE, n.d.) is an effort to support interoperability between US and Europe Grid Projects. It presents description of core Grid resources at the conceptual level by defining an information model. It is used for both monitoring and discovery purposes and describes the state and functionalities of Grid resources.

2.2.1. Discussion

In this research, we propose a system architecture that meets the interoperability guidelines suggested by the OGF GIN work group. To this end, we integrate the Glue Schema into our design to be able to interoperate with GIN activity participating information services. With this study, we also intend to build an architecture that would address a wide range of Web Service applications and provide an interoperation-bridge across the existing implementations of information services. Thus, we implement two widely used and WS-I compatible grid information services: Extended UDDI XML Metadata Service and WS-Context XML Metadata Service.

2.3. The Index Service

The Index Service (Index, n.d.) is a semantic metadata registry provided by the Globus Toolkit (Globus, n.d.), which is an open source software toolkit used for building Grid systems and applications. The Globus Toolkit utilizes the The WS-Resource Framework (WSRF) (Czajkowski, 2004) that is a set of six Web Services specifications that define modeling and managing state in Web Services. In WSRF approach, a resource is an entity that encapsulates the state (metadata) of a stateful Web Service and metadata items are exposed as ResourceProperties by the WSRF capable grid services. Such metadata can be queried using standard web service operations as defined by the WSRF. The Globus-provided Index Service is designed for WSRF capable grid services and provides repository for both stateful and stateless medatata in Grid infrastructures. It contains a registry of grid resources and collects information from them, making it accessible and queryable from one location. caGrid (Tan et al., 2008) is an open source middleware that enables secure data sharing and analysis among institutions and utilizes an extended version of the Index Service for semantic metadata discovery.

2.3.1. Discussion

In this research, we propose a hybrid registry that supports integration of the widely used WS-I compatible service metadata repositories: UDDI and WS-Context. We use the WS-Context Specification, which is different from the Index Service, to model and manage state in Web Services. Point-to-point methodologies provide service conversation with metadata only from the two services that exchange information. However, by utilizing the WS-Context approach, the Hybrid Service provides communication among many services based on the third-party metadata management strategy.

2.4. The Universal Description, Discovery, and Integration (UDDI) Specification

The Universal Description, Discovery, and Integration (UDDI) Specification (Bellwood et al., 2003) is a widely used standard that enables services to advertise themselves and discover other services. It is a WS-Interoperability (WS-I) compatible standard. UDDI Specification is designed as a domain-independent, standardized method for publishing/discovering information about Web Services. It also offers users a unified and systematic way to find service providers through a centralized registry of services. A number of studies extend and improve the out-of-box UDDI Specification. Open Geographical Information Systems Consortium (OGC, 2009), for example, introduced a set of design principles, requirements, and spatial discovery methodologies for the discovery of OGC services through an UDDI interface (OWS1.2, 2003). The methodologies that OGC introduced have since been implemented by various organizations such as (Sycline, n.d.). The Syncline experiment implemented a UDDI discovery interface on an existing OGC Catalog Service data model so that UDDI users can discover services registered through OGC Registries.

This capability showed that spatial discovery and content discovery through UDDI Specification is possible. Other projects such as UDDI-M (Dialani, 2002) and UDDIe (ShaikhAli et al., 2003) introduced the idea of associating metadata and lifetime with UDDI Registry service descriptions, where retrieval relies on the matches of attribute name-value pairs between service descriptions and service requests. METEOR-S (Verma, 2005) leveraged UDDI Specification by utilizing semantic web languages and identifying different semantics when describing a service, such as data, functional, quality of service, and executions. Grimories (GRIMOIRES, n.d.) extends the functionalities of UDDI to provide a semantic enabled registry designed and developed for the MyGrid project (MyGrid, n.d.). The Grimories project supports third-party attachment of metadata about services and represents all published metadata in the form of RDF triples, either in a database, in a file, or in a memory.

2.4.1. Limitations

We find following limitations in the existing out-of-box UDDI specifications: First, UDDI introduces a keyword-based retrieval mechanism and does not allow advanced metadata-oriented query capabilities. Second, UDDI does not take into account the volatile behavior of services. Third, UDDI does not provide domain-specific query capabilities such as geospatial queries. We find the following limitations in the OGC's UDDI approach: First, the UDDI introduced by the OGC is designed for and limited to geospatial specific usage. Second, the OGC approach does not define a data model rich enough to capture descriptive metadata that might be associated with service entries. We also find limitations in the existing UDDI-Extensions: These approaches have investigated a generic and centralized metadata service that focus on domain-independent metadata management problems. However, because they are generic, these solutions do not solve the domain-specific metadata management problems as we see in the geographical information system domain.

2.4.2. Discussion

The UDDI Specification is promising as a widely used WS-I compatible standard to manage semi-static metadata associated to Web Services. For this research, we built a UDDI XML Metadata Service to address the aforementioned limitations of previous UDDI solutions. This implementation manages both prescriptive and descriptive metadata associated with Grid/Web Services and addresses metadata management requirements of geospatial services.

2.5. The Web Services Context (WS-Context) Specification

The Web Services Context (WS-Context) Specification (Bunting, 2003) defines a simple mechanism to share and keep track of common information shared between multiple participants in Web Service interactions. It is a lightweight storage mechanism, which allows participants of an activity to propagate and share context information. WS-Context Specification defines an activity as a unit of distributed work involving one or more parties (services, components). In order for an activity to extend over a number of Web Services, certain information has to flow among the participants of the application. This specification refers to such information as context and focuses on its management. The WS-Context Specification defines three main components: a) context service, b) context, and c) an activity lifecycle service. The context service is the core service and is concerned with managing the lifecycle of context propagation. The context defines information about an activity and is referenced with a URI. It allows a collection of actions to take place for a common outcome. The minimum required context information (such as the context URI) is

exchanged among Web Services in the header of SOAP messages to correlate the distributed work in an activity. This way, a participant service obtains the identifier and makes a key-based retrieval on the context service. Thus, a typical search with the WS-Context is based mainly on key-based retrieval/publication capabilities. The activity of lifecycle service defines the scope of a component activity. Note that activities can be nested. An activity may be a component activity of another. In this case, additional information (such as security metadata) to a basic context may be kept in a component service, which is registered with the core context service and participates in the lifecycle of an activity.

2.5.1. Limitations

We find following limitations in WS-Context Specification. First, the context service, a component defined by WS-Context to provide access/storage to state information, has limited functionalities, such as its two primary operations: GetContext and SetContext. However, traditional and Semantic Grid applications present extensive metadata needs, which in turn, require advanced search/access/store interface to distributed session state information. Second, the WS-Context Specification focuses only on defining stateful interactions of Web Services. It does not define a searchable repository for interaction-independent information associated with the services involved in an activity. There is a need for a unified specification, which can provide an interface not only for stateful metadata but also for the stateless, interaction-independent metadata associated with Web Services.

2.5.2. Discussion

The WS-Context Specification is a promising approach for tackling the problem of managing distributed session state, since it models a session metadata repository as an external entity where more than two services can easily access/ store highly dynamic, shared metadata. For this research, we implemented a prototype of the WS-Context – Context Manager Service by expanding the out-of-box WS-Context Specifications. This implementation manages dynamically generated session-related metadata.

2.6. Information Security

Information security is a fundamental issue in Grid Information Services, as the Grid/Web Service metadata may not be open to anyone. Thus, an information security mechanism is needed. Managing information security deals with managing access rights. The capability-based access control is a commonly used approach for managing access rights. It is used to give each user a list of capabilities to give the access rights related to the metadata (Tanenbaum & Van Steen, 2002). In this scenario, a user can access the metadata only if he or she has sufficient access rights. A protection domain is another approach in which the system grants the request and carries out the operation first by checking with the protection domain associated with that request (Saltzer, 1975).

2.6.1. Discussion

In this study, we leave the investigating and leveraging of information security research for future work, and instead concentrate on the unification, federation, and interoperability aspects of the system.

2.7. TupleSpaces

TupleSpaces is an associated memory paradigm. A TupleSpace forms an associated shared memory through which two or more processes can exchange/share data. It provides mutual exclusive access, associative lookup and persistence for a repository of tuples that can be accessed concurrently. Thus, a tuplespace can be used to coordinate

events of processes. A tuplespace is comprised of a set of tuples: data structures containing typed fields where each field contains a value. A small example of a tuple would be: ("context_id", Context), which indicates a tuple with two fields: a) a string, "context_id" and b) an object, "Context". The tuplespace was first introduced by Gelernter and Carriero at Yale University (Carriero, 1989) as a part of Linda programming language. Linda consists fundamentally of four operations ("in", "rd", "out" and "eval") through which tuples can be added, retrieved or taken from a tuplespace. The JavaSpaces (Sun Microsystems, 1999) project by Sun extends and implements Linda. Linda has been extended to support different types of communication and coordination between systems and has increased some interest in diverse communities such as the ubiquitous computing (sTuples (Khushraj et al., 2004)) and Semantic Web (Triple Spaces, see Krummenacher et al., 2005).

2.7.1. Discussion

The tuplespaces paradigm provides mutually exclusive access, which in turn enables data sharing between processes. This way both the shared memory and the processes are temporarily and spatially uncoupled. We take as a requirement that our design should employ the tuplespaces paradigm as an in-memory storage to meet aforementioned performance requirement of the system. A java implementation of the TupleSpaces concept, JavaSpaces, was released by Sun MicroSystems. However, JavaSpaces requires a number of daemon services to run including a naming service, a restart service, and the JavaSpaces service. These services add complexity to the systems employing JavaSpaces. MicroSpaces (Coleman et al., 2004), an open-source implementation of TupleSpaces paradigm, is an alternative collection of java libraries and provides same API semantics identical with JavaSpaces. MicroSpaces is a multi-threaded application and dependent on RMI to provide interactions with JavaSpaces. Apart from the existing implementation approaches, we take as a requirement that our design should support a lightweight implementation of JavaSpaces that does not require RMI-based communication protocol or other daemon services to run.

3. HYBRID SERVICE

We designed and built a novel Grid Information Service Architecture called Hybrid Grid Information Service (Hybrid Service), which provides unification, federation, and interoperability of Grid Information Services. The Hybrid Service forms an add-on architecture that interacts with the local information services and unifies them in a higher-level hybrid system. In other words, it provides a unifying architecture, where one can assemble metadata instances of different information services. We built a prototype implementation that showed that the Hybrid Service achieves unification of the two local information service implementations, WS-Context and Extended UDDI, and support their communication protocols. We also showed that the Hybrid Service achieves information federation by utilizing a global schema, which integrates local information service schemas, and user-provided mapping rules, which provides transformations between the metadata instances of the global schema and the local schemas. With these capabilities, the Hybrid Service enables different Grid Information Service implementations to interact with each other and share each other's metadata. Furthermore, the Hybrid Service provides the ability to issue integrated queries on the heterogeneous metadata space, where metadata comes from different information service providers. In turn, this enables the system to support an integrated access to not only quasi-static, rarely changing interaction-independent metadata, but also highly updated, dynamic interaction-dependent metadata associated with Grid/Web Services. We discuss

semantics of the Hybrid Service in the following section followed by a section in which we discuss the architecture of the system.

4. SEMANTICS

In this section, we discuss four information service specifications: extended UDDI Specification, which extends the existing out-of-box UDDI Specification to address its aforementioned limitations (see Section 1); WS-Context Specification, which improves existing out-of-box Web-Service Context Specification to meet the aforementioned requirements of the Hybrid Service (see Section 1); Glue Schema Specification, which is used as-is to support interoperability with US and Europe Grid projects; and Unified Schema Specification, which integrates the first three information service specifications. We also discuss two Hybrid Service Schemas: Hybrid Schema and SpecMetadata Schema, which define the necessary abstract data models to achieve a generic architecture for unification and federation of different information service implementations in the Hybrid Service. The documentation related to the Hybrid Service Specifications and XML Schemas can be accessed from the project website at Aktas (2009).

4.1. The Extended UDDI Specification

We designed extensions to the out-of-box UDDI Data Structure to associate both prescriptive and descriptive metadata with service entries. An earlier version of our approach to extending UDDI semantics is briefly discussed in (Aktas et al, 2008a). In this way the system can interoperate with existing UDDI clients without requiring an excessive change in the implementations. UDDI-M and UDDIe projects introduced the idea of associating simple (name, value) pairs with service entities. This methodology is promising because it provides a generic metadata catalog and also has its own merits of simplicity in implementation. Thus, we adopt this approach and expand on existing UDDI Specifications as described in the following section.

4.1.1. Extended UDDI Schema

We introduced an extended UDDI data model (see Figure 1) to address the metadata requirements of Geographical Information System/Sensor Grids. This data model includes the two additional/modified entities: a) extended business service entity (businessService) and b) service attribute entity (serviceAttribute). Here, each businessService entity is associated with one-to-many serviceAttribute entities. We describe the additional/modified data model entities (both the businessService and serviceAttribute entities) below.

Business service entity structure: The UDDI's business service entity structure contains descriptive yet limited information about Web Services. A comprehensive description of the out-of-box business service entity structure defined by UDDI can be found in Bellwood (2003). Here, we only discuss the additional XML structures introduced to expand on the existing business service entity. (The structure diagram for the business service entity is illustrated in Figure 2.) These additional XML elements are a) service attribute and b) lease. The service attribute XML element corresponds to a static metadata (e.g., WSDL of a given service). Similar to the session entity, a business service entity may have a lifetime associated with it. A lease structure describes a period of time during which a service can be discoverable.

Service attribute entity structure: A service attribute (serviceAttribute) data structure describes information associated with service entities. The structure diagram for the serviceAttribute entity is illustrated in Figure 2. Each service attribute corresponds to a piece of metadata, and it is simply expressed with (name, value) pairs. Apart from similar (Dialani, 2002), (ShaikhAli et al., 2003) in the proposed system, a service attribute

includes a) a list of abstractAtttributeData, b) a categoryBag and c) a boundingBox XML structures. An abstractAttributeData element is used to represent metadata that is directly related with functionality of the service and store/maintain these domain specific auxiliary files as-is. This allows us to add third-party data models such as "capabilities.xml" metadata file describing the data coverage of domain-specific services such as the geospatial services. An abstractAttributeData can be in any representation format such as XML or RDF. This data structure allows us to pose domain-specific queries on the metadata catalog. Say, an abstractAttributeData of a geospatial service entry contains "capabilities.xml" metadata file. As it is in XML format, a client may conduct a find_service operation with an XPATH query statement to be carried out on the abstractAttributeData, i.e. "capabilities.xml". In this case, the results will be the list of geospatial service entries that satisfy the domain-specific XPATH query. The categoryBag is used to provide a custom classification scheme to categorize serviceAttribute elements. A simple classification could be whether the service attribute is prescriptive or descriptive. A boundingBox element is used to describe both temporal and spatial attributes of a given geographic feature. This way the system enables spatial query capabilities on the metadata catalog.

4.1.2. Extended UDDI Schema XML API

We present extensions/modifications to the existing UDDI XML API set to standardize the additional capabilities of our implementation. These additional capabilities can be grouped under two XML API categories: Publish and Inquiry.

The Publish XML API is used to publish metadata instances belonging to different entities of the extended UDDI Schema. It extends the UDDI Publish XML API Set and consists of the following functions: *save service:* Used to extend

Figure 1. Extended UDDI service schema

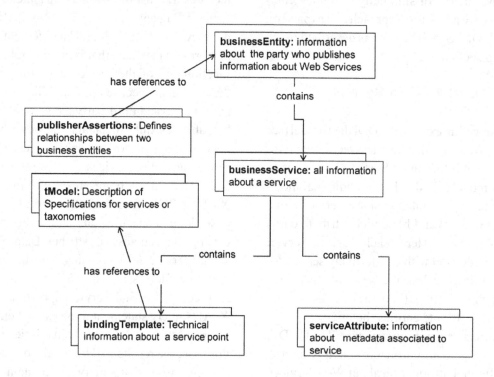

Figure 2. The figure on the left shows the partial structure diagram for businessService entity. The figure on the right shows the structure diagram for serviceAttribute entity.

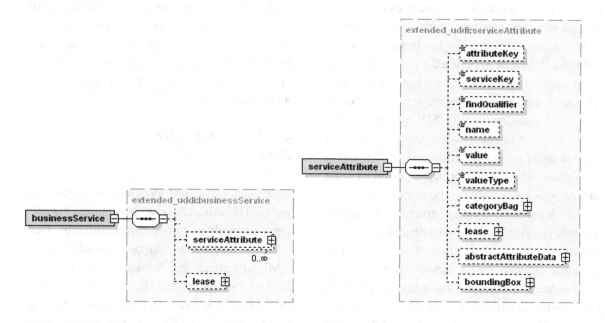

the out-of-box UDDI save service functionality. The save service API call adds/updates one or more Web Services into the service. Each service entity may contain one-to-many serviceAttribute elements and may have a lifetime (lease). *save serviceAttribute:* Used to register or update one or more semi-static metadata associated with a Web Service. *delete service:* Used to delete one or more service entity structures. *delete serviceAttribute:* Used to delete existing serviceAttribute elements from the service. The Inquiry XML API is used to pose inquiries and to retrieve metadata from the Extended UDDI Information Service. It extends the existing UDDI Inquiry XML API set, and consists of the following functions: *find service:* Used to extend the out-of-box UDDI find service functionality. The find service API call locates specific services within the service. It takes additional input parameters, such as serviceAttributeBag and Lease, to facilitate the additional capabilities. *find serviceAttribute:* Used to find the aforementioned serviceAttribute elements. The find serviceAttribute API call returns a list of serviceAttribute structures that match the conditions specified in the arguments. *get serviceAttributeDetail:* Used to retrieve semi-static metadata associated with a unique identifier. The get serviceAttributeDetail API call returns the serviceAttribute structure corresponding to each of the attributeKey values specified in the arguments. *get serviceDetail:* Used to retrieve service entity structure associated with a unique identifier.

4.1.3. Using Extended UDDI Schema XML API

Given the capabilities of the Extended-UDDI Service, one can simply populate metadata instances by using the Extended-UDDI XML API, as in the following scenario. Say, a user publishes a new metadata to be attached to an already existing service in the system. In this case, the user constructs a serviceAttribute element. Based on

aforementioned extended UDDI data model, each service entry is associated with one or more serviceAttribute XML elements. A serviceAttribute corresponds to a piece of interaction-independent metadata that is expressed with (name, value) pair. We can illustrate a serviceAttribute as in the following example: ((throughput, 0.9)). A serviceAttribute can be associated with a lifetime and categorized based on custom classification schemes. A simple classification could be whether the serviceAttribute is prescriptive or descriptive. In the aforementioned example, the throughput service attribute can be classified as descriptive. In some cases, a serviceAttribute may correspond to a domain-specific metadata where service metadata could be directly related with functionality of the service. For instance, OGC compatible Geographical Information System services provide a "capabilities.xml" metadata file describing the data coverage of geospatial services. We use an abstractAttributeData element to represent such metadata and store/maintain these domain specific auxiliary files as-is. As the serviceAttribute is constructed, it can then be published to the Hybrid Service by using "save_serviceAttribute" operation of the extended UDDI XML API. On receiving a metadata publish request, the system extracts the instance of the serviceAttribute entity from the incoming requests, assigns a unique identifier to it and stores in in-memory storage. Once the publish operation is completed, a response is sent to the publishing client.

4.2. The WS-Context Specification

WS-Context tackles the problem of managing distributed session state. Unlike the point-to-point approaches, WS-Context models a third-party metadata repository as an external entity where more than two services can easily access/store highly dynamic, shared metadata. We investigated semantics for a XML Metadata Service that would expand on the WS-Context approach for managing distributed session state information. An earlier version of our approach to extending WS-Context semantics is briefly discussed in (Aktas et al., 2008a).

4.2.1. WS-Context Schema

We introduced an information model comprised of the following entities: sessionEntity, session-Service, and context entities. Figure 3 illustrates the data model for the WS-Context Service. A sessionEntity describes information about a session under which a service activity takes place. A sessionEntity may contain one-to-many session-Service entities. A sessionService entity describes information about a Web Service participating in a session. Both sessionEntity and sessionService may contain one-to-many context entities. A context entity contains information about interaction-dependent, dynamic metadata associated with either sessionService or sessionEntity, or both. Each entity represents specific types of metadata. Instances of these structures have system-defined unique identifiers. An instance of an entity gets its identifier when it is first published into the system. All entities have a lifetime during which the entity instances are expected to be up-to-date. In the sections that follow we discuss the core entities of the WS-Context Service Schema.

Session entity structure: A sessionEntity describes a period of time devoted to a specific activity, associated contexts, and sessionService involved in the activity. A sessionEntity can be considered an information holder for the dynamically generated information. The structure diagram for sessionEntity is illustrated in Figure 4. An instance of a sessionEntity is uniquely identified with a session key. A session key is generated by the system when an instance of the entity is published. If the session key is specified in a publication operation, the system updates the corresponding entry with the new information. When retrieving an instance of a session, a session key must be presented. A sessionEntity may have a name and description associated with it. A name is a user-defined identifier and its uniqueness is determined by the session publisher.

A user-defined identifier is useful to information providers for managing their own data. A description is optional textual information about

Figure 3. WS-Context service schema

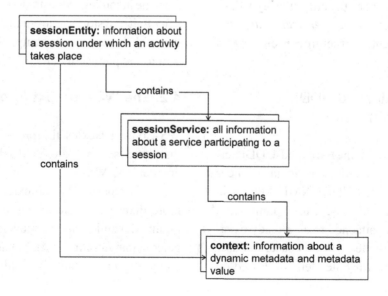

Figure 4. The figure on the left shows the structure diagram for sessionEntity. The figure in the middle shows the structure diagram for sessionService. The figure on the right shows the structure diagram for context entity.

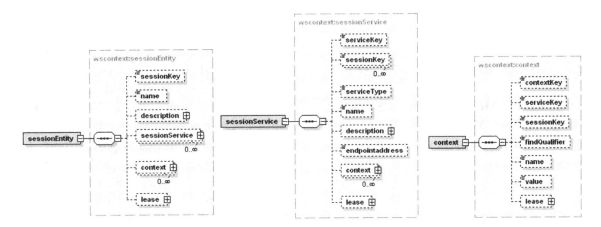

a session. Each sessionEntity contains one-to-many context entity structures. The context entity structure contains dynamic metadata associated with a Web Service or a session instance, or both. Each sessionEntity is associated with its participant sessionServices. The sessionService entity structure is used as an information container for holding limited metadata about a Web Service participating to a session. A lease structure describes a period of time during which instances of a sessionEntity, a sessionService, or a context entity can be discoverable.

Session service entity structure: The sessionService entity contains descriptive, yet limited information about Web Services participating to a session. The structure diagram for the sessionService entity is illustrated in Figure 4. A service key identifies a sessionService entity. A sessionService may participate in one or more sessions, and there is no limit to the number of sessions in which a service can participate. These sessions are identified by session keys. Each sessionService has a name and description associated with it. This entity has an endpoint address field, which describes the endpoint address of the sessionService. Each sessionService may have one

or more context entities associated with it. The lease structure identifies the lifetime of the sessionService under consideration.

Context entity structure: A context entity describes dynamically generated metadata. The structure diagram for a context entity is illustrated in Figure 4. An instance of a context entity is uniquely identified with a context key, which is generated by the system when an instance of the entity is published. If the context key is specified in a publication operation, the system updates the corresponding entry with the new information. When retrieving an instance of a context, a context key must be presented.

A context is associated with a sessionEntity. The session key element uniquely identifies the sessionEntity that is an information container for the context under consideration. A context has also a service key, since it may also be associated with a sessionService participating in a session. A context has a name associated with it. A name is a user-defined identifier and its uniqueness is determined by context publisher. The information providers manage their own data in the interaction-dependent context space by using this user-defined identifier. The context value can be in any representation format, such as binary, XML or RDF. Each context has a lifetime. Thus, each context entity contains the aforementioned lease structure that describes the period of time during which it can be discoverable.

4.2.2. WS-Context Schema XML API

We present an XML API for the WS-Context Service. The XML API sets of the WS-Context XML Metadata Service can be grouped as Publish, Inquiry, Proprietary, and Security.

The Publish XML API is used to publish metadata instances belonging to different entities of the WS-Context Schema. It extends the WS-Context Specification Publication XML API set, and consists of the following functions: *save session:* Used to add/update one or more session entities into the hybrid service. Each session may contain one-to-many context entities, have a lifetime (lease), and be associated with service entries. *save context:* Used to add/update one or more context (dynamic metadata) entities into the service. *save sessionService:* Used to add/update one or more session service entities into the hybrid service. Each session service may contain one-to-many context entities and have a lifetime (lease). *delete session:* Used to delete one or more sessionEntity structures. *delete context:* Used to delete one or more contextEntity structures. *delete sessionService:* Used to delete one or more session service structures. The Inquiry XML API is used to pose inquiries and to retrieve metadata from the service. It extends the existing WS-Context XML API. The extensions to the WS-Context Inquiry API set are outlined as follows: *find session:* Used to find sessionEntity elements. The find session API call returns a session list matching the conditions specified in the arguments. *find context:* Used to find contextEntity elements. The find context API call returns a context list matching the criteria specified in the arguments. *find sessionService:* Used to find session service entity elements. The find sessionService API call

returns a service list matching the criteria specified in the arguments. *get sessionDetail:* Used to retrieve sessionEntity data structure corresponding to each of the session key values specified in the arguments. *get contextDetail:* Used to retrieve the context structure corresponding to the context key values specified. *get sessionServiceDetail:* Used to retrieve sessionService entity data structure corresponding to each of the sessionService key values specified in the arguments. The Proprietary XML API is implemented to provide find/add/modify/delete operations on the publisher list, i.e., authorized users of the system. We adapt semantics for the proprietary XML API from existing UDDI Specifications. This XML API is as follows: *find publisher:* Used to find publishers registered with the system that match the conditions specified in the arguments. *get publisherDetail:* Used to retrieve detailed information regarding one or more publishers with given publisherID(s). *save publisher:* Used to add or update information about a publisher. *delete_publisher:* Used to delete information about a publisher with a given publisherID from the metadata service. The Security XML API is used to enable authenticated access to the service. We adopt the semantics from existing UDDI Specifications. The Security API includes the following function calls. *get_authToken:* Used to request an authentication token as an 'authInfo' (authentication information) element from the service. The authInfo element allows the system implement access control. To this end, both the publication and inquiry API set include authentication information in their input arguments. *discard_authToken:* Used to inform the hybrid service that an authentication token is no longer required and should be considered invalid.

4.2.3. Using WS-Context Schema XML API

Given the capabilities of the WS-Context Service, one can simply populate metadata instances using the WS-Context XML API, as in the following scenario. Say, a user publishes a metadata under an already created session. In this case, the user first constructs a context entity element. Here, a context entity is used to represent interaction-dependent, dynamic metadata associated with a session or a service, or both. Each context entity has both system-defined and user-defined identifiers. The uniqueness of the system-defined identifier is ensured by the system itself, whereas the user-defined identifier is used simply to enable users to manage their memory space in the context service. As an example, we can illustrate a context such as in ((system-defined-uuid, user-defined-uuid, "Job completed")). A context entity also can be associated with a service entity, and it has a lifetime. Contexts may be arranged in parent-child relationships. One can create a hierarchical session tree where each branch can be used as an information holder for contexts with similar characteristics. This capability enables the system to be queried for contexts associated with a session under consideration and also enables the system to track the associations between sessions. As the context elements are constructed, they can be published with the save_context function of the WS-Context XML API. On receiving publishing metadata request, the system processes the request, extracts the context entity instance, assigns a unique identifier, stores in the in-memory storage, and returns a respond back to the client.

4.3. The Glue Schema Specification

The Grid Laboratory Uniform Environment (Glue) Schema is a collaboration effort to support interoperability between US and Europe Grid projects. It presents description of core Grid resources at the conceptual level by defining an information model. The Glue Schema has the following core entities: site, computing element, storage element, service. The site entity is used to aggregate services and resources installed and managed by the same people. The computing element entity is a concept that captures information related computing

resources. The storage element entity presents a data model for abstracting storage resources. The service entity captures all the common attributes associated to Grid Services. A site can aggregate one to n computing elements, one to n storage elements, one to n services. Here, each service may contain one to n service data.

In order to be compatible with the Grid Interoperation Now (GIN) research activity and its participating Grid projects, we integrate the Glue Schema and its communication protocol with the Hybrid Service. Note that in the prototype implementation, we showed that the proposed architecture supports the two information service implementations: Extended UDDI and WS-Context. Based on experimental study with prototype implementation and on the generic architecture of the Hybrid Service, we think that existing implementations of Glue Schema Specification can be easily integrated with the proposed architecture. Thus, we do not provide an implementation for the Glue Schema. For an extensive discussion on the Glue Schema Information Model, we refer the readers to the Glue Schema Specification document, which is available in (GLUE, n.d.).

4.4. The Unified Schema Specification

We introduced an abstract data model and query/publish XML API for a Unified Schema Specification. We achieved the Unified Schema, which integrates the extended UDDI, the WS-Context, and the Glue Schemas by using the schema integration technique.

Schema integration is an activity of providing a unified representation of multiple data models (Rahm & Bernstein, 2001). The schema integration consists of two core steps: *schema matching* and *schema merging* (Bernstein, 2003). The *schema matching* step identifies mapping between the similar entities of schemas. Matching between different schema entities is based on semantic relationships according to the comparison of their intentional domains. To provide schema matching we have two steps: a) finding the matching concepts, b) finding the semantic relationship and constructing partial integrated schemas among the matching concepts. The *schema-merging* step merges different schemas and creates an integrated schema based on the mappings identified during schema matching step. The schema-merging step also identifies the mappings between the integrated schema and local schemas.

We consider the schemas ExtendedUDDI, Glue, and WS-Context as a motivating example to create the Unified Schema. We start the schema integration between the ExtendedUDDI and Glue Schemas. In the first step (schema matching), we find the following correspondences between the entities of these schemas. The first mapping is between ExtendedUDDI.businessEntity and Glue.site entities: The ExtendedUDDI. businessEntity is used to aggregate one-to-many Web Services managed by the same people or organization. Similarly, the Glue.site entity is used to aggregate services and resources managed by same people. Therefore, businessEntity and site are matching concepts, as their intentional domains are similar. The cardinality between the site and businessEntity differs, as the businessEntity may contain one-to-many site entities. For example, Indiana University could be an instance of the businessEntity, while the Community Grids Laboratory could be an instance of the site entity. Indiana University contains one-to-many research labs. The second mapping is between ExtendedUDDI.businessService and Glue.service entities: These entities are equivalent, as the set of real objects that they represent are the same. The cardinality between these entities is also the same. In the integrated schema, we unify these entities as a service entity. The third mapping is between ExtendedUDDI. serviceAttribute and Glue.serviceData: These two entities can be considered as equivalent because both describe attributes associated with Grid/Web Services. The cardinality between these entities is also the same. In the integrated schema, we

unify the entities as metadata. After the schema matching is completed, we merge the two schemas and create an integrated schema (ExtendedUDDI &Glue) based on the mappings that we identified.

We continue with the schema integration by integrating the WS-Context Schema with the newly constructed ExtendedUDDI&Glue Schema. In the schema-matching step, we find the following mappings: First mapping is between (ExtendedUDDI&Glue).businessEntity, (ExtendedUDDI&Glue).site and WS-Context. sessionEntity: The businessEntity is used to aggregate one-to-many services and sites managed by the same people. The site entity aggregates grid resources, including services, computing, and storage elements. The sessionEntity is used to aggregate session services participating in a session. Therefore, businessEntity and site (from ExtendedUDDI&Glue schema) can be considered to be matching concepts with the sessionEntity (from WS-Context schema), as their intentional domains are similar. The cardinality between these entities differs, as the businessEntity may contain one-to-many sessionEntities. The site entity also may contain one-to-many sessionEntities. The second mapping is between: (ExtendedUDDI&Glue).service and WS-Context. sessionService: These entities are equivalent, as the intentional domains that they represent are the same. The cardinality between these entities is also the same. In the integrated schema, we unify these entities as a service entity. The third mapping is between (ExtendedUDDI&Glue). metadata and WS-Context.context: These entities are equivalent as the intentional domains that they represent are the same. The cardinality between these entities is also the same. In the integrated schema, we unify these entities as a metadata entity. Finally, we merge the two schemas based on the mappings that we identified and create a unified schema (see Figure 5 for illustration) that integrates the Extended UDDI, WS-Context, and Glue Schemas.

Figure 5. Unified schema

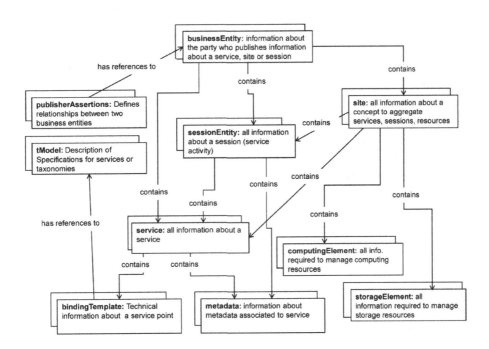

The Unified Schema captures both interaction-dependent and interaction-independent information associated with Grid/Web Services. The Unified Schema unifies matching and disjoint entities of different schemas.

As illustrated in Figure 5, it is comprised of the following entities: businessEntity, sessionEntity, site, service, computingElement, storageElement, bindingTemplate, metadata, tModel, publisherAssertions. A businessEntity describes a party that publishes information about a session (i.e. service activity), site, or service. The publisherAssertions entity defines the relationship between the two businessEntities. The sessionEntity describes information about a service activity that takes place. A sessionEntity may contain one-to-many service and metadata entities. The site entity describes information about services, their sessions, and the resources installed and is managed by the same people. The site entity may contain information about Grid resources, such as services, computingElements, and storageElements. The service

entity provides descriptive information about a Grid/Web Service family. It may contain one-to-many bindingTemplate entities that define the technical information about a service end-point. A bindingTemplate entity contains references to tModel that define descriptions of specifications for service end-points. The service entity may also have one-to-many metadata attached to it. A metadata contains information about both interaction-dependent, interaction-independent metadata and service data associated to Grid/Web Services. A metadata entity describes the information pieces associated with services, sites, or sessions as (name, value) pairs.

4.4.1. The Unified Schema XML API

To facilitate testing of the federation capability, we introduce a limited Query/Publish XML API that can be carried out on the instances of the Unified Schema. We can group the Unified Schema XML API under two categories: Publish and Inquiry.

The Publish XML API is used to publish metadata instances belonging to different entities of the Unified Schema and consists of the following functions: *save business:* Used to add/update one or more business entities into the hybrid service. *save session:* Used to add/update one or more session entities into the hybrid service. Each session may contain one-to-many metadata, one-to-many service entities, and have a lifetime (lease). *save service:* Used to add/update one or more service entries into the hybrid service. Each service entity may contain one-to-many metadata element and may have a lifetime (lease). *save metadata:* Used to register or update one or more metadata associated with a service. *delete business:* Used to delete one or more business entity structures. *delete session:* Used to delete one or more sessionEntity structures. *delete service:* Used to delete one or more service entity structures. *delete metadata:* Used to delete existing metadata elements from the hybrid service. The Inquiry XML API is used to pose inquiries and to retrieve metadata from the service. It consists of the following functions: *find business:* This API call locates specific businesses within the hybrid services. *find session:* Used to find sessionEntity elements. The find session API call returns a session list matching the conditions specified in the arguments. *find service:* Used to locate specific services within the hybrid service. *find metadata:* Used to find service entity elements. The find service API call returns a service list matching the criteria specified in the arguments. *get businessDetail:* Used to retrieve businessEntity data structure of the Unified Schema corresponding to each of the business key values specified in the arguments. *get sessionDetail:* Used to retrieve sessionEntity data structure corresponding to each of the session key values specified in the arguments. *get serviceDetail:* Used to retrieve service entity data structure corresponding to each of the service key values specified in the arguments. *get metadataDetail:* Used to retrieve the metadata structure corresponding to the metadata key values specified.

4.4.2. Using the Unified Schema XML API

Given these capabilities, one can simply populate the Hybrid Service with Unified Schema metadata instances as in the following scenario. Say, a user wants to publish both session-related and interaction-independent metadata associated with an existing service. In this case, the user constructs a metadata entity instance. Each metadata entity has both system-defined and user-defined identifiers. The uniqueness of the system-defined identifier is ensured by the system itself; whereas, the user-defined identifier is used simply to enable users to manage their memory space in the context service. We can illustrate a context as in the following examples: a) ((throughput, 0.9)) and b) ((system-defined-uuid, user-defined-uuid, "Job completed")). A metadata entity also can be associated with the site or sessionEntity of the Unified Schema, and it has a lifetime. As the metadata entity instances are constructed, they can be published with the "save_metadata" function of the Unified Schema XML API. On receiving a publishing metadata request, the system processes the request, extracts the metadata entity instance, assigns a unique identifier, stores in the in-memory storage, and returns a respond back to the client.

4.5. The Hybrid Service Semantics

The Hybrid Service introduces an abstraction layer of a uniform access interface to support one-to-many information service specifications (such as WS-Context, Extended UDDI, or Unified Schema).

To achieve the uniform access capability, the system presents two XML Schemas: a) Hybrid Schema and b) Specification Metadata (SpecMetadata) Schema. The Hybrid Schema defines the generic access interface to the Hybrid Service. The SpecMetadata Schema defines the necessary information required by the Hybrid Service to process instances of supported information service schemas. We discuss the semantics of the Hybrid Schema and the SpecMetadata Schema in the following sections.

4.5.1. The Hybrid Schema

The Hybrid Service presents an XML Schema, called the Hybrid Schema, to enable uniform access to the system. This Schema is designed to achieve a unifying access interface to the Hybrid Service. Thus, it is independent from any of the local information service schemas supported by the Hybrid Service. It defines a set of XML API to enable clients/providers to send specification-based publish/query requests (such as WS-Context's "save_context" request) in a generic way to the system. The XML API consists of the following functions: *hybrid_function:* This XML API call is used to pose inquiry/publish requests based on any specification. With this function, the user can specify the type of the schema and the function. This function allows users to access an information service back-end directly. The user also specifies the specification-based publish/query request in XML format based on the specification under consideration. On receiving the hybrid_function request call, the system handles the request based on the schema and function specified in the query. *save_schemaEntity:* This API call is used to save an instance of any schema entities of a given specification. The save_schemaEntity API call is used to update/add one or more schema entity elements into the Hybrid Grid Information Service. On receiving a save_schemaEntity publication request message, the system processes the incoming message based on information given in the mapping file of the schema under consideration. Then, the system stores the newly-inserted schema entity instances into the in-memory storage. *delete_schemaEntity:* The delete_schemaEntity is used to delete an instance of any schema entities of a given specification. The delete_schemaEntity API call deletes existing service entities associated with the specified key(s) from the system.

On receiving a schema entity deletion request message, the system processes the incoming message based on information given in the mapping file of the schema under consideration. Then the system deletes the correct entity associated with the key. *find_schemaEntity:* This API call locates schemaEntities whose entity types are identified in the arguments. This function allows the user to locate a schema entity among the heterogeneous metadata space. On receiving a find_schemaEntity request message, the system processes the incoming message based on information given in the schema mapping file of the schema under consideration. Then the system locates the correct entities matching the query under consideration. *get_schemaEntity:* The get_schemaEntityDetail is used to retrieve an instance of any schema entities of a given specification. It returns the entity structure corresponding to key(s) specified in the query. On receiving a get_schemaEntityDetail retrieval request message, the system processes the incoming message based on information given in the mapping file of the schema under consideration. Then the system retrieves the correct entity associated with the key. Finally, the system sends the result to the user.

To illustrate the Hybrid Service access interface, we discuss the "save_schemaEntity" element (see Figure 6), which is used to publish metadata instances into the Hybrid Service. One utilizes the "save_schemaEntity" element to publish metadata instances for the customized implementations of information service specifications. The "save_schemaEntity" element includes an "authInfo" element, which describes the authentication information; a "lease" element, which is used to identify the lifetime of the metadata instance; a "schemaName" element, which is used to identify a specification schema (such as Extended UDDI Schema); a "schemaFunctionName", which is used to identify the function of the schema (such as "save_serviceAttribute"); and a "schema_SA-VERequestXML", which is an abstract element used for passing the actual XML document of the specific publish function of a given specification. The Hybrid Service requires a specification metadata document that describes all necessary information to process XML API of the schema under consideration. We discuss the specification metadata semantics in the following section.

4.5.2. The SpecMetadata Schema

The SpecMetadata XML Schema is used to define all necessary information required for the Hybrid Service to support an implementation of information service specification. The structure diagram for specification metadata is illustrated in Figure 6. The Hybrid System requires an XML metadata document, which is generated based on the SpecMetadata Schema, for each information service specification supported by the system. The SpecMetadata XML file helps the Hybrid System determine how to process instances of a given specification XML API.

The SpecMetadata includes Specname, Description, and Version XML elements. These elements define descriptive information to help the Hybrid Service to identify the local information service schema under consideration. The FunctionProperties XML element describes all required information regarding the functions that will be supported by the Hybrid Service.

The FunctionProperties element consists of one-to-many FunctionProperty sub-elements. The FunctionProperty element consists of function name, memory-mapping, and information-service-backend mapping information. Here the memory-mapping information element defines all necessary information to process an incoming request for in-memory storage access. The memory-mapping information element defines the name, user-defined identifier, and system-defined identifier of an entity. The information-service-backend information is needed to process the incoming request and to execute the requested operation on the appropriate information service backend. This information defines the function name, its arguments, return values, and the class, which needs to be executed in the information service backend. The *MappingRules XML element* describes all required information regarding the mapping rules that provide mapping between the Unified Schema and the local information service schemas such as extended UDDI and WS-Context. The MappingRules element consists of one-to-many MappingRule sub-elements. Each MappingRule describes information on how to map a unified schema XML API to a local information service schema XML API. The MappingRule element contains the necessary information to identify functions that will be mapped to each other.

Figure 6. The figure on the left shows the Hybrid Service XML Schema for the Hybrid Service metadata publish function (save_schemaEntity). The figure on the right shows the structure diagram for Spec-Metadata Schema.

Given these capabilities, one can simply populate the Hybrid Service as in the following scenario. Say, a user wants to publish a metadata into the Hybrid Service using WS-Context's "save_context" operation through the generic access interface. In this case, the user first constructs an instance of the "save_context" XML document (based on the WS-Context Specification) as if s/he wants to publish a metadata instance into the WS-Context Service. Once the specification-based publish function is constructed, it can be published into the Hybrid Service by utilizing the "save_schemaEntity" operation of the Hybrid Service Access API. As for the arguments of the "save_schemaEntity" function, the user needs to pass the following arguments: a) authentication information, b) lifetime information, c) schemaName as "WS-Context", d) schemaFunctionName as "save_context", and e) the actual save_context document that was constructed based on the WS-Context Specification. Recall that for each specification, the Hybrid Service requires a SpecMetadata XML document (an instance of the Specification Metadata Schema). On receipt of the "save_schemaEntity" publish operation, the Hybrid Service obtains the name of the schema (such as WS-Context) and the name of the publish operation (such as save_context) from the passing arguments. In this case, the Hybrid Service consults with the WS-Context SpecMetadata document and obtains necessary information about how to process incoming "save_context" operation. Based on the memory mapping information obtained from the user-provided SpecMetadata file, the system processes the request, extracts the context metadata entity instance, assigns a unique identifier, stores in the in-memory storage, and returns a response back to the client.

5. ARCHITECTURE

The Hybrid Service is an add-on system that interacts with local information service implemen-

tations and unifies them in a higher-level architecture. Figure 7 illustrates the detailed architectural design and abstraction layers of the system. The clients interact with the system through the uniform access interface. *The Uniform Access layer* imports the XML API of the supported Information Services. The Hybrid Information Service prototype supports XML API for Extended UDDI, WS-Context, and Unified Schema (the Unified Schema integrates different local schemas into one global schema for federation of information services). This layer is designed as generic as possible so that it can support one-to-many XML API, as the new information services are integrated with the system. *The Request-processing layer* is responsible for extracting incoming requests and processing operations on the Hybrid Service. It is designed to support two capabilities: notification and access control. The notification capability enables the interested clients to be notified of the state changes happening in a metadata. It is implemented by utilizing the publish-subscribe based paradigm. The access control capability is responsible for enforcing controlled access to the Hybrid Grid Information Service. The investigation and implementation of the access control mechanism for the decentralized information service is omitted here for future study. *TupleSpaces Access API* allows access to in-memory storage. This API supports all query/publish operations that can take place on the Tuple Pool. The *Tuple Pool* implements a lightweight implementation of JavaSpaces Specification (Sun Microsystems, 1999) and is a generalized in-memory storage mechanism. It enables mutually exclusive access and associative lookup to shared data. The *Tuple Processor layer* is designed to process metadata stored in the Tuple Pool. Once the metadata instances are stored in the Tuple Pool as tuple objects, the system starts processing the tuples and provides the following capabilities. The first capability is LifeTime Management. Each metadata instance may have a lifetime defined by the user. If the metadata lifetime is exceeded, then it is evicted from the TupleSpace. The second capability is Persistency Management. The system checks with the tuple space every so often for newly added/updated tuples and stores them into the database for persistency of information. The third capability is Fault Tolerance Management. The system checks with the tuple space every so often for newly added/updated tuples and replicates them in other Hybrid Service instances using the publish-subscribe messaging system. This capability also provides consistency among the replicated datasets. The fourth capability is Dynamic Caching Management. With this capability, the system keeps track of the requests coming from the pub-sub system and replicates/migrates tuples to other information services where the high demand is originated. The *Filtering layer* supports the federation capability. This layer provides filtering between instances of the Unified Schema and local information service schemas, such as WS-Context Schema, based on the user-defined mapping rules to provide transformations. The *Information Resource Manager layer* is responsible for managing low-level information service implementations. It provides decoupling between the Hybrid Service and sub-systems. The *Pub-Sub Network layer* is responsible for communication between Hybrid Service instances.

5.1. Execution Logic Flow

The execution logic for the Hybrid Service happens as follows. Firstly, on receiving the client request, the request processor extracts the incoming request. The request processor processes the incoming request by checking it with the specification-mapping metadata (SpecMetadata) files. For each supported schema, there is a Spec-Metadata file, which defines all the functions that can be executed on the instances of the schema under consideration. Each function defines the required information related with the schema entities to be represented in the Tuple Pool (e.g., entity name, entity identifier key, etc.). Based on

this information, the request processor extracts the inquiry/publish request from the incoming message and executes these requests on the Tuple Pool. We apply the following strategy to process the incoming requests. First off all, the system keeps all locally available metadata keys in a table in the memory. On receipt of a request, the system first checks if the metadata is available in the memory by checking with the metadata-key table. If the requested metadata is not available in the local system, the request is forwarded to the Pub-Sub Manager layer to probe other Hybrid Services for the requested metadata. If the metadata is in the in-memory storage, then the request processor utilizes the Tuple Space Access API and executes the query in the Tuple Pool. In some cases, requests may require to be executed in the local information service back-end. For an example, if the client's query requires SQL query capabilities, it will be forwarded to the Information Resource Manager, which is responsible of managing the local information service implementations.

Second, once the request is extracted and processed, the system presents abstraction layers for some capabilities, such as access control and notification. First capability is the access control management. This capability layer is intended to provide access control for metadata accesses. As the focus of our investigation is distributed metadata management aspects of information services, we leave out the research and implementation of this capability as future study. The second capability is the notification management. Here, the system informs the interested parties of the state changes happening in the metadata. In this way the requested entities can keep track of information regarding a particular metadata instance.

Third, if the request is to be handled in the memory, the Tuple Space Access API is used to enable the access to the in-memory storage. This API allows us to perform operations on the Tuple Pool. The Tuple Pool is an in-memory storage. The Tuple Pool provides a storage capability where

Figure 7. This figure illustrates the execution flow of the Hybrid Grid Information Service from top-to-bottom. Each rectangle shape identifies a layer of the system with its particular purpose.

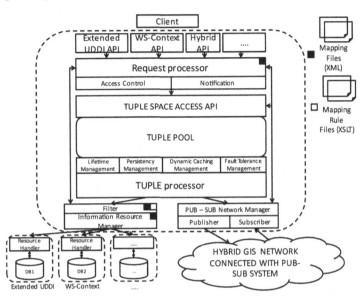

the metadata instances of different information service schemas can be represented.

Fourth, once the metadata instances are stored in the Tuple Pool as tuple objects, the tuple processor layer is used to process tuples and to provide a variety of capabilities. The first capability is Life-Time Management. Each metadata instance may have a lifetime defined by the user. If the metadata lifetime is exceeded, then it is evicted from the Tuple Pool. The second capability is Persistency Management. The system checks with the tuple space every so often for newly added/updated tuples and stores them into the local information service back-end. The third capability is Dynamic Caching Manager. The system keeps track of the requests coming from the other Hybrid Service instances and replicates/migrates metadata to where the high demand is originated. The fourth capability is Fault Tolerance Management. The system again checks with the tuple space every so often for newly added/updated tuples and replicates them in other information services using the pub-sub system. This service is also responsible for providing consistency among the replicated

datasets. As the main focus of this paper is to discuss information federation in Grid Information Services, a detailed discussion on replication, distribution, and consistency enforcement aspects of the system is omitted here.

The Hybrid Service supports a federation capability to address the problem of providing integrated access to heterogeneous metadata. To facilitate the testing of this capability, a Unified Schema is introduced by integrating different information service schemas. If the metadata is an instance of the Unified Schema, such metadata needs to be mapped into the appropriate local information service back-end. To achieve this, the Hybrid Service utilizes the filtering layer. This layer does filtering based on the user-defined mapping rules to provide transformations between the Unified Schema instances and local schema instances. If the metadata is an instance of a local schema, then the system does not apply any filtering, and backs up this metadata to the corresponding local information service back-end.

Fifth, if the metadata is to be stored to the information service backend (for persistency of information), the Information Resource Management layer is used to provide connection with the back-end resource. The Information Resource Manager handles the management of local information service implementations. It provides decoupling between the Hybrid Service and sub-systems. With the implementation of Information Resource Manager, we have provided a uniform, single interface to sub-information systems. The Resource Handler implements the sub-information system functionalities. Each information service implementation has a Resource Handler that enables interaction with the Hybrid Service.

Sixth, if the metadata is to be replicated/stored into other Hybrid Service instances, the Pub-Sub Management Layer is used for managing interactions with the Pub-Sub network. On receiving the requests from the Tuple Processor, the Pub-Sub Manager publishes the request to the corresponding topics. The Pub-Sub Manager may also receive key-based access/storage requests from the pub-sub network. In this case, these requests will be carried out on the Tuple Pool by utilizing TupleSpace Access API. The Pub-Sub Manager utilizes publisher and subscriber sub-components in order to provide communication among the instances of the Hybrid Services.

5.2. Modular Structure

The Hybrid Grid Information Service prototype implementation consists of various modules such as Query and Publishing, Expeditor, Filter and Resource Manager, Sequencer, Access, and Storage. This software is an open-source project and available at (Aktas, n.d.). The *Query and Publishing* module is responsible for processing the incoming requests issued by end-users. The *Expeditor* module forms a generalized in-memory storage mechanism. The *Filter and Resource Manager* modules provide decoupling between the Hybrid Information Service and the sub-systems. The *Sequencer* module is responsible for labeling each incoming context with a synchronized time-stamp. Finally, the *Access and Storage* modules are responsible for actual communication between the distributed Hybrid Service nodes to support the functionalities of a replica hosting system.

The *Query and Publishing* module is responsible for implementing a uniform access interface for the Hybrid Grid Information Service. This module implements the Request Processing abstraction layer with access control and notification capabilities. On completing the request processing task, the Query and Publishing module utilizes the Tuple Space API to execute the request on the Tuple Pool. On completion of operation, the Query and Publication module sends the result to the client. As discussed earlier, context information may not be open to anyone, thus there is a need for an information security mechanism. We leave out the investigation and implementation of this mechanism as a future study. We must note that to facilitate testing of the centralized Hybrid Service in various application use domains, we implemented a simple information security mechanism. Based on this implementation, the centralized Hybrid Service requires an authentication token to restrict who can perform an inquiry/publish operation. The authorization token is obtained from the Hybrid Service at the beginning of the client-server interaction. In this scenario, a client can only access the system if he/she is an authorized user by the system and his/her credentials match. If the client is authorized, he/she is granted an authentication token, which needs to be passed in the argument lists of publish/inquiry operations. The Query and Publishing module also implements a notification scheme. This is achieved by utilizing a publish-subscribe based messaging scheme. This enables users of the Hybrid Service to utilize a push-based information retrieval capability where the interested parties are notified of the state changes. This push-based approach reduces the server load caused by continuous information polling. We use the NaradaBrokering software (Pallickara & Fox, 2003) as the messaging infrastructure and its libraries to implement subscriber and publisher components.

The *Expeditor* module implements the Tuple Spaces Access API, Tuple Pool and Tuple-processing layer. The Tuple Spaces Access API provides an access interface on the Tuple Pool. The Tuple Pool is a generalized in-memory storage mechanism. Here, to meet the performance requirement of the proposed architecture, we built an in-memory storage based on the TupleSpaces paradigm (Carriero, 1989). The Tuple-processing layer introduces a number of capabilities: Life-Time Management, Persistency Management, Dynamic Caching Management, and Fault Tolerance Management. Here, the LifeTime Manager is responsible for evicting those tuples with expired leases. The Persistency Manager is responsible for backing-up newly stored/updated metadata into the information service back-ends. The Fault Tolerance Manager is responsible for creating replicas of the newly added metadata. The Dynamic Caching Manager is responsible for replicating/migrating metadata under high demand onto replica servers where the demand originated.

The *Filtering* module implements the filtering layer, which provides a mapping capability based on the user defined mapping rules. The Filtering module obtains the mapping rule information from the user-provided mapping rule files. As the mapping rule file, we use the XSL (stylesheet language for XML) Transformation (XSLT) file. The XSLT provides a general purpose XML transformation based on pre-defined mapping rules. Here, the mapping occurs between the XML APIs of the Unified Schema and the local information service schemas (such as WS-Context or extended UDDI schemas).

The *Information Resource Manager* module, illustrated in Figure 8, handles the management of local information service implementations such as the extended UDDI. The Resource Manager module separates the Hybrid System from the sub-system classes. It identifies which sub-system classes are responsible for a request and what methods need to be executed by processing the specification-mapping metadata file that belongs to the local information service under consideration. On receipt of a request, the Information Resource Manager checks with the corresponding mapping file and obtains information regarding the specification-implementation. Such information could be a class (which needs to be executed), it's function (which needs to be invoked), and the function's input and output types, so that the Information Resource Manager can delegate the handling of incoming request to the appropriate sub-system. By using this approach, the Hybrid Service can support one-to-many information services as long as the sub-system implementation classes and the specification-mapping metadata (SpecMetadata) files are provided. The Resource Handler is an external component to the Hybrid Service. It is used to interact with sub-information systems. Each specification has a Resource Handler, which allows interaction with the database. The Hybrid System classes communicate with the sub-information systems by sending requests to the Information Resource Manager, which forwards the requests to the appropriate sub-system implementation. Although the sub-system object (from the corresponding Resource Handler) performs the actual work, the Information Resource Manager, from the perspective of the Hybrid Service inner-classes, appears to do the work. This approach separates the Hybrid Service implementation from the local schema-specific implementations.

The *Resource Manager* module is also used for recovery purposes. We have provided a recovery process to support persistent in-memory storage capability. This type of failure may occur if the physical memory is wiped out when power fails or a machine crashes. This recovery process converts the database data to in-memory storage data (from the last backup). It runs at the bootstrap

Figure 8. We implemented an Information Resource Manager, which separates specification-implementations from the implementation of the Hybrid Service.

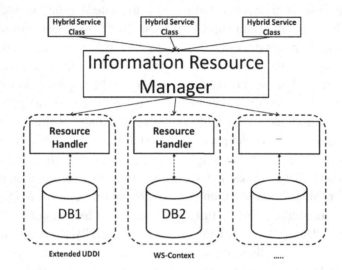

of the Hybrid Service. This process utilizes user-provided "find_schemaEntity" XML documents to retrieve instances of schema entities from the information service backend. Each "find_schemaEntity" XML document is a wrapper for schema specific "find" operations. First, at the bootstrap of the system, the recovery process applies the schema-specific find functions on the information service backend and retrieves meta-data instances of schema entities. Second, the recovery process stores these metadata instances into the in-memory storage to achieve persistent in-memory storage.

To impose an order on updates, each context must be time-stamped before it is stored or updated in the system. The responsibility of the *Sequencer* module is to assign a timestamp to each metadata, which will be stored into the Hybrid Service. To do this, the Sequencer module interacts with Network Time Protocol (NTP)-based time service implemented by NaradaBrokering software. This service achieves synchronized timestamps by synchronizing the machine clocks with atomic timeservers available across the globe.

6. EVALUATION

In our previous studies, we performed evaluations on our implementations of two WS-I compatible Web Service Specifications: the UDDI XML Meta-data Service and the WSContext XML Metadata Service (Aktas et al., 2008a). Initial evaluation results of the Hybrid Service were presented in the Semantics, Knowledge and Grid (SKG-2008) Conference (Aktas et al, 2008b). In this paper, we investigate the performance and scalability aspects of the Hybrid Service with respect to information federation and present an extensive evaluation of the system. We explore the effectiveness and scalability of the proposed add-on hybrid system under increasing message rates. We present an evaluation of the prototype implementation of the proposed system architecture for the Unified Schema XML API standard operations. In this section, the following research questions are ad-dressed: What is the performance of the Hybrid Service prototype with federation capability as far as the Unified Schema XML API standard operations?, How do Unified Schema XML API functions compare with other supported Schema

XML APIs such as WS-Context XML API?, What is the scalability of the Hybrid Service prototype for Unified Schema XML API standard operations under increasing work load or message sizes?

The investigations are conducted using various nodes of a cluster located at the Community Grids Laboratory at Indiana University. This cluster consists of eight Linux machines that have been setup for experimental usage. The configuration of the cluster nodes is given in Table 1, while the software environment for the experiments is listed in Table 2. In the experiments, the performance is evaluated with respect to response time at client applications. The response time is the average time from the point a client sends off a query until the point the client receives a complete response. Note that the client/server architecture, with all machines on the same network, is setup to measure an approximation of the optimal system performance. The results measured in this environment will be the optimal upper bound of the system performance. Analyzing the results gathered from the experiments, we encountered some outliers. External effects, such as network and server, mainly cause these outliers; we did not see these abnormal values in the internal timing-data, which is obtained by measuring the plain processing time. To avoid abnormalities in the results, we removed the outliers by utilizing the Z-filtering methodology that discards the anomalies.

We conducted two experiments to understand the behavior of the system with respect to information federation. These are performance and scalability experiments.

The *performance experiment* is conducted to understand the baseline performance of the prototype implementation of the Hybrid Service. This evaluation investigates the performance of the system for standard Unified Schema operations and compares it against the performance of WS-Context Schema operations when there is no additional traffic. To do this the following testing cases are completed: a single client sends publish/query requests to an echo service, which receives

a message and then sends it back to the client with no processing applied; a single client sends publish/query requests to a Hybrid Service, which grants the request with memory access; a single client sends publish/query requests to a Hybrid Service, which grants the request with database access. In the experiment, both the Hybrid Service and testing client application were located in two different servers located in the Linux cluster. The design of these experiments is depicted in Figure 9. This experiment was repeated five times and we recorded the average response time.

We investigated the best possible backup-interval period to provide persistency at a high performance response rate. In this investigation, we observed a trade-off in choosing the value for backup-time-interval. If the backup frequency is too high, such as every 10 milliseconds, then the time required for a publish function is ~ 10.2 milliseconds. If the backup frequency is every 10 seconds or lower, then the time required for a publish function is stabilized to ~7.5 milliseconds. Therefore, we chose the value for backup frequency as every 10 sec. Here, for testing purposes, we used WS-Context Schema primary operations: save_context and get_context and the equivalent Unified Schema primary operations: save_metadata and get_metadata. We used metadata size of 1.7KB. Note that metadata examples used in these experiments can be accessed from (Aktas, n.d.). The registry size was 5000. We used 200 observations at each testing and calculated average execution time.

Table 1. Summary of the cluster node - machine configurations

Hardware configuration	
Processor	*Intel® Xeon™ CPU (2.40GHz)*
RAM	*2GB total*
Network Bandwidth	*100 Ambits/sec.[1] (among the cluster nodes)*
OS	*GNU/Linux (kernel release 2.4.22)*

Figure 9. Testing cases of responsiveness experiment for Unified Schema and WS-Context standard operations

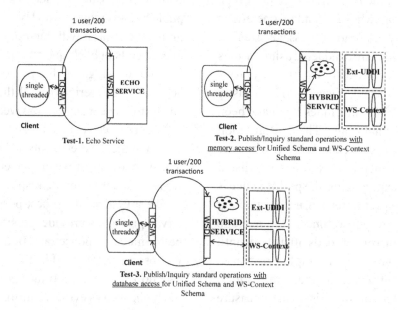

Analyzing the results depicted in Figure 10, we observe that the Hybrid Service has negligible processing overheads when the federation capability is used. This experimental study indicates that the Hybrid Service achieves noticeable performance improvements in metadata management for standard operations by simply employing an in-memory storage mechanism, while preserving a certain persistency level. (The standard deviation values remained the same for different testing cases of each experiment and ranged between 1.4 and 2 milliseconds.) We also observe that the Unified Schema operations require more time (as opposed to WS-Context Schema operations) for database accesses. This is because the system keeps the Unified Schema metadata in the relevant local information service (in this case WS-Context XML Metadata Service) for persistency reasons. In turn, the system requires additional time for database accesses to perform transformation between the Unified Schema and WS-Context Schema instances.

In the *scalability experiment*, we investigated two research questions: a) how well does the Hybrid Service perform when the context size is increased; b) how well does the Hybrid Service perform when the message rate per second is increased. In this experiment we investigated the performance of the Unified Schema XML API to understand the system behavior under increasing workloads while the federation capability is being used.

Table 2. Software environment configuration

Software configuration	
Compiler	Java 2 Standard Edition v.1.5 with maximum heap size of 1024 MB using the –Xmx1024m option
Servlet container	Tomcat Apache Server v.5.5.8 with max. multiple thread number of 1000
Web Service container	Apache Axis v.2.0
Database	MYSQL with v.4.1
Timing function	Java 2 with v.1.5 – timing function "nanoTime()"

Figure 10. The figure on the left shows the round trip time chart for metadata publish requests. The figure on the left shows the round trip time chart for metadata inquiry requests.

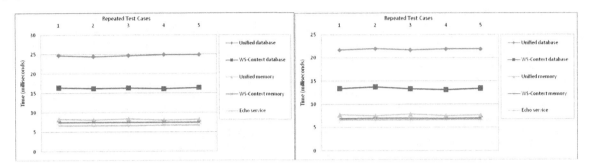

To answer the first research question, as illustrated in Test-A in Figure 11, we increased the context sizes at each step of the experiment until we observed the degradation in the response times. To answer the second question, as illustrated in Test-B in Figure 11, we ramped-up the work load (number of messages sent per second) until the system performance degraded.

The results of this experiment are depicted in Figure 12. Analyzing the results, we conclude that Hybrid Service Unified Schema XML API standard operations performed well for increasing

message sizes. (The standard deviation values ranged between 1.6 and 2.4 milliseconds.) By comparing the performance values from an Echo Service and Hybrid Service, we observe that pure server processing time is negligible and remains the same as the size of the messages increases. We also conclude that Hybrid Service Unified Schema XML API standard operations performed well under increasing message rates. For inquiry request messages, we observe a threshold value after which the system performance starts decreasing due to high message rate. This threshold is

Figure 11. Testing cases of scalability experiment for Unified Schema inquiry and publish functionalities.

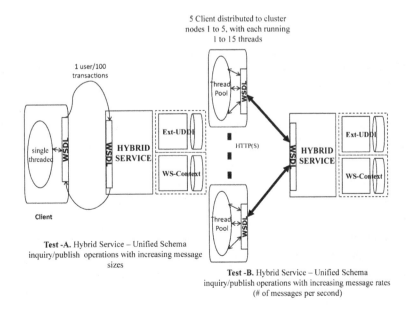

Figure 12. The figure on the left shows the round trip time chart for publish requests for increasing metadata payload sizes. The figure on the right shows the Unified Schema inquiry/publish response time at various levels of message rates per second.

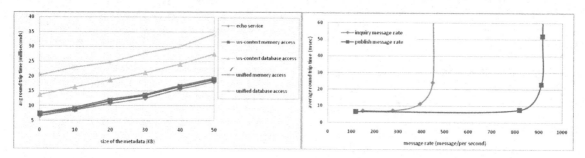

mainly due to the limitations of the Web Service container, as we observe the similar threshold when we test the system with an echo service that returns the input parameter passed to it with no message processing applied. For publish request messages, we observe another threshold value where the system performance starts dropping down. The reason for this is the following: As the publish message-rate is increased, the number of updated or newly written metadata in the Tuple Pool is also increased. In turn, the action that writes the larger number of updates into the default local information service back-end affects the system performance and causes higher fluctuations in the response times for increasing number of simultaneous publish requests.

7. CONCLUSION AND FUTURE RESEARCH DIRECTIONS

We introduced a novel architecture for a Hybrid Grid Information Service (Hybrid Service) that supports handling and discovery of not only quasi-static, stateless metadata, but also session related metadata. The Hybrid Service is an add-on architecture that runs one layer above existing information service implementations. It provides unification, federation, and interoperability of Grid Information Services.

To achieve unification, the Hybrid Service is designed as a generic system with front and back-end abstraction layers supporting one-to-many local information systems and their communication protocols. To achieve federation, the Hybrid Service is designed to support an information integration technique in which metadata from several heterogeneous sources are transferred into a global schema and queried with a uniform query interface. To manage both quasi-static and dynamic metadata and to provide interoperability with wide-range of Web Service applications, the Hybrid Service is integrated with two local information services: WS-Context XML Metadata Service and Extended UDDI XML Metadata Service. The WS-Context Service is implemented based on WS-Context Specification to manage dynamic, session related metadata. It is an implementation of the Context Manager component of the WS-Context Specification. The Extended UDDI Service is implemented based on an extended version of the UDDI Specification to manage semi-static, stateless metadata. We performed a set of experiments to evaluate the performance and scalability of the Hybrid Service to understand whether it can achieve information federation with acceptable costs. This evaluation pointed out the following results. First, the Hybrid Service achieves information federation with negligible processing overheads for accessing/storing metadata. Second, the Hybrid Service achieves noticeable performance improvements in standard operations by employing in-memory storage while preserving persistency of information. Third, the Hybrid Service scales to high message rates and message sizes while supporting information integration where metadata comes from heterogeneous data-systems.

With this research, we revisited distributed data management techniques to achieve integrated access to heterogeneous metadata coming from a limited number of local information services. We intend to further improve this approach to be able to scale up to a high number of local metadata sources. An additional area that we intend to research is an information security mechanism for the distributed Hybrid Service.

ACKNOWLEDGMENT

The Advanced Information Systems Technology Program of NASA's Earth-Sun System Technology Office supported this research.

REFERENCES

Aktas, M. S. (2004). iSERVO: Implementing the International Solid Earth Research Virtual Observatory by Integrating Computational Grid and Geographical Information Web Services. *Pure and Applied Geophysics, 163*(11-12), 2281–2296. doi:10.1007/s00024-006-0137-8

Aktas, M. S. (2008a). XML Metadata Services. *Concurrency and Computation, 20*(7), 801–823. doi:10.1002/cpe.1276

Aktas, M. S., et al. (2008b, December 3-5). Information federation in Grids. In *Proceedings of the 4th International Conference on Semantics, Knowledge and Grid (SKG 2008)*, Beijing, China. Aktas, M. S. (n.d.). *Fault Tolerant High Performance Information Service - FTHPIS - Hybrid WS-Context Service*. Retrieved July 2009 from http://www.opengrids.org/wscontext

Bellwood, T., Clement, L., & von Riegen, C. (2003). *UDDI Version 3.0.1: UDDI Spec Technical Committee Specification*. Retrieved July 2009 from http://uddi.org/pubs/uddi-v3.0.1-20031014.htm

Bernstein, P. (2003). Applying model management to classical meta data problems. In *Proceedings of CIDR* (pp. 209-220).

Bunting, B., Chapman, M., Hurley, O., Little, M., Mischinkinky, J., Newcomer, E., et al. (2003). *Web Services Context (WS-Context) version 1.0*. Retrieved from http://www.arjuna.com/library/specs/ws_caf_1-0/WS-CTX.pdf

Carriero, N., & Gelernter, D. (1989). Linda in context. *Communications of the ACM, 32*(4), 444–458. doi:10.1145/63334.63337

Coleman, R., Bhardwaj, A., Dellucca, A., Finke, G., Sofia, A., Jutt, M., et al. (2004). *MicroSpaces software with version 1.5.2*. Retrieved July 2009 from http://microspaces.sourceforge.net

Czajkowski, K., et al. (2004). *The WS-Resource framework*. Retrieved October 2009 from http://www.globus.org/-wsrf/specs/ws-wsrf.pdf

Dialani, V. (2002). *UDDI-M Version 1.0 API Specification*. Southampton, UK: University of Southampton.

EGEE. (n.d.). *The Enabling Grids for E-science (EGEE) project*. Retrieved October 2009 from http://www.eu-egee.org

Florescu, D., Levy, A., & Mendelzon, A. (1998). Database techniques for the world-wide web: A survey. *SIGMOD Record, 27*(3), 56–74. doi:10.1145/290593.290605

Globus. (n.d.). *The Globus Toolkit*. Retrieved October 2009 from http://www.globus.org

GLUE. (n.d.). *The GLUE Schema*. Retrieved October 2009 from http://infnforge.cnaf.infn.it/glueinfomodel

GRIMOIRES. (n.d.). *GRIMOIRES UDDI compliant Web Service Registry with metadata annotation extension.* Retrieved from http://sourceforge.net/projects/grimoires

Index Service. (n.d.). *Index Service caGrid.* Retrieved October 2009 from http://cagrid.org/display/metadata13-/Index+Service

Khushraj, D., Lassila, O., & Finin, T. (2004). sTuples: Semantic Tuple Spaces. In *Proceedings of the First Annual IEEE International Conference on Mobile and Ubiquitous Systems: Networking and Services (MobiQuitous'04)* (pp. 268-277). Washington, DC: IEEE Computer Society.

Krummenacher, R., Strang, T., & Fensel, D. (2005, March). *Triple spaces for and ubiquitous web of services.* Paper presented at the W3C Workshop on the Ubiquitous Web, Tokyo.

Lenzerini, M. (2002). Data integration: A theoretical perspective. *PODS*, 243-246. MyGrid. (n.d.). *UK e-Science project.* Retrieved October 2009 from http://www.mygrid.org.uk

NGS. (n.d.) *The National Grid Service (NGS).* Retrieved October 2009 from http://www.gridsupport.ac.uk

OGC. (n.d.). *The Open Geospatial Consortium (OGC).* Retrieved July 2009 from http://www.opengis.org

OGF. (n.d.). *Open Grid Forum.* Retrieved October 2009 from http://www.ogf.org

OGF-GIN. (n.d.). *Grid Interoperation Now Community Group (GIN-CG).* Retrieved from https://forge.gridforum.org/projects/gin

OWS1. 2. (2003). *UDDI Experiment, OpenGIS Interoperability Program Report OGC 03-028.* Retrieved from http://www.opengeospatial.org/docs/03-028.pdf

Ozsu, T., & Valduriez, P. (1999). *Principles of distributed database* systems (2nd ed.). Upper Saddle River, NJ: Prentice Hall.

Pallickara, S., & Fox, G. (2003). NaradaBrokering: A middleware framework and architecture for enabling durable peer-to-peer grids. In *Proceedings of Middleware 2003.*

Rahm, E., & Bernstein, P. (2001). A survey of approaches to automatic schema matching. *The VLDB Journal*, 334–350. doi:10.1007/s007780100057

Saltzer, J., & Schroeder, M. (1975). The protection of information in computer systems. *Proceedings of the IEEE*, *63*(9), 1278–1308. doi:10.1109/PROC.1975.9939

ShaikhAli. A., Rana, O., Al-Ali, R., & Walker, D. (2003). UDDIe: An extended registry for web services. In Proceedings of the Service Oriented Computing: Models, Architectures and Applications, Orlando, FL. Washington, DC: IEEE Computer Society. Sun_Microsystems. (1999). *JavaSpaces specification revision 1.0.* Retrieved July 2009 from http://www.sun.com/jini/specs/js.ps

Sycline. (n.d.). *Home page.* Retrieved July 2009 from http://www.synclineinc.com

Tan, W., Foster, I., & Madduri, R. (2008). Scientific workflows that enable Web scale collaboration: Combining the power of Taverna and caGrid. *IEEE Internet Computing*, *12*(6), 30–37. doi:10.1109/MIC.2008.120

Tanenbaum, A., & Van Steen, M. (2002). *Distributed Systems Principles and Paradigms.* Upper Saddle River, NJ: Prentice Hall.

Verma, K., Sivashanmugam, K., Sheth, A., Patil, A., Oundhakar, S., & Miller, J. (2005). METEOR-S WSDI: A scalable P2P infrastructure of registries for semantic publication and discovery of web services. *Journal of Information Technology and Management.*

Wu, W., et al. (2005). Grid Service Architecture for Videoconferencing. In M. P. Bekakos, G. A. Gravvanis, & H. R. Arabnia (Eds.), *Grid Computational Methods*.

Zanikolas, S. (2005). A taxonomy of Grid Monitoring Systems. *Future Generation Computer Systems*, *21*(1), 163–188. doi:10.1016/j.future.2004.07.002

Ziegler, P., et al. (2004). Three decades of data integration - all problems solved? *WCC*, 3-12

ENDNOTE

[1]   The bandwidth measurements were taken with Iperf tool for measuring TCP and UDP bandwidth performance. (http://dast.nlanr.net/Projects/Iperf)

This work was previously published in the International Journal of Web Services Research, Volume 7, Issue 1, edited by Liang-Jie (LJ) Zhang, pp. 65-98, copyright 2010 by IGI Publishing (an imprint of IGI Global).

Section 2
Matchmaking and Substitution

Chapter 5
Specifying and Composing Web Services with an Environment Ontology-Based Approach

Puwei Wang
Renmin University of China, China

Zhi Jin
Peking University and Chinese Academy of Sciences, China

Lin Liu
Tsinghua University, China

Budan Wu
Beijing University of Posts and Telecommunications, China

ABSTRACT

Precise capability specification is the key for identifying and composing the right Web services. This paper specifies service capabilities in terms of the environment entities from the application domain and the effects imposed by the Web service on these entities. An environment ontology for Web services is adopted to provide formal sharable representations of the domain-specific environment entities. A hierarchical state machine is constructed for each environment entity to describe its behaviors, and the effects imposed by a Web service are described as the state transitions traces of environment entities, which define the capability of the Web service. Web service composition that satisfies a set of requested effects is then conducted by reasoning on the effects of services. The proposed approach emphasizes the external manifestation of Web services and service composition based on the effect reasoning. An example of online travel service illustrates the proposed approach.

DOI: 10.4018/978-1-4666-1942-5.ch005

1. INTRODUCTION

Web services technology has gained momentum and adopted as one of the major form of Internet applications. Web services have added a new level of functionality to the current Web, as an important step towards achieving seamless integration of distributed components, which are autonomous and self-contained (Benatallah, 2003). Web service composition takes place when a request cannot be satisfied by any single Web service individually. It composes some elementary Web services to form a new and composite Web service so that the composite Web service has the required capabilities. Thus, capability specifications of Web services are fundamental for the outcome of service composition. Also as pointed by McIlraith (2001) "fundamental to implementing reliable, large-scale interoperation of Web services is the need to make such services computer interpretable – to create a semantic Web of services whose properties, capabilities, interfaces, and effects are encoded in an unambiguous, machine-understandable form."

Earlier efforts on the XML-based service standards, such as Web Service Description Language (WSDL2.0, 2007) are designed to provide descriptions of message exchange mechanisms for describing the service interface. However, the kind of keyword-based approach supported by WSDL2.0 is not sufficient for effective service discovery and composition. Ontology Web Language for Web services (OWL-S1.2, 2008) takes up the challenge of representing the capabilities of Web services by bridging the gap between the semantic Web and Web services. The OWL-S capability model assumes a Web service as a stateless one-step atomic process, which includes the information transformation performed by service and the state transition as consequence of the execution of the service by using four parameters, i.e., Input, Output, Precondition and Result (IOPR). However, the four parameters do depict the capability of a Web service to a certain extent,

but still show limitations in certain elaborated situations. Refer to the Web services as a one-step process, those services with intermediate states can not be described in due process.

In our previous work (Wang, Jin, & Liu, 2006; Wang et al., 2008; Wang & Jin, 2006; Hou, Jin, & Wu, 2006), an environment ontology-based approach is proposed for Web services. The capabilities of a Web service should be grounded on the environment entities surrounding this service and the effects on these entities imposed by the service. The conceptualization of the environment entities, i.e., the environment ontology, is given as the sharable understanding for specifying the capabilities of Web services. After grounding the capabilities of Web services onto the environment ontology, we can infer the capabilities of Web services, as the environment ontology is shared and machine-understandable. A state-based mechanism is introduced to be viewed as the capability specification of Web services, which captures the effects of Web services on the environment. Along this line, this paper introduces when a request is given, how the Web service composition is conducted by reasoning on the effects of candidate Web services to get the desired effects of the request.

The rest of this paper is structured as follows. Section 2 introduces briefly the environment ontology. An example is given for illustrating the environment ontology. Section 3 describes an environment ontology-based approach for specifying capabilities of Web services semantically. Section 4 presents the Web service composition which is conducted by reasoning on the effects of Web services to satisfy the requested effects. Section 5 discusses related work. Finally, we conclude the paper in section 6.

2. ENVIRONMENT ONTOLOGY

The environment of a Web service is a set of stateful real world entities surrounding the Web service.

Moreover, environment entities are domain-relevant and independent to any Web service. Therefore, the conceptualization of environment entities, i.e., the environment ontology, constitutes the sharable domain knowledge of environment for Web services. The state transitions of any environment entity are caused by the actions of Web services. For example, *ticket* is an environment entity in online travelling arrangement domain. It has two states: *available* and *sold*. A Web service can change its state from *available*, i.e., ticket is available, to *sold*, i.e., ticket is sold. In this sense, the state transitions depict the capabilities of Web services.

We extend the general ontology structure, i.e., the ontology structure in (Maedche, 2002), in the following aspects. First, we extend concept node in the general ontology structure with a state machine for specifying its states and the state transitions. Second, we propose to use the hierarchical state machine for supporting different granularity of the conceptualization inspired by the work of Heimdahl (1996). For reducing the computational complexity, our hierarchical state machine is assumed to be with a tree-like structure.

2.1. Environment Ontology

The environment ontology will be described briefly in the section. An environment ontology is a 6-tuple:

$$EnvO := \{Rsc, X^c, H^c, HSM, res, inter\}$$

in which,

- *Rsc is a finite set of the environment entities. An environment entity is described as* $\{eid, Attrs\}$*, in which* eid is the identifier of the environment entity and $Attrs$ is the set of attributes;
- $X^c \subseteq Rsc \times Rsc$ *is an ingredient relation between the environment entities.*

$\forall e_1, e_2 \in Rsc$, $\langle e_1, e_2 \rangle \in X^c$ means that e_1 is a part of e_2;

- $H^c \subseteq Rsc \times Rsc$ *is a taxonomic relation between the environment entities,* $\forall e_1, e_2 \in Rsc$, $\langle e_1, e_2 \rangle \in H^c$ means that e_1 is a subclass of e_2;
- *HSM is a finite set of tree-like hierarchical state machines (called "THSM");*
- $res : Rsc \leftrightarrow HSM$ *is a bijective function.* $\forall e \in Rsc$, there is one and only one $hsm \in HSM$, $hsm = res(e)$ and hsm is called the THSM of e;
- $inter \subseteq HSM \times HSM$ *is a state-trigger-transition relation between the THSMs. The relation means that output of a state in a THSM can trigger a state transition in another THSM.*

Here, the THSM is designed for life cycle description of an environment entity in a particular domain. Normally, the THSM in the environment ontology is called the domain THSM. The effects of Web services are modeled based on the domain THSMs. A THSM may contain two kinds of states, i.e., the ordinary states and the super-states. A super-state can be further subdivided into another basic state machine. THSM assumes that each basic state machine has one and only one super-state. Moreover, the domain THSM of an environment entity can be divided into some different parts according to the function properties, and each part is called a function area that consists of a set of hierarchical state transitions. This division is similar with the functional phase partition of the life-cycle THSM description of an environment entity. The function area is for bridging abstract requirement and specific state transitions of the environment entities.

Before detailing the domain THSMs, we first introduce the basic state machine (called "BSM"). In the following, $e \in Rsc$ is an environment entity and $States(e)$ is the set of states of environment entity e. A basic state machine of environment entity e is a 5-tuple:

$$N := \{S, \Sigma, T, f, \lambda_0\}$$

in which,

- $S \subseteq States(e)$ is a finite *set of states;*
- $\pounds$ is *a finite set that is partitioned into two subsets:* $\pounds^{in}$ and $\pounds^{out}$ for describing inputs and outputs respectively;
- $T \subseteq S \times \pounds^{in} \times S$ is a set of *state transitions;*
- $f : S \rightarrow \pounds^{out}$ is *an output function;*
- $\lambda_0 \in S$ is *the start state.*

For including the hierarchy of the state machines, we define $\preceq$ as a tree-like partial ordering with a topmost state in the set of states of an environment entity. This relation defines the hierarchy relation on the states ($x \preceq y$ means that x is a descendant of y ($x \prec y$), or x and y are equal ($x = y$)). Tree-like means that $\preceq$ has the following property:

$$\neg(a \preceq b \vee b \preceq a) \Rightarrow \neg\exists x : (x \preceq a \wedge x \preceq b)$$

If the state x is a descendant of y ($x \prec y$), and there is no state z such that $x \prec z \prec y$, we say that state x is a *child* of state y (x *child* y) and state y is parent of state x. If $\exists s, N$, $s \notin S(N)$ ($S(N)$ denotes the set of states in BSM N), and $\forall s' \in S(N)$, s' *child* s, we say that state s is a super-state that can be refined to be a sub-BSM N (or N has a super-state s), and $\langle s, N \rangle$ is a *subdivision*. The start state in sub-BSM N is called *default child* of super-state s. Because that $\preceq$ is a tree-like partial ordering, each BSM have one and only one super-state.

Let $e \in Rsc$ be an environment entity, $BSM(e) = \{N_1, ..., N_n\}$ ($n \geq 1$) be the set of BSMs of e and D is the set of subdivisions. A

tree-like hierarchical state machine (called "THSM") of environment entity e is a 2-tuple:

$$hsm(e) := \{BSM(e), D\}$$

in which,

- *There is a special basic state machine in* $BSM(e)$ *that is called the* root *(denoted by* N_{root} *) of the THSM;*
- *The remaining basic state machines are partitioned into* $m \geq 1$ *disjoint sets* $B_1, ..., B_m$, *Each* B_i ($1 \leq i \leq m$) *also constitutes a tree-like hierarchical state machine, i.e.,* $hsm_i = \{B_i, D_i\}$, $D_i \subseteq D$. *If* $N_{root}^{B_i} \in B_i$ *is the* root *of* hsm_i, *then* $\exists s \in S(N_{root})$, *such that* $\langle s, N_{root}^{B_i} \rangle \in D$ (hsm_i *is called the sub-THSM of* s).

With the tree-like hierarchical state machine, the state-trigger-transition relation *inter* can be given. Let hsm_1 and hsm_2 be two THSMs, $S(hsm_i)$ be the set of states in hsm_i and $T(hsm_i)$ be the set of state transitions in hsm_i ($i = 1, 2$). The state-trigger-transition relation between these two THSMs is as follows:

$$inter := \{\langle hsm_1, hsm_2 \rangle \mid \exists s \in S(hsm_i), t \in T(hsm_j),$$
$$i \neq j, s \uparrow t\}$$

in which $s \uparrow t$ is called a state-trigger-transition and it means that output of the state s can trigger the state transition t.

For example, in the domain of online traveling arrangement, there are two environment entities ticket and creditcard. The output of state *valid* of creditcard can trigger a state transition of ticket from *ordered* to *sold*, i.e., *valid*↑(*ordered*→*sold*). The output of state *valid* of creditcard can trigger a state transition of ticket from *available* to *sold*, i.e., *valid*↑(*available*→*sold*). And the output of state *sold* of ticket can trigger a state transition of creditcard from *non-charged* to *charged*, i.e., *sold*↑(*non-charged*→*charged*). Therefore, there exists a state-trigger-transition relation between *hsm*(*creditcard*) and *hsm*(*ticket*).

2.2. An Example of Environment Ontology

Segment of the *Budget Travelling Environment Ontology* (called "BTO") is given to illustrate our ideas. In BTO, there are five environment entities *hotelroom, creditcard, ticket, merchandise* and *itinerary*. The environment entity *ticket* is for taking travelers to their destinations, environment entity *hotelroom* is for accommodating travelers, and environment entity *creditcard* is a method of payment. Both *ticket* and *hotelroom* are subclasses of *merchandise*. Moreover, environment entity *itinerary* describes a trip from a departure to a destination. A *ticket* includes an *itinerary*. Table 1 details the environment ontology *BTO*.

3. CAPABILITY SPECIFICATION OF WEB SERVICES

Based on our environment-based approach, a capability profile of a Web service is described by its environment entities and the effects of the Web service on the environment entities. With the help of the environment ontology, a state machine-based capability specification can be generated by adding semantics into the capability profile.

3.1. Capability Profile

For a specific Web service, its environment entities are derived from the environment ontology by assigning specific values to attributes of the environment entities. An environment entity of a Web service is described as
$$e := eid\,[attr_1\,?\,v_1, attr_2\,?\,v_2, ..., attr_n\,?\,v_n]\,, \quad \text{in}$$
which eid is a name of the environment entity, $attr_i \in Attrs$ is an attribute of the environment entity and v_i is a value of the attribute $attr_i$ $(i \in [1, n])$. For example, for a specific Web service that provides an online ticket-selling service, *ticket*[*departure?beijing, destination?shanghai*] is an environment entity *ticket* of the Web service that means a ticket from *beijing* to *shanghai*.

An effect of a Web service on an environment entity is described as a state change of the environment entity caused by the Web service. It can be described as
$effect(e) := \{Input, Output, change\}$, in which *Input* is a set of inputs to environment entity e from the Web service, *Output* is a set of outputs from environment entity e to the Web service and *change* is a state change of environment entity e caused by the Web service. A state change means that the state of an environment entity changes from an initial state to a target state via a set of middle states. For example, an effect of a simple ticket-selling service on environment entity *ticket* can be described as *ticket*:{{*orderInfo,accountInfo*}, {*soldInfo*}, <*available, {ordered},sold*>}. It means that the Web service has the inputs {*orderInfo,accountInfo*} and the outputs {*soldInfo*} with the environment entity *ticket*, and a state change of *ticket* caused by the Web service is from the initial state, i.e., *available*, to the target state, i.e., *sold*, via the middle state, i.e., *ordered*.

Therefore, a capability profile to advertise capability of a Web service can be described based on the effects that the Web service imposes on its environment entities. A capability profile of a Web service is described as follows.

$CapabilityProfile := \{Entity, Effect\}$

in which,

- $Entity = \{e_1, ..., e_n\}$ is a set of *environment entities of the Web service;*

Table 1. Budget Traveling Environment Ontology (BTO)

Environment Entity
merchandise is the goods in business. It has the attribute *price*.
itinerary is a trip from a departure to a destination. It has the attributes *departure* and *destination*.
ticket is for taking travelers to their destinations. It has the attributes *departure-time* and *arrival-time*.
hotelroom is for accommodating travelers. It has the attributes *location*, *checkin-time* and *checkout-time*.
creditcard provides a method of payment. It has the attribute *validity-period* and *type*.
Taxonomic Relation:
<ticket, merchandise> $\in H^c$. It means that ticket is merchandise, and ticket inherits the attributes from merchandise. Hence, ticket also has the attribute *price*.
<hotelroom, merchandise> $\in H^c$. It means that hotel room is merchandise, and hotelroom inherits the attributes from merchandise. Hence, hotelroom also has the attribute *price*.
Ingredient Relation:
<itinerary, ticket> $\in X^c$. A ticket includes an itinerary, and then ticket has the attributes *itinerary.departure* and *itinerary.destination*.
Domain THSM:
ticket↔hsm(ticket)   *hsm(ticket)* is the domain THSM of ticket. Ticket has two function areas {*ticket manufacture, ticket circulation*}. One part of *hsm(ticket)* represents the ticket producing, the other part represents ticket circulation.
hotelroom↔hsm(hotelroom)   *hsm(hotelroom)* is the domain THSM of hotelroom. Hotelroom has two function areas {*room vacancy, room use*}. One part of *hsm(hotelroom)* represents the hotel room in vacancy, the other part represents the hotel room in use.
creditcard↔hsm(creditcard)   *hsm(creditcard)* is the domain THSM of creditcard. Creditcard has two function areas {*card validity, card invalidity*}. One part of *hsm(creditcard)* represents the card is invalid for use, the other part represents the card is valid for use.
merchandise↔hsm(merchandise)   *hsm(merchandise)* is the domain THSM of merchandise.
itinerary↔hsm(itinerary)   *hsm(itinerary)* is the domain THSM of itinerary.
State Trigger Transition Relation:
<hsm(ticket), hsm(creditcard)> $\in inter$. It means that ticket can be paid by credit card.
<hsm(hotelroom), hsm(creditcard)> $\in inter$. It means that hotelroom can be paid by credit card

- $Effect = \{effect\ (e_1),...,effect\ (e_n)\}$ is a set of *effects which the Web service imposes on the environment entities*.

The capability profile is a light-weight profile, because the provider of a Web service can only describe simply a set of environment entities of the Web service and a set of effects of the Web service on the environment entities. Moreover, with the help of the environment ontology, a state machine-based capability specification can be generated automatically by adding some kind of semantics (i.e., state transitions) to the capability profile. Concretely, by traversing the domain THSM of an environment entity, traces from the initial state to the target state via a set of the middle states triggered by a series of inputs can be generated. Actually, these traces, which may include the state transitions in a basic state machine, or the transitions from a state to its default child, or the transitions from a state to its parent, can constitute a THSM. Normally, the THSM generated from a domain THSM is called specific THSM. Each specific THSM is corresponding to an effect on an environment entity.

We use a forest communicating hierarchical state machine (called "FCHM") to cluster the set of specific THSMs corresponding to a set of effects and the state-trigger-transition relation between them. A forest-structured communicating hierarchical state machine (FCHM) of a Web service is described as follows:

$$chm := \{ \check{s} , inter_{\check{s}} \}$$

in which,

- $\check{s}$ is a set of *specific THSMs corresponding to a set of effects of the Web service,*
- $inter_{\check{s}}$ is a set of *the state-trigger-transitions among $\check{s}$.*

The FCHM is viewed to be a capability specification of Web service. The capability specification is based on a process model and will not be entangled by implementation of Web services.

3.2. An Example of Capability Profile

Let us consider a specific Web service *Budget Traveling Agency* (called "BTA"). It can provide the traveling arrangement for travelers. BTA is supposed to have the basic capability: ticket selling and hotel-room ordering in China. The environment in which BTA is situated has been depicted as BTO (shown in Table 1). There are three

environment entities *ticket[departure?China, destination?China]*, *hotelroom[location?China]* and *creditcard[type?MasterCard]* of the service BTA. The XML-style capability profile of BTA is described in Exhibit 1.

This capability profile can be translated to statements in natural language: BTA provides ticket selling and delivering service for travelers in China. Before purchasing tickets, ordering service is provided. If the ordered tickets are not appropriate, the orders can be cancelled by travelers. Moreover, BTA provides hotel room service. Similarly, if the ordered rooms are not appropriate, the orders can be cancelled by travelers. The tickets and hotel rooms can be paid by MasterCard credit card.

3.3. The Generation of FCHM

Constructing FCHM contains two steps. They are constructing specific THSMs and identifying the state-trigger-transitions among these specific THSMs. The procedure *createSpecificTHSM* is designed for constructing the specific THSMs. The generation of FCHM is described in Exhibit 2.

Figure 1 is the screenshot for showing the FCHM of *BTA* generated by using the ALGO-RITHM.1. In Figure 1, the rectangular box titled *hotelroom[location?China]* depicts a specific THSM (denoted by $k(hotelroom)$), which is generated based on the effect that *BTA* imposes on the environment entity *hotelroom[location?China]*. Similarity, $k(ticket)$ and $k(creditcard)$ denote the specific THSMs of environment entity *ticket[departure?China,destination?China]* and *creditcard[type?MasterCard]*. There are state-trigger-transitions among these THSMs $k(ticket)$, $k(hotelroom)$ and $k(creditcard)$. The generated FCHM of *BTA* from its capability profile is given as follows:

Exhibit 1.

```
<capability_profile ID="Budget_Travelling_Agency">
xmlns:resource="http://www.ecf4ws.org/bto"
<entity ID="ticket@bto">
 <value attribute="departure">China</value>
 <value attribute="destination">China</value>
</entity>
<entity ID="hotelroom@bto">
 <value attribute="location">China</value>
</entity>
<entity ID="creditcard@bto">
 <value attribute="type">MasterCard</value>
</entity>
<effect ID="ticket_selling">
 <entity>ticket</entity>
 <inputs>orderInfo,orderCancelInfo,reAvailableInfo,accountInfo,deliveryInfo</inputs>
 <outputs>deliveredInfo</outputs>
 <state_change>
  <initial_state func_area="ticket_circulation">available</initial_state>
  <middle_states func_area="ticket_circulation">ordered,cancelled</middle_states>
  <target_state func_area="ticket_circulation">delivered<target_state>
 </state_change>
</effect>
<effect ID="hotel_reservation">
 <entity>hotelroom</entity>
 <inputs>orderInfo,orderCancelInfo,accountInfo,reVacancyInfo</inputs>
 <outputs>paidInfo</outputs>
 <state_change>
  <initial_state func_area="room_vacancy">vacancy</initial_state>
  <middle_states func_area="room_use">ordered,cancelled</middle_states>
  <target_state func_area="room_use">paid<target_state>
 </state_change>
</effect>
<effect ID="creditcard_payment">
 <entity>creditcard</entity>
 <inputs>chargeInfo<iutput>
 <outputs>chargedInfo<outputs>
 <state_change>
  <initial_state func_area="card_validity">valid</initial_state>
  <target_state func_area="card_validity">charged<target_state>
 </state_change>
</effect>
</capability_profile>
```

$chm_{Ma} = \{\{k(ticket), k(hotelroom), k(creditcard)\}, \{\langle k(ticket), k(creditcard)\rangle,$

$$\langle k(hotelroom), k(creditcard)\rangle\}\}$$

4. WEB SERVICE COMPOSITION

Web service composition combines some available elementary Web services to create a new and composite Web service so that the new Web service can satisfy the user's request. In our ap-proach, firstly, capabilities of the available Web services are specified by using their effects on the environment entities; secondly, the request is also specified by using the desired effects on the environment entities; thus, Web service composition finally can be performed by reasoning on the effects of the candidate Web services to get the desired effects of the request.

In this section, an example is used to illustrate the Web service composition. We assume that there are four Web services, *ticket-selling*

Exhibit 2.

ALGORITHM 1 FCHM-Generator

Inputs: Environment Ontology $EnvO$, Capability Profile $\{Entity,\ Effect\}$:

$$Entity = \{e_1,...,e_n\} \subseteq Rsc$$

$$Effect = \{effect\ (e_1),...,effect\ (e_n)\}$$

Outputs: FCHM $chm = \{\check{s}\ ,inter_{\check{s}}\ \}$

Instantiating $chm : \check{s}\ = \varphi,\ inter_{\check{s}} = \varphi$:

$runhsm = \{hsm(e_i)\ |\ e_i \in Entity\}$; //*obtaining the domain THSMs* $hsm(e_i)$ *of the environment entity* e_i from the environment ontology $EnvO$

$readyhsm = \varphi$; //those tree-*like hierarchical state machines have been processed. It is initialized to be null*

while ($runshm \neq \varphi$) **do**

  $hsm(e) = getDomainTHSM(runhsm)$;

$runshm = runhsm - \{hsm(e)\}$; //*getting a domain THSM* $hsm(e)$ *from* $runhsm$

  $effect(e) = getEffect(e, Effect)$; //*getting the effect on the environment entity* e

$k(e) = createSpecificTHSM(hsm(e), effect(e))$; //*obtaining a new specific THSM* $k(e)$ by pruning the domain THSM $hsm(e)$ according to $effect(e)$

  $readyhsm = readyhsm \cup \{k(e)\}$;

end while

$\check{s}\ = readyhsm$; //the construc*ted specific THSMs under effects of the Web service*

$inter_{\check{s}} = createInter(K, EnvO)$; //*creating the state-trigger-transitions among the constructed specific THSMs in* K according to the environment ontology $EnvO$.

return $chm = \{\check{s}\ ,inter_{\check{s}}\ \}$

end

Figure 1. Screenshot: the FCHM generated from the capability profile of BTA

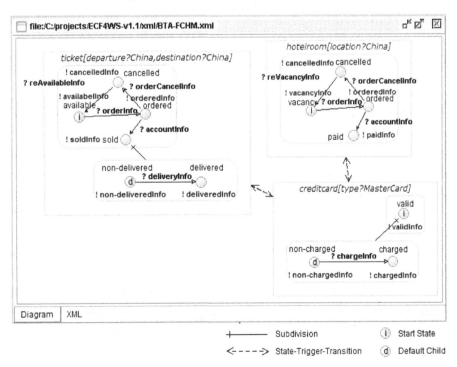

service (*TSA*), *ticket-delivery service* (*TDS*), *hotel service* (*HOS*) and *payment service* (*PAS*) respectively. They have three shared environment entities, *ticket*[*departure?China,destination?Chi na*], *hotelroom*[*location?China*] and *creditcard* [*type?MasterCard*] derived from the environment ontology BTO (see Table 1). Given the goal G_{travel} that needs *budget traveling service* (*BTA*) for travelers (its FCHM is given in Figure 1). This goal can be represented as a set of desired effects on the three environment entities. Obviously, any of the four Web services can not satisfy G_{travel} by its own. There should be a possibility to combine the four Web services together in order to fulfill the goal G_{travel}. The composition is conducted by combining their effects on the three environment entities in terms of the satisfiability of the desired effects of G_{travel}.

The desired effects of the goal G_{travel} is given in Table 2, and its FCHM which is generated based on the effects has been shown in Figure 1.

Moreover, the effects of the four available Web services (*TSA, TDS, HOS* and *PAS*) are listed in Table 3.

With the help of the environment ontology *BTO* (see Table 1), the FCHMs (Figure 2) of the four Web services are generated based on the effects. They are viewed as the capability specifications of the four available Web services.

Given the four available Web services $W = \{TSA, TDS, HOS, PAS\}$, a composition of W is a FCHM chm_{bta} such that chm_{bta} delegates all state transitions in the FCHMs chm_{tsa}, chm_{tds}, chm_{hos} and chm_{bas} of the four Web services. Given the goal G_{travel} which can not be satisfied by any available Web services in W, Web service composition for satisfying the goal G_{travel} is to check whether there exists a composition chm_{bta} of W which is the FCHM of the goal G_{travel}.

Formally, given two FCHMs chm_1 and chm_2, the task to get a desired composition chm of chm_1 and chm_2 can be decomposed to the following two sub-tasks. First, we compose the

specific THSMs in chm_i (i=1, 2) which are of same environment entity. For example, in the two FCHMs $chm_{tsa} = \{\{k_{ticket}^{tsa}\}, \varphi\}$ (Figure 2(a)) and $chm_{tds} = \{\{k_{ticket}^{tds}\}, \varphi\}$ (Figure 2(b)), k_{ticket}^{tsa} and k_{ticket}^{tds} are of the same environment entity *ticket*, we need to check whether or not there exists a target THSM k_{ticket}^{bta} (shown in Figure 1) by composing the two THSMs k_{ticket}^{tsa} and k_{ticket}^{tds}. Second, state-trigger-transitions among these composed specific THSMs are constructed according to the sharable domain knowledge, i.e., the environment ontology. For example, we suppose that $k_{creditcard}^{bta}$ is a composition of $k_{creditcard}^{bta}$ and φ (There is not another specific THSM of *creditcard* except for $k_{creditcard}^{bta}$ in elementary FCHMs). It is described in the environment ontology BTO that a state *valid* in $k_{creditcard}^{bta}$ can trigger a state transition from *ordered* to *sold* in k_{ticket}^{bta}. Therefore, there is a state-trigger-transition relation between $k_{creditcard}^{bta}$ and k_{ticket}^{bta}.

Concretely, we present here how to compose the FCHMs, chm_{tsa}, chm_{tds}, chm_{hos} and chm_{pas}, of four available Web services (Ticket-Selling Service (*TSA*), Ticket-Delivering Service (*TDS*), Hotel Service (*HOS*) and Payment Service (*PAS*), see Figure 4) to get the desired FCHM chm_{bta} (see Figure 1).

First, we present how to check whether there exists a target THSM k_{ticket}^{bta} by composing the two THSMs k_{ticket}^{tsa} and k_{ticket}^{tds}. Berardi (2003) has developed a technique for composition of finite state machines in terms of the satisfiability of a formula of Deterministic Propositional Dynamic Logic (DPDL). We translate the THSMs k_{ticket}^{bta}, k_{ticket}^{tsa} and k_{ticket}^{tds} into a set of DPDL formulas (Wang & Jin, 2006), and a DPDL formula Φ_{ticket} that captures the composition can be built as a conjunction of these formulas. We formulate the problem on composition existence of the target THSM k_{ticket}^{bta} based on the Berardi's proposition (Berardi, 2003): *The DPDL formula* Φ_{ticket} *is*

Table 2. Desired effects

Budget Traveling Service *(BTA)*
ticket[*departure?China,destination?China*]:{
{*orderInfo,orderCancelInfo,reAvailableInfo,accountInfo,deliveryInfo*},{*deliveredInfo*},
<*available,{ordered,cancelled},delivered*>}
hotelroom[*location?China*]:{
{*orderInfo,orderCancelInfo,reVacancyInfo,accountInfo*},{*paidInfo*},
<*vacancy,{ordered,cancelled},paid*>}
creditcard[*type:MasterCard*]:{
{*chargeInfo*},{*chargedInfo*},<*valid, φ ,charged*>}

Table 3. Effects of the four available services

Ticket-Selling Service *(TSA)*
ticket[*departure?China,destination?China*]:{
{*orderInfo,orderCancelInfo,reAvailableInfo,accountInfo*},{*soldInfo*},
<*available,{ordered,cancelled},sold*>}

Ticket-Delivery Service *(TDS)*
ticket[*depature?China,destination?China*]:{
{*deliveryInfo*},{*deliveredInfo*},<*sold, φ ,delivered*>}

Hotel Service *(HOS)*
hotelroom[*location?China*]:{
{*orderInfo,orderCancelInfo,reVacancyInfo,accountInfo*},{*paidInfo*},
<*vacancy,{ordered,cancelled},paid*>}

Payment Service *(PAS)*
creditcard[*type:MasterCard*]:{
{*chargeInfo*},{*chargedInfo*},<*valid, φ ,charged*>}

Figure 2. Screenshot: FCHMs of the four available web services

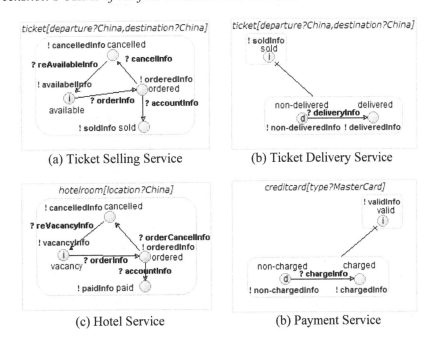

(a) Ticket Selling Service   (b) Ticket Delivery Service

(c) Hotel Service   (b) Payment Service

Figure 3. Architecture of the ECF4WS

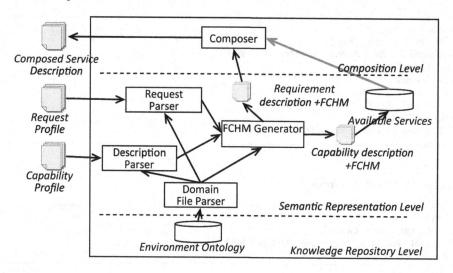

Figure 4. Screenshot: the composite FCHM

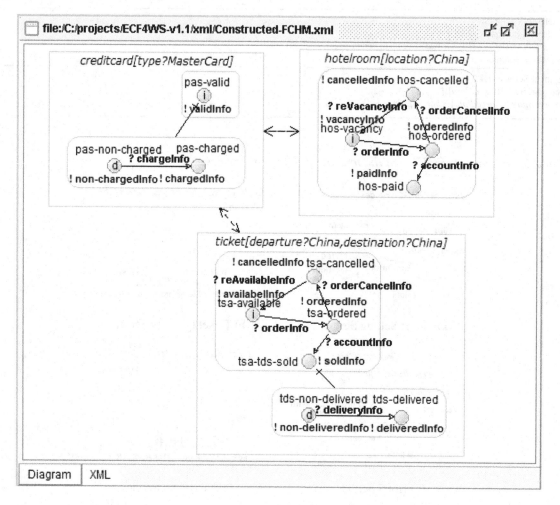

satisfiable if and only if there exists the target THSM k_{ticket}^{bta} by composing the two THSMs k_{ticket}^{tsa} and k_{ticket}^{tds}. Based on the standard Tableau Algorithm, we can construct the target THSM k_{ticket}^{bta} by composing k_{ticket}^{tsa} and k_{ticket}^{tds} after validating the satisfiability of formula Φ_{ticket}. Moreover, because there is one and only one $k_{creditcard}^{pas}$ which is a specific THSM of *creditcard* in the four elementary FCHMs, $k_{creditcard}^{bta}$ is just $k_{creditcard}^{pas}$. Similarly, $k_{hotelroom}^{bta}$ is also just $k_{hotelroom}^{hos}$.

Second, the two state-trigger-transitions in the environment ontology *BTO* between environment entities *ticket* and *creditcard* are given as follows. We can get $\langle k_{creditcard}^{bta}, k_{hotelroom}^{bta} \rangle \in inter_{bta}$ and $\langle k_{creditcard}^{bta}, k_{ticket}^{bta} \rangle \in inter_{bta}$.

creditcard-valid$_{bta}$ $\uparrow$ $\langle$ *ticket-ordered$_{bta}$*, *accountInfo*, *ticket-sold$_{bta}$* $\rangle$

ticket-sold$_{bta}$ $\uparrow$ $\langle$ *creditcard-non-charged$_{bta}$*, *feeInfo*, *creditcard-charged$_{bta}$* $\rangle$

Finally, a target Web service (*BTA*, its capability specification is chm_{bta}) that satisfies goal G_{travel} is constructed by composing the FCHMs of the four available Web services, i.e., *TSA* (chm_{tsa}), *TDS* (chm_{tds}), *HOS* (chm_{hos}) and *PAS* (chm_{pas}).

We have developed a prototype (ECF4WS, Environment ontology-based Capability specification Framework for Web Services) for specifying and composing Web services. Figure 3 shows the three-level architecture of the prototype. In the knowledge repository level, the environment ontologies are constructed by domain experts and are deposited in a repository. They are viewed as the sharable environment knowledge to support the semantic capability specification of Web services and the Web service composition. In the semantic representation level, the FCHMs are generated from the Web service capability profile or request profile. There are the four modules in this level: 1)

DomainFileParser. When using the Web service capability profile or request profile, DomainFileParser is invoked. It retrieves an environment ontology from the repository, and parses the environment ontology to get the structured data. 2) DescriptionParser and RequestParser. They read the capability profile or request profile, and build the semantic links between the profiles and the environment ontology. 3) FCHM-Generator. It generates the FCHM from the capability profile or the request profile. The capability profile and its FCHM are put into the repository of the available services, and the request profile and its FCHM are submitted to composer for service composition. Finally, in the composition level, the composer takes the responsibility to obtain the request and to generate the desired service by composing the available services in the repository.

The result of composing the FCHMs of these four Web services in our prototype system is shown in Figure 4. Concretely, *TSA* changes environment entity *ticket* from state *available* to state *sold* via two middle states {*ordered, cancelled*}. And *PAS* changes environment entity *creditcard* from state *valid* to state *charged*. These two services are synchronous by using two state-trigger-transitions: output of *creditcard*'s state *valid* triggers state transition of *ticket* from state *ordered* to state *sold*, and output of ticket's state *sold* triggers the state transition of *creditcard* from state *non-charged* to state *charged*. Sequentially, *TDS* changes environment entity *ticket* from state *sold* to state *delivered*. Moreover, *HOS* changes environment entity *hotelroom* from state *ordered* to state *paid* by using state-trigger-transitions with *PAS*.

Based on the composite FCHM, we can learn how the four Web services (*TSA, TDS, HOS, PAS*) collaborate to satisfy the given goal G_{travel}. *TSA* provides the ticket selling service. Sequentially, *TDS* provides the ticket delivery service. *TSA* and *PAS* are synchronous by using state-trigger-transitions, i.e., ticket is paid by credit card. *HOS* provides the hotel room service. *HOS* and *PAS* are also synchronous by using state-trigger-transitions,

Exhibit 3.

```
<service_composition>
  <service name="TSA">
   <input>orderInfo,orderCancelInfo,reAvailableInfo,accountInfo</input>
   <output>soldInfo</output>
  </service>
  <service name="TDS">
   <input>deliveryInfo</input>
   <output>deliveredInfo</output>
  </service>
  <service name="HOS">
   <input>orderInfo,orderCancelInfo,reVacancyInfo,accountInfo</input>
   <output>paidInfo</output>
  </service>
  <service name="PAS">
   <input>chargeInfo</input>
   <output>chargedInfo</output>
  </service>
  <sequence>
   <invoke partnerName="TSA"/>
   <invoke partnerName="TDS"/>
  </sequence>
  <synchronization>
   <invoke partnerName="TSA"/>
   <invoke partnerName="PAS"/>
   <state_trigger_transition ID="pay_ordered_ticket">
   <state_trigger_transition ID="ticket_charge_creditcard">
  </synchronization>
  <synchronization>
   <invoke partnerName="HOS"/>
   <invoke partnerName="PAS"/>
   <state_trigger_transition ID="pay_ordered_hotelroom">
   <state_trigger_transition ID="hotelroom_charge_creditcard">
  </synchronization>
</service-composition>
```

i.e., hotel room is paid by credit card. The result of composition then is given in the XML style presented in Exhibit 3.

Figure 5 shows the screenshot of the service composition of the four available Web services, which is generated from the constructed FCHM.

5. RELATED WORK

Web service technology is a growing and hot research area. Capability specification of Web services is a necessary step for publishing services and for requesting services. In this field, earlier efforts include the XML-based standards, such as Web Service Description Language (WSDL2.0, 2007). It is designed to provide the descriptions

of message exchange mechanisms for describing the service interface. However, the keyword-based approach is not very helpful for the automatic service discovery. Universal Description Discovery Integration (UDDI3.0, 2004) provides a registry of Web services. It describes Web services by their physical attributes such as name, address and the services that they provide. As UDDI dose not touch service capabilities, it is of no help to search for services on the basis of what they provide.

OWL-S (OWL-S Coalition, 2004) takes up the challenge of representing the functionalities of Web services. It attempts to bridge the gap between the semantic Web and Web services. The main contribution of the OWL-S approach is its service ontology, which builds on the pile of Semantic Web standards. OWL-S capability model is based

Figure 5. Composition of the four available web services

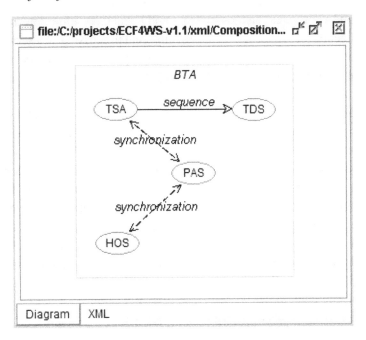

on a one-step atomic process which includes the information transformation performed by service and the state transition as consequence of the execution of the service, i.e. IOPR schema. Bansal et al. (2003) argue that a limitation of OWL-S arises due to the lack of logical relationships underlying the inputs and outputs of its capability model. They propose the OWL-S process model, which is primarily designed for specifying how a Web service works, to be the capability specification of Web services. By allowing describing the constraints between inputs and outputs and allowing creating incrementally concepts directly with the advertisements and requests, LARKS (Sycara, 2002) makes improvement to OWL-S. LARKS is a matching engine that allows matching of advertisements and requests on the basis of the capabilities that they describe to some extent. WSDL-S (2005) is a lightweight Web service description by annotating the WSDL documents with semantics. Like to OWL-S, WSDL-S also uses the inputs, outputs, preconditions and results to capture service capability.

Currently, behavioral description for services has also attracted much attention. Wombacher (2004, 2005) proposes using an extended finite state automata as description of Web services. However, side-effects arise due to the reason that a process description should be globally predefined to ensure consistency during service matchmaking. The loosely coupled Web services are often developed by different teams, and are described in different conceptual framework without prior agreement. Hence, key problem of such efforts is that process description of a Web service should be understood by other Web services without prior knowledge. Shen (2005) proposes a behavior model for Web services using automata and logic formalisms. It adopts the IOPR schema in OWL-S to describe activities of Web services. Grigori (2005) proposes a solution for service retrieval based on behavioral description using a graph representation formalism for services. It assumes that the semantic information including name of operation, inputs and outputs of activities has been attached to each service. Moreover, Salaun (2004) argues that essential facets of Web services are described using process algebraic notations, i.e., capability description and message exchanges are specified by process algebra.

Fensel (2007) proposes the ontology-based elements of the interface definition of a WSMO Web service description for service choreography and orchestration. These elements depict the behavior of the service as state-based mechanisms from the external views which are separate abstractions of the actual implementation of the services. Therefore, they also offer the state-based mechanisms describing services' capabilities for service discovery. The Choreography interface describes the behavior of the service from the client's point of view. WSMO has made successful steps towards state-based mechanisms in semantic Web services. These efforts agree on the capabilities of Web services are the behaviors of the services in terms of their internal structure.

Based on different service descriptions, many approaches for Web service composition are proposed. McIlraith (2002) proposes an approach to the automated composition of Web services. It first translates the OWL-S service description into the assertions in situation calculus and composes the services by using the situation reasoning. Sirin (2004) proposes a framework which uses a Hierarchical Task Network planner called SHOP2 to compose Web services. SHOP2 provides algorithms for translating an OWL-S service description to a SHOP2 domain. This kind of efforts assumes that Web service can be described as interface-based model. However, only interface description is not enough for capturing service capabilities. The OWL-S process model (Pistore, 2005) is proposed for Web service composition. Other representative composition efforts (Narayanan 2002; Hamadi, 2003; Yu, 2004) use Petri net. And, state machine is popularly proposed for representing Web service. In Berardi (2005), the *Roman* model focuses on *activities* of services, and the services are represented as finite state automata with transitions labeled by these activities. The Conversation model (Bultan, 2003)

focuses on messages passed between Web services, and again uses finite state automata to model the internal processing of a service. WSMO (Fensel, 2007) specifies internal and external choreography of Web services using abstract state machines. In Ye (2009), a state-based process model of Web service also is proposed for service composition. This kind of efforts assumes that Web service is described as its local behavior. They have many contributions to collaboration model to achieving Web service composition. However, although the process-based model is more expressive than the interface-based model, it may be too tied with the implementation of services. Generally, these kinds of efforts emphasize the implementation information in the actual execution of Web services. They may not capture service capability description at higher-level of abstraction.

Moreover, WS-Resources (2006) and WS-Context (2007) approaches also focus on environment (or called context) information in the actual implementation of Web services for coordinating and collaborating. Both WS-Context and WS-Resource approaches support stateful interactions. WS-Context provides a structuring mechanism, and a software service definition for organizing and sharing context across multiple execution endpoints. These efforts emphasize the actual execution of Web services, and they do not consider the abstract descriptions of Web services.

Different from these approaches, we use the environment entities for capturing the semantics of Web services capabilities and specify the capabilities of Web services based the environment-based view. We express the environment as a set of stateful environment entities with which Web services interact, and the effects of the Web service are specified as life-cycle descriptions of these environment entities. Capabilities of Web services are expressed by the effects of the services imposed on their environment entities. As a result, Web service composition can be performed by composing the effects of candidate services to get the desired effects.

6. CONCLUSION

This paper proposes an approach for specifying and composing Web services based on the environment ontology. It enables automated generation of semantic capability specification from the effects that Web services impose on environment entities. The THSMs in the environment ontology are used to specify such effects. The FCHMs are natural capability specification of Web services. The main feature of our work is constructing semantic state machine-based capability specification from the environment ontology. It is a process model but is irrelevant to the actual implementation of Web services. The capability specification is expected to be an extension of existing semantic Web services. Based on this capability specification, the environment entities can play the role of collaborating Web services. Web service composition therefore is conducted by reasoning on the effects of the candidate Web services in terms of the satisfiability of the desired effects of the requests.

The main contributions of this paper include that:

- The state transitions of the environment entities are conceptualized as sharable knowledge in environment ontology which produces the state transition-based capability specification. That assures that the specification will be unambiguous and machine-understandable.
- A lightweight and explicit effects-based capability profile of Web services has been designed. Lightweight means that capability specification can be generated by adding the semantics (i.e., state transitions) automatically to the capability profile from environment ontology.
- Service composition has been characterized to be a combination of the effects imposed by the candidate Web services on their environment entities while the

requestor only needs to give a high-level request profile.

In our future work, the environment ontology-based capability specification of Web services will be related to current popular semantic description language of Web services. Moreover, more efficient algorithm for automated Web service composition will be proposed. The validation and verification of the Web service composition also will be given.

ACKNOWLEDGMENT

This work was supported financially by the National Natural Science Fund for Distinguished Young Scholars of China (Grant No. 60625204) the National Basic Research and Development 973 Program (Grant No. 2009CB320701), the Key Projects of National Natural Science Foundation of China (Grant Nos. 90818026, 60736015) and Scientific Research Fund of Renmin University of China (Grant No. 22382075).

REFERENCES

Bansal, S., & Vidal, J. M. (2003). Matchmaking of Web Services Based on the DAML-S Service Model. In *Proceedings of the International joint conference on Autonomous Agents and Multi-Agent Systems (AAMAS'03)* (pp. 926-927).

Benatallah, B., Sheng, Q. Z., & Dumas, M. (2003). The Self-Serve Environment for Web Services Composition. *IEEE Internet Computing, 7*(1). doi:10.1109/MIC.2003.1167338

Berardi, D., et al. (2003). Automatic Composition of E-Services That Export Their Behavior. *International Conference on Service Oriented Computing (ICSOC 2003)* (LNCS 2910, pp. 43-58).

Berardi, D., et al. (2005). Automatic Composition of Transition based Semantic Web Services with Messaging. In *Proceedings of the International Conference on Very Large DataBases (VLDB 2005)* (pp. 613-624).

Bultan, T., Fu, X., Hull, R., & Su, J. (2003). Conversation Specification: A New Approach to Design and Analysis of E-Service Composition. In *Proceedings of the International World Wide Web Conference (WWW 2003)* (pp. 403-410).

Fensel, D., Polleres, A., & Bruijn, J. (2007). *Ontology-based Choreography of WSMO Services, WSMO Final Draft*. Retrieved from http://www.wsmo.org/TR/d14/v0.4/

Grigori, D., & Bouzeghoub, M. (2005). Service retrieval based on behavioral specification. In *Proceedings of the IEEE International Conference on Services Computing (SCC'05)* (pp. 333-363).

Hamadi, R., & Benatallah, B. (2003). A Petri Net-based Model for Web Service Composition. In *Proceedings of the Australasian Database Conference (ADC 2003)* (pp. 191-200).

Heimdahl, M. P. E., & Leveson, N. G. (1996). Completeness and Consistency in Hierarchical State-Based Requirements. *IEEE Transactions on Software Engineering, 22*(6), 363–377. doi:10.1109/32.508311

Hou, L., Jin, Z., & Wu, B. (2006). Modeling and Verifying Web Services Driven by Requirements: An Ontology-based Approach. *Science in China Series F: Information Sciences, 49*(6), 792–820. doi:10.1007/s11432-006-2031-5

Maedche, A. (2002). *Ontology learning for the semantic Web*. Dordrecht, The Netherlands: Kluwer.

Mahleko, B., & Wombacher, A. (2005). A grammar-based index for matching business processes. In *Proceedings of the International Conference on Web Services (ICWS'05)* (pp. 21-30).

McIlraith, S., & Son, T. C. (2002). Adapting Golog-r Composition of Semantic Web Services. In *Proceedings of the International Conference on Principles of Knowledge Representation and Reasoning (KR 2002)* (pp. 482-496).

McIlraith, S. A., Son, T. C., & Zeng, H. (2001). Semantic Web Services. *IEEE Intelligent Systems, 16*(2), 46–53. doi:10.1109/5254.920599

Narayanan, S., & McIlraith, S. (2002). Simulation, Verification and Automated Composition of Web Services. In *Proceedings of the International World Wide Web Conference (WWW 2002)* (pp. 77-88).

OWL-S1.2. (2008). *OWL-S: Semantic Markup for Web Services version 1.2*. Retrieved from http://www.daml.org/services/owl-s/1.2/overview/

Pistore, M., et al. (2005). Process-Level Composition of Executable Web Services: On the fly Versus Once-for-all Composition. In *Proceedings of the European Semantic Web Conference (ESWC 2005)* (LNCS 3532, pp. 62-77).

Salaun, G., Bordeaux, L., & Schaerf, M. (2004). Describing and Reasoning on Web Services using Process Algebra. In *Proceedings of the International Conference on Web Services (ICWS'04)* (pp. 43-50).

Shen, Z., & Su, J. (2005). Web Service Discovery Based on Behavior Signatures. In *Proceedings of the IEEE International Conference on Services Computing (SCC'05)* (pp. 279-286).

Sirin, E. (2004). HTN planning for Web Service Composition using SHOP2. *Journal of Web Semantics, 1*(4), 377–396. doi:10.1016/j.websem.2004.06.005

Sycara, K., et al. (2002). LARKS: Dynamic Matchmaking Among Heterogeneous Software Agents in Cyberspace. In *Proceedings of the International Joint conference on Autonomous Agents and Multi-Agent Systems (AAMAS'02)* (pp. 173-203).

UDDI3. 0. (2004). *Universal Description Discovery Integration (UDDI) version 3.0.* Retrieved from http://uddi.org/pubs/uddi v3.htm

Wang, P. (2008). Building Towards Capability Specifications of Web Services Based on an Environment Ontology. *IEEE Transactions on Knowledge and Data Engineering, 20*(4), 547–561. doi:10.1109/TKDE.2007.190719

Wang, P., & Jin, Z. (2006). Web Service Composition: An Approach Using Effect-based Reasoning. In *Proceedings of the International Workshop on Engineering Service Oriented Applications: Design and Composition* (*WESOA 2006*) (LNCS 4652, pp. 62-73).

Wang, P., Jin, Z., & Liu, L. (2006). An Approach for Specifying Capability of Web Services based on Environment Ontology. In *Proceedings of the IEEE International Conference on Web Services (ICWS'06)* (pp. 365-372).

Wombacher, A. (2004). Matchmaking for Business Processes Based on Choreographies. *International Journal of Web Services Research, 1*(4), 14–32.

Wombacher, A., Fankhuaser, P., & Neuhold, E. (2004). Transforming BPEL into annotated Deterministic Finite State Automata for Service Discovery. *International Conference on Web Services (ICWS'04)* (pp. 316-323).

WS-Context. (2007). *Web Services Context Specification (WS-Context) Version 1.0.* Retrieved from http://docs.oasis-open.org/ws-caf/ws-context/v1.0/wsctx.html

WS-Resource. (2006). *Web Services Resource 1.2.* Retrieved from http://docs.oasis-open.org/wsrf/wsrf-ws_resource-1.2-spec-os.pdf

WSDL2. 0. (2007). *Web Services Description Language (WSDL) Version 2.0.* Retrieved from http://www.w3.org/TR/wsdl20

WSDL-S. (2005). *Web Service Semantics - WSDL-S.* Retrieved from http://www.w3.org/Submission/WSDL-S/

Ye, C. (2009). Atomicity Analysis of Service Composition across Organizations. *IEEE Transactions on Software Engineering, 35*(1), 2–28. doi:10.1109/TSE.2008.86

Yu, T., Luon, C., & Kai-Tao, H. (2004). SRN: An Extended Petri-Net-Based Workflow Model for Web Service Composition. In *Proceedings of the IEEE International Conference on Web Services (ICWS'04)* (pp. 591-599).

This work was previously published in the International Journal of Web Services Research, Volume 7, Issue 3, edited by Liang-Jie (LJ) Zhang, pp. 72-91, copyright 2010 by IGI Publishing (an imprint of IGI Global).

Chapter 6
Managing the Replaceability of Web Services Using Underlying Semantics

Dunlu Peng
University of Shanghai for Science and Technology, Shanghai, China

Xiaoling Wang
East China Normal University, Shanghai, China

Aoying Zhou
East China Normal University, Shanghai, China

ABSTRACT

In the context of web services, service replaceability refers to the ability of substituting one service for another. With the bloom of service-oriented computing, the effective management of service replaceability is important to make the applications unaffected once the requested service cannot work. This work studies the quantitative aspect of the replaceability of web services. FCA (Formal Concept Analysis) method is applied to reveal the pairwise replaceable relationship among web services. A novel structure, called RSLattice, is proposed to index web services on the basis of the underlying semantics, and the replaceability among services at the operation level is represented accurately. It ensures that the services having mutual replaceability are organized in the same path of RSLattice. Based on this property, we can greatly reduce the search space when retrieving the replaceable services in RSLattice. Experimental evaluation shows that RSLattice is an efficient and flexible structure for service replaceability management.

1. INTRODUCTION

The replaceability of web services refers to the ability of using one service to substitute another in such a way that the change is transparent to service consumers' applications. This issue is

quite important to keep the stability of the service-oriented applications, especially in the case that the invoked service cannot work. Currently, if one service is unavailable, this exception will be propagated to its consumers' applications and makes the consumers' applications suspend or abort. To solve this problem, a straightforward

DOI: 10.4018/978-1-4666-1942-5.ch006

solution is to find a service to replace the unavailable one. Intuitively, it seems that it is a simple job of checking whether the operations of one service contain those of the service being replaced based on WSDL (Brogi, Canal, & Pimental, 2004). However, the checking is quite time consuming if the number of services is large and the services are deployed by different companies or organizations. Thus, to select the replaceable services at runtime is critical to reach the transparency of service applications. In this article, we study this problem and develop a novel data structure, which can be built on-line at the initialization phase, to represent the replaceability among services. We also verify the benefits of this approach from the theoretical and experimental aspects.

Currently, UDDI servers, as the brokers for advertising web services over the Internet, provide great support to find partners, products and services (Kleijnen & Raju, 2003). But its category-based service discovery method puts more human effort for consumers and providers. The providers need to publish their services in the appropriate UDDI categories, and the consumers are responsible for browsing the 'right' categories in order to find the potentially relevant services. Such an approach is very costly, and may produce low-precision results if the number and categories of web services are becoming very large (Bernstein & Klein, 2002). Moreover, it does not offer any support for the selection of the best services among many alternative services. The prioritization of the candidates is again the responsibility of consumers. Therefore, it can be concluded that the current service discovery approach is inapplicable to retrieve the replaceable services for a given service efficiently. This drawback is caused by the categorization of web service at the UDDI server, for it does not take into account the replaceable relationship among web services.

In this article, to represent the relationship among services, we present a novel structure, called *RSLattice*, which is formed by applying FCA (Formal Concept Analysis) to a collection of web services. *RSLattice* effectively indexes web services on the basis of the underlying semantics and accurately represents the replaceability among services at the operation level. This property ensures that once a *RSLattice* has been built for a specific service collection, searching replaceable services for the given service contained in the collection through the *RSLattice* will be very efficient. It is because the quantitative metrics of the replaceability can be pre-computed, and not necessary to compute the replaceability among services at query time. *RSLattice* can be used in conjunction with current UDDI service discovery method to support more automatic replaceable service discovery by distinguishing the potential alternatives from the possibly irrelevant services and ranking the candidates according to their quantified replaceability. For the sake of conciseness, we use 'service' to stand for 'web service' in following sections.

The remained parts of this article are organized as follows. Section 2 reviews the related work in the literature. Section 3 gives the problem description and some basic definitions. In Section 4, we describe how to organize the replaceable services using FCA and propose a new structure, called *RSLattice*, to reveal and represent the underlying semantics among services. Some algorithms which can retrieve the replaceable services for a specific service in a *RSLattice* are presented in Section 5. Section 6 is experimental evaluation of the proposed approach. Finally, concluding remarks are given in Section 7.

2. RELATED WORK

One of the most important objectives of the replaceability management is to support the discovery of the replaceable services for a specific service. The most related work in this area is service discovery. In this section, we will offer a brief survey on this topic.

Service discovery is to find desired services according to the requirements of the consumers. Researchers have done much work on service discovery. As a very important approach for software reuse, signature matching could be used for the selection of services. However, signature matching itself is error-prone because it considers only data types but ignores the functions; furthermore, two services with the same signature may have completely different functions. Zaremski and Wing solved this problem by examining signature (data types of input/output messages) matching and specification matching (Zaremski & Wing, 1997). In addition, this approach needs to analyze the data types and post-conditions which cannot be obtained from current service description. In Coalition (2002), Heβ & Kushmerick (2003), and Paolucci, Kawmura, Payne and Sycara (2002), the authors proposed some methods to annotate the traditional services with some additional semantic information and then employed this semantics to improve the performance of service discovery.

Dong et al. developed a clustering algorithm (Dong, Halevy, Madhavan, Nemes & Zhang, 2004) that groups the names of service operation parameters into semantically meaningful concepts. The concepts were leveraged to determine similarity of inputs (or outputs) of web-service operations. Wang et al. obtained the similar services based on the similarity among services measured with information retrieval and structure matching (Wang & Stroulia, 2003).

The aforementioned work contributes to service discovery from different aspects; however, they are not so helpful to solve the service replaceability problem, for none of them posts underlying semantics to characterize the replaceability among services. This makes searching replaceable services with these off-the-shelf approaches be quite inefficient and inaccurate. Our proposed method overcomes this disadvantage by taking sufficient consideration of the underlying relationship among services when managing service replaceability. The implementation shows that with our approach, the tasks of retrieving replaceable services can be accomplished in an efficient way.

3. PROBLEM DESCRIPTION

Before introducing our approach, we give some basic definitions and the formal description of the problem.

Replaceable Service and Service Replaceability

In SOA applications, once a service S cannot work, a possible solution is to find another one, say, S', to substitute S, then, it is said that S' is a alternative of S. Service replaceability is to study which service is the alternative for a specific one. From the consumers' perspective, the alternative can satisfy their requirements or can offer all the functions provided by the original one.

In the literature, each service is described by WSDL document, and it can be defined as a set of operations where each operation is represented by input/out messages and its functions (Zhuge & Liu, 2004). Now, we give the formal definitions of replaceable services and service replaceability.

Definition 3.1 *(Replaceable services): Suppose that D is the collection of services, and $ws_i(oplist_i)$,$ws_j(oplist_j) \in D$ are two individual services, where $oplist_i$ and $oplist_j$ are the sets of operations provided by ws_i and ws_j, respectively. If $cop_{i,j} = oplist_i \cap oplist_j \neq \varnothing$, then, $ws_j(oplist_j)$ is said to be a replaceable service of ws_i w.r.t $cop_{i,j}$ in D. Here, 'w.r.t' means that service ws_i can be replaced by ws_j if the invoked operation of ws_i is an operation in the set of $cop_{i,j}$. Otherwise, if the invoked operation is not in $cop_{i,j}$, ws_i can not be replaced by ws_j.*

Definition 3.1 shows that if ws_j is a replaceable service of ws_i, there is at least one common operation between ws_i and ws_j. According to the proportion of common operations among the total operations in services, we define the service replaceability of ws_j to ws_i as follows.

Definition 3.2 *(Service replaceability): Given two services, $ws_i(oplist_i)$ and $ws_j(oplist_j)$, and $cop_{i,j} = oplist_i \cap oplist_j$ is their common operations. The replaceability of ws_j to ws_i, which is denoted as $Rep_{i,j}$, can be quantified by*

$$Rep_{i,j} = \frac{|cop_{i,j}|}{|oplist_i|} \tag{1}$$

Where $|cop_{i,j}|$ and $|oplist_i|$ are the numbers of operations contained in $cop_{i,j}$ and $oplist_i$. Notice that the replaceability of service ws_j to service ws_i may not be equal to that of service ws_i to service ws_j.

It seems that the definition of replaceability is something like that of conventional similarity. But these two concepts are different in essence: similarity is symmetrical, while replaceability is unsymmetrical. For instance, given two services, ws_1 and ws_2, *Similarity*(ws_1, ws_2) is equal to *Similarity*(ws_2, ws_1). But the replaceability of ws_1 to ws_2 may not be equal to that of ws_2 to ws_1. The following classification of replaceable services for a given service shows the above difference: ws_1 is a complete replaceable service of ws_2, does not mean that ws_2 is also a complete replaceable service of ws_1. This is not a feature of similarity between two services. For convenience, in following section we use the fraction rather than the percentage of $Rep_{i,j}$ without declaring explicitly.

Clearly, the service replaceability measures the substitutional ability of one service to another. According to the value of $Rep_{i,j}$, we classify the replaceable services into three types:

1. **Complete replaceable service (CRS):** If $Rep_{i,j} = 1$, which means that ws_i can be completely replaced by ws_j, then ws_j is a Complete Replaceable Service (or CRS) of ws_i.

2. **Partial replaceable service (PRS):** If $Rep_{i,j} < 1$, which implies that only the partial operations of wsi are provided by ws_j, then ws_j is a Partial Replaceable Service (or PRS) of ws_i w.r.t $cop_{i,j}$, where $cop_{i,j} = oplisti \cap oplistj$.

3. **Unreplaceable service (URS):** If $Rep_{i,j} = 0$, in other words, there is no common operations between ws_i and ws_j, then ws_j is an Un-Replaceable Service (or URS) of ws_i.

Although ws_j is a CRS of ws_i does not mean that ws_i is also a CRS of ws_j, ws_i must be a PRS of ws_j. Let us see an example:

Example 1 Let $ws_1(op_2, op_3)$ and $ws_2(op_1, op_2, op_3, op_4)$ be two services, it is obvious that ws_2 is a CRS of ws_1 because of $Rep_{1,2} = \frac{|\{op_2, op_3\}|}{|\{op_2, op_3\}|} = \frac{2}{2} = 1.0$, and ws_1 is a PRS of ws_2 because of

$$Rep_{2,1} = \frac{|\{op_2, op_3\}|}{|\{op_1, op_2, op_3, op_4\}|} = \frac{2}{4} = 0.5.$$

Sometimes, we also say ws_2 is more general than ws_1 or ws_1 is more specific than ws_2. Similarly, this example indicates that if ws_j is a PRS of ws_i, ws_i can be a CRS or PRS of ws_j.

Definition 3.1 and 3.2 illustrate that, for a specific service $ws_i(oplist_i)$, the replaceable services form a set Rws_i where each $ws_j(oplist_j) \in Rws_i$ satisfies $oplist_i \cap oplist_j \neq \emptyset$. In other words, a service will be added into the set as long as it has one or more common operation with the service being replaced. This restriction is too loose to keep a reasonable number of replaceable services in Rws_i. In order to remove redundant replaceable services in Rws_i, we employ the following model to evaluate the optimal replaceable service set.

Definition 3.3 *(Optimal replaceable service set): Suppose that Rws_r is a set of replaceable services of ws_i in the service collection D, that is, every*

$ws_j(oplist_j) \in Rws_r$ *is a replaceable service of* ws_i. *If* Rws_r *satisfies: i) the replaceability of* Rws_r *to* ws_i, *denoted as* $Rep_{i,r}$ *is the greatest one in all the replaceable service subsets; ii) there does not exist any subset of* Rws_r, *that is* $Rwsr' \subset Rws_r$, *whose replaceability to* ws_i *equals to* $Rep_{i,r}$, *then* Rws_r *is said to be an optimal replaceable service set of* ws_i *in D, denoted as* $SORS_i$.

Definition 3.3 implies that an optimal replaceable service set has the smallest number of services providing the highest replaceability to a specific service in the given service collection. Although there may be many replaceable service subsets for a given service, only the optimal ones are meaningful to reduce the complexity of the consumers' application and the manual efforts of service-oriented application developers. Therefore, the goal of service replaceability management is to build an effective data structure to organize the replaceable services. This structure provides great support for the system to find the optimal replaceable service sets. Based on this idea, the problem of service replaceability management is given in next subsection.

Management of Service Replaceability

When a service provides multiple operations, it is very common that different service requestors invoke different operations of a service. This fact means that, from the perspective of service requestors, the replaceable services of the invoked service may be different from each other. On the other hand, the above discussion illuminates that the replaceability management of services is to organize services with an effective structure which enables user to retrieve the replaceable service efficiently and accurately. However, we need to take into account the following three considerations when building the structure.

1. Replaceable services are for the invoked operations, rather than the entire service being replaced. This implies that managing the replaceability among services at the operation level has precedence over at the service level.

2. For a specific service, if it supports several different operations, it has a great possibility for different requestors invoking different operations. Therefore, the replaceable service set varies with the requestors even though they invoke the same service.

3. Searching replaceable service is different from the general service searching. The latter can be accomplished by keyword-based methods (Dong, Halevy, Madhavan, Nemes, & Zhang, 2004). Applying these approaches directly to retrieve the replaceable services is quite time-consuming because it needs to execute too much similarity evaluation between services at the service level, and thus it is infeasible for real time execution. According to definition 3.1 and 3.2, the possible replaceable services of a specific service are those whose replaceability to the service being replaced is greater than zero. Therefore, to retrieve the replaceable services efficiently, the search space can be bounded to the services which have some common operations with the service to be replaced. Furthermore, in order to improve the searching performance, we need to organize the search space with an effective structure.

Based on the above considerations, we give a formal description of the problem of managing service replaceability.

Problem statement: Given a service $ws_i(oplist_i)$ and a service collection D, where

$$ws_i(oplist_i) \in D, ws_j(oplist_j)$$

is a replaceable service of ws_i in D. The common operations between ws_i and ws_j is $cop_{i,j} = oplist_i \cap oplist_j$ and the replaceability of ws_j to ws_i is

$$Rep_{i,j} = \frac{|cop_{i,j}|}{|oplist_i|}.$$

The problem of managing service replaceability is to organize the services in D using an effective structure by considering the replaceability $Rep_{i,j}$ and the common operations among services $cop_{i,j}$. This structure needs to guarantee the efficiency for searching the replaceable services of a given service.

A naive approach for solving this problem is to build a structure to index the replaceable services for each service. When the number of services is small, it is not difficult to build such a structure and keep the high efficiency of retrieving replaceable service because very few joins are needed in the process of retrieving. However, in real applications, the population and categories of services are both very large, and the mutual replaceability between the services is not high enough. Under such circumstance, if this naive approach of managing the replaceable services is adopted, the execution of searching will be costly for a large number of join operations.

In this article, by considering their common operations and the value of replaceability, we employ FCA (formal concept analysis) to analyze the relationship among services, and a novel structure, called *RSLattice*, is designed to manage the replaceability among services by navigating the relationship among services in a semantic way.

4. APPLYING FCA TO SERVICES

In this section, the fundamentals of formal concepts analysis for services are introduced.

Brief Introduction of FCA

FCA (Formal Concept Analyis) is a mathematic approach used to analyze the conceptual data and knowledge processing (Ganter & Wille, 1999; Godin, Missaoui, &Alaoui, 1991). Its mathematical foundation is the theory of concept lattice (Birkhok, 1993). In which, the formal concept is formulated as unit of thought for modeling a domain, and comprises its intension and extension. The objects to which a concept applies form the extension of the concept and the attributes characterizing the objects compose the intension of the concept. FCA can be used to generate a concept lattice by finding all the possible concepts to reveal the implicit relationship between objects. It has been successfully applied to a wide range of applications. Here, we only introduce how to employ FCA in service context using its fundamental theory.

Generally, FCA analyzes data in three steps. The first one is to determine formal concept context, which is composed of three parts: objects, attributes, and their relationship. The second one is to extract the formal concepts from the context. A formal concept represents a dual relationship between a subset of objects and a subset of attributes. The final one is to arrange the formal concepts into a hierarchical order, say, *RSLattice*, in our work, to reveal the underlying relationship among services. The formal concept context, formal concept and *RSLattice* for services are defined as follows.

Definition 4.1 (Formal concept context of services): *Suppose that D is a service collection, the formal concept context of the services contained in D is a triple and denoted as FCC(Ws, Ao, R), where Ws is the object set which is formed by the services in D, Ao is the attribute set which is composed of the operations provided by the services in Ws, and R represents the relationship among the elements of Ws and those of Ao, that is, $r_{i,j} = ws_i \times op_j$ where $ws_i \in$ Ao and $op_j \in$ Ao.*

Numerically, $r_{i,j}$ is set to 1 if op_j is provided by ws_i, otherwise, it is set to 0.

This definition is described with following equations:

$$Ws = \left\{ws_1, ws_2, ..., ws_n \mid ws_i \subset D\right\} \tag{2a}$$

$$Ao = \left\{op_1, op_2, ..., op_m \mid \forall op_i, \exists ws_j \in Ws \text{ and } ws_j.prod. \ op_i\right\} \tag{2b}$$

and the relationship R is mathematically represented as:

$$r_{i,j} = \begin{cases} 1 & \text{if } ws_i.prod.op_j \\ 0 & \text{otherwise} \end{cases} \tag{3}$$

where $ws_i.prod.op_j$ means ws_i provides operation op_j. Equation 3 indicates that the formal concept context of services in a service collection can be represented as a binary table.

Example 2 In our example service collection, there are six services providing eight operations totally. Table 1 is the corresponding formal concept context of the services computed with Equation 2. The value of $r_{i,j}$ indicates whether operation op_j is provided by service ws_i, i.e, 1 is for the positive answer and 0 is for the negative answer. For instance, $r_{1,3} = 1$ means that ws_1 provides op_3, and $r_{1,2}=0$ implies that op_2 is not provided by ws_1.

After defining the formal concept context of services, now we are at the point to define the formal concepts in a specific context.

Definition 4.2 (Formal concept of services) *Let FCC(Ws,Ao,R) be a formal concept context of services. The formal concept of services is a binary relation, represented as FC(CWs,CAo), where CWs ⊂ Ws, CAo ⊂ Ao, and CWs, CAo satisfy:*

$$CAo = \left\{op \mid op \in Ao, \forall ws \in CWs \text{ and } ws.prod. \ op\right\} \tag{4a}$$

$$CWs = \left\{ws \mid ws \in Ws, \forall op \in CAo \text{ and } ws.prod. \ op\right\} \tag{4b}$$

Table 1. Formal Concept Context

service	op_1	op_2	op_3	op_4	op_5	op_6	op_7	op_8
ws_1	1	0	1	0	0	0	1	1
ws_2	1	1	0	0	0	0	0	0
ws_3	0	0	0	0	1	0	1	0
ws_4	1	0	1	0	0	0	0	0
ws_5	0	0	1	1	0	0	0	0
ws_6	0	0	0	1	0	1	0	0

where $ws.prod.op$ means operation op is provided by services ws. Generally, CAo is referred as the intension of FC, and CWs is referred as the extension of FC. They can be formally represented as $CAo = in(FC)$ and $CWs = ex(FC)$, respectively.

Example 3 Figure 1(a) describes the formal concepts computed with Equation 4 in the formal concept context of service shown in Table 1. Each row represents the information of a same formal concept, including its label (first column), its extension (second column) and its intension (last column). For every formal concept, each service in the extension provides all the operations in the intension, and vice versa. For instance, $ex(FC_6)= \{ws_1,ws_4\}$ and $in(FC_6)=\{op_1,op_3\}$. According to Table 1, it is clear that both ws_1 and ws_4 can provide op_1 and op_3.

The last step of FCA is to build the concept lattice which reveals the underlying relationship among services. In our context, the concept lattice is named as *RSLattice*, which actually uses concept lattice to organize services. Researchers have already proposed several efficient algorithms for building and updating concept lattice, such as Ganter and Wille (1999), Godin, Missaoui and Alaoui (1991), Birkhok (1993), and Peng, Huang, Wang and Zhou (2005). These approaches can be employed to build and maintain our *RSLattice*. The research of these algorithms is out of the scope of this article, and no description is given in detail.

Figure 1. The RSLattice and formal concepts of Web services w.r.t the formal concept context in Table 1

(a) Examples of formal concepts of services

(b) Example of RSLattice

FCoWS	extent	intent
FC_1	$ws_1, ws_2, ws_3, ws_4, ws_5, ws_6$	NULL
FC_2	ws_1, ws_2, ws_4	op_1
FC_3	ws_1, ws_3	op_7
FC_4	ws_1, ws_4, ws_5	op_3
FC_5	$ws_5 ws_6$	op_4
FC_6	ws_1, ws_4	op_1, op_3
FC_7	ws_2	$op_1 op_2$
FC_8	ws_3	$op_5 op_7$
FC_9	ws_5	$op_3 op_4$
FC_{10}	ws_6	$op_4 op_8$
FC_{11}	ws_1	op_1, op_3, op_7, op_8
FC_{12}	NULL	$op_1, op_2, op_3, op_4, op_5, op_6, op_7, op_8$

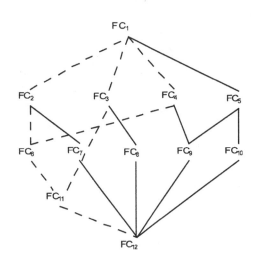

Service Relationship Representation – *RSLattice*

As discussed above, in FCA, the conceptual structure of data, which describes the relationship between objects and attributes, is represented as concept lattice. When applying FCA to service context, *RSLattice* is given to represent the relationship between services and operations.

Suppose that $FCC(Ws,Ao,R)$ is a formal concept context of services. The corresponding *RSLattice*, which gives a semantic description of relationship among services in $ex(FCC)$, is denoted as $RSL(Ws,Ao,R)$ (or briefly *RSL*). It is obvious that each formal concept in the *FCC* corresponds to a node of *RSL*, and each node of *RSL* represents a formal concept in *FCC*. Therefore, in following sections, we do not discriminate the two terms, formal concepts and nodes, in *RSLattice*.

Given two formal concepts $FC_i(CWs_i, CAo_i)$, $FC_j(CWs_j, CAo_j)$ in a formal concept context. If FC_i and FC_j satisfy the partial order, $CWs_i \subseteq CWs_j \Leftrightarrow CAo_i \supseteq CAo_j$, then FC_i and FC_j are Ancestor-Descendant Relationship (or **ADR**) concepts,

denoted as $FC_i \leq FC_j$. FC_i is a descendant of FC_j and FC_j is an ancestor of FC_i. More specially, if there does not exist another concept, say, FC_k, which satisfies $FC_i \leq FC_k \leq FC_j$, then, FC_i and FC_k are Parent-Child Relationship (or PCR) concepts. That is, FC_j is a parent of FC_i and FC_i is a child of FC_j.

Definition 4.3 (Fundamental concepts in *RSLattice*): *Suppose that RSL is a RSLattice and FC_i, FC_j are two nodes in RSL. The number of nodes (or formal concepts) is the size of RSL, denoted as $|RSL|$. If FC_i and FC_j are PCR nodes, then there is an edge between and denoted as $E(FC_i, FC_j)$. All the edges connected together from Top(RSL) to a specific node, say, FC_i, forms a path arriving at FC_i, denoted as Path(FC_i). The length of a path refers to the number of edges in the path. The longest path from Top(RSL) to Bottom(RSL) through FC_i is the chain of node FC_i, and represented as Chain(FC_i). The longest chain of all the nodes in RSL is the chain of RSLattice, and denoted as Chain(RSL). The number of edges in Chain(FC_i) from the Top(RSL) to FC_i is referred as the level of*

131

FC_j. The length of Chain(RSL) is also called the layers of the RSLattice. The distance between two nodes is the number of edges between them, and denoted as $Dist(FC_i, FC_j)$. Specially, $Dist(FC_i, FC_i) = 0$, and $Dist(FC_i, FC_j) = \infty$ if there is no path from FC_i to FC_j. The node which has the maximal extension and the minimal intension is the top node of RSL and denoted as Top(RSL), and the node with the minimal extension and the maximal intension is the bottom node of RSL and represented as Bottom(RSL).

Example 4 Figure 1(b) is the *RSLattice* generated by considering the partial order relationship between the formal concepts in Figure 1(a). According to the figure, FC_2 and FC_6 are PCR nodes because they satisfy the partial order: i) $ex(FC_2) \supset ex(FC_6)$, because $ex(FC_2) = \{ws_1, ws_2, ws_4\}$ and $ex(FC_6) = \{ws_1, ws_4\}$; ii) $in(FC_2) \subset in(FC_6)$, because $in(FC_2) = \{op_1\}$, $in(FC_6) = \{op_1, op_3\}$, and there is no other node between FC_2 and FC_6. Therefore, FC_2 and FC_6 are PCR nodes, and there is an edge between them. Similarly, FC_2 and FC_{11} are ADR nodes for $FC_2 \geq FC_6 \geq FC_{11}$ and thus there is a path from FC_2 to FC_{11}. There are three paths through FC_{11}, $P_1: FC_1 \rightarrow FC_2 \rightarrow FC_6 \rightarrow FC_{11} \rightarrow FC_{12}$, $P_2: FC_1 \rightarrow FC_4 \rightarrow FC_6 \rightarrow FC_{11} \rightarrow FC_{12}$ and $P_3: FC_1 \rightarrow FC_3 \rightarrow FC_{11} \rightarrow FC_{12}$. There are shown as dotted edges in the figure. The length of P_1, P_2 and P_3 are 4, 4 and 3, respectively. Obviously, P_1 and P_2 are the chains of FC_{11} and the level of FC_{11} is 3. It is also observed that P_1 and P_2 are the chains of the *RSLattice,* and thus the layer of the *RSLattice* is 4. The bottom node of the *RSLattice* is FC_{12} and the top node is FC_1.

Proposition 4.1: *The nodes in the RSLattice satisfy the following properties:*

Proof: *Obviously, i) is true; for ii), according to the description of RSLattice, it follows that $FC_1 \leq FC_2 \Leftrightarrow CWs_2 \supseteq CWs_1 \Leftrightarrow CAo_2 \subseteq CAo_1$. Similarly, $FC_2 \leq FC_1 \Leftrightarrow CWs_2 \subseteq CWs_1 \Leftrightarrow CAo_1 \subseteq CAo_2$. Therefore, $CWs_1 = CWs_2$ and $CAo_1 = CAo_2$, that*

is, $FC_1 = FC_2$. In property iii, $FC_1 \leq FC_2 \Leftrightarrow CAo_2 \subseteq CAo_1$ and $FC_2 \subseteq FC_3 \Leftrightarrow CAo_3 \subseteq CAo_2$, thus, $CAo_3 \subseteq CAo_1$. $CWs_1 \subseteq CWs_3$ can be obtained in the same way. This means $FC_1 \leq FC_3$.

According to the lattice theory, in a given formal concept context, the corresponding concept lattice is not unique. This claim also exists in the service context, that is, the *RSLattice* is not unique in a given formal concept context of web services. In our approach, for brevity, we only discuss the minimal *RSLattice* which is defined as follows:

Definition 4.4 *(**Minimal RSLattice**): Given a service collection D and a RSLattice, RSL(Ws,Ao,R), which is corresponding to the formal concept context of D. $FC_1(CWs_1, CAo_1)$ and $FC_2(CWs_2, CAo_2)$ are two arbitrary nodes in RSL(Ws,Ao,R). If FC_1 and FC_2 satisfy the following two conditions: i) $CWs_1 = CWs_2$ implies $CAo_1 = CAo_2$; ii) $CAo_1 = CAo_2$ implies $CWs_1 = CWs_2$, then RSLattice is the minimal RSLattice of D, and is denoted as Min(RSL).*

Definition 4.4 implies that in minimal *RSLattice*, if two nodes have same intension, they also have the same extension and vice versa. This merit reduces the redundant nodes in the *RSLattice* and improves the performance of retrieving replaceable service in the *RSLattice*.

In Section 1, we mentioned that the structure, *RSLattice*, representing the replaceability among services can be built offline at the initialization phase. Of course, it can also be built online. However, the process of computing the replaceability among services is costly, especially when the number of services in the collection is very large. Therefore, we suggest that the replaceability initially be built offline. Some previous work, such as Service-Oriented Monitoring Registry (Kalali, Alencar, & Cowan, 2003) and watchdong like model (Liu, Jia, & Pui, 2002) can be used to monitor the availability of a service. If a service is not available, a notification will be sent to the system, and the service will be marked in *RSLattice*. On the other hand, if the service changes from unavailable to available, the mark will be removed. When retrieving the replaceable services, only unmarked replaceable services are returned to the users. This method guarantees the replaceable services appeared in the result set are always available. By this way, we can make the proposed structure more adaptive.

5. SEARCHING REPLACEABLE SERVICES IN *RSLattice*

To retrieve the replaceable services online, we have to compute the similarity between these semi-structure documents, and it is too time-consuming. We show that *RSLattice* is an efficient approach to support the retrieval of replaceable services. At first, let us see how to search the replaceable services for a specific service in the *RSLattice*.

Correspondence between Replaceable Services and *RSLattice* Nodes

Before discussing the searching strategy, some concepts and theorems are introduced.

Definition 5.1 *(RSNN and CRSNN): Suppose that D is the service collection, RSL is the RSLattice corresponding to the formal concept context of services contained in D, and $ws_i(oplist_i) \in D$ is a specific service. For any node FC_j in RSL, if $in(FC_j) \cap oplist_i \neq \phi$, then, FC_j is a RSNN Replaceable Service Nested Node (or RSNN) of ws_i. A RSNN FC_j is a Complete Replaceable Service Nested Node (or CRSNN) of ws_i, if and only if*

$$Rep_{i,FCi} = \frac{|in(FC_i) \cap oplist_i|}{|oplist_i|} = 1.$$

Definition 5.1 means that, in the *RSLattice*, the set of common operations among the services in the extension of the CRSNN is the same as

that of the service being replaced. According to the definition of formal concept of services (see Definition 4.2), it is obvious that the service being replaced is contained in the extension of the CRSNN. If there are any other services in the extension besides the service being replaced, they must be the complete replaceable services and should appear in the optimal replaceable service set (see Definition 3.3).

In Section 3.2, we mentioned that the replaceable services are with respect to the invoked service operations, rather than the entire service. Thus, we propose the definition of the RSNNs for a specific service with respect to a set of requested operations.

Definition 5.2 *(RSNN and CRSNN w.r.t a set of requested service operations): Let FC_j be a RSNN of ws_i, $oplist_i$ be the operation set of ws_i, and $r_k \subseteq oplist_i$ be a requested operation set of ws_i. If $in(FC_j) \cap r_k \neq \phi$, then FC_j is a RSNN w.r.t r_k. Particularly, if $Rep_{FC_j, r_k} = \frac{|in(FC_j) \cap r_k|}{|r_k|} = 1$ is satisfied, then FC_j is a CRSNN of ws_i w.r.t r_k.*

According to the properties of *RSLattice*, if a CRSNN with respect to a set of requested operations r_k of the service being replaced (say, $ws_i(oplist_i)$) exists in the *RSLattice*, it must be an ancestor of the CRSNN. It is because $r_k \subseteq oplist_i$.

Example 5 In the *RSLattice* shown in Figure 1(b), the intension of node FC_{11} is {op_1, op_3, op_7, op_8} which is equal to the operation set of ws_1. Thus, FC_{11} is the CRSNN of ws_1. Suppose that r_1 = {op_7} is a requested operation set of ws_1, FC_3 is a CRSNN of ws_1 w.r.t r_1, because $in(FC_3) = \{op_7\} = r_1$.

Theorem 5.1: *For any service ws_i in a service collection D, there exists exactly one CRSNN of ws_i, say, FC_j, which satisfies $in(FC_j) = oplist_i$, in the corresponding RSLattice of D.*

Proof: *Firstly, let us give the proof of the existence. Assume that there is no CRSNN of ws_i in the corresponding RSLattice (RSL) of D, that is, there is no node in RSL whose intension contains $oplist_i$. Any node in RSL whose extension contains wsi should satisfy one of the following two conditions: i) $in(FC_j) \supset oplist_i$ or ii) $in(FC_j) \subset oplist_i$. According to the definition of formal concept of web services (Definition 4.2), for a given formal concept $FC_j(CWs_j, CAo_j)$, each service in CWs_j provides all the operations contained in CAo_j. If $in(FC_j) \supset oplist_i$ means at least one operation in CAo_j can not be provided by ws_i, it conflicts with the Definition 4.2. If $in(FC_j) \subset oplist_i$, that is, there is at least one operation, $op_k \in oplist_i$ which meets $op_k \in in(FC_j)$. Because op_k is provided by ws_i, so it should be contained in the intension of some nodes whose extension contains ws_i. Therefore, there must exist at least one node whose intension equals $oplist_i$, i.e., $in(FC_j) = oplist_i$.*

Secondly, we prove there are only one CRSNN in the *RSLattice* for ws_i. Assume that there are two or more CRSNNs in the *RSLattice*, whose intensions are exactly the same as the operation set of the service being replaced. We define two different nodes, FC_1 and FC_2, as the CRSNNs of ws_i in RSL which satisfy $in(FC_1) = in(FC_2) = oplist_i$. Here, we only discuss the minimal RSLattice (Definition 4.4), so, $FC_1 = FC_2$. This fact conflicts with our assumption.

Theorem 5.2: *Suppose that RSL is a RSLattice and FC_j is the CRSNN of a specific service $ws_i(oplist_i)$ in RSL, namely, $in(FC_j) = oplist_i$. Then, FC_j is the nearest node, whose extension contains ws_i, in the chain of FC_j to the bottom of the RSL .*

Proof: *Let FC_k be a node in the chain of FC_j between FC_j and Bottom(RSL), and its extension contains ws_i. This means that $ws_i \in ex(FC_j)$, $ws_i \in ex(FC_k)$ and $Dist(FC_j , Bottom(RSL)) > Dist(FC_k, Bottom(RSL))$.*

According to Definition 4.3, any two ADR nodes satisfy $ex(FC_j) \supset ex(FC_k)$ and $in(FC_j) \subset in(FC_k)$. From the above, it follows that $in(FC_j) = oplist_i$, thus, $opslit_i \subset in(FC_k)$. Similarly, $ws_i \in ex(FC_k)$ implies that ws_i provides all the operations contained in $in(FC_k)$, i.e., $oplist_i \supseteq in(FC_k)$. From above discussion, it is easy to get $oplist_i = in(FC_k)$. Therefore, $in(FC_j) = in(FC_k)$ implies $FC_i = FC_j$ (see Definition 4.4), that is to say, FC_i and FC_j refer to the same node of RSL.

Theorem 5.3: *Suppose that RSL is a RSLattice, and FC_j is the CRSNN of a specific service $ws_i(oplist_i)$ in RSL, i.e., $in(FC_j) = oplist_i$. In RSL, all the replaceable services of ws_i must appear in the extension of some nodes in the paths through FC_j.*

Proof: *Let $ws_j(oplist_j)$ be a replaceable service of ws_i, i.e., $Rep_{i,j} = \dfrac{|oplist_i \cap oplist_j|}{|oplist_i|} > 0$. We prove that ws_j must appear in the extension of some nodes in paths through FC_j. We make an assumption that ws_j does not appear in any path through FC_j. According to the definition of replaceable services (Definition 3.1), it follows that $cop_{i,j} = oplist_i \cap oplist_j \neq \phi$. If $cop_{i,j} = oplist_i$, then ws_j must be contained in the extension of FC_j, but it conflicts with our assumption. If there is $cop_{i,j} \subset oplist_i$, a node FC_k can be found to satisfy $\{ws_i, ws_j\} \subseteq ex(FC_k)$, $cop_{i,j} = in(FC_k)$ and $in(FC_k) \subset oplist_i = in(FC_j)$ in RSL; therefore, FC_j and FC_k are two ADR nodes and they must be in the same path.*

Example 7 From Figure 1(b), it can be seen that all the replaceable services of ws1 are in the extension of some nodes in the path through FC_{11}, which is the CRSNNs of ws_1 in the *RSLattice*. In detail, all the replaceables service of ws1 are in the extension of some nodes in following paths, $FC_1 \rightarrow FC_2 \rightarrow FC_6 \rightarrow FC_{11} \rightarrow FC_{12}$, $FC_1 \rightarrow FC_4 \rightarrow FC_6 \rightarrow FC_{11} \rightarrow FC_{12}$ and $FC_1 \rightarrow FC_3 \rightarrow FC_{11} \rightarrow FC_{12}$.

Theorem 5.3 also means that URSes (unreplaceable replaceable services, see Section 3.1) are not in the paths through the CRSNN in the *RSLattice*. This guarantees that when searching the replaceable services for a specific service being replaced in the *RSLattice*, we only need to visit the nodes in the paths through the CRSNN of the service being replaced.

Algorithms

Before describing the algorithms for searching replaceable services (see Figure 2) in the *RSLattice*, let us see how to accomplish the selection of optimal replaceable service set (see Definition 3.3) for a specific service being replaced in a service collection through the *RSLattice*. According to the replaceability and the importance of a replaceable service to the service to be replaced, the replaceable services fall into four categories.

Definition 5.3 *(Types of replaceable services):* *Suppose that D is the service collections; RSL is the corresponding RSLattice; ws_i is the service being replaced, FC_j be a replaceable nested node of ws_i. $Rws_{i,j} = ex(FC_j) - \{ws_i\}$ is the set of replaceable services of ws_i which provide the operations in $in(FC_j)$. If there is only one service, say $ws_k \in Rws_{i,j}$, then ws_k is the Required Replaceable Service (or RRS) w.r.t the operations in $in(FC_j)$. If there are more than one services in $Rws_{i,j}$, these services are Optional Replaceable Services (or ORS) of ws_i w.r.t the operations in $in(FC_j)$. For any $ws_k \in ORS$, if it has more common operations with ws_i than any other replaceable services, then ws_k is a Preferential Replaceable Service (or PRS) w.r.t the operations in $in(FC_j)$. If $ws_k \in ORS$ does not belong to any above types, then it is a Discardable Replaceable Service (or DRS) of ws_i.*

The categorization of replaceable services in Definition 5.3 is very useful for the selection of S_{ORS_i} (the optimal replaceable service set of ws_i,

see Definition 3.3). We impose the following order when selecting the S_{ORS_i}: $RRS \rightarrow PRS \rightarrow ORS$. Notice that in each step, we only select the service which has not existed in the result set.

Example 8 Taking searching S_{ORS_1} in *RSLattice* (see Figure 1(b)) as an example. By using Theorem 5.3, we know that the RSNNs of ws_1 are in the paths through FC_{11}. They are FC_2, FC_3, FC_4 and FC_6, and the replaceable service set of ws_1 is $\{ws_2, ws_4, ws_3, ws_5\}$. According to Definition 5.3, it follows that ws_3 and ws_4 are the RRSes of ws_1 because $ex(FC_3) - ws_1 = ws_3$, $ex(FC_6) - ws_1 = ws_4$. Therefore, ws_3 and ws_4 are firstly selected as the members of $S_{ORS_1} \circ \{ws_2, ws_4\}$ is the set of ORSes of $ws1$ with respect to op_1 and $\{ws_4, ws_5\}$ is the set of ORSes of ws_1 with respect to op_3. But ws_4 has already existed in the result set, thus, ws_2 and ws_5 can be regarded as a DRS of ws_1. Finally, $S_{ORS_1} = \{ws_3, ws_4\}$ is obtained.

According to Theorem 5.3, to search all the replaceable services we only need to transverse the nodes in the paths through the CRSNNs of the service being replaced. And Definition 5.3 can be used to filter the results when computing the optimal replaceable service sets.

Algorithm Searching_ORS, as shown in Algorithm 1, is to compute the S_{ORS_i} by transversing the *RSLattice* in DFS(Depth-First Search)-manner. To avoid accessing a node repeatedly, we use a integral numerical array *visited_node*[ ] to identify the visited node. The algorithm obtains a S_{ORS_i} by two steps. At first, invokes Searching_RS to compute all the replaceable services of ws_i, Rws_i. Then, it gets the S_{ORS_i} by calling algorithm Optimizing_RS (Algorithm 3) to filter DRSes (the discardable replaceable services) in Rws_i. For the convenient maintenance of S_{ORS_i}, a hash table can be used to index the services in S_{ORS_i} by taking the operations as the keys and the services providing the operations appeared in the keys as the values.

Figure 2. Algorithms for searching replaceable services in RSLattice

---

Algorithm 1: *Searching Optimal Replaceable Services (Searching_ORS)*

Input: $(RSL; ws_i)$, where $ws_i(oplist_i)$ is the service been replaced and *RSL* is the *RSLattice* corresponding to the service collection in which ws_i is contained.

Output: S_{ORSi} is an optimal replaceable service set of ws_i discovered in *RSL*.

1 begin

2     $visited\_node[|RSL|] \leftarrow 0$;

3   for $vnode = 1$ to $|RSL|$ do

4         $Rwsi \leftarrow Searching\_RS(RSL, vnode, visited\_node, ws_i, oplist_i)$;

5   end for

6 $SORS_i \leftarrow Optimizing\_RS(Rwsi; oplisti)$;

7 return $SORS_i$;

8 end

Algorithm 2: Searching Replaceable Services (*Searching_RS*)

Input: $(RSL, lnode, visited\_node, ws_i, oplist_i)$, where *RSL* is the *RSLattice* corresponding to the service collection which contains ws_i, *lnode* is the node from which the algorithm transverses the *RSLattice* ; ws_i is the service being replaced and $oplist_i$ is its operation set;

Output: *Rwsi* is the set of replaceable services of *wsi*.

1 begin

2   if $visited\_node[lnode] = 0$ then

3         $FC_{lnode} \leftarrow GetConcept(lnode)$;

4         $FC_{lnode+1} \leftarrow GetConcept(lnode + 1)$;

5         $cop_{lnode} \leftarrow in(FC_{lnode}) \cap oplist$;

The idea behind algorithm Search RS is that if a non-visited node FC_k satisfying $in(FC_k) \cap oplist_i \neq \varnothing$, then the members in $ex(FC_k) - ws_i$ are the replaceable services of ws_i; if $in(FC_i) \cap oplist_i = \varnothing$, then stop searching the node and its descendants. We continue to visit the node in the paths till arriving at the CRSNN (see Definition 5.1) and returning to the non-visited nodes at above level. Finally, all the replaceable services of ws_i can be obtained. In this way, we only visit the nodes in the paths through the CRSNN whose intension equals $oplist_i$. In the algorithm, the re-

Algorithm 3: *Computing an Optimal Replaceable Service Set of ws (Optimizing_ RS)*

Input: (Rws_i, $oplist_i$), where Rws_i is the set of hash tables containing the replaceable services of ws_i. For each hash table in $el_i \in Rws_i$, el_i.
    key is the operation that can be provided by the services in $el_i.value$. $oplist_i$ is the operations of ws_i;
Output: S_{ORSi} is the hash table containing a set of optimal replaceable service set of ws_i.
1 begin
2 foreach $el_i \in Rws_i$ do
3 if $|el_i.value| = 1$ then
$S_{ORSi}.add(el_i.value)$; $oplist_i \leftarrow oplist_i - el_i.key$;
5 continue;
6 $el_i \leftarrow Rws_i.get(max(oplist_i \cap el_i.key))$;
7 while $oplisti \neq \varnothing$ and $el_i \neq null$ do
$S_{ORSi}.add(el.value)$;
9 $oplist_i \leftarrow oplist_i - el_i.key$;
10 $el_i \leftarrow Rws_i.get(max(oplist_i \cap el_i.key))$;
11 endwhile
12 endfor
13 return S_{ORSi};
14 end

---

lationship between *lnode* and *lnode + 1* is PCR (Parent-Child relationship). The idea is described clearly in Algorithm 2.

After obtaining all the replaceable services of ws_i, we now compute the S_{ORS_i} using *Optimizing_RS* (see Algorithm 3). Algorithm 3 firstly chooses the RRSes (see Definition 5.3) and puts them into the result set. Then, a greedy idea is employed to select the PRSes. In each iteration, it only chooses the service which can provide more common operations with the service being replaced than any other services. This is accomplished by function $Rws_i.get(max(oplist_i \cap el_i.key))$. Such a process stops when every operation of the replaced service is provided by at least one replaceable service in the result set or all the elements in Rws_i are visited.

When searching the replaceable services in a *RSLattice*, it invokes only once the algorithm Searching_ORS. The reason is that if a node has been marked as visited, it will not be visited again. We only need to search its neighbor nodes. The complexity depends on the number of operations provided by the service being replaced, the physical data type, and the size of the structure for storing the *RSLattice*. For example, if we exploit 2-dimensional array to store *RSLattice*, we need $O(n^2)$ to search all the neighbor nodes,

where n is the number of nodes in the *RSLattice*. For Algorithm 3, the complexity of algorithm Optimizing_RS is $O(l * m)$, where l is the number of operations of the replaced service and m is the size of Rws_i. Compared with n, l and m are much smaller, thus, the complexity of the whole algorithm is $O(n^2)$.

6. EXPERIMENTS

To demonstrate the performance of the proposed algorithms, we implement the proposed approach and conduct a series of experiments on real data sets. The experimental settings and results are described as follows. All the experiments were run on a 1.4GHz Pentium III PC with 256MB memory running Windows 2000 professional.

Experimental Settings

For the data set, a service corpus is built by gathering the services from the main authoritative UDDI repositories, including IBM, BEA, XMethod and Microsoft etc. This corpus contains 693 WSDL files and 2734 operations in total. The WSDL files associated with each service in the corpus can be accessed from the Web.

The describing information of each service includes the detailed description of its functions, its input/output messages, the name of service and its operations, and the textual description service and its operations. This textual information is preprocessed by performing word stemming, removing stop-words and splitting synthetical words by the TF/IDF method (Salton & Buckley, 1998).

To test the performance of the approach, we conduct two groups of experiments. Although there are lots of services providing the same functionalities on the Web, few of them have the exact same description documents. During the procedure of generating the formal concepts for services, the preprocessed service operations are vectorized at first, and then the similar operations using the cosine similarity function are determined. Therefore, one group of our experiments is to measure the value of similarity threshold impact on the performance of generating *RSLattice*.

In above discussion, we mentioned that the most important objective of this work is to develop an effective structure which can support searching replaceable service in an efficient way. Thus, our second group of experiments is to investigate the performance of querying S_{ORS} in the *RSLattices*.

Performance Measures

Besides adopting the conventional performance measures in information retrieval areas, i.e., precision (p), recall (r) and F_1-measure (Ricardo & Berthier, 1999), we also use other metrics, such as the time for generating formal concept of services, response time of executing a set of queries and the size of *RSLattice* varying with the size of service corpus to evaluate the proposed method.

Precision (p) is the number of actual positive S_{ORS_i} (c) returned by the system among all predicted positive S_{ORS_i} (t) returned by the system. Recall (r) is the proposition of actual positive S_{ORS_i} (c) returned by the system among all actual positive S_{ORS_i} (tc) in the corpus. The computation of them are shown as below:

$$p = \frac{|c|}{|t|} ; \ r = \frac{|c|}{tc} \tag{5}$$

F_1-measure measures the harmonic average of precision and recall and is determined using the following formula:

$$F_1 = \frac{2 \times p \times r}{p + r} \tag{6}$$

Evaluation of *RSLattice* Generation

The performance of generating *RSLattice* is evaluated by investigating the size of *RSLattice* varying with the different similarity threshold (s) between service operations. The real-application shows that few services having exactly the same textual descriptions although they provide the same functions. Therefore, before building the *RSLattice*, a quantitative definition of similar service operations are needed. Because current services are described in textual manner, such as WSDL documents, it is reasonable to index them at the operation level in TF/IDF method and evaluate their similarity with some distance measuring approaches. In our experiments, the cosine similarity function is employed to measure the similarity between service operations. If the similarity of any two service operations is greater than the predefined threshold (s), they are regarded as the same when computing the formal concepts. Therefore, it is meaningful to determine the effects of s on the size of *RSLattice* and the time needed to compute the formal concept of services.

The size of *RSLattice* (i.e. the number of nodes in the *RSLattice*) and the time for generating the formal concepts using different similarity threshold (s) over different size of service operation corpus are measured. The similarity threshold (s)

is decreased from 0.8 to 0.2, and the size of service operation corpus is increased from 400 to 2734. Figure 3(a) illustrates the size of *RSLattice* varies with the different value of *s* over different size of service operation corpus. As the figure shows, the similarity threshold (*s*) decreases, the size of *RSLattice* is increased slightly. This is due to the fact that the pairs of similar service operations increase as *s* decreases. According to the definition of formal concept of services, it is observed that the number of formal concepts, which equals the size of *RSLattice*, also becomes larger. Figure 3(b) reflects the effects in a different way. Note that the increase in time needed to compute the formal concepts when *s* is decreased. It is because the number of common operations increases as *s* decrease, which leads to the greater number of formal concepts.

Evaluation of Searching *RSLattice*

We choose a benchmark of 257 services and generate a workload of 1000 zipf ($\alpha = 0.6$) distributed requested operations of the services. The experiments try to find all the optimal replaceable service sets for each service in the service corpus w.r.t the requested operations. According to the above theorems and algorithms, to search the replaceable service for a given web service in the *RSLattice*, it only needs to visit the nodes in the paths which pass through the CRNSN (complete replaceable service nested node, see Definition 5.2) whose intension equals the operation set of the service. For a specific query, because the replaceable services must appear in the extension of some ancestor nodes of the CRSNN of the corresponding service, so it is enough to visit the ancestor nodes of the CRSNN rather than all the nodes in the paths through the CRSNN. The *RSLattice* itself does not introduce any noise into the searched results, thus, the precision chiefly depends on the similarity threshold *s* which is used to determine the similar operations. The value of similarity threshold is set to 0.3, 0.5 and 0.8 respectively, to study its impact on the performance of the proposed approach.

The contemporary semantic based service retrieving approaches mostly need services (such as DAML-S based services and OWL-S based services) having the ontological description. However, these semantic approaches are infeasible to the WSDL-based services which are lack of ontological description. Although there are many WSDL-based service retrieving

Figure 3. The effects of different similarity threshold on the performance of generating RSLattice

(a) Size of RSLattice

(b) Time for Computing Formal Concept of Services

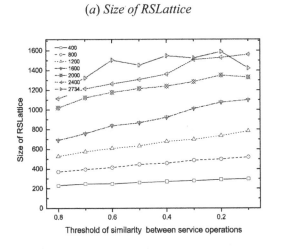

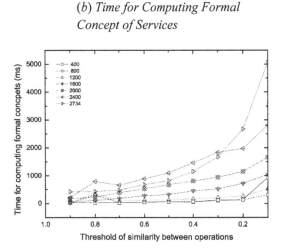

approaches (Wang & Stroulia, 2003; Dong, Halevy, Madhavan, Nemes & Zhang, 2004), few of them aim to find the replaceable services. Full-Text search (FT) and Pure-Similarity search (PS), whose features are more or less used in current WSDL-based service retrieval approaches, are the fundamental and most likely the methods used to search the replaceable services. Therefore, in our experiments, we compare our approach with this two traditional information retrieval approaches.

The experiments are run over 400, 800, 1200, 1600, 2000, 2400 and 2734 operations. The experimental results, including the precision, *F*1- measure and the time of each approach for executing the queries, are presented in Figure 4. Figure 4(a) depicts the precision of different approaches. The trend of the histogram illustrates that the precision of our approach increases with the increases of *s*. When *s* = 0.5 and *s* = 0.8, the precision is better than that of full-text search and pure similarity search. Figure 4(b) shows the F_1-

Figure 4. The Performance of Querying Optimal Replaceable Service sets in RSLattice

(a) Precision

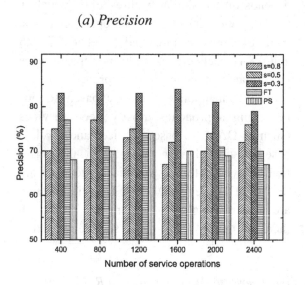

(b) F1-measure of Searching Optimal Rreplaceable Service Sets

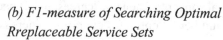
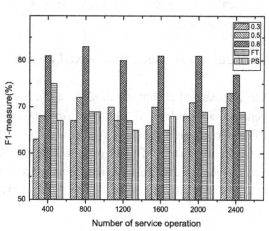

(c) Time for Execution of Queries

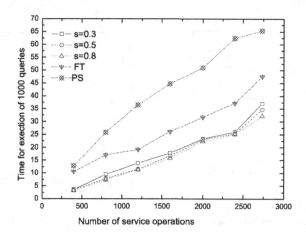

measures of different approaches. We know that $F1$-measure is the harmonic average of precision and recall. Figure 4(b) indicates that if s is greater enough, such as 0.8 in the figures, our approach can balance precision and recall at a higher level than that of other two approaches.

The response time for searching optimal replaceable services is also tested, and the results are shown in Figure 4(c). The figure shows that, with the increase of the size of service operation corpus, the execution time increases for all the approaches. However, there are different trends for different approaches. The performance of *RSLattice* is very stable for different values of s and the different size of service operation corpus. The time cost is less than that of full-text search and pure similarity search. The main reason is that, when searching the optimal replaceable services in the *RSLattice* for a specific service, it only needs to visit the nodes in the paths through the CRSNN of the service. These experiments demonstrate that *RSLattice* can be used to search the replaceable services for a given service in an efficient way.

7. CONCLUSION

Service replaceability is a very important issue to make the technology of service computing more practical. We quantitate the replaceability among services by considering the common operations between them and propose a novel structure, *RSLattice*, which is designed by applying FCA to service collection. *RSLattice* reveals the replaceable relationship among services by maintaining the underlying semantics.

Experimental results show that our approach performs better than any other traditional methods for searching the replaceable services. For the future work, we plan to extend this work in following directions. Firstly, we would like to combine our approach with ontology, such as OWLS (W3C, 2004), to improve the search accuracy. Secondly, some extra information, such as QoS, will be considered during the selection of the optimal replaceable service for a specific service. Finally, we want to further exploit more strategies for clustering services according to underlying semantics.

ACKNOWLEDGMENT

This work was partially supported by the National Natural Science Foundation of China under Grant No. 60773075, State Key Development Program of Basic Research of China (973 Program) under Grant No. 2010CB328106, Natural Science Foundation of Shanghai under Grant No. 10ZR1421100 and Innovation Program of Shanghai Education Commission under Grant No. 08YZ98.

REFERENCES

W3C. (2004). *OWL-S: Semantic Markup for Web Services*. Retrieved from http://www.w3.org/Submission/OWL-S

Bernstein, A., & Klein, M. (2002). *Discovering services: Towards high-precision service retrieval*. Paper presented at CaiSE, Toronto, ON, Canada.

Birkhok, G. (1993). *Lattice theory* (3rd ed.). Providence, RI: American Mathematical Society.

Brogi, A., Canal, C., & Pimental, E. (2004). Formalizing web service choreographies. *Electronic Notes in Theoretical Computer Science, 105,* 73–94. doi:10.1016/j.entcs.2004.05.007

Coalition, D. S. (2002). *DAML-S: Web Service description for Semantic Web*. Paper presented at the International Semantic Web Conference (ISWC), Sardinia, Italy.

Dong, X., Halevy, A., Madhavan, J., Nemes, E., & Zhang, J. (2004, August 31-September 3). Similarity Search for Web Services. In *Proceedings of the 13th International Conference on Very Large Data Bases VLDB*, Toronto, ON, Canada (pp. 372-383).

Ganter, B., & Wille, R. (1999). *Formal concept analysis: Mathematical foundations*. Heidelberg, Germany: Springer Verlag.

Godin, R., Missaoui, R., & Alaoui, H. (1991). Learning algorithms using a Galois lattice structure. In *Proceedings of the Third International Conference on Tools for Artificial Intelligence*, San Jose, CA (pp. 22-29). Washington, DC: IEEE Computer Society. Heß, A., & Kushmerick, N. (2003). *Learning to attach semantic metadata to web services*. Paper presented at the 2nd International Semantic Web Con-ference (ISWC), Sanibel Island, FL.

Kalali, B., Alencar, P., & Cowan, D. (2003). *A service-oriented monitoring registry*. Paper presented at the Conference on the Centre for Advanced Studies on Collaborative Research.

Kleijnen, S., & Raju, S. (2003). *An open web services architecture*. New York: ACM Press.

Liu, W., Jia, W., & Pui, O. A. (2002). *Add exception notification mechanism to web services*. Paper presented at the Fifth International Conference on Algorithms and Architectures for Parallel Processing (ICA3PP).

Paolucci, M., Kawmura, T., Payne, T., & Sycara, K. (2002). *Semantic matching of Web Services Capabilities*. Paper presented at the International Semantic Web Conference (ISWC).

Peng, D., Huang, S., Wang, X., & Zhou, A. (2005). *Concept-based retrieval of alternate web services*. Paper presented at the 10th Conference on Database Systems for Advanced Applications (DASFAA), Beijing, China.

Ricardo, B., & Berthier, R. (1999). *Modern information retrieval*. New York: ACM Press.

Salton, G., & Buckley, C. (1998). Term weighting approaches in automatic retrieval. *Information Processing & Management*, 24(5), 513–523. doi:10.1016/0306-4573(88)90021-0

Wang, Y., & Stroulia, E. (2003). *Flexible interface matching for web-service discovery*. Paper presented at the Fourth International Conference on Web Information Systems Engineering (WISE'03), Rome, Italy.

Zaremski, A. M., & Wing, J. M. (1997). Specification matching of software components. *ACM Transactions on Software Engineering and Methodology*, 6(4), 333–369. doi:10.1145/261640.261641

Zhuge, H., & Liu, J. (2004). Flexible retrieval of web service. *Journal of Systems and Software*, 70(1-2), 107–116. doi:10.1016/S0164-1212(03)00003-7

This work was previously published in the International Journal of Web Services Research, Volume 7, Issue 1, edited by Liang-Jie (LJ) Zhang, pp. 46-64, copyright 2010 by IGI Publishing (an imprint of IGI Global).

Chapter 7
Similarity Measures for Substituting Web Services

Maricela Bravo
Centro de Investigación y de Estudios Avanzados, Mexico

Matias Alvarado
Centro de Investigación y de Estudios Avanzados, Mexico

ABSTRACT

Web service substitution is one of the most advanced tasks that a composite Web service developer must achieve. Substitution occurs when, in a composite scenario, a service operation is replaced to improve the composition performance or fix a disruption caused by a failing service. To move the automation of substitution forward, a set of measures, considering structure and functionality of Web services, are provided. Most of current proposals for the discovery and matchmaking of Web services are based on the semantic perspective, which lacks the precise information that is needed toward Web service substitution. This paper describes a set of similarity measures to support this substitution. Similarity measurement accounts the differences or similarities by the syntax comparison of names and data types, followed by the comparison of input and output parameters values of Web service operations. Calculation of these measures was implemented using a filtering process. To evaluate this approach, a software architecture was implemented, and experimental tests were carried on both private and public available Web services. Additionally, as is discussed, the application of these measures can be extended to other Web services tasks, such as classification, clustering and composition.

INTRODUCTION

In the last two decades, there has been a growing interest for developing Web service- based projects and for generating Web service interfaces from legacy software. This growing interest corresponds to the evolution of telecommunications, the emergence of open and interoperable protocols, the development of XML-based standard languages, and the increasing usage of Internet as a public wide area net for connecting users, businesses and software agents. As a result, many Web service providers (software vendors) have taken the advantage of using Internet as an

DOI: 10.4018/978-1-4666-1942-5.ch007

open window to the entire world to offer their services through public repositories. Currently, many applications are being developed with the composition of multiple Web services to solve complex problems. Web service composition is the information technology, which full realization is expected for automating the intense information interchange among users and businesses. Many challenging tasks are involved in Web service composition, ranging from classification, clustering, search, discovery, substitution, among others. In particular, in this paper the main stress is on Web service substitution.

Web service substitution is one of the most advanced tasks that a composite Web service developer must achieve. Substitution occurs when in a composite scenario a service operation is replaced to improve the composition performance or to fix a disruption caused by a failing service. In order to take a step forward the automation of substitution, a set of measures, considering structure and functionality, should be provided.

Considering the use of different formats for names and parameters, the following service data should be measured:

- Similarity of the Web service operation names.
- Syntax equivalence on the operation parameters type.
- Equal number of the input/output parameters.

Many existing solutions have approached the problem of discovering and classifying Web services from a semantic perspective. From this perspective, many authors use natural language processing techniques to obtain the semantics from the documentation provided by the developers of Web services. Another approach consists of annotating or enhancing semantically Web service repositories by generating manually or semi-automatically domain ontologies (Sykara et al., 2003; Heb & Kushmerick, 2003; Dong et al., 2004; Bener et al., 2009). There are proposals which address Web service composition by matching their input and output parameters. The outputs of two or more Web services are combined as the compound input of another Web service, and so on in a kind of Web service chain (Sanchez & Sheremetov, 2008). This is a promising research approach, but needs to be fully proved regarding the particular format and implementation of the diverse Web service providers. Actually, in order to overcome the bottle neck for Web services substitution, and facilitate its effective automation, the structural and functional plain match of Web services is needed. Development of parsing tools for matchmaking is ongoing (Hull & Su, 2006). The parsers construction based on finite state automata provide the formal fundament to overcome this challenge in accurate and precise manner (Shwentick, 2007).

Although the existence of multiple Web service developers, user communities, as many public and private service repositories; few computational solutions for automated extraction, identification and classification of Web services have been proposed, with the main goal of clustering functional-based substitutable services.

The main contribution of this work is on the definition and test of similarity measures for the structural and functional comparison among Web services, fundamental aspects for the automated identification of substitutable Web services. Differentiating with majority of works that use semantic approaches, useful for domain-based searchers, but inefficient for substitution match.

The organization of this paper is as follows: first, a Web service architecture is presented, describing the major tasks and the relationships among them. Then a review of related work is described in addition to an analytical comparison among the different approaches. The set of structural, functional and substitution measures are presented, followed by the architecture for experimentation. Experimental results are described and their significance is evaluated according to Recall and Precision measures, and finally conclusions.

WEB SERVICE MAJORS

Currently Web services are at the core of many applications and solutions. In Figure 1 a set of related Web service tasks is presented. The layers represent from the basic and more generalized tasks (bottom) to more complex and specialized tasks (top). Similarity measurement represents an essential building block to more specialized and complex tasks such as classification, clustering, composition, substitution and optimization. Without measuring, it would not be possible to classify a set of Web services, or to select particular services to execute composition, neither substitute a non functional service from a workflow, nor substitute to improve the performance of a supply chain, etc. This is the main topic of this paper, aiming at designing the required computational infrastructure to support further intensive and complex tasks such as composition, substitution and optimization of sets of Web services.

Among the main tasks concerning Web services are:

1. *Search* consists of browsing through public repositories to find a specific Web service solution based on a set of key words.
2. *Discovery* consists of exploring public Web repositories to encounter and identify specific Web services. According to (Sycara et al., 2003), to discover a Web service, a service infrastructure should be able to represent the capabilities and recognize the similarity between capabilities provided and functionalities requested.
3. *Matchmaking* consists of comparing consumer requests against offered services, to find potential matches among them, in order to provide a set of valuable Web services for substitution or composition (Bener et al., 2009).
4. *Invocation* is done after the client has found the Web service, by obtaining a copy of the public service interface and constructing a communication proxy for the particular service provider. The client sends a request to the provider with the input parameters specified in the interface. The provider receives the request, executes the service remotely and returns the result to the invoking client. Recent research efforts are focusing on

Figure 1. Web service tasks

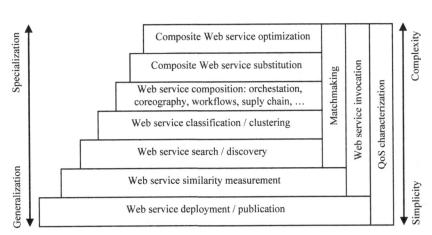

the automated invocation of Web services (Domingue et al., 2008).

5. *Quality characterization* is made by identifying and recording the relevant quality characteristics of sets of public services, as well as by eliminating false or fraudulent information provided by the service owners. Some examples of QoS (quality of service) characteristics are: cost, availability, usability, scalability, testability, auditability, security, throughput, latency, among others, (Menasce, 2002) and (O'Brien, Bass, & Merson, 2005).

6. *Classification* and *clustering* consists of identifying the class to which a specific service belongs to, it has been approached using different techniques (Heb & Kushmerick, 2003). Clustering of Web services consists of generating a representative set of clusters obtained from the set of evaluated services.

7. *Composition* is the task for harmonizing multiple services to solve a complex problem beyond the particular facilities of a sole Web service. Composition requires the plan generation previous to the online/offline composition design. Two of the most used Web service architectures are: orchestration, which sets a centralized control of the compound Web service execution, and choreography a decentralized control.

8. *Substitution* is the task for replacing a compound Web service piece by another with the equivalent structure and functionality.

9. *Optimization* specifies an objective function to be maximized or minimized, subject to a set of relevant constraints.

The outlined Web service tasks do not represent an exhaustive list, but a reference for ongoing research. Other reference architectures have been presented, for example, Yu et al. (2008) describe a Web service stack highlighting the key dimensions of interoperability.

The Web Service Substitution Challenge

Web service substitution occurs when in a composite scenario a service operation is replaced to improve the composition performance or to fix a disruption caused by a failing service. In order to automate substitution, similarity measures are the basis to find a suitable substitute service. The possible applications of these measures are: search and selection of components, improve a Web service composition, classify or cluster a Web service public repository for ontology construction, enhance a QoS repository with structural and functional data to support dynamic composition of Web services during execution time, and reduce the cost of failures in composite scenarios, among others.

Most of Web service measures have been proposed for the deployment of domain-based search engines, which frequently fail for substitution purposes because they classify domain-based similar services but with different functionalities. In this work the aim is to measure similarity in order to substitute a particular operation of a Web service by another with the same functionality, and as long as possible with equivalent performance. To strength Web services matchmaking, the functional similarity definition (see Formula 10) considers the input values (domain) that the operation requires as part of the preconditions before the service is invoked, and the output values (range) that the operation provides as effects after the service is invoked. This inclusion of the domain and range values of the services allows the basic automation needed to interoperate Web services beyond the parameters type and structure, at the level of the functional capabilities, fundamental for services classification, composition and substitution.

The logic-based semantic match extended by syntactic derivative tools are recent solution approaches to deal with Web service classification and composition difficulties (Klush & Kaufer, 2009; Klush et al., 2009). These hybrid approaches that incorporate the IOPE (input, output, preconditions, effects) during Web services discovery, classification and composition, could eventually be used for substitution purposes.

Aiming at giving a wider perspective on Web services substitution challenges, promising trends in Web service composition research is related to complex distributed configurations, namely Workflow-based Composition, (Belhajjame et al., 2006), and Web service-based Supply chain, (Xu & Qiu, 2004; Piak, 2004). Further efforts on these approaches are due; among the most relevant is the assumption of the engineering models to manage the provider-consumer connections through the slave chain in the presence of abnormal or unexpected events (Adhitya, Srinivasan, & Karimi, 2007). Characterization of dynamic connections among service providers and consumers through industrial chains provide experience models that can be extended to deal with complex interaction environments like those present in typical Web service community of practice.

RELATED WORK

Many reported solutions had taken as input for processing and classification of Web services, WSDL description files, or Web service public repositories, or information sources and formats such as OWL-S profile and model description files. However, to obtain such types of service description files, they need to be generated manually or semi-automatically using specific tools (WSDL2OWLS), which is not a generalized and common task among Web service developers. Another used source of information is the source code of the Web service, considering that only the owners or developers of the services may use these files to extract information.

Dong et al. (2004), provide a similar approach for supporting Web service similarity search and clustering. They also consider name and text description, operation description, and input/output descriptions. Jeong et al. (2008) present a functional quality of service approach to discover and compose interoperable Web services, they consider as functional attributes: the service category, the service name, the operation name, the input and output messages and the annotation of the service. They provide a tree similarity based on structure matching of XML schema documents, but we consider this is a costly task. In this paper we report the extraction of particular elements of XML schema documents, instead of comparing the entire documents. None of these works consider for functional evaluation the input and output value instances and do not consider substitution requirements.

Reported measures have different purposes and use different techniques, some measure the semantic similarity, others measure the service interface structure, and others provide execution performance measures. Considering the different approaches used to measure sets of services, we can classify them into the following not disjoint set of measure classes:

1. **Text-based measures:** Represent the set of measures that use natural language processing (NLP) techniques, information extraction (IE) techniques, or linguistic analysis (LA) techniques. These techniques take as input source the names of services, the UDDI descriptions of public Web services, and any description of the service included in the documentation tag of the WSDL file. These techniques are commonly based on word sense algorithm disambiguation through public dictionaries or thesaurus, such as Wordnet, or domain ontologies, for reference see the Element Level Match measure presented in (Patil et al., 2004), (Kim & Candan, 2006).

2. **Structural-based measures:** These measures are based on the extraction of the service XML structural information published in the Web service description files; see the

ASSAM tool presented by (Heb, Johnston, & Kushmerick, 2004). These kinds of measures consider specifically the input data, output data, parameter names and number of parameters provided by the service interface (Dong et al., 2004). Any structural information obtained from the service descriptions, using as source WSDL files.

3. **Ontology-based measures:** These measures use as source for evaluating similarity between service operations particular ontological process models (Bernstein & Klein, 2002), such as DAML-S in (Srivastava & Koehler, 2003; Sivashanmugam et al., 2003), OWL-S (Sánchez & Sheremetov, 2008a) or WSMO ontologies in (Bener et al., 2009).

4. **Performance-based measures:** This measurement approach consists of the service behavior evaluation. They measure performance aspects, execution time, execution cost, quality of service, etc. For reference see the works reported by (Le-Hung, Hauswirth, & Aberer, 2005; Li, Du, & Tian, 2007). To obtain this information, the following options exist:

   ○ Generating a valid value interval to invoke the service operation, in order to discover its functionality through the resulting.

   ○ Incorporating a monitoring system to continuously evaluate and log the invocation and execution of the service operations.

   ○ Obtaining this information from the Web service provider or developer.

   ○ Obtaining this information from the Web service client or consumer.

5. **Hybrid measures:** These kinds of measures involve two or more of the mentioned measures. Zheng and Bouguettaya (2007) described an operation similarity measure which considered structural information (input and output parameters) and ontology-based aspects from OWL-S.

Analytical Comparison

Even though the existence of multiple ways for measuring similarity between Web services, they pose some particularities. In Table 1 we present a comparison between the different approaches, indicating their advantages, disadvantages and possible applications.

The different approaches used for measuring service similarity described and compared above, which were applied to discovery, classification and composition of Web services, could be extended to attend substitution in some way. As well as, the similarity measures introduced in this paper for substitution purposes can be used for Web service discovery, classification and composition as explained in Discussion.

Measures Design Criteria

The set of similarity measures for sets of Web service operations, were designed according to the following criteria:

1. They should measure the structural elements of the Web service operation such as input and output parameters, data type parameters and values of parameters.

2. They should measure the functionality of the service operation obtained by executing it and evaluating the input and output value instances.

3. They should be easy to calculate to avoid overloading the server where Web services are located nor overloading the providers execution.

4. The calculus of the similarity measures should be based on the only public available Web service information source that is WSDL files from service repositories.

5. They should be developed for supporting substitution and optimization of composed Web services.

Table 1. Approaches for measuring service similarity

Measurement approach	Advantages	Disadvantages
Text-based	Use of NLP techniques to extract, classify and organize a set of Web services, published in dynamic and heterogeneous repositories. It is suitable for generation of ontologies that represent the domain of the evaluated set of services. Represents the base for developing domain-based search engines.	The computational cost is too high. Classification results is error prone due to the erroneous or lack of documentation of Web services. Does not facilitate automatic composition and substitution.
Structural	There are public APIs that facilitate the extraction of structural information from service descriptor files. These files can be treated with tree structure algorithms, facilitating its computational analysis. It is suitable for service composition based on well specified problems, where the requester knows a priori the service call template. Suitable for implementation in private networks where service developers will integrate and operate the Web service composition.	The structural information is semantically or functionally hard treatable. It is hard to discover the internal logics of the service, because the information access is by the software interface. The service consumer needs to know a priori the service interface details, in order to do specific searches and execute the selected service. Domain based searches are not easy to achieve with this approach.
Process model ontology	They provide enhanced semantic information related to the Web service interface, such as pre-conditions and effects (OWL-S), and facilitate the matchmaking process.	There are not enough published ontologies of Web services with OWL-S and WSMO, in order to use them as input sources. Requires that the services to be modeled using one of these formal models.
Performance	Offers accurate information about the service, after its execution. Service functionality can be modeled after the execution of the service, in order to obtain a formal representation of the behavior of the service. Generation of a classification or ontology clustering sets of services based on their performance quality. These kinds of measures are valuable to generate QoS data repositories and their importance relationships to the client side.	It depends on the execution and monitoring of the service that can be processed by a local monitoring system or the client feedback. The computational cost for monitoring service execution is high and requires the implementation of a transactional server separated from the architecture.

MEASURES

In this section a set of measures to evaluate similarity aspects between Web service operations are introduced. These measures aim at helping the developer of composite Web services in the arduous task of selecting a set of service operations for composition purposes, and the set of services operations that may substitute a failed one during execution of the composite scenario or for optimization.

In a composite service scenario when a substitution is required, independently of maintaining or improving (optimizing) the current composition process performance, the important aspects to evaluate are the structure and functionality of both,

the substitute and the substituted service operations. Structure refers to the input and output elements of the service operation piece: the substitute service should exactly fit the substituted service operation template; functionality refers that the substitute service operation should show the same behavior than the substituted in order to keep the composition process execution equal or better as it was before the disruption. This way the execution results of the substitute operation will remain the same, equivalent, or improved, compared to the results of the substituted operation.

To measure similarity between multiple Web service operations, it is necessary to extract the only public information provided by a WSDL description file, normally located in public repositories. A WSDL description file consists of a set of tags used for describing the elements of a Web service interface. The important elements that a WSDL describes are:

1. *types*, which provide data type definitions used to describe the messages exchanged;
2. *message*, which represents an abstract definition of the data being transmitted;
3. *portType*, which is a set of abstract operations;
4. *binding*, which specifies concrete protocol and data format specifications for the operations and messages defined by a particular portType;
5. *port*, which specifies an address for a binding;
6. *service*, which is used to aggregate a set of related ports; and
7. *document*, which is an optional element used to represent human readable documentation.

Structural Measures

The information of the service interface is obtained from the published description WSDL file. The description of a service represents the interface of communication of a set of software functions or methods located in a particular node. The information contained in a WSDL file is used by the service consumer, in order to implement a proxy client for invoking the service operations at the remote node. Any function or method may be executed through its communication interface, which is commonly known in the programming language area as the function or method template. The method template is represented by the operation name, the name and data type of the returned variable or object and the names and data types of the input parameters. For this work, it is being considered that the structural information of a service operation defined through its communication interface consists of three basic elements: operation names, input parameters and output parameters.

a) Operation Name Similarity

The name of each operation of a service frequently provides useful information because there is a real connection between the operation intentions or semantics with its name syntactically expressed. This connection is generated when the programmer of the service selects and defines the name given to operations, aiming at offering a name representing what the service operation offers. Therefore, the comparison of the name of operations to obtain a more precise measure of the similarity between service operations is considered. The following measure is defined for this purpose.

Let P_1 and P_2 be two compound names. P_1 consists of a set of n lexical tokens identified by $Tokens_1$. P_2 consists of a set of m lexical tokens identified by $Tokens_2$. The lexical similarity measure between them represents the ratio of dividing the absolute value of the intersection of both sets of name tokens by the union of both sets of name tokens.

$$LexicalSim(P_1, P_2) = |Tokens_1 \cap Tokens_2| / |Tokens_1 \cup Tokens_2| \qquad (1)$$

The lexical similarity measure will return a value in the range from 0 to 1, where a 0 value represents a null lexical similarity between the names, and returned value of 1 sets a full lexical name similarity. Based on the previous definition, a particular measure to evaluate the lexical similarity between operation names is defined.

Let $Oname_1$, $Oname_2$, be two operation names from different services, each consisting of a set of n lexical tokens identified by $OnameTokens_1$ and $OnameTokens_2$, respectively. The name lexical similarity between them is calculated by:

$$OperationNameLexicalSim(Oname_1, Oname_2) = |OnameTokens_1 \cap OnameTokens_2| / |OnameTokens_1 \cup OnameTokens_2| \qquad (2)$$

b) Input Parameter Similarity

Input parameters represent the invocation template of the service operation, so they must be implemented exactly as they have been defined in the service communication interface. For composition and substitution purposes, they should be attended, because a substitute service operation has to fit with another service operation following this input template.

Let $O_1 = (Oname_1, Ip_1)$, $O_2 = (Oname_2, Ip_2)$ be two operations from different services, where $Oname_m$ is the operation name and Ip_m is the set of input parameters of operation m. The respective sets of input parameters as follows:

$Ip_1 = \{ (nameP_1, typeP_1), (nameP_2, typeP_2), \ldots, (nameP_i, typeP_i) \}$,

$Ip_2 = \{ (nameP_1, typeP_1), (nameP_2, typeP_2), \ldots, (nameP_i, typeP_i) \}$.

Each parameter is given by a pair of name and data type, where $nameP_i$ is the name of parameter i and $typeP_i$ denotes the data type of parameter i. In order to get a numerical representation of the input level of similarity the following measure is proposed.

The input parameter similarity measures the ratio of dividing the cardinalities of the intersection by the union of both sets of input parameters.

$$InputParSim(O_1, O_2) = |Ip_1 \cap Ip_2| / |Ip_1 \cup Ip_2| \tag{3}$$

The input parameter similarity measure will return a value in the range from 0 to 1, where a 0 value represents a total difference between the input parameters, and a returned value of 1 represents a total similarity.

c) Output Parameter Similarity

On defining this measure, the first intuition is to calculate output parameter similarity as input parameter similarity. However, this is not possible. The public operation service descriptions offer enough detail about the set of input parameters, but lack of detailed specification for output parameters. Output specification of service operations generally refer to objects containing complex type definitions, which are not always public available. The service provider specifies the required input parameters in order to execute the particular operation, no matter what output type of object will return to the client. The returned object data type treatment is responsibility of the client invoking the service.

A combined approach for calculating output parameter similarity between two different operations is proposed. Based on Equation 1, a measure to evaluate the lexical similarity between output parameter names, is defined.

Let $OPname_1$, $OPname_2$, be two output parameter names from different services, each consisting of a set of n lexical tokens identified by $OPnameTokens_1$ and $OPnameTokens_2$, respectively. The output parameter name lexical similarity is calculated by:

$$OPnameLexicalSim(OPname_1, OPname_2) = |OPnameTokens_1 \cap OPnameTokens_2| / |OPnameTokens_1 \cup OPnameTokens_2| \tag{4}$$

The lexical similarity measure will return a value in the range from 0 to 1, where a 0 value represents a totally different lexical similarity between the names of output parameters, and a returned value of 1 represents a fully lexical name similarity

Let $OPtype_1$, $OPtype_2$, be two output parameter data types from different operations. The output parameter data type similarity between them is calculated by:

$$OPtypeSim\left(OPtype_1, OPtype_2\right) = \begin{cases} 1, & if\, OPtype_1 = OPtype_2 \\ 0, & otherwise \end{cases} \tag{5}$$

The data type similarity measure will return a value of 1 if both data types are equal and a value of 0 if data types are different. The final output parameter similarity is calculated using the lexical parameter name and the data type similarities between output parameter names. Therefore, the final computing results in:

- **Output Similarity.** Let $O_1 = (Oname_1, Op_1)$, $O_2 = (Oname_2, Op_2)$, be two operations from different services. Where $Oname_m$ represents the operation name and Op_m represents the output parameter object of operation m. Each output parameter, in turns consists of name and data type, $Op_1 = (OPname_1, OPtype_1)$, and $Op_2 = (OPname_2, OPtype_2)$.

As a particular case of similarity, O_1 and O_2 are output equivalent if, $((OPname_1 = OPname_2)$ **and** $(OPtype_1 = OPtype_2))$.

The general output parameter similarity is given by the mean of output parameter name lexical similarity and output parameter data type similarity.

$$OutputParSim(O_1, O_2) = \\ OPnameLexicalSim(OPname_1, OPname_2) + \\ OPtypeSim(OPtype_1, OPtype_2) / 2 \tag{6}$$

The output parameter similarity measure will return a value in the range from 0 to 1, where a 0 value represents a total difference between the output parameters, and a returned value of 1 represents a total similarity.

d) Structural Similarity

The structural similarity measure is the mean of the parameter name similarity (Equation 2), input parameter similarity (Equation 3) and out-

put parameter similarity (Equation 6). Let $O_1 = (Oname_1, Ip_1, Op_1)$, $O_2 = (Oname_2, Ip_2, Op_2)$, be two service operations, with their respective sets of parameters, the level of structural similarity is given by:

$$StructuralSim(O_1, O_2) = OperationNameLexicalSim(Oname_1, Oname_2) + InputParSim(O_1, O_2) + OutputParSim(O_1, O_2) / 3 \tag{7}$$

Functional Measures

The functional similarity evaluation is defined considering the execution of the operations of the Web services being compared. According to the mathematical definition of function, in order to evaluate functional similarity between the service operations O_1 and O_2, the input domain set as well as the output range of values are introduced.

Let D be the input value domain for the service operations being compared, R be the output value range throughout the execution evaluation of the service operations, and $R' \subseteq R$. Notice that, in general, O_1 and O_2 can be operations from different services, with their respective set of input values D_1 and D_2, and output values R_1 and R_2.

a) Input Value Similarity

Let O_1 and O_2 be two different service operations, the input value similarity between them is defined by:

$$InputValueSim(O_1, O_2) = |D_1 \cap D_2| / |D_1 \cup D_2|$$

The similarity value measure is in the range $[0, 1]$, where 0 sets the null similarity between the values of input parameters, and 1 the full similarity.

b) Output Value Similarity

Let O_1 and O_2 be two different service operations, O_1 and O_2 are R' **functional similar** if $\forall$ $d \in D$, the evaluation of both service operations are elements of R', i.e., O_1 (d), O_2 (d) $\in R'$. The generalization regarding different ranges R_1, and R_2 is with respect the intersection $R_1 \cap R_2$. Thus, the output value similarity between O_1 and O_2 is calculated by:

$$OutputValueSim(O_1, O_2) = \begin{cases} |R_1' \cap R_2|/|R_1 \cap R_2| & \text{if } |R_1 \cap R_2| \neq \varnothing \\ 0, & \text{if } |R_1 \cap R_2| = \varnothing \end{cases} \tag{9}$$

The output value similarity is in the range [0 1], where 0 sets the null similarity between the returned values of the operation execution, and 1 the full similarity.

c) Functional Similarity

The functional similarity between them is calculated by:

$$FunctionalSim(O_1, O_2) = InputValueSim(O_1, O_2) + OutputValueSim(O_1, O_2) / 2 \tag{10}$$

The functional similarity measure value is in [0, 1], where 0 sets the null similarity between the returned values of the operation execution, and 1 the full similarity.

This functional similarity measure considers the input values (domain) that the operation requires as part of the preconditions before the service is invoked, and the output values (range) that the operation provides as effects after the service is invoked. The similarity measurement between the input/output values of the services to be compound is fundamental to overcome the interoperability difficulties during the automation of Web services composition and substitution.

Substitution Measure

Substitution is the task of finding a service operation with equivalent functionality to replace another service operation. This highly complex task involves identifying the relevant elements for the substitution process. Herein the substitution approach is based on the evaluation of structural and functional aspects of service operations. The structural similarity measures include the operation name, the input parameter and the output parameter. However, the operation name similarity evaluation is omitted considering that the names of operations do not real impact on the composed service functionality. Thus, the relevant attributes to account when selecting a substitute operation are: the set of input parameters, the returned output parameter and the functional similarity.

Let $O_1 = (Oname_1, Ip_1, Op_1)$, $O_2 = (Oname_2, Ip_2, Op_2)$, be two service operations, with their respective sets of parameters. O_2 **is a full substitute operation of O_1** if and only if,

$StructuralSim(O_1, O_2) = 1$, and
$FunctionalSim(O_1, O_2) = 1$.

In a general perspective the **level of substitution** between O_1 and O_2 operations, is a numerical value given by the sum of the weighed products of structural similarity and functional similarity as follows.

$LevelOfSubstitution(O_1, O_2) =$
$StructuralSim(O_1, O_2) * w_1 +$
$FunctionalSim(O_1, O_2) * w_2 \tag{11}$

Coefficients w_1, and w_2 represent the respective weights of similarities, according to their importance, with the restriction that $w_1 + w_2 = 1$. A level of substitution 1 sets a full structural and functional equivalence in between O_1 and O_2, while a level 0 sets null similarity and the impossibility of substitution. Most cases, the value of similarity is not 0 or 1, but the closeness to each of them is a useful data to learn on the plausible substitution.

EXPERIMENTAL ARCHITECTURE

In order to evaluate this proposal, the software architecture depicted in Figure 2 was implemented and experimental cases executed. The first case uses a set of local Web services that were implemented to show the applicability of structural, functional and substitution measures. For the second case, a set of Web services were selected from the http://seekda.com public Web service repository, to show the calculation of structural measures with public Web services. The overall architecture consists of the following modules: service repository, service data extraction, operation name lexical similarity, output parameter similarity; input parameter similarity, client for invoking service operations, functional similarity, structural similarity and level of substitution.

The implementation technologies are the following:

1. The service repository consists of a Web server (Tomcat), a SOAP implementation API (Axis), and a set of published Web services.

2. The service data extraction module is a Java class based on the UDDI4J and WSDL4J API's; the main functionality is for connecting Web service repositories and for extracting the WSDL files information.

3. The operation name lexical similarity module is a Java method, which computes a lexical similarity comparison between two service operation names.

4. The input parameter similarity module is a Java method for comparing two input parameter sets.

5. The output parameter similarity module integrates Java methods for calculating the final output parameter similarity; one calculates the parameter name lexical similarity and the other the data type parameter similarity.

6. The client for invoking Web services operations is a Java program that uses the Axis API for invoking Web services.

Figure 2. Experimentation architecture

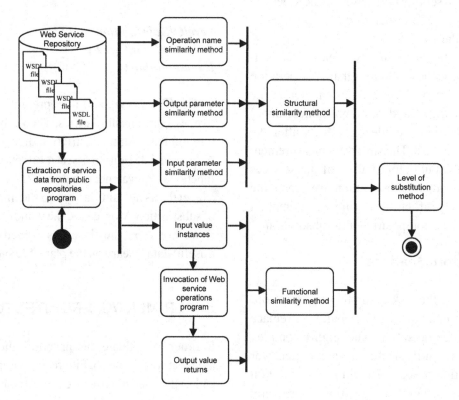

7. The functional similarity module is a Java method, which compares the returned values of execution of service operations.
8. The structural similarity module is a Java method which combines the execution of the operation name lexical similarity and the output parameter similarity.
9. The level of substitution module is a Java method which combines the execution results of the structural similarity and the functional similarity.

Implementation of Web Services

In order to calculate structural and functional similarity between Web service operations, a set of Web services and their respective operations were developed. These services correspond to the airline booking domain. In Table 2, the implemented service operations and their particular details are described, such as input and output parameters.

EXPERIMENTAL RESULTS

The process for calculating the measures was implemented with a filtering approach, see Figure 3: from the less costly structural extraction and comparison measures, to the more costly direct invocation and comparison of returned values. First the structural similarity was applied to obtain a reduced set. Then the functional similarity was calculated by invoking the operations, and finally the level of substitution. For the first phase, the entire set of service operations were used for the calculus of the structural similarity. To reduce the set of operations pairs, the pairs that resulted in null similarity were not considered for the second phase, such that a reduced number of operation pairs were used to calculate the functional similarity. And finally, the last phase resulted in less operation pairs. The reason for applying this approach was to minimize the number of invocations during the functional evaluation, with the goal of comparing a reduced number of operations with

Table 2. Implemented service operations and details

Id	Operation name	Input parameters	Output parameters
Op_0	*getFlightPrice*	$Ip_0 = \{$ (*cityArrival, string*), (*cityDeparture, string*), (*dateArrival, string*), (*dateDeparture, string*)$\}$	$Op_0 = \{$ (*getFlightPriceReturn, float*) $\}$
Op_1	*getAvailability*	$Ip_1 = \{$ (*cityArrival, string*), (*cityDeparture, string*), (*dateArrival, string*), (*dateDeparture, string*)$\}$	$Op_1 = \{$ (*getAvailabilityReturn, float*) $\}$
Op_2	*getCapacity*	$Ip_2 = \{$ (*flight, int*) $\}$	$Op_2 = \{$ (*getCapacityReturn, int*)$\}$
Op_3	*getPrice*	$Ip_3 = \{$ (*departureCity, string*), (*landingCity, string*), (*flight, int*) $\}$	$Op_3 = \{$ (*getPriceReturn, float*) $\}$
Op_4	*getTimeDeparture*	$Ip_4 = \{$ (*flight, int*) $\}$	$Op_4 = \{$ (*getTimeDepartureReturn, string*) $\}$
Op_5	*getTimeLanding*	$Ip_5 = \{$ (*flight, int*) $\}$	$Op_5 = \{$ (*getTimeLandingReturn, string*) $\}$
Op_6	*getItineraries*	$Ip_6 = \{ \}$	$Op_6 = \{$ (*getItinerariesReturn, array*) $\}$
Op_7	*calcPrice*	$Ip_7 = \{$ (*departureCity, string*), (*landingCity, string*) $\}$	$Op_7 = \{$ (*calcPriceReturn, float*)$\}$
Op_8	*getAvailableSits*	$Ip_8 = \{$ (*flightNum, int*) $\}$	$Op_8 = \{$ (*getAvailableSitsReturn, int*) $\}$
Op_9	*getLandingTime*	$Ip_9 = \{$ (*flightNum, int*) $\}$	$Op_9 = \{$ (*getLandingTimeReturn, string*) $\}$
Op_{10}	*getDepartureTime*	$Ip_{10} = \{$ (*flightNum, int*) $\}$	$Op_{10} = \{$ (*getDepartureTimeReturn, string*) $\}$
Op_{11}	*getFlights*	$Ip_{11} = \{ \}$	$Op_{11} = \{$ (*getFlightsReturn, array*) $\}$

a higher probability for resulting with high level of substitution.

Using Local Web Services

To calculate the set of similarity measures between the set of service operations, the number of different operation pairs were obtained as follows. Considering a set of *n* service operations, the possible number of different pairs among them is n^2. However, recalling that the objective is to measure similarity between different service operations, the number of pairs where operations are equal is extracted, which is *n*. It is also considered that a pair of operations (*a, b*) has the same similarity as a pair of operations (*b, a*), thus the number of different operation pairs is reduced dividing by 2. Therefore, for a given set of 12 service operations, the number of different operation pairs is 66.

$Pairs = (n^2-n)/2$

$Pairs = (12^2-12)/2 = 66$ (12)

Structural Measures

With the set of 66 operation pairs, the Java methods for calculating the *Operation name similarity*, the *Input parameter similarity* and the *Output parameter similarity* were executed. After combining these measures, the set of operation pairs that resulted with a structural similarity greater than 0, were selected. In Table 3, this structural calculus is shown.

However, some operation pairs with nothing in common but the set of input parameters were noising the results. The decision was then to exclude the *Input parameter similarity* only for filtering the number of potential similar operation pairs; the new resulting set of structural similar operation pairs is shown in Table 4.

The resulting set of operation pairs that obtained a degree of structural similarity is shown in Table 4. There are two operation pairs that

Figure 3. Filtering approach for calculating the set of measures

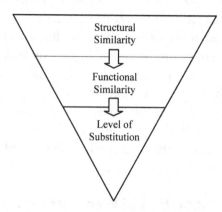

resulted with the highest degree of similarity; operation 4 compared with operation 10 and operation 5 with operation 9. This result can be read as follows:

- Service operations *getTimeDeparture* and *getDepartureTime* are structurally similar.
- Service operations *getTimeLanding* and *getLandingTime* are structurally similar.

Other operation pairs resulted in different degrees of structural similarity. They must be executed in order to know their level of functionality. For now, this is a filtered set of operation pairs with a potential substitution similarity.

Functional Measures

The set of operation pairs returned with a degree of structural similarity were the basis for functional evaluation. From the 66 original operation pairs, 13 operation pairs were obtained, which represent a reduction of 80%. This reduction helps the functional evaluation; there is no case of evaluating service operations that have nothing in common. Another important aspect that has to be considered for evaluating functional similarity is the set of input values. To calculate the functional similarity

Table 3. Operation pairs that obtained a degree of structural similarity

Id	Operation names	Operation names	Operation name similarity	Input parameter similarity	Output parameter similarity	Structural
Op0 Op1	getFlightPrice	getAvailability	0.0000	1.0000	0.0000	0.33333
Op0 Op3	getFlightPrice	getPrice	0.5000	0.0000	0.7500	0.41667
Op0 Op7	getFlightPrice	calcPrice	0.3333	0.0000	0.6667	0.33333
Op1 Op2	getAvailability	getCapacity	0.0000	0.0000	0.5000	0.16667
Op1 Op8	getAvailability	getAvailableSits	0.0000	0.0000	0.5000	0.16667
Op2 Op3	getCapacity	getPrice	0.0000	0.3333	0.0000	0.11111
Op2 Op4	getCapacity	getTimeDeparture	0.0000	1.0000	0.0000	0.33333
Op2 Op5	getCapacity	getTimeLanding	0.0000	1.0000	0.0000	0.33333
Op2 Op8	getCapacity	getAvailableSits	0.0000	0.0000	0.5000	0.16667
Op3 Op4	getPrice	getTimeDeparture	0.0000	0.3333	0.0000	0.11111
Op3 Op5	getPrice	getTimeLanding	0.0000	0.3333	0.0000	0.11111
Op3 Op7	getPrice	calcPrice	0.5000	0.6667	0.7500	0.63889
Op4 Op5	getTimeDeparture	getTimeLanding	0.3333	1.0000	0.6667	0.66667
Op4 Op9	getTimeDeparture	getLandingTime	0.3333	0.0000	0.6667	0.33333
Op4 Op10	getTimeDeparture	getDepartureTime	1.0000	0.0000	1.0000	0.66667
Op5 Op9	getTimeLanding	getLandingTime	1.0000	0.0000	1.0000	0.66667
Op5 Op10	getTimeLanding	getDepartureTime	0.3333	0.0000	0.6667	0.33333
Op6 Op11	getItineraries	getFlights	0.0000	1.0000	0.5000	0.50000
Op8 Op9	getAvailableSits	getLandingTime	0.0000	1.0000	0.0000	0.33333
Op8 Op10	getAvailableSits	getDepartureTime	0.0000	1.0000	0.0000	0.33333
Op9 Op10	getLandingTime	getDepartureTime	0.3333	1.0000	0.6667	0.66667

Table 4. Filtered operation pairs that obtained a degree of structural similarity

Operation pairs	Operation names	Operation names	Operation name similarity	Output parameter similarity	Structural similarity
Op0 Op3	getFlightPrice	getPrice	0.5000	0.7500	0.6250
Op0 Op7	getFlightPrice	calcPrice	0.3333	0.6667	0.5000
Op1 Op2	getAvailability	getCapacity	0.0000	0.5000	0.2500
Op1 Op8	getAvailability	getAvailableSits	0.0000	0.5000	0.2500
Op2 Op8	getCapacity	getAvailableSits	0.0000	0.5000	0.2500
Op3 Op7	getPrice	calcPrice	0.5000	0.7500	0.6250
Op4 Op5	getTimeDeparture	getTimeLanding	0.3333	0.6667	0.5000
Op4 Op9	getTimeDeparture	getLandingTime	0.3333	0.6667	0.5000
Op4 Op10	getTimeDeparture	getDepartureTime	1.0000	1.0000	**1.0000**
Op5 Op9	getTimeLanding	getLandingTime	1.0000	1.0000	**1.0000**
Op5 Op10	getTimeLanding	getDepartureTime	0.3333	0.6667	0.5000
Op6 Op11	getItineraries	getFlights	0.0000	0.5000	0.2500
Op9 Op10	getLandingTime	getDepartureTime	0.3333	0.6667	0.5000

between the set of service operations, exactly the same input values should be provided, therefore similar scenarios for the execution of the service operations should be defined. In Table 5, the set of input value formats and instances are shown, as well as the returned value of each service operation after invocation.

Input Value Similarity

The resulting input value similarity for each operation pair is presented in Table 6.

Output Value Similarity

The resulting output value similarity for each operation pair is presented in Table 7.

Functional Similarity

With the set of 13 operation pairs, the *Output value similarity*, the *Input value similarity* and the *Functional similarity* were calculated. The set of operation pairs that resulted with a functional are shown in Table 8 and Figure 4.

Substitution Measure

Finally, to evaluate the level of substitutability, structural and functional measures are computed. The resulting level of substitutability for each operation pair is shown in Table 9.

Two operation pairs resulted in the highest level of substitution, so can be exchanged with any modification. The relationships of these operation pairs can be interpreted as follows:

- Service operations *getTimeDeparture* and *getDepartureTime* are fully substitutable.
- Service operations *getTimeLanding* and *getLandingTime* are fully substitutable.

Is remarkable the relationships obtained with operations Op0, Op3 and Op7. The results of the measures indicate the closeness between them. Their relationships can be interpreted as follows:

- Service operations *getFlightPrice* and *getPrice* is substitutable with some changes.
- Service operations *getFligthPrice* and *calcPrice* is substitutable with some changes.
- Service operations *getPrice* and *calcPrice* is substitutable with some changes.

The information provided with these measures indicates what aspect of the operation is required to overcome to get full substitutability. When a low structural similarity is obtained, then further analysis should be done with the structural detailed measures to evaluate if modifications are feasible. On the contrary, when a low functional similarity is obtained, then the mismatching result is beyond the Web service consumer, and he should evaluate if the result would be acceptable or select a different service provider.

Using Public Web Services

For the second case, a set of six public Web services were selected from the public repository Seekda.com. These services correspond to the currency conversion domain. Table 10 shows the list of selected services, and Table 11 shows the operation names, input and output parameters of selected operations from these services.

Using Formula 12, a total of 231 operation pairs were used to calculate de structural similarity. As this operation list is too long, a filtered list is shown in Table 12. The filtered list shows those operation pairs that resulted in structural similarity equal or higher than 0.4.

There is one operation pair that resulted in the highest structural similarity; this is the case of operation pair Op5 and Op11. The resulting relationship can be interpreted as follows:

Table 5. Invocation data of all service operations

Operation names	Input value format	Input values	Returned value	Operation names	Input value format	Input values	Returned value
getFlightPrice	String cityArrival, String cityDeparture, String dateArrival, String dateDeparture	"Guadalajara", "México", "15/01/09", "15/01/09"	$1,230	getPrice	String departureCity, String landingCity, int flight	"México", "Guadalajara", 125	$3,600
getFlightPrice	String cityArrival, String cityDeparture, String dateArrival, String dateDeparture	"Guadalajara", "México", "15/01/09", "15/01/09"	$1,230	calcPrice	String departureCity, String landingCity	"México", "Guadalajara"	$2,300
getAvailability	String cityArrival, String cityDeparture, String dateArrival, String dateDeparture	"Guadalajara", "México", "15/01/09", "15/01/09"	250	getCapacity	int flight	125	300
getAvailability	String cityArrival, String cityDeparture, String dateArrival, String dateDeparture	"Guadalajara", "México", "15/01/09", "15/01/09"	250	getAvailableSits	int flightNum	125	300
getCapacity	int flight	125	300	getAvailableSits	int flightNum	125	300
getPrice	String departureCity, String landingCity, int flight	"México", "Guadalajara", 125	$3,600	calcPrice	String departureCity, String landingCity	"México", "Guadalajara"	$2,300
getTimeDeparture	int flight	125	10:30 a.m.	getTimeLanding	int fligh	125	
getTimeDeparture	int flight	125	10:30 a.m.	getLandingTime	int flightNum	125	
getTimeDeparture	int flight	125	10:30 a.m.	getDepartureTime	int flightNum	125	10:30 a.m.
getTimeLanding	int flight	125	12:20 p.m.	getLandingTime	int flightNum	125	
getTimeLanding	int flight	125	12:20 p.m.	getDepartureTime	int flightNum	125	10:30 a.m.
getItineraries			Set of flights	getFlights			Set of flights
getLandingTime	int flightNum	125	12:20 p.m.	getDepartureTime	int flightNum	125	10:30 a.m.

Service operations *conversionRate* and *getConversion* are structurally similar.

There are two operation pairs that resulted in high structural similarity of 0.7222, operation pairs Op5, Op9 and Op9, Op11. This result means that these operation pairs could be fully structural

Table 6. Resulting input value similarity

Operation names	Input values	Operation names	Input values	Input value similarity
getFlightPrice	"Guadalajara", "México", "15/01/09", "15/01/09"	getPrice	"México", "Guadala-jara", 125	0.40
getFlightPrice	"Guadalajara", "México", "15/01/09", "15/01/09"	calcPrice	"México", "Guada-lajara"	0.50
getAvailability	"Guadalajara", "México", "15/01/09", "15/01/09"	getCapacity	125	0.00
getAvailability	"Guadalajara", "México", "15/01/09", "15/01/09"	getAvailableSits	125	0.00
getCapacity	125	getAvailableSits	125	1.00
getPrice	"México", "Guadala-jara", 125	calcPrice	"México", "Guada-lajara"	0.67
getTimeDeparture	125	getTimeLanding	125	1.00
getTimeDeparture	125	getLandingTime	125	1.00
getTimeDeparture	125	getDepartureTime	125	1.00
getTimeLanding	125	getLandingTime	125	1.00
getTimeLanding	125	getDepartureTime	125	1.00
getItineraries	none	getFlights	none	1.00
getLandingTime	125	getDepartureTime	125	1.00

similar if minor changes were made. The operation pairs that resulted in high structural similarity are:

- Service operations *conversionRate* and *getConversionRate* require minor changes to be fully structurally similar.
- Service operations *GetConversionRate* and *GetConversionRate* require minor changes to be fully structurally similar.

As observed in these results, the operation pairs that resulted in high degree of similarity (Op5, Op11), (Op5, Op9) and (Op9, Op11) are all related, which corroborates the consistency of the measures.

EVALUATION

Using local Web services

To evaluate experimental results, *Precision* and *Recall* measures were calculated (Baeza-Yates & Ribeiro-Neto, 1999), two widely used information retrieval evaluation techniques. For this case the *Precision* is defined as the number of relevant operation pairs with a measure result >= 0.5, divided by the total number of operation pairs with a measure result > 0. And *Recall* is defined as the number of relevant operation pairs with a measure result >= 0.5, divided by the total number of existing relevant operation pairs (which should have been selected).

Table 7. Resulting output value similarity

Operation names	Output values	Operation names	OutputValues	Expected value range	Expected data type	Output value similarity
getFlightPrice	1230	getPrice	3600	1000 - 5000	numeric	1.00
getFlightPrice	1230	calcPrice	2300	1000 - 5000	numeric	1.00
getAvailability	250	getCapacity	300	0 - 1000	numeric	1.00
getAvailability	250	getAvailableSits	300	0 - 1000	numeric	1.00
getCapacity	300	getAvailableSits	300	0 - 1000	numeric	1.00
getPrice	3600	calcPrice	2300	1000 - 5000	numeric	1.00
getTimeDeparture	10:30 a.m.	getTimeLanding	12:20 p.m.	time	time	1.00
getTimeDeparture	10:30 a.m.	getLandingTime	12:20 p.m.	time	time	1.00
getTimeDeparture	10:30 a.m.	getDepartureTime	10:30 a.m.	time	time	1.00
getTimeLanding	12:20 p.m.	getLandingTime	12:20 p.m.	time	time	1.00
getTimeLanding	12:20 p.m.	getDepartureTime	10:30 a.m.	time	time	1.00
getItineraries		getFlights	result set	data set array	array of complex type	unreachable
getLandingTime	12:20 p.m.	getDepartureTime	10:30 a.m.	time	time	1.00

Therefore, in order to obtain the performance measures, it is necessary to define the total number of relevant operation pairs. This set of pairs was selected by human observation, based on a semantic sound and prior knowledge of the operation names and real functionality, aiming at using a valid set of operation pairs and contrast with the set of measures. The resulting set of relevant operation pairs is given in Exhibit 1.

An *F-measure* (Rijsberjen, 1979) was also calculated. The *F-measure* represents the accuracy of a test, in this case of a measure. It considers the *Precision* and the *Recall* values; it can be interpreted as a weighted average of the precision and recall, where F-measure reaches its best value at 0. The traditional *F-measure* is the harmonic mean of precision and recall. Its formalism follows:

$$F = 2 * (Precision * Recall) / (Precision + Recall)$$

Based on the experimental results, *Precision*, *Recall* and *F-measure* were calculated, Table 13 shows the results of these calculations. Figure 5 shows graphically these results. The meaning of a *Precision* on the measures is the number of correct related operation pairs, divided by the number of the related operation pairs. The best *Precision* result of the measures is the functional, while the worst is the structural. The meaning of a *Recall* number on the set of measures is defined as the number of correct related operation pairs, divided by the total number of operation pairs that actually should be related. The best *Recall* result is the functional. The *F-measure* represents the average of *Precision* and *Recall*, obviously the functional measure has the best *F-measure* result.

Table 8. Resulting functional similarity

	Operation names	Operation names	Output value similarity	Input value similarity	Functional similarity
Op0 Op3	getFlightPrice	getPrice	1.00	0.40	0.70
Op0 Op7	getFlightPrice	calcPrice	1.00	0.50	0.75
Op1 Op2	getAvailability	getCapacity	1.00	0.00	0.50
Op1 Op8	getAvailability	getAvailableSits	1.00	0.00	0.50
Op2 Op8	getCapacity	getAvailableSits	1.00	1.00	1.00
Op3 Op7	getPrice	calcPrice	1.00	0.67	0.83
Op4 Op5	getTimeDeparture	getTimeLanding	1.00	1.00	1.00
Op4 Op9	getTimeDeparture	getLandingTime	1.00	1.00	1.00
Op4 Op10	getTimeDeparture	getDepartureTime	1.00	1.00	1.00
Op5 Op9	getTimeLanding	getLandingTime	1.00	1.00	1.00
Op5 Op10	getTimeLanding	getDepartureTime	1.00	1.00	1.00
Op6 Op11	getItineraries	getFlights		1.00	0.50
Op9 Op10	getLandingTime	getDepartureTime	1.00	1.00	1.00

The *Precision*, *Recall* and *F-measure* have been presented for the *structural, functional* and *substitution* measures. However, it has to be noted, that the *substitution* measure is a mean representation of *structural* and *functional* measures. Therefore, the *Precision* and *Recall* results for *substitution* will always result between the *structural* and *functional* range values.

The important conclusions that can be obtained from these measures are: while *structural* and *functional* information extraction from the WSDL service interfaces do not offer the highest accuracy that is desirable, they do offer important information relative to the selection of a substitutable operation service, contrasting in this aspect with majority of semantic approaches, which are

Figure 4. Graphical representation of the level of structural and functional similarity

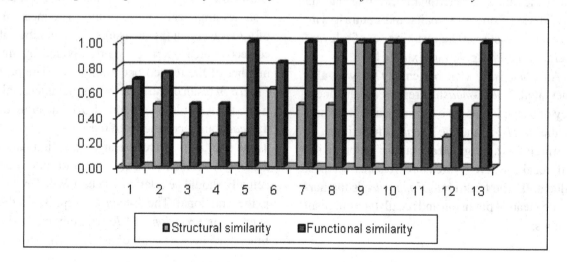

Table 9. Resulting level of substitution

	Operations	Structural similarity	Functional similarity	Level of substitution
Op0 Op3	getFlightPrice getPrice	0.63	0.70	0.66
Op0 Op7	getFlightPrice calcPrice	0.50	0.75	0.63
Op1 Op2	getAvailability getCapacity	0.25	0.50	0.38
Op1 Op8	getAvailability getAvailableSits	0.25	0.50	0.38
Op2 Op8	getCapacity getAvailableSits	0.25	1.00	0.63
Op3 Op7	getPrice calcPrice	0.63	0.83	0.73
Op4 Op5	getTimeDeparture getTimeLanding	0.50	1.00	0.75
Op4 Op9	getTimeDeparture getLandingTime	0.50	1.00	0.75
Op4 Op10	getTimeDeparture getDepartureTime	1.00	1.00	**1.00**
Op5 Op9	getTimeLanding getLandingTime	1.00	1.00	**1.00**
Op5 Op10	getTimeLanding getDepartureTime	0.50	1.00	0.75
Op6 Op11	getItineraries getFlights	0.25	0.50	0.38
Op9 Op10	getLandingTime getDepartureTime	0.50	1.00	0.75

based on finding semantic relations leaving apart structural and functional aspects.

Using Public Web Services

The results obtained with the operations of public Web services, should be interpreted as the measure indicates; if a structural similarity of 1 is obtained, this means that the service operations are fully structural similar, in case of a substitution, these operations would not need to be structurally re-

designed to be plugged into a composition chain. If a 0.6 structural similarity was obtained, then a further analysis should be done in order to know the reason of the difference, which would be on the operation names, or the input parameters or the output parameters. Obtaining detailed information of these particulars is another benefit of the calculated measures. A developer or system integrator could know the exact source of the syntactic differences and evaluate the cost of modifications and decide if a modification is the

Table 10. Public Web service details

Service	Country	Provider	WSDL File
WS01	United States	serviceobjects.net	http://ws2.serviceobjects.net/ce/CurrencyExchange.asmx?WSDL
WS02	United States	webservicex.com	http://www.webservicex.com/currencyconvertor.asmx?WSDL
WS03	United States	kowabunga.net	http://currencyconverter.kowabunga.net/converter.asmx?WSDL
WS04	Germany	petermeinl.de	http://www.petermeinl.de/CurrencyConverter/CurrencyConverter.asmx?wsdl
WS05	United States	cloanto.com	http://fx.cloanto.com/webservices/CurrencyServer.asmx?wsdl
WS06	Costa Rica	ic-itcr.ac.cr	http://www.ic-itcr.ac.cr/asp/1.1/webservice/ConverterService.asmx?wsdl

Table 11. Public Web service details

Service	OpId	Operation name	Input parameters	Output Parameters
WS01	Op0	GetAllCurrencies	LicenseKey, string	GetAllCurrenciesResult, ArrayOfCurrency-NameResponse
WS01	Op1	GetAllCountryCurrencies	LicenseKey, string	GetAllCountryCurrenciesResult, ArrayOf-CountryCurrencyResponse
WS01	Op2	GetExchangeRate	ConvertFromCurrency, string ConvertToCurrency, string LicenseKey, string	ConvertFromCurrency, string ConvertToCurrency, string ExchangeRate, double Error, string
WS01	Op3	ConvertCurrency	Amount, string ConvertFromCurrency, string ConvertToCurrency, string LicenseKey, string	ConvertFromCurrency, string ConvertToCurrency, string Amount, string ConvertedAmount, double Error, string
WS01	Op4	GetCountryCurrency	Country, string LicenseKey, string	GetCountryCurrencyResult, CountryCurren-cyResponse
WS02	Op5	ConversionRate	FromCurrency, Currency (string) ToCurrency, Currency (string)	ConversionRateResult, double
WS03	Op6	GetCurrencies	GetCurrencies, void	GetCurrenciesResult, ArrayOfString
WS03	Op7	GetCurrencyRate	Currency, string RateDate, dateTime	GetCurrencyRateResult, decimal
WS03	Op8	GetCurrencyRates	RateDate, dateTime	GetCurrencyRatesResult
WS03	Op9	GetConversionRate	CurrencyFrom, string CurrencyTo, string RateDate, dateTime	GetConversionRateResult, decimal
WS03	Op10	GetConversionAmount	CurrencyFrom, string CurrencyTo, string RateDate, dateTime Amount, decimal	GetConversionAmountResult, decimal
WS04	Op11	GetConversionRate	fromCurrency, string toCurrency, string	GetConversionRateResult, double
WS04	Op12	GetConversionRateList	timeStamp, string countryList, ArrayOfString currencySymbolList, ArrayOfString usdConversionRateList, ArrayOf-Double	timeStamp, string countryList, ArrayOfString currencySymbolList, ArrayOfString usdConversionRateList, ArrayOfDouble
WS05	Op13	ConvertToNum	LicenseKey, string fromCurrency, string toCurrency, string amount, double rounding,boolean date, string type, string	ConvertToNumResult, double
WS05	Op14	CountryToCurrency	licenseKey, string country, string activeOnly, boolean	CountryToCurrencyResult, string
WS05	Op15	Currencies	licenseKey, string	CurrenciesResult, string
WS05	Op16	CurrencyCustom	licenseKey, string country, string locale, string	CurrencyCustomResult, string

continued on following page

Table 11. Continued

Service	OpId	Operation name	Input parameters	Output Parameters
WS05	Op17	CurrencyName	licenseKey, string currency, string locale, string titleStyle, boolean	CurrencyNameResult, string
WS05	Op18	CurrencySymbol	licenseKey, string country, string locale, string	CurrencySymbolResult, string
WS05	Op19	LocaleToCurrency	licenseKey, string country, string locale, string	LocaleToCurrencyResult, string
WS05	Op20	RateNum	licenseKey, string baseCurrency, string toCurrency, string rounding,boolean date, string type, string	RateNumResult, double
WS06	Op21	Convert	sourceCurrency, string targetCurrency, string value, double	ConvertResult, double

Table 12. Public Web service details

Operation pairs	Operation names	Operation names	Operation name similarity	Input parameter similarity	Output parameter similarity	Structural similarity
Op0 Op1	GetAllCurrencies	GetAllCountryCur-rencies	0.6667	1.0000	0.3333	0.6667
Op0 Op15	GetAllCurrencies	Currencies	0.5000	1.0000	0.2500	0.5833
Op1 Op15	GetAllCountryCur-rencies	Currencies	0.3333	1.0000	0.1667	0.5000
Op2 Op3	GetExchangeRate	ConvertCurrency	0.0000	0.7500	1.0000	0.5833
Op4 Op14	GetCountryCurrency	CountryToCurrency	0.6667	0.6667	0.3333	0.5556
Op5 Op9	**ConversionRate**	**GetConversionRate**	**1.0000**	**0.6667**	**0.5000**	**0.7222**
Op5 Op11	**ConversionRate**	**GetConversionRate**	**1.0000**	**1.0000**	**1.0000**	**1.0000**
Op6 Op15	GetCurrencies	Currencies	1.0000	0.0000	0.5000	0.5000
Op9 Op10	GetConversionRate	GetConversionAmount	0.3333	0.7500	0.6667	0.5833
Op9 Op11	**GetConversionRate**	**GetConversionRate**	**1.0000**	**0.6667**	**0.5000**	**0.7222**
Op13 Op20	ConvertToNum	RateNum	0.2500	0.6250	0.6250	0.5000
Op14 Op16	CountryToCurrency	CurrencyCustom	0.2500	0.5000	0.6250	0.4583
Op14 Op18	CountryToCurrency	CurrencySymbol	0.2500	0.5000	0.6250	0.4583
Op14 Op19	CountryToCurrency	LocaleToCurrency	0.5000	0.5000	0.7500	0.5833
Op16 Op17	CurrencyCustom	CurrencyName	0.3333	0.4000	0.6667	0.4667
Op16 Op18	CurrencyCustom	CurrencySymbol	0.3333	1.0000	0.6667	0.6667
Op16 Op19	CurrencyCustom	LocaleToCurrency	0.2500	1.0000	0.6250	0.6250
Op17 Op18	CurrencyName	CurrencySymbol	0.3333	0.4000	0.6667	0.4667
Op17 Op19	CurrencyName	LocaleToCurrency	0.2500	0.4000	0.6250	0.4250
Op18 Op19	CurrencySymbol	LocaleToCurrency	0.2500	1.0000	0.6250	0.6250

Table 13. Precision and recall of measures

Measure	No. retrieved pairs	No. existing relevant pairs	Relevant retrieved pairs	Precision	Recall	F-measure
Structural	9	8	5	0.56	0.63	0.59
Functional	13	8	8	0.62	1.00	0.76
Substitution	10	8	6	0.60	0.75	0.67

Exhibit 1.

```
Relevant Pairs = {(getFlightPrice, getPrice),
                  (getFlightPrice, calcPrice),
                  (getAvailability, getCapacity),
                  (getAvailability, getAvailableSits),
                  (getPrice, calcPrice),
                  (getCapacity, getAvailableSits),
                  (getTimeDeparture, getDepartureTime),
                  (getTimeLanding, getLandingTime)}
|Relevant Pairs| = 8
```

best option to get the highest structural similarity or search for another operation substitute or develop a new one.

To evaluate these pairs of operations with the functional similarity measure, there is an important requirement to fulfill, that is, the input and output values must be instantiated. In the case of public available Web services, from public repositories, this information is not provided, regardless of the name and data type defined in WSDL files, no input and output values data requirements or exemplars are provided, making very difficult the instantiation of parameters for invocation and output values comparison. Additionally, some operations require a license key to be invoked.

Figure 5. Graphical representation of precision and recall

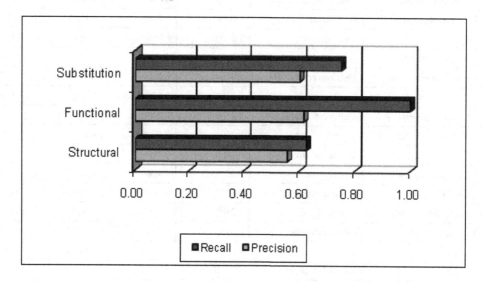

DISCUSSION

The structural information of a Web service that is obtained from its public available description –and used in this paper–, is a detailed source of information. Besides, the cost for extracting and analyzing this information is less than the cost of applying NLP techniques or constructing ontologies. Until now, majority of reported works on Web services matchmaking have stressed the semantic approach, leaving apart the pure structural information. Experimental results show that, without using a semantic approach, the use of structural measures offers significant information for the substitution of Web services.

The similarity measures defined are relevant for Web service substitution, which strongly depends on a structural and functional match. These measures can be used as the foundation for constructing Web service quality testers, facilitating the constant monitoring of Web services execution. In addition, the syntactical precision of the substitution definition acting on a pair of services, guaranties the automated replacement of a service operation at run time; actually, during the continuous execution of a composition. As well, this substitution measure can be used for design decision making, in the way that provides a realistic clue about the required effort for service modifications regarding an eventual match: it is a straightforward measure of the cost of re-programming an operation template.

Actually, in spite of the existence of various techniques and algorithms to select, search, find, discover, match, multiple Web services, which are based on different approaches ranging from syntactic, semantic, and pragmatic, among others; there are still many issues that must be addressed to fully automate composition.

The numerical similarity measures introduced above are useful to the complex Web service tasks currently under research and deployment. The basic syntactic design and automation of the similarity measures facilitate the incorporation on matchmaking task, which is a requirement for Web services classification, composition or substitution. The following list calls for direct extensions or eventual applications of the defined similarity measures:

1. For automated *classification or clustering* of Web services: the introduced measures provide structural and functional information, which used in combination with machine learning algorithms, will help with automated classification and cluster generation.

2. Once the services are classified or the clusters identified, *ontology learning* solutions may be integrated to automatically generate a domain ontology which represents a semantic classification of the set of analyzed services. Automated population of the ontology and relation generation can be executed with the structural and functional information obtained with the measures.

3. Once the Web services have been analyzed, classified and represented with an ontology, an intelligent *selector or search engine*, can look up for specific Web service requests, for matchmaking with template specifications, which can be coped with the similarity measures.

4. Mapping functional relationships with ontology models based on IOPE, such as DAML-S (Srivastava & Koehler, 2003; Sivashanmugam et al., 2003), OWL-S (Sánchez & Sheremetov, 2008a), WSMO (Bener et al., 2009) and WSMO-MX (Klush & Kaufer, 2009). Considering that an input parameter value instance is part of the pre-conditions, as well as the output value is an effect of the execution of the service, the IOPE ontology models can use the similarity measures, integrated with the syntactic extensions, for matchmaking purposes on Web services.

The last observation ranges the similarity measures applicability on hybrid matchmaker tools integrating semantic and syntactic matching. The modeling of ontologies support the semantic match whereas the syntactical analysis of structured input/output parameters is hold by the derivatives tools that describe the constraints through Web services; (Klush et al., 2009) is another recent hybrid Web services matchmaker. The IOPE approaches apply to Web services discovery, classification and composition, and they could eventually be used for substitution purposes.

Additionally, considering the existence of legacy software in any public or private enterprise, rapid construction of Web service ontology-models can benefit from the use of the structural and functional measures, obtaining useful information towards the inter-enterprise service-based supply chain interoperability.

The Functional Similarity

In order to complete the Web services functional evaluation, the comparison on the input and output parameter values is required. However, the common situation is that this information is not coded within the WSDL files. Currently, by using public Web services, is not possible to overcome this restriction easily – impacting agile usage and selection of public Web services. Actually, the design and implementation of Web service operations is coded in private software libraries, as well as workflow processes inside the information systems supporting complex supply chains of providers and customers, are all closed to external users for commercial and security reasons. Extension to current standards to include required data exemplars will facilitate the analysis of functional similarity and interoperation among public Web services.

Moreover, in order to make exhaustive the Web services functional match, the comparison on the design and implementation of the mathematical operation is required, in addition to the input and output parameters values. Actually, in the community of open source software, where the Web service operation code is public available, the similarity measurement can be directly extended to the design and implementation of the mathematical operations, the engineering processes or the workflow processes.

CONCLUSION

In this paper a set of structural and functional measures towards Web service substitution are introduced. The set of structural measures let to identify when a service operation fulfills the substitution structural requirement, such that the operation template includes the input parameters names, data types and output parameter. The process for calculating these measures is implemented using a filtering approach: structural-syntactical and functional. Experimental results show that the obtained information is significantly enough to support the substitution of operations from an unordered set of Web services, even public ones. Additionally, this approach can be applied to other Web services tasks, such as: classification, clustering and composition. There are still many issues that must be addressed to fully automate the functional comparison of Web services. One of the most difficult is the evaluation of output values, because different formats, data sizes and naming conventions can be obtained from similar services, manual comparison is arduos an error prone. Therefore, research on the development of efficient algorithms should go in this direction.

ACKNOWLEDGMENT

Thanks to the postdoctoral program of CONACYT, Mexico, for the financial support to carry on this research.

REFERENCES

Adhitya, A., Srinivasan, R., & Karimi, I. A. (2007). A Model-based Rescheduling Framework for Managing Abnormal Supply Chain Events. *Computers & Chemical Engineering, 31*(5/6), 496–518. doi:10.1016/j.compchemeng.2006.07.002

Baeza-Yates, R., & Ribeiro-Neto, B. (1999). *Modern Information Retrieval*. New York: ACM Press.

Belhajjame, K., Embury, S. M., Paton, N. W., Stevens, R., & Globe, C. A. (2006). *Automatic Annotation of Web Services based on Workflow Definitions*.

Bener, A., Ozadali, V., & Ilhan, E. S. (2009). Semantic matchmaker with precondition and effect matching using SWRL. *International Journal of Expert Systems with Applications*, 9371-9377.

Bernstein, A., & Klein, M. (2002). Discovering Services: Towards High-Precision Service Retrieval. In *Proceedings of the Web Services, E-Business, and the Semantic Web* (LNCS 2512, pp. 260-275).

Domingue, J., Cabral, L., Galizia, S., Tanasescu, V., Gugliotta, A., Norton, B., & Pedrinaci, C. (2008). IRS-II: A broker-based approach to semantic Web services. *Journal of Web Semantics: Science, Services and Agents on the World Wide Web, 6*(1).

Dong, X., Halevy, A., Madhavan, J., Nemes, E., & Zhang, J. (2004). Similarity Search for Web Services. In *Proceedings of the 30th VLDB Conference* (pp. 372-383).

Heb, A., Johnston, E., & Kushmerick, N. (2004). ASSAM: A Tool for Semi-automatically Annotating Semantic Web Services. In *Proceedings of the International Semantic Web Conference* (pp. 320-334).

Heb, A., & Kushmerick, N. (2003). Learning to Attach Semantic Metadata to Web Services. In *Proceedings of the International Semantic Web Conference* (pp. 258-273).

Hull, R., & Su, J. (2005). Tools for composite web services: A short overview. *SIGMOD Record, 34*(2), 86–95. doi:10.1145/1083784.1083807

Jeong, B., Cho, H., & Lee, C. (2008). On the functional quality of service (FQoS) to discover and compose interoperable Web services. *International Journal of Expert Systems with Applications*, 5411-5418.

Kim, J. W., & Candan, K. S. (2006). CP/CV: Concept Similarity Mining without Frequency Information from Domain Describing Taxonomies. In *Proceedings of the 15th ACM International Conference on Information and Knowledge Management* (pp. 483-492).

Klusch, M., Benedik, F., Khalid, M., & Sykara, K. (2009). OWLS-MX: Hybrid OWL-S Service Matchmaker. *Journal of Web Semantics, 7*(2), 121–133. doi:10.1016/j.websem.2008.10.001

Klusch, M., & Kaufer, F. (2009). WSMO-MX: A Hybrid Semantic Web Service Matchmaker. *Web Intelligence and Agent Systems, 7*(1), 23–42.

Le-Hung, V., Hauswirth, M., & Aberer, K. (2005). Towards P2P-based Semantic Web Service Discovery with QoS Support. In *Proceedings of the Business Process Management Workshops* (pp. 18-31).

Li, H., Du, X., & Tian, X. (2007). Towards Semantic Web Services Discovery with QoS Support using Specific Ontologies. In *Proceedings of the Third International Conference on Semantics, Knowledge and Grid* (pp. 358-361).

Menasce, D. A. (2002). QoS issues in Web services. *IEEE Internet Computing*, 72–75. doi:10.1109/MIC.2002.1067740

O'Brien, L., Bass, L., & Merson, P. (2005). *Quality Attributes and Service-Oriented Architectures* (Tech. Rep. No. CMU/SEI-2005-TN-014). Pittsburgh, PA: Carnegie Mellon University.

Paik, I. (2004). Intelligent Agent to Support Design in Supply Chain Based on Semantic Web Services. In *Proceedings of the Fourth International Conference on Hybrid Intelligent Systems*. Washington, DC: IEEE Computer Society.

Patil, A., Oundhakar, S., Seth, A., & Verma, K. (2004). METEOR-S Service Annotation Framework. In *Proceedings of the 13th international conference on World Wide Web* (pp. 553-562).

Rijsbergen, V. (1979). *Information Retrieval* (2nd ed.). Oxford, UK: Butterworth.

Sanchez, C., & Sheremetov, L. (2008a). A Model for Service Discovery with Incomplete Information. In *Proceedings of 5th International Conference on Electrical Engineering, Computing Science and Automatic Control* (pp. 340-345). Washington, DC: IEEE Computer Society Press.

Sanchez, C., & Sheremetov, L. (2008b). A Model for Semantic Service Matching with Leftover and Missing Information. In *Proceedings of 8th International Conference on Hybrid Intelligent Systems* (pp. 198-203). Washington, DC: IEEE Computer Society Press.

Shwentick, T. (2007). Automata for XML – A survey. *Journal of Computer and System Sciences*, *73*(3), 289–315.

Sivashanmugam, K., Verna, K., Seth, A., & Miller, J. (2003). Adding Semantics to Web Service Standards. In *Proceedings of the International Conference on Web Services* (pp. 395-401). CS-REA Press, 395-401.

Srivastava, B., & Koehler, J. (2003). Web Service Composition- Current Solutions and Open Problems. In *Proceedings of the Workshop on Planning for Web Services*.

Sycara, K., Paolucci, M., Ankolekar, A., & Srinivasan, N. (2003). Automated Discovery, Interaction and Composition of Semantic Web Services. *Journal of Web Semantics*, *1*(1), 27–46. doi:10.1016/j.websem.2003.07.002

Xu, Q., & Qiu, R. G. (2004). Integration of Web Services and Agents for Supply Chain System Collaboration. In *Proceedings of the IEEE International Conference on Systems, Man and Cybernetics* (pp. 2079-2083).

Yu, Q., Liu, X., Bouguettaya, A., & Medjahed, B. (2008). Deploying and managing Web services: issues, solutions, and directions. *The VLDB Journal*, *17*(3), 537–572. doi:10.1007/s00778-006-0020-3

Zheng, G., & Bouguettaya, A. (2007). A Web Service Mining Framework. In *Proceedings of the IEEE International Conference on Web Services* (pp. 1096-1103).

This work was previously published in the International Journal of Web Services Research, Volume 7, Issue 3, edited by Liang-Jie (LJ) Zhang, pp. 1-27, copyright 2010 by IGI Publishing (an imprint of IGI Global).

Chapter 8
Service Flavors:
Differentiating Service Offerings in a Services Marketplace

Harshavardhan Jegadeesan
SAP Labs, India

Sundar Balasubramaniam
BITS, India

ABSTRACT

In a services marketplace where a particular service is provided by multiple service providers, service offerings have to be differentiated against competitor services in order to gain market share. Differentiation of services is also needed for different markets and for different consumer segments. Strategies to differentiate service offerings have to be unintrusive—without requiring major changes to the existing service realization mechanisms. In this article, the authors present Service Flavors, a strategy for service providers to differentiate services. By using this strategy, it is possible to analyze and adapt various aspects of a service that help differentiate it from that of the competitors. The authors model differentiating aspects as policies and also provide a mechanism for enforcing these policies in the middleware.

1 INTRODUCTION

Service-oriented computing paradigm deals with organizing and utilizing distributed capabilities under the control of different ownership domains (Oasis, 2005). A service represents an underlying capability of a provider which meets the goals of a consumer. In the services marketplace (Papazoglou & Georgakopoulos, 2003) context, a service could be a commoditized service, a specialized service or a monopolistic service based on the number of service providers providing that service.

Specialized services are provided by very few service providers in the services marketplace (e.g. payroll & benefits services). A service offered by a single service provider is a monopolistic service.

DOI: 10.4018/978-1-4666-1942-5.ch008

Examples of monopolistic services are *Apply for Driving License* and *File Tax Returns* services offered by the state department (service provider). The citizen (service consumer) uses these services to apply for a motor vehicle driving license or to file his tax returns. Normally eGovernance services are monopolistic in nature as they are provided by a single service provider—the government (Press, 2003).

In contrast, commoditized services are always provided by multiple competing service providers in a services marketplace. For example, consider a *Shipping Service* in the context of an e-marketplace such as eBay®. It is provided by multiple providers such as UPS®, USPS®, DHL®, OverniteExpress® or FedEx®. More often than not, the underlying capabilities represented by these services remain the same due to standardization of messages and interfaces. Standardization leads to business layer interoperability; efforts such as Universal Business Language (UBL) (Meadows & Seaburg, 2004), ebXML (Kotok, 2001), RosettaNet (Damodaran, 2004) and UN/CEFACT (Hofreiter, Huemer, & Naujok, 2004) address business layer interoperability. The standardization of these competing services is a result of market compulsions. For customers, standardization supports easy migration from one provider to another. However, standardization takes away provider lock-in advantages for service providers. As a result, every service provider is faced with the dilemma of balancing standardization and differentiation of their service offerings. Given that standardization is a necessity, service providers of commoditized services must still differentiate their service offerings from that of the competition in order to sustain as well as gain market share. The differentiation strategy used to differentiate services in a services marketplace must be unintrusive, i.e. without requiring major alterations to already existing service realization mechanisms.

The context of this article is a service development and delivery platform that enables the service providers to differentiate their service offerings. Our main contributions in this article are the following:

- We present *Service Flavors*—a strategy for unintrusive differentiation of service offerings.
- We provide means to identify and specify differentiating aspects of service offerings. We propose a way to document these aspects in a catalog.
- We propose a model-based approach for domain experts to specify differentiating aspects of service offerings as service policies.
- We describe how differentiation is achieved at runtime through policy enforcement during service invocation and execution.

1.1 Example: *ShippingService*

We use the example of a fictitious[1] *ShippingService*—a commoditized service provided by FedEx®. A commoditized shipping service in an e-marketplace like eBay® would be provided by multiple service providers such as UPS®, USPS®, DHL® etc. The schemas of the messages could either be similar or different across service providers, but the underlying capability is the same. The service capability model below represents the *ShippingService* (Figure 1). The service capability model is based on a services metamodel described in (Harshavardhan Jegadeesan, 2008). The corresponding WSDL 2.0 (Chinnici, Gudgin, Moreau, Schlimmer, & Weerawarana, 2004) snippet (Figure 2) shows the functional service description of the fictitious shipping service. The shipping service defines a *ShipItem* operation which supports shipping a package from one place to another.

The rest of the article is organized as follows: Section 2 introduces the concept of differentiating aspects (i.e. flavoring aspects); we identify specific flavoring aspects and document them in a catalog. Section 3 describes how the flavoring aspects are modeled as service policies using a

Figure 1. Service capability model

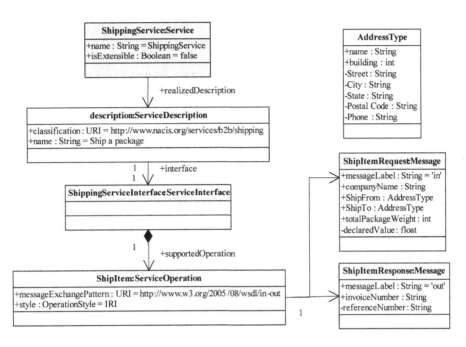

Figure 2. WSDL 2.0 snippet for shipping service

```
- <description xmlns="http://www.w3.org/ns/wsdl" xmlns:tns="http://service.fictitious.com/shipping/fedex"
    targetNamespace="http://service.fictitious.com/shipping/fedex">
    <documentation>Fictitious FedEx Shipping Service</documentation>
  - <types>
    - <xsd:schema xmlns:soap="http://schemas.xmlsoap.org/wsdl/soap/" xmlns:xsd="http://www.w3.org/2001/XMLSchema"
        xmlns:wsdl="http://schemas.xmlsoap.org/wsdl/" elementFormDefault="qualified"
        targetNamespace="http://service.fictitious.com/shipping/fedex">
      - <xsd:element name="AddressType">
        + <xsd:complexType>
        </xsd:element>
      - <xsd:element name="ShipItemRequest">
        - <xsd:complexType>
          - <xsd:sequence>
            <xsd:element minOccurs="0" maxOccurs="1" name="CompanyName" type="xsd:string" />
            <xsd:element minOccurs="0" maxOccurs="1" name="ShipFrom" type="tns:AddressType" />
            <xsd:element minOccurs="0" maxOccurs="1" name="ShipTo" type="tns:AddressType" />
            <xsd:element minOccurs="0" maxOccurs="1" name="TotalPackageWeight" type="xsd:integer" />
            <xsd:element minOccurs="0" maxOccurs="1" name="DeclaredValue" type="xsd:float" />
          </xsd:sequence>
        </xsd:complexType>
        </xsd:element>
      - <xsd:element name="ShipItemResponse">
        - <xsd:complexType>
          - <xsd:sequence>
            <xsd:element minOccurs="0" maxOccurs="1" name="InvoiceNumber" type="xsd:string" />
            <xsd:element minOccurs="0" maxOccurs="1" name="Reference Number" type="xsd:string" />
          </xsd:sequence>
        </xsd:complexType>
        </xsd:element>
      </xsd:schema>
    </types>
  - <interface name="ShippingServiceInterface">
    - <operation name="ShipItem" pattern="http://www.w3.org/ns/wsdl/in-out">
      <documentation>Ship Item Operation</documentation>
      <input element="tns:ShipItemRequest" />
      <output element="tns:ShipItemResponse" />
    </operation>
  </interface>
  + <binding xmlns:wsoap="http://www.w3.org/ns/wsdl/soap" name="ShippingServiceEndpoint" interface="tns:ShippingServiceInterface"
      type="http://www.w3.org/ns/wsdl/soap" wsoap:version="1.2" wsoap:protocol="http://www.w3.org/2006/01/soap11/bindings/HTTP/">
  + <service name="ShippingService" interface="tns:ShippingServiceInterface">
</description>
```

generic policy metamodel. Section 4 describes how the policy models are translated to executable specification. Section 5 describes how these policies and thereby service flavors are enforced in the SOA middleware. Section 6 discusses related work. Section 7 discusses conclusions and future work.

2 FLAVORING ASPECTS: DIFFERENTIATING ASPECTS OF A SERVICE

In order to differentiate service offerings, it is important to understand the *changing parts* across service offerings. By understanding the changing parts, we could arrive at aspects of a service that help in differentiating the service against competing services. Every service description has a functional part representing the underlying *capability on offer* and a non-functional part representing the terms in which the capability is offered—the *terms of offer*. The terms of offer represents aspects such as price, quality of service, discounts and promotions offered etc. The *capability on offer* satisfies a goal of the consumer under the constraints of the *terms of offer*. A service description must describe both the functional capability on offer as well as the non-functional terms of offer for automatic selection and consumption of a service (O'Sullivan, Edmond, & Ter Hofstede, 2002).

In the case of the *ShippingService*, the underlying capability is to ship items from one place to another. Given that the capability on offer is the same across competing services, how does a service provider differentiate his shipping service from that of the competition? On what basis does a service consumer choose a particular shipping service? Consider the examples of a websites such as www.redroller.com and iShip™ that compare the shipping services provided by various providers such as USPS®, DHL® and OverniteExpress®. It is interesting to note the dimensions in which these services are compared—delivery date (quality of service) and shipping rates (price). Therefore, given that the capability on offer is the same, consumers would choose a particular service based on *attractiveness* of the terms of offer. Certain aspects of the terms of offer—aspects such as cost (pricing), discounts (promotions), availability, quality of service, convenience of use, packaging, and so forth (Toma, Roman, & Fensel, 2007)—that make service offerings attractive to consumers become differentiating aspects, we call these *Flavoring Aspects*. The important criteria to determine if an aspect is a flavoring aspect or not is to answer this question—'would the aspect make the terms of offer attractive to the consumer and differentiate the service offering from that of competition?' We call this the *attractiveness of terms of offer* criterion. It is important to note that, there are other aspects such as service reputation (Maximilien & Singh, 2002), market perception and service rating (by rating agencies), and so forth, which also significantly impact the choice of a service by a consumer. However, these are not under the direct influence of the service provider and are not considered in this article. Our service flavors strategy supports two use-cases to differentiate service offerings:

UC#1: Creation of *competitive service offerings* by unintrusively varying flavoring aspects and attractively positioning services to consumers.

UC#2: Creation of *targeted service offerings* by offering the same capability on-offer under different terms of offer. Each targeted offering represents a discrete variation of a service or a *Service Flavor*.

2.1 A Catalog of Flavoring Aspects

The flavoring aspects identified during the early-stage services development have to be precisely documented in a catalog as they are reusable assets in services development. We propose a standard schema to document the flavoring aspects. The standard schema would facilitate better communication among stakeholders during the design and modeling activities. The schema is presented (see Table 1) along with a pictorial XML Schema (Fallside, 2000) representation below (see Figure 3):

We use this schema to catalog flavoring aspects. The advantage of documenting these flavoring aspects in the early-stage services development is that it helps in separation of concerns. Most importantly, note that the catalog presented below (Figure 4) is not complete. It is extensible to support specification of various other flavoring aspects. New flavoring aspects could be added to the catalog, for example *Dispute Resolution* could be another flavoring aspect that could be added to the catalog. Dispute Resolution mechanisms

Table 1. Standard schema for flavoring aspects catalog

Name of Concern	The name of the concern
Type of Aspect	Denotes the aspect type
Related Aspects	Denotes related aspects for this aspect
Context	Denotes the context in which the aspect applies
Rationale & Discussion	Provides a brief description of the aspect and its application
Quantification	Denotes applicability of the aspect. It could be: 1. List of services in the services portfolio, a random list of services 2. Select services/service operations or service interaction points (end-points) 3. Ownership Domain (a physical or administrative partition for services). 4. A particular customer or a customer segment.
Vocabulary	Vocabulary defines a set of vocabulary items which are used to describe the aspect

Figure 3. XML schema (pictorial representation) for flavoring aspects

Figure 4. Extensible catalog of flavoring aspects

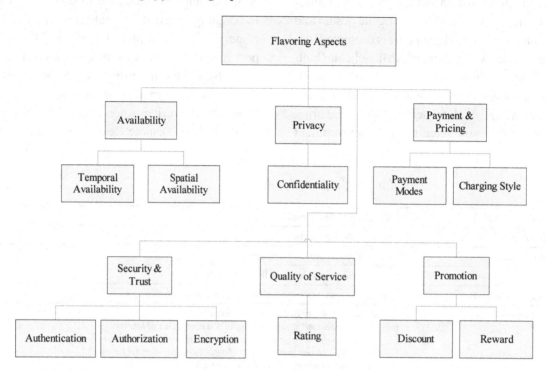

between the provider and consumer could be different in different markets and geographies (ombudsman, courts, special appellate tribunal) etc.

Further we document selected flavoring aspects below using the schema described in Table 1. (See Tables 2, 3, 4, 5, 6 and 7)

Our approach enables identification and specification of flavoring aspects irrespective of how the service would eventually be realized—completely automated implementation, human

task or a hybrid. Our *ShippingService* is an example of hybrid service realization consisting of two parts—the shipping request, which is fully automated and the physical shipment of goods, which is a human task. While flavoring aspects such as *Pricing* and *Promotion* impact the automated part (i.e. shipping request), a quality of service aspect such as *Delivery Time* impacts the human task (i.e. physical shipment of goods). However, it is important to model all flavoring

Table 2. Flavoring aspect: Service availability

Name of Concern	Service Availability
Type of Aspect	Availability
Related Types	Temporal Availability, Spatial Availability
Context	Service consumer trying to consume a service should be aware of the time (temporal) and location (spatial) the service would be available.
Rationale and Discussion	Service Availability in terms of time (temporal) and location (spatial) determines when and where a service consumer interacts with the service provider to accesses the service offering. Availability of a service is determined by a host of factors such as provisioning of the service, the availability constraints of the service provider.
Quantification	Any service consumption scenario is affected by the availability concern of the service.

Table 3. Flavoring aspect: Service pricing

Name of Concern	Service Pricing
Type of Aspect	Pricing &Payment
Related Aspects	Payment Mode, Charging Style
Context	A Service offering from a provider could have a cost associated with it.
Rationale and Discussion	Payment is a concern during access of a paid service. Payment for a service is determined by cost of service access, the charging style and the payment modes.
Quantification	Payment is a concern across a set of paid services.

Table 4. Flavoring aspect: Service promotion

Name of Concern	Service Promotion
Type of Aspect	Promotion
Related Aspects	Discounts & Rewards
Context	A Service provider would promote his service by offering discounts and rewards to service consumers
Rationale and Discussions	Promotion is a concern which deals with promoting the use of a service offering among the service consumers. Promotion schemes could provide discounts on using the service, waive cost for a fixed time-period and offer reward points which could be redeemed.

Table 5. Flavoring aspect: Service privacy

Name of Concern	Service Privacy
Type of Aspect	Privacy
Related Aspects	Confidentiality
Context	A Service provider must guarantee the service consumers confidentiality of service access information and exchanged information.
Rationale and Discussions	Privacy must be guaranteed to the service consumer by securing and preventing misuse of information provided by the user. Privacy deals with providing confidentiality of service access and user information.

Table 6. Flavoring aspect: Service security & trust

Name of Concern	Service Security & Trust
Type of Aspect	Security & Trust
Related Aspects	Authentication, Authorization, Encryption
Context	A Service provider must guarantee the service consumers security and trust while accessing the service offering
Rationale and Discussions	Security deals with authentication (identifying consumer) authorization (validating consumer access rights) and encryption of communication between the provider and consumer.

Table 7. Flavoring aspect: Service quality

Name of Concern	Service Quality
Type of Aspect	Quality of Service
Related Aspects	Rating
Context	A Service provider must guarantee acceptable and agreed upon quality of service to the service consumer.
Rationale and Discussions	Service quality is determined by response time of the service (execution time). Quality of Service is also reflected by service rating provided by rating agencies or by other service users. Rating of the service by other service users reflects the perception of the service in the marketplace.

aspects irrespective of the impacted part(s) because these aspects capture the terms of offer of the service irrespective of the realization.

3 MODELING FLAVORING ASPECTS AS SERVICE POLICIES

After identifying and documenting the flavoring aspects, we need to specify semantics and associated operational behavior of flavoring aspects. We need to define a vocabulary for each flavoring aspect with a set of vocabulary items along with types and domain of applicable values for each of these vocabulary items.

3.1 Specifying Vocabulary for Flavoring Aspects

As a first step in specifying vocabulary, *vocabulary items* associated with each flavoring aspect has to be identified and defined. Each vocabulary item would have a type and applicable values (domain) associated with it. The set of vocabulary items for a flavoring aspect provide a controlled vocabulary to define that flavoring aspect. For example, the pricing flavoring aspect can have vocabulary items such as type of price (*applicable values:* absolute price, proportional price, dynamic price), price, credit period etc. We define vocabulary items for six selected flavoring aspects we identified and defined above. The vocabulary items could also be extended to suit specific scenario and business

needs. We present vocabulary items, their type and applicable values below (Table 8):

The vocabulary of flavoring aspects could standardize across service providers as an industry standard over time. For example, *cost* (price) and *execution time* (delivery time) are now standardized vocabulary items in the package shipping industry. Consensus on vocabulary of flavoring aspects could also be achieved using ontologies (Noy & McGuinness, 2001). QoSOnt is an effort to achieve consensus on quality of service vocabulary for service-centric systems (Dobson, Lock, & Sommerville, 2005). Creating ontologies for flavoring aspects will support automatic inference, reasoning and semantic interoperability of vocabulary items across flavoring aspects and service providers in the marketplace. However, presently, we have defined flavoring aspects vocabulary as simple XML schemas (See *Service Pricing.xsd* in a pictorial form) (see Figure 5). Nevertheless, it is possible to document these aspects as separate ontologies, using a web ontology language like OWL.

3.2 Use of Service Policies

While the service description languages like WSDL specify service capability, service interfaces and messages, the service policy languages are used to specify the non-functional terms of offer. In our Service Flavors approach, we use service policies to define the terms of offer of a service offering. The service policy mechanism is based on prepositional logic and allows specifying

Table 8. Vocabulary items, their type and applicable values for flavoring aspects

No.	Aspect	Vocabulary Items	Type	Applicable Values
1	Service Availability			
		Availability Period	Validity	
		Geographical Location	Location	
2	Service Pricing			
		Pricing Period	Validity	
		Applicable Location	Location	
		Price Type	String	Absolute price, Proportional price Dynamic price
		Price	Amount	
		Additional Price Type	String	Tax, Shipping, Commission, Octoroi, Surcharge
		Additional Price	Amount	
		Credit Period	Duration	
		Payment Mode	String	Cheque, Cash, Credit Card, Bank Transfer, Gift Coupon
		Charging Style	String	Pay-per-use, Rental, Subscription
3	Service Promotion			
		Promotion Period	Validity	
		Applicable Location	Location	
		Reward Type	String	Reward points, Coupons
		Reward Value	Integer	
		Discount Percent	Integer	
		Discount Value	Float	
4	Service Privacy			
		Use of Personal Information	String	Internal, External
		Is Shared with Third-Party Partners	Boolean	
5	Service Security & Trust			
		isIdentificationRequired	Boolean	
		Identification Type	String	PIN, Password, Membership Card, National Identification Card
		isdigitalCertificateRequired	Boolean	
		Digital Certificate Type	String	
		isEncryptionRequired	Boolean	
		Encryption Type	String	
6	Service Quality			
		Execution time	Duration	
		Rating	Integer	
		rating type	String	Positive, Neutral, Negative
		rating agency	String	

Figure 5. Vocabulary items for service pricing flavoring aspect

```xml
<?xml version="1.0" encoding="utf-8" ?>
- <xs:schema xmlns="http://www.fictitious.com/servicepricing" elementFormDefault="qualified"
    targetNamespace="http://www.fictitious.com/servicepricing"
    xmlns:xs="http://www.w3.org/2001/XMLSchema">
    <xs:include schemaLocation="Common.xsd" />
  - <xs:element name="Pricing">
    - <xs:complexType>
      - <xs:sequence>
          <xs:element xmlns:q1="www.fictitious.com" name="ApplicablePeriod"
            type="q1:Validity" />
          <xs:element xmlns:q2="www.fictitious.com" name="ApplicableLocation"
            type="q2:Location" />
          <xs:element name="CreditPeriod" type="xs:duration" />
        - <xs:element xmlns:q3="www.fictitious.com" name="Price">
          - <xs:complexType>
            - <xs:sequence>
              - <xs:element name="PricingMechanism">
                + <xs:simpleType>
                </xs:element>
              - <xs:element name="PriceType">
                + <xs:simpleType>
                </xs:element>
                <xs:element name="Amount" type="xs:float" />
                <xs:element name="CurrencyCode" type="xs:string" />
              </xs:sequence>
            </xs:complexType>
          </xs:element>
        - <xs:element name="ChargingStyle">
          - <xs:simpleType>
            - <xs:restriction base="xs:string">
                <xs:enumeration value="pay-per-use" />
                <xs:enumeration value="subscription" />
              </xs:restriction>
            </xs:simpleType>
          </xs:element>
      </xs:sequence>
    </xs:complexType>
  </xs:element>
</xs:schema>
```

assertions (constraints) on vocabulary, an ability to combine these assertions using conjunction or disjunction into service policies. A service policy represents the terms of offer of a service offering. The terms of offer is associated with the capability on offer by attaching the service policy to the service description using policy attachment mechanisms, offering separation of concerns. The 'terms of offer' of the service is essentially a set of assertions – constraints on the vocabulary items of different flavoring aspects.

Technically, competitive service offerings (UC#1) are created by altering the terms of offer by varying the assertions in the corresponding service policy. Targeted service offerings (UC#2) are created by conditionally attaching different terms of offer (different service policies) to service offerings.

3.3 Service Policy Metamodel

Normally domain experts (business experts) independently define the terms of offer (service policies) and associate them to service offerings. Domain experts prefer a visual syntax to specify terms of offer. We provide a service policy metamodel to support model-driven development of service policies. The service policy metamodel must support modeling of four functional layers of a generic policy model(Anderson & Balasubramanian, 2005):

- **Vocabulary specification:** Specification of vocabulary items associated with various flavoring aspects and their applicable values which would then be used in service policies.
- **Constraint specification:** Specification of assertions (constraints), which would normally be constraints on the applicable values of vocabulary items.

- **Policy specification:** Specification of acceptable combinations of the constrained vocabulary items.
- **Bindings specification:** Specification of application of the service policies on various policy subjects (services).

The service policy metamodel we present in this article is a MOF2 (OMG, 2006) based metamodel. The 'Core' in the figure represents the UML2: Infrastructure (OMG, 2007) package. We explain the key classes, associations and constraints if any, in the metamodel (Figure 6):

- **Service policy:** A service policy defines a set of enforceable constraints which would be applied on a policy subject (Oasis, 2005). It reflects the point of view of a service participant who is the owner of the policy.
- **Service participant:** A service participant could be a service provider or a consumer.

Figure 6. Service policy metamodel

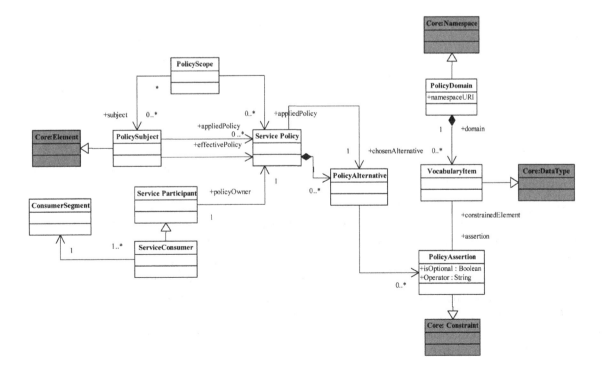

A service provider policy is communicated to the consumer along with the service description. In our case, where we represent terms of offer through policies, the service participant is the service provider.

- **Policy subject:** A policy subject represents an entity on which a policy is applied. A policy subject extends the *Core: Element*. The policy subjects could be Ownership Domain (supports physical or administrative partition of services); Service, Service Interface, Service Operation, Message and Interaction Point (end point), Consumer and Consumer Segment. If a set of policies are applicable on a single policy subject, these are reconciled and represented as an 'effective policy'.

- **Policy scope:** A policy scope represents a set of policy subjects on which a policy could be applied. It is a mechanism to group policy subjects together in order to apply the same policy on them. More than one policy could also be applied on the policy scope.

- **Policy alternative:** Each policy has a set of policy alternatives out of which at least one has to be honored. The policy alternative which is honored is called the 'chosen alternative'. Every policy alternative would have more than one policy assertion.

- **Policy assertion:** Every policy alternative would have one or more policy assertions. A policy assertion is a constraint applied on a vocabulary item (constrained element) of a particular domain. The policy assertion specifies the allowable range, range of values, or set of values for a vocabulary item. The policy assertion could be optional in nature. It also has an operator associated with it. The operator is a predicate operator used to describe constraints.

- **Policy domain:** A policy domain represents a grouping of assertions belonging to a particular aspect such as pricing, avail-

ability, security, trust, etc. It is representative of a flavoring aspect. A policy domain is identified by a name and a namespace URI and it extends the *Core: Namespace*.

- **Vocabulary item:** A vocabulary item represents semantics associated with a particular flavoring aspect and belongs to a policy domain. Every vocabulary item has a set of applicable values. The vocabulary items for a particular domain (aspect) are defined by the domain expert. It extends the *Core: DataType*.

- **Service consumer:** A service consumer is a service participant. A consumer can be a policy owner and the consumer policy has to have a suitable intersection with the service provider policy for the consumer and provider to collaborate. The consumer also belongs to a particular consumer segment. It could also be a policy subject. By associating a service policy to a consumer we could model consumer specific SLAs.

- **Consumer segment:** A consumer segment is used to group related consumers together. It represents a market segment of customers. A consumer segment could be a policy subject on which segment specific policies can be applied. That applied service policy would hold good for consumers belonging to that consumer profile. Service offering can be targeted to a specific customer segment.

We use the metamodel to model the service pricing policy (Figure 7) and apply it to our shipping service. Consider the following *Subscription Pricing Policy* the provider adopts to differentiate against competing shipping services and also increase subscription customers in order to gain predictability in monthly revenues. Assertions are created on vocabulary items credit period, price and charging style of the pricing flavoring aspect, represented as a policy domain.

Figure 7. Service pricing policy model

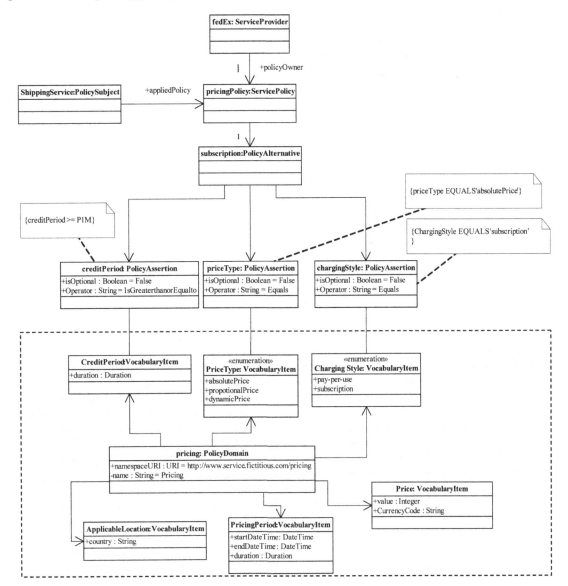

Subscription Pricing Policy

The service provider of the fictitious shipping service (FedEx®) provides a one-month credit period for its subscription customers.

3.3 Consumer Context-Aware Service Policies

Segmenting customers and targeting those customer segments with promotions is a good service differentiation strategy. We create targeted offerings (UC#2)—*Service Flavors*—by offering the same service with different terms of offer. For example, a pricing or promotion policy could be different for members of an alliance from that of other consumers., say, like *members of Star Alliance in the aviation sector can redeem frequent flyer miles (reward points) across alliance partners* Terms of offer for specific consumer segments can be created by creating different service policies for each of those segments. The service consumers could be segmented based on various customer segmentation schemes—based on customer characteristics such as small businesses, business partners, or members of an alliance or based on qualitative characteristics such as gold, silver or platinum customers derived based on previous engagements or revenues from the customer. These schemes are based on existing business imperatives and are different across industries and businesses. The domain expert defines consumer segments and associates specific service policies to each segment. Consider, for example, the *USFSB Member Discount Policy* that provides a flat 10% discount to members of the US Small Businesses federation (customer segment). A new consumer segment (*USFSB*: Consumer Segment) is created to represent the small business customers belonging to the USFSB. A service policy is created which has a promotion alternative with a constrained value for vocabulary item (Discount Percent = 10%) for the service promotion policy domain. This example is modeled using our service policy metamodel in Figure 8.

Figure 8. Service promotion policy model for USFSB customer segment

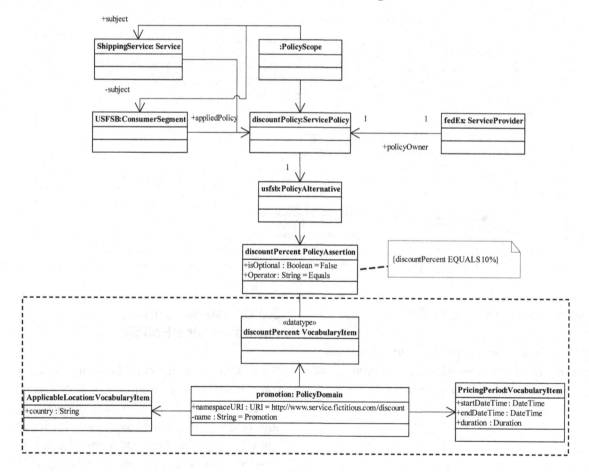

4 CONVERTING SERVICE POLICY MODELS TO EXECUTABLE POLICY SPECIFICATIONS

Once the service policies are modeled to represent the terms of offer, they have to be converted to appropriate executable standards for them to be incorporated into the service description. In the *ShippingService* example, the service capability model (in Figure 1) was converted to a standard WSDL 2.0 service description (in Figure 2). In the same manner, the policies described using our service policy models have to be transformed to appropriate industry accepted open-standards. Since there are multiple and sometimes competing standards, we look at different standards available in each of the four layers of the generic policy model (Table 9).

Technically the policy models created using our service policy metamodel could be transformed to any of these specifications using MOF2 Model to Text Transformation Language (MTL) (Oldevik, Neple, Grønmo, Aagedal, & Berre, 2005) standard mappings. But we have made certain choices for the standards.

For the purpose of vocabulary specification, we use domain-independent XML schemas.

While specifying vocabulary as ontologies has obvious advantages, we prefer XML schemas for simplicity. For specifying assertions, we prefer domain-independent assertion specification using WS-Policy Constraints (see Section 4.1). For the purpose of policy specification, we choose to use the industry accepted standard WS-Policy. The assertions that are part of every alternative in the WS-Policy specification would be domain-independent assertions specified using WS-Policy-Constraints language. For the purpose of binding, we use the WS-Policy Attachment specification. Currently we support intrinsic attachment of policies to WSDL 2.0 elements. Attaching policies to a service consumer or a consumer segment is outside the scope of WS-PolicyAttachment and is realized in the SOA middleware.

4.1 Domain-Dependent vs. Domain-Independent Specification

Vocabulary and assertions (constraints) can be defined using either domain-dependent or domain-independent specifications (Anderson, 2004). Industry standard specification languages such as WS-Security, WS-Trust, WS-ReliableMessaging (WS-RM) (Bilorusets, Bosworth, & Box, 2004)

Table 9. Standards relevant to generic policy model layers

Generic Policy Model Layer	Specifications
Vocabulary Specification	Domain-Dependent Specification
	WS-Security (Atkinson et al., 2002), WS-Trust (Anderson et al., 2005), WS-ReliableMessagingPolicy), domain-dependent assertions for pricing, promotion etc.
	Domain-Independent Specification
	XML Schema (Fallside, 2000), Web Ontology Language (OWL) (Smith, Welty, & McGuinness, 2004) to support specification of domain ontologies for flavoring aspects
Constraint Specification (Specification of Assertions)	Domain-Dependent Specification
	WS-Security, WS-Trust, WS-ReliableMessagingPolicy
	Domain-Independent Specification
	WS-PolicyConstraints, XACML (Anderson & Balasubramanian, 2005)
Policy Specification	WS-Policy (Bajaj et al., 2004), WSPL (Anderson, 2004)
Binding Specification	WS-Policy Attachment (Bajaj et al., 2006)

etc. provide *domain-specific* assertions on a rigid and restricted vocabulary for the technical domains such as security, trust and reliable messaging. Moreover, it is possible to define domain-specific vocabulary and assertions for domains such as availability, pricing etc. based on the policy author guidelines (Yendluri & Yalçinalp, 2007).

However, we prefer domain-independent specifications to specify vocabulary and assertions for flavoring aspects. Our preference is due to the flexible vocabulary requirements presented by flavoring aspects. Especially, the vocabulary for certain flavoring aspects such as pricing and promotions not only evolve, but also significantly vary across industries – in contrast to the rigid vocabulary of technical domains such as security. For example, promotions could be based on *reward points* in the logistics domain, but based on *flyer miles* in the aviation domain. Hence the vocabulary items (*reward points / flyer miles*) for promotions domain vary when compared to a rigid vocabulary item (*securityToken*) in the security domain. In order to support flexible vocabulary specification, we prefer to use domain-independent specifications. Consequently, we choose a *domain-independent* policy assertion language (WS-PolicyConstraints) to specify assertions. WS-PolicyConstraints uses XACML (Godik & Moses, 2003) based functions to specify constraints on the vocabulary items. Even technical domains such as security can be expressed using WS-PolicyConstraints (Anderson, 2004). In summary, our decision to use domain-independent specification is based on the following:

- To support flexibility of vocabulary for flavoring aspects.
- Absence of domain-specific specifications for aspects such as availability, pricing, promotions etc.
- Advantage of using a single generic policy handling logic for parsing policies in the SOA middleware. Domain-specific assertions require domain-specific policy handling in the SOA middleware to enforce these policies.

Going back to our *Subscription Pricing Policy* modeled in Figure 7, the constraint specified on the vocabulary item *creditPeriod* in the model is converted to a WS-PolicyConstraints below (Figure 9):

In Figure 10, we show the enhanced service description for the Shipping Service. The WSDL 2.0 is enhanced with the *Subscription Pricing Policy*. The *SubscriptionPricingPolicy* is specified with a single alternative which has domain-independent assertions on vocabulary items 'creditPeriod', 'priceType', and 'chargingStyle' specified using WS-PolicyConstraints. The policy is intrinsically referenced in the <service/> using <wsp: Policy Reference />.

4.2 Flavored Service Consumption

The enhanced service description describes the combination of the capability on offer (service interface, types and messages) and the relevant terms of offer (service policy). The enhanced

Figure 9. Specification of constraints using WS-PolicyConstraints

```
<Apply
    FunctionId="&wspc;function:is-less-than-or-equal">
<AttributeValue
    DataType="&xsd;duration">P1M</AttributeValue>
<ResourceAttributeDesignator
    AttributeId="creditPeriod"
    DataType="&xsd;duration"/>
</Apply>
```

Figure 10. Service description enhanced with subscription pricing policy

```
<description xmlns="http://www.w3.org/ns/wsdl"
             xmlns:tns="http://service.fictitious.com/shipping/fedex"
             xmlns:xsd="http://www.w3.org/2001/XMLSchema"
             xmlns:wsp="http://www.w3.org/ns/ws-policy"
             xmlns:xacml="urn:oasis:names:tc:xacml:1.0:policy"
             xmlns:wspc="http://research.sun.com/ns/ws-policyconstraints"
             xmlns:wsu="http://docs.oasis-open.org/wss/2004/01/oasis-200401-wss-wssecurity-utility-1.0.xsd"
             targetNamespace="http://service.fictitious.com/shipping/fedex">

  <documentation>Fictitious FedEx Shipping Service</documentation>
  <types> .... </types>
  <wsp:Policy wsu:Id = "SubscriptionServicePolicy">
      <wsp:ExactlyOne>
          <wsp:All>
              <Apply FunctionId="&wspc;function:is-greater-than-or-equal">
              <AttributeValue DataType="&xsd;duration">P1M</AttributeValue>
              <ResourceAttributeDesignator AttributeId="creditPeriod" DataType="&xsd;duration"/>
              </Apply>

              <Apply FunctionId="&wspc;function:equals">
              <AttributeValue DataType="&xsd;string">absolutePrice</AttributeValue>
              <ResourceAttributeDesignator AttributeId="priceType" DataType="&xsd;string"/>
              </Apply>

              <Apply FunctionId="&wspc;function:equals">
              <AttributeValue DataType="&xsd;string">Subscription</AttributeValue>
              <ResourceAttributeDesignator AttributeId="chargingStyle" DataType="&xsd;string"/>
              </Apply>

          </wsp:All>
      </wsp:ExactlyOne>
  </wsp:Policy>

  <interface name="ShippingServiceInterface"> ... </interface>
  <binding> ... </binding>

  <service name="ShippingService" interface="tns:ShippingServiceInterface">
      <documentation>Fictitious FedEx Shipping Web Services.</documentation>
      <endpoint name="ShippingServiceEndpoint" binding="tns:ShippingServiceEndpoint
                address="http://service.fictitious.com/shipping/fedex.asmx"/>
      <wsp:PolicyReference URI="#SubscriptionPricingPolicy" />
  </service>
</description>
```

service description represents a discrete variation of the service—a *Service Flavor*. For a Service Consumer, an appropriate service flavor (i.e. an enhanced service description with a specialized service policy) is presented by the services registry based on the consumer segment, during service look-up. If no specific service flavor is available (i.e. if no special terms of offer are available for the consumer segment) the enhanced service description contains the default terms of offer. The consumers use the enhanced service description to invoke the service.

5 ENFORCING SERVICE POLICIES IN THE SOA MIDDLEWARE

To support service differentiation, the terms of offer expressed as service policies have to be enforced in the SOA middleware during service invocation. The most important criterion for policy enforcement is that it has to be *unintrusive*—without requiring any changes to the existing service realization mechanisms. Earlier we mentioned that our service flavors approach is agnostic to service realization mechanisms i.e. our flavoring aspect could impact the automated part of service realization, the human task or both wherever applicable. In case of a fully automated realization, complete policy enforcement happens in the middleware. Suppose the realization is through a hybrid model (partly automated, partly human task). Then partial policy enforcement happens in the middleware. In our *Shipping Service* example, the realization is a hybrid model—the shipping request is automated, whereas the physical shipment of goods is a human task. Consider a Quality of Service flavoring aspect such as *delivery time* that impacts the human task. In this case, the enforcement of *delivery time* cannot be done in the middleware during service invocation.

The service consumer constructs a SOAP request message based on the enhanced service description. The policy preferences are expressed in the SOAP header using SOAP header extensions for each flavoring aspect. Figure 11 presents a sample SOAP request for the *ShippingService* (the SOAP body is not presented for brevity).

The header extension element *Consumer Profile* provides enough consumer information to associate the consumer with a consumer segment. The header extension *Pricing* provides the *charging style* and the *price type* from the pricing flavoring aspect. For each service invocation, the SOAP request has to be processed in stages: first, the consumer has to be associated to a segment using the *Consumer Profile* header element, then each of the header extensions have to be processed to enforce the terms of offer. To support extensibility, each flavoring aspect is associated with a

handler, which will process related header extensions. We assume that our flavoring aspects are orthogonal and can be handled in any order.

We realize policy enforcement using an active SOAP intermediary (Mitra, 2003) which we call the *Flavoring Intermediary* (Figure 12). The flavoring intermediary is configured to play the role (*soap: role=*http://fictitious.com/role/policyEnforcement*)* of a Policy Enforcement Point (PEP) for flavoring service policies. The flavoring intermediary works on the SOAP header extensions associated with flavoring aspects specially tagged with the *soap: role* attribute (see Figure 11). We use Apache Axis 2.0 (hereon Axis2) SOAP engine (Perera et al., 2006) as the SOAP intermediary.

We take advantage of the extensible SOAP processing model of Axis2 that allows user-defined Phases and Handlers. A *flavoring handler* is defined for the enforcement of each flavoring aspect. Enforcement of policies takes place in a *flavoring*

Figure 11. Sample SOAP request for the shipping service

```
- <soap:Envelope xmlns:soap="http://www.w3.org/2003/05/soap-envelope"
    soap:encodingStyle="http://www.w3.org/2001/12/soap-encoding">
- <soap:Header>
    xmlns:p="http://fictitious.com/servicepricing"
    soap:role="http://fictitious.com/role/policyEnforcement" soap:mustUnderstand="true">
- <consumer:ConsumerProfile xmlns:consumer="http://fictitious.com/consumerprofile"
    xmlns:common="http://fictitious.com/common"
    soap:role="http://fictitious.com/role/policyEnforcement" soap:mustUnderstand="true">
    <consumer:reference scheme="UUID">00300571-cecb-1dec-978d-
      559058888227</consumer:reference>
    <consumer:FormattedName>Generic Co.</consumer:FormattedName>
    <common:accessTime>2008-03-29T13:20:00.000</common:accessTime>
- <common:Location>
    <common:Country>US</common:Country>
  </common:Location>
  </consumer:ConsumerProfile>
- <p:Pricing xmlns:p="http://fictitious.com/Pricing"
    xmlns:common="http://fictitious.com/common"
    soap:role="http://fictitious.com/role/policyEnforcement" soap:mustUnderstand="true">
    <p:priceType>regular</p:priceType>
    <p:chargingStyle>subscription</p:chargingStyle>
  </p:Pricing>
  </soap:Header>
  <soap:Body>..</soap:Body>
  </soap:Envelope>
```

Figure 12. Flavoring intermediary to enforce flavoring service policies

phase (a user-defined phase in Axis2) that invokes the flavoring handlers. Figure 13 describes the flavoring phase and the associated handlers packaged in a flavoring module.

We also have a Consumer Profiling Handler (CPH), which is configured to be the first handler that gets invoked in the flavoring phase. The CPH deals with profiling the consumer and associating the consumer with a consumer segment. The consumer segment information may be useful for other flavoring handlers to enforce their specific policies. In our example (Figure 11), the Pricing Handler would need to know the consumer segment to apply the *Subscription Pricing Policy*. We use the Axis 2 *MessageContext* to share the consumer segment information from the CPH with the other handlers. In our example, the header elements *ConsumerProfile* and *Pricing*

are handled by CPH and Pricing Handler respectively.

When a new flavoring aspect is needed, a new instance of a policy domain is added in the policy model and a corresponding flavoring handler is generated and automatically added to the end of the flavoring phase. Since the policies are based on domain-independent assertions the semantics of any policy could be understood by a generic processing logic (a standard XACML policy processor).

6 RELATED WORK

Service Flavors presents a strategy to differentiate services in the service marketplace from the perspective of the provider. The closest related work is the Web Services Offering Language

Figure 13. The flavoring module with flavoring phase and flavoring handlers in Axis2

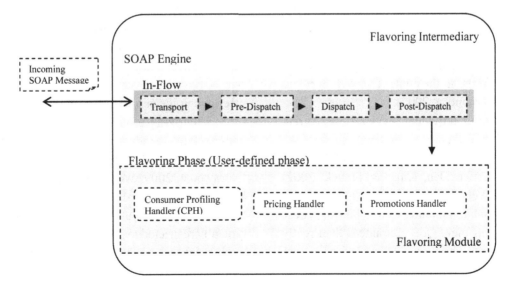

(WSOL) (Tosic, Patel, & Pagurek, 2002). The WSOL presents the concept of 'class of service' which relates to our discrete service variation, the service flavor. The WSOL specification presents a WSDL1.1-compatible XML language to describe a service offering which is a class of a web service. The class of service concept could be used to differentiate services. An important thing to note is that WSOL is not specifically intended for differentiating services, but is designed to support management of services, expressing constraints (pre-, post-conditions) etc.

In comparison, Service Flavors is a complete strategy and not just a language like WSOL. It supports the entire life-cycle from early-stage identification, definition and documentation of differentiating (flavoring) aspects as well as the vocabulary items associated with them. The service flavors approach is also open-standards compliant, whereas the WSOL is not an approved standard. Service Flavors use open-standards such as WS-Policy, WS-PolicyAttachment and WS-PolicyConstraints which have industry backing to define discrete variations of a service. The service flavors approach also prescribes a model-driven approach to create discrete variations of a service. Our approach also uses standard SOAP header extensions to specify terms of offer during service invocation. This is common practice in domain-dependent specifications such as WS-RM, WS-Trust, WS-Security etc. Others have also used SOAP headers to specify non-functional properties in the context of Grid Services (Foster et al., 2005) and in the in the context of Web Services (Ortiz, & Hernandez, 2007).

For defining individual Service-Level Agreements (SLAs), there are languages such as the IBM's Web Service-Level Agreement (WSLA) (Ludwig, Keller, Dan, King, & Franck, 2002) and HP's Webservice Management Language (WSML) (Sahai, Durante, & Machiraju). These SLAs support mere QoS guarantees than really define discrete variations. These languages are mature, high-quality and proven, but inherently lack the capability to express discrete service variations as they were not meant for flavoring. WS-QoS (Tian, 2005) is a QoS specification language which has a notion of *class of service*; however it is more centered on network-level QoS and is not useful to flavor services.

The flavoring aspects such as pricing, availability etc. are essentially non-functional properties of services. O'Sullivan et al. (2002) has done extensive work on non-functional properties in service description; O'Sullivan, Edmond, and Ter Hofstede (2005) also presents formal syntax of service properties. Though some of our non-functional aspects are inspired from this work, our focus is a subset influencing flavoring of a service.

A striking feature of these flavoring aspects is that they represent crosscutting service-level concerns from the perspective of the service provider. Aspect-Oriented Software Development (AOSD) (Filman, Elrad, Clarke, & Aksit 2005) offers an elegant way to handle cross-cutting concerns in software development by modularizing these concerns as aspects. The flavoring aspects represent crosscutting concerns such as availability, quality of service, pricing and promotions which are largely service-level provider concerns. There could be other crosscutting concerns in services development such as domain-level concerns, technical middleware concerns, service realization concerns (implementation and composition concerns) which are not addressed by flavoring aspects. The focus of flavoring aspects is to create service flavors and support differentiating service offerings in the services marketplace.

Modularizing cross-cutting concerns is also addressed in the industry through Business Rules in the context of business process management (Narayanan, 2009; WebSphere, 2008). Business Rules are conceptually similar to Aspects—in the AOSD sense—but the use case scenarios are typically restricted to process management i.e. to modularize the changes in a process implementation so that a change in a business rule does not change the process. In contrast flavoring aspects typically capture service properties based on the *attractiveness of terms of offer* criterion.

7 CONCLUSION AND FUTURE WORK

In this article, we presented a strategy to support unintrusive differentiation of services in a service marketplace. We identified terms of offer of a service to be the changing part in a service description in the context of differentiation. The terms of offer was represented by the non-functional aspects which we identified as flavoring aspects. These flavoring aspects were expressed as service policies defined by the domain expert using a service policy metamodel. These flavoring service policies were enforced by a flavoring SOAP intermediary acting as a policy enforcement point. By adopting the service flavors strategy, a service provider can unintrusively differentiate his services from that of competing services in the marketplace. The service flavors strategy could also be effectively employed to target specific customer segments. It could also be used to provide services to business partners or consumers based on custom SLAs. The future work would involve the following:

- Understanding the dependency of one flavoring aspect on another (e.g. impact of promotions over pricing) and providing a way to specify this dependency.
- Developing MOF2 to Text Language (MTL) based templates for converting policy models to open-standard specifications.
- In addition to using service flavoring to differentiate services, providers could also package service offerings with other related services to augment their value and convenience of use. The related services could be either from them or from their business partners. For example, the *Ship*

Item service could be packaged with a free *Shipment Pickup* service, which picks up shipment from the premises of the customer to create a Service Bundle. In our future work, we would enhance the service flavoring strategy with the service bundling strategy to support service differentiation.

REFERENCES

Anderson, A., & Balasubramanian, D. (2005). *XACML-Based Web Services Policy Constraint Language (WS-PolicyConstraints)*. Santa Clara, CA: Sun Microsystems.

Anderson, A. H. (2004). An introduction to the Web Services Policy Language (WSPL). In *Proceedings of the Fifth IEEE International Workshop on Policies for Distributed Systems and Networks: POLICY 2004* (pp. 189-192).

Anderson, S., Bohren, J., Boubez, T., Chanliau, M., Della-Libera, G., Dixon, B., et al. (2005). *Web Services Trust Language (WS-Trust)*. IBM.

Atkinson, B., Della-Libera, G., Hada, S., Hondo, M., Hallam-Baker, P., Klein, J., et al. (2002). *Web Services Security (WS-Security). Version, 1*. IBM.

Bajaj, S., Box, D., Chappell, D., Curbera, F., Daniels, G., Hallam-Baker, P., et al. (2004). *Web Services Policy Framework (WS-Policy)*. Retrieved from http://www-106.ibm.com/developerworks/library/specification/ws-polfram

Bajaj, S., Box, D., Chappell, D., Curbera, F., Daniels, G., Hallam-Baker, P., et al. (2006). *Web Services Policy Attachment (WS-PolicyAttachment)*. Retrieved from http://msdn.microsoft.com/webservices/default.aspx

Bilorusets, R., Bosworth, A., & Box, B. D. (2004). *Web Services Reliable Messaging Protocol (WS-ReliableMessaging)*. IBM.

Chinnici, R., Gudgin, M., Moreau, J. J., Schlimmer, J., & Weerawarana, S. (2004). Web Services Description Language (WSDL) Version 2.0 Part 1: Core Language. *W3C Working Draft, 3*.

Damodaran, S. (2004). B2B integration over the Internet with XML: RosettaNet successes and challenges. In *Proceedings of the 13th International World Wide Web Conference, Alternate Track Papers & Posters* (pp. 188-195).

Dobson, G., Lock, R., & Sommerville, I. (2005). QoSOnt: A QoS Ontology for Service-Centric Systems. In *Proceedings of the 31st EUROMICRO Conference on Software Engineering and Advanced Applications 2005* (pp. 80-87).

Fallside, D. C. (2000). *XML Schema Part 0: Primer (W3C Candidate Recommendation CR-xmlschema-0-20001024)* World Wide Web Consortium (W3C).

Fasbinder, M. (2008). *WebSphere Process Server business rules lifecycle*. IBM DeveloperWorks.

Filman, R. E., Elrad, T., Clarke, S., & Aksit, M. (2005). *Aspect-oriented software development*. Reading, MA: Addison-Wesley.

Foster, I., Czajkowski, K., Ferguson, D. E., Frey, J., Graham, S., & Maguire, T. (2005). Modeling and managing state in distributed systems: The role of OGSI and WSRF. *Proceedings of the IEEE, 93*(3), 604–661. doi:10.1109/JPROC.2004.842766

Godik, S., & Moses, T. (2003). *eXtensible Access Control Markup Language (XACML) Version 1.0*. OASIS.

Harshavardhan Jegadeesan, S. B. (2008). A MOF2-based Services Metamodel. *Journal of Object Technology*.

Hofreiter, B., Huemer, C., & Naujok, K. D. (2004). UN/CEFACT's business collaboration framework-motivation and basic concepts. In *Proceedings of MKWI* (pp. 4).

Kotok, A. (2001). *Ebxml: The new global standard for doing business over the internet*. New York: New Riders Publishing.

Ludwig, H., Keller, A., Dan, A., King, R. P., & Franck, R. (2002). *Web Service Level Agreement (WSLA) Language Specification*. IBM.

Maximilien, E. M., & Singh, M. P. (2002). Conceptual model of web service reputation. *SIGMOD Record, 31*(4), 36–41. doi:10.1145/637411.637417

Meadows, B., & Seaburg, L. (2004). *Universal Business Language 1.0*. OASIS.

Mitra, N. (2003). SOAP Version 1.2 Part 0: Primer. *W3C Recommendation, 24*.

Narayanan, R. (2009). Business rules change all the time, but your applications don't have to. *SAP Insider, 10*(2).

Noy, N. F., & McGuinness, D. L. (2001). *Ontology development 101: A guide to creating your first ontology* (Tech. Rep. KSL-01-05 and SMI-2001, 880). Palo Alto, CA: Stanford Knowledge Systems Laboratory Stanford Medical Informatics.

O'Sullivan, J., Edmond, D., & Ter Hofstede, A. (2002). What's in a service? Towards accurate description of non-functional service properties. *Distributed and Parallel Databases, 12*(2), 117–133. doi:10.1023/A:1016547000822

O'Sullivan, J., Edmond, D., & ter Hofstede, A. H. M. (2005). *Formal description of non-functional service properties*. WSMO Working Group.

OASIS. (2005). Reference Model TC (OASIS Reference Model for Service Oriented Architectures Working Draft 10).

Oldevik, J., Neple, T., Grønmo, R., Aagedal, J., & Berre, A. J. (2005). Toward Standardised Model to Text Transformations. In *Proceedings of the Model Driven Architecture-Foundations and Applications, First European Conference (ECMDA-FA 2005)*, Nuremberg, Germany (LNCS 3748, pp. 239-253).

OMG. (2006). *Meta Object Facility (MOF) Core Specification Version 2.0.* Needham, MA: Author.

OMG. (2007). *UML 2.0 Infrastructure Specification.* Needham, MA: Author.

Ortiz, G., & Hernandez, J. (2007, May 13-19). A case study on integrating extra-functional properties in web service model-driven development. In *Proceedings of the Second International Conference on Internet and Web Applications and Services, 2007 (ICIW '07)* (pp. 35-35).

Papazoglou, M. P., & Georgakopoulos, D. (2003). Service-oriented computing. *Communications of the ACM, 46*(10), 25–28. doi:10.1145/944217.944233

Perera, S., Herath, C., Ekanayake, J., Chinthaka, E., Ranabahu, A., & Jayasinghe, D. (2006). Axis2, middleware for next generation web services. In *Proceedings of ICWS, 2006,* 833–840.

Press, I. O. S. (2003). Electronic government-design, applications, and management, by å Grönlund. *Information Polity, 8*(3), 193–199.

Sahai, A., Durante, A., & Machiraju, V. (2001). *Towards automated SLA management for web services.* (Tech. Rep. HPL-2001-310 R. 1). Palo Alto, CA: Hewlett Packard.

Smith, M. K., Welty, C., & McGuinness, D. L. (2004). OWL Web Ontology Language Guide. *W3C Recommendation, 10.*

Tian, M. (2005). *QoS integration in Web services with the WS-QoS framework.* Berlin, Germany: Department of Mathematics and Computer Science, Freie Universität.

Toma, I., Roman, D., & Fensel, D. (2007). On describing and ranking services based on non-functional properties. *NWESP,* 61-66.

Tosic, V., Patel, K., & Pagurek, B. (2002, May 27-28). *WSOL-Web Service Offerings Language.* Paper presented at International Workshop on Web Services, E-Business, and the Semantic Web: CAiSE 2002, WES 2002, Toronto, Canada.

Yendluri, P., & Yalçinalp, Ü. (2007). *Web Services Policy 1.5-Guidelines for Policy Assertion Authors.* W3C.

ENDNOTE

[1]   All services and scenarios described in the paper are fictitious.

This work was previously published in the International Journal of Web Services Research, Volume 7, Issue 1, edited by Liang-Jie (LJ) Zhang, pp. 22-45, copyright 2010 by IGI Publishing (an imprint of IGI Global).

Section 3
Quality of Services (QoS)

Chapter 9
Flexible Probabilistic QoS Management of Orchestrations

Sidney Rosario
INRIA Centre Rennes Bretagne Atlantique, France

Albert Benveniste
INRIA Centre Rennes Bretagne Atlantique, France

Claude Jard
ENS Cachan Bretagne, IRISA, Bruz, France

ABSTRACT

In this paper, the authors develop a comprehensive framework for QoS management based on soft probabilistic contracts. The authors approach also encompasses general QoS parameters, with "response time" as a particular case. In addition, the authors support composite QoS parameters, for example, combining timing aspects with "quality of data" or security level. They also study contract composition (how to derive QoS contracts for an orchestration from the QoS contracts with its called services), and contract monitoring.

INTRODUCTION

Web services and their orchestrations are now considered an infrastructure of choice for managing business processes and workflow activities over the Web infrastructure (van der Aalst, 2002). BPEL (WSBPEL, 2007) has become the industrial standard for specifying orchestrations. Besides BPEL, the Orc formalism has been proposed to specify orchestrations, by W. Cook and J. Misra at Austin (Misra, 2007) (Kitchin, 2009). Orc is a

simple and clean academic language for orchestrations with a rigorous mathematical semantics. For this reason, our study in this paper relies on Orc. Its conclusions and approaches, however, are also applicable to BPEL.

When dealing with the management of QoS, the commitments of each subcontractor with regard to the orchestration are specified via contracts in the form of Service Level Agreements, SLA (Bohj, 2001). Most SLAs commonly tend to have QoS parameters which are mild variations of the following: response time (latency); availability; maximum allowed query rate (throughput); and

DOI: 10.4018/978-1-4666-1942-5.ch009

security (Keller, 2003). From QoS contracts with sub-contractors, the overall QoS contract between orchestration and its clients can be established. This process is called contract composition. Then, since contracts cannot only rely on trusting the sub-contractors, monitoring techniques must be developed for the orchestrator to be able to detect possible violation of a contract, by a sub-contractor. Finally, upon contract violation, the orchestrator may consider reconfiguration, i.e., replacing some called services by alternative, "equivalent" ones — we do not address this last task here.

To the best of our knowledge, with the noticeable exception of (Liu, 2001) and (Hwang, 2007), all composition studies consider performance related QoS parameters of contracts in the form of hard bounds. For instance, response times and query throughput are required to be less than a certain fixed value and validity of answers to queries must be guaranteed at all times. When composing contracts, hard composition rules are used. Typical examples are addition or maximum (for response times), or conjunction (for validity of answers to queries). Whereas this results in elegant and simple composition rules, this general approach by using hard bounds does not fit the reality well and may lead to over pessimistic promises. Indeed, real measurements of response times for existing Web services reveal that they vary a lot and are better represented through their histogram. Thus we have proposed in (Rosario, 2008) using soft probabilistic contracts instead. In such contracts, hard bounds are replaced by probabilistic obligations, i.e., a QoS parameter is considered probabilistic and a distribution probability is agreed for it. The obligation is that the called service should behave "no worse" than this agreed distribution regarding this QoS parameter, in a sense that we formalize in this paper.

Adopting a probabilistic approach for QoS has many advantages, but also raises some issues when performing contract composition and contract monitoring. Analytical solutions for deriving the distribution of the composition from the distribution of its components exist for simple cases where the control flow of the composition is not affected by the data values of the queries and their responses, and other timing issues. Queuing network techniques can be used in simple cases like this. More sophisticated stochastic Petri nets can also be used, but they require restricting to exponential distributions. These elegant analytical approaches, however, are not applicable in general to services orchestrations where responses to queries and timing (via timeouts) interfere with the control flow – The CarOnLine example in the next section is an instance of this. We thus need to develop new techniques to perform contract composition and contract monitoring, adapted to probabilistic contracts.

Contributions: In this paper we extend and systematize the approach of (Rosario, 2008) and (Bouillard, 2009) by extending it beyond the case of soft probabilistic contracts for Response Time.

Our first contribution consists in proposing a comprehensive approach for Soft Probabilistic QoS Contracts encompassing a large class of QoS parameters taking values in partially ordered domains, together with means to build composite QoS parameters and contracts and reason about them.

A second contribution consists in a procedure to perform flexible contract composition, which consists in relating the obligations binding the pair {client, orchestration}, to the obligations binding the different pairs {orchestration, called service}.

A third (minor) contribution consists in the extension of the technique proposed in (Rosario, 2008) for contract monitoring to our generalized case. This extension turns out to be straightforward, as we shall see.

Last but not least, we discuss languages features that are useful in making our approach effective. Not surprisingly, QoS domains must be declared along with their characteristics allowing to perform contract composition. We also found it very useful to introduce a language feature that is generic with respect to the various QoS domains and performs a filtering of responses from called services or from pools thereof, according to best QoS performance. We illustrate this with the Orc language.

Our whole approach is supported by the TOrQuE tool (Tool for Orchestration Quality of Service Evaluation), from which experimental results for contract composition are derived.

Organization of the paper: Our study is illustrated by the "CarOnLine" example that we present in the next section. Based on this example, we discuss in particular why QoS domains should be partially, not totally, ordered. Then we develop our general framework for flexible QoS management, including the procedure for contract composition. Experiments are reported in the last section. An appendix gathers the complete formal model.

OUR APPROACH

In this section we outline our approach. Corresponding key elements are detailed in subsequent sections. To motivate our approach we first discuss a representative case of an orchestration, the CarOnLine example.

The "CarOnLine" Motivating Example

The CarOnLine example is shown in Figure 1. In search for a car, a client calls the CarOnLine orchestration with a car type — small car, family car, SUV, etc — as the input. The orchestration calls two garages, GarageA and GarageB, in parallel, with the client's car type as an input parameter. The garages respond with their price quote for that car and best offer is selected. The calls to the garages are guarded by a Timeout. If only one garage has responded when a timeout occurs, its response is taken as the best offer and any eventual response of the other garage is simply ignored. If no garage

responds before timeout, then a Fault message is returned to the client, indicating an exception.

After selecting the best offer for the car, CarOnLine finds insurance and credit offers for this car. For credit offers, two services AllCredit and AllCreditPlus are called in parallel and the offer having the best (lowest) interest rate is chosen. The insurance services called depend on the type of car which needs to be insured. If the car requested by the client is of some "deluxe" category, then only one service — GoldInsure — can offer insurance for such cars, and any offer made by it is taken. If the car is not a "deluxe" car, then two services, InsureAll and InsurePlus are called in parallel and the best insurance, i.e., the one that costs the least amongst the two offers, is selected. In the end, the tuple (price, credit, insurance) is returned to the client.

In this example, we regard the tuple (time, price, credit, insurance) as a composite QoS parameter for optimization by the orchestration. The usual practice in dealing with composite parameters consists in synthesizing a single parameter by combining their components using, e.g., linear combination with user selected weights, see (Zeng, 2004) for typical examples. We think that this makes little sense in most cases including the present one. Thus we prefer keeping the different QoS parameters as such and order them individually. As a consequence, the composite parameter can be only partially, not totally, ordered.

A formal description of CarOnLine using the Orc language is given in Figure 2. Orc offers three primitive operators, see (Misra, 2007) and (Kitchin, 2009) for details. For Orc expressions f, g, expression "f | g" executes f and g in parallel. Expression "f >x> g" evaluates f first and for every value returned by f, a new instance of g is launched with variable x assigned to this return value; in particular, "f >> g" (which is a special case of the former where returned values are not assigned to any variable) causes every value returned by f to create a new instance of g. Expression "f **where** x:∈ g" executes f and g in parallel. When g returns

Figure 1. Schematic representation of the CarOnLine example

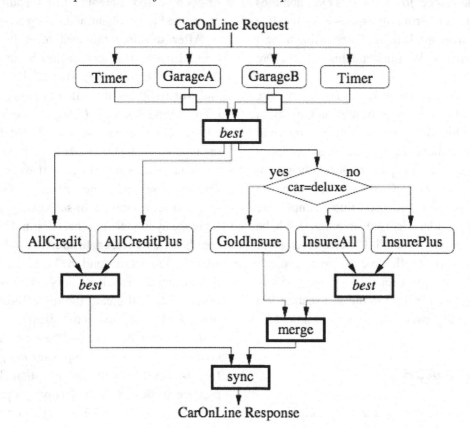

its first value, x is assigned to this value and the computation of g is terminated. All site calls in f having x as a parameter are blocked until x is defined (i.e., until g returns its first value).

The operator $:\in_Q$ is a new operator *introduced for our QoS studies, where Q is the (static) parameter of this operator. Q is a QoS parameter whose domain is a partially ordered set $(D_Q, \leq)$* that is an upper and lower lattice. By convention, "best" will refer to a minimal element among a set. The expression "f**where** $x :\in_Q g$" does not take the first value returned by g as x. Instead it waits for a "best quality" response among all responses from g to that call, irrespective of the time taken to generate them — since the domain of Q is only partially ordered in general, a best response may not be unique, so nondeterministic choice is performed in this case. Observe that: $\in$

is a particular case of $:\in_Q$ by taking for Q the latency or response time of the call — in this case it is not needed to wait for all the responses from g to get the best one, since the first one received will, by definition, be the best.

Summary of Our Approach for QoS Management

Our objective is to develop the needed framework and tools to support the following tasks in QoS management:

- **Task 1:** To give a QoS-enhanced description of the orchestration: this is best illustrated by the Orc specification of the CarOnLine example in Figure 2. QoS parameters are declared together with their

Figure 2. CarOnLine in Orc. We show in red the add-ons to Orc to handle QoS

Assumptions QoS parameters :
δ : inter-query time, $D_\delta = \mathbb{R}_+$
Guarantees QoS parameters :
d : latency, $D_d = \mathbb{R}_+$
p : car price, $D_p = \mathbb{R}_+$
i : insurance costs, $D_i = \mathbb{R}_+$
c : credit rate, $D_c = \mathbb{R}_+$

$$CarOnLine(car) \;\triangle\; CarPrice(car) \;>p>\; \mathbf{let}(p, c, i)$$
$$\mathbf{where} \quad c :\in_d GetCredit(p)$$
$$i :\in_d GetInsur(p, car)$$

$$Best_Q(E_1, \ldots, E_n) \;\triangle\; \mathbf{let}(a) \;\; \mathbf{where}\; a :\in_Q \{E_1 \mid E_2 \ldots \mid E_n\}$$

$$CarPrice(car) \;\triangle\; \{\; Best_{(\ell, p)}($$
$$Best_d(GarageA[d, p](car), RTimer[d](T)),$$
$$Best_d(GarageB[d, p](car), RTimer[d](T))$$
$$)\}$$
$$>p>\; \{\; \mathbf{if}(p \neq Fault)) \gg \mathbf{let}(p)\; \}$$

$$GetCredit(p) \;\triangle\; Best_c(AllCredit[d, c](p), AllCreditPlus[d, c](p))$$

$$GetInsur(p, car) \;\triangle\; \{\; \mathbf{if}(car = deluxe) \gg GoldInsure[d, i](p)\} \mid$$
$$\{\; \mathbf{if}(car \neq deluxe) \gg$$
$$Best_i(InsurePlus[d, i](p), InsureAll[d, i](p))$$
$$\}$$

type. The Orc expressions describe how the services are orchestrated. Special operators related to QoS are provided. Such a specification should allow for complex interactions between control, response values of the services called, and values of the QoS parameters. For example, in CarOnLine the QoS parameter tuple {latency, price, credit, insurance} interacts with the value of parameter "car".

- **Task 2:** To specify probabilistic contracts with explicit obligations of the different actors: A contract usually involves two parties and consists of assumptions and guarantees: provided that one party (the client) respects certain assumptions, it is assured certain guarantees from the other party

(the provider). For example, the orchestration is a client of the services it calls, and a provider of a service to its own clients. We thus have a contract binding each called service to the orchestration, and a contract binding the orchestration to its client. For the first type of contract, the guarantee involves the QoS of the called services, and for the second type of contract, the guarantee involves the overall QoS of the orchestration. Now, to account for the high variability in performance of Web services, we consider the QoS parameters to be random. So the guarantee part of a contract specifies a worst case probability distribution for the different QoS parameters affected by the service.[1]

- **Task 3:** To model how QoS parameters evolve while the query is processed: As an example consider the QoS parameter latency for CarOnLine. By observing how the query travels through the orchestration and knowing the latency of the service calls, we can use max-plus algebraic rules to derive the orchestration's end-to-end latency for that query. We need to develop a similar algebra and the associated operations for generic QoS parameters, which model how the QoS parameters of a query evolve while being processed by the orchestration. Moreover, the treatment of the QoS parameters for assumptions and guarantees differ. Guarantee QoS parameters (like latency) are associated with individual queries but assumptions (like inter-query time) are derived from a flow of queries). This task is addressed in detail in the section on "QoS Computing".

- **Task 4:** To perform Monte-Carlo simulations for contract composition: We need a procedure to derive the probabilistic contract between the orchestration and its clients from the probabilistic contracts agreed between the orchestration and the services it calls. As mentioned in the introduction, the analytical techniques for composing probability distributions are not applicable to generic orchestrations where control, data and time may interfere in possibly complex ways. In this case, Monte-Carlo simulation techniques are a powerful alternative. They rely on the mathematically sound basis of statistical inference and law of large numbers. In such simulations, the computations mentioned in Task 3 are repeated sufficiently, to derive an empirical estimate of the probability distribution for the overall QoS of the orchestration. This technique is developed in detail in the section on "Probabilistic Contract Composition".

- **Task 5:** To monitor probabilistic contracts: We must monitor, on-line, whether the services called by the orchestration actually meet the agreed probabilistic contract. The techniques for monitoring probabilistic contracts must be based on statistical testing procedures. We treat this task in the section on "Probabilistic Contract Monitoring".

The next two sections are devoted to the study of the Tasks 3 and 4 mentioned above.

QoS COMPUTING

In this section we review the algebra needed for reasoning about the evolution of QoS parameters. Since the treatment of the guarantee QoS parameters differ from that of the assumption QoS parameters, we consider each case separately.

QoS Domains and the Algebra of QoS Computing for Guarantee Parameters

Our discussion on the evolution of the guarantee QoS parameters involves an abstract toy orchestration example, with no concrete meaning attached to it. The example uses Petri net unfoldings or occurrence nets to model the executions of the orchestration seen as a concurrent system.[2] Corresponding formal material is developed in the Appendix.

An input query to the orchestration is represented by a set of (initial) input tokens, and the processing of the query is modeled by the flow of the tokens in the net. We attach the guarantee QoS parameters to the tokens to model how these parameters evolve when the query is processed. The tokens are thus equipped with a color consisting of a pair

$$(v,q) = (\text{data}, \text{QoS value})$$

Figure 3 depicts our toy example. In this figure, pre- and post-sets of a transition t are denoted by $^{\bullet}t$ *and* $t^{\bullet}$ respectively. The following rules are sufficient to describe the evolution of the QoS parameters of a query while being processed by the orchestration:

QoS increments are captured by $\oplus$: When traversing a transition, each token gets its QoS value incremented. For example, the left most token has initial QoS value q_0, *which gets incremented as* $q_1 = q_0 \oplus \delta q_1$ *when traversing* t_1.

Synchronizing tokens: A transition t is enabled when all places in its preset have tokens. For the transition to fire, these tokens must synchronize, which results in the "worst" QoS value, denoted by supremum $\vee$ associated to a given order $\leq$, where smaller means better. For example, when the two input tokens of t_2 *get synchronized, the resulting synchronized pair has QoS value* $q_0'' \vee q_1$. This is depicted on Figure 3 with this QoS value attached to the shaded area.

Dealing with conflicts, competition policy: Let us first focus on the conflict following place q_0'. *The QoS alters the usual semantics of the conflict by using a competition policy that is reminiscent of the classical race policy (Marsan, 1989). The*

competition between the two conflicting transitions in the post-set is solved by using order $\leq$ also used for token synchronization: test whether $q_1' \leq q_1''$ holds for the resulting QoS values, or the converse. Any smallest among the two can win the competition — nondeterministic choice can thus occur, in particular when the alternatives are not comparable.

However, comparing $q_1' = q_0' \oplus \delta q_1'$ and $q_1'' = q_0' \oplus \delta q_1''$ generally requires knowing the two alternatives, which in general can affect the QoS of the winner. This is taken into account by introducing a special operator "$\lhd$": If two transitions t and t' are in competition and would yield tokens with respective QoS values q and q' in their post-sets, the cost of comparing them to set the competition alters the QoS value of the winner in that — assuming the first wins — q is modified and becomes q'. For the case of the figure, we get

$$
\begin{aligned}
&if\ q_0' \oplus \delta q_1' \leq q_0' \oplus \delta q_1'',\ then\ t_1'\ fires\ and\\
&\qquad q_1' = \left(q_0' \oplus \delta q_1' \right) \lhd \left(q_0' \oplus \delta q_1'' \right)\\
&if\ q_0' \oplus \delta q_1' \geq q_0' \oplus \delta q_1'',\ then\ t_1''\ fires\ and\\
&\qquad q_1'' = \left(q_0' \oplus \delta q_1'' \right) \lhd \left(q_0' \oplus \delta q_1' \right)
\end{aligned}
\tag{1}
$$

Figure 3. A simple example. Only QoS values are mentioned — with no data. Each place comes labeled with a QoS value q which is the q-color of the token if it reaches that place.

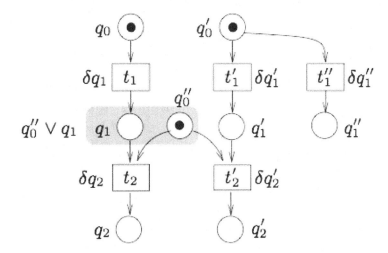

Now, another conflict may occur between t_2 and t_2'. Now, if t_1'' actually wins the first competition, then t_2' will never be enabled and this second potential conflict does not occur. In this case, t_2 fires and we get $q_2 = (q_o'' \vee q_1) \oplus \delta q_2$. The other case is handled in a way similar to (1).

We now instantiate our generic famework by reviewing some examples of QoS domains, with their associated relations and operators $\oplus$, $\leq$, and $\lhd$. *It is kindly suggested that the reader re-scans the above items, for each instance:*

Latency or Response Time: QoS value of a token gives the accumulated latency d, or "age" of the token since it was created when querying the orchestration. Corresponding QoS domain is R_+, *equipped with* $\oplus_d = +$, and $\leq_d =$ the usual order on R_+. Regarding operator, for the case of latency with race policy, comparing two dates via does not impact the QoS of the winner: answer to this predicate is known as soon as one of the two events is seen, i.e., at time $\min(d_1; d_2)$. Hence, for this case, we take $d_1 \ d_2 = d_1$, i.e., d_2 does not affect d_1. This is the basic example, which was studied in (Bouillard, 2009).

Security level: QoS value s of a token belongs to ({high, low}, $\leq_s$), *with high* $\leq_s$ low. Each transition has a security level encoded in the same way, and we take $\oplus_s = \vee_s$, reflecting that a low security service processing a high security data yields a low security response. Regarding operator $\lhd_s$, again, comparing two values via $s_1 \leq_s s_2$ does not impact the QoS of the winner: QoS values are strictly "owned" by the tokens, and therefore do not interfere when comparing them. Hence, we take again $s_1 \lhd_s s_2 = s_1$, i.e., s_2 does not affect s_1. More generally, Quality of Response, which has several instances in the CarOnLine example, is handled in the same way as security level, by using various domains.

Composite QoS, first example: we may also consider a composite QoS parameter consisting of the pair (s,r), where s is as above and r is some

Quality of Response with domain D_r, *equipped with* $\leq_r$ and $\lhd_r$. Since the two components s and r are similar in nature, we simply take $\leq = \leq_s \times \leq_r$ and $\lhd = (\lhd_s, \lhd_r)$.

Composite QoS, second example, illustrating operator $\lhd$: So far the special operator $\lhd$ did not play *any role. We will need it, however, for the coming case. Consider a composite QoS parameter (s,d), where s and d are as above, and priority is given to security s. Accordingly, we take $\leq$ to be the lexicographic order obtained from the pair* $(\leq_s, \leq_d)$ *by giving priority to s.*

Focus on operator $\lhd$. *Consider the marking resulting after firing t_1 and t_1' in Figure 3, enabling transitions t_2 and t_2', which are in conflict. Now, suppose that the QoS value $q_2 = (q_o'' \vee q_1) \oplus \delta q_2$ of the token in postset of t_2 is equal to $q_2 = (low, d_2)$. Similarly, suppose that the QoS value $q_2' = (q_o'' \vee q_1) \oplus \delta q_2'$ of the token in postset of t_2' is equal to $q_2' = (low, d_2')$, where $d_2' >_d d_2$. From the competition rule, transition t_2 wins the conflict and the outgoing token has QoS value $q_2 = (low, d_2)$.*

However, the decision to select t_2 *can only be made when q_2' is known, that is, at time d_2'*. The reason for this is that, since at time d_2 a token with security level low is seen at place following t_2, it might happen that a token with security level high later enters place following t_2'. The latter would win the conflict according to our competition policy – security level prevails. Observing that the right most token indeed has priority level low can only be seen at time d_2'. Thus it makes little sense assigning $q_2 = (low, d_2)$ to the outgoing token; it should rather be $q_2 = (low, d_2')$.

This is why a non-trivial operator $\lhd$ *is needed, namely, writing* $\leq$ *for short instead of* $\leq_d$:

$$(s,d) \lhd (s',d') = (s, \max(d,d')) \qquad (2)$$

QoS Domains and the Algebra of QoS Computing for Assumptions

We now look at the case of assumption QoS parameters. Unlike the guarantee parameters which are attached to the individual tokens, the assumption parameters values are derived from a stream of tokens.

A typical example of an assumption parameter is the client's inter-query rate (or throughput) [3] that we develop next. Again, because of the complex interactions between control, response values of the services called, and values of the QoS parameters, it is not possible in general to relate directly the query throughput at the orchestration, to the query throughput for each service called by the orchestration. To overcome this, we will handle instead the delay α *between two successive queries to a service – actually, query throughput is equal to the inverse of the average of delay α*.

Referring to the the example of Figure 3, evaluation of α *is performed as follows. In the following analysis, dates will be generically denoted by symbol d*. Let d and $^\bullet d$ denote the date of the current query and previous query to the orchestration. The three initial tokens shown in Figure 3 are available at date d, and their previous occurrences were available at date $^\bullet d$. On the other hand, we have $\alpha = d - {}^\bullet d$. Depending on choices occurring in places q_0' and q_0'', different transitions can fire. As an example, consider the case where t_1, t_2 and t_1'' fire when the considered three tokens associated to the query are processed by the orchestration. Denote by α_1, α_2 and α_1'' the corresponding values for the delay between two successive calls to the services represented by transitions t_1, t_2 and t_1''. Then, we have $\alpha_1 = d_1 - {}^\bullet d_1$ and similarly for the other cases. Observe that the "previous" operator represented by the prefixing bullet is local to each considered transition, since not all transitions are fired when a query is processed by the orchestration. To summarize, by running the orchestration, it is possible to get the dates of the different service calls when processing this query. By storing current and previous dates of each service call, the values of the delay between successive queries of each service can be inferred.

PROBABILISTIC CONTRACTS AND THEIR COMPOSITION

In this section we first study QoS contracts in a probabilistic setting, that is, contracts when QoS parameters are considered random. We then study contract composition, i.e., the process by which the orchestration can derive the contract it can offer to its clients from the contracts agreed with the services it calls.

Probabilistic Contracts

Since we decided to consider QoS parameters as random, we can specify them via their cumulative distribution function (or distribution function for short), defined by $F_Q(x) = \mathbf{P}(Q \leq x)$, *where x ranges over all possible values of the domain of parameter Q. This notion is classical for the case where the domain of QoS parameter Q can be totally ordered. We can still use it when the domain of Q is only partially, not totally, ordered. The reason is that the family of sets of trials* $\{\omega \mid Q(\omega) \leq x\}$, *where x ranges over all possible values of the domain of Q, is still rich enough to fully specify the probabilistic behavior of Q.*

Probabilistic contract: Formally, a probabilistic contract is thus a pair

$$\left(F_A, F_Q\right)$$

of distribution functions, representing the assumed distribution for the random assumption A and the guaranteed distribution for the random QoS parameter Q.

What "better" means: When dealing with performance related contracts (such as QoS contracts), it is expected that it is valid, for an actor, to perform better than specified in the agreed contract. At this point it is worth formalizing what it means for a called site to perform better under our probabilistic setting, i.e., when QoS parameters are considered random. To this end, we shall use the notion of stochastic (partial) ordering $\geq_S$, *induced by partial order* $\leq$ defined on a domain D (Kamae, 1977). Recall that, for Q a random QoS parameter taking its values in partially ordered domain $(D, \leq)$, $F(x) = \mathbf{P}(Q \leq x)$ denotes its distribution function, where x ranges over all possible values of the domain D of Q. For F and F' two different distribution functions for Q, say that $F' \leq_S F$ (we say that F' is stochastically smaller than F) if $F'(x) \geq F(x)$ holds for all possible values x in domain D – note the opposite directions of the inequalities. Using stochastic ordering, say that that a called service performs better regarding its QoS parameter Q if its actual distribution function F' is stochastically smaller than its nominal distribution function F.

We are now ready to formalize what it means for a called service to satisfy its contract in our probabilistic setting.

Contract satisfaction: Pair (A, Q), *consisting of an actual random parameter A for the assumption and an actual random parameter Q for the guaranteed QoS, satisfies contract* (F_A, F_Q) *if*

$$A \geq_S^A F_A \text{ and } Q \leq_S^Q F_Q \text{ both hold,}$$

where $\leq^A$ *and* $\leq^Q$ denote the partial orders defined on the domains of A and Q, and $\leq_S^A$ and $\leq_S^Q$ are corresponding stochastic orders as defined above. The reason for using different directions for the orders in assumptions and guarantees is that "better" translates as $\geq_S^A$ for assumptions and $\leq_S^Q$ for guarantees.

The Issue of Monotonicity

It is usually expected that, if a called service performs better than what its contract specifies, this can only improve the overall QoS performance of the orchestration. Such monotonicity property is indeed the very basis for QoS management in networks.

Unfortunately, as already pointed out, orchestrations can involve complex interactions between the control specified by the orchestration, the parameters of the queries, and the dates at which answers to queries are returned by the called services. As observed, e.g., by (Bouillard, 2009), such complex interactions can impair monotonicity. That is, it can happen that an improvement in the QoS performance of some called service will result in a decrease of the QoS overall performance of the orchestration. Indeed, monotonicity does not always hold for orchestrations. In (Bouillard, 2009), conditions ensuring monotonicity of an orchestration are stated for the restricted case of latency or response time. Such conditions are extended to the general QoS framework studied the present paper in (Rosario, 2009-2).

Contract Composition

We are now ready to investigate contract composition, which consists in inferring from the contracts the orchestration has with its called services, the overall contract the orchestration can offer to its clients. Throughout this section all orchestrations we consider are probabilistically monotonic. Each service t will be assigned a probabilistic contract ($F_{A,t}$, $F_{Q,t}$) i.e., a pair consisting of a probabilistic QoS guarantee $F_{Q,t}$, and a probabilistic QoS assumption $F_{A,t}$ that any client of this service must comply with.

If assumptions $F_{A,t}$ are ignored, probabilistic contract composition is straightforward and proceeds as follows:

Each query to the orchestration generates calls to (a subset of) the services of the orchestration. For each such call to as service t, a value of the guaranteed QoS parameters is drawn from $F_{Q,t}$. *The QoS values of the different services called are then composed to give the end-to-end guaranteed QoS value of the orchestration for that particular query. Computing this end-to-end guaranteed QoS value is achieved by attaching QoS parameters to the tokens traversing the orchestration as discussed in the previous section.*

Following Monte-Carlo simulation principles, the above step is done repeatedly, randomly drawing values for the QoS parameters of the services called. This results in randomly distributed values for the end-to-end QoS of the orchestration. If the above step is repeated sufficiently many times, then a good empirical estimate of the probability distribution of the end-to-end QoS of the orchestration is obtained.

Such a Monte-Carlo procedure was proposed in (Rosario, 2008), for the restricted case of latency or response time. Observe that, in this case, end-to-end QoS contracts for the orchestration are derived from the individual contracts between the orchestration and the called sites.

Unfortunately, this simple composition procedure fails to apply to the general case where both guarantees and assumptions are jointly considered. The reason is that, whereas dependencies for guarantees are outward directed (from called sites to orchestration), they are inward directed (from orchestration to called sites) for assumptions. For example, from knowing the delay between two successive queries to the orchestration, the delay between two successive queries to each service called by the orchestration is inferred. The fact that dependencies are directed in opposite ways for assumptions and guarantees causes the failure of the above simple composition procedure. To overcome this we propose a more elaborated two-phase procedure:

Contract composition procedure when handling both assumptions and guarantees. The procedure proceeds in three phases:

1. **Initial conditions:** They consist of F_A^0, *the assumed distribution for the orchestration, and* $F_{Q,t}^0$, the guaranteed distribution offered by each service t of the model.

2. **Simulation Phase:** it consists of the following successive steps:
   - Draw random calls to the orchestration according to distribution F_A^0; each call to t *the orchestration generates zero, one, or several calls to each service t of the orchestration;*
   - For every such call to a service t: record the value α_t *of the assumption of the call to t, draw random QoS increment* ξ_t from distribution $F_{Q,t}^0$, and compute the QoS parameters of token when entering $t^\bullet$ using competition policy;
   - For each call to the orchestration, record the resulting end-to-end QoS.
   - Performing step 2.b for successive calls to t yields an empirical estimate $F_{A,t}^1$ for t *the actually occurring assumptions for t. Recording the end-to-end QoS for the successive calls to t yields an empirical estimate* F_Q^1 of the actual end-to-end QoS of the orchestration.

3. **Negotiation Phase:** At this point, two cases may occur:
   - For the good case, pair $\left(F_{A,t}^1, F_{Q,t}^0\right)$ *is a contract considered acceptable by every service t*. The orchestration can then propose the contract $\left(F_A^0, F_Q^1\right)$ to its client and the procedure terminates at this step.
   - For the bad case, pair $\left(F_{A,t}^1, F_{Q,t}^0\right)$ *is a contract considered not acceptable*

$by\, t \in T'$, for some set $T' \subseteq T$ of services. The guarantees may be too demanding considering the assumptions. In this case we will re-run the above iterative process with new inputs. We have two alternative approaches to do this, depending on which inputs we choose to update:

In the first approach, we keep $F_{Q,t}^0$ *unchanged for every service* t. Then, we update the assumed distribution F_A^0 for the orchestration to a distribution F_A^1 such that $F_A^1 >_s^A F_A^0$, i.e., F_A^1 is more demanding for client and more favorable for the orchestration than F_A^0 is. When running the simulation phase using F_A^1 instead of F_A^0, a new assumed distribution $F_{A,t}^2$ results for t that is more favorable than $F_{A,t}^1$ for service t. Having sufficiently weakened F_A^1 should then yield an assumed distribution $F_{A,t}^2$ such that $\left(F_{A,t}^2, F_{Q,t}^0\right)$ is now considered acceptable by every service t.

In the second approach, we do not change the assumed distributions F_A^0 *and* $F_{A,t}^1$, but we relax the guaranteed distribution $F_{Q,t}^0$ for every $t \in T'$ to $F_{Q,t}^1$. The guaranteed distributions are relaxed till $\left(F_{A,t}^1, F_{Q,t}^1\right)$ is an acceptable contract for every $t \in T'$.

To prove the convergence of this iterative procedure we will need the following assumptions:

1. For any contract $\left(F_A, F_Q\right)$, there exists a weaker contract $\left(F_A', F_Q'\right)$ – meaning that $F_A' \leq_s^A F_A$ and $F_Q' \geq_s F_Q$ – that is acceptable to both parts involved in the negotiation.
2. The considered probabilistic model of the orchestration is strictly monotonic w.r.t the assumptions, meaning that, for any service t and any given $F_{A,t}'$, there exists a QoS assumption F_A for the orchestration that generates a QoS assumption $F_{A,t}$ for a service

t such that $F_{A,t} \geq_s^A F_{A,t}'$, i.e., $F_{A,t}$ is better than $F_{A,t}'$ for service t.

Assumption 1 is "societal" because it is an assumption about the behavior of the "agents" that undertake contract negotiation. This assumption is not of a mathematical nature, unlike the second one, which is a strenghtening of monotonicity. We successively study the first and the second approach for the negotiation phase.

For the first approach, observing convergence is simple. We observe that using assumption 1, we can find assumption distribution $F_{A,t}^2$ *such that* $\left(F_{A,t}^2, F_{Q,t}^1\right)$ is an acceptable contract for t. Now using assumption 2, we can strengthen the assumptions F_A^1 sufficiently enough, such that the assumptions that t is subject to is $F_{A,t}^2$.

For the second approach, use assumption 2 to find $F_{Q,t}^1 \geq_s F_{Q,t}^0$ *such that* $\left(F_{A,t}^1, F_{Q,t}^1\right)$ is now an acceptable contract for service t. Now, re-running the simulation phase with initial conditions F_A^0 and $F_{Q,t}^1$, yields $F_{A,t}^1$ as an assumption for each service t, and F_Q^2 as an updated guaranteed QoS for the orchestration. Since contract $\left(F_{A,t}^1, F_{Q,t}^1\right)$ is acceptable to t, the orchestration can offer to its client F_Q^2 as a guaranteed QoS. Observe that we do not need the stronger assumption *2 for the second approach*.

PROBABILISTIC CONTRACT MONITORING

Once contracts have been agreed, they must be monitored by the orchestration for possible violation. Contract monitoring is studied in detail in (Rosario, 2008) for the case of a single QoS parameter, namely the latency. The same technique, however, extends without change, to our case. We nevertheless reproduce it here because QoS domains can be partially, not totally, ordered in our case. Monitoring applies to each contracted distribution F individually, where F is the distribution associated to some QoS parameter Q having partially ordered domain D. By monitoring the considered service, the orchestration can get an estimate of the actual distribution of Q, we call it G. The problem is, for the orchestration, to decide whether or not G complies with F, where compliance is defined according to formula

$$\sup_{x \in D} F(x) - G(x) \leq 0 \qquad (3)$$

However, G(x) in (3) is not given to the orchestration; it can only be estimated by collecting actual values for QoS parameter Q. To this end, we consider the following basic empirical estimate for G(x), namely:

$$\widehat{G}_\Lambda(x) \;=\; \frac{\left|\{q \in \Delta \mid q \leq x\}\right|}{|\Delta|}$$

where Δ *is a sample of values q for Q collected at run time by the orchestration and* $|A|$ *is the cardinal of set A.* Estimate $\widehat{G}_\Delta$ converges toward G when the size of Δ grows to infinity. In practice, successive values for $\widehat{G}_\Delta$ are updated on-line at run time by collecting in Δ buffered values for Q in a buffer of size N large enough. If Δ_τ is the content of the buffer at time τ, we thus get an estimate $\widehat{G}_{\Delta_\tau}$, which we denote by $\widehat{G}_\tau$ for simplicity. Then, the indicator in (3) is replaced by:

$$\chi_\tau =_{def} \sup_{x \in D} F(x) - \widehat{G}_\tau(x)$$

At a first sight, a violation should be declared at the first instant τ when $\chi_\tau > 0$ *occurs. The problem is that estimate* $\widehat{G}_t(x)$ can randomly fluctuate around G(x), especially for N not large enough. Hence, applying the brute force stopping rule $\chi_\tau > 0$ will inevitably result in many false alarms. A counter-measure consists in having a tolerance zone above the critical value 0. This yields the following stopping rule for declaring

violation: $\chi_\tau \geq \lambda$, where $\lambda > 0$ is a design parameter of the procedure, defining the tolerance zone. We do not provide here the details of how monitoring is implemented, the reader is referred to (Rosario, 2008), section V for this.

EXPERIMENTS

In our experiments, we implement the contract composition procedure on the CarOnLine example. We use Orc to model the orchestration. The Orc program for CarOnLine is given in Figure 2. Our tool for performing contract composition is built upon an interpreter of Orc in Java, developed by members of the Orc team at the University of Texas at Austin (ORC, 2009).

- **Initial conditions**: The first input for the contract composition procedure, i.e., the assumed distribution F_A^0 *is taken to be the inter-query time distribution of the calls to orchestration by its clients. We assume* F_A^0 to be an exponential distribution with a rate parameter equal to 5 (i.e., 5 requests/sec). The second input is the guaranteed distributions $F_{Q,t}^0$ offered by each of the contracted services of the orchestration. We see in Figure 2 that a given service (for e.g. GarageA) affects multiple QoS parameters. In the experiments we assume independence of these parameters and take distribution $F_{Q,t}^0$ to be a product of the distributions of each of the QoS parameters. The guaranteed distribution for the latency parameter for the services is shown in Figure 4.[4] The guaranteed distributions for the other QoS parameters of the CarOnLine example are given in Table 1.

- **Simulation phase:** With these initial conditions, we ran the simulation phase with 100,000 calls to the orchestration. In every call, the inter-query time for each service

Figure 4. Cumulative distribution functions of latency, for the services of CarOnLine, and end-to-end latency. The result of the re-negotiation is shown in GarageBNego and CarOnLineNego.

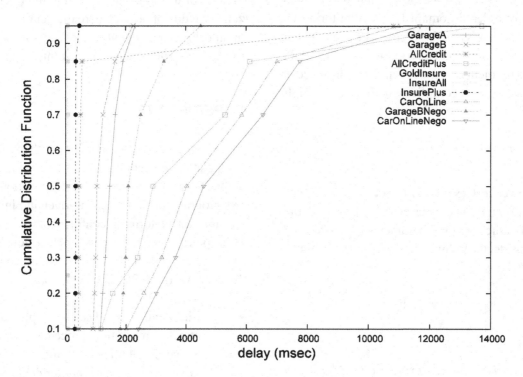

Table 1. Guaranteed distribution functions for the QoS parameters p, i and c of Figure 2. The first column of each table gives the QoS parameter and its values. The other columns give a service of CarOnLine, and the probability of getting a QoS value for that service. GA, GB, AC, ACP, GI, IP and IA are abbreviations for the services GarageA, GarageB, AllCredit, AllCreditPlus, GoldInsure, InsurePlus and InsureAll respectively. Columns labelled O represent the corresponding QoS value for the end-to-end orchestration

p	GA	GB	O	i	GI	IP	IA	O	c	AC	ACP	O
10,000	0.15	0.18	0.17	100	0.2	0.22	0.2	0.21	1	0.25	0.2	0.2
12,000	0.15	0.14	0.14	300	0.2	0.23	0.25	0.22	2	0.2	0.2	0.2
15,000	0.2	0.23	0.23	350	0.3	0.2	0.15	0.23	3	0.15	0.25	0.24
20,000	0.25	0.15	0.16	500	0.15	0.15	0.25	0.16	4	0.2	0.15	0.16
25,000	0.25	0.3	0.3	800	0.15	0.2	0.15	0.18	5	0.2	0.2	0.2

Table 2. Average throughput for each of the contracted sites

Site Name	GarageA	GarageB	AllCredit	AllCreditPlus	GoldInsure	InsureAll	InsurePlus
Throughput	5.028	5.028	5.028	5.028	1.679	3.342	3.342

was observed and the resulting the end-to-end latency for the orchestration was recorded. The resulting distribution for the assumptions $F_{A,t}^1$ — *the inter-query time — for each of the services is given in Table 2. The orchestration's end-to-end QoS for the response time,* F_Q^1, *is shown in Figure 3 by the CarOnLine curve.*

- **Negotiation Phase:** Now suppose that for GarageB, the inter-query distribution $F_{A,t}^1$ *is too strong for the guarantees* $F_{Q,t}^0$ it offers. The contract with GarageB has to be re-negotiated. We adopt the "second approach" for negotiation, keeping the assumptions unchanged, but relaxing the guarantees for GarageB. We show in the Figure 4 the new guarantee distribution by the GarageBNego curve and we show the result of the re-negotiation by the CarOnLineNego curve.

RELATED WORK

Proposals for QoS-based SLA composition are few and no well-accepted standard exists to date. (Menascé, 2002) discusses QoS issues in Web services, introducing the response times, availability, security and throughput as QoS parameters. He also talks about the need of having SLAs and monitoring them for violations. He does not however, advocate a specific model to capture the QoS behaviour of a service, or a composition approach to compose SLAs. (Agarwal, 2004) views QoS based SLA composition as a constraint satisfaction/optimization problem solved by linear programming. (Cardoso, 2004) follows a rule based approach to derive QoS parameters for a workflow, given the QoS parameters of its component tasks. (Zeng, 2004) and (Zeng, 2007) use Statecharts to model composite services and use linear programming techniques such that it optimizes some specific global QoS criterion. In

(Nguyen, 2006), the authors propose using fuzzy distributed constraint satisfaction programming (CSP) techniques for finding the optimal composite service. (Canfora, 2005) uses Genetic Algorithms for deriving optimal QoS compositions. Compared to the linear programming method of (Cardoso, 2004), the genetic algorithm is typically slower on small to moderate size applications, but is more scalable.

A distinguishing feature of our proposal is that we deviate from using hard bounds and handle soft probabilistic contracts. In (Chandrasekaran, 2002) the authors use WSFL (Web Service Flow Language) and enhance it with the capability to specify QoS attributes. Web service Performance Analysis Center (sPAC) (Song, 2005), is another similar approach for performance evaluation of services and their compositions. For both works, probabilistic models are translated into simulation engines for performance analysis. The fundamental difference from our approach is that the approach assumes a "closed world" scenario, assuming that the services of the orchestration can be instrumented with measurement code to get information about its performance. We rely on contracts, instead.

The notion of probabilistic QoS has been introduced and developed in (Hwang, 2004) and (Hwang, 2007) with the ambition to compute an exact formula for the composed QoS, which is only possible for restricted forms of orchestrations without any data dependency. We propose using simulation techniques to analyze the QoS of a composite service, this allows us to use non-trivial distributions as models for performance and also permits analysis of orchestrations whose control flow have data and time related dependencies. A distinct feature of our approach is that the quality domains can be partially ordered which allows expressing rich and possibly complex QoS parameters.

Automated SLA negotiation can also be modelled as a constraint satisfaction problem (CSP). The QoS demands of each of the party involved are expressed in the form of constraints on QoS variables. The negotiation succeeds if the constraint problem admits a solution, i.e., there is atleast one assignment to the QoS variables that satisfy all the constraints. In (Bistarelli, 2009) the authors consider soft constants, by assigning a preference value to each constraint. The domain of these preference values is an absorptive semi-ring, where the values are partially ordered. The negotiating entities are then modeled as processes which interact with each other through a central store, to which they add or remove constraints. Individual constraints of the processes are composed into a global constraint using the operator of the semi-ring, which can be seen as a conjunction operator. Processes can also retract constraints from the store, as a result of which the global constraint gets relaxed. The negotiation terminates when all the processes have reached a final success state. The use of the semi-ring structure and the associated partial orders here is different from our approach in which the domain of the QoS parameters, and not their contracts, is partially ordered. Note that these SLA negotiation methods are related, but quite different from what we propose. Contracts can be negotiated by any two entities, and there is no reference to an underlying orchestration. The negotiation procedure moreover does not involve the use of simulation as in our case.

CONCLUSION AND PERSPECTIVES

In this paper we have proposed a framework for QoS management based on soft probabilistic contracts. This work is a step forward toward establishing QoS management of Web services on a mathematically sound basis. Our vision is targeted to the use of Web services for business processes, in a semi-open world such as multi-tier supplier chains. According to this vision, Web services provider interact via contracts.

More precisely, Web service interfaces must expose information regarding the following:

1/ how they should be queried — this involves conformance of the query with regard to data types, semantic aspects of data, and, for more sophisticated services involving complex, dynamic, interaction, the allowed dialogs between the service and the client who queries it; but this also involves QoS aspects, e.g., maximal query throughput or allowed complexity of the submitted query; 2/ how they respond when properly queried—this involves conformance of the return with regard to data types, semantic aspects of data, and, for more sophisticated services involving complex, dynamic, interaction, the possible dialogs between the service and the client who queries it; but this also involves QoS aspects, e.g., maximal latency, quality of response, etc. Today, Web service interfaces are mostly poor in many of these aspects — emphasis is on typing issues and data semantics and QoS issues are handled in a primitive way.

Orchestrations allow composing services to form new services. This immediately raises the issue of how to compose contracts. Contract composition was the heart of this paper. To account for variability in Web servers and networks, QoS parameters were considered to be random. This is still not common, but we strongly believe it should be like this. In such a probabilistic framework, QoS contracts consist in exposing percentiles for the QoS parameter in consideration, e.g., 95% of responses better than…, 75% of responses better than…, etc. Our main contribution is a general procedure for multi-QoS contract composition in such a probabilistic context.

QoS relates to performance. Therefore it makes sense assuming that a Web service outperforming its contract should do well for the orchestration — actually all SLA are designed with this implicit assumption in mind. Formal study of monotonicity of orchestrations w.r.t. QoS parameters is the subject of other ongoing work.

ACKNOWLEDGMENT

This work was partially funded by the ANR national research program DOTS (ANR-06-SETI-003), DocFlow (ANR-06-MDCA-005) and the project CREATE ActivDoc.

REFERENCES

Abbes, S., & Benveniste, A. (2006). True-concurrency Probabilistic Models: Branching Cells and Distributed Probabilities for Event Structures. *Information and Computation, 204*(2), 231–274. doi:10.1016/j.ic.2005.10.001

Aggarwal, R., Verma, K., Miller, J. A., & Milnor, W. (2004). Constraint Driven Web Service Composition in METEOR-S. IEEE International Conference on Services Computing, 23-30.

Bhoj, P., Singhal, S., & Chutani, S. (2001). SLA Management in Federated Environments. *Computer Networks, 35*(1), 5–24. doi:10.1016/S1389-1286(00)00149-3

Bistarelli, S., & Santini, F. (2009). A Nonmonotonic Soft Concurrent Constraint Language for SLA Negotiation. *Electronic Notes in Theoretical Computer Science, 236*, 147–162. doi:10.1016/j.entcs.2009.03.020

Bouillard, A., Rosario, S., Benveniste, A., & Haar, S. (2009). *2009 (LNCS 5606* (pp. 263–282). Monotonicity in Service Orchestrations. In Proceedings of Petri Nets.

Canfora, G., Di Penta, M., Esposito, R., & Villani, M.-L. (2005). An Approach for QoS-aware Service Composition based on Genetic Algorithms. Genetic and Evolutionary Computation Conference, 1069-1075.

Cardoso, J., Sheth, A. P., Miller, J. A., Arnold, J., & Kochut, K. (2004). Quality of Service for Workflows and Web Service Processes. *Journal of Web Semantics, 1*(3), 281–308. doi:10.1016/j.websem.2004.03.001

Chandrasekaran, S., Silver, G. A., Miller, J. A., Cardoso, J., & Sheth, A. P. (2002). XML-based Modeling and Simulation: Web Service Technologies and their Synergy with Simulation. Winter Simulation Conference, 606-615.

Hwang, S.-Y., Wang, H., Srivastava, J., & Paul, R. A. (2004). A Probabilistic QoS Model and Computation Framework for Web Services-Based Workflows. Conceptual Modeling - ER, 596-609.

Hwang, S.-Y., Wang, H., Tang, J., & Srivastava, J. (2007). A Probabilistic Approach to Modeling and Estimating the QoS of Web-Services-based Workflows. *Information Science, 177*(23), 5484–5503. doi:10.1016/j.ins.2007.07.011

Kamae, T., Krengel, U., & O'Brien, G. L. (1977). Stochastic Inequalities on Partially Ordered Spaces. *Annals of Probability, 5*(6), 899–912. doi:10.1214/aop/1176995659

Keller, A., & Ludwig, H. (2003). The WSLA Framework: Specifying and Monitoring Service Level Agreements for Web Services. *Journal of Network and Systems Management, 11*(1). doi:10.1023/A:1022445108617

Kitchin, D., Quark, A., Cook, W., & Misra, J. (2009). The Orc Programming Language. In *Proceedings of FMOODS/FORTE* (LNCS 5522, pp. 1-25). New York: Springer Verlag.

Liu, Z., Squillante, M., & Wolf, J. (2001). On Maximizing Service-Level-Agreement profits. ACM Conference on Electronic Commerce, 213-223.

Marsan, M. A., Balbo, G., Bobio, A., Chiola, G., Conte, G., & Cumani, A. (1989). The Effect of Execution Policies on the Semantics and Analysis of Stochastic Petri Nets. *IEEE Transactions on Software Engineering, 15*(7), 832–846. doi:10.1109/32.29483

Menascé, D. A. (2002). Qos issues in web services. *IEEE Internet Computing, 6*(6), 72–75. doi:10.1109/MIC.2002.1067740

Misra, J., & Cook, W. (2007, March). Orchestration: A Basis for Wide-Area Computing. Journal of Software and Systems Modeling.

Murata, T. (1989). Petri Nets: Properties, Analysis and Applications. *Proceedings of the IEEE,* (77): 541–580. doi:10.1109/5.24143

Nguyen, X. T., Kowalczyk, R., & Phan, M. T. (2006). Modelling and Solving QoS Composition Problem Using Fuzzy DisCSP. International Conference on Web Services, 55-62.

ORC Language Project. (2009). Retrieved from http://orc.csres.utexas.edu

Rosario, S., Benveniste, A., Haar, S., & Jard, C. (2008). Probabilistic QoS and Soft Contracts for Transaction based Web Services Orchestrations. *IEEE Transactions on Service Computing, 1*(4), 187–200. doi:10.1109/TSC.2008.17

Rosario, S., Benveniste, A., & Jard, C. (2009). Flexible Probabilistic QoS Management of Transaction based Web Services Orchestrations. International Conference of Web Services, 107-114.

Rosario, S., Benveniste, A., & Jard, C. (2009-2). A Theory of QoS for Web Service Orchestrations (Inria Research Rep. No. 6951). Retrieved from http://hal.archives-ouvertes.fr/docs/00/39/15/92/PDF/RR-6951.pdf

Rosario, S., Kitchin, D., Benveniste, A., Cook, W. R., Haar, S., & Jard, C. (2007, September 28-29). Event Structure Semantics of Orc. In Proceedings of the Web Services and Formal Methods, 4th International Workshop (WS-FM 2007), Brisbane, Australia (pp. 154-168).

Song, H. G., & Lee, K. (2005). sPAC (Web Services Performance Analysis Center): Performance Analysis and Estimation Tool of Web Services. Business Process Management, 109-119.

van der Aalst, W. M. P. (1997). Verification of Workflow Nets. International Conference on Application and Theory of Petri Nets, 407-426.

van der Aalst, W. M. P. (1998). The Application of Petri Nets to Workflow Management. The Journal of Circuits. *Systems and Computers, 8*(1), 21–66.

van der Aalst, W. M. P., & van Hee, K. M. (2002). *Workflow Management: Models, Methods, and Systems.* Cambridge, MA: MIT Press.

WSBPEL. (2007, April 11). Web Services Business Process Execution Language Version 2.0. OASIS Standard. Retrieved from http://docs.oasis-open.org/wsbpel/2.0/OS/wsbpel-v2.0-OS.html

Zeng, L., Benatallah, B., Ngu, A. H. H., Dumas, M., Kalagnanam, J., & Chang, H. (2004). QoS-Aware Middleware for Web Services Composition. *IEEE Transactions on Software Engineering, 30*(5), 311–327. doi:10.1109/TSE.2004.11

Zeng, L., Lei, H., & Chang, H. (2007). Monitoring the QoS for Web Services. International Conference on Service Oriented Computing, 132-144.

ENDNOTES

[1] Alternatively, when no such contract can be established (for e.g. if the called service is offered by a popular provider such as Google), a distribution can be estimated from measurement records.

[2] The reader not familiar with Occurrence Nets needs only to know that they are 1-safe Petri nets (having at most 1 token in each place) with no loops and no backward conflict (the preset of each place consists of exactly one transition). As such, they represent the possible finite executions of any 1-safe Petri net. They can also be used to model the executions of a Workflow net (van der Aalst and van Hee 2002). Note also that occurrence nets were already used as a semantic domain for Orc in (Rosario et al. 2007).

[3] Observe that the same arise in QoS in the context of networks and IP. For example, there is typically a limit in how frequently a same IP-address can call some free Web services. In this context, QoS involves parameters that are obligations for the network, e.g., jitter and latency, whereas not exceeding maximal throughput is an obligation for the user of the network.

[4] The (cumulative) distributions for latency were derived from measurements made by calling six web services, published in the XMethods repository http://www.xmethods.net.

[5] In the example of Figure 3, transitions t_1' and t_1'', along with their pre and post sets form one of the branching cells of the net.

APPENDIX: THE ORCHESTRATION FORMAL MODEL

In this appendix we first formalize QoS domains and then we present OrchNets as our model for QoS enhanced orchestrations. OrchNets are a special form of colored occurrence nets (CO-nets) in which explicit provision is offered for QoS management. Note that the executions of Workflow Nets (van der Aalst, 1997) and (van der Aalst, 1998) are also CO-nets.

QoS Domains

- **QoS domains for guarantees**: A QoS domain for guarantees is a tuple $Q = (D, \leq, \oplus, \lhd)$ *where:*

  $(D, \leq)$ is a partial order that is a complete upper lattice, meaning that every subset $S \subseteq D$ has a unique least upper bound denoted by $\vee S$. By convention, we interpret synchronization order $\leq$ as "better". Hence operator $\vee$ amounts to taking the "worst" QoS and is used while synchronizing tokens.

  Operator $\oplus : D \times D \to D$ captures *how a transition increments the QoS value; it satisfies the following conditions:*

  - there exists some neutral element 0 such that $\forall q \in D \Rightarrow q \oplus 0 = 0 \oplus q = q$;
  - $\oplus$ is monotonic: $q_1 \leq q_1'$ *and* $q_2 \leq q_2'$ imply $(q_1 \oplus q_2) \leq (q_1' \oplus q_2')$. 3. $\forall q, q' \in D, \exists \delta q \in D$ such that $q \leq q' \oplus \delta q$.

  The competition function $\lhd : D \times D^* \to D$, *where* $D^* = \bigcup_{k=0}^{\infty} D^k$ and $D^0 = \varnothing$, maps a pair consisting of 1/ the QoS resulting from the synchronization of the input tokens, and 2/ the tuple of the QoS of other tokens that must be considered when applying competition. We require the following regarding $\lhd$:

  - $q \lhd \varepsilon = q$ where ε *denotes the empty tuple, that is, if no competition occurs, then* q *is not altered;*
  - $\lhd$ is monotonic, meaning that $q \leq q'$ *and* $q_1 \leq q_1', ..., q_n \leq q_n'$ together imply $(q \lhd (q_1, ..., q_n)) \leq (q' \lhd (q_1', ..., q_n'))$.

  The actual size of the second component of competition function $\lhd$ *is dynamically determined while executing the net, this is why the domain of $\lhd$ is $D \times D^*$.*

- **QoS domains for assumptions**: A QoS domain for assumption is a pair $(A, \leq^A)$, *where:*

  $A = R_+ \times B$, R_+, *the set of positive real numbers is equipped with its usual order $\leq$, B is equipped with some partial order $\leq_B$;*

  $\leq^A$ *is the product order, and* $(A, \leq^A)$ *is a complete lower lattice, meaning that every subset $S \subseteq D$* has a unique least lower bound denoted by $\wedge S$.

For t a service, an assumption is a pair $\alpha = (\tau, \beta)$ *where* τ is the elapsed time since the last token was received, and β collects the other assumptions attached to the tokens. Observe that $\tau \leq \tau'$ must be interpreted as "τ is worse than τ'" from the point of view of t, because this amounts to increasing the load on t. We take the same interpretation for $\leq_B$, and also for partial order $\leq^A$ on A; thus "better" translates as "$\geq^A$" for assumptions, which is the converse of guarantees.

If some QoS parameter Q of the orchestration is irrelevant to a service it involves, we take the convention that this service acts on tokens with a 0 increment on the value of Q. With this convention we can safely assume that the orchestration, all its called services, and all its tokens use the same QoS domain. This assumption will be in force in the sequel. Before providing the formal definition of OrchNets, we need some background on occurrence nets.

Background on Petri Nets and Occurrence Nets

We assume that the reader is familiar with the basics of Petri nets (Murata, 1989). A Petri net is a tuple $N = (P, T, F, M_0)$, *where: P is a set of places, T is a set of transitions such that* $P \cap T = \varnothing$, $F \subseteq (P \times T) \cup (T \times P)$ is the flow relation, $M_0 : P \to \mathbf{N}$ is the initial marking. For a node $x \in P \cup T$, we call $\bullet x = \{y \mid (y, x) \in F\}$ the preset of x, and $x \bullet = \{y \mid (x, y) \in F\}$ the postset of x. For N a net the causality relation $\leq$ is the transitive and reflexive closure of F. For a node x, the set of causes of x is $\lceil x \rceil = \{y \in P \cup T \mid y \leq x\}$. Two nodes x and y are in conflict, denoted by $x \# y$, if there exist distinct transitions $t, t' \in T$, such that $t \leq x$, $t' \leq y$ and $\bullet t \cap \bullet t' \neq \varnothing$. Nodes x and y are said to be concurrent if neither $x \leq y$ nor $y \leq x$ nor $x \# y$. A configuration of N is a subnet κ of nodes of N such that: 1/ if $x < x'$ and $x' \in \kappa$ then $x \in \kappa$; and, 2/ for all nodes $x, x' \in \kappa$, $x \# x'$ is false. For convenience, we require that the maximal nodes in a configuration are places.

Occurrence nets: A Petri net is safe if all its reachable markings M satisfy $M(P) \subseteq \{0, 1\}$. *A safe net is an occurrence net (O-net) iff*

- $x \# x$ is false for every $x \in P \cup T$;
- $\leq$ is a partial order and $\lceil t \rceil$ *is finite for any* $t \in T$;
- for each place $p \in P$, $| \bullet p | \leq 1$;
- $M_0 = \{p \in P \mid \bullet p = \varnothing\}$ holds.

Occurrence nets are a good model for representing the possible executions of a concurrent system.

Branching cells: We need to consider, dynamically while execution progresses, the set of transitions that are both enabled and in conflict with a considered transition. This was studied by (Abbes, 2006) with the notion of branching cell, which we recall now. Let N be an occurrence net. Two transitions $t, t' \in T$ *are in minimal conflict, written* $t \#_m t'$, if and only if $(\lceil t \rceil \times \lceil t' \rceil) \cap \# = \{(t, t')\}$. A prefix M of N is a causally closed subnet of N whose maximal nodes are places; formally, M is closed under operations $t \to \lceil t \rceil$ and $t \to t \bullet$. Prefix M is called a stopping prefix if it is closed under minimal conflict: $(t \in M \wedge t' \#_m t) \Rightarrow t' \in M$. Branching cells of occurrence net N are inductively defined as follows: 1/ every minimal (for prefix relation) stopping prefix of N is a branching cell, and, 2/ let B be any such branching cell and κ any maximal configuration of it, then any branching cell of N^κ is a branching cell of N, where N^κ, the future of κ, is defined by

$$N^\kappa = \{x \in N \setminus \kappa \mid \forall x' \in \kappa, \, x \# x' \text{ is false}\} \cup \max Places(\kappa)$$

where $\max Places(\kappa)$ *is the set of maximal nodes of* κ (which are all places).[5] A result regarding branching cells that we will need is that the minimal branching cells of an occurrence net are pairwise concurrent.

OrchNets: Formal Definition and Semantics

In this section we assume QoS domains $(D, \leq, \oplus, \triangleleft)$, *for guarantees, and* $(A, \leq^A)$ for assumptions.

Orchnets: An OrchNet is a tuple $N = (N, V, A, Q, Q_{init})$ *consisting of*

A finite occurrence net N with token attributes

$$c = (v, \beta, q) = (data, assumption, QoS\ value)$$

A family $V = (v_t)_{t \in T}$ of value *functions, mapping the data values of the transition's input tokens to the data value of the transition's output token.*

A family $A = (\alpha_t)_{t \in T}$ *of assumptions, where* $\alpha_t = (\tau_t, \beta_t)$ for each $t \in T$, τ_t is the time elapsed since the previous token traversed transition t, and β_t is the value set for the assumptions by transition t when the considered token traverses it.

A family $Q = (\xi_t)_{t \in T}$ of QoS *functions, mapping the data values of the transition's input tokens to a QoS increment.*

A family $Q_{init} = (\xi_p)_{p \in min(P)}$ of ini*tial QoS functions for the minimal places of N.*

Values, assumptions, and QoS functions can be nondeterministic. We introduce a global, invisible, daemon variable ω *that resolves this nondeterminism and we denote by* Ω its domain. That is, for $\omega \in \Omega$, $v_t(\omega)$, $\alpha_t(\omega)$, $\xi_t(\omega)$, and $\xi_p(\omega)$ are all deterministic functions of their respective inputs.

Competition Policy: We will now explain how the presence of QoS values attached to tokens affects the semantics of OrchNets. Assumptions play no role in the competition policy. Thus, in the following analysis, we can safely ignore α. *So, when talking about a "QoS value" in this subsection, we mean a QoS value for guarantees. Accordingly, we will consider that any place p of occurrence net N has a pair* $(v_p, q_p) = $ (data, QoS value) assigned to it, which is the color held by a token reaching that place.

Let $\omega \in \Omega$ *be any value for the daemon. The continuation of any finite configuration* $\kappa(\omega)$ is constructed by performing the following steps, where we omit the explicit dependency of $\kappa(\omega)$, $v_t(\omega)$, and $\xi_t(\omega)$, with respect to ω, for the sake of clarity:

Choose nondeterministically a minimal branching cell B in the future of κ.

For t any minimal transition of B, compute: $q_t = \left(\vee_{p' \in \bullet t} q_{p'} \right) \oplus \xi_t(v_{p'} \mid p' \in \bullet t)$

Competition step: select nondeterministically a minimal transition t_* *of B such that no other minimal transition t of B exists such that* $q_t < q_{t_*}$.

Augment κ *to* $\kappa' = \kappa \cup \{t_*\} \cup t_*^\bullet$, and assign, to every $p \in t_*^\bullet$, the pair (v,q), where

$$v = v_t(v_{p'} \mid p' \in \bullet t)$$
$$q = q_{t_*} \triangleleft (q_t \mid t \in B, t\ minimal, t \neq t_*)$$

Observe that the augmented configuration κ' *as well as the pair (v,q) are dependent on* ω.

Step 4 of competition policy simplifies for the first three examples of the paper, since $q \triangleleft (q_1, ..., q_n) = q$ *in these cases. On the other hand, a non-trivial operator* $\triangleleft$ was needed to address example 4.

Since occurrence net N is finite, the competition policy terminates in finitely many steps when $N^{\kappa(w)} = \varnothing$. *The total execution thus proceeds by a finite chain of nested configurations:* $\varnothing = \kappa_0(\omega) \subset \kappa_1(\omega)... \subset \kappa_n(\omega)$. Hence, $\kappa_n(\omega)$ is a maximal configuration of N that can actually occur according to the competition policy, for a given $\omega \in \Omega$; such actually occurring configurations are denoted by $\kappa(N, \omega)$.

For the particular case of latency, our competition policy boils down to the classical race policy (Marsan, 1989). Our competition policy bears some similarity with the "preselection policies", except that the continuation is selected based on QoS values in our case, not on random selection. We will also need to compute the QoS for any configuration of N, even if it is not a winner of the competition policy. We do this using the same procedure as above, but without the competition step:

Let $\kappa_{\max}$ *be any maximal configuration of N and* $\kappa \subseteq \kappa_{\max}$ a prefix of it. With reference to the previous procedure, *perform the following: step 1 with B any minimal branching cell in* $\kappa_{\max} \setminus \kappa$, step 2 with no change, and then step 4 for any t as in step 2. Performing this repeatedly yields the pair (v_p, q_p) for each place p of $\kappa_{\max}$.

We are now ready to define what the QoS value of an OrchNet is, thus formalizing what we mean by "the QoS of an orchestration".

For κ *any configuration of occurrence net N, and* ω any value for the daemon, the end-to-end QoS of κ is defined as

$$E_\omega(\kappa, N) = \vee_{p \in \mathrm{maxPlaces}(\kappa)} q_p(\omega)$$

The end-to-end QoS $E_\omega(N)$ *and loose end-to-end QoS* $F_\omega(N)$ of OrchNet N are given by

$$E_\omega(N) = E_\omega(\kappa(N, \omega), N)$$
$$F_\omega(N) = \max\{E_\omega(\kappa, N) \mid \kappa \in V(N)\}$$

where $V(N)$ is the *set of all maximal configurations of net N.*

Observe that $E_\omega(N) \leq F_\omega(N)$ *holds and* $E_\omega(N)$ is indeed naturally observed when the orchestration is executed. Pessimistic bound $F_\omega(N)$ can be obtained by simulating, for all drawn outcome of the QoS parameters for each transition t, all possible choices irrespective of actual data.

The reason for considering $F_\omega(N)$ *instead of* $E_\omega(N)$ is when the orchestration is not monotonic. Since the map $N \rightarrow F_\omega(N)$ is always monotonic, one can base contract composition on the pessimistic evaluation $F_\omega(N)$ and then apply contract composition as before.

This work was previously published in the International Journal of Web Services Research, Volume 7, Issue 2, edited by Liang-Jie (LJ) Zhang, pp. 21-42, copyright 2010 by IGI Publishing (an imprint of IGI Global).

Chapter 10
Optimal Fault Tolerance Strategy Selection for Web Services

Zibin Zheng
The Chinese University of Hong Kong, China

Michael R. Lyu
The Chinese University of Hong Kong, China

ABSTRACT

Service-oriented systems are usually composed by heterogeneous Web services, which are distributed across the Internet and provided by organizations. Building highly reliable service-oriented systems is a challenge due to the highly dynamic nature of Web services. In this paper, the authors apply software fault tolerance techniques for Web services, where the component failures are handled by fault tolerance strategies. In this paper, a distributed fault tolerance strategy evaluation and selection framework is proposed based on versatile fault tolerance techniques. The authors provide a systematic comparison of various fault tolerance strategies by theoretical formulas, as well as real-world experiments. This paper also presents the optimal fault tolerance strategy selection algorithm, which employs both the QoS performance of Web services and the requirements of service users for selecting optimal fault tolerance strategy. A prototype is implemented and real-world experiments are conducted to illustrate the advantages of the evaluation framework. In these experiments, users from six different locations perform evaluation of Web services distributed in six countries, where over 1,000,000 test cases are executed in a collaborative manner to demonstrate the effectiveness of this approach.

1. INTRODUCTION

Web services are self-contained, self-describing, and loosely-coupled computational components designed to support machine-to-machine interaction by programmatic Web method calls, which

allow structured data to be exchanged with remote resource. In the environment of service-oriented computing (Zhang et al., 2007), complex service-oriented systems are usually dynamically and automatically composed by distributed Web service components. Since the Web service components are usually provided by different organizations and

DOI: 10.4018/978-1-4666-1942-5.ch010

may easily become unavailable in the unpredictable Internet environment, it is difficult to build highly reliable service-oriented systems employing distributed Web services. However, reliability is a major issue when applying service-oriented systems to critical domains, such as e-commerce and e-government. There is thus an urgent need for practical reliability enhancement techniques for the service-oriented systems.

By tolerating component faults, software fault tolerance is an important approach for building reliable systems and reducing the expensive roll-back operations in the long-running business processes. One approach of software fault tolerance, also known as design diversity, is to employ functionally equivalent yet independently designed program versions for tolerating faults (Lyu, 1995). This used-to-be expensive approach now becomes a viable solution to the fast-growing service-oriented computing arena, since the distributed Web services with overlapping or equivalent functionalities are usually independently developed by different organizations. These alternative Web services can be obtained from the Internet and employed for the construction of diversity-based fault tolerant service-oriented systems. By fault tolerance techniques, long-running business process roll-backs can be reduced since failures of the components can be tolerated by employing alternative candidates (other Web services). Although a number of fault tolerance strategies have been proposed for establishing reliable traditional systems (Lyu, 1995), in the fast-growing field of service computing, systematic and comprehensive studies on software fault tolerance techniques to transactional Web services are still missing.

When applying fault tolerance techniques to the service-oriented systems, several challenges need to be addressed:

- The commonly-used fault tolerance strategies should be identified and their performance needs to be investigated and com-

pared extensively by theoretical analysis and real-world experiments.

- Quality-of-service (QoS) values of the Web services are needed for determining the optimal fault tolerance strategy. However, some nonfunctional performance of the Web services (e.g., response-time and failure-rate) is location-dependent and difficult to obtain.

- Feasible optimal fault tolerance strategy selection approaches are needed since the Internet is highly-dynamic and the performance of Web services are changing frequently. However, the optimal fault tolerance strategy is application dependent subject to the user preference.

In this paper, we present a distributed fault tolerance strategy evaluation and selection framework for Web services, which is designed and implemented as WS-DREAM (Distributed REliability Assessment Mechanism for Web Service) (Zheng & Lyu, 2008b, a). In WS-DREAM, the QoS performance of Web services can be obtained via user-collaboration and the optimal fault tolerance strategy is determined in such a way to optimize the performance of the service-oriented system with a given set of user requirements. The contributions of the paper are threefold:

- Identify various commonly-used fault tolerance strategies and design a distributed evaluation framework for Web services.
- Propose a dynamic optimal fault tolerance strategy selection algorithm, which can be automatically reconfigured at runtime.
- Implement a working prototype and conduct large-scale real-world experiments. More than 1,000,000 Web service invocations are executed by 6 distributed service users different locations on 8 Web services located in different countries.

Let's consider motivating example that user named Ben plans to build reliable service-oriented application using available fault tolerance strategies. He faces several challenges:

1. What are the commonly-used fault tolerance strategies?
2. How to know the performance of the remote Web services?
3. How to select the optimal fault tolerance strategy based on the user preference?
4. How to dynamically reconfigure the fault tolerance strategy when the performance of remote Web services is changed?

To address these challenges, this paper first identifies the commonly-used fault tolerance strategies with systematic mathematical formulas in Section 2. Then, a user-collaborated evaluation framework is proposed for obtaining QoS values of Web services efficiently in Section 3. A dynamic optimal fault tolerance selection algorithm with user-requirement models is subsequently proposed in Section 4. To illustrate the evaluation framework and to study the performance of various fault tolerance strategies, a prototype is designed and implemented in Section 5, and detailed experimental results are presented in Section 6. Finally, related-work is introduced in Section 7 and conclusion is provided in Section 8.

2. FAULT TOLERANCE STRATEGIES

Due to the compositional nature of Web services, reliability of the service-oriented systems becomes a formidable challenge. Software fault tolerance by design diversity (Lyu, 1995) is a feasible approach for building reliable service-oriented systems. The major fault tolerance strategies can be divided into *time-redundancy* and *space-redundancy* (Leu et al., 1990; Salatge & Fabre, 2007), where *time-redundancy* uses extra computation/communication time to tolerate faults, and *space-redundancy* employs extra resources, such as hardware or software, to mask faults.

Space-redundancy includes *active-replication* and *passive-replication*. *Active-replication* is performed by invoking all service candidates at the same time to process the same request, and employing the first returned response as the final outcome (Chan et al., 2007). *Passive-replication* invokes a primary candidate to process the request first. Backup candidates will be invoked only when the primary candidate fails. The *time-redundancy*, *active-replication*, and *passive-replication* are named *Time*, *Active*, and *Passive*, respectively, in this paper.

As shown in Table 1, combining the basic strategies (*Time*, *Active*, and *Passive*) can produce more feasible fault tolerance strategies. As shown in Figure 1, a strategy named *A(B)* means that Strategy *B* is employed at the lower level and Strategy *A* at the higher level. As discussed in the work (Leu et al., 1990), we assume the remote Web services are failed in a fixed rate, and the Web service candidates are independent with each other.

In the following, we provide detailed introduction and the mathematical formulas for calculating the *failure-rate* and *response-time* of these fault tolerance strategies. Failure-rate (f) is the

Table 1. Combination of the basic fault tolerance strategies

	Active	Time	Passive
Active	1. Active	5. Active(Time)	7. Active(Passive)
Time	4. Time(Active)	2. Time	9. Time(Passive)
Passive	6. Passive(Active)	8. Passive(Time)	3. Passive

probability that a service request is incorrectly responded within the maximum expected time, and response-time (t) is the time duration between sending a request and receiving a response of a service user.

1. **Active:** All the n Web service candidates are invoked in parallel and the first successfully returned response will be selected as final result. The formulas for calculating the *failure-rate* (f) and *response-time* (t) of this strategy are defined as:

$$f = \prod_{i=1}^{n} f_i; \quad t = \begin{cases} \min\{T_c\} :| T_c |> 0 \\ \max\{T_f\} :| T_c |= 0 \end{cases};$$ (1)

where n is the number of candidates, T_c is a set of Round-Trip Times (RTT) of the successful invocations, and T_f is a set of RTT of the unsuccessful invocations. When all the parallel invocations are failed ($| T_c |= 0$), the maximal RTT value is employed as the response-time.

2. **Time:** The original Web service will be retried for a certain times if it fails. The

formulas for calculating *failure-rate* and *response-time* are defined as:

$$f = (f_1)^m; \quad t = \sum_{i=1}^{m} t_i (f_1)^{i-1};$$ (2)

where m is the retried times, f_1 is the *failure-rate* of the remote Web service, and t_i is the *response-time* of the ith Web service invocation.

3. **Passive:** Another backup Web service will be tried sequentially if the primary Web service fails. The formulas for calculating *failure-rate* and *response-time* are defined as:

$$f = \prod_{i=1}^{m} f_i; \quad t = \sum_{i=1}^{m} (t_i \prod_{k=1}^{i-1} f_k);$$ (3)

where m is the recovery times, t_i is the invocation response-time of the ith Web service, and f_i is the *failure-rate* of the ith Web service.

4. **Time (Active):** As shown in Figure 1 (4), the first v best performing candidates are invoked in parallel. The whole parallel block

Figure 1. Fault tolerance strategies

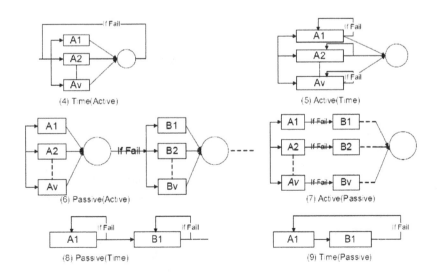

will be retried if all parallel invocations fail. The formulas for *failure-rate* and *response-time* are defined as:

$$f = (\prod_{i=1}^{v} f_i)^m ; t = \sum_{i=1}^{m} t_i'(\prod_{j=1}^{v} f_j)^{i-1}; \qquad (4)$$

where v is the parallel invocation number, m is the retry times, t_i' is the response-time of the ith time of invoking the whole parallel block. t_i' can be calculated by

$$t_i' = \begin{cases} \min\{T_c^i\} : | T_c^i | > 0 \\ \max\{T_f^i\} : | T_c^i | = 0 \end{cases}, \text{ where}$$

$T_c^i \cup T_f^i = \{t_i\}_{i=1}^{v}$.

5. **Active(Time):** As shown in Figure 1 (5), the v best performing candidates are invoked in parallel. The candidates will be retried individually if they fail. The formulas are defined as:

$$f = \prod_{i=1}^{v} (f_i)^m; \quad t = \begin{cases} \min\{T_c\} : | T_c | > 0 \\ \max\{T_f\} : | T_c | = 0 \end{cases}; \qquad (5)$$

where m is the retried times, $T_c \cup T_f = \{t_i'\}_{i=1}^{v}$, and $t_i' = \sum_{j=1}^{m} t_{ij}(f_i)^{j-1}$.

6. **Passive(Active):** As shown in Figure 1 (6), another set of backup candidates will be tried if all of the primary v candidates fail. The formulas are defined as:

$$f = \prod_{i=1}^{m} \prod_{j=1}^{v} f_{ij}; \quad t = \sum_{i=1}^{m} (t_i' \prod_{k=1}^{i-1} \prod_{j=1}^{v} f_{kj}); \qquad (6)$$

where m is the recovery times and

$$t_i' = \begin{cases} \min\{T_c^i\} : | T_c^i | > 0 \\ \max\{T_f^i\} : | T_c^i | = 0 \end{cases}.$$

7. **Active(Passive):** As shown in Figure 1 (7), the best performing v candidates are invoked in parallel. Each individual candidate in the primary v candidates will try another

backup candidate sequentially if it fails. The formulas are defined as:

$$f = \prod_{j=1}^{v} \prod_{i=1}^{m} f_{ij}; \quad t = \begin{cases} \min\{T_c\} : | T_c | > 0 \\ \max\{T_f\} : | T_c | = 0 \end{cases}; \qquad (7)$$

where m is the recovery times,

$$T_c \cup T_f = \{t_i'\}_{i=1}^{v}, \text{ and } t_i' = \sum_{j=1}^{m} (t_{ij} \prod_{k=1}^{j-1} f_{ik}).$$

8. **Passive(Time):** As shown in Figure 1 (8), the primary candidate will retry itself for m times before trying other backup candidates. Only a set of u best performing candidates are employed as backup candidates among all the n replicas. The formulas are defined as:

$$f = \prod_{i=1}^{u} (f_i)^m; \quad t = \sum_{i=1}^{u} (t_i' \prod_{k=1}^{i-1} (f_k)^m); \qquad (8)$$

where $t_i' = \sum_{j=1}^{m} t_i f_i^{j-1}$.

9. **Time(Passive):** As shown in Figure 1 (9), a replica will try another backup candidate first if it fails. After trying u candidate without success, all the u candidates will be retried sequentially. The formulas are as:

$$f = (\prod_{i=1}^{u} f_i)^m; \quad t = \sum_{i=1}^{m} (t_i' (\prod_{j=1}^{u} f_j)^{i-1}); \qquad (9)$$

where m is the retried times and

$$t_i' = \sum_{j=1}^{u} (t_j \prod_{k=1}^{j-1} f_k).$$

These fault tolerance strategies can be divided into three types:

- **Parallel (Strategy 1):** All Web service candidates are invoked at the same time. Parallel type strategies can be employed to obtain good response-time performance, although it consumes a considerable amount of computing and networking resources.

- **Sequential (Strategies 2, 3, 8 and 9):** The Web service candidates are invoked sequentially. Sequential strategies consume fewer resources, but suffer from bad response-time performance in erroneous environments.

- **Hybrid (Strategies 4, 5, 6 and 7):** A subset of the Web service candidates are invoked in parallel. Hybrid strategies consume fewer resources than parallel strategies and have better response time performance than the sequential strategy.

3. DISTRIBUTED EVALUATION FRAMEWORK

For calculating the response-time and failure-rate of various fault tolerance strategies, the QoS performance (response-time and failure-rate) of target Web services are needed. Without accurate QoS values of the Web services, it is really difficult to calculate the performance of different fault tolerance strategies and make optimal fault tolerance strategy selection.

Since the service providers may not deliver the QoS they declared and some QoS properties (e.g., response-time and failure-rate) are highly related to the locations and network conditions of service users, Web service evaluation can be performed at the client-side to obtain more accurate QoS performance (Wu et al., 2007; Zeng et al., 2004). However, several challenges have to be solved when conducting Web service evaluation at the client-side: (1) It is difficult for the service users to make professional evaluation on the Web services themselves, since the service users are usually not experts on the Web service evaluation, which includes WSDL file analysis, test case generation, evaluation mechanism implementation, test result interpretation and so on; (2) It is time-consuming and resource-consuming for the

service users to conduct a long-duration evaluation on many Web service candidates themselves; and (3) The common time-to-market constraints limit an in-depth and accurate evaluation of the target Web services.

To address these challenges, we propose a distributed evaluation framework for Web services, together with its prototyping system WS-DREAM (Zheng & Lyu, 2008b, a), as shown in Figure 2. This framework employs the concept of *user-collaboration*, which has contributed to the recent success of BitTorrent (Bram, 2003) and Wikipedia (www.wikipedia.org). In this framework, users in different geographic locations share their observed QoS performance of Web services by contributing them to a centralized server. Historical evaluation results saved in a data center are available for other service users. In this way, QoS performance of Web services becomes easy to be obtained for the service users.

As shown in Figure 2, the proposed distributed evaluation framework includes a centralized server with a number of distributed clients. The overall procedures can be explained as follows.

1. **Registration:** Service users submit evaluation requests with related information, such as the target Web service addresses, to the WS-DREAM server.
2. **Client-side application loading:** A client-side evaluation application is loaded to the service user's computer.
3. **Test case generation:** The *TestCase Generator* in the server automatically creates test cases based on the interface of the target Web Services (WSDL files).
4. **Test coordination:** Test tasks are scheduled based on the number of current users and test cases.
5. **Test cases retrieval:** The distributed client-side evaluation applications get test cases from the centralized server.

Figure 2. Distributed evaluation framework

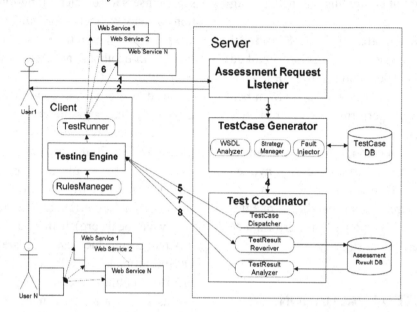

6. **Test cases execution:** The distributed client-side applications execute the test cases to conduct testing on the target Web services.

7. **Test result collection:** The distributed client-side applications send back the test results to the server, and repeat the steps 5, 6 and 7 to retrieval and execute more test cases.

8. **Test result analysis:** The *TestResult Analyzer* in the server-side is engaged to process the collected data and send back the detailed evaluation results to the service user.

The advantages of this user-collaborated evaluation framework include:

1. This framework can be implemented and launched by a trust-worthy third-party to help service users conduct accurate and efficient Web service evaluation in an easy way, without requiring service users to have professional knowledge on evaluation design, test case generation, test result interpretation, and so on.

2. The historical evaluation results on the same Web services can be reused, making

the evaluation more efficient and save resource for both the service users and service providers.

3. The overall evaluation results from different service users can be used as useful information for optimal Web service selection. The assumption is that the Web service, which has good historical performance observed by most of the service users, has higher probability to provide good service to the new service users.

By this framework, evaluation on Web services becomes accurate, efficient and effective.

4. FAULT TOLERANCE SELECTION

In this section, we propose an algorithm for dynamic optimal fault tolerance strategy selection.

4.1 Notations and Utility Function

The notations used in the remainder of this paper are defined where t is an abstract task and $\{ws\}_{i=1}^{n}$

is a set of Web service candidates for t; q^1, q^2, and q^3 are three QoS properties which present *response-time*, *failure-rate*, and *parallel-invocation-number*, respectively. All of these three QoS properties are negative, where smaller value stands for better quality. Q^1, Q^2, and Q^3 are the user requirements on these three QoS properties, respectively. The values of Q^1, Q^2, and Q^3 are set by the service users. For example, $Q^1 = 1000$ms means that the task t must be finished within one second. As a result, the Web service candidates with response-time (q^1) larger than 1 second will not be selected. Q^3 presents the user-requirement on the *parallel-invocations-number*. For example, the parallel Web service invocation can be disabled by setting Q^3 to be 1 when the Web service invocations are payment-oriented.

To quantize performance of different Web service candidates, a utility function is defined as:

$$u = \sum_{j=1}^{m} w_j \times \frac{q^j}{Q^j} \tag{10}$$

where w_j is the user-defined weights for setting the priorities of QoS properties, m is the number of QoS properties, and a smaller value of utility value u means better performance. The value of m is three in this paper, since we consider three quality properties in our selection algorithm. More QoS properties can be added to our algorithm easily in the future without fundamental changes.

The design consideration of the utility function is that response-time performance (q^1) of a particular Web service is related to the corresponding user requirement (Q^1). For example, 100 ms is a large latency for the latency-sensitive applications, while it is neglectable for the non-latency-sensitive applications. By using $\frac{q^1}{Q^1}$, we have a more personalized representation of the response-time performance of Web services. Failure-rate (q^2) and parallel invocation number (q^3) are similarly considered.

4.2 Selection Algorithm

The target of the selection algorithm is to find out the optimal fault tolerance strategy for an abstract task t based on the objective QoS performance of Web service candidates as well as subjective requirements of service users. To determine the optimal fault tolerance strategy, we first rank the Web service candidates based on their QoS performance using the utility function. Then, the optimal parallel invocation number is determined by solving an optimization problem. Finally, the optimal fault tolerance strategy is determined.

4.2.1 Web Service Candidate Ranking

The Web service candidates $\{ws\}_{i=1}^{n}$ for the task t are ranked by their utility values, which can be calculated by $u_i = \sum_{j=1}^{3} w_j \times \frac{q_i^j}{Q^j}$, where u_i is the utility value of the ith candidate, q_i^j is the jth quality property of the candidate, and $q_i^3 = 1$ since there are no parallel invocations when ranking the candidates. After the ranking, $\{\tilde{w}s\}_{i=1}^{n}$ is a set of ranked Web service candidates, where $\tilde{w}s_1$ is the best performing Web service with the smallest utility value.

4.2.2 Parallel Invocation Number Determination

By finding out the optimal parallel invocation number v, the optimal fault tolerance strategy type can be determined as: Sequential ($v = 1$), Hybrid ($1 < v < n$) and Parallel ($v = n$). The value of v can be obtained by solving the following optimization problem:

Problem 1

Minimize:

$$\sum_{i=1}^{n} \tilde{u}_i x_i \tag{11}$$

Subject to:

$$\sum_{i=1}^{n} \tilde{q}_i^k x_i \leq Q^k (k=1,2,3) \qquad (12)$$

$$\sum_{i=1}^{n} x_i = 1 \qquad (13)$$

$$x_i \in \{0,1\} \qquad (14)$$

In Problem 1, Equation 11 is the objective function, where $\tilde{u}_i$ is the utility value of invoking the first i best performing Web service candidates in parallel ($\{\tilde{w}s\}_{j=1}^{i}$). There are totally n solutions to this problem, which are $i = 1, ..., i = n$. Equation 12 is the constraint function which makes sure the QoS performance of the solution meets the requirements of service users. In Equation 12, $\tilde{q}_i^1$ and $\tilde{q}_i^2$ is the overall response-time performance and overall failure-rate performance of invoking the first i Web service candidates in parallel, which can be calculated by employing the Equation 1 in Section 2, $\tilde{q}_i^3$ is the parallel invocation number ($\tilde{q}_i^3 = i$) and Q^k is the user requirements. Equation 13 and Equation 14 are to make sure that only one solution will be selected for the task, where x_i is set to 1 if the first i service candidates are invoked in parallel and 0 otherwise. Algorithm 1 is designed to solve Problem 1. For each potential solution, we first use Equation 1 in Section 2 to calculate the overall QoS values. Then the solutions which cannot meet the user-requirements are excluded. After that, the utility values of the remanding solutions are calculated by using the utility function in Equation 10. Finally, the solution with smallest utility value u_x will be selected as the final solution for Problem 1 by setting $v = x$.

4.2.3 Sequential Fault Tolerance Strategy Determination

If $v = 1$, sequential strategies (Strategies 2, 3, 8 and 9) will be selected. To determine the optimal sequential strategy, the poor performing candidates, which will greatly influence the response-time performance of sequential strategies, will be excluded. A set of good performing candidates W will be selected out by using:

$$W = \{\tilde{w}s_i \mid u_i \leq a, 1 \leq i \leq n\} \qquad (15)$$

where a is the threshold on candidate performance and u_i is the utility value of the candidate $\tilde{w}s_i$. If there is no candidate meet the performance threshold ($|W| = 0$), the service user needs to provide more candidates or devalue the performance threshold a. When $|W| = 1$, strategy 2 (*Time*) is employed, since all other strategies need redundant candidates. When $|W| = n$, strategy 3 (*Passive*) is employed. Otherwise, strategy 8 (*Passive(Time)*) or strategy 9 (*Time(Passive)*) will be employed.

$p_1 = u_2 - u_1$, which is the performance degradation between $\tilde{w}s_1$ and $\tilde{w}s_2$, is employed to find out the optimal strategy between strategy 8 and strategy 9. When the performance degradation is large ($p_1 \geq b$, where b is the threshold of performance degradation), retrying the original Web service ($\tilde{w}s_1$) first is more likely to obtain better performance (strategy 8) than invoking the backup candidate (strategy 9).

4.2.4 Hybrid Fault Tolerance Strategy Determination

If $1 < v < n$, hybrid fault tolerance strategies will be selected. p_2 represents the performance difference between the primary v candidates and the secondary v candidates. p_2 can be calculated by

$$p_2 = \frac{1}{v} \sum_{i=1}^{v} (u_{i+v} - u_i) \qquad (16)$$

Figure 3. Algorithm 1- parallel invocation number calculation

```
Data: Ranked service candidates {w̄s}ⁿᵢ₌₁, user-requirements
        Qᵏ(1 ≤ k ≤ 3)
Result: Optimal parallel invocation number v.
for (i = 1; i ≤ n; i++) do
  | if ∀k(qᵢᵏ ≤ Qᵏ) then
  |   | uᵢ = utility(qᵢ);
  | end
end
if no solution available then
  | Throw exception;
end
uₓ = min{uᵢ};
v = x ;
```

where v is the parallel invocation number. If the performance difference is large ($p_2 \geq b$), retrying the original parallel candidates first is more likely to obtain better performance (Strategies 4 and 5) than invoking the secondary v backup candidates (Strategies 6 and 7).

p_3 is the failure frequency of the first v candidates, which can be calculated by

$$p_3 = \frac{1}{v}\sum_{i=1}^{v} q_i^2 \qquad (17)$$

where q^2 is the failure-rate of the ith candidate. In the erroneous environment ($p_3 \geq c$), strategy 5 and strategy 7 will be selected, since strategy 4 and strategy 6 need to wait for all responses of the parallel candidates before retrying/recovering, which will greatly degrade the response-time performance.

4.2.5 Parallel Fault Tolerance Strategy Determination

If $v = n$, strategy 1 (Active) will be selected. Strategy Active invokes all the candidates in parallel. Figure 4 shows the whole fault tolerance strategy selection procedures discussed above. First, the sequential, hybrid, and parallel types

are determined based on the parallel invocation number v. Then, the detailed strategy will be determined based on the values of W, p_1, p_2, and p_3.

4.3 Dynamic Fault Tolerance Strategy Reconfiguration

The performance of Web services may change dramatically or the services may even become unavailable in the unpredictable Internet environment. Moreover, the user-requirements of the optimal fault tolerance strategy may change from time to time. To enable dynamic reconfiguration of the optimal fault tolerance strategy, we propose a dynamic reconfiguration approach as shown in Figure 5. The reconfiguration procedures are as follows: (1) the initial optimal fault tolerance strategy is calculated by employing the selection algorithm in Section 4.2. (2) The service-oriented application invokes the remote Web services with the selected fault tolerance strategy, and records the QoS performance (e.g., response-time, failure-rate) of the invoked Web services. (3) If the performance of the fault tolerance strategy is unacceptable or the renewal time is come, the service-oriented application will update the user requirements and employed the updated infor-

Figure 4. Fault tolerance strategy selection procedure

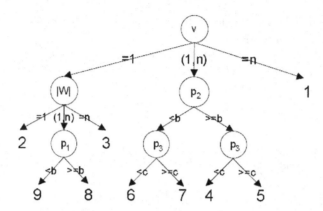

mation for recalculating the new optimal fault tolerance strategy.

By the above reconfiguration approach, service users can handle the frequently context information changes by recalculating optimal fault tolerance strategy using updated QoS performance of the target Web services as well as updated user-requirements. The recalculation frequency is application-dependent and controlled by the service users based on their preference, which is out of the scope of this paper.

5. IMPLEMENTATION

To illustrate the distributed evaluation framework and the fault tolerance strategy selection algorithm, a prototype (www.wsdream.net) is implemented. The client-side of WS-DREAM is realized as a Java Applet, which can be loaded and run automatically by the Internet browsers of the service users. The server-side of WS-DREAM is implemented as several components, including a *HTML Web site* (www.wsdream.net), a *TestCaseGenerator* (Java application), a *TestCoodinator* (Java Servlet), and a data center for recording evaluation results and test-cases (MySQL).

To study the performance of the nine fault tolerance strategies presented in Section 2 and the strategy selection algorithm proposed in Section 4,

a large-scale real-world experiment is conducted. In the experiment, a set of 8 real-world Web services are employed. As shown in Table 2, these Web services include 6 functionally equivalent Amazon Web services located in 6 countries, a *GlobalWeather* Web service located in US and a *IPService* located in US. More than 1,000,000 Web service invocations are executed by these service users and the detailed experimental results will be reported in Section 6.

Figure 5. Optimal fault tolerance strategy reconfiguration procedures

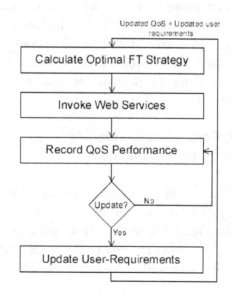

6. EXPERIMENTS

6.1 Individual Web Services

Figure 6 and Figure 7 show the experiment results from the six distributed service users (*US, HK, SG, CN, TW and AU*) on the six Amazon Web services (*a1–a6*). In Figure 6, under the Location column, *U* stands for user-locations and WS presents the Web services. *cn, tw, au, sg, hk, us* present the six user-locations conducting the evaluation. As shown in Table 2, *a1, a2, a3, a4, a5 and a6* stand for the six Amazon Web Services, which are located in US, Japan, Germany, Canada, France, and UK, respectively. The Cases column shows the failure-rate (*F%*), which is the number of failed invocations (*Fail*) divided by the number of all invocations (*All*). The RTT column shows the average (*Avg*) and standard deviation (*Std*) of the response-time/ Round-Trip-Time (RTT) performance. The *ProT* column shows the average (*Avg*) and standard deviation (*Std*) of the process-time (*ProT*), which is the time consumed by the Web service server for processing the request (time duration between the Web service sever receives and request and sends out the corresponding response).

The experimental results in Figure 6 and Figure 7 show:

Table 2. Locations of the web services

WS Names	Providers	Locations
ECommerceService	Amazon	US
ECommerceService	Amazon	Japan
ECommerceService	Amazon	Germany
ECommerceService	Amazon	Canada
ECommerceService	Amazon	France
ECommerceService	Amazon	UK
GlobalWeather	WebserviceX.net	US
GeoIP	WebserviceX.net	US

- As shown in Figure 7 (a), the response-time (RTT) performance of the target Web services change dramatically from user to user. For example, invoking a-us only needs 74 milliseconds on average from the user location of us, while it requires 4184 milliseconds on average from the user-location of cn.

- As indicated by the *Std* values in Figure 6, even in the same location, the RTT performance vary drastically from time to time. For example, in the user-location of *cn*, the RTT values of invoking a1 vary from 562 milliseconds to 9906 milliseconds in our experiment. The unstable RTT performance degrades service quality and makes the latency-sensitive applications easy to fail.

- The ProT values in Figure 6 indicate that the response-times of the Amazon Web services are mainly consist of network-latency rather than server processing-time. Since the average process-times of all the six Amazon Web services are all less than 50 milliseconds, which is very small compared with the RTT values shown in Figure 6.

- Users under poor network conditions are more likely to suffer from unreliable service, since unstable RT T performance degrades service quality and even leads to timeout failures. Figure 7 (b), which illustrates the failure-rates of the Web services, shows that the service user with the worst RTT performance (*cn*) has the highest failure rate, while the service user with the best RTT performance (*us*) has the lowest failure-rate.

Figure 8 and Figure 9 show the experimental results of the *GlobalWeather* and *GeoIP* Web services. The same as Figure 6, Figure 8 and Figure 9 shows that performance of the Web services is quite different from location to location. Com-

Figure 6. Experimental results of the Amazon web services

Location		Cases			RTT (ms)		ProT(ms)	
U	WS	All	Fail	F%	Avg	Std	Avg	Std
cn	a1	484	109	22.52	4184	2348	42	19
	a2	482	128	26.55	3892	2515	46	27
	a3	487	114	23.40	3666	2604	42	17
	a4	458	111	24.23	4074	2539	45	21
	a5	498	96	19.27	3654	2514	43	18
	a6	493	100	20.28	3985	2586	45	20
au	a1	1140	0	0	705	210	42	16
	a2	1143	0	0	577	161	44	29
	a3	1068	0	0	933	272	45	115
	a4	1113	0	0	697	177	42	17
	a5	1090	0	0	924	214	44	23
	a6	1172	3	0.25	921	235	44	24
hk	a1	21002	81	0.38	448	304	42	21
	a2	20944	11	0.05	388	321	44	33
	a3	21130	729	3.45	573	346	43	18
	a4	21255	125	0.58	440	286	43	20
	a5	21091	743	3.52	575	349	44	20
	a6	20830	807	3.87	570	348	43	20
tw	a1	2470	0	0	902	294	44	22
	a2	2877	1	0.03	791	315	44	40
	a3	2218	0	0	1155	355	44	17
	a4	2612	5	0.19	899	300	43	20
	a5	2339	0	0	1144	370	44	21
	a6	2647	1	0.03	1150	363	45	23
sg	a1	1895	0	0	561	353	44	19
	a2	1120	0	0	503	322	43	33
	a3	1511	0	0	638	409	43	20
	a4	1643	0	0	509	240	44	15
	a5	1635	0	0	638	310	44	24
	a6	1615	0	0	650	308	43	16
us	a1	3725	0	0	74	135	42	18
	a2	3578	0	0	317	224	43	33
	a3	3766	0	0	298	271	43	16
	a4	3591	0	0	239	260	43	19
	a5	3933	0	0	433	222	44	30
	a6	3614	0	0	293	260	44	19

paring with the *GlobalWeahter* and *GeoIP* Web services, the *ECommerceService* Web services provide better failure-rate performance. This may related to the fact that the ECommerceService Web services are provided by big company (*Amazon*) and are built for e-business purpose.

6.2 Fault Tolerance Strategies

Real-world experiments are conducted to study the performance of different fault tolerance strate-gies. Figure 10 shows the experimental results of various fault tolerance strategies employing the six functionally equivalent Amazon Web services (*a1,...,a6*) as redundant service candidates. Figure 10 shows that Strategy 1 (Active) has the best RTT performance. This is reasonable, since Strategy 1 invokes all the six candidates at the same time and employs the first returned response as the final result. However, its failure-rate is high compared with other strategies, which may be caused by opening too many connections simultaneously.

Figure 7. Response-time and failure-rate performance

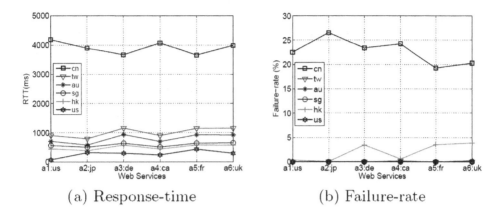

(a) Response-time   (b) Failure-rate

Figure 8. Experimental results of the GlobalWeather web services

Location		Cases			RTT (ms)			
U	WS	All	Fail	F%	Avg	Std	Min	Max
cn	GW	409	337	82.39	6643	2003	2094	9969
tw	GW	1981	35	1.76	1105	1401	343	9844
au	GW	1104	5	0.45	503	544	234	9375
sg	GW	1363	0	0	1403	1544	265	9937
hk	GW	21148	1426	6.74	1563	1560	406	9999
us	GW	3837	0	0	1290	1346	125	9828

Nevertheless, the failure rate of 0.027% is relatively small compared with the failure rate incurred without employing any fault tolerance strategies, as shown in Figure 6. RTT performance of sequential type strategies (Strategies 2, 3, 8 and 9) is worse than other strategies, because they invoke candidates one by one. The reliability performance of these strategies is the best (without any failure). Hybrid type strategies (Strategies 4, 5, 6 and 7) achieve good RTT performance, although not the best. The reliability performance is also in the middle, better than parallel type strategy but worse than sequential type strategies. All the 15 failures shown in Figure 10 are due to timeout of all the six Web service candidates, which may be caused by client-side network problems.

6.3 Optimal FT Strategy Selection Scenarios

6.3.1 Scenario 1: Commercial Application

In Section 1, we present a scenario that a service user named Ben plans to build a reliable service-oriented application and faces several challenges. More specifically, we assume that Ben's service-oriented application will be deployed in Hong Kong and the Amazon Web services will be invoked for book displaying and selling in this commercial Web application. The followings are the performance requirements of Ben:

Figure 9. Experimental results of the GeoIP web services

Location		Cases			RTT (ms)			
U	WS	All	Fail	F%	Avg	Std	Min	Max
cn	GIP	540	32	5.92	2125	1927	531	9781
tw	GIP	2822	60	2.12	732	1270	265	9875
au	GIP	1125	0	0	355	609	234	9360
sg	GIP	1312	0	0	571	878	265	9594
hk	GIP	21007	1263	6.01	849	1582	203	9999
us	GIP	3621	0	0	675	1348	125	9938

1. Response-time. Ben sets the requirement on response-time Q^1 as 500 ms, since too large response latency will lead to loss of business.
2. Failure-rate. Since the application is commercial, the failure-rate requirement Q^2 is set to be 0.5% by Ben.
3. Parallel invocation number. Invoking too many parallel candidates will consume significant computing and networking resources. Therefore, Ben sets Q^3 to be 3.

Employing the optimal fault tolerance strategy selection algorithm proposed in Section 4.2 and the QoS performance of the Amazon Web services shown in Figure 6, the selection procedures are shown in Figure 11. In Figure 11, for ease of discussion, we set $w_1 = w_2 = w_3 = 1 / 3$, which are the weights for different quality properties. The values of the thresholds a, b, and c are set as $a = 2$; $b = 1$; $c = 1\%$ empirically. Q^1, Q^2 and Q^3 are set based on the user-requirements. $\{ws_i\}_{i=1}^6$ is a set of Web service candidates. The response-time (q^1) and failure-rate (q^2) of these candidates are shown in Figure 6. After calculating the utility values of these candidates using Equation 10, the candidates are ranked as $\{\tilde{ws}_i\}_{i=1}^6$. For determining the optimal parallel invocation number (v), Algorithm 1 is employed. The utility values of invoking different number of parallel candidates are shown in $\{\tilde{u}_i\}_{i=1}^6$. The smallest utility value is selected out and v is set to be 1 accordingly.

Figure 10. QoS performance of the fault tolerance strategies

Type	Cases			RTT(ms)			
	All	Fail	F%	Avg	Std	Min	Max
1	21556	6	0.027	279	153	203	3296
2	22719	0	0	389	333	203	17922
3	23040	0	0	374	299	203	8312
4	21926	4	0.018	311	278	203	10327
5	21926	1	0.004	312	209	203	10828
6	21737	2	0.009	311	225	203	10282
7	21737	2	0.009	310	240	203	13953
8	21735	0	0	411	1130	203	51687
9	21808	0	0	388	304	203	9360

Figure 11. Selection procedures of scenario 1

$$a = 2; b = 1; c = 1\%; w_1 = w_2 = w_3 = 1/3;$$

$$n = 6; Q^1 = 500ms; Q^2 = 0.5\%; Q^3 = 3;$$

$$\{ws_i\}_{i=1}^6 = \{\text{a-us, a-jp, a-de, a-ca, a-fr, a-uk}\};$$

$$\{q_i^1\}_{i=1}^6 = \{448, 388, 573, 440, 575, 570\};$$

$$\{q_i^2\}_{i=1}^6 = \{0.38\%, 0.05\%, 3.45\%, 0.58\%, 3.52\%, 3.87\%\};$$

$$\{q_i^3\}_{i=1}^6 = \{1, 1, 1, 1, 1, 1\};$$

$$\{u_i\}_{i=1}^6 = \{0.66, 0.4, 2.79, 0.79, 2.84, 3.07\};$$

$$\{\tilde{u}s_i\}_{i=1}^6 = \{\text{a-jp, a-us, a-ca, a-de, a-fr, a-uk}\};$$

$$\{\tilde{u}_i\}_{i=1}^6 = \{0.4, 0.44, 0.53, 0.63, 0.74, 0.85\};$$

$$v = 1;$$

$$W = \{ws_i | u_i = \leq 2\} = \{\text{a-jp, a-us, a-ca}\};$$

$$|W| = 3;$$

$$p_1 = u_2 - u_1 = 0.66 - 0.4 = 0.26;$$

$$v = 1 \& 1 < |W| < 6 \& p_1 < b \Rightarrow \text{Strategy 9};$$

Since $v = 1$, sequential type strategy will be selected (Strategy 2, 3, 8, and 9). Because $|W| = 3$ (only the top three best performing candidates are selected), and $p_1 < 1$ (the difference between the primary candidate and secondary candidate is not significant), Strategy 9 (*Time(Passive)*) is selected (backup candidates will be invoked if the primary candidate fails, and all the three candidate will be retried if all of them fail).

As shown in Figure 6, from the location of Hong Kong, network condition is good and the failure-rate is low. The response-time improvement of invoking candidates in parallel is limited. Therefore, sequential strategies for this scenario are reasonable.

6.3.1 Scenario 2: Noncommercial Web Page

In scenario 2, we assume another service user named Tom in the location of *cn* also plans to employ the Amazon Web services to provide book information query service in his personal home page. The performance requirements of Tom are as follows:

1. Response-time. Since the Web page of Tom is noncommercial, the response-time requirement Q^1 is set to be 3000 milliseconds.
2. Failure-rate. Since the Web page of Tom is not for critical purposes, the failure-rate Q^2 is set to be 5%.
3. Parallel invocation number. Q^3 is set to be 3.

After conducting the selection procedures shown in Figure 12, Strategy 7 (*Active(Passive)*) with three parallel invocations is selected as the optimal strategy for Tom. In this scenario, the failure-rates of individual Web services are high. Hybrid strategy with suitable number of parallel invocations can be employed to improve the failure-rate performance as well as response-time performance. Our algorithm provides suitable fault tolerance strategy selection result for this scenario.

Figure 12. Selection procedures of scenario 2

$$a = 2; b = 1; c = 1\%; w_1 = w_2 = w_3 = 1/3;$$
$$n = 6; Q^1 = 3000ms; Q^2 = 5\%; Q^3 = 3;$$
$$\{ws_i\}_{i=1}^6 = \{\text{a-us, a-jp, a-de, a-ca, a-fr, a-uk}\};$$
$$\{q_i^1\}_{i=1}^6 = \{4184, 3892, 3666, 4074, 3654, 3985\};$$
$$\{q_i^2\}_{i=1}^6 = \{22.52\%, 26.55\%, 23.4\%, 24.23\%, 19.27\%, 20.28\%\};$$
$$\{q_i^3\}_{i=1}^6 = \{1, 1, 1, 1, 1, 1\};$$
$$\{u_i\}_{i=1}^6 = \{2.08, 2.31, 2.08, 2.18, 1.8, 1.91\};$$
$$\{\tilde{w}s_i\}_{i=1}^6 = \{\text{a-fr, a-uk, a-us, a-de, a-ca, a-jp}\};$$
$$\{\tilde{u}_i\}_{i=1}^6 = \{1.8, 0.82, 0.65, 0.67, 0.74, 0.83\};$$
$$v = 3;$$
$$p_2 = \tfrac{1}{3} \times \sum_{i=1}^3 u_{i+v} - u_i = 0.26;$$
$$p_3 = \tfrac{1}{3} \times \sum_{i=1}^3 q_i^2 = 20.69\%;$$
$$1 < v < 6 \& p_2 < b \& p_3 \geq c \Rightarrow \text{Strategy 7.}$$

7. RELATED WORK AND DISCUSSION

A number of fault tolerance strategies for Web services have been proposed in the recent literature (Salatge & Fabre, 2007; Chan et al., 2007; Foster et al., 2003; Moritsu et al., 2006; Vieira et al., 2007). The major approaches can be divided into sequential strategies and parallel strategies. Sequential strategies invoke a primary service to process the request. The backup services are invoked only when the primary service fails. Sequential strategies have been employed in FT-SOAP (Fang et al., 2007) and FT-CORBA (Sheu et al., 1997). Parallel strategies invoke all the candidates at the same time, which have been employed in FTWeb (Santos et al., 2005), Thema (Merideth et al., 2005) and WS-Replication (Salas et al., 2006). In this paper, we provide systematic introduction on the commonly-used fault tolerance strategies. Moreover, we present the hybrid fault tolerance strategies, which are the combination of the basic strategies.

A great deal of research effects have been performed in the area of Web service evaluation. Various approaches, such as Qos-aware middleware (Zeng et al., 2004), reputation conceptual model (Maximilien & Singh, 2002), and Bayesian network based assessment model (Wu et al, 2007), have been proposed. Some recent work (Rosario et al., 2008; Zeng et al., 2004; Wu et al., 2007; Deora et al., 2003) also take subjective information, such as provider reputation, user rating and user requirement, into consideration to make evaluation more accurate. For presenting the non-functional characteristics of the Web services, QoS models of Web services have been discussed in a number of recent literature (Ardagna & Pernici, 2007; Jaeger et al., 2004; O'Sullivan et al., 2002; Ouzzani & Bouguettaya, 2004; Thio & Karunasekera, 2005). The QoS data of Web services can be measured from either the service user's perspective (e.g., response-time, success-rate, etc.) or the service provider's perspective (e.g., price, availability, etc.). In this paper, we consider the most representative QoS properties (response-time, failure-rate, and parallel-invocation-number). QoS measurement of Web services has been used in the Service Level Agreement (SLA) (Ludwig et al., 2003), such as IBMs WSLA framework (Keller & Ludwig, 2002) and the work from HP (Sahai et al., 2002). In SLA, the QoS data are mainly for the service providers to maintain a certain level of service to their clients and the QoS data are not available to others. In this paper, we introduce the concept of user-collaboration and provide a framework to enable the service users to share their individually-obtained Web service QoS values for the best fault tolerance strategy. The experimental prototype is shown to make Web service evaluation and selection effcient, effective and optimal.

Recently, dynamic Web service composition has attracted great interests, where complex applications are specified as service plans and the optimal service candidates are dynamically determined at runtime by solving optimization problems. Although the problem of dynamic Web service selection has been studied by a number of research tasks (Ardagna & Pernici, 2007; Bonatti & Festa, 2005; Yu et al., 2007; Zeng et al., 2004; Sheng et al., 2009), very few previous work focuses on the problem of dynamic optimal fault tolerance strategy selection. In this paper, we address this problem by proposing an optimal fault tolerance strategy selection algorithm, which can dynamically update the optimal fault tolerance strategy to deal with the frequent context information changes.

The WS-Reliability (OASIS, 2005) can be employed in our overall Web services framework for enabling reliable communication. The proposed WSDREAM framework can be integrated into the SOA runtime governance framework (Kavianpour, 2007) and applied to industry projects.

9. CONCLUSION

This paper proposes a distributed fault tolerance strategy evaluation and selection framework for Web services. Based on this framework, we study and compare various fault tolerance strategies by theoretical formulas as well as experimental results. Based on both objective QoS performance of Web services as well as subjective user requirements, an optimal strategy selection algorithm is designed. Motivated by the lack of large-scale real-world experiments in the field of service-oriented computing, a prototype (WS-DREAM) is implemented and comprehensive real-world experiments are conducted by distributed service users all over the world. The experimental results are employed for performance study of the individual Web services, the fault tolerance strategies, and the proposed strategy selection algorithm. With the facility of the proposed framework, accurate evaluation of Web services and fault tolerance strategies can be acquired effectively through user-collaboration, and optimal fault tolerance strategy can be obtained dynamically at runtime.

Currently, this distributed evaluation framework can only work on stateless Web services. More investigations are needed to apply it to stateful Web services. Our future work will also include the tuning of the selection algorithm (e.g., the values of the thresholds a, b and c), the investigation of more QoS properties, and better use of historical Web service evaluation results.

ACKNOWLEDGMENT

The work described in this paper was fully supported by a grant from the Research Grants Council of the Hong Kong Special Administrative Region, China (Project No. CUHK4158/08E).

REFERENCES

Ardagna, D., & Pernici, B. (2007). Adaptive service composition in flexible processes. *IEEE Transactions on Software Engineering*, 369–384. doi:10.1109/TSE.2007.1011

Bonatti, P. A., & Festa, P. (2005). On optimal service selection. In Proceedings of the WWW (pp. 530-538).

Bram, C. (2003). Incentives build robustness in bittorrent. In *Proceedings of the First Workshop on the Economics of Peer-to-Peer Systems.*

Chan, P. P., Lyu, M. R., & Malek, M. (2007). Reliable web services: Methodology, experiment and modeling. In *Proceedings of the ICWS* (pp. 679-686).

Deora, V., Shao, J., Gray, W. A., & Fiddian, N. J. (2003). A quality of service management framework based on user expectations. In *Proceedings of the ICSOC.*

Fang, C. L., Liang, D., Lin, F., & Lin, C. C. (2007). Fault tolerant web services. *Journal of Systems Architecture*, *53*(1), 21–38. doi:10.1016/j.sysarc.2006.06.001

Foster, H., Uchitel, S., Magee, J., & Kramer, J. (2003). Model-based verification of web service compositions. In *Proceedings of the ASE.*

Jaeger, M. C., Rojec-Goldmann, G., & Muhl, G. (2004). Qos aggregation for web service composition using workflow patterns. In *Proceedings of the EDOC* (pp. 149-159).

Kavianpour, M. (2007). Soa and large scale and complex enterprise transformation. In *Proceedings of the ICSOC* (pp. 530-545).

Keller, A., & Ludwig, H. (2002). The wsla framework: Specifying and monitoring service level agreements for web services. In *Proceedings of the IBM Research Division.*

Leu, D., Bastani, F., & Leiss, E. (1990). The effect of statically and dynamically replicated components on system reliability. *IEEE Transactions on Reliability*, *39*(2), 209–216. doi:10.1109/24.55884

Ludwig, H., Keller, A., Dan, A., King, R., & Franck, R. (2003). A service level agreement language for dynamic electronic services. *Electronic Commerce Research*, *3*(1-2), 43–59. doi:10.1023/A:1021525310424

Lyu, M. R. (1995). *Software Fault Tolerance. Trends in Software.* New York: Wiley.

Maximilien, E., & Singh, M. (2002). Conceptual model of web service reputation. *SIGMOD Record*, *31*(4), 36–41. doi:10.1145/637411.637417

Merideth, M. G., Iyengar, A., Mikalsen, T., Tai, S., Rouvellou, I., & Narasimhan, P. (2005). Thema: Byzantine-fault-tolerant middleware forweb-service applications. In *Proceedings of the SRDS* (pp. 131-142).

Moritsu, T., Hiltunen, M. A., Schlichting, R. D., Toyouchi, J., & Namba, Y. (2006). Using web service transformations to implement cooperative fault tolerance. In *Proceedings of the ISAS* (pp. 76-91).

O'Sullivan, J., Edmond, D., & ter Hofstede, A. H. M. (2002). What's in a service? *Distributed and Parallel Databases*, *12*(2/3), 117–133. doi:10.1023/A:1016547000822

OASIS. (2005). *Web services reliable messaging*. Retrieved from http://specs.xmlsoap.org/ws/2005/02/rm/ws-reliablemessaging.pdf

Ouzzani, M., & Bouguettaya, A. (2004). Efficient access to web services. *IEEE Internet Computing*, *8*(2), 34–44. doi:10.1109/MIC.2004.1273484

Rosario, S., Benveniste, A., Haar, S., & Jard, C. (2008). Probabilistic qos and soft contracts for transaction-based web services orchestrations. *IEEE Trans on Services Computing*, *1*(4), 187–200. doi:10.1109/TSC.2008.17

Sahai, A., Durante, A., & Machiraju, V. (2002). Towards automated sla management for web services. In *Proceedings of the HP Laboratory*.

Salas, J., Perez-Sorrosal, F., Marta Pati, M., & Jim'enez-Peris, R. (2006). Wsreplication: a framework for highly available web services. In *Proceedings of the WWW* (pp. 357-366).

Salatge, N., & Fabre, J. C. (2007). Fault tolerance connectors for unreliable web services. In *Proceedings of the DSN* (pp. 51-60). DOI http://dx.doi.org/10.1109/DSN.2007.48

Santos, G. T., Lung, L. C., & Montez, C. (2005). Ftweb: A fault tolerant infrastructure for web services. In *Proceedings of the EDOC* (pp. 95-105).

Sheng, Q. Z., Benatallah, B., Maamar, Z., & Ngu, A. H. (2009). Configurable composition and adaptive provisioning of web services. *IEEE Trans on Services Computing, 2*(1), 34–49. doi:10.1109/TSC.2009.1

Sheu, G. W., Chang, Y. S., Liang, D., Yuan, S. M., & Lo, W. (1997). A fault-tolerant object service on corba. In *Proceedings of the ICDCS* (p. 393).

Thio, N., & Karunasekera, S. (2005). Automatic measurement of a qos metric for web service recommendation. In *Proceedings of the ASWEC* (pp. 202-211).

Vieira, M., Laranjeiro, N., & Madeira, H. (2007). Assessing robustness of web-services infrastructures. In *Proceedings of the DSN* (pp. 131-136). DOI http://dx.doi.org/10.1109/DSN.2007.16

Wu, G., Wei, J., Qiao, X., & Li, L. (2007). A bayesian network based qos assessment model for web services. In *Proceedings of the SCC*.

Yu, T., Zhang, Y., & Lin, K. J. (2007). Efficient algorithms for web services selection with end-to-end qos constraints. *ACM Trans Web, 1*(1), 6. DOI http://doi.acm.org/10.1145/1232722.1232728

Zeng, L., Benatallah, B., Ngu, A. H., Dumas, M., Kalagnanam, J., & Chang, H. (2004). Qos-aware middleware for web services composition. *IEEE Trans Softw Eng, 30*(5), 311-327. DOI http://dx.doi.org/10.1109/TSE.2004.11

Zhang, L. J., Zhang, J., & Cai, H. (2007). *Services Computing*. New York: Springer.

Zheng, Z., & Lyu, M. R. (2008a). A distributed replication strategy evaluation and selection framework for fault tolerant web services. In *Proceedings of the ICWS* (pp 145-152).

Zheng, Z., & Lyu, M. R. (2008b). Ws-dream: A distributed reliability assessment mechanism for web services. In *Proceedings of the DSN* (pp. 392-397).

This work was previously published in the International Journal of Web Services Research, Volume 7, Issue 4, edited by Liang-Jie (LJ) Zhang, pp. 21-40, copyright 2010 by IGI Publishing (an imprint of IGI Global).

Chapter 11
Satisfying End User Constraints in Service Composition by Applying Stochastic Search Methods

Freddy Lecue
The University of Manchester, UK

Nikolay Mehandjiev
The University of Manchester, UK

ABSTRACT

Semantic web service compositions must be aligned with requirements from the target users in terms of quality requirements. Given a set of quality requirements, one can choose to either find the optimal composition or a "good enough" composition, which satisfies these requirements. Since optimizing compositions of semantic services under quality constraints is known to be NP-hard, it is unsuitable for realistic problems within large search spaces. The authors address the issue by using the "good enough" approach, selecting the first composition that passes their quality threshold. Firstly, this paper defines quality constraints within an innovative and extensible model designed to balance semantic fit (or functional quality) with quality of service (QoS) metrics. The semantic fit criterion evaluates the quality of semantic links between the semantic descriptions of Web services parameters, while QoS focuses on non-functional criteria of services. User quality requirements are met by selecting a valid composition. To allow the use of this model with a large number of candidate services as foreseen by the strategic EC-funded project SOA4All the authors formulate the selection problem as a Constraint Satisfaction Problem and test the use of a stochastic search method.

DOI: 10.4018/978-1-4666-1942-5.ch011

INTRODUCTION

Service composition aims to create new services out of existing ones, to satisfy needs for which there are no existing services. If we tag services with semantic information as found in the Semantic Web (Berners-Lee et al., 2001), we can automate composition since the description of functionality, inputs and outputs of services are now machine-processable, or we can now automate the reasoning with the semantics of services (Sycara et al., 2003). For example, the Web Ontology Language (OWL) (Smith et al., 2004), is based on concepts from Description Logics (Baader & Nutt, 2003) and uses formal conceptualizations of a particular domain (ontologies).

Composing semantic services under realistic assumptions of scale whilst under time constraints is the focus of this work. Scale comes from the current trends of growth in Internet and the Internet of Services, indeed we can expect thousands of candidate component services to choose from when composing. Time may be limited because people who compose services using mash-up environments expect to see results of their actions in a short time-frame to give them the needed feedback of their actions in a visual interactive mode of development.

Under these assumptions we can no longer search for optimal solution in respect to some quality and functional requirements. We have to resort to "good enough" composition, where we take the first composition to pass a minimum threshold of quality and functionality requirements. In this paper we demonstrate how this can be done when considering the semantic similarities between input and output parameters as indicators of service functionality, or functional aspects of service composition (Lecue et al., 2008), combined with non functional parameters such as Quality of Services (QoS) (Canfora et al., 2005; Berbner, 2006; Yu & Lin, 2005). To measure semantic similarity, we use the concept of (functional) semantic link (Lecue & Leger, 2006), defined as

a semantic connection between an output and an input parameter of two services. Here we propose to unify both types of criteria in an innovative and extensible model that could be used to estimate, select and optimize the quality of any semantic Web service composition.

Maximizing the quality of service composition using this model is essentially a multi-objective optimization problem with constraints on quality of services and their semantic links. Such a problem is known to be NP-hard (Papadimtriou & Steiglitz, 1982) and intractable (Lecue et al., 2008; Zeng et al., 2004) in a context of a large number of services. Indeed most approaches have been shown to have poor scalability in terms of time taken to compute optimal compositions when the size of the initial set of services grows. Such a case can arise in the future semantic web, where millions of semantic services will be accessible globally. This is the vision of SOA4All, a strategic EC-funded project aiming to create the tools, languages and conceptual techniques where scalability is one of its main objectives.

Rapid computation of (non necessarily optimal) compositions is especially important for interactive systems providing service composition facilities for end users, where long delays may be unacceptable. A typical scenario would involve an end-user retrieving a template for a desired composition, and specifying some constraints in addition to the ones already in the template. The software should then propose a combination of services which satisfies these constraints. This should happen in real-time even for a very complex composition template with a large number of alternative matching services. In this work we address this scalability issue by selecting a composition (among a large number achieving the same goal) satisfying some constraints (defined along the innovative quality model) rather than computing the optimal composition. To this end we i) formulate quality-driven semantic web service composition as a Constraint Satisfaction Problem (CSP) and ii) test the use of a stochastic search method. Finally we compare the latter with state-of-the-art approaches.

In the remainder of this paper, we describe the proposed approach and offer some experimental results of its application. We start by commenting on related work and aligning our contributions with key results in the field. Then in the "Preliminaries" section we briefly review i) semantic links, ii) their common descriptions and iii) the web service composition model. The "Quality Model" section introduces the quality criteria for quality driven semantic web service composition. The "A Scalable Approach for Quality Driven Semantic Web Service Composition" section details its CSP formalization and tests the use of a stochastic search method. The "Implementation and Experiments" section reports and discusses results from the experimentations. Finally, "Conclusion" draws some conclusions and talks about possible future directions.

RELATED WORK

Starting from an initial set of available services, we define web service composition according to Definition 1.

Definition 1. *(Web Service Composition): Web service composition aims at selecting and interconnecting web services provided by different partners in order to achieve a particular goal.*

Automating web service composition aims to overcome the problem where no single service can satisfy the goal specified by the service consumer. A number of different approaches have been proposed, including Logic-based (Rao et al., 2003; Rao et al., 2006) Matchmaking-based (Lassila & Dixit, 2004), Graph-Theory-based (Zhang et al., 2003), Golog-based (McIlraith et al., 2001), and AI-Planning-based (Wu et al., 2002). However, very few approaches have addressed the constraints-based composition (Definition 2).

Definition 2. *(Constraints-based Web Service Composition): Constraints-based composition of web service represents a set of compositions that satisfy a set of constraints as quality criteria. Computing such compositions aims at selecting compositions according to some constraints on a set of pre-defined metrics.*

In this section we appraise the existing approaches to compute constraints-based compositions and especially most specific approaches that optimize different levels of quality along the constraints that need to be met.

Despite considerable work in area of service composition, no effort has specifically addressed selection of service composition constrained by both QoS and semantic similarities in a context of large domains. Indeed main approaches focus on either QoS (Ardagna & Pernici, 2007; Canfora et al., 2005; Zeng et al., 2004) such as price, reliability and execution time (hence independence between web services), or functional criteria such as semantic links (Lecue et al., 2008), but no both criteria in the same model. In addition all of the latter approaches do not consider computation of composition that scales the web, mainly because they aims at computing the most optimal compositions in terms of different levels of criteria.

Indeed solving such an optimization problem falls in the category of search problems, which are NP-hard. Most of these approaches focus on optimizing the composition by mapping it to a multi-criteria optimization problem. Despite some scalability issues, the latter can be approached using IP (Zeng et al., 2004; Lecue et al., 2008), GA (Canfora et al., 2005), or Constraint Programming (Hassine et al., 2006).

Contrary to IP (Zeng et al., 2004), Genetic Algorithms are better at handling non linearity of aggregation functions, and provide better scaling up to a large number of candidate services per task (actually 16 tasks and 25 candidate services per tasks). Even if this approach has been shown to scale well in a bound environment, the approach suffers from its static and predefined number of individuals and generation, which need to be known at design time. In addition the latter predefined numbers could restrict the optimal composition to be local rather than global.

The selection problem can be also modelled as a knapsack problem (Yu & Lin, 2005), wherein (Arpinar et al., 2005) performed dynamic programming to solve it. Unfortunately the previous QoS-driven service composition approaches consider only links (or connections between services parameters) valued by Exact matching types, hence they do not take into account the semantic quality of compositions. The latter issue is addressed by (Lecue et al., 2008), who introduce a general and formal model to evaluate such a quality. From this they formulate an optimization problem which is solved by adapting the IP-based approach of (Aggarwal et al., 2004; Zeng et al., 2004). All quality criteria are used for specifying both constraints and objective function.

According to the latter approaches, Table 1 summarizes the main optimization-based approaches related to our work along four dimensions:

- **Quality Model:** this dimension describes the optimization approach used to select the most appropriate composition;
- **Quality Attributes:** Properties of the criteria involved in the quality model;

- **Optimization Type:** Is the optimal composition local or global?;
- **Scalability of the Approach:** Does the approach scale well in large domains i.e., large number of services in the composition.

Our Contribution

Review of existing approaches reveals that no approach has specifically addressed constraints based service composition using both QoS and semantic similarities dimensions in a context of significant scale.

In contrast to the previous approaches and mainly the methods presented in Table 1, we present an innovative model that addresses both types of quality criteria (i.e., functional and QoS criteria) for selecting web service composition, the whole in large scale domains such as the Web. In this direction we follow (Hassine et al., 2006) and suggest the use of CSP to model quality-driven semantic web service composition. In contrary, our approach presents:

1. A stochastic search method to compute a single composition that meets initial constraints rather than computing the optimal composition.

Moreover we also extend their model by:

Table 1. Comparison of optimization based web service composition approaches (no = not supported, yes = fully supported)

	(Canfora et al., 2005)	**(Zeng et al., 2004)**	**(Lecue et al., 2008)**
Composition Approach	Genetic Algorithm (GA) based	Integer Programming (IP) based	Integer Programming (IP) based
Quality Model	Non Functional Properties (QoS)	Non Functional Properties (QoS)	Functional Fit (Semantic Link)
Quality Attributes	Non Linear	Linear (Linearization required)	Linear (Linearization required)
Optimization Type	Possible local optimum	Global	Global
Scalability of the Approach	Limited by the number of individuals and generations.	No	No

2. Using semantic links to consider data flow in composition; and

3. Considering not only QoS but also semantic quality (and constraints) of composition.

PRELIMINARIES

We describe how semantic links[1] introduced in (Lecue & Leger, 2006) can be used to model web service composition and how the concept of Common Description can be used to measure the semantic fit of the links.

Semantic Links between Web Services

In the semantic web, input and output parameters of services referred to concepts in a common terminology or ontology[2] O, where the OWL-S profile (Ankolenkar et al., 2004), WSMO capability (Fensel et al., 2005) or SA-WSDL (Kopecky et al., 2007) can be used to describe them (through semantic annotations). At functional level, web service composition consists in retrieving some semantic links (Lecue & Leger, 2006) noted $sl_{i,j}$ (Figure 1) i.e.,

$$sl_{i,j} := \langle s_i, Sim_O(Out\_s_i, In\_s_j), s_j \rangle \qquad (1)$$

between output parameters $Out\_s_i \in O$ of services s_i and input parameters $In\_s_j \in O$ of other services s_j. Thereby s_i and s_j are partially linked according to a matching function Sim_T between their functional parameters. Given an ontology O, (Paolucci et al., 2002; Li & Horrocks, 2003) value the range of the latter function Sim_O onto five matching types:

- Exact i.e., If the output parameter Out_s_i of s_i and the input parameter of In_s_j of s_j are equivalent concepts. Formally $O \models Out\_s_i \equiv In\_s_j$,

- PlugIn i.e., If the output parameter Out_s_i of s_i is sub-concept of the input parameter In_s_j of s_j. Formally $O \models Out\_s_i \subset In\_s_j$,

- Subsume i.e., If the output parameter Out_s_i of s_i is super-concept of the input parameter In_s_j of s_j. Formally $O \models Out\_s_i \supset In\_s_j$,

- Intersection i.e., If the intersection of the output parameter Out_s_i of s_i and the input parameter of In_s_j of s_j is satisfiable. Formally $O \models \neg(Out\_s_i \cap In\_s_j \sqsubseteq \perp)$,

- Disjoint i.e., Otherwise the output parameter Out_s_i of s_i and the input parameter of Out_s_j of s_j are incompatible. Formally $O \models Out\_s_i \cap In\_s_j \sqsubseteq \perp$.

Figure 1. A Semantic Link $sl_{i,j}$ between Services s_i and s_j

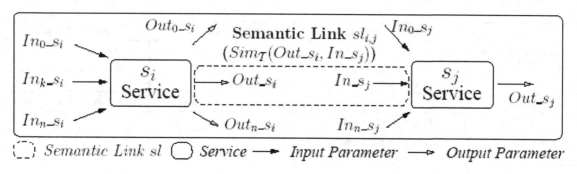

Example 1. *(Semantic Link and Matching Type):* *Suppose* $sl_{1,2}$ *(Figure 4) is a semantic link between two services* s_1 *and* s_2 *such that the output parameter NetworkConnection of* s_1 *is (semantically) linked to the input parameter SlowNetworkConnection of* s_2 *. According to Figure 2 and the definition of matching types, this link is valued by a Subsume matching type since NetworkConnection* $\supset$ *SlowNetworkConnection.*

The matching function Sim_O enables, at design time, the discovery of certain levels of semantic compatibilities (i.e., Exact, PlugIn, Subsume, Intersection) and incompatibilities (i.e., Disjoint) among independently defined service descriptions.

Common Description of a Semantic Link

Besides computing the matching type of a semantic link, (Lecue et al., 2007) suggest computing a finer level of information i.e., the Extra and Common Descriptions between Out_s_i and In_s_j of a semantic link $sl_{i,j}$. They adapt the definition of Concept Abduction (Colucci et al., 2005) (Definition 3) in the context of web service composition. Then, they compare the service parameters defined in ALN Description Logic (DL).

Definition 3. *(Concept Abduction): Let* L *be a DL,* C *,* D *be two concepts in* L *, and* O *be a set of axioms in* L *. A Concept Abduction Problem (CAP), denoted as* $\langle L, C, D, O \rangle$ *is finding a concept* $H \in L$ *such that* $O \models C \cap H \subseteq D$ *.*

This produces a compact representation of the "difference" H between descriptions Out_s_i and In_s_j of a semantic link $sl_{i,j}$. The Extra Description H is defined by $O \models Out\_s_j \cap H \subseteq In\_s_i$, hence it provides a

solution of the Concept Abduction problem $\langle L, Out\_s_j, In\_s_i, O \rangle$. In other words H refers to information required by In_s_j but not provided by Out_s_i to ensure a correct data flow between services s_i and s_j. The Common Description of Out_s_i and In_s_j, defining as their Least Common Subsumer (Baader et al., 2004) lcs, refers to information required by In_s_j and effectively provided by Out_s_i.

Example 2. *(Extra & Common Description): Suppose the semantic link* $sl_{1,2}$ *between* s_1 *and* s_2 *(Example 1 and Figure 3), valued by a Subsume matching type (Example 3). According to Definition 3 and Figure 3, such a link requires a semantic refinement to be applied in a composition of web services. In the first hand the description missing in NetworkConnection to be plugged in the input parameter SlowNetworkConnection is referred by the Extra Description* H *of the Concept Abduction Problem* $\langle L, \text{NetworkConnection}, \text{SlowNetworkConnection}, O \rangle$ *i.e.,* $\forall netSpeed.Adsl1M$ *. In the other hand the Common Description defined by the Least Common Subsumer of the output parameter of* s_1 *and the input parameter of* s_2 *is referred by the information required by SlowNetworkConnection and effectively provided by NetworkConnection i.e.,* $lcs(\text{SlowNetworkConnection}, \text{NetworkConnection})$ *i.e., NetworkConnection.*

Remark 1. *(Alternative for Extra Description): Other approaches such as the Difference operator (Teege, 1994; Brandt et al., 2002) can be used to remove from a given description all the information contained in another description. Actually the difference operator introduced by (Brandt et al., 2002) is a refinement of Teege's (1994) difference that considers the syntactic minimum (with respect to a subdescription ordering) between incomparable ALE descriptions instead of*

Figure 2. Sample of an ALN terminology T

$$NetworkConnection \equiv \forall netPro.Provider \sqcap \forall netSpeed.Speed$$
$$NoNetworkConnection \equiv NetworkConnection \sqcap \forall netSpeed.NoAdsl$$
$$SlowNetworkConnection \equiv NetworkConnection \sqcap \forall netSpeed.Adsl1M$$
$$FastNetworkConnection \equiv NetworkConnection \sqcap \forall netSpeed.AdslMax$$
$$Speed \equiv \geq 0\,mBytes, \quad NoAdsl \equiv Speed \sqcap \leq 0\,mBytes$$
$$Adsl1M \equiv Speed \sqcap \geq 1\,mBytes, \quad AdslMax \equiv Speed \sqcap \geq 8\,mBytes$$
$$IPAddress \equiv Address \sqcap \forall protocol.IP$$
$$VoIPId \equiv Address \sqcap \forall network.FTLocal$$
$$VideoDecoder \equiv Decoder \sqcap \forall decrypt.Video$$
$$ZipCode \sqsubset \top, EMail \sqsubset \top, Address \sqsubset \top, Invoice \sqsubset \top, PhonNum \sqsubset \top$$
$$OutAction \sqsubset Action, InterAction \sqsubset Action$$
$$orderAction \equiv OutAction \sqcap \geq 1\,PhonNum \sqcap \geq 1\,IPAddress \sqcap \geq 1\,Decoder$$
$$findOfferAction \equiv InterAction \sqcap \geq 1\,PhonNum \sqcap \geq 1\,ZipCode \sqcap \geq 1\,EMail$$

a semantic maximum (ordering according to the subsumption operator). Teege (1994) and Brandt et al. (2002) perform equivalence between two concept descriptions whereas the concept abduction computes a subsumption of concept descriptions.

Modeling Web Service Composition

The process model of web service composition and its semantic links is specified by a statechart (Harel & Naamad, 1996). This choice has been motivated by several reasons. First, statecharts possess formal semantics, which is essential for analysing com-

Figure 3. A semantic link valued by a subsume matching type

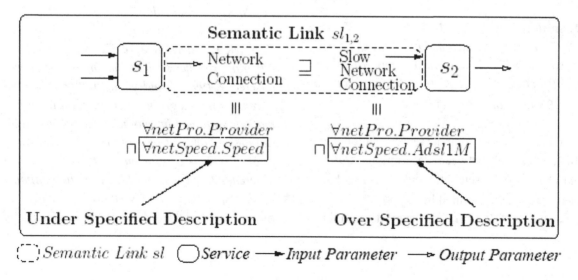

Figure 4. A (concrete) web service composition

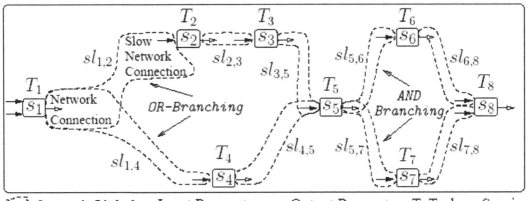

posite service specifications. Second, statecharts are a well-known and well supported behaviour modelling notation. Finally, statecharts offer most of the control-flow constructs found in existing process modelling languages and they have been shown to be suitable for expressing typical control flow dependencies. Hence, it is possible to adapt the semantic-based service selection mechanisms developed using statecharts to fit other alternative languages. In more details, each state refers to a service being activated, whereas its transitions coincide with semantic links. In addition some basic composition constructs such as sequence, conditional branching (i.e., OR-Branching), structured loops, concurrent threads (i.e., AND-Branching), and inter-thread synchronization can be found. To simplify the presentation, we initially assume that all considered statecharts are acyclic and consists of only sequences, OR-Branching and AND-Branching. In case of cycle, a technique for *unfolding* statechart into its acyclic form needs to be applied beforehand. The method (Zeng et al., 2004) used to unfold the cycles of statecharts is to examine the logs of past executions in order to determine the average number of times that each cycle is taken.

Example 3. *(Process Model of a Web Service Composition): Suppose a composition (Figure 4) extending Example 1 with six more services $s_{i,1 \leq i \leq 8}$, eight more semantic links $sl_{i,j}$. Its process model consists of sequences, OR-Branching and AND-Branching.*

The Example 3 and Figure 4 illustrate a composition wherein tasks T_i and abstract semantic link $sl_{i,j}^A$ (i.e., a semantic link between Tasks, not services; here between Tasks T_i and T_j) have been respectively concretized by one of their n candidate services (e.g., s_i) and n^2 candidate links (e.g., $sl_{i,j}$). Indeed some services with common functionality, preconditions and effects although different input, output parameters and quality (e.g., QoS) can be selected to perform a target goal T_i and obtaining a concrete composition. Such a selection will have a direct impact on semantic links involved in the concrete composition.

In the following, we address the issue of selecting and composing a large and changing collection of services. We will make the choice of services at composition time, based on both quality of i) services and ii) their semantic links.

QUALITY MODEL

Firstly we present a quality criterion to value semantic links. Then we proposed how it can be extended to also cover non-functional QoS, thus allowing us to estimate both quality levels of any compositions.

Quality of Semantic Link

We consider two generic quality criteria for semantic links $sl_{i,j}$ defined by $\langle s_i, Sim_O(Out\_s_i, In\_s_j), s_j \rangle$:

- **Common Description rate** $q_{cd}(sl_{i,j}) \in (0,1]$ is defined by:

$$q_{cd}(sl_{i,j}) := \frac{|lcs(Out\_s_i, In\_s_j)|}{|H| + |lcs(Out\_s_i, In\_s_j)|} \quad (2)$$

wherein the Extra Description H is a solution of the Concept Abduction problem $\langle L, Out\_s_j, In\_s_i, O \rangle$ (Definition 3): the difference between service parameters Out_s_i and In_s_j. In other words q_{cd} estimates the rate of descriptions which is well specified for ensuring a correct data flow between s_i and s_j. In more details |.| refers to the size of *ALN* concept descriptions (Kusters, 2001(p.17) i.e., |T|, |⊥|, |A|, |¬A|, |∃r| are 1; |C⊓ D|:= |C|+|D|; |∀r.C| is 1 + |C|; $|(\geq nr)|$ and $|(\leq nr)|$ are 2+log(n+1) (binary encoding of n). For instance |Adsl1M| is 1+2+log(2) i.e., 4 in Figure 2.

- **Matching Quality** q_m of a semantic link $sl_{i,j}$ is a value in (0; 1] defined by $Sim_O(Out\_s_i, In\_s_j)$ i.e., either 1 (Exact), $\frac{3}{4}$ (PlugIn), $\frac{1}{2}$ (Subsume) and $\frac{1}{4}$ (Intersection). Contrary to q_{cd}, q_m does not estimate similarity between the parameters of semantic links but gives a general over-

view (discretized values) of their semantic relationships.

In case we consider $Out\_s_i \cap In\_s_j$ to be not satisfiable, it is straightforward to extend and adapt our quality model by i) computing contraction (Colucci et al., 2003) between Out_s_i and In_s_j, and ii) valuing the Disjoint matching type. Thus, the two quality criteria can be update in consequence.

Given the above quality criteria, the quality vector of a semantic link $sl_{i,j}$ is defined as follows:

$$q(sl_{i,j}) := (q_{cd}(sl_{i,j}), q_m(sl_{i,j})) \quad (3)$$

Example 4. *(Quality of Semantic Links): Suppose the composition in example 3. Let s_2' be another candidate service for T_2 in Figure 4 with Network-Connection as an input parameter. The semantic link $sl_{1,2}'$ between s_1 and s_2' is valued by $Sim_O(Out\_s_1, In\_s_2')$ i.e., an Exact matching type between respectively the output and input parameters of s_1 and s_2'. In addition the common description rate (2) is valued by 1 since the size of the Abduction between the output and input parameters of s_1 and s_2' is 0. Therefore $q(sl_{1,2}')$ is $(1,1)$ whereas $q(sl_{1,2})$ is $(\frac{2}{7}, \frac{1}{2})$. Therefore the quality of $sl_{1,2}'$ is better than the quality of $sl_{1,2}$ on both criteria, then $q(sl_{1,2}') > q(sl_{1,2})$.*

Remark 2. *(Non Comparable Quality Vector): We can compare a weighted average of their normalized components in case the value of the first element of semantic link $sl_{1,2}'$ is better than the first element of $sl_{1,2}$ but worse for the second element (Hwang & Yoon, 1981).*

Remark 3. *(Multiple Semantic Links between Two Services): In case s_i and s_j are related by more than one link, the value of each criterion is retrieved by computing their average.*

Quality of Semantic Link and QoS

Here we extend the latter quality model by also exploiting the non functional properties of services (also known as QoS attributes (O'Sullivan et al., 2002)) involved in each semantic link. We simplify the presentation by considering only:

- Execution Price $q_{pr}(s_i) \in R^+$ of service s_i i.e., the fee requested by the service provider for invoking it.
- Response Time $q_t(s_i) \in R^+$ of service s_i i.e., the expected delay between the request and result moments.

The latter values of execution price and response time are given by service providers or third parties e.g., by means of some logs of previous executions. Note that the method for computing the value of q_{pr} and q_t (which is not the scope of the paper) is not unique. Indeed different computation methods can be designed to fit the needs of specific applications (Cardoso et al., 2004; Zeng et al., 2004).

A quality vector of a service s_i is then defined as follows:

$$q(s_i) := (q_{pr}(s_i), q_t(s_i)) \qquad (4)$$

Thus a QoS-extended quality vector of a semantic link $sl_{i,j}$:

$$\overset{*}{q}(sl_{i,j}) := (q(s_i), q(sl_{i,j}), q(s_j)) \qquad (5)$$

Given an abstract link between goals T_i and T_j, one may select the link with the best matching quality, common description rate, the cheapest and fastest services, or may be a compromise between the four by coupling (3) and (4) in (5). Moreover, the selection could be influenced by predefining some constraints e.g., a service response time lower than a given value.

Example 5. *QoS-Extended Quality of Semantic Link: Suppose T_2 and its two candidate services s_2 and s_2' wherein $q(s_2') < q(s_2)$. According to the Example 4, s_2' should be preferred regarding the quality of its semantic link with s_1, whereas s_2 should be preferred regarding its QoS. So what about the best candidate for $sl_{1,2}^A$ regarding both criteria: $\overset{*}{q}$?*

Quality of Composition

Here we present Definitions 4 and 5, which are required to compare and rank different compositions along the common description rate and matching quality dimension. The rules for aggregating quality values for any concrete composition, given the quality of its underlying services and semantic links (here s and sl stand respectively for s_i and $sl_{i,j}$) are provided in Table 2 and Table 3. The approach for computing semantic quality of such a composition c is adapted from the application-driven heuristics of (Lecue et al., 2008), while the computation of its non functional QoS is similar logic to (Cardoso et al., 2004).

Definition 4. *(Common Description rate of a Composition): The Common Description rate of a composition measures the average degree of similarity between all corresponding parameters of services linked by a semantic link.*

Definition 4 motivates how to compute such a rate for sequential, AND-Branching and OR-Branching compositions. The Common Description rate Q_{cd} of both a sequential and AND-Branching composition c is defined as the average of its semantic links' common description rate $q_{cd}(sl)$. Therefore the overall common description rate of any compositions is a linear function of semantic links' common description rate. The

Table 2. Semantic quality aggregation rules for service composition

Composition Construct	Semantic Quality Criterion	
	Q_{cd}	Q_m
Sequential/ AND- Branching	$\dfrac{1}{|sl|}\sum_{sl} q_{cd}(sl)$	$\Pi_{sl} q_m(sl)$
OR- Branching	$\sum_{sl} q_{cd}(sl)\cdot p_{sl}$	$\sum_{sl} q_m(sl)\cdot p_{sl}$

rates for different links are all considered with the same importance.

The common description rate of an OR-Branching composition is a sum of $q_{cd}(sl)$ weighted by p_{sl} i.e., the probability that semantic link sl be chosen at run time. Such probabilities are initialized by the composition designer, and then eventually updated considering the information obtained by monitoring the workflow executions.

Definition 5. *(Matching Quality of a Composition): The matching quality of a composition estimates the overall matching quality of semantic links involved in the composition. Contrary to the common description rate, this criterion aims at easily distinguishing and identifying between very good and very bad matching quality.*

Table 3. Non functional quality aggregation rules for service composition

Composition Construct	Non Functional Quality Criterion	
	Q_t	Q_{pr}
Sequential/	$\sum_s q_t(s)$	$\sum_s q_{pr}(s)$
AND- Branching	$\max_s q_t(s)$	
OR- Branching	$\sum_s q_t(s)\cdot p_s$	$\sum_s q_{pr}(s)\cdot p_s$

Definition 5 motivates how to compute such a level of quality for sequential, AND-Branching and OR-Branching compositions.

The matching quality Q_m of a sequential and AND-Branching composition c is defined as a product of $q_m(sl)$. All different (non empty) matching qualities involved in such compositions require to be considered together in such a (non-linear) aggregation function to make sure that compositions containing semantic links with low or high matching quality will be more easily identified, and then pruned for the set of potential solutions.

The matching quality of an OR-Branching composition c is defined as the same way as its common description rate by replacing $q_{cd}(sl)$ by $q_m(sl)$ - see Table 2.

Besides considering functional qualities of a composition, we also consider its non functional properties. In this direction the Execution Price Q_{pr} of a sequential and AND-Branching composition c is a sum of every service's execution price $q_{pr}(s)$. The execution price of an OR-Branching composition c is defined in the same way as $Q_{cd}(c)$, by changing $q_{cd}(c)$ by $q_{pr}(s)$. Regarding the Response Time $Q_t(c)$ of a composition c of a sequential and AND-Branching composition c is a sum of the response time $q_t(s)$ of the services s that participate in the composition c whereas the $Q_t(c)$ of an AND-Branching composition c is bound by the highest response time of its AND-Branches (because of the design-time composition). The response time of an OR-Branching composition c is defined in the same way as $Q_{cd}(c)$, by changing $q_{cd}(c)$ by $q_t(s)$.

Using the above aggregation rules described in Table 2 and Table 3, the quality vector of any concrete composition can be defined by (7). Contrary to QoS criteria $Q_{l,l\in\{t,pr\}}$, the higher $Q_{l,l\in\{cd,m\}}$ the higher its lth quality for semantic criterion.

$$Q(c) := (Q_{cd}(c), Q_m(c), Q_t(c), Q_{pr}(c)) \qquad (6)$$

Equalities (3), (4), (5) as well as (6) can be extended by considering further quality of semantic links (e.g., their robustness (Lecue et al., 2007)) and services (e.g., reputation, reliability, availability (O'Sullivan et al., 2002)).

A SCALABLE APPROACH FOR QUALITY DRIVEN SEMANTIC WEB SERVICE COMPOSITION

Since scalability is one of our main concerns we suggest to compute a single concrete composition (by assigning a services to each task; Figure 4) among a set of potential solutions rather than computing the optimal composition (impractical in large domains). The selection process of such a concrete composition will be driven by constraints on i) the quality of component services and ii) the quality of their semantic links. To this end the quality model (5) is used to model local constraints on both semantic links and services whereas (6) is considered to model global constraints.

Example 6. *(Compositions and Constraints): Given a composition of tasks (e.g., in Figure 4) achieving a specific goal, the end-user is requested to provide some constraints on the composition she expects. For example, the end-user may have a limited budget and thus the execution price Q_{pr} is constrained, or he/she cannot accept a matching quality Q_m below a given limit. We can also imagine local constraints on specific tasks and semantic links.*

Towards this issue we formalize the problem as a *Constraint Satisfaction Problem* (CSP) and apply a stochastic search method to compute a solution that meets constraints. In this section, compositions refer to their concrete form.

CSP Formalization

CSP (Tsang, 1993) is a key formalism for many combinatorial problems such as ours. The success of this paradigm is due to its simplicity, its natural fit to a number of several real-world applications and especially the efficiency of existing underlying solvers. In addition such formalism allows a generic representation of any Web service composition problem with constraints. Hence, we formalize Web service composition as a CSP (Definition 6) with local and global constraints.

Definition 6. *(Composition-Driven CSP): A Composition-Driven CSP is defined as a triple (T, D, C):*

- *T is the set of tasks (variables) $\{T_1, T_2, ..., T_n\}$ defined in the composition;*
- *D is the set of domains $\{D_1, D_2, ..., D_n\}$. D_i represents possible concrete services that fulfill the task T_i;*
- *C is the set of constraints i.e., local C_L and global C_G. Unlike constraints C_L need to be satisfied for any given assignment (i.e., services and semantic links) to specific tasks T, constraints C_G need to be met by the overall concrete composition.*

Solving a composition-driven CSP consists in finding one (or all complete in more general cases) assignment of services $s_{i,1 \leq i \leq n} \in D_1 \times ... \times D_n$ to tasks $T_{i,1 \leq i \leq n}$ that satisfy all the constraints C.

In particular C_G and C_L can be defined according to some end-users profiles (e.g., preferences). On the one hand the end-user can define a global constraint C_G for each quality dimension, hence constraints regarding both the semantic and non functional quality of composition. On the other hand the end-user may also describe local constraints C_L on any service or semantic link, respectively regarding their non functional and semantic quality. For instance some constraints in C_G can be formalized according to (7), (8). Thus (7) constrains the common description rate of a sequential and AND-Branching composition to not be lower than a given value v (predefined by the end-user to model her constraints), whereas (8) constrains its execution price to not be upper than v.

$$\frac{1}{|sl_{i,j}^A|}\sum_{sl_{i,j}^A} q_{cd}(sl_{i,j}^A) \geq v, v \in [0,1] \quad (7)$$

$$\sum_{T_i} q_{pr}(T_i) \leq v, v \in R^+ \quad (8)$$

In case the local matching quality of a semantic link $sl_{i,j}$ is required to be higher than a given value $v \in [0,1]$ such a constraint can be defined by $q_m(sl_{i,j}^A) > v$. Similar local constraints can be applied on execution price (e.g., less than \$5, where 5 refers to the value $v \in [0,1]$) and response time of services (e.g., less than 1500 ms, where 1500 refers to the value $v \in [0,1]$).

Local constraints are enforced during service selection. Those which violate them are filtered from the list of candidate services, reducing its number and the size of the CSP.

A Stochastic Search Method

The composition-driven CSP is solved by adapting a *stochastic search method* (Tsang, 1993). Such a method sacrifices completeness (i.e., all solutions) for speed by computing "a single" solution. More precisely we adapt the *Hill Climbing algorithm* (Rich, 1991; Papadimtriou & Steiglitz, 1991), which is the most appropriate for a large number of services in domains $D_{i,1 \leq i \leq n}$. The Hill Climbing algorithm requires two functions:

- An *evaluation function* f which maps every composition c in the search space to a value according to (9). f assigns a better value to compositions c with high semantic quality attributes and low QoS attributes.

$$f(c) = \frac{\omega_{cd}\tilde{Q}_{cd}(c) + \omega_m \tilde{Q}_m(c)}{\omega_{pr}\tilde{Q}_{pr}(c) + \omega_t \tilde{Q}_t(c)} \quad (9)$$

where $\tilde{Q}_{l \in \{pr,cd,m\}}$ refer to Q_l normalized in the interval $[0,1]$. $\omega \in [0,1]$ is the weight assigned to the lth quality criterion and $\sum_{l \in \{pr,t,cd,m\}}\omega_l = 1$. In this way preferences on quality of the desired concrete compositions can be done by simply adjusting ω_l e.g., the Common Description rate could be weighted higher. Therefore unsatisfied constraints which have higher priority in (9) than others enforce the overall quality of the composition to be weakened.

- An *adjacency function* which maps every composition in the search space to some other compositions. Here two compositions are considered to be adjacent to each other if they differ in exactly one assignment (S,T) between them.

From this formalization the Hill Climbing algorithm starts with a random composition (let's say c_{final}) in the search space. All the compositions which are *adjacent* to c_{final} are evaluated using the *evaluation function*. In case some of its adjacent compositions have higher values than c_{final}, then one is picked non-deterministically to become the new final composition. Heuristics can be used for choosing from among the higher composition values when more than one exists. The algorithm iterates until all the constraints are satisfied by c_{final}, even if the algorithm can climb to a higher composition (in the sense of f). A solution to the composition-driven CSP is the first set of assignments which does not violates constraints.

In case no solution exists, users may revise and relax constraints. Instead, fuzzy logic could be used to address the imprecision in specifying quality constraints, estimating quality values and expressing composition quality.

All the CSP based search methods have worst case complexity which is exponential to the number of variables. However the stochastic search method such as the Hill Climbing algorithm scales better (in general cases) since it focuses on the first composition that met constraints.

IMPLEMENTATION AND EXPERIMENTS

In this section, we discuss the prototype tool that we developed to compute constraints-based semantic Web service composition in our framework. Moreover we give a preliminary evaluation of the suggested approach by analyzing some results obtained with the prototype developed.

Architecture and Implementation

Our technique of "Automated generation of scalable and QoS-aware semantic web service compositions" is implemented and integrated on top of a FLC model: the SLM (Semantic Link Matrix) model (Lecue et al., 2009). Our approach extends the latter model by performing the automated composition of web services by i) considering non-functional properties of their services (i.e., their QoS), and ii) the semantic similarity between parameters of incoming and outgoing services, the whole in a iii) scalable way and iv) by considering end user constraints on the expected composition result. Here we briefly overview the prototype architecture and discuss its extension to support quality of services and their quality of semantic links. The prototype architecture (Figure 5) consists of five main modules:

- The Web-based Interface the end-user will interact with,
- The Service Discovery and Selection module,

Figure 5. Architecture and implementation: from an integration point of view

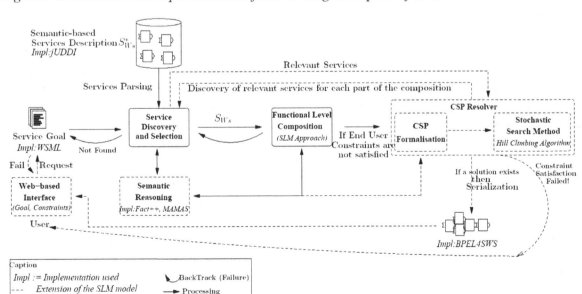

- A Functional Level Composition (FLC) module together with a pool of semantic-based services,
- A Semantic Reasoning component, and
- The whole extended by the stochastic search method to resolve the CSP.

From a *Web-based interface* the end user describes its goal she wants a service (or a composition) achieve. Such a goal is rendered in the so called service goal (Fensel et al., 2005), described in terms of its input and output parameters. In addition the end user is requested to provide the level of quality the final (composite) service will expose in term of non functional quality (Execution Price, Response Time) and semantic quality (Common Description rate, Matching Quality). The latter information has been formalized as constraints in previous sections, and they are provided by means of a profile of constraints.

From this the *Service Discovery and Selection module* facilitates the advertisement and location of relevant web services. It is implemented using i) a semantic extension of Java implementation of the Universal Description, Discovery and Integration (UDDI with its TModel), and ii) the Web Service Modelling Language (WSML) for describing semantic web services together with their domain ontologies. Note that WSML services have been also annotated by their Non Functional Properties NFP in terms of response time and execution price. This has been achieved according to the WSMO ontology for specifying QoS[3]: a set of ontologies (i.e., locative, temporal, availability, price, trust, security, etc.) providing the terminology needed to specify QoS aspects of services.

Once relevant web services are retrieved, the *Functional Level Composer FLC module* (i.e., SLM-based model which consider only stateless and semantic web services) aims at retrieving a partial order of these services by means of the Semantic Reasoning component. Roughly speaking the SLM model aims pre-composing and chaining services at design time according to their semantic links. However the computed composition does not necessarily match the constraints requested by the end user. Therefore a new step of constraints satisfaction is requested. This step requires a new and relevant allocation of services in the composition computed by the SLM-based model.

Then the *CSP solver* consists in assigning the most relevant service to each task (in term of the stochastic search method presented earlier in this paper) by first formalizing the CSP problem and then retrieving solutions to the latter problem. To this end this module interacts with the *Service Discovery and Selection module* in order to discover services that could fit the tasks of the composition. Finally the *CSP solver* either i) moves to the serialization of the service composition in case the *CSP solver* finds an appropriate solution (in terms of constraints satisfied) or ii) go back to the end user, asking less restricting constraints to achieve.

The architecture is completed by a *Semantic Reasoning Module*, which provides a vital infrastructural support to three components of the architecture i.e., the *Service Discovery and Selection Module*, the *Functional Level Composition Module*, and the *CSP Solver* module. The main function of this module is to infer some properties on input and output parameters of Web services. For instance the latter module standard ensures DL reasoning inference such as subsumption satisfiability or subsumption of Web service parameters by means of a DL reasoner. These are achieved by means of a DL reasoner Fact++[4] (Horrocks, 1998) whereas Abduction (required for computing difference between output and input parameters of services) is performed by MAMAS-tng[5]. In our approach we use the open source Fact++ reasoner to compute standard reasoning and the MAMAS-tng to compute non standard reasoning such as Concept Abduction. The power of such a module is therefore crucial to the performance of the overall architecture.

Experimental Results

First of all we expose our approach in three realistic scenarios to show the practical to use of our approach. To this end we:

1. Test the whole architecture in Figure 5 and comparing our approach with the other components (in term of execution time) i.e., mainly the *Service Discovery and Selection module* and the *Functional Level Composer module,*

In addition to test the applicability of the approach to problems of realistic complexity, we analyze its performance[6] through numerical simulation by:

2. Observing the evolution of constraints satisfaction over the iterations of the stochastic search method (here Hill Climbing algorithm),
3. Observing the evolution of the composition quality (9) over the iterations of the stochastic search method,
4. Decoupling the stochastic search method and the (offline) DL reasoning process required in our approach,
5. Comparing our approach with state-of-the-art approaches such as *Genetic Algorithm (GA)* (Canfora et al., 2005) and *Integer Programming (IP)* (Zeng et al., 2004) based approaches.

For the experiments (*Evolution of Constraints Satisfaction, Evolution of Composition Quality, and Search Process and DL Reasoning* sections) we have generated the descriptions of 300 tasks, and 350 alternative semantic service descriptions for each task (350^2 candidate semantic links between 2 tasks). We use an actual industrial (telecoms) ontology described in ALN with 1880 concepts and 560 properties, and estimate values

for price and response time. Common description rate and matching quality of semantic links are computed according to a DL reasoning process.

We conducted experiments using the implemented prototype system to evaluate our approach. In the experiments the PC used for running the prototype system had the configuration of Intel(R) Core(TM)2 CPU, 2.4GHz with 2GB RAM. The PC runs Linux-gnu (2.6.12-12mdk). Our approach is implemented in Java, extending an open source library[7].

Evaluating Constraints based Service Composition in Realistic Scenario

The constraints based service composition has been evaluated on three scenarios in use in France Telecom (Lecue et al., 2009):

*   One in the Telecom domain where the number of potential web services (i.e., $\#S_{Ws}^*$) is 35 and the ALN Ontology consists of 305 defined concepts and 117 object properties;
*   Another in the E-Tourism domain where $\#S_{Ws}^*$ is 45 and the ALN Ontology consists of 60 defined concepts and 19 object properties;
*   And finally one in the E-HealthCare domain where $\#S_{Ws}^*$ is 12 and the ALN Ontology consists of 105 defined concepts and 37 object properties.

The purpose of this experiment is to value the scalability of our approach in realistic scenario, and then compare it with the other components of the architecture (Figure 5).

The whole execution of the architecture takes at worst 0.201 second. This is much faster than it would take for a user to discover relevant services, compose them and then assign the most relevant service to each task, the whole satisfying some quality constraints.

From the Table 4 (testing on simple scenario in use i.e., no simulation based experimentation), we can see that the CSP Solving process (i.e., CSP Formalisation and Stochastic Search Method) are more time consuming than the FLC and Discovery processes. More particularly the execution time of the search method is constant in each scenario. This is caused by the small size of the scenario, but still real use cases in application. The CSP Solving process is mainly depending of the CSP formalisation, i.e., computing the adjacency function that links compositions.

Evolution of Constraints Satisfaction

Figure 6 reports the evolution of satisfaction constraints over the iterations[8] (also known as the number of nodes expanded in the search tree) of the stochastic search method, by varying the (average) number of tasks, i.e., 100, 200, 300.

Figure 6 illustrates different levels of convergence to a composition that meets the constraints by iteratively maximizing the common description and matching quality while minimizing price and response time (i.e., maximizing f).

Table 5 presents the computation costs and the number of iterations required to obtain a composition that met initial constraints. According to this and Figure 6 the more tasks, services the more time consuming to converge to a solution.

All constraints in the CSP problem have been equally considered. It is obvious that unsatisfied constraints with a higher priority could weaken the composition quality.

Evolution of Composition Quality

Figure 7 reports the evolution of the composition quality (9) (i.e., f with equal weights assigned to the different quality criteria) over the iterations of the stochastic search method, by varying the number of tasks, i.e., 100, 200, 300.

According to Figure 7 and Table 6, retrieving an (local) optimal composition is very time consuming, and then cannot be considered in large scale domains. However computing compositions

Table 4. Evaluating constraints based service composition in realistic scenario

Parameters and Processes	Detailed Parameters	Application Domain		
		Telecom (nbConcept:305)	E-Tourism (nbConcept:60)	E-HealthCare (nbConcept:105)
Initial Number of Web Services	$\# S_{Ws}^*$ (see Figure 5)	35	45	12
Discovery	Time Exec. (ms)	39.1	58.2	12.5
	$\# S_{Ws}$ (see Figure 5)	7	13	6
FLC	Time Exec. (ms)	8.8	49.5	6.3
CSP Solver	Constraints	Non Functional and Semantic Level	Non Functional and Semantic Level	Non Functional and Semantic Level
	Number of candidate services per task	5	3	2
	CSP Formalisation (Time Execution in ms)	40.1	90.6	15.2
	Stochastic Search method (Time Execution in ms)	2.6	3.1	2.4

Figure 6. Constraints satisfaction evolution

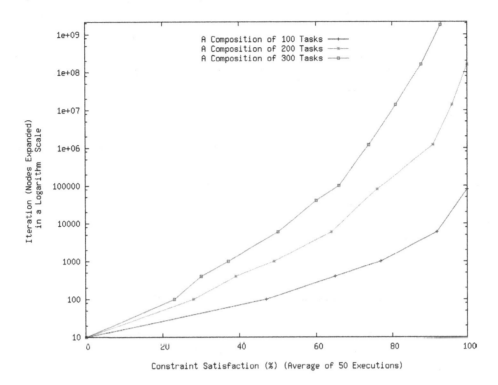

Figure 7. Composition quality evolution

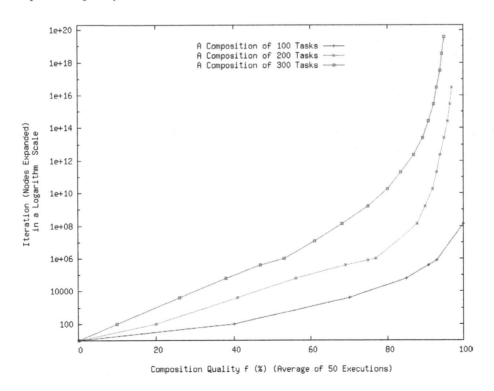

Table 5. Evaluating constraints satisfaction

Tasks Num	Const. Satisfaction (%)	Iterations	Time (ms)
100	99	8.10^4	2912
200	97	16.10^7	4850
300	95	22.10^{11}	8142

that simply satisfied initial constraints is more scalable. Note that compositions with an average quality of 53% met the initial constraints in our experiments.

Search Process and DL Reasoning

Contrary to QoS given (in general) by providers, the quality of semantic links are estimated according to DL reasoning (i.e., Subsumption for q_m; Abduction and lcs for q_{cd}). Since our approach is depending of the latter reasoning and the stochastic search method, we suggest decoupling and detailing their computation costs in Figure 8.

DL reasoning is the most time consuming process in large-scale problem of quality-driven semantic web service composition (i.e., number of tasks and candidate services greater than 100 and 350). This is caused by i) the large number of potential semantic links between tasks and ii) the critical complexity of q_{cd} computation through DL Abduction (even in ALN DL).

Table 6. Evaluating composition quality

Tasks Num	Comp. Quality (%)	Iterations	Time (s)
100	99	14.10^7	845
200	97	3.10^{16}	9531
300	95	36.10^{18}	>10 hours

Comparison with Other Approaches

We compare our approach with alternatives based on IP (Zeng et al., 2004) and GA (Canfora et al., 2005) by upgrading their quality criteria with quality of semantic links. To this end we focus on the computation (or convergence) time of these approaches to satisfy a given set of quality constraints of a composition. Here 90% of constraints should be satisfied.

In more details, the evaluation function (9) requires to be maximized with the IP and GA based approaches. (9) is restricted to quality criteria $\tilde{Q}_{cd}$, $\tilde{Q}_{pr}$ in order to satisfy the linearity constraint attached to the IP approach.

The IP-based optimization problem is solved by running CPLEX, a state of the art IP solver based on the branch and cut technique[9] (Wolsey, 98) whereas the GA approach is implemented in Java, extending a GPL library[10]. As a case study we considered a composition of 300 tasks where the number of candidate services varies from 1 to 500.

Even if our stochastic search method does not compute optimal composition, the results of this experimentation (Figure 9) confirm its adoption for large domains such as the web since it outperforms both GA and IP for a large number of candidate services per task (from 280).

Such results of IP and GA based approaches are, in parts, explained by the exponential search required to compute the optimal composition.

CONCLUSION

In this work we studied quality-driven semantic web service composition. Our approach has been directed to meet the main challenges facing this problem, i.e., how to effectively compute compositions of QoS-driven web services by considering their semantic links in large domains such as the Web. First of all we have presented an innovative

Figure 8. DL reasoning and search method

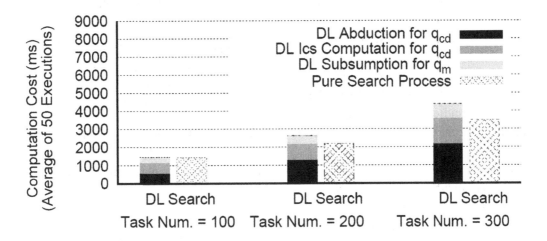

and extensible model to evaluate quality of i) web services (QoS), ii) their semantic links, and iii) their compositions. In regards to the latter criteria, the problem is formalized as a CSP problem with multiple constraints. Since one of our main concerns is about selection of large-scale web service compositions (i.e., many services can achieve a same functionality), we suggested to follow a

Figure 9. Comparing state-of-the-art approaches

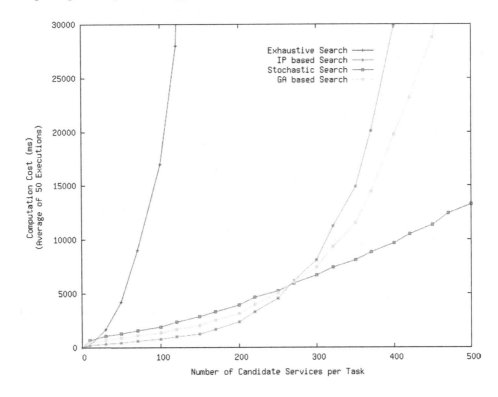

stochastic search method which is faster than optimizing them. The experimental results have confirmed the latter and have shown acceptable computations cost of our approach despite the time consuming process of the off-line DL reasoning. In addition our approach has been implemented and tested in a more complete architecture where service discovery and composition are present. This overall architecture has also been tested in three realistic scenarios in use.

The main direction for future work is to consider a finer abduction operator, which is easy-to-compute in expressive DLs. We also plan to extend the quality model by considering domain-specific/dependent QoS criteria (e.g., a temperature service could have QoS attributes such as precision or refresh frequency) for which the aggregation function has to be user-specified. We will also focus on an extension of the semantic link definition, by considering the type assigned to input and output variable at run time. Finally the dynamic distribution of the CSP on different peers needs also to be studied to improve the convergence time of our approach.

ACKNOWLEDGMENT

This work is conducted within the European Commission VII Framework IP Project Soa4All (Service Oriented Architectures for All) (http://www.soa4all.eu/), Contract No. IST-215219.

REFERENCES

Aggarwal, R., Verma, K., Miller, J. A., & Milnor, W. (2004). Constraint Driven Web Service Composition in METEOR-S. In *Proceedings of the International Conference on Services Computing* (pp. 23-30).

Ankolenkar, A., Paolucci, M., Srinivasan, N., & Sycara, K. (2004). *The OWL-S coalition* (Tech. Rep. OWL-S 1.1). OWL.

Ardagna, D., & Pernici, B. (2007). Adaptive service composition in flexible processes. *IEEE Transactions on Software Engineering, 33*(6), 369–384. doi:10.1109/TSE.2007.1011

Arpinar, I. B., Zhang, R., Aleman-Meza, B., & Maduko, A. (2005). Ontology-driven web services composition platform. *Inf. Syst. E-Business Management, 3*(2), 175199.

Baader, F., & Nutt, W. (2003). In *the Description Logic Handbook: Theory, Implementation, and Applications*.

Baader, F., Sertkaya, B., & Turhan, A.-Y. (2004). Computing the least common subsumer w.r.t. a background terminology. In *Proceedings of the DL*.

Berbner, R., Spahn, M., Repp, N., Heckmann, O., & Steinmetz, R. (2006). Heuristics for QoS-aware Web Service Composition. In *Proceedings of the ICWS* (pp. 72-82).

Berners-Lee, T., Hendler, J., & Lassila, O. (2001). The semantic web. *Scientific American, 284*(5), 34–43. doi:10.1038/scientificamerican0501-34

Brandt, S., Kusters, R., & Turhan, A. (2002). Approximation and difference in description logics. In *Proceedings of the KR* (pp. 203-214).

Canfora, G., Penta, M. D., Esposito, R., & Villani, M. L. (2005). An approach for qos-aware service composition based on genetic algorithms. In *Proceedings of the GECCO* (pp. 10691075).

Cardoso, J., Sheth, A. P., Miller, J. A., Arnold, J., & Kochut, K. (2004). Quality of service for workflows and web service processes. *Journal of Web Semantics, 1*(3), 281–308. doi:10.1016/j.websem.2004.03.001

Colucci, S., Noia, T. D., Sciascio, E. D., Donini, F., & Mongiello, M. (2005). Concept abduction and contraction for semantic-based discovery of matches and negotiation spaces in an e-market-place. In *Proceedings of the ECRA, 4,* 41–50.

Fensel, D., Kifer, M., de Bruijn, J., & Domingue, J. (2005). Web Service Modeling Ontology. *W3C.*

Harel, D., & Naamad, A. (1996). The STATE-MATE semantics of Statecharts. *ACM Transactions on Software Engineering and Methodology, 5*(4), 293–333. doi:10.1145/235321.235322

Hassine, A. B., Matsubara, S., & Ishida, T. (2006). A constraintbased approach to web service composition. In *Proceedings of the ISWC* (pp. 130-143).

Horrocks, I. (1998). Using an expressive description logic: Fact or fiction? In *Proceedings of the KR* (pp. 636-649).

Hwang, C.-L., & Yoon, K. (1981). *Multiple Criteria Decision Making.* LNEMS.

Kopecky, J., Vitvar, T., Bournez, C., & Farrell, J. (2007). SAWSDL: y Semantic annotations for WSDL and XML schema. *IEEE Internet Computing, 11*(6), 60–67. doi:10.1109/MIC.2007.134

Kusters, R. (2001). *Non-Standard Inferences in Description Logu ics (LNCS 2100).* New York: Springer. doi:10.1007/3-540-44613-3

Lassila, O., & Dixit, S. (2004, March). Interleaving discovery and composition for simple workflows. In *Semantic Web Services, AAAI Spring Symposium Series* (pp. 22-26).

Lecue, F., Boissier, O., Delteil, A., & Leger, A. (2009, March). Web service composition as a composition of valid and robust semantic links. *IJCIS, 18*(1).

Lecue, F., Delteil, A., & Leger, A. (2007). Applying abduction in semantic web service composition. In *Proceedings of the ICWS* (pp. 94 101).

Lecue, F., Delteil, A., & Leger, A. (2008). Optimizing causal link based web service composition. In *Proceedings of the ECAI* (pp. 45-49).

Lecue, F., & Leger, A. (2006). A formal model for semantic web service composition. In *Proceedings of the ISWC* (pp. 385398).

Li, L., & Horrocks, I. (2003). A software framework for matchmaking based on semantic web technology. In Proceedings of the WWW (pp. 331-339).

McIlraith, S. A., Son, T. C., & Zeng, H. (2001). Semantic web services. *IEEE Intelligent Systems, 16*(2), 46–53. doi:10.1109/5254.920599

O'Sullivan, J., Edmond, D., & ter Hofstede, A. H. M. (2002). What's in a service? *Distributed and Parallel Databases, 12*(2/3), 117–133. doi:10.1023/A:1016547000822

Paolucci, M., Kawamura, T., Payne, T., & Sycara, K. (2002). Semantic matching of web services capabilities. In *Proceedings of the ISWC* (pp. 333347).

Papadimtriou, C. H., & Steiglitz, K. (1982). *Combinatorial Optimization: Algorithms and Complexity.* Upper Saddle River, NJ: Prentice-Hall.

Rao, J., Kungas, P., & Matskin, M. (2003, June). Application of linear logic to web service composition. In *Proceedings of the 1st International Conference on Web Services* (pp. 3-10).

Rao, J., Kungas, P., & Matskin, M. (2006). Composition of semantic web services using linear logic theorem proving. *Information Systems, 31*(4-5), 340–360. doi:10.1016/j.is.2005.02.005

Rich, K. K. (1991). *E. Artifice Intelligence.*

Russell, S., & Norvig, P. (1995). *Artificial Intelligence: a modern approach.* Upper Saddle River, NJ: Prentice-Hall.

Smith, M. K., Welty, C., & McGuinness, D. L. (2004). OWL web ontology language guide. In *Proceedings of the W3C recommendation*.

Sycara, K. P., Paolucci, M., Ankolekar, A., & Srinivasan, N. (2003). Automated discovery, interaction and composition of semantic web services. *Journal of Web Semantics*, *1*(1), 27–46. doi:10.1016/j.websem.2003.07.002

Teege, G. (1994). In Doyle, J., Sandewall, E., & Torasso, P. (Eds.), *Making the difference: A subtraction operation for description logics* (pp. 540–550). San Francisco, CA: Morgan Kaufmann.

Tsang, E. (1993). *Foundations of Constraint Satisfaction*.

Wolsey, L. (1998). *Integer Programming*. New York: John Wiley and Sons.

Wu, D., Parsia, B., Sirin, E., Hendler, J. A., & Nau, D. S. (2003). Automating DAML-S web services composition using SHOP2. In *Proceedings of the International Semantic Web Conference* (pp. 95-210).

Yu, T., & Lin, K.-J. (2005). Service selection algorithms for composing complex services with multiple QoS constraints. In *Proceedings of the ICSOC* (pp. 130143).

Zeng, L., Benatallah, B., Ngu, A. H. H., Dumas, M., Kalagnanam, J., & Chang, H. (2004). Qos-aware middleware for web services composition. *IEEE Transactions on Software Engineering*, *30*(5), 311–327. doi:10.1109/TSE.2004.11

Zhang, R., Arpinar, I. B., & Aleman-Meza, B. (2003). Automatic composition of semantic web services. In *Proceedings of the ICWS* (pp. 38-41).

ENDNOTES

[1] In this paper we introduce the term Semantic Link as equivalent to Causal Link in (Lecue and Leger, 2006).

[2] Distributed ontologies are not considered here but are largely independent of the problem addressed in this work.

[3] http://www.wsmo.org/ontologies/nfp/

[4] http://owl.man.ac.uk/factplusplus/

[5] http://dee227.poliba.it:8080/MAMAS-tng/DIG

[6] Here, we do not report cases where no solution is retrieved.

[7] http://opensource.arc.nasa.gov/software/javagenes/

[8] An iteration occurs in case the current composition c does not meet the constraints and some of its adjacent compositions c' have the following property: $f(c) < f(c')$.

[9] LINDO API v5.0, Lindo Systems Inc. http://www.lindo.com/

[10] http://jgap.sourceforge.net/

This work was previously published in the International Journal of Web Services Research, Volume 7, Issue 4, edited by Liang-Jie (LJ) Zhang, pp. 41-63, copyright 2010 by IGI Publishing (an imprint of IGI Global).

Chapter 12
The MACE Approach for Caching Mashups

Osama Al-Haj Hassan
University of Georgia, USA

Lakshmish Ramaswamy
University of Georgia, USA

John A. Miller
University of Georgia, USA

ABSTRACT

In recent years, Web 2.0 applications have experienced tremendous growth in popularity. Mashups are a key category of Web 2.0 applications, which empower end-users with a highly personalized mechanism to aggregate and manipulate data from multiple sources distributed across the Web. Surprisingly, there are few studies on the performance and scalability aspects of mashups. In this paper, the authors study caching-based approaches to improve efficiency and scalability of mashups platforms. This paper presents MACE, a caching framework specifically designed for mashups. MACE embodies three major technical contributions. First, the authors propose a mashup structure-aware indexing scheme that is used for locating cached data efficiently. Second, taxonomy awareness into the system is built and provides support for range queries to further improve caching effectiveness. Third, the authors design a dynamic cache placement technique that takes into consideration the benefits and costs of caching at various points within mashups workflows. This paper presents a set of experiments studying the effectiveness of the proposed mechanisms.

INTRODUCTION

Web 2.0 is drastically changing the landscape of the World Wide Web by empowering end-users with new tools for enhanced interaction and participation. Among Web 2.0 applications, mashups

DOI: 10.4018/978-1-4666-1942-5.ch012

(Programmable Web, 2009) are becoming increasingly popular as they provide end-users with high degrees of personalization. Conceptually, mashups are Web services that are created by end-users who also *consume* their results. They offer high level of personalization because they are developed by end-users themselves as opposed to regular Web services which are designed by professional developers. (Throughout this paper, the term Web services refer to traditional Web service model in which a service provider creates and deploys Web services).

Mashups basically collect data from several data sources distributed across the Web, which would then be aggregated, processed, and filtered to generate output which would be sent to end-user. Several mashup platforms exist on the Web including Yahoo Pipes (Yahoo Inc., 2007) and Intel MashMaker (Intel Corp., 2007). The unique features of mashups, represented in high personalization and end-user participation, pose new scalability challenges. First, giving end-users the privilege of designing their own mashups causes a mashup platform to host a large volume of mashups which implies that the scalability requirement for mashup platforms is much higher when compared with Web services portals. Second, large volumes of mashups also imply that the opportunities for data reuse are minimal unless specialized mechanisms to boost data reuse are adopted. Third, mashups fetch data from several data sources across the Web; these data sources differ in their characteristics and their geographical distribution. Finally, mashups may be designed by non-technical-savvy end-users, and hence they are not necessarily optimized for performance. Unfortunately, scalability and performance challenges of mashups received little attention from the research community. Although there have been some studies on the performance of traditional orchestrated Web service processes (Chandrasekaran, 2003), to our best knowledge, no studies have investigated efficiency and scalability aspects of mashups or proposed techniques to tackle them.

This paper explores caching as a mechanism to alleviate the scalability challenges of mashups. Caching is a proven strategy to boost performance and scalability of Web applications. For example, Web content delivery and Web services have long adopted caching (Wang, 1999). Several caching techniques have been specifically developed for

Web services (Tatemura, 2005; Terry, 2003). However, most of these techniques cannot be directly used for mashups because of some significant differences between Web services and mashups. We need a caching framework that not only takes into account the structural characteristics of mashups but is also adaptive to the various dynamics of the mashup platform.

Contributions

This paper describes the design and evaluation of MACE (**ma**shup **c**ache) - a server-side cache framework for the mashup domain. MACE is sensitive to the structural composition of the mashups, and it can store results at intermediate stages of mashup workflows. The design of the MACE framework embodies three original contributions.

- We design a mashup structure-aware scheme for indexing cached data which enables MACE to efficiently discover whether any of the currently cached data can be reused in the execution of a newly created mashup.
- We incorporate taxonomy-awareness and provide support for range queries to further increase reuse of cached data.
- We present a dynamic cache point selection scheme that estimates the benefits and costs of caching data at different stages of mashup trees. Our approach selects a set of points that collectively maximize the benefit-to-cost ratio of caching data at those points.

We have evaluated the MACE framework through several sets of experiments. Our experiments demonstrate that MACE significantly improves the scalability and efficiency of mashup platforms. In the following sections, we discuss our motivations for doing this research and describe our mashup model and architecture. We follow that by proposing our index structure that eases accessing mashups. We then introduce two techniques to increase the utilization of our index, namely support of range queries and taxonomy awareness. Further, we describe our caching scheme for mashups. Finally, we investigate our model by discussing a detailed set of experiments.

MACE: BACKGROUND AND DESIGN OVERVIEW

In this section, we outline the challenges that need to be addressed in developing an effective cache framework for the mashup domain. Further, we develop a formal model for mashups which serves as an analytical framework for studying their performance.

Motivation

Although mashups are in-essence Web services, there are significant differences between mashups and traditional Web services. As exemplified by Yahoo Pipes (Yahoo Inc., 2007), mashup platforms typically host several thousands of distinct mashups, whereas the number of *distinct* Web services in a typical Web services portal is relatively small. The frequency of execution of most individual mashups is expected to be modest (the request rate experienced by the mashup platforms may still be very high due to the large number of

mashups they host). Thus, the data generated in a mashup platform is substantially greater than its Web services counterpart, whereas the opportunity for data reuse is much lower.

As Web services are authored by professional developers, they are optimized for performance, and they usually adhere to certain broad guidelines with respect to their overall structures. Therefore, it is possible for a human to identify the stages of Web services at which the results should be cached. On the other hand, mashups can be extremely heterogeneous in terms of their structure, as they are created by large sets of individuals with varying degrees of technical expertise. Further, most mashups require data from external sources, which implies that the costs of executing them depend upon external conditions upon which the mashup platform has little control. A comparison between Web service portals and mashup platforms is summarized in Table 1.

Because of these differences, traditional Web service caching schemes are inadequate for mashups. Mashups demand a more dynamic caching strategy, wherein: (a) the intermediate results of mashup computations can be stored for future use; (b) the cache enables the intermediate results of one mashup to be used in another; and (c) the caching decisions are based upon dynamic benefit-cost analysis which also take into account the external conditions.

Table 1. Comparison between Web service portals and mashup platforms

Comparison Criteria	Web Service Portals	Mashup Platforms
Created By	Developers	End-users
Number of distinct Web services/ mashups	Several hundreds	Several thousands
Degree of personalization	Limited	High
Adherence to design guidelines	Strong	Weak
Ease of data reuse	High	Low
Optimized at design time	Typical	Rare
Data sources	Mostly internal	Mostly external

Mashup Model

In this section, we develop a formal model for mashups. A mashup platform can be thought of as a system that contains a set of mashups; a mashup fetches data from sources that are distributed across the Internet, processes the fetched data in ways specified by the end-users, and dispatches the processed data to the end-users who again are distributed over a wide-area network. $MpSet = \{Mp_0, Mp_1, ..., Mp_{N-1}\}$ represents the mashups existing in the mashup platform at a given point in time. The mashup platform includes a set of classes of basic processing operators such as *filter*, *sort*, *join*, *truncate*, *count*, *location-extraction*, *reverse*, *subelement*, *tail*, and *unique*. For ease of modeling, we introduce two special classes of operators. The *fetch* operator class corresponds to the function of retrieving data required for a mashup from an external or an internal source, and a *dispatch* operator class represents the function of dispatching the mashup results to the end-user. . $OpSet = \{op_0, op_1, ..., op_{M-1}\}$. denotes the set of classes of operators available in the mashup platform. Without loss of generality, operators classes op_{M-2} and op_{M-1} correspond to the fetch (represented as fo) and dispatch (do) operators classes, respectively. The rest of the $OpSet$ elements are data processing operators classes. Each operator class may specify certain requirements on the number of inputs that are fed into it and the type and formats of these inputs. Also, each operator class always produces the same type of output. For example, the sort operator class expects a single table with possibly multiple rows and columns as input, and produces a table with the same number of rows and columns as output.

A mashup comprises of a set of operators instances chosen from the $OpSet$. Every mashup contains one or more instance of the fetch operator class and one instance of the dispatch operator class. Specifically, a mashup is modeled as a *tree* with each node corresponding to a mashup operator instance. In this tree, the output of an operator node forms (one of the) inputs of its parent node. Furthermore, the dispatch operator instance always forms the root of the tree, and each leaf node corresponds to a fetch operator instance. $\{nd_0^l, nd_1^l, ..., nd_{Q-1}^l\}$ represent the nodes in the tree of the mashup Mp_l, where each node corresponds to an instance of operator class from $OpSet$. We note that while an individual mashup is modeled as tree, multiple mashups might share data sources, thus forming directed acyclic graphs (DAGs). Although some mashups update the original data sources, this work focuses on those that process data from remote sources rather than the ones that update them.

Each operator in $OpSet$ is associated with two functions. The *cost function*, represented as $CF^{op_j}(s_0, s_1, ..., s_{q-1})$ for operator op_j represents the cost of performing the operation. The parameters $s_0, s_1, ..., s_{q-1}$ represent the sizes of the inputs to the operator op_j. The concept of cost function is generic, and it can be measured in a variety of ways including latency involved in performing the operation and the computational/communication load imposed by the operation. In this paper, we quantify the cost of an operator instance through its latency. The output size estimation function, represented as $OSF^{op_j}(s_0, s_1, ..., s_{q-1})$ captures the size of the output of the operator instance op_j, where $s_0, s_1, ..., s_{q-1}$ are the sizes of the inputs. The *cost value* of a node nd_i^l (denoted as $CV^{nd_i^l}$) in the mashup Mp_l is the value of the cost function of the corresponding operator instance on the specific inputs indicated in the mashup tree. Similarly, the output size value $OSV^{nd_i^l}$ of the node nd_i^l is output size function of the corresponding operator instance evaluated on the inputs specified by the mashup tree.

The total cost of executing the mashup Mp_l is the sum of the cost values of all its operators instances. Similarly, the output size of mashup

Mp_i is *OSV* of its root node. Henceforth, for ease of representation, we refer to instances of operators classes as operators.

High Level Architecture

Figure 1 illustrates the architecture of the MACE system. The MACE system is co-located with the mashup platform. However, it is designed such that the mashup platform itself would require minimal modifications to work in conjunction with MACE.

In order for MACE to select stages at which data will be cached, it continuously observes the execution of mashups, and collects statistics such as request frequencies, update rates and costs and output size values at various nodes of the mashups. It then performs cost-benefit analysis of caching at different nodes of mashups, and chooses a set of nodes that are estimated to yield best benefit-cost ratios. An operator node in a mashup tree that is chosen for caching by MACE (i.e., the results until that stage of the mashup execution would be stored) is called a *cache point*. Any node in the mashup tree except the root of the tree (corresponding to the dispatch operator) can potentially be chosen as a cache point. This set of nodes is called the *potential cache point set*

(*PcpSet*), and each individual node in this set is referred to as *potential cache point*.

MACE also interacts with the mashup editor to obtain newly created mashups. For each new mashup, the MACE platform analyzes whether any of the cached results can be substituted for part of the mashup workflow. If so, the mashup is modified so that cached data is re-used, and only the additional operations required for completing the mashup are performed. The modified mashup is then provided to the mashup platform for execution. In addition to these two main features, the MACE platform also incorporates the basic cache functionalities such as replacement scheme and data consistency mechanism. This paper focuses on the design of a dynamic cache point determination technique and mechanism to re-use the cached data for substituting parts of incoming mashups. The next sections describe these two unique features of the MACE platform.

CACHE INDEXING FOR EFFICIENT DATA REUSE

Determining points of data reuse in newly created mashups is not a straightforward task. Notice that a cache point represents the results of com-

Figure 1. MACE architecture

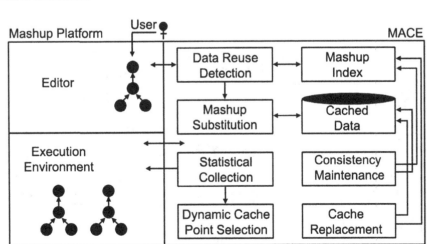

putations occurring in a *subtree* of the mashup tree. This subtree itself might have one or more branches with fetch operators at the leaves. The results at a particular cache point Cp_h can be reused for a new mashup Mp_l if and only if the subtree represented by Cp_h *exactly matches* a subtree in Mp_l. By exact matching, we mean that a subtree of the incoming mashup has the same structure as that of the subtree represented by Cp_h, and parameters of operators in both subtrees are the same. Since mashup platforms support large numbers of mashups, we need a scalable mechanism to find out whether one or more subtrees of a new mashup match existing cache points. MACE includes a novel cache point indexing scheme to address this issue, which is explained later in this section. If one or more subtrees of a new mashup Mp_l are found to match existing cache points in MACE system, Mp_l is modified as follows. For each subtree that matches an existing cache point, the subtree is replaced with a fetch operator that references the cached data corresponding to the cache point. For example, if an arbitrary subtree St_q of a Mp_l, matches an existing cache point Cp_h, St_q is replaced with a fetch operator that refers to the cached data corresponding to Cp_h. The modified mashup is then sent to the mashup platform which executes it. Figure 2 illustrates the modification of a new mashup to reuse data available in the cache. We now explain our mashups representation and indexing that enables efficient discovery of cache points.

B+ Tree Mashup Index

We use the B+ tree structure to index cache points. Each operator in *OpSet* is given a unique identification string. A mashup workflow is represented by concatenating its operators' unique identification strings. Unlike other operators, join operators have two components to be joined and that makes its representation a little bit different than regular operators. A Join operator starts with special character SU: starts a join block, followed by the first component, followed by a special character MU: comes in the middle between joined components, followed by the second component, followed by a special character EU: ends a join block. Figure 3 shows an example of a mashup representation. The dashes in index keys are not part of mashup representation; they are introduced as separators between attributes for more clarity.

The index nodes' entries of the B+ tree are substring of mashups identification strings. They are entered to the index based on their lexicographical order. Consider the following mashup example, Fetch data source "buycars.cars.com", filter data based on model="Honda", sort on

Figure 2. Cached data reuse in MACE

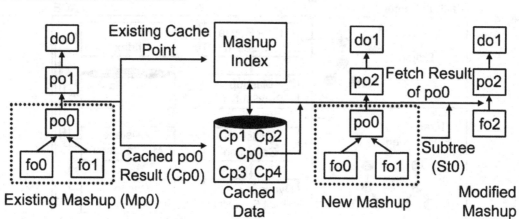

Figure 3. Mashup representation and index

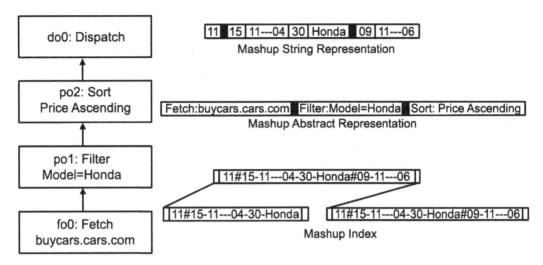

"price", if we decide to cache after the filter operator is executed, then "11#15-11-04-30-Honda" will be inserted into the index. However, if we decide to cache after the whole mashup execution flow is done, then "11#15-11-04-30-Honda#09-11-06" is inserted into the index. Figure 3 shows the mashup index if we decided to cache after both of the previous 2 points. The numbers in identification strings are IDs of the data sources, operators and attributes forming a mashup, for example, the filter operation (15-11-04-30-Honda) is interpreted as follows, "15" is the ID of the filter operator, "11" is the data source ID from which attribute "04" is taken, "30" is the ID of the equality operator and "Honda" is the value on which the attribute "04" is filtered. In the previous identification strings # represents a special character which works as a separator between operators. Notice that each operator's identification string reflects the operators which precede it in the mashup workflow; this enables us to index mashups without losing order of execution of mashup operators.

RANGE QUERIES AND TAXONOMY AWARENESS

Until now, our design of the indexing scheme is focused on lookups for *exact matches*. However, supporting lookups for inexact matches can considerably increase the reuse of cached data. Consider the case when the cache contains superset of data needed for an incoming mashup. In this case, the data in the cache can be appropriately filtered and reused for the new mashup. Unfortunately, looking up for exact matches would fail to even locate the existence of the superset, thereby precluding the possibility of data reuse.

Towards addressing this issue, we enhance our indexing mechanism to support two specific kinds of inexact matching, namely, range queries and hierarchical taxonomies. Our strategy relies on the fact that the keys in the leaf level of the B+ tree index are sorted, which implies that mashups that are lexicographically close by to one another are stored either in the same index node or in a nearby node.

Supporting Range Queries

Suppose that a new mashup requires data with parameter "p" being in the range interval [x,y]. With exact matching, if the mashup index does not contain the precise range [x,y], a *cache miss* occurs and the new mashup is executed end-to-end. Consider the scenario when the cache contains the results of an earlier mashups that is similar to the new one except that parameter "p" is in the range [a,b]. Now the question is whether this data can be reused for the new mashup? In order to determine this, we need to consider three distinct cases. First, if "x≥a and y≤b", then this means that range interval [x,y] is fully included within range interval [a,b] which also means that the result of the new mashup is fully contained within the result of the existing mashup. In this case, a cache hit is declared and a local search within the result of the existing mashup is performed to extract the result of the new mashup. Second, if "x≥a and y>b" or "x<a and y≤b" or "x<a and y>b", then the range interval [x,y] is partially included in the range interval [a,b]. Here, because the result of the new mashup cannot be completely satisfied by the existing cached mashup result, then a cache miss is declared and the new mashup is executed end-to-end. It is noteworthy that this partial inclusion relationship can be useful in two situations. First, the case where partial results can be extracted from cached data and we query for missing data, then the missing data and partial results are combined. Second, the case where the new mashup cannot be executed due to difficulties in communicating with data sources. In such a situation, the data available in the cache is reused to provide the end-user with a valid but incomplete result. For example, if we consider the "x≥a and y>b" scenario, the result satisfying the range interval [x,b] can be provided for the end-user from cached data. Such a result is not complete, but it is still valid and may be useful to the end-user. Third, if "x<a and y<a" or "x>b and y>b", then the range [x,y] is totally outside the range [a,b]. In this case, a cache miss is declared and the new mashup is executed end-to-end.

The inherent capability of the B+ tree structure to lookup range values can be leveraged for the above purpose. The following example illustrates how this is achieved in the MACE framework. Suppose the following mashup result is cached in the system: Fetch data from "buycars.cars.com" then filter data based on "price < 5000". Based on our mashup string representation, this mashup is represented in the cache as "11#15-11-06-32-5000" where the last 4 digits correspond to the value on which data is filtered (5000). Now, suppose an end-user asks for a new mashup which is described as follows, fetch data from "buycars.cars.com" then filter data based on "price < 4000", the new mashup is represented as "11#15-11-06-32-4000". This case represents case 1 where the range interval of the new mashup is fully included within the range interval of the existing mashup. We can see that the two mashups have some common part (11#15-11-06-32) in their string representation. Without using range query improvement, a search for the new mashup representation "11#15-11-06-32-4000" results in a cache miss, this happens because we make exact matching between index keys and the mashup representation we are looking for. When using range query awareness, the search process for previous mashup (11#15-11-06-32-4000) in the tree explores through index levels based on lexicographical order of keys and eventually arrives at the existing mashup key "11#15-11-06-32-5000". Now, instead of declaring a cache miss, we detect that this key (11#15-11-06-32-5000) and the key we are looking for (11#15-11-06-32-4000) represent the same mashup except that the value on which data is filtered is different. Here, we do not have to execute the new mashup right from its starting point, instead, we search items that the previous key points to and then exclude items with price between 4000 and 5000. Accordingly, we achieve better utilization of out mashup index. As an example of case 2, suppose the new mashup is filtering data based on "price<6000", here the result of the new mashup is partially included in the existing mashup cached result. Normally, we declare a cache miss and execute the new mashup from scratch, but if the new mashup execution is interrupted due to communication problems, then a cache hit is declared and the end-user is provided with the result of car items cheaper than $5000. One might argue that providing incomplete result is not accurate. Although this is true, the partial result can satisfy end-user demands in many cases, here in the car example, the end-user might find a suitable car within the incomplete list of cars.

Note that when MACE caches mashup results, it may so happen that two results sets (of two distinct mashups) overlap without anyone of them being a subset of the other. In such a scenario, we do not make duplicate copies of data that is common to both sets. We maintain a single copy of the common items but store the pointer at two distinct locations in the index. This maximizes the utility of the available storage.

Supporting Hierarchical Taxonomies

The range query technique presented in the previous section works well for numeric parameters. However, in many cases, end-users can create mashups that extract general information, while others might create mashups that extract more specific information with respect to parameters that are non-numeric. Consider the case when the mashup platform caches the results of a mashup that extracts all sports related stories from "sports. yahoo.com". Now, suppose another end-user creates a mashup that extracts all stories related to tennis from "sports.yahoo.com". Clearly, the results of the new mashup are more specific and constitute a subset of the results of the existing mashup. The previous range query mechanism cannot be used for this case as the parameter is keyword-based.

We have developed a mechanism to detect these types of generic/specific relationships among mashups in terms of keyword parameters. The central idea is to build a hierarchical taxonomy that defines relationship between various keywords or categories. The assumption is that a keyword at a higher level in the hierarchy subsumes all keywords which reside underneath it. This hierarchical taxonomy is used to enhance data reuse and minimize cache misses. When a new mashup is created, our strategy is not to just search the index for earlier mashups with exactly matching keywords, but also to look for existing mashups that have *ancestors* of the keywords in the incoming mashup. Specifically, suppose an existing mashup filters data based on non-numeric keyword-valued parameter "p" being equal to "X", and suppose this result is cached. Later, suppose a new mashup which is identical to the existing mashup except that "p" equals "Y" is created. Normally, a cache miss is declared and the new mashup is executed end-to-end. However, providing that a hierarchical taxonomy exists, we can use it to look for a possible relationship between X and Y. If X is an ancestor (direct or indirect parent) of Y, then the result of new mashup is a subset of the cached result. However, the cached results cannot be directly used for the new mashup. The cached results have to be locally filtered to the actual result of the new mashup. As an example, suppose the cache contains the result of the mashup that fetches data from "sports.yahoo.com", then filter data based on the criterion "category = sport". The index has the key "09#15-09-02-32-sport" corresponding to this data in the cache, where "sport" is the value on which data is filtered. Now, suppose an end-user creates a mashup to fetch data from "sports.yahoo.com", then filter data based on "category = tennis". The key for the new mashup is "09#15-09-02-32-tennis", where "tennis" is the value on which data is filtered. The search process for the new mashup in the cache starts by exploring the index until we reach the level containing the key "09#15-09-02-32-sport". If we are going to use exact matching to look for the new mashup in the cache, we will end up with a cache miss. Instead, we detect that the part "09#15-09-02-32" is common between the new mashup and the cached mashup, so we extract the value on which the cached mashup is filtered (sport) and we extract the value on which the new mashup is filtered (tennis), then we consult the taxonomy to look for a possible relationship between these two keywords. Since "tennis" is a child of "sport" in the taxonomy, we conclude that the result of the new mashup is contained in the result of the previously cached mashup. Consequently, the result of the new mashup can be found by locally filtering the cached data of the first mashup. Figure 4 illustrates the above example.

CACHE POINT SELECTION TECHNIQUE

In this section, we describe our dynamic cache point selection technique. We formulate the dynamic cache point selection as an optimization problem following which we provide efficient algorithms for cache point selection.

Problem Formulation

This section formulates the cache point selection as a cost-benefit optimization problem. We provide two flavors of the cost-benefit optimization problem. The first one models a scenario wherein the storage-space availability at MACE is unlimited and the second corresponds to the scenario in which the MACE system has limited storage capacity. We begin by introducing terminology and notation that are employed in the problem formulation.

Potential cache point set $\left(PcpSet = \{Pcp_0, Pcp_1, ..., Pcp_{M-1}\}\right)$ represents the *unique* potential cache points corresponding to the mashups existing in the *MpSet*. Recall that every operator node in a mashup except the root is a potential cache point. The members of *PcpSet* are unique in the sense that the potential cache points that represent subtrees which exist in multiple mashups are included only once. The sum of the cost values of all the descendant nodes of a potential cache point Pcp_k including the cost value of Pcp_k is called the *cumulative cost value* of Pcp_k

$$\left(CCV^{Pcp_k} = CV^{Pcp_k} + \sum_{Pcp_h \in Descendent(Pcp_k)} (CV^{Pcp_h})\right).$$

Figure 4. Taxonomy support in MACE

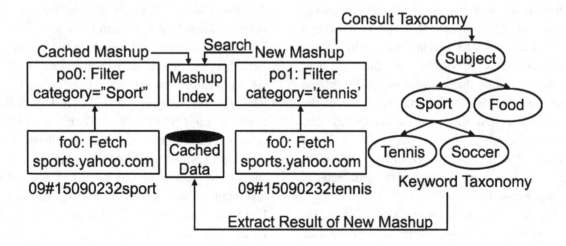

Cost-Benefit Analysis

The benefits of caching the results at a particular potential cache point Pcp_k is that the cached data would be reused for any future requests of all mashups that Pcp_k is part of, thus avoiding the re-executions of Pcp_k and all of its descendant nodes. Let *request frequency* of Pcp_k (represented as RF^{Pcp_k}) denote the number of times Pcp_k needs to be executed per unit time to satisfy end-user requests if the output of Pcp_k is not cached. Note that RF^{Pcp_k} is the total sum of the request frequencies of all the individual mashups that the subtree under Pcp_k is part of. Thus, the benefits per unit time obtained by caching at Pcp_k is $RF^{Pcp_k} \times CCV^{Pcp_k}$.

Caching at a potential cache point Pcp_k involves two distinct costs, namely *consistency costs* and *storage costs*. Consistency costs are the costs involved in maintaining the consistency of cached data in the face of updates to the data from external sources that are used in computing the output of Pcp_k. Notice that the data cached at Pcp_k becomes invalid, and would need to be updated anytime the data obtained through any of the fetch operators below Pcp_k changes. Each time the output of Pcp_k needs to be recomputed, Pcp_k and all of its descendant nodes need to be re-executed. Thus, the consistency costs per unit time of caching at Pcp_k can be quantified as $UF^{Pcp_k} \times CCV^{Pcp_k}$, where UF^{Pcp_k} represents the sum of the update frequencies of all the external data sources fetched by the operators below Pcp_k.

The storage costs of caching at Pcp_k are directly proportional to the size of the output (OSV^{Pcp_k}). However, notice that the storage costs only matter when available storage is limited. Furthermore, storage costs and consistency costs are inherently different, and cannot be combined into a single equation in meaningful way. We model the storage costs as constraint rather than optimization criterion.

$RF^{Pcp_k} \times CCV^{Pcp_k} - UF^{Pcp_k} \times CCV^{Pcp_k}$ is called the *cost-benefit trade-off* for Pcp_k (represented as CBT^{Pcp_k}). CBT^{Pcp_k} quantifies the net cost-savings obtained by caching at Pcp_k. Note that in this formulation of CBT^{Pcp_k}, the computational overheads incurred at the time of serving end-user requests and those incurred to maintain consistency of cached data, are of equal importance. In scenarios where one is more important than the other, the two terms of CBT^{Pcp_k} have to be appropriately weighted to reflect their relative importance.

Scenario 1 -- No storage limitations: As stated earlier, the objective of the dynamic cache point selection scheme is to select a set of cache points such that the benefit-cost tradeoff is maximized. Let X^{Pcp_k} be a $\{0,1\}$ variable denoting whether Pcp_k is selected as a cache point (X^{Pcp_k} is 1 if Pcp_k is chosen and 0 otherwise). Therefore, the optimization criterion would be to assign X^{Pcp_k} values to each potential cache point $Pcp_k \in PcpSet$ such that $\sum_{Pcp^k \in PcpSet} X^{Pcp_k} \times CBT^{Pcp_k}$ is *maximized*. However, notice that the optimization problem, as it stands, can lead to *duplicate-caching* (caching same or interdependent data multiple times thus wasting resources). In order to avoid this, we introduce the following constraint. For any pair of potential cache points $\{Pcp_k, Pcp_i\}$ such that $Pcp_k \in Descendent(Pcp_i)$ or vice-versa, $X^{Pcp_k} + X^{Pcp_i} \leq 1$.

Scenario 2 -- Limited storage: The optimization problem for the limited storage scenario is similar to the previous case, but the total storage requirements of cached data should not exceed the storage available in the MACE system. Suppose Sg denote amount of storage available. The optimization problem can be stated as follows. Assign values to decision variables $\{X^{Pcp_0}, X^{Pcp_1},...,X^{Pcp_{(M-1)}}\}$ corresponding to the potential cache points $\{Pcp_0, Pcp_1,..., Pcp_{M-1}\}$ such that $\sum_{Pcp^k \in PcpSet} X^{Pcp_k} \times CBT^{Pcp_k}$ is *maximized* while ensuring that the following constraints are not violated:

$$X^{Pcp_k} \in \{0,1\}, \forall Pcp_k \in PcpSet \qquad (1)$$

$$\forall \{Pcp_k, Pcp_i\} \qquad (2)$$

such that

$$Pcp_k \in Descendent(Pcp_i) \, || $$
$$Pcp_i \in Descendent(Pcp_k), X^{Pcp_k} + X^{Pcp_i} \leq 1;$$

and

$$\sum_{Pcp_k \in PcpSet} X^{Pcp_k} \times OSF^{Pcp_k}(ips) \leq Sg, \qquad (3)$$

where the variable ips represent the inputs to the operator at Pcp_k as specified in the mashups. This is a constrained discrete optimization problem solving which requires exhaustive search of the solution space. In the next section, we present a greedy strategy-based algorithm for this problem.

Cache Point Selection Algorithms

First, we consider the scenario wherein the storage space is not a constraint. Statistics such as the request frequencies and update frequencies of all potential cache points are collected, and the corresponding cumulative cost values are calculated. For each mashup in the platform, our algorithm searches for the best cache point as follows. The algorithm starts searching from the potential cache point that is shared across many other mashups, and at the same time is located at lower-levels of the mashup tree. This can be achieved by starting at a node that has the maximum value for $\frac{SMCount}{Height}$, where $SMCount$ (sharing mashups count) indicates the number of mashups that share the potential cache point and $Height$ indicates its height in the mashup. The rationale for starting the search at such a node is that it is likely to yield

maximum reuse (thereby maximizing the benefits) at low consistency maintenance costs. Suppose the algorithm starts from the potential cache point Pcp_k. The node that is currently being searched is called the *current search point (CSP)*. We calculate CBT^{CSP} as $RF^{CSP} \times CCV^{CSP} - UF^{CSP} \times CCV^{CSP}$. We then compare the value of CBT^{CSP} to the CBT value of its ancestor in the mashup and the CBT value of its descendant in the mashup (if Pcp_k has multiple descendants, we consider the sum of their CBT values). If the CBT value of the ancestor is higher than that of Pcp_k, the ancestor is initialized as the new CSP, and the algorithm continues searching upwards from that point. If, on the other hand, the descendant node had a higher CBT value, the descendant is initialized as the new CSP and the algorithm continues searching downwards. If Pcp_k has multiple descendants, the algorithm continues searching downwards from each of them. The search terminates when we reach one or more nodes such that the CBT values of their respective descendants and ancestors are lower than their CBT values[1]. The potential cache point(s) at which the search terminates are chosen as the cache points and included in the *cache point set (CPSet)*. The algorithm searches each mashup in a similar fashion to discover all the cache points. This algorithm yields optimal solution to the scenario with no storage limitations. The algorithm is linear in terms of the number of potential cache points in the platform.

We now extend the above algorithm for the limited storage scenario. Recall that discovering optimal solutions for this scenario requires exhaustive search of the solution space. Therefore, our objective is to design an efficient algorithm that yields close to optimal solutions. The algorithm for the limited storage scenario works in two stages. The first stage is exactly similar to the algorithm described above for the scenario wherein the storage space is not a limitation.

However, the storage requirements for *CPSet* obtained at this step may exceed the available storage (Sg). The second stage of the algorithm performs additional level of pruning as follows. For each cache point Pcp_k in the *CPSet* produced at the end of first step, it calculates the ratio

$$BCS^{Pcp_k} = \frac{CBT^{Pcp_k}}{OSV^{Pcp_k}}$$. This ratio quantifies the

per-byte cost savings obtained by caching the results of Pcp_k. The cache points are sorted in the descending order of their *BCS* values. The algorithm then progressively eliminates the cache points from the end of this sorted list (i.e., the cache points with the least *BCS* values are eliminated first) until the results of the cache points remaining in the *CPSet* can fit into the available storage. The rationale for this elimination strategy is to retain cache points that provide maximum benefits for the amount of storage space they consume. Once the *CPSet* is computed, the MACE engine starts storing the outputs of the cache points.

EXPERIMENTS AND RESULTS

Our experimental study has three objectives: 1) Study the impact of MACE's dynamic cache point selection on the performance of the mashup platform. 2) Evaluate the benefits and overheads of the proposed cache point indexing scheme. 3) Test the impact of range queries and taxonomy awareness support on our system. First, we describe the experimental setup.

Experimental Setup

Our experimental setup simulates a mashup environment with a mashup server, 80 data sources and 100000 end-users spread out on the Internet. The mashup server in our setup is, to a considerable extent, based upon the Yahoo Pipes environment (Yahoo Inc., 2007). Similar to Yahoo pipes, our mashup platform contains 10 distinct operators namely, *filter*, *sort*, *join*, *truncate*, *count*, *location-extraction*, *reverse*, *subelement*, *tail*, and *unique*. End-users continuously create mashups which are executed on the mashup server. The mashup server executes the mashup and disseminates the results to the end-user.

We use two datasets for our experiments -- a real dataset and a synthetic dataset. In the real dataset, we build our mashup to closely reflect reality. In this dataset, we have 5000 mashups which pull data from 80 real data sources over the Web. These data sources are extracted from syndic8 (Barr, 2008) feeds repository. This repository is a directory of RSS and Atom feeds existing on the Web. When a mashup is executed, an actual connection to data sources is made to fetch data and the communication time needed to fetch data is measured. We also implemented a set of operators so that they process the real fetched data and therefore their execution time is also measured. In our real mashup set, the mean value for latency to extract data from data sources is 0.6 seconds and the average number of items in these sources is 21 items. The number of subscriptions to a data source is representative of its popularity. In Figure 5, we plot the popularities of various feeds. To study the characteristics of the feed popularity, we also show a curve depicting the Zipfian distribution with α (exponent value) = 0.9. The diagram shows that feeds popularity closely resembles the Zipfian distribution. Similarly, Figure 6 indicates that the feed sizes also resemble Zipfian distribution with α = 0.9. Figure 7, on the other hand, plots the relationship between feed popularity and feed data sizes. The figure shows that most feeds have small data sizes and low popularity.

Our synthetic dataset contains simulated operators where the execution time for each of these operators is estimated by performing a number of experiments on Yahoo pipes wherein we evaluated the latencies and output sizes of individual operators on XML feeds with sizes varying from 100 KB to 3 MB. As a result, we have real-

Figure 5. Feeds popularity compared to Zipfian distribution

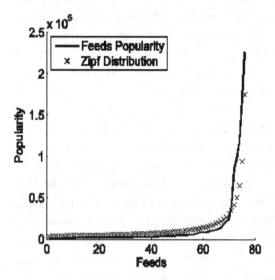

Figure 6. Feeds sizes compared to Zipfian distribution

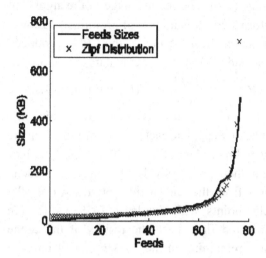

istic cost functions and output size functions. The number of distinct mashups existing at the platform in the synthetic dataset varies with the experiment, and it ranges from 1000 to 5000. The mean value for latency to extract data from data sources is 15 seconds and the average number of items in these sources is 536 items. For our synthetic dataset, the network topology is based upon the measurement by DIMES (Shavitt, 2005) on the actual Internet in 2008. We use BRITE (Medina, 2001) and BRITE extension (Wahlisch, 2008) to transform DIMES data into a more convenient form. Our topology has 378444 nodes.

Evaluation of the Dynamic Cache Point Selection Scheme

In the first set of experiments, we quantify the performance benefits of the dynamic cache point selection scheme. The dynamic cache point selection scheme is compared to two other schemes: *End-results caching* wherein only the end-results of the mashups are cached, and *No caching* wherein the mashup platform does not employ any type of caching. These three schemes are compared with

respect to the total cost incurred by the mashup platform in serving the end-user requests. For an individual mashup, the cost is quantified as the associated computational latency at the mashup platform.

In the first experiment, we compare the three schemes as the mean of the request rates of all mashups varies from 20 requests per unit time

Figure 7. Relationship between feeds popularity and feeds data sizes

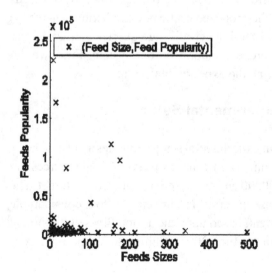

Figure 8. Total cost when request frequency is variable

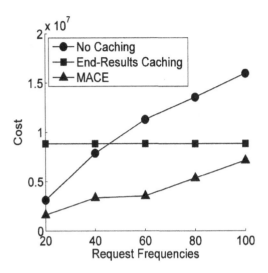

Figure 9. Total cost when update frequency is variable

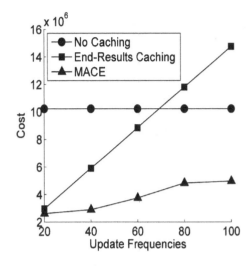

to 100 requests per unit time. The total number of mashups at the server is 5000 (therefore, the cumulative request rate at the mashup server varies from 10,000 and 500,000). In the synthetic dataset, a Zipfian distribution with $\alpha = 0.9$ is used to model the popularity variations among the individual mashups, while in the real dataset, popularity variations among individual mashups is extracted from syndic8 feeds repository. The mean of the update frequencies of the data sources (henceforth referred to as update frequency) is set to 60. This experiment is conducted on the synthetic dataset. The cache is assumed to have enough storage to hold the results (intermediate or final) of all mashups. Thus, we use the dynamic cache point selection algorithm for the no-storage limitations scenario. Figure 8 shows the total costs per unit time for the results of the experiments. As the results indicate, the cost incurred by the MACE's dynamic cache point is lower than the other two schemes throughout the simulated request rate range. The cost incurred by the End-results caching scheme is essentially constant as requests are served using cached data not requiring additional computations. In End-results caching, costs are mainly due to re-calculation of the

cached results when one or more inputs used in a mashup changes[2]. At very low request rates, the costs of no-caching scenario are comparable to those of the MACE system. However, the costs of no-caching scenario rises quickly with increasing request rates. It is to be noted here that although the costs of the dynamic cache point selection scheme increases with increasing request rates, it does not rise indefinitely; its curve becomes flat once upon reaching the End-results caching cost levels.

In the second experiment (Figure 9) which is also conducted on the synthetic dataset, we study effect of update frequencies of data sources on the performances of the three schemes. The setup is very similar to that of the previous one except that the mean mashup request rate is fixed at 60 requests per unit time whereas the update frequency of all data sources is varied from 20 to 100 per unit time. Again, we see that the MACE system yields significantly better performance than the other two schemes. However, in this experiment, the costs of the no-caching scenario remain constant. This is because, there is no cached data that needs to be recomputed when the input data changes.

Figure 10. Total cost in the cases of synthetic and real data when request frequency is variable

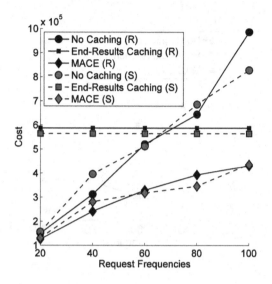

Figure 11. Total cost in the cases of synthetic and real data when update frequency is variable

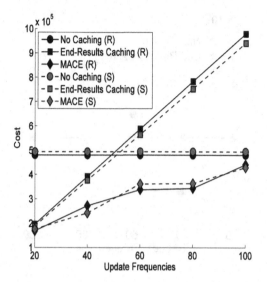

In the third experiment, we aim to compare the results of experiments of the synthetic dataset with the results obtained from the real dataset. So, we measure the total cost per unit time required for executing our mashup set in both cases. First, we fix update rate to 60 updates per unit time and we vary request rate in the range of 20 to 100 requests per unit time. After that we fix request rate to 60 requests per unit time and we vary update rate in the range of 20 to 100 updates per unit time. In Figure 10 and Figure 11, "R" refers to real dataset and "S" refers to synthetic dataset, these two figures show that the patterns we have for the real dataset are similar to the patterns we have for the synthetic dataset, the only thing different is the scale of cost values. The cost values for real data set in Figure 10 and Figure 11 reflect the real world and make our experiments more realistic.

The better performance of the dynamic cache point selection scheme is essentially due to its ability to adapt to the changing update and request frequencies by moving the cache point to upper or lower levels of the tree. Figure 12 demonstrates this phenomenon by plotting the average level of the cache points as the update frequency varies from 20 to 100. The mean mashup request rate remains constant at 60. As the results indicate, as the update rate increases, MACE selects cache points that are located at lower-levels of the tree thereby reducing the costs of recomputing the cached results. The End-results caching, on the other hand, always caches at the same level (just before the dispatch operator).

In the next experiment, we use our synthetic dataset to evaluate the three scenarios when the storage available at the caches is limited. In this experiment, we fix the total request rate at 60 and update frequency at 180. The storage availability is varied from 10% to 100% of the storage needed for caching entire result set for the particular caching strategy. Least Recently Used cache replacement is employed for all schemes. As Figure 13 demonstrates, MACE results in better performance by selecting cache points that provide higher per-byte cost savings.

Figure 12. Level of cache points when update frequency is variable

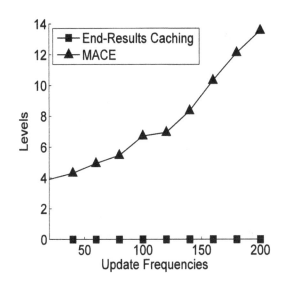

Figure 13. Total cost when available storage is variable

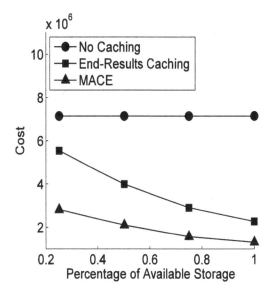

Mashup Index Analysis

In the second set of experiments, we use our synthetic dataset to study the scalability and performance of MACE's indexing mechanism by measuring the average latency involved in accessing a cache point stored in the B+ tree index. In the first experiment in this set, we evaluate the effects of request rate on the index access time. The mashup server has 5000 mashups with each mashup having 11 operators. The update frequency of all data sources is held constant at 60. As Figure 14 shows, index access time decreases as request frequency increases. This is due to two factors. First, when request frequency increases, MACE tends to select cache points near the roots of the respective mashup trees. As we move closer to the root, the width of the tree shrinks and the number of cache points in the index decreases. Second, MACE analyzes a new mashup starting from its root and goes down the tree looking for matching cache points. At high request frequencies, the cache points are closer to the root, and hence the search for matching cache points concludes faster. This result shows an important strength

of our indexing scheme - it responds faster when the request rates are higher thereby improving the mashup platform's scalability.

Next, we study the effect of the mashup depth on index access time. The server again contains 5000 mashups. The mean mashup request rate

Figure 14. Total index access time when request frequency is variable

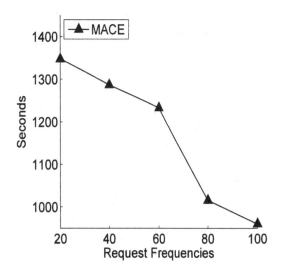

and the update frequency are both set to 60. Figure 15 shows the index access times when the depth of the mashups is varied from 5 to 20. Initially, the index access time increases linearly with mashup depth. The reason for this behavior is that probability of selecting cache points from lower levels of the tree increases as the mashup depth increases, and hence the search for matching cache points takes more time to conclude. However, the index access time becomes flat when the mashup depth reaches around 15.

Evaluation of Range Queries and Taxonomy Awareness

In this experiment which is conducted on the real dataset, we study the effect of using partial matching on mashup index utilization. The mashup server has 5000 mashups with each mashup having 11 operators. The update frequency of all data sources is held constant at 60. Figure 16 shows that using support for range queries decreases the total cost for executing mashups by 9 percent. This effect happens because mashup index hit rate increases as Figure 17 shows. In the case where range queries are not supported, an index search might result in a cache miss. On the other hand, when range queries are supported, the probability of having a cache hit from searching the index increases. For the experiment of range queries, wherever we have a filter operator that filters data based on a numeric attribute, we use a numeric value between 1000 and 5000 upon which data is filtered (e.g., price<3000). The numeric value is selected randomly from the range 1000-5000. The effect of taxonomy awareness is shown in Figure 18 where we notice that the total cost for executing mashups decreases when taxonomy awareness is used. This also occurs because of the increase in mashup index hit rate which is shown in Figure 19. An index lookup might result in a cache miss when taxonomy awareness is not used, but when it is used, the probability of having cache hits increases. We build our taxonomy by

Figure 15. Total index access time when mashup depth is variable

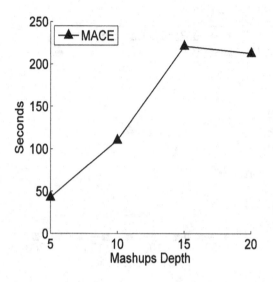

extracting keywords from Google search-based keyword tool (Google Inc., 2008). This tool classifies the keywords people search for and put it in categories. The tool enables its users to search for keywords as well as download keywords categories and keyword lists as CSV files. When we build our mashups, wherever a filter operator is used, a random keyword or category name from the taxonomy is used as the parameter upon which data is filtered. We believe that the percentage of improvement resulted from using the feature of range queries and taxonomy awareness is affected by the following. First, such a feature can only be applied to a subset of the operators that can be used to build mashups. For example, range queries support can be used for filter, truncate, and tail operators, but it cannot be used for fetch, reverse, and unique operators. Second, the number of keywords end-users can choose from and the number of numeric values the end-users can use in their operators is high; therefore, the possibility of detecting operators where range query and taxonomy support can be used is low. Further improvement can be reached by considering the patterns end-users follow for selecting keywords

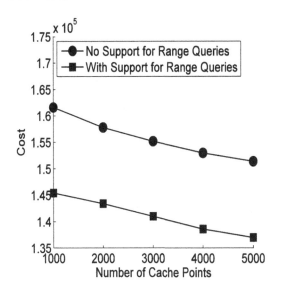

Figure 16. The effect of for range queries support on the total cost

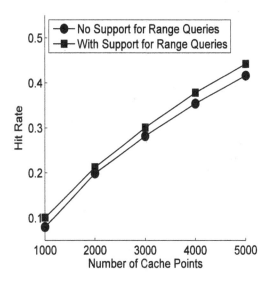

Figure 17. The effect of range queries support on index hit rate

and selecting numeric values in different domains. For example, if more end-users are interested in car prices below $5000, this can be an indication that most of end-user mashups related to filtering car results might contain "price < 5000". The same principle is applied to taxonomy awareness, if end-users care most about food, then more mashups are expected to use keywords related to food domain. Incorporating end-user patterns in building mashups is expected to produce more realistic results.

RELATED WORK

Research in the area of mashups is still in its nascent stages. MARIO (Riabov, 2008) is a recent mashup editing tool in which mashups are built from tags and executed using a planning algorithm. DAMIA (IBM Corp, 2007) is a data integration service for situational applications in the enterprise domain. Kulathuramaiyer (2007) describes a mashup for digital journals which enables its users to explore digital libraries using semantic-rich meta-data. Subspace (Jackson, 2007) adopts the sandboxing

principle to isolate applications into trust layers. Marmite (Wong, 2007) is a mashup tool implemented as a Firefox plug-in using Java Script and XUL, it enables end-users to aggregate and filter data from several Web contents and services. It also has the capability of directing mashups output to several sources such as websites, text files, or even compliant source code that can be customized. MashMaker (Ennals, 2007) is a mashup Web tool that enables end-users to manipulate data from other websites and define their visualized queries over it; it also provides sharing of mashups as widgets among end-users. Liu (2007) provides a mashup architecture that is based on an extension of the Service Oriented Architecture (SOA). Similar to (provider, broker, and consumer) SOA roles, their system presents roles of mashup component builder, mashup server, and mashup consumer, such that these roles interact together to facilitate data and services composition to end-users through a Web based interface. Karma (Tuchinda, 2008) is another mashup platform that enables end-users to build mashups by example. They argue that using widgets as building blocks

Figure 18. The effect of taxonomy awareness on total cost

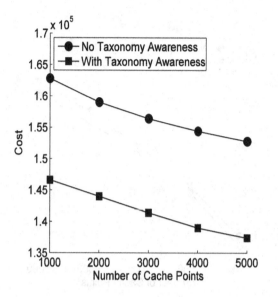

Figure 19. The effect of taxonomy awareness on Index hit rate

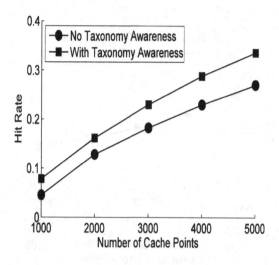

of mashups is not convenient for end-users because as a mashup platform grows, the number of widgets grows as well and that will confuse the end-user on which widget he needs to perform his task. Based on that, the authors let end-users extract data they want from websites. The data is stored behind the scenes as DOM trees and it is visualized to the end-user as tables, then the end-user can visually work on the data with the help of their system. Their system allows end-users to fix and integrate data and define rules between attributes of data, these attributes are stored in the system as XPath rules and the system intelligently applies the rules on data containing the previous attributes. SMash (Dekeukelaere, 2008) is a security model that can be integrated in Web browsers in order to make mashup applications secure. The Authors state that current browsers security models are not appropriate for mashups, because mashups require interaction between different data sources while regular browsers usually disallow such interactions between links coming from different sources. SMash defines a security model so that scripts coming from different data

sources are not allowed to change each others data. At the same time, the model does not allow such scripts to spy on end-user data banks. The model applies component isolation in mashups while at the same time guaranteeing communication between components using authenticated communication channels. The model also defines security rules on which types of interactions are allowed between components. To our best knowledge, the previous mashup platforms do not use caching while in MACE we introduce caching for mashups.

Web content caching in general has received considerable research attention (Iyengar, 1997; Wang, 1999; Ramaswamy, 2005; Yin, 2002). Issues such as caching granularity, caching architectures, consistency maintenance and data placement and replacement strategies have been extensively investigated. Various caching techniques are proposed to optimize several parameters in Web caching. One category of those schemes is cache routing schemes (Thaler, 1998; Valloppillil, 1997) where hashing is used to map files to cooperative caches groups. A second category is multicast-based schemes (Michel, 1998) where communication and coordination between caches is performed using IP level multicasting. A third category is directory-based schemes (Fan, 1998; Tewari, 1999) where a subset of contents of cooperative caches is stored in every cache. Ninan (2003) proposes a lease based scheme called cooperative leasing in which a lease based technique is used to maintain document consistency. Gao (2005) proposes a scheme for edge caching where different levels of object consistency have been taken into account in order to minimize consistency maintenance costs. A dynamic scheme for disseminating data is presented in (Shah, 2004) where each data object has its own dissemination tree which is built based on coherency requirements of caches.

Web services, have been an active area of research in which aspects such as description, discovery, composition, and efficiency of Web services are addressed (Benatallah, 2006; Ardagna, 2007; Aoyama, 2002). Web services caching in particular gained interest from the research community. In WReX (Tatemura, 2005), a caching middleware architecture for caching XML Web services responses is proposed. Terry (2003) discusses caching XML Web services for mobile clients. Caching Web services by utilizing proxy caches is used to minimize communication in mobile ad hoc networks (Artail, 2006). Dorn (2006) proposes a scheme to maintain Web services availability in cases of communication link interruptions; their scheme utilizes a cache proxy to increase the availability of Web services. Ramasubramanian (2004) explains that WSDL which is used to describe Web services lacks information to support caching, so authors extend WSDL to include information about what operations are cacheable in a way that is transparent to clients and servers. Challenges on caching Web services in PDAs is discussed in (Liu, 2007) where the authors provide a caching scheme that helps alleviate problems resulting from loss of connectivity and

their scheme is adaptable to bandwidth changes. However, as we remarked earlier, most of the existing Web service caching schemes store results at fixed stages of the Web services, and hence are less effective for the mashup domain.

CONCLUSION

Traditional Web service caching schemes are not effective for mashup domain due to its unique characteristics. In this paper, we presented the design and evaluation of MACE $--$ a dynamic caching framework for mashups. MACE is based upon a formal mashup model wherein an individual mashup is represented as a tree of operators. MACE's design includes a dynamic mashup cache point selection scheme which maximizes the benefit of mashup caching. We have also proposed a novel indexing mechanism that supports efficient discovery of mashup cache points. Our indexing mechanism not only supports queries for exact matches but also range queries and hierarchical taxonomy-based queries. Through a detailed experimental study, we showed that MACE can significantly improve performance and scalability of mashup platforms.

REFERENCES

Aoyama, M., Weerawarana, S., Maruyama, H., Szyperski, C., Sullivan, K., & Lea, D. (2002). Web services engineering: promises and challenges. In *Proceedings of the International Conference on Software Engineering* (pp. 647-648).

Ardagna, D., & Pernici, B. (2007). Adaptive service composition in flexible processes. *IEEE Transactions on Software Engineering, 33*(6), 369–384. doi:10.1109/TSE.2007.1011

Artail, H., & Al-Asadi, H. (2006). A Cooperative and Adaptive System for Caching Web Service Responses in MANETs. In *Proceedings of the International Conference on Web Services* (pp. 339-346).

Barr, J., & Kearney, B. (2001). *syndic8 feeds repository*. Retrieved from http://www.syndic8.com

Benatallah, B., & Motahari-Nezhad, H. R. (2006). Servicemosaic project: modeling, analysis and management of web services interactions. In *Proceedings of the Asia-Pacific conference on Conceptual modeling* (pp. 53-79).

Chandrasekaran, S., Miller, J. A., Silver, G., Arpinar, I. B., & Sheth, A. P. (2003). Performance Analysis and Simulation of Composite Web Services. *Electronic Markets: The International Journal, 13*(2), 120–132. doi:10.1080/1019678032000067217

Corp, I. B. M. (2007). *Damia*. Retrieved from http://services.alphaworks.ibm.com/damia/

Dekeukelaere, F., Bhola, S., Steiner, M., Chari, S., & Yoshihama, S. (2008). SMash: secure component model for cross-domain mashups on unmodified browsers. In *Proceedings of the WWW* (pp. 535-544).

Dorn, C., & Dustdar, S. (2006). Achieving Web Service Continuity in Ubiquitous Mobile Networks the SRR-WS Framework. In *Proceedings of the International Workshop on Ubiquitous Mobile Information and collaboration Systems (UMICS)*.

Ennals, R. J., & Garofalakis, M. N. (2007). MashMaker: mashups for the masses. In *Proceedings of the ACM SIGMOD international conference on Management of data* (pp. 1116-1118).

Fan, L., Cao, P., Almeida, J., & Broder, A. (1998). Summary Cache: A Scalable Wide-Area Web Cache Sharing Protocol. *ACM SIGCOMM, 28*(4), 254–265. doi:10.1145/285243.285287

Gao, L., Dahlin, M., Nayate, A., Zheng, J., & Iyengar, A. (2005). Improving Availability and Performance with Application-Specific Data Replication. *IEEE Transactions on Knowledge and Data Engineering, 17*(1).

Google Inc. (2008). *Search-based keyword tool*. Retrieved from http://www.google.com/sktool/

Intel Corp. (2007). *Mash Maker*. Retrieved from http://mashmaker.intel.com/web/

Iyengar, A., & Challenger, J. (1997). Improving web server performance by caching dynamic data. In *Proceedings of the USENIX Symposium on Internet Technologies and Systems* (pp. 49-60).

Jackson, C., & Wang, H. J. (2007). Subspace: secure cross-domain communication for web mashups. In Proceedings of the *WWW* (pp. 611-620).

Kulathuramaiyer, N. (2007). Mashups: Emerging application development paradigm for a digital journal. *Journal of Universal Computer Science, 13*(4), 531–542.

Liu, X., & Deters, R. (2007). An efficient Dual Caching Strategy for Web Service-Enabled PDAs. In *Proceedings of the ACM Symposium on Applied Computing* (pp. 788-794).

Liu, X., Hui, Y., Sun, W., & Liang, H. (2007). Towards Service Composition Based on Mashup. In *Proceedings of the 2007 IEEE Congress on Services* (pp. 332-339).

Medina, A., Lakhina, A., Matta, I., & Byers, J. (2001). Brite: an approach to universal topology generation. In *Proceedings of the International Symposium on Modeling, Analysis and Simulation of Computer and Telecommunication Systems* (pp. 346-353).

Michel, S., Nguyen, K., Rosenstein, A., Zhang, L., Floyd, S., & Jacobson, V. (1998). Adaptive Web Caching: Towards a New Global Caching Architecture. *Computer Networks and ISDN Systems, 30*(22-23), 2169–2177. doi:10.1016/S0169-7552(98)00246-3

Ninan, A., Kulkarni, P., Shenoy, P., Ramamritham, K., & Tewari, R. (2003). Scalable Consistency Maintenance in Content Distribution Networks Using Cooperative Leases. *IEEE Transactions on Knowledge and Data Engineering, 15*(4), 813–828. doi:10.1109/TKDE.2003.1209001

Programmable Web. (2009). Retrieved from http://www.programmableweb.com

Ramasubramanian, V., & Terry, B. (2004). *Caching of XML Web Services for Disconnected Operation* (Tech. Rep. No. MSR-TR-2004-139). Microsoft Corp.

Ramaswamy, L., Iyengar, A., Liu, L., & Douglis, F. (2005). Automatic Fragment Detection in Dynamic Web Pages and Its Impact on Caching. *IEEE TKDE, 17*(6), 859–874.

Riabov, A., Bouillet, E., Feblowitz, M., Liu, Z., & Ranganathan, A. (2008). Wishful search: interactive composition of data mashups. In *Proceedings of the WWW* (pp. 775-784).

Shah, S., Ramamritham, K., & Shenoy, P. (2004). Resilient and Coherence Preserving Dissemination of Dynamic Data Using Cooperating Peers. *IEEE Transactions on Knowledge and Data Engineering, 16*(7), 799–812. doi:10.1109/TKDE.2004.1318563

Shavitt, Y., & Shir, E. (2005). Dimes: let the internet measures itself. *ACM SIGCOMM, 35*(5), 71–74. doi:10.1145/1096536.1096546

Tatemura, J., Po, O., Sawires, A., Agrawal, D., & Candan, K. S. (2005). Wrex: A scalable middleware architecture to enable xml caching for web-services. *Middleware*, 124-143.

Terry, D. B., & Ramasubramanian, V. (2003). Caching xml web services for mobility. *ACM Queue; Tomorrow's Computing Today, 1*(3), 70–78. doi:10.1145/846057.864024

Tewari, R., Dahlin, M., Vin, H., & Kay, J. (1999). Beyond Hierarchies: Design Considerations for Distributed Caching on the Internet. In *Proceedings of the International Conference on Distributed Computing Systems*.

Thaler, D., & Ravihsankar, C. (1998). Using Name-Based Mappings to Increase Hit Rates. *IEEE/ACM Transactions on Networking, 6*(1), 1-14.

Tuchinda, R., Szekely, P., & Knoblock, C. (2008). Building Mashups by Example. In *Proceedings of the International Conference on Intelligent User Interfaces* (pp. 139-148).

Valloppillil, V., & Ross, K. W. (1997). *Cache Array Routing Protocol v1.0*. Internet Draft.

Wahlisch, M., Schmidt, T. C., & Spat, W. (2008). What is happening from behind? - making the impact of internet topology visible. *Campus-Wide Information Systems, 25*(5), 392–406. doi:10.1108/10650740810921529

Wang, J. (1999). A survey of web caching schemes for the internet. *ACM SIGCOMM, 29*(5), 36–46. doi:10.1145/505696.505701

Wong, J., & Hong, J. (2007). Making mashups with marmite: towards end-user programming for the web. In *Proceedings of the SIGCHI conference on Human factors in computing systems* (pp. 1435-1444).

Yahoo Inc. (2007). *Yahoo pipes*. Retrieved from http://pipes.yahoo.com/

Yin, J., Alvisi, L., Dahlin, M., & Iyengar, A. (2002). Engineering Web Cache Consistency. *ACM Transactions on Internet Technology*, *2*(3), 224–259. doi:10.1145/572326.572329

ENDNOTES

[1] The search may also terminate when we reach the end of the mashup tree (in either direction)

[2] First-time mashup executions also contribute towards the total costs in End-results caching but these costs are comparatively very small.

This work was previously published in the International Journal of Web Services Research, Volume 7, Issue 1, edited by Liang-Jie (LJ) Zhang, pp. 64-88, copyright 2010 by IGI Publishing (an imprint of IGI Global).

Section 4
Security and Privacy

Chapter 13

Enhancing Security Modeling for Web Services Using Delegation and Pass-On

Wei She
University of Texas at Dallas, USA

I-Ling Yen
University of Texas at Dallas, USA

Bhavani Thuraisingham
University of Texas at Dallas, USA

ABSTRACT

In recent years, security issues in web service environments have been widely studied and various security standards and models have been proposed. However, most of these standards and models focus on individual web services and do not consider the security issues in composite services. In this article, the authors propose an enhanced security model to control the information flow in service chains. It extends the basic web service security models by introducing the concepts of delegation and pass-on. Based on these concepts, new certificates, certificate chains, delegation and pass-on policies, and how they are used to control the information flow are discussed. The authors also introduce a case study from a healthcare information system to illustrate the protocols.

1 INTRODUCTION

Service oriented architecture (SOA) is a popular paradigm for system integration and interoperation. Web service is the current standard for SOA. While SOA has many benefits, security is still a major concern. Because the web service environ-ment is open, distributed, heterogeneous, and integrated in nature, and involves new processes and messages, new security requirements arise. To fulfill these requirements, a lot of research works have been conducted in recent years to provide better security mechanisms for web service environment. The most notable work is the set of WS security specifications (OASIS, 2006; IBM, 2006) proposed by a group of organizations including

DOI: 10.4018/978-1-4666-1942-5.ch013

OASIS, WS-I, IBM, Microsoft, etc. SAML provides an XML-based standard for the exchange of authentication, entitlement, and attribute information. XACML is the core XML schema defined to represent access control policies. WS Security specifies an abstract web service security model including security tokens with digital signatures to protect and authenticate SOAP messages. WS Trust defines extensions to WS Security, including the methods to issue, renew and validate security tokens, and the way to exchange and broker trust relationships. WS Federation further defines how trust relationships are managed and brokered in a heterogeneous federated environment. WS Trust also supports extended features such as simple delegation and forwarding of security tokens between different parties and exchange of policies. WS Policy specifies a framework for expressing web service constraints and requirements as policies using policy assertions. WS Security Policy extends WS Security by specifying the policy assertions to describe security policies.

The specification models discussed above address the basic security requirements in web services. There have also been other research works that propose innovative security models and extensions to address new security issues in web services. Bhatti et al. proposed to incorporate contextual information, such as time, location, or environmental state, into WS access control models (Bhatti, Bertino, & Ghafoor, 2005). In this model, they also proposed the dynamic trust level of a user, which is initialized by a trust establishing procedure, and adjusted by context in the access. Bertino et al. (2006) proposed to carry on negotiation in an access by specifying the message types and contents exchanged based on the agreement about security requirements and services reached by the requestor and the service provider. In an open environment where unknown users may present, negotiations may also be conducted upon missing credentials or even security policies. Koshutanski et al. (2003) proposed a model that allows the derivation of necessary credentials from a given set of policies. With derived credentials, it is possible to conduct negotiations for privileges. Xu et al. (2006) proposed a framework which allows the negotiation on security policies; that is, even if the user violates part of the policy rules of the service provider, or vice versa, it is still possible to generate a positive access decision if both parties come to an agreement. Skogsrud et al. (2003) proposed to apply the solutions of trust negotiation into web service environments to secure the interactions among unknown users. Rao et al. proposed a security model to secure the process of publishing, searching, and binding a service (2004). In web service environment, security control may also be put on third party brokers (Carminati, Ferrari, & Hung, 2005, 2006), which perform security matchmaking before making further service invocation.

However, most of the existing works focus on individual web services and do not consider service composition. Advanced WS security techniques allow a service to effectively control the accesses to its resources, but do not provide mechanisms to let the services control their further information flows. Consider an online cooperative diagnosis system which involves a patient, several cooperating doctors and counselors, and multiple medical databases. The patient P contacts his family doctor F for help. The symptom of P is unusual and F contacts a specialist S to co-diagnose the disease. After confirmed the diagnosis, S contacts a counselor C to obtain the treatment information and the records of other patients with the same disease, intending to help P understand the disease and treatment implications. C, in turn, accesses several medical databases $D_1, D_2, ...,$ to retrieve the desired information. Assume that C has the full rights to access all the information in the medical databases D_i, for some i. C trusts S and will pass all obtained results to the specialist S. S trusts her college family doctor F and F trusts her patient P and the retrieved medical records will be passed from S to F and to P. However, the database D_i may have a policy that the personal medical records for disease x can only be released to any counselor, the specialists for disease x, and the patients contracted disease x. In current web service security models, D_i cannot control its information flow in the chain and the involved personal medical records may be uncontrollably revealed to the family doctor F. Also, D_j may have a policy that confines the medical records of children with disease x should only be revealed to someone who has kids with disease x. Similarly, D_j has no control on how the information flows after the records are released to C. As can be seen, it is desirable to have a better security model in service chains such that the flow of sensitive information can be controlled.

Another problem in current WS security framework is the lack of direct support of delegation. Also consider the online cooperative diagnosis system given above. Suppose that to help the diagnosis, the specialist S needs to have the patient P's historical medical record, which is stored in a medical database D_i. S may either access the medical database by himself/herself, or acquire the assistance from his physician S. As the patient may consider his medical record as private and never authorized any sharing, the medical database D_i may simply deny S's access request. A natural solution is to let P delegate his access rights to S to enable the access. Delegation has been studied in many areas, including multi-agent systems (Yialelis & Sloman, 1996), role-based access control (Barka & Sandhu, 2000; Zhang, Ahn, & Chu, 2003; Zhang, Oh, & Sandhu, 2003; Yin, Wang, Shi, Jia, & Teng, 2004), grid security (Welch, 2004; Gasser & McDermott, 1990; Kortesniemi & Hasu, 2000), workflow management systems (Atluri & Warner, 2005), web service (Wang, Vecchio, & Humphrey, 2005), etc. Delegation authorizes someone the access to the resources that he/she is usually not entitled to access; therefore, it is risky and needs to be strictly controlled. Constraints can be defined in delegation certificates to support the desired control (Aura, 2001; Zhang, Ahn, & Chu, 2003).

Also, in service composition, it is necessary to control re-delegation; that is, delegate delegated privileges to others. Re-delegation is highly risky if the privileges are re-delegated to some party through a long delegation chain. Although many research works in delegation consider constraining the delegation and re-delegation, none of them provide a comprehensive solution. In order to carry out delegation securely under the web service context, delegation constraints must be specified properly to have its scope correctly controlled. Also, policies have to be defined to provide further control.

This article proposes to use delegation and pass-on concepts to secure interactions in a composed web service. We first examine the global service environment from the perspective of the conventional "individualized" WS architecture, and develop a generalized system model consisting domains, services, and resources. The global system is assumed to be formed by several disjoint domains. We assume the non-existence of third party mediators, and the mediation (authentication and verification) is done by interactions between CAs and VEs of the attending domains. Then, we formally define an enhanced WS security model which incorporates additional types of certificates to express delegation (She, Thuraisingham, & Yen, 2007) and pass-on (She, Yen, & Thuraisingham, 2008). In a service chain, delegation and pass-on certificates can also form a certificate chain whose eligibility is the basis of the access decision in our system. We also provide the definition of our policy system, and explain how delegation and pass-on policies can be represented using existing policy languages. We give a detailed system flow which describes how an access request is generated and evaluated. We also provide brief discussions about the verification of a certificate chain and the issue of revocation.

The organization of the rest of the article is as follow. A general model of web service system and a service chain model are introduced in Section 2. In Section 2, we also provide some prerequisite definitions including claims and constraints, and basic access model using credentials. The key constructs of the enhanced WS security model are discussed in details in Section 3, including the definitions of delegation and pass-on certificates, delegation and pass-on chains, and the delegation and pass-on policies. In Section 4, we provide a general system flow, and in Section 5, we present a case study to illustrate our protocols. The article is concluded in Section 6.

2 SYSTEM MODEL

2.1 A Model of WS System

We consider a WS system as comprised of a set of domains, a set of services, and a set of resources. Each service and resource is managed in a specific domain. And by service invocations, resources of one service are used by another. We focus on information resources, which can be any types of raw or processed data in arbitrary forms. Domains are disjoint, and each domain contains a certificate authority (CA) that issues certificates and a verifier (VE) that validates certificates and enforces security policies. A domain defines a set of domain-specific knowledge, which includes all types of policies and other supporting information. Our system model is formally defined as follows.

Definition 2.1. *A WS system W is a triple (D, S, R) in which,*

- *D is a set of disjoint domains. Each domain $d \in D$ has a certificate authority $d.CA$ which makes assertions and issues certificates, a verifier $d.VE$ which verifies accesses to the resources in domain d, and a set of knowledge $d.K$. A knowledge, $k \in d.K$, is either a policy or a piece of supporting information in domain d that can be used for producing an access decision.*

- *S is a set of services. The domain of service $s \in S$ is denoted by $dom(s)$, where $dom(s) \in D$. s owns a set of certificates/credentials $s.C$ issued by a $d'.CA$, where $d' \in D$.*

- *R is a set of resources. A resource $r \in R$ is an identifiable data object stored in a domain and has atomic access. The domain of resource $r \in R$ is denoted by $dom(r)$, where $dom(r) \in D$. □*

2.2 A Model of Service Chain

When several individual services are composed together, it is called a composite service and those services that compose it are called the component services. When discussing the security issues, we only consider one request served by the composite service. Multiple requests can be handled the same way, one at a time. The component services, and the service invocations form a service graph, in which each component service is represented by a vertex, and service invocation by a directed edge from an invoker to an invokee. We also assume that a component service is not a composite one. In this article, we further simplify a service graph into a service chain. This simplification is only for making the discussion clearer. The solution we provide is applicable to general service graphs.

Definition 2.2. *A service chain $CH_{1,n}$ is a sequence of services $<s_1, s_2, ..., s_n>$ ($\forall 1 \leq i \leq n, s_i \in S$) which satisfies:*

- s_1 *is the initial requesting service.*
- $\forall i, j, 1 \leq i, j \leq n, i \neq j \Rightarrow s_i \neq s_j;$
- *Service invocation only occurs between s_i and s_{i+1} ($1 \leq i < n$). □*

2.3 Prerequisite Definitions

This subsection provides some prerequisite definitions including expression, claim, and constraint. All certificates/credentials that we consider in this article are defined based on claim and/or constraint. Claims and constraints are essentially expressions. The formal definitions are given in the following.

Definition 2.3. *An expression E has the form attr c val, where attr is a string describing a certain attribute, val is a value, and c is any relational operator. A claim is an expression made by a certificate authority to assert a property of a service. A constraint is an expression made by a certificate authority to state a precondition that must hold for a certificate to be valid.* □

Claims and constraints are different that a claim specifies a certain property of a service, whereas a constraint specifies a condition under which a certificate can be valid. More specifically, a claim simply states a truth, such as service_provider_name = "utdlib"; while, a constraint specifies a requirement that may not always hold. For example, the constraint delegation_chain_length ≤ 10 specifies that the length of the delegation chain must be no greater than 10. When a certificate is verified by a VE, the included constraints are first evaluated. If the validation of any of the constraints fails, then the certificate will be ignored.

2.4 Access Using Credentials

The basic access control mechanism we consider is as follows. The VE makes access decisions by evaluating the credentials presented by the invoker and the properties of the requested resources against security policies. A credential includes a set of claims that specify some properties of the service such as service name, service provider name, role, clearance level, etc. The access privileges granted to a service can also be specified as the properties of the service. The formal definition of the credential is as follows.

Definition 2.4. *An credential cd is issued from a CA to a service to assert that the service holds certain properties. cd is defined as (CA, s, clm),*

in which CA is the issuer, s is a service who owns ac, and clm is a set of claims that describe the properties of s. □

For convenience, we assume that a credential is always issued by a single CA. Generally, a local CA of s_i, $Dom(s_i).CA$, may issue credentials to s_i to certify its identity, related properties, and local access privileges. The CA from another domain, $D_j.CA$, $D_j \neq Dom(s_i)$, may issue credentials to s_i to grant s_i accesses to the services/resources in D_j. We use $cd(s_i)$ to represent a set of credentials owned by service s_i. Figure 1 is an example credential which specifies the service name, clearance level, user type and delegability for service S1.

3 ENHANCED SECURITY MODEL FOR SERVICE CHAIN

In conventional web service security models, each service invocation in a service chain is treated as an independent event. Consider a service chain $<s_1, s_2, s_3, s_4>$. Suppose that s_1 has the privileges to access s_3 and s_4, but s_2 does not have the privilege to access s_3 and s_3 does not have the privilege to access s_4. Under existing WS security architecture, there is no way to let s_2 access s_3 or let s_3 access s_4. On the other hand, if s_1 does not have the privileges to access s_3 or s_4 but s_2 does, then s_2 can access critical information of s_3 and s_4 and pass it on to s_1 in raw or processed forms without concerning whether revealing this information to s_1 is fine for s_3 and s_4. In other words, the two directions of information flows in conventional service invocation protocols are not symmetric; the service invocation direction has strict constraints while the returning direction is fully unprotected. If for the second case, s_1 has the privilege to access s_2 implies s_2 can trust s_1 and pass the execution results derived from the critical data (or even the raw data) of s_3 and s_4 to s_1, then for the first case, s_1 should be allowed to delegate its privilege to s_2 and s_3 to allow their invocations to s_3 and s_4,

Figure 1. Example credential

```
<Credential id = "S1-CD-0001">
    <IssuedBy id = "S1-CA"/>
    <IssuedTo id = "S1"/>
      <ClaimSet>
      <Claim ea = "service_name" op = "equal_to" ev = "utdlib"/>
      <Claim ea = "clearance_level" op = "equal_to" ev = "public"/>
      <Claim ea = "user_type" op = "equal_to" ev = "librarian"/>
      <Claim ea = "delegability" op = "equal_to" ev = "true"/>
      </ClaimSet>
</Credential>
```

respectively. If such delegation requires special certificates, then passing back the data derived from the critical information of s_3 and s_4 to s_1, who had no privilege to access the critical data of s_3 and s_4, should only be allowed when a special certificate is issued to consent the pass on action.

In this article, we design a new protocol for service invocations that empowers the services and their domains to control the accesses more effectively. A service chain embeds the information flow. In the forward flow, the information of the requesters cumulates and flows toward the service providers. For the service chain $<s_1, s_2, s_3, s_4>$, the request s_2 sends to s_3 may contain information computed from s_1's request. On the return path, the information returned from the service providers cumulates and flows toward the requesters. For $<s_1, s_2, s_3, s_4>$, the information returned from s_2 to s_1 may contain data that can be used to derive the information returned from s_4 to s_3 and from s_3 to s_2. In our protocol, we design two types of certificates, delegation and pass-on certificates, to support delegation and control the passing of data objects. The delegation certificate allows the service s_1 to delegate its credentials to s_2 such that s_2 can act on behalf of s_1. In this case, if s_1 is authorized to certain resources, then s_2 is also authorized. The pass-on certificate is introduced to allow a service, say s_3 to authorize another service s_2 to pass on its returned information to

other services. Relative to existing protocols, the delegation mechanism makes it possible to establish some service chains that are impossible in conventional protocols; and the pass-on mechanism takes away the default power of passing on returned information to unknown services and makes the pass-on of information a specifically given instead of a default privilege.

In the first example given above, s_1 can issue a delegation certificate to s_2 to allow s_2 to access s_3, and s_2 needs to delegate the privileges obtained from s_1 to s_3 to allow s_3 to access s_4. These two correlated delegation certificates form a delegation chain. In the return direction, s_3 needs to issue a pass-on certificate to allow the information to be sent to s_2 and s_1, and s_4 needs to issue a pass-on certificate to allow the information to be sent to s_3, s_2, and s_1. These pass-on certificates form a pass-on chain. In order for s_3 and s_4 to make access decisions, s_2 needs to send a pass-on request to s_3 to inform s_3 about the pass-on relationship between s_2 and s_1. And similarly, s_3 also needs to send a pass-on request to s_4. These pass-on requests form a requester chain.

In our protocol, by default, a service accesses another by presenting its own credentials. It may also use the credentials delegated from others. In this case, a delegation certificate must be issued; and such a delegation can only be activated in the negotiation phase, that is, when the access with a service's own credentials fails. In the default case, the service needs to include a pass-on request within its access request to inform the invokee about the pass-on relationship. Consider service chain $<s_1, s_2, s_3, s_4>$. Assume that s_2 has the privileges to access s_3 and s_4, but s_1 does not have the privileges to access s_3 and s_4, and s_3 does not have the privilege to access s_4. Note that s_1 does not generate a pass-on request as it is the initial requester. On receiving s_1's access request, s_2 generates a pass-on request and invokes s_3 with its own credentials, and similar, s_3 sends a pass-on request to s_4. On checking s_2 and s_1 against s_3's security policies, s_3 may generate two possible decisions. On generating a positive decision, the service invocation will continue to s_4; whereas if a negative decision is generated, then the transaction goes to negotiation phase, in which attribute requests may be returned from s_3 to s_2, and s_2 may either provide other credentials or request s_1 for delegation. In this example, as s_2 has the privileges for accessing s_3, a positive decision is generated, and the service invocation continues to s_4. Similarly, s_3 includes a pass-on request within its access request by default. For s_3's access, s_4 will generate a negative decision due to insufficient privileges. In this case, the negative decision is returned to s_3, and an attribute request may be created. On receiving an attribute request, s_3 decides to either still present its own credentials or request delegation from s_2. Suppose that s_3 requests delegation from s_2. A special delegation request is created and returned to s_2. s_2 may request its CA to issue a delegation certificate, or simply return a negative decision to s_1. This is also decided by evaluating on its security policies. If s_2's CA agrees to issue the delegation certificate, then this delegation certificate and s_2 and s_3's pass-on requests will be evaluated by s_4 against s_4's security policies, and the requested data will be returned all the way back to s_1 if a positive decision is made. In the return direction, all of s_4, s_3, and s_2 will attach a pass-on certificate within the response, which authorizes all the prior services.

This section formally defines the above concepts. Section 3.1 introduces pass-on request and pass-on certificate. Section 3.2 introduces attribute request and delegation certificate. Section 3.3 introduces our policy system which defines delegation and pass-on policies.

3.1 Pass-On Request and Pass-On Certificate

We introduce the pass-on request to represent the pass-on relationship between two services. In a service chain $<s_1, s_2, ..., s_n>$, each service s_i, $1 < i < n$, presents a pass-on request pr_i to s_{i+1}. pr_i represents the pass-on relationship between s_i and s_{i-1} where, s_i is the sender of the data and s_{i-1} is the receiver. The pass-on requests accumulate from service requesters to service providers, and thus form a requester chain. We formally define the pass-on request in Definition 3.1.

Definition 3.1. *In a service chain $< s_1, s_2, ..., s_n >$, a pass-on request pr_i $(1 < i < n)$ is a request sent from s_i to s_{i+1} that informs s_{i+1} about the pass-on relationship between s_i and s_{i-1}. pr_i is defined as a tuple (s_i, s_{i-1}) where s_i is called the sender, and s_{i-1} is called the receiver. The pass-on requests in the service chain form a requester chain $RCH_{1,i} = <(pr_2, cd(s_1, s_2)), ..., (pr_{i-1}, cd(s_{i-2}, \underline{s}i_{-1})> (2 < i < n)$, where $cd(s_{i-2}, s_{i-1})$ denotes the set of credentials that s_{i-2} provides to access s_{i-1}.* □

Each access request in our protocol contains a requester chain. On returning the requested information, each service s_i checks all the services included in the requester chain $RCH_{1,i-1}$ against s_i's security policies. If this results in a positive decision, then a pass-on certificate pc_i is issued to authorize all the services in $RCH_{1,i-1}$. The pass-on certificate may also specify a set of constraints that must be satisfied for it to be valid. For example, the issuer may define a duration constraint in the pass-on certificate to make it only valid for a certain period. Also, one may specify a session id or transaction id in the pass-on certificate to prevent it from being used in other sessions or transactions. More sophisticated constraints may be included in a pass-on certificate. For example, the issuer may specify that the computed data in next service node must at least have certain security properties for the pass-on to be valid. Defining constraints in the pass-on certificate provides a means for the data owner to flexibly control the flow of the data. We formally define the pass-on certificate as follows.

Definition 3.2. *In a service chain $<s_1, s_2, ..., s_n>$, a pass-on certificate pc_i ($1 < i \le n$) is a certificate that is issued by s_i's CA to allow the data requested by s_i to be revealed to all s_i's prior services. pc_i is defined as ($Dom(s_i).CA$, $CH_{1,i-1}$, $cnstrnt_i$) where $Dom(s_i).CA$ is the issuer, $CH_{1,i-1}$ is a partial service chain $<s_1, s_2, ..., s_{i-1}>$, and $cnstrnt_i$ is a set of constraints that have to be satisfied for pc_i to be valid, called the pass-on constraint.* □

Figure 2 is an example pass-on certificate which authorizes two services, S1 and S2 to pass on S3's response. It also specifies a duration constraint and a session constraint.

The pass-on certificates issued in a service chain form a certificate chain, called a pass-on

chain. In a service chain $<s_1, s_2, ..., s_n>$, each service s_i receives a pass-on chain which starts from pc_n and ends up to pc_{i+1}. Such a pass-on chain underlies s_i's access decision, and must be validated before s_i sends out the requested data. To validate such a pass-on chain, s_i has to verify all the included pass-on certificates pc_k ($i < k \le n$). We formally define the pass-on chain as follows.

Definition 3.3. *In a service chain $<s_1, s_2, ..., s_n>$, the issued pass-on certificates form a pass-on chain. Each service s_i ($1 \le i < n$) receives a pass-on chain $PCH_{n,i} = <pc_n, pc_{n-1}, ..., pc_{i+1}>$.* □

3.2 Delegation Certificate and Delegation Chain

By sending prior services' information within the requests and pass-on certificates within the response, a service can effectively control the flow of its critical information. That is, if s_2 has the privileges to access s_3's critical information, but s_1 is not, s_3 may still be able to make a negative decision if passing this information to s_1 is risky. However, this requires that s_2 is authorized to s_3, which may not be the case. If s_2 is not authorized to s_3, but s_1 is, then there is no way for the current

Figure 2. Example pass-on certificate

```
<PassOnCertificate id = "S3-PC-0001">
    <IssuedBy id = "S3-CA"/>
    <IssuedTo>
      <ServiceSet>
        <Service id = "S2"/>
        <Service id = "S1"/>
      </ServiceSet>
    </IssuedTo>
    <ConstraintSet>
      <Constraint ea = "system_date" op = "less_equal_to" ev = "11/1/2008"/>
      <Constraint ea = "session_id" op = "equal_to" ev = "000001"/>
    </ConstraintSet>
</PassOnCertificate>
```

WS security architecture to allow such accesses. In this case, delegation is required.

We define delegation certificate to represent the delegation relationship between two services. A delegation certificate specifies a set of credentials that is delegated from a delegator to a delegatee. For simplicity, we assume that a delegation certificate is issued by a single CA to represent the delegation relationship from a single delegator to a single delegatee. Similar to the pass-on certificate, a delegation certificate may also specify a set of constraints which is first validated. If any of the constraints specified in a delegation certificate is invalid, then the delegation certificate will be ignored. In some cases, a service may further delegate another one. This service has two alternatives, either delegating its own credentials, or delegating the delegated credentials. For the latter case, we need to support re-delegation. With continuous re-delegations, a delegation chain is formed. Unlike the pass-on chain which is simply a sequence of certificates, the delegation certificates presented in a delegation chain are correlated. That is, if s_1 delegates s_2, and s_2 re-delegates s_3, the credentials that s_2 delegates to s_3 must be a subset of the credentials that s_1 delegates to s_2. Also, the constraints specified in s_2's delegation certificate must be more restrictive than those in s_1's delegation certificate. For simplicity, we do not allow the accesses using mixed credentials. That is, s_2 can access s_3 with either s_2's own credentials or s_1's credentials by delegation, but not both. Access with credentials of multiple services may bring other difficulties for making access decisions. For example, if the credentials owned by n different services are presented for an access, and all these credentials are delegated credentials, then the invoked service needs to consider all the delegation chains including these credentials. Also, if any of these services is malicious, then it may be difficult for the invoked service to determine which service behaves maliciously. To support the construction of such a delegation chain, a delegation certificate

need specify its prior delegation certificate if it is presented in a delegation chain. We formally define delegation certificate as follows.

Definition 3.4. *In a service chain $<s_1, s_2, ..., s_n>$, a delegation certificate dc_i ($1 < i \le n$) is a certificate that is issued by s_i's CA to delegate a set of credentials to s_{i+1}. dc_i is defined as ($Dom(s_i).CA$, $s_i, s_{i+1}, cd_i, cnstrnt_i, pred_i$), where $Dom(s_i).CA$ is the issuer, s_i is the delegator, s_{i+1} is the delegatee, cd_i is a non-empty set of credentials that is delegated to s_{i+1}, $cnstrnt_i$ is a set of constraints that have to be satisfied for dc_i to be valid, called the delegation constraint, and $pred_i$ is an identifier that refers to the previous delegation certificate if dc_i is presented in a delegation chain. The delegation certificate has the following properties:*

- If s_i delegates its own credentials to s_{i+1}, then $cd_i \subseteq cd(s_i)$, and $pred_i = nil$.
- If s_i re-delegates the credentials delegated from s_{i-1}, then the $cd_i \subseteq cd_{i-1}$, $pred_i = cd_{i-1}$, and $cnstrnt_i \Rightarrow cnstrnt_{i-1}$. □

Figure 3 is an example delegation certificate which describes the delegation from service S1 to S2. S2 is delegated the credential S1-CD-0001 which certifies the service name, clearance level, and user type. This delegation certificate is only valid if the following conditions hold: (1) the system date is before 11/1/2008; (2) the session id is 000001; (3) the length of the delegation chain is no greater than 10.

By re-delegation, several delegation certificates form a delegation chain. In a service chain, each service s_i ($1 < i < n$) may receive several delegation chains $DCH_{j,k}$ ($1 \le j \le k < i$), which are first validated. We define a delegation chain as follows.

Definition 3.5. *In a service chain $<s_1, s_2, ..., s_n>$, a delegation chain $DCH_{i,j}$ ($1 \le i \le j < n$) is a sequence of delegation certificates $<dc_i, ..., dc_j>$ which satisfies the following properties:*

Figure 3. Example delegation certificate

```
<DelegationCertificate id = "S1-DC-0001">
    <IssuedBy id = "S1-CA"/>
    <IssuedFrom id = "S1"/>
    <IssuedTo id = "S2"/>
    <DelegatedCredential>
        <Credential id = "S1-CD-0001">
            <IssuedBy id = "S1-CA"/>
            <IssuedTo id = "S1"/>
            <ClaimSet>
                <Claim ea = "service_name" op = "equal_to" ev = "utdlib"/>
                <Claim ea = "clearance_level" op = "equal_to" ev = "public"/>
                <Claim ea = "user_type" op = "equal_to" ev = "librarian"/>
            </ClaimSet>
        </Credential>
    </DelegatedCredential>
    <ConstraintSet>
        <Constraint ea = "system_date" op = "less_equal_to" ev = "11/1/2008"/>
        <Constraint ea = "session_id" op = "equal_to" ev = "000001"/>
        <Constraint ea = "delegation_chain_length" op = "less_equal_to" ev = "10"/>
    </ConstraintSet>
</DelegationCertificate>
```

- $pred_i = nil$, and $\forall k, i \leq k < j, dc_k = pred_{k+1}$.
- $\forall k, i < k \leq j, cd_k \subseteq cd_{k-1}$.
- $\forall k, i < k \leq j, cnstrnt_k \Rightarrow cnstrnt_{k-1}$. $\square$

3.3 Delegation and Pass-on Policies

In our model, the requester chain and a set of delegation chains presented to a service are first checked against security policies. The delegation certificates that are issued along the service chain are checked against delegation policies to ensure that all these certificates are correctly issued, and not abused by any service. Delegation policy is introduced in Section 3.3.1. Also, all the services presented in the requester chain must be checked against pass-on policies to ensure that passing data to these services does not cause undesired information leakage. Pass-on policy is discussed in Section 3.3.2.

3.3.1 Delegation Policy

Delegation allows a service s_1 to temporarily hand over its privileges to another service, say s_2, such that s_2 can be allowed to access the protected resources on service s_3 if s_1 is authorized to these resources. As we support re-delegation in our model, privileges may "travel" through a delegation chain and be passed to some service, say s_2', which is trusted neither by s_1 nor s_3. In this situation, sensitive information of s_3 may be revealed to s_2', which is undesired for s_3. Moreover, delegation may violate the principle of least privilege, that is, if delegating the credentials that are not necessary for the access. To control the scope of the delegation chain and/or prevent risky and/or unnecessary delegations, a special policy is required, which is called delegation policy. Delegation policy is enforced by the VE when the CA intends to issue a delegation certificate.

Moreover, as in the above example, $dom(s_1)$ and $dom(s_3)$ may be different domains, and may not be fully trusted to each other, the delegation certificate issued by $dom(s_1).CA$ need also be checked when s_2 or s_2' invokes s_3, against s_3's delegation policies. The delegation policies enforced in these two situations are slightly different; that is, their decisions have different security meanings, and the former may have a side effect, which is a delegation certificate. However, we discuss them together as their major parts are the same; that is, both define a set of constraints for a specific pair of delegator and delegatee. In this sense, the delegation constraints defined in a delegation certificate can somehow be regarded as a delegation policy. Actually, in our model, a delegation policy may generate not only a positive/negative decision, but also a set of obligations, which is essentially a set of delegation constraints. We formally define a delegation policy as follows.

Definition 3.6. *A delegation policy dp is defined as* $(C_{dtor}, C_{dtee}, C_{dcd}, dec, oblg)$ *where:*

- C_{dtor}, C_{dtee}, and C_{dcd} are the sets of constraints for delegator, delegatee, and the delegated credentials.
- *dec* is the delegation decision which is either positive or negative.
- *oblg* is the obligation which contains a set of delegation constraints. □

In the delegator's site, the delegation policy specifies a set of conditions under which the requested delegation certificate can or cannot be issued, and also a set of delegation constraints that must be taken into the delegation certificate if a positive decision is generated. In writing these delegation constraints into a delegation certificate, a service essentially propagates its delegation policies to others. And by specifying re-delegation constraints in a delegation certificate, a service may be able to further control the scope of the delegation. Various re-delegation constraints

may be specified in a delegation certificate. For example, the delegation policy may simply ban the re-delegation by specifying the following constraint: re-delegability = false. Or, we may also specify the maximal depth/length of the delegation chain by defining, say, delegation_depth = 10. More sophisticated delegation constraints can be defined such that the better control of the delegation can be achieved.

In our model, we assume that all the services on a service chain are semi-honest. That is, they all follow the protocol and ensure the validity of the delegation constraints. But some of the services may attempt to derive sensitive information from the data that they receive. Also, we do not consider the cross-domain vocabulary mapping which is an open issue in multi-domain systems. For simplicity, we assume that there is a unified vocabulary defined for all the services on a service chain, such that the constraints specified in a delegation certificate can always be understood. Figure 4 is an example delegation policy, which specifies the following constraints for the delegation certificate to be issued: (1) the delegator must be delegable, and not in {S2, S3, S4}; (2) the delegatee must be trusted services; (3) delegated privileges cannot be at TopSecret level. It also specifies three delegation constraints that are exactly the same as the constraints included in the example delegation certificate in Section 3.2.

3.3.2 Pass-On Policy

The pass-on policy is slightly different from the conventional access control policies. That is, the former usually specifies how a data object can be passed to a set of services. A pass-on policy may consider all the potential receivers of the data instead of one. This actually has similar effect to the access control policies. Moreover, pass-on policies can be used to specify more sophisticated constraints. For example, we may define that data cannot be passed in their raw forms. Or, we can define that if the probability of deriving a service's

Figure 4. An example delegation policy

```
<DelegationPolicy id = "S1-DP-0001" dec = "positive">
    <Delegator>
        <ConstraintSet op = "and">
            <Constraint ea = "delegability" op = "equal_to" ev = "true"/>
            <Constraint op = "not_in">
                <Eattribute ea = "service_name"/>
                <EvalueSet>
                    <Evalue ev = "S2"/>
                    <Evalue ev = "S3"/>
                    <Evalue ev = "S4"/>
                </EvalueSet>
            </Constraint>
        </ConstraintSet>
    </Delegator>
    <Delegatee>
        <Constraint ea = "trust_level" op = "equal_to" ev = "trusted"/>
    </Delegatee>
    <Credential>
        <Constraint ea = "clearance_level" op = "not_equal_to" ev = "TopSecret"/>
    </Credential>
    <Obligation>
        <ConstraintSet op = "and">
            <Constraint ea = "system_date" op = "less_equal_to" ev = "11/1/2008"/>
            <Constraint ea = "session_id" op = "equal_to" ev = "000001"/>
            <Constraint ea = "delegation_chain_length" op = "less_equal_to" ev = "10"/>
        </ConstraintSet>
    </Obligation>
</DelegationPolicy>
```

input data from its output data, then passing the output data to others is not allowed. In our model, how a specific data object is passed among services is called the passing context. And the above constraints are called passing context constraints. We formally define the pass-on policy as follows.

Definition 3.7. *A pass-on policy pp is defined as* $(C_{rcvr}, C_{data}, C_{pcntxt}, dec)$ *where:*

- C_{rcvr}, and C_{data} are the set of constraints defined for the receiving services and passed data.
- C_{pcntxt} is the set of passing context constraints.
- *dec* is the pass-on decision which is either positive or negative. □

Figure 5 is an example pass-on policy which specifies two passing context constraints: (1) data cannot be passed between services in raw forms; (2) if the risk of deriving the input data from output data is high, then the pass-on action is disallowed.

3.4 Certificate Revocation

We consider two types of revocations: automatic revocation, and manual revocation. The simplest example for automatic revocation is to specify a duration constraint in the certificate, such that when the time is out, the certificate will be automatically disabled. In a service chain environment, we consider another type of automatic revocation; that is, by specifying a session/transaction constraint, which is usually the case for pass-on

Figure 5. An example pass-on policy

```
<PassOnPolicy id = "S3-PP-0001" dec = "negative">
   <PassingContext>
      <ConstraintSet>
         <Constraint ea = "pass_on_form" op = "equal_to" ev = "raw"/>
         <Constraint ea = "derivation_risk" op = "equal_to" ev = "high"/>
      </ConstraintSet>
   </PassingContext>
</PassOnPolicy>
```

and delegation certificates. When a session or transaction terminates, then all the certificates in this session or transaction will be automatically revoked. Usually, there is no need to manually revoke a pass-on or delegation certificate. However, we do allow such a manual revocation. Manual revocation can be either instant or dilatory. For an instant revocation, all the services in the service chain will be aware of the revocation immediately. That is by propagating a revocation message to all the services on the chain. For a dilatory revocation, the services will not learn about the revocation until next time the certificate is used. The revocation of the delegation certificate is cascaded in the sense that all the follow-up delegation certificates in the delegation chain need also be revoked. Consider the service chain $<s_1, s_2, ..., s_n>$. Assume that $dom(s_1).CA$ issues a delegation certificate dc_1 to s_2, and in turn s_2 re-delegates the credentials included in dc_1 to s_3, which results in the delegation certificate dc_2. If dc_1 is revoked, then dc_2 also needs to be revoked since the credentials that s_2 delegates to s_3 are delegated from s_1. These two revocations together form a cascaded revocation.

3.5 Certificate Chain Verification

In a service chain $<s_1, s_2, ..., s_n>$, each delegation certificate dc_i needs to be repeatedly validated by all the services s_k, $i+2 \leq k \leq n$. This is because that a delegation certificate may be revoked at any time during the transaction. Also, because

different domains enforce different delegation policies, the access decision that is based on the validity of the delegation chain may be different at different sites.

The verification of a pass-on certificate is simply authenticating the certificate. Hence, the verifications of the same pass-on certificate at different sites usually return the same result. Although, such verification procedures may also be repeated among different services, we may probably ignore some of them if two domains are trusted to each other to a certain degree. That is, if $dom(s_i).CA$ trusts $dom(s_j).CA$, $i<j$, then $dom(s_i).CA$ can simply accept the verification result of $dom(s_j).CA$, and ignore all the pass-on certificates pc_k, $j < k \leq n$. If this is case, the verification procedure of pass-on certificates can be significantly simplified. The best case is that, each service s_i (s_i's local CA essentially) only needs to verify pc_{i+1}.

4 ENHANCED SYSTEM MODEL AND GENERAL SYSTEM FLOW

4.1 An Enhanced System Model

In this section, an enhanced system model is formally defined to achieve better security control in WS systems. This definition is an enhancement of the system model given in Definition 2.1. It is also based on the definitions given in the above sections. In the enhanced system, the certificate set

C is divided into three disjoint subsets for authorization, delegation, and pass-on certificates. All the entities in our system are described by claims and conditions. Also, each domain defines a set of delegation policies and a set of pass-on policies. We present our formal definition in the following.

Definition 4.1. *An enhanced WS system W is a triple (D, S, R) in which:*

- *D is a set of disjoint domains. Each domain $d \in D$ has a certificate authority $d.CA$ which makes assertions and issues certificates, a verifier $d.VE$ which verifies accesses to the resources in domain d, a set of delegation policies $d.DP$, and a set of pass-on policies $d.PP$.*
- *S is a set of services. The domain of service $s \in S$ is denoted as $dom(s)$, where $dom(s) \in D$.*
- *R is a set of resources. A resource $r \in R$ is an identifiable data object stored in a domain and has atomic access. The domain of resource $r \in R$ is denoted as $dom(r)$, where $dom(r) \in D$.*
- *C is a set of certificates/credentials. C is defined as a triple (CD, PC, DC) where CD is a set of credentials, PC is a set of pass-on certificates, and DC is a set of delegation certificates. A credential $cd \in CD$ is owned by a service $s \in S$, and issued by $d'.CA$, where $d' \in D$. □*

4.2 General System Flow

In this section, we show how the flow of sensitive information can be controlled in service chain by providing a general system flow. We consider service $(1 < i < n)$ in the service chain $<s_1, s_2, ..., s_n>$ which attempts to invoke s_{i+1}. All the consequent interactions, between s_i and s_{i+1}, and between s_i and s_{i-1}, are discussed. Note that s_1's and s_n's flows may have some minor difference, which will be explained after the system flow.

Algorithm 1. Forward Flow

1. On receiving a requester chain $RCH_{1,i-1}$, and a set of delegation chains $DCHS_i = \{DCH_{k_1, j_1}, ..., DCH_{k_m, j_m}\}$, $\forall\, 1 < l \le m$, $j_{l-1} < k_l$, and $j_m < i-1$, s_i intends to invoke s_{i+1}.
2. s_i checks all the delegation chain in $DCHS_i$ against delegation policies, if a negative decision is made, the return a negative decision to s_{i-1}, otherwise, continue.
3. s_i sends pass-on request pr_i, $RCH_{1,i}$, and $cd(s_i)$ within its access request to s_{i+1}.

Note that in step 1, m is the number of delegation chains, and we have $m \ge 0$. If $m = 1$, then there is only 1 delegation chain; however, if $m = 0$, then there is no delegation chain. By $j_m < i-1$, we ensure that s_{i-1} did not delegate s_i. This is because s_{i-1} cannot predict whether s_i will invoke s_{i+1} or which s_{i+1} will be invoked.

Algorithm 2. Backward Flow

1. On receiving a pass-on chain $PCH_{n,i}$, and s_{i+1}'s response, s_i intends to pass the response to s_{i-1}.
2. s_i validates all the pass-on certificate in $PCH_{n,i}$, if a negative decision is made, then generates a negative decision and go to 5, otherwise, continue.
3. s_i computes its own response using s_{i+1}'s response.
4. s_i evaluates all the services contained in $RCH_{1,i-1}$ against its pass-on policies, if a negative decision is made, then generates a negative decision and go to 5, otherwise, creates its own pass-on certificate pc_i and prepares $PCH_{n,i-1}$, and sends response to s_{i-1}.
5. If the negative decision is made due to insufficient credentials, then s_i generates an attribute request and sends to s_{i-1} and enters negotiation flow, otherwise, sends a negative decision to s_{i-1}.

Note that in step 5, s_i generates an attribute request to inform s_{i-1} about the required attributes for accessing the requested data. This may concern the issue of metadata privacy, which is not discussed in this article. However, this can be decided by s_i before returning the decision.

Algorithm 3. Negotiation Flow

1. On receiving an attribute request from s_i, s_{i-1} decides whether s_{i-1} can have the access by presenting the required credentials, if yes, then sends the credentials to s_i, otherwise, continue.
2. s_{i-1} generates a delegation request to s_{i-2}.
3. If s_{i-2} holds the required credentials, then evaluates s_{i-1} against its delegation policy and continue, otherwise, sends the delegation request back to s_{i-3}.
4. If a positive decision is made, then sends the issued delegation certificate dc_{i-2} to s_{i-1}, otherwise, sends back the negative decision.

5 CASE STUDY

In this section, we introduce a case study system, an online cooperative diagnosis system, to illustrate our security model for service chains. The system has been introduced in Section 1. Here we introduce the system with some variations and discuss it more formally. In this system, several doctors and/or counselors cooperate with each other to make diagnosis for a patient. Note that the doctor, counselor, and patient are human beings that participate in this activity and all employ an agent system to facilitate this online diagnosis. Here, we only consider the agents which are the representatives of these human entities and do not concern about the security issues between the agents and the actual human participators. Let *Patient* denote the patient, *Doctor$_i$*, for some *i*, denote the doctor, and *Counselor$_j$*, for some *j*, denote the counselor. We also introduce several medical databases into our case study system, and

essentially, most of the security concerns are for these databases. Let MDB_k, for some k, denote the medical database. All these participators may be located in different administrative domains. For simplicity, we assume that they are distributed in domain D_1 to D_5 as shown in Figure 6. Note that Figure 6 only shows an example scenario in which the direction of the arrow denotes the direction of the flow of requests. Also note that, in this article, we do not consider the cross-domain vocabulary mapping issue, and simply assume that all these entities have their vocabularies aligned in advance.

In this online cooperative diagnosis system, the medical databases store a large volume of sensitive data, which include the medical records of the patients, the historical treatment archives, lab test reports, reports of clinical trial of new drugs, etc. The patient has private data that may require high-level protection, including his/her identities, medical records, insurance documents, and other medical-related data. Also, the doctors and/or counselors may store some sensitive data that should be kept away from unauthorized accesses. In the following sub sections, we present several examples to show how our protocols can be used to control the flow of sensitive data and facilitate the establishment of some special service chains which cannot be built up in conventional systems. Section 5.1 shows how we manipulate pass-on certificates to control the flow of data. And Section 5.2 shows how a service can delegate its privileges to others to temporarily enable their accesses to certain data.

5.1 Pass-on Flow

In this section, we show how pass-on requests and pass-on certificates can be used to control the information flow in a service chain. Note that while discussing the pass-on flow, we do not consider the delegation which is discussed in Section 5.2. Consider an example in which, the personal physician of the patient, *Doctor$_1$*, acquires the assistance from a specialist, *Doctor$_2$*, who in turn, requests

Figure 6. Architecture of the online cooperative diagnosis system

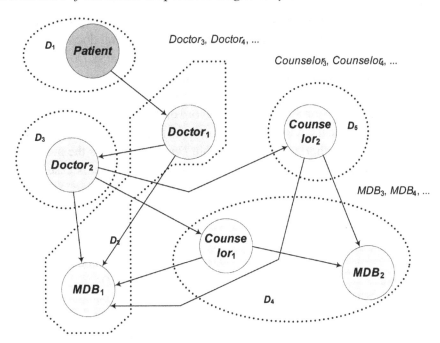

several counselors, $Counselor_1$, to retrieve helpful historical treatment archives from a medical database, say MDB_2. In this example, the service chain $<Patient, Doctor_1, Doctor_2, Counselor_1, MDB_2>$ is formed. As can be seen from Figure 6, both $Counselor_1$ and MDB_2 are in domain D_4. Practically, they may be run by the same hospital, and thus $Counselor_1$ should be authorized to some resources in MDB_2. Also, $Patient$, $Doctor_1$, and $Doctor_2$ are all not in domain D_4, and thus may not be allowed to access the resources in MDB_2. If this is the case, then revealing the sensitive data of MDB_2 to $Doctor_2$, or $Doctor_1$, or the patient, is not desired for the hospital that runs MDB_2, and in conventional systems, such an information leakage cannot be avoided. In the following, we show how such an undesired information flow can be prevented by letting the services consider indirect requesters and specify more flexible access control policies. We consider the last service node, MDB_2, to illustrate how an access control decision is made by checking pass-on policies for all the prior services, and how pass-on certifi-

cates are issued and validated to ensure that the information flow is under control. Note that, we assume that the services are semi-honest; that is, they all conform to the protocols, but may infer or retrieve unauthorized data.

Figure 7 shows the requester chain received by MDB_2. The requester chain has several <Requester> sections, with each corresponding to a service. In each requester section, a pass-on request subsection, and a credential subsection are included. The pass-on request informs other services about the pass-on relationship represented by this certificate, and the credentials are used for making access control decisions. On receiving this requester chain and the set of credentials associated with it, MDB_2 checks all the requesters' credentials against its pass-on policy which is shown in Figure 8. This pass-on policy confines that if the historical treatment data are for special diseases and are classified at secret level or above, then revealing them in their raw forms to general doctors or the doctors who are not working for the hospital should be denied. It can be seen from

Figure 7 that $Doctor_1$ is a general doctor, thus if $Counselor_1$ requests for the historical treatment archives for some special disease, then a negative decision will be drawn. On the other hand, if both $Doctor_1$ and $Doctor_2$ are specialists, then it is possible that MDB_2 generates a positive decision.

If a positive access control decision is generated, then MDB_2 will request its local CA to issue a pass-on certificate to explicitly authorize all the prior services. This pass-on certificate will be validated repeatedly at $Counselor_1$'s, $Doctor_2$'s, and $Doctor_1$'s sites. This pass-on certificate is shown in Figure 9. It also specifies a session constraint.

5.2 Delegation Flow

In this section, we show how delegation certificates are used to enable the establishment of some service chains which are not achievable in conventional systems. Consider an example in which the personal physician of the patient, $Doctor_1$, is a general doctor who acquires the assistance of a specialist, $Doctor_2$, for the diagnosis. The hospital that $Doctor_1$ works for manages a medical database MDB_1, which stores the medical record of the patient. To facilitate the cooperation between these participators, it is necessary to enable $Doctor_2$ to access the medical record of the patient in MDB_1. In this case, the service chain $<Patient, Doctor_1, Doctor_2, MDB_1>$ should be built up. Under conventional WS security framework, there is no way to establish such a service chain, if $Doctor_2$ does not have the required privileges. However in our protocol, we can enable this access by letting $Doctor_2$ request a delegation certificate from $Doctor_1$. Note that $Doctor_1$'s access privileges to the patient's medical record is also delegated, that is, from the patient. If this is the case, then requesting the delegation from

Figure 7. Requester chain received by MDB_2

```
<RequesterChain>
  <Requester>
    <PassonRequest sndr = "Patient" rcvr = "Nil"/>
    <Credential id = "Patient-CD-001" by = "Some CA" to = "Patient">
      <ClaimSet>
        <Claim ea = "user_id" op = "equal_to" ev = "**********"/>
        <Claim ea = "name" op = "equal_to" ev = "**********"/>
        ......
      </ClaimSet>
    </Credential>
  </Requester>
  <Requester>
    <PassonRequest sndr = "Doctor1" rcvr = "Patient"/>
    <Credential id = "Doctor1-CD-001" by = "D2-CA" to = "Doctor1">
      <ClaimSet>
        <Claim ea = "occupation" op = "equal_to" ev = "general"/>
        <Claim ea = "affiliation" op = "equal_to" ev = "*********"/>
        ......
      </ClaimSet>
    </Credential>
  </Requester>
  ......<PassonRequest sndr = "Doctor2" rcvr = "Doctor1"/> ......
  ......<PassonRequest sndr = "Counselor1" rcvr = "Doctor2"/> ......
</RequesterChain>
```

Figure 8. Pass-on policy of MDB₂

```
<PassOnPolicy id = "MDB2-PP-0001" dec = "negative">
  <Receiver>
    <ConstraintSet op = "or">
        <Constraint ea = "occupation" op = "equal_to" ev = "general"/>
        <Constraint ea = "affiliation" op = "not_equal_to" ev = "******"/>
    </ConstraintSet>
  </Receiver>
  <Data>
    <ConstraintSet op = "and">
      <Constraint ea = "security_level" op = "greater_equal_to" ev = "Secret"/>
      <Constraint ea = "type" op = "equal_to" ev = "special"/>
    </ConstraintSet>
  </Data>
  <PassingContext>
    <Constraint ea = "pass_on_form" op = "equal_to" ev = "raw"/>
  </PassingContext>
</PassOnPolicy>
```

Doctor₁ involves the issue of re-delegation which needs to be strictly controlled. First, the owner of the privilege may specify whether the delegated privilege can be re-delegated to others, or how many times it can be re-delegated. Such constraints are usually specified in <Obligation> section in the delegation policy, and later on taken into the issued delegation certificate. Also, re-delegation can be controlled by the resource owner, by speci-

fying in the delegation policy whether delegated or re-delegated privileges can be used to access certain resources. Figure 10 shows the delegation policies of the patient and *MDB₁*.

On delegating *Doctor₁* the access privilege to the medical record, the patient will write the delegation constraints specified in the delegation policy into the issued delegation certificate. These delegation constraints include a duration constraint

Figure 9. Pass-on certificate of MDB₂

```
<PassOnCertificate id = "MDB2-PC-0001" by = "D5-CA">
    <IssuedTo>
      <ServiceSet>
        <Service id = "Counselor1 "/>
        <Service id = "Doctor2"/>
        <Service id = "Doctor1"/>
        <Service id = "Patient"/>
      </ServiceSet>
    </IssuedTo>
    <ConstraintSet>
      <Constraint ea = "session_id" op = "equal_to" ev = "000001"/>
    </ConstraintSet>
</PassOnCertificate>
```

defined for the delegation certificate issued to *Doctor*$_1$, and a set of constraints which confines that re-delegation is allowed but only when the delegatee is a specialized doctor, and the delegation chain is no longer than 5 (re-delegated for 5 times). If *Doctor*$_2$ satisfies these constraints, then *Doctor*$_1$ can re-delegate him/her the patient's credentials without communicating with the patient. However, if the patient's delegation policy does not allow automatic re-delegation, then *Doctor*$_1$ must send *Doctor*$_2$'s information back to the patient for the decision. Suppose that *Doctor*$_2$ is a specialist; then in this case, the delegation certificate that is shown in Figure 11 will be issued.

On receiving the above delegation certificate, *MDB*$_1$ validates the delegation constraints and the delegated credentials, and checks them against its delegation policies. If success, then a positive access control decision is made and the requested data are sent. Note that, *MDB*$_1$ may specify more restrictive conditions for re-delegation. As can be seen from Figure 10, *MDB*$_1$ only allows the credentials used for the accesses to be re-delegated

at most once (e.g., the patient delegates *Doctor*$_1$, and *Doctor*$_1$ delegates *Doctor*$_2$). Suppose that *Doctor*$_2$ wants to involve *Doctor*$_i$, for some *i*, in the diagnosis, and delegates *Doctor*$_i$ the patient's credentials. Although this is eligible for the patient, yet such an access will be simply denied by *MDB*$_1$ according to its delegation policies.

6 CONCLUSION

Web service security is a challenging area in SOA environment. Conventional SOA security models focus on individual services and exhibit some problems. In this article, we present an enhanced security model to provide better control of the information flow among services. We design a protocol to support the delegation and pass-on actions between services, and the decision process is based on the verification of a certificate chain. We also provide a detailed discussion of our policy system including the concepts of delegation and pass-on policies.

Figure 10. Delegation policies of the patient and MDB$_1$

```
<DelegationPolicy id = "Patient-DP-0001" dec = "positive">
   <Obligation>
      <ConstraintSet>
         <Constraint ea = "system_date" op = "less_equal_to" ev = "1/1/2009"/>
         <Constraint ea = "redelegability" op = "equal_to" ev = "true"/>
         <Constraint ea = "delegation_chain_length" op = "less_equal_to" ev = "5"/>
         <Constraint ea = "occupation" op = "equal_to" ev = "specialist"/>
      </ConstraintSet>
   </Obligation>
</DelegationPolicy>

<DelegationPolicy id = "MDB2-DP-0001" dec = "positive">
   <Delegatee>
      <Constraint ea = "occupation" op = "equal_to" ev = "specialist"/>
   </Delegatee>
   <Obligation>
      <Constraint ea = "delegation_chain_length" op = "less_equal_to" ev = "2"/>
   </Obligation>
</DelegationPolicy>
```

Figure 11. Delegation certificate issued from Doctor₁ to Doctor₂

```
<DelegationCertificate id = "Doctor1-DC-0001" by = "D2-CA" from =
"Doctor1" to = "Doctor2">
  <DelegatedCredential>
    <Credential id = "Patient-CD-001" by = "Some CA" to = "Patient">
      <ClaimSet>
        <Claim ea = "user_id" op = "equal_to" ev = "**********"/>
        <Claim ea = "name" op = "equal_to" ev = "**********"/>
        ......
      </ClaimSet>
    </Credential>
  </DelegatedCredential>
  <ConstraintSet>
    <Constraint ea = "system_date" op = "less_equal_to" ev = "1/1/2009"/>
    <Constraint ea = "redelegability" op = "equal_to" ev = "true"/>
    <Constraint ea = "delegation_chain_length" op = "less_equal_to" ev = "5"/>
    <Constraint ea = "occupation" op = "equal_to" ev = "specialist"/>
  </ConstraintSet>
</DelegationCertificate>
```

The work in this article provides a foundation for further research and development of a comprehensive security paradigm for well-controlled secure web service interactions. In this article, we only consider the control of the flow of the information contained in responses. In practice, the information contained in the requests may also require high level protection. And, if the service chain is dynamically composed, the flow of the information contained in the requests becomes more difficult to be controlled. We plan to develop a sophisticated web service security model to consider comprehensive information flow control. Also, this article develops general delegation and pass-on mechanisms for composite services. Some issues such as negotiation can be considered in depth to enhance the model. For example, if the patient does not know in advance what privileges are required for the doctors, then the doctors may get insufficient privileges to access the database or get unnecessary privileges and cause possible privilege misuse. Thus, it is necessary to confine the delegation at the needed level while starting a negotiation phase when the privileges are not sufficient. Similarly, pass-on negotiation should also be supported. For example, in case a medical database does not allow its medical records to flow to a patient due to lack of the knowledge to the patient credentials, then a negotiation protocol between the database and the patient can be established dynamically. We plan to further develop delegation negotiation and pass-on negotiation protocols to provide powerful security support for web service composition.

REFERENCES

Atluri, V., & Warner, J. (2005). Supporting conditional delegation in secure workflow management systems. In *Proceedings of the Tenth ACM Symposium on Access Control Models and Technologies* (pp. 49-58).

Aura, T. (2001). Distributed access-rights management with delegation certificates. In *secure internet programming* (LNCS 1603, pp. 211-235).

Barka, E. S., & Sandhu, R. S. (2000). *A role-based delegation model and some extensions.* Paper presented at the 23rd National Information Systems Security Conference.

Bertino, E., Squicciarini, A. C., Paloscia, I., & Martino, L. (2006). Ws-AC: A fine grained access control system for web services. *World Wide Web (Bussum), 9*(2), 143–171. doi:10.1007/s11280-005-3045-4

Bhatti, R., Bertino, E., & Ghafoor, A. (2005). A trust-based context-aware access control model for web-services. *Distributed and Parallel Databases, 18*(1), 83–105. doi:10.1007/s10619-005-1075-7

Carminati, B., Ferrari, E., & Hung, P. C. K. (2005). Web service composition: A security perspective. In *Proceedings of the 2005 International Workshop on Challenges in Web Information Retrieval and Integration* (pp. 248-253).

Carminati, B., Ferrari, E., & Hung, P. C. K. (2006). Security conscious web service composition. In *Proceedings of the IEEE International Conference on Web Services* (pp. 489-496)

Fenser, D., & Bussler, C. (2002). The Web Service Modeling Framework WSMF. *Electronic Commerce Research and Applications, 1*(2), 113–137. doi:10.1016/S1567-4223(02)00015-7

Gasser, M., & McDermott, E. (1990). An architecture for practical delegation in a distributed system. In *Proceedings of the IEEE Symposium on Security and Privacy* (pp. 20).

IBM. (2006). *Microsoft, RSA, and Verisign.* Retrieved from http://specs.xmlsoap.org

Kortesniemi, Y., & Hasu, T. (2000). *A revocation, validation and authentication protocol for SPKI based delegation systems.* Paper presented at the Network and Distributed Systems Security Symposium.

Koshutanski, H., & Massacci, F. (2003). An access control framework for business processes for web services. In *Proceedings of the 2003 ACM Workshop on XML Security* (pp. 15-24).

OASIS. (2006). *Index.* Retrieved from http://docs.oasis-open.org

Rao, Y., Feng, B., Han, J., & Li, Z. (2004). SX-RSRPM: A security integrated model for Web services. In *Proceedings of the 2004 International Conference on Machine Learning and Cybernetics* (Vol. 5, pp. 26-29).

She, W., Thuraisingham, B. M., & Yen, I. (2007). Delegation-based security model for web services. In *Proceedings of the IEEE International Symposium on High Assurance Systems Engineering* (pp. 82-91).

She, W., Yen, I., & Thuraisingham, B. M. (2008). Enhancing security modeling for web services using delegation and pass-on. In *Proceedings of the IEEE International Conference on Web Services* (pp. 545-552).

Skogsrud, H., Benatallah, B., & Casati, F. (2003). Model-driven trust negotiation for web services. *IEEE Internet Computing*, 45–51. doi:10.1109/MIC.2003.1250583

Wang, J., Vecchio, D. D., & Humphrey, M. (2005). Extending the security assertion markup language to support delegation for web services and grid services. In *Proceedings of the IEEE International Conference on Web Services* (pp. 67-74).

Welch, V., Foster, I., Kesselman, C., Mulmo, O., Pearlman, L., Tuecke, S., et al. (2004). *X.509 proxy certificates for dynamic delegation.* Paper presented at the 3rd Annual PKI R&D Workshop.

Xu, W., Venkatakrishnan, V. N., Sekar, R., & Ramakrishnan, I. V. (2006). A framework for building privacy-conscious composite web services. In *Proceedings of the IEEE International Conference on Web Services* (pp. 655-662).

Yialelis, N., & Sloman, M. (1996). A security framework supporting domain-based access control in distributed systems. In *Proceedings of the Symposium on Network and Distributed System Security* (p. 26).

Yin, G., Wang, H., Shi, D., Jia, Y., & Teng, M. (2004). A rule-based framework for role-based constrained delegation. In *Proceedings of the 3rd International Conference on Information Security* (pp. 186-191).

Zhang, L., Ahn, G.-J., & Chu, B.-T. (2003). A rule-based framework for role-based delegation and revocation. *ACM Transactions on Information and System Security*, 6(3), 404–441. doi:10.1145/937527.937530

Zhang, X., Oh, S., & Sandhu, R. S. (2003). PBDM: A flexible delegation model in RBAC. In *Proceedings of the 8th ACM symposium on Access Control Models and Technologies* (pp. 149-157).

This work was previously published in the International Journal of Web Services Research, Volume 7, Issue 1, edited by Liang-Jie (LJ) Zhang, pp. 1-21, copyright 2010 by IGI Publishing (an imprint of IGI Global).

Chapter 14
Behavioral Attestation for Web Services Based Business Processes

Masoom Alam
Institute of Management Sciences, Pakistan

Tamleek Ali
Institute of Management Sciences, Pakistan

Mohammad Nauman
Institute of Management Sciences, Pakistan

Patrick C. K. Hung
University of Ontario Institute of Technology, Canada

Xinwen Zhang
Samsung Information Systems America, USA

Quratulain Alam
Institute of Management Sciences, Pakistan

ABSTRACT

Service Oriented Architecture (SOA) is an architectural paradigm that enables dynamic composition of heterogeneous, independent, multi-vendor business services. A prerequisite for such inter-organizational workflows is the establishment of trustworthiness, which is mostly achieved through non-technical measures, such as legislation, and/or social consent that businesses or organizations pledge themselves to adhere. A business process can only be trustworthy if the behavior of all services in it is trustworthy. Trusted Computing Group (TCG) has defined an open set of specifications for the establishment of trustworthiness through a hardware root-of-trust. This paper has three objectives: firstly, the behavior of individual services in a business process is formally specified. Secondly, to overcome the inherent weaknesses of trust management through software alone, a hardware root of-trust devised by the TCG, is used for the measurement of the behavior of individual services in a business process. Finally, a verification mechanism is detailed through which the trustworthiness of a business process can be verified.

DOI: 10.4018/978-1-4666-1942-5.ch014

1. INTRODUCTION

Service Oriented Architecture (SOA) with underlying technologies like web services and web service orchestration facilitates smooth interaction among independent, multivendor data sources and legacy applications running on heterogeneous platforms across distributed information networks. Such interactions require intelligently interfaced application software and dynamic integration with other connected cooperative environments. As a result, more applications and services have been deployed which bring new businesses and pervasive information sharing.

With these trends, the paradigm of SOA opens new vistas for businesses in the form of dynamic collaborations, where services comprise unassociated, loosely coupled units of functionality and call to other services are not embedded in them. This means that there are no hardcore calls to each other in their source code. Instead a number of protocols are defined that describe how these services can pass and parse messages. These protocols e.g., Business Process Execution Language (BPEL) (Weerawarana, 2005) define the patterns based on which these service calls are composed to form a business process.

Services provide interface to the individual components of a software. However, abstracting the internals behind a single interface makes SOA more prone to security vulnerabilities. For example, it is extremely difficult to verify that an electronic health record or credit card number input into a service is updated or used in a trustworthy way. A prerequisite for the realization of SOA based inter-organizational workflows is the establishment of trustworthiness. However, according to current best practices, trustworthiness is mostly achieved through nontechnical measures such as legislation, or social consent that businesses, or organizations simply pledge themselves to adhere. All existing approaches

for secure composition of business processes are focused on the issues of authentication and authorization only. Authentication and authorization are primarily concerned with the verification of service identity and checking permissions for calling a specific service.

Existing approaches for secure composition of business processes (Bertino, 2001), (Gudes, 1999), (Huang, 1999), (Wainer, 2003), (Anderson, 2002) do not take the behavior of individual services into account while composing business processes. Behavioral attestation of a service is concerned with the question that whether a service is consuming the input in a trusted way and as a result producing the trusted output or not. It is a third dimension that goes well beyond the traditional view of authentication and authorization.

We have laid down the following three requirements for the behavioral attestation of business processes. Firstly, a framework is needed that can explicitly specify the behavior of individual services in a business process. A formal means of specification helps to abstract the complex details of the underlying hardware and software.

Secondly, a mechanism is needed that can measure the dynamic behavior of services in a trustworthy way. Existing approaches for platform protection through software alone – by their very principle – are uncompromising and have inherent weaknesses (Pearson, 2002),(Grawrock, 2006),(Alam, 2007). Trusted Computing Group (TCG) has taken a quantum leap in security, "a hardware root of trust", which provides secure storage for data and cryptographic keys. Remote attestation is an essential characteristic of Trusted Computing that provides a hardware supported evidence in enciphered form that a trusted environment actually exists on a remote platform (Pearson, 2002), (Grawrock, 2006). This feature can be used in reporting the behavior of a service to a remote authority. However, existing approaches for the realization of remote attestation measure

309

the trustworthiness from binaries, configurations and properties. All of these techniques are low-level attestation techniques only and none of them define what a trusted behavior actually is and how to specify it (Alam, Zhang, Nauman, & Ali, 2008). Thus, these approaches cannot be used as a ready-made solution for the behavioral attestation of business processes.

Finally, trusted third parties are needed that can play a role beyond traditional certification authorities and Privacy CAs (Graz, 2008). These attestation authorities should be able to attest the behavior of a business process and can issue credentials based on their behavior.

We define the behavior of a service as a set of observable actions or reactions of the service in response to its *execution environment*. The execution environment comprises input data and the security policy associated with a service. In our viewpoint, a given business process is trustworthy if the data input to services is trustworthy and if all services in the business process enforce their security policies in a trustworthy manner.

In this paper, we present Behavioral Attestation for Business Processes (BA4BP), which is a framework for the identification, specification, and verification of different behaviors associated with a business process. It is the process of verification of 1) the integrity of the input data – service intake – and 2) correct enforcement of the security policy attached to a service – service processing. The framework is realized in three steps 1) behavior specification, 2) behavior measurement and; 3) behavior verification.

In Step 1 (cf., Section 4), the framework specifies the behavior of a service in a formal way. Each service is characterized by a set of attributes, which include the data, input as parameters to a service. A change in the values of these attributes can influence the overall behavior of a service. Note that this change should be in accordance with the security policy attached to the service.

In Step 2 (cf., Section 5), the framework uses the Trusted Platform Module (TPM) for measuring the dynamic behavior of the services in a business process. The measurements are stored in the secure storage provided by the TPM.

In Step 3 (cf., Section 6), the framework uses a verification mechanism for the attestation of different recorded behaviors – called enforcement behaviors. In order to prove the trustworthiness of different services in a business process, the framework compares the expected behaviors with the enforcement behaviors and draws conclusions regarding the trustworthiness of individual services.

Our contributions in this paper are threefold: Firstly, we define a mechanism for explicitly specifying the criteria for the trustworthiness of a service platform. Secondly, we create an abstraction layer at the web services level through which existing low-level attestation techniques can be combined to specify the expected behavior of a service platform. Finally, our approach enables a predictive analysis of the behavior of a service platform.

- **Outline**: Some background information about Trusted Computing and Remote Attestation is provided in Section 2. Section 3 presents the methodology of our framework and takes a bird eye view of our behavioral attestation framework. In Section 4, we formally define the semantics of services behavior. Section 5 presents our reference architecture and section 6 covers the measurement of these behaviors. Section 7 describes the verification of the measured behaviors. Section 8 presents the implementation details and Section 9 highlights some of the related works carried out in the past in this area. Finally, Section 10 provides an outlook on this contribution.

2. BACKGROUND

2.1 Trusted Computing and Remote Attestation

The Trusted Computing Group (Mitchell, 2005) has devised a mechanism for bringing trust to the different aspects of computing including the PC client, mobile platforms and storage media. The hardware chip is called the Trusted Platform Module (TPM) and is a secure co-processor responsible for providing a root of trust. Each TPM is uniquely identified by its Endorsement Key (EK) that is burned in to it by its manufacturer.

According to (Yoshihama, 2007), the endorsement key is a 2,048-bit RSA public and private key pair, which is created randomly on the chip at manufacture time and cannot be changed. The private key never leaves the chip, while the public key is used for attestation and for encryption of sensitive data sent to the chip". An Attestation Identity Key (AIK) generated by the TPM and signed by a trusted third party, uniquely identifies the particular users of a target platform.

TPM has the capability of storing platform configurations in shielded memory locations called the Platform Configuration Registers (PCRs). PCRs are special purpose registers that designed to store cryptographic hashes, specifically SHA-1 hashes of software loaded for execution. PCRs are tamper resistant as they can only be set using a special operation called PCR extend. The irreversibility of SHA-1 ensures that once a hash has been saved in a PCR, it cannot be removed by any software loaded after the extend operation has been performed. Therefore, the hashes in the PCR can be used to report the configurations of a platform to a challenging party in a trusted way.

Each PCR can store a 160-bit hash value and at each reboot, the PCRs are reset. Each software component of the platform is mapped to 160-bit hash value that represents its good state. Each new hash is concatenated with an existing hash in the PCR and the new hash is stored in the same PCR. In this way, a small number of PCRs can be used to measure all the components of a platform. Further, a Stored Measurement Log (SML) is used to keep track of the sequence of measurements in the PCRs.

This concept of reporting the platform configurations to a challenger in order to provide trust in the behavior of a target platform is termed as *remote attestation*. Remote attestation is an important feature of Trusted Computing (Mitchell, 2005), which allows a remote party to verify the integrity of another platform through trust tokens submitted by the TPM on the target platform. In a typical remote attestation scenario, a service provider verifies the integrity of the platform, before dispatching a resource to it. For example, a hospital verifies the integrity of the client platform before dispatching medical record of a patient to it.

The underlying idea in remote attestation is to present the PCR measurements within its TPM to a challenger. In a typical remote attestation scenario, a platform's TPM collects the requested PCR values with their indices, signs them with an AIK and returns them to the challenger along with the SML. Using SML and PCR measurement values, it is possible for a challenger to re-compute the PCR values and compare them with their expected values. Based on the comparison, the challenger can make a decision whether the target platform is in a valid state or not. For a comprehensive introduction to remote attestation and trusted computing, we refer the reader to Mitchell (2005).

There are four prominent approaches proposed in the literature for the realization of remote attestation. Configuration based attestation requires that a service platform present the trusted configurations of its platform to a challenger. Trusted configurations mean that, for example, the service platform provides a proof signed by the TPM that a particular security module is installed on the service platform. Based on these evidences, the challenger evaluates the trustworthiness of the service platform.

Another approach, Integrity Measurement Architecture (IMA) (Sailer, 2003), uses binary attestation. In IMA, a service platform presents the binary hashes of all its components loaded after booting. A challenger verifies the sequence of these binary hashes and concludes as to the trustworthiness of the target platform using this information.

PRIMA (Jaeger, 2006) enhances the IMA approach by taking the hash of the required components only. Moreover, it also analyzes the information to and from the target application using SELinux (Loscocco, 2001) policies.

Reporting all system components through binary hashes or revealing all system configurations might give rise to severe efficiency problems and security threats, respectively. To overcome these limitations, property-based attestation (Chen, 2006; Kühn, 2007; Poritz, 2004; Sadeghi, 2004) proposes to map a set of related system configurations to some meaningful properties. For example, the property, Multi Level Security (MLS) enabled" can be mapped to system configurations such as the support of MLS in SELinux policies. In this way, the configurations of a target platform are not disclosed to a challenger.

Each of these existing low-level remote attestation techniques is useful in some scenarios but becomes infeasible in others. For example, revealing all system configurations in a highly critical environment may cause a denial of service attack (Shi, 2005). Moreover, none of these approaches specify an explicit benchmark with which the trustworthiness of a target platform can be compared.

Model-based Behavioral Attestation (MBA) (Alam, Zhang, Nauman, & Ali, 2008) which combines these existing low-level techniques and uses them in a supporting manner so that the weaknesses of one can be addressed by another. BA4WS (Alam, Zhang, Nauman, & Ali, 2008) is a step forward in this direction. It uses behavioral attestation at the web services level allowing for the incorporation of low level attestation techniques in a supporting manner using existing web services security standards.

2.2 WS-Attestation

In order to leverage the concept of remote attestation at the web services level, a new mechanism – called WS-Attestation – has been proposed. The proposal extends WS-Trust (Anderson, 2002) to define how an service provider and service requestor interact with each other for attestation purposes. The main entities involved in WS-Attestation are a Service Provider (SP) – which needs to attest the integrity of a platform, a Service Requester (SR) – the target platform which reports its integrity and a Validation Service (VS) – the trusted third-party which can perform attestation on behalf of the SP.

The main idea behind the introduction of VS is to address privacy issues involved in revealing system configurations via PCRs and SML. After attestation, a VS advocates about certain properties of an SR like PlatformIntegrity = true etc.

In order to support flexible communication between service provider, service requestor and validation service, WS-Attestation proposes three different architectural models (cf., Figure 1).

In the *Pushed Model* (cf., Figure 1a), a service requestor takes an attestation credential from a validation service and presents it to the service provider. In the *Pulled Model* (cf., Figure 1b), the service requestor sends its PCRs and SML along with the service request. The service provider then requests the validation service for the verification of different properties of the service requestor using its sent PCRs. Finally, in the *Delegated Model* (cf., Figure 1c), the service provider requests the validation service to perform attestation on its behalf. Depending on the underlying attestation scenario, any combination of these three models can be utilized.

Figure 1. WS-attestation architectural models

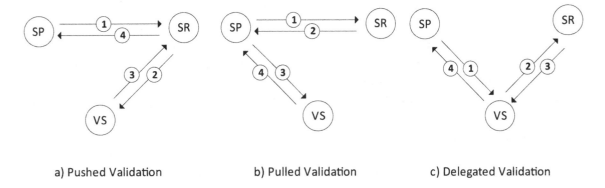

a) Pushed Validation   b) Pulled Validation   c) Delegated Validation

However, WS-Attestation provides only a structural paradigm on which more fine-grained attestation frameworks can be developed. More specifically, in WS-Attestation, the specification of an explicit criterion for the trustworthiness of a service requestor platform is left unspecified. In the following sections, our approach is presented in detail.

3. METHODOLOGY

Mayer (2006) defines reference monitor as a tamperproof, non-by passable and a small component or module responsible for mediating all accesses to data or objects or devices by a particular software. It provides an abstract model of the necessary and sufficient properties that must be achieved by any system claiming to have securely enforced access controls. It can be used as a tool for the design and implementation of secure systems.

An organization can articulate the reference monitor as part of its security requirements. The basic function of a reference monitor is to verify the nature of the request against a set of already defined policies. A reference monitor is an abstract component that can be implemented within an operating system, virtual machine, or an application. According to its level of abstraction where the concept of reference monitor is realized,

the job functions of the corresponding reference monitor might change. Within a software application for example, healthcare, the job functions of a reference monitor are to mediate the access control between medical subjects such as Doctor and Nurse, and medical records. Similarly, a reference monitor within an operating system will mediate access between processes and devices and other processes. Thus, the level of abstraction of a reference monitor decides upon the level of granularity, it mediates access control.

There are three main principles for the design and development of a secure system. Firstly, any access to internal or external data objects within a software component should be mediated by its reference monitor. This makes the reference monitor *non-by-passable* and assures that security policy is indeed enforced. The degree of security assurance that can be assigned to a software is based on how much it is dependent on its reference monitor for accessing data or objects. This also indicates the control and security features enabled within an application. Thus, an application having a very loose relationship with its reference monitor will allow most of the job functions without the prior approval of its reference monitor and hence, it may not be the best candidate to be ranked as a good security application. On the other hand, having tightly coupled with its reference monitor, an application can be ranked as a secure application.

Secondly, special mechanism shall be employed so that the access mediation mechanism is tamperproof. This means that, it should be impossible to penetrate an attack on the reference monitor of a software component. In order to prevents such attacks, existing software based solutions for enabling security such as Anti Viruses have inherent weaknesses (Alam, 2007).

Finally, the reference monitor shall be small enough in order to perform analysis and formal verification. Formal specification and verification of the behavior of the reference monitor can demonstrate that whether a reference monitor enforces a security policy in a trustworthy way or not.

Having these points in mind, we have devised an approach for hardware assisted attestation of services using their reference monitors. We identify reference monitors as integral part of a service platform. In our approach, we attest or verify the behavior of the reference monitor of a service. In the context of service oriented architecture (cf., Figure 2), a reference monitor is responsible for mediating access control between service invokers and service providers. A business

process is composed of a set of services in which each service can play the role of service invoker as well as service provider. In order to provide secure and trustworthy environment at the service platform, its reference monitor should be tightly coupled – mediates each and every service call, tamper proof – hardware assisted security and formally verified business logic.

- *Tightly coupled* means that all service calls along with their input parameters are intercepted by the reference monitor. These parameter values – also called attributes, are then used by the reference monitor for the evaluation of its policies which dictate the set of rules for mediating access control. In our settings, no service calls can bypass its reference monitor.
- *Tamper proof* refers to the property that a reference monitor has a trusted behavior. In this regard, we use hardware assisted security mechanism to verify the behavior of a reference monitor. In our approach, the behavior of a reference monitor is measured

Figure 2. Service reference monitor

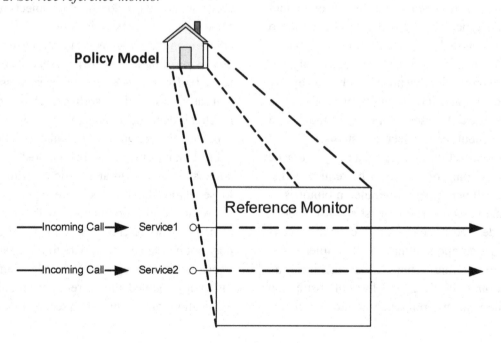

in two steps. In the first step, all configurations files, libraries a reference monitor is dependent on are measured. Secondly, the attribute values input to a reference monitor through service calls are also measured.

- *Formal verification* refers to the property that the behavior of a reference monitor shall be formally specified. Since a reference monitor is influenced by a policy model rather than relying on the underlying security policies that are implemented by a reference monitor, we target the policy model of the corresponding reference monitor. A policy model defines a set of access control requirements that a reference monitor should fulfill. In this way, we focus at a higher level of abstraction covering a range of security policies. A business process may be composed of a set of services each of which are running across geographical boundaries and thus having different implementations for their reference monitors. A policy model is composed of a set of components. Each of these components needs to be analyzed thoroughly to identify a general set of behaviors associated with its distinct components. This identification helps to categorize the trusted components of a policy model. Afterwards, the behavior of the policy model is formally specified. An attestation authority uses these behaviors to determine the trustworthiness of the service platform at which the policy model is realized. Working at this higher level of abstraction, the behavior analysis need to be performed only once and results can be used for different services implementing the same policy model. In the following sections, our approach is detailed.

4. SERVICE BEHAVIOR

A Business Process (BP) is composed of a finite number of services denoted by

$$\{s_1, s_2 .... s_n\}$$

where $s_i \in S$. A service is defined as a function call, which may take a number of inputs and may return any number of output values. Formally:

$$s : x_1, x_2, ... x_n \mapsto y_1, y_2, ... y_j$$

where $s \in S$, x_i are input parameters to the service s and y_j are the output values.

An activity within a business process is defined as a scenario in which a service s_1 can access another service s_2 and is denoted by $s_1 \rightarrow s_2$ where $\rightarrow$ sign indicates that s_1 can access s_2 one or more times in a single (authenticated) session. Depending on the role of a service in an activity, it can be treated as a subject or object service. For example, in activity $s_1 \rightarrow s_2$, s_1 is treated as a subject service and s_2 as an object service.

Example 1 *An online hospital service calls a laboratory service for further investigation regarding some patient. In this activity, we write* $hospital \rightarrow lab1$ *where hospital is the subject service and lab1 is the object service.*

Each service in an activity has a finite number of attributes $ATT = \{a_1, a_2, ... a_n\}$, associated with it. Each attribute is defined as a (name, value) pair and a particular attribute a of a service s is referred to as $s.a$ where $s \in BP$ and $a \in ATT$. Attributes of a service are categorized as internal or external attributes. Attributes that are generated from the service platform such as internal data, service configurations, system time etc., are called internal attributes. External attributes are the service parameters or the response data, a service may get as an output from another service.

Example 2 *The laboratory service (introduced in Example 1) forwards the electronic health record to another laboratory service as input and retrieves test results for specific diseases as output from the* second laboratory service. In this case, the health record is a parameter of the service and is thus treated as an attribute.

Each service within an activity has a reference monitor responsible for the evaluation and execution of its security policies. Each reference monitor is influenced by a policy model and a policy model is generally composed of a set of components each of which has an associated behavior. We define a policy model as follows:

Definition 1 *A policy model M is a 3-tuple: M = (P,C, A_u). Where:*

- P is a set of instance policies,
- C is a finite set of authorization conditions or predicates built from the internal or external attributes and,
- A_u is a finite set of attribute update actions

An instance policy $p \in P$ is a 3-tuple, each element of which is a subset of the corresponding element in M. In general, an access control system of a service consists of a set of subjects S – service invokers, a set of objects O – service providers, a set of rights R – usually refer to the execution of a service, a set of attributes ATT – parameters and output of a service, and a set of access policies P.

A service security policy or simply policy p associated with it defines a set of conditions C, under which a subject service s_1 can access object service s_2. Each $c \in C$ is composed of a set of subject service and object service attributes. All attributes, which are used in the security policy of a service, affect the overall behavior of the corresponding service. Attributes trustworthiness is captured by the *Attribute Behavior* (cf., Section 4.2).

Example 3 *The laboratory service can have a policy that requires the verification of the supplied credit card information for sufficient credit. For this purpose, the laboratory service may call a billing service to verify that the supplied credit card number is valid.*

Example 4 *The billing service (introduced in Example 3), before supplying the credit card information, verifies that the laboratory service is authorized to access this information. If the authorization conditions hold, the laboratory service is allowed to access the billing service.*

A service policy also contains a set of attribute update actions A_u, which update the attributes of services involved in the activity. Attribute update actions are treated as internal or external service calls. *Attribute Update Behavior* (cf., Section 4.2) keeps track of all service attribute updates mentioned in the security policy of a service.

Example 5 *The laboratory service (introduced in Example 1) may update the input medical record using an internal service.*

In general, for each of these behaviors, the formal specification takes the following form. First, the behavior itself is defined. Afterwards, the trustworthiness of the corresponding behavior is specified.

4.1 Attribute Behavior

A service policy contains a set of conditions that are primarily dependent on the service internal and external attributes. These attributes play a key role in sorting out access decisions for a service. We define attribute behavior as follows:

Definition 2 *(Attribute Behavior) Let s_1 be a service called by another service s_2 such that $s_2 \rightarrow s_1$ and C be the set of conditions associated* with the service s_1. *Access to s_1 is allowed if an only if all conditions based on internal/external attributes return true.*

An attribute of a service is defined as a (name, value) pair. In order to include the behavior property, it is treated as a triple (name, value, behavior). We define the trustworthiness of state transition behavior as:

Definition 3 *(Attribute Behavior Trustworthiness) ATT is a set of attributes of services s_1 and s_2 where $s_1 \rightarrow s_2$. A policy can evaluate in a trustworthy manner if and only if the behavior of all attributes involved in the condition C is trustworthy and all conditions are true. Formally,*

$$\forall j.s.attr_j.behavior = trusted \wedge C = TRUE$$

where $attr_j \subset ATT$ and C is the set of conditions associated with the service s_1.

4.2 Attribute Update Behavior

Attribute update actions are an integral part of the service behavior. We define attribute update behavior as follows:

Definition 4 (Attribute Update Behavior) *Given an attribute $s.a_i$, and an update service 'update', the attribute update behavior is defined as the application of an internal update service on the attribute. The application of the service yields a new value which is assigned to the attribute. Formally:*

$$update : s.a_i \mapsto s.a_i'$$

We define the trustworthiness of internal attribute update behavior as:

Definition 5 (Internal Attribute Update Behavior Trustworthiness) *an attribute update behavior*

is trustworthy if the corresponding attribute is in a trusted state and the service updating it is also trusted. Formally:

$$s.a'.behavior = upate.behavior \wedge s.a.behavior$$

We conclude that a behavior process can only be trustworthy if all its services are trustworthy. The behavior of an individual service is defined as follows:

Definition 6 (Service Behavior Trustworthiness) *A service behavior is trustworthy if its input is trustworthy—attribute behavior and if its attribute update behavior is trustworthy.*

However, a case exists where updates to the service attributes may be performed by calling other services. The trustworthiness of the external updates can be verified by measuring the integrity of the corresponding service. We define the external attribute update as follows:-

Definition 7 (External Attribute Update Behavior Trustworthiness) *an external attribute update behavior is trustworthy if the behavior of the producing service is trustworthy. Formally:*

if $s : x_1, x_2, ... x_n \mapsto y_1, y_2, ... y_j$

then each y_j behavior is trurstworthy if

$$s.behavior = TRUSTED \wedge x_i.behavior = TRUSTED$$

In the above definition, the behavior of the output of the service s is trustworthy if and only if the input x_i is trustworthy and the service s is trustworthy. For the service behavior, the same criteria will be used as described in Section 4.1 and 4.2. Below, we describe our target architecture and a framework for the measurement of these behaviors. Afterwards, their verification mechanism is detailed.

5. TARGET ARCHITECTURE

A business process is composed of a set of services each of which can call each other in order to achieve a common objective or task. These services can be distributed across different systems that are connected with each other over a network. In case, services are located within an organization, a single attestation authority can take care of their behavioral attestation. In a distributed environment, however, multiple attestation authorities can be given the task for the attestation of different services. In this section, we detail the attestation of a single service. The same procedure can be applied to multiple services in a business process.

An attestation authority provides an attestation service that can be called by different services periodically for their attestation. The attestation service takes the various logs as input – called enforcement behavior logs of a service as input and after processing sends a certificate describing the integrity of the corresponding service. The certificate contains an integrity level that can be verified, before calling a service and supplying some confidential data. The integrity level is assigned based on the verification the supplied inputs to a service and then verifying the different behaviors associated with the policy of the subject service. Hence, it is verified that whether a service will process the input in a trustworthy manner or not. In addition to the assignment of integrity levels, within an organization, an attestation service can also call an appropriate authority, if found a malicious code within a service.

In our target architecture, the role of reference monitor is played by the data flow model of XACML. An XACML data flow model provides a classical example of access control mechanism implemented in a distributed and platform independent web services platform. Its dataflow describes how different components of an access control system can be designed within a web service. Within the data flow model, the context handler insulates outer implementation environment from the access control system. Thus, XACML can be realized in a variety of web services platforms for example, .NET, J2EE, and so forth. This motivates us to choose XACML data flow model as a standard for the realization of the reference monitor concept.. Secondly, its policy enforcement point clearly separates the enforcement point from the policy decision point which is responsible for the evaluation of access control polices. A policy information point is responsible for gathering attributes of the subject, object and environment and thus, all the outer information to the reference monitor comes with the help of attributes. Each policy of the XACML represents an instance of the policy model, enforced by the XACML reference monitor. In our target architecture, the policy decision point, policy enforcement point and all its constituent components are termed as reference monitor.

Figure 3 describes our target architecture. After authentication, each service is assigned a unique ID. All subsequent calls from the service are treated as being in a single authenticated session. After authentication, the Policy Enforcement Point forwards the request to the Policy Decision Point for access evaluation. We assume that a proper authentication mechanism has been employed such as public key infrastructure or biometric devices for service authentication. The Policy Decision Point retrieves the applicable policy and required attributes for policy evaluation through the Context Handler. After successful evaluation, the Policy Decision Point sends the result of the policy evaluation to the Policy Enforcement Point. The Policy Enforcement Point maintains a separate session for each respective activity. In our target architecture, a reference monitor is a component responsible for the evaluation and enforcement of an activity policy. Thus, the Policy Decision Point, the Policy Enforcement Point and the Context Handler all together are referred to as a reference monitor. The Context Handler is responsible for adhering attributes from various sources and for performing updates on these attributes.

Figure 3. Target architecture

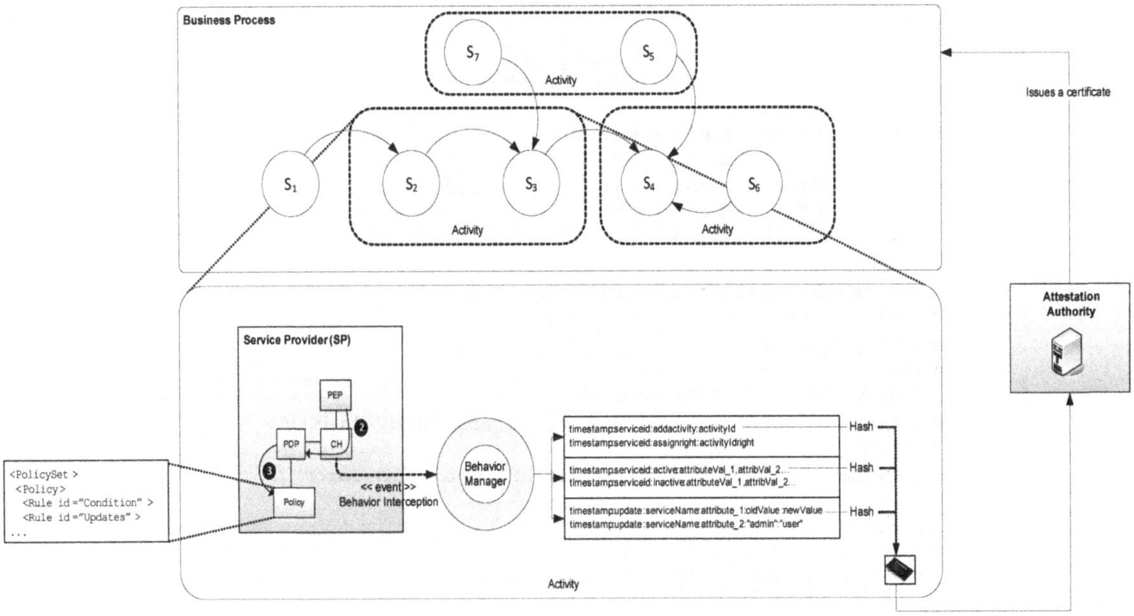

An XACML policy consists of four main constructs. These are 1) <PolicySet>, 2) <Policy>, 3) <Rule> and The <PolicySet> acts like a container in which various policies (<Policy>) can be placed. These policies define the main access control conditions, a web service want to enforce. These conditions are described using the <condition> element and are enclosed in the <Rule> element. Each XACML construct contains a <Target> element that can be used to the policy the credentials of the subject in a access control scenario. For example, <target> might refer to a service s_1, in which case, the associated policy will be applied if the subject is asking for service s_1.

Figure 4 shows an XACML policy that formalizes the following high-level security requirement.

The lab service can be accessed by supplying a valid medical record and a valid credit card or insurance number.

Note that the policy is described in high-level syntax. Line 4 describes the target of the policy which is a lab service. This means that whenever, lab test service is called this policy will be enforced by the reference monitor.

Line 5-29 defines two conditions base on various external attributes such as medical record which is an input parameter of the lab service and thus categorized as an external attribute.

The behavior of these attributes is vital for the trustworthy evaluation of the aforementioned policy. In section 6, we describe that how the behavior of these attributes is measured.

With reference to our target architecture, WS-Attestation provides three models namely pulled, pushed and delegated model. These models formalize the communication aspects between a service provider, service requestor, and validation service. However, generally, all WS-Attestation models verify the integrity of the service requestor platform only. For example, in the pulled model, a service provider pulls the integrity metrics from a service requestor and sends it to an appropriate attestation authority for attestation (Alam, Zhang,

Figure 4. An example XACML Policy

```
1)  <PolicySet>…
2)    <Policy RuleCombiningAlgId="permit-overrrides">      ...
3)     <Rule Effect="Permit" RuleId="ba4ws:rule1">
4)       <Target>Lab</Target>
5)      <Condition FunctionId="boolean-and">
6)       <Apply FunctionId="boolean-or">
7)        <Apply FunctionId="urn:vs1.ims.edu:validInsurance">
8)         <AttributeSelector
9)            RequestContextPath="/request/SML/medicalRecord" />
10)        </Apply>
11)       <AttributeValue DataType="boolean">
12)          true
13)       </AttributeValue>
14)      </Apply>
15)     <Apply FunctionId="boolean-equal">
16)       <Apply FunctionId="urn:vs1.ims.edu:creditCardValidity">
17)        <AttributeSelector
18)           RequestContextPath="/request/SML/medicalRecord" />
19)       </Apply>
20)      <AttributeValue DataType="boolean">
21)         true
22)      </AttributeValue>
23)     </Apply>
24)     <Condition>
25)     <Apply FunctionId="update">
26)       <AttributeSelector
27)          RequestContextPath="/request/SML/medicalRecord" />
28)      </Apply>
29)     </Condition>
30)     </Rule>
31)    </Policy>
32) </PolicySet>
```

Nauman, & Ali, 2008). In the pushed model, a service provider pushes the service requestor for attestation before allowing access to her service. Similarly, in the delegated model, the service provider delegates the responsibility of attestation to an appropriate attestation authority. We note that WS-Attestation devised models are not suitable for the attestation of a business process. More specifically, a service requestor cannot force a service provider for the attestation of its services. For example, a service requestor cannot push a service provider for the attestation from a specific attestation authority. At best, a service request can choose to opt for a service based on its integrity requirements.

6. BEHAVIOR MEASUREMENT

Behavior measurement refers to a mechanism in which the behavior of the services is measured while the activities are being performed. Each service in an activity has an associated security policy that dictates how the activity should be performed in a business process. Basically, in this step, the trustworthiness of the execution environment of a service, which comprises input data and security policy, is measured. In our target architecture, XACML (Lorch, 2003) dataflow model is used as an abstract representation of the execution environment of a service policy. We have extended the dataflow model of XACML in order to capture the behavior of an activity. The reason is that, XACML is a de-facto standard for the specification of complex access control scenarios.

There are two levels at which the behavior measurement of a service platform will take place. The first one – termed as static measurement – in which the execution environment of a service will be measured (cf., Section 6.1). In the dynamic measurement all the external attribute values are measured as they come in the reference monitor of a service (cf., Section 6.2). The high-level objective is, to ensure that a service is operating on valid inputs and its execution environment is processing the input in a trustworthy manner.

6.1 Static Measurements

The execution environment of a service includes all its internal attributes such as libraries, binaries and configuration files that are necessary for the execution of the corresponding service. In our target architecture, integrity measurement architecture is used to measure the execution environment of a service. It is a solution for the measurement and reporting of integrity of Linux based systems and has been developed by IBM T.J. Watson Research Center. The proposed technique is commonly known as the Integrity Measurement Architecture (IMA) (Sailer, 2003). It is based on verifying the status of the software and code executed on the

system by taking a hash of the binaries before they are executed.

If the hashes correspond to known good hashes then the system is of high integrity. In this approach, integrity indicates the status of the binary. If the binary has not been modified in an unauthorized manner the binary is said to be of high integrity.

IMA extends the trusted boot process of the Trusted Computing Group beyond the bootstrapping of the loader. IMA establishes a chain of trust from the TPM to the application. IMA measures all the code that is executed on the host system. The kernel of the Linux system has been modified so that all the code that is loaded into the memory for execution is measured by taking a SHA1 hash of the code just before it is executed. A measurement list is maintained which contains all of the measurements that were taken (Figure 5).

There are three major components that work together to make up the Integrity Measurement Architecture of IBM Watson labs. These are a) the Measurement Mechanism on the host system which takes measurements as executables are loaded in to the memory b) an Integrity Challenge Mechanism c) an Integrity Validation Mechanism that validates the measurements and determines that the measurements taken were correct and that they have not been tampered with.

Figure 5. Integrity measurement architecture showing the complete mechanism of measurement of execution environment

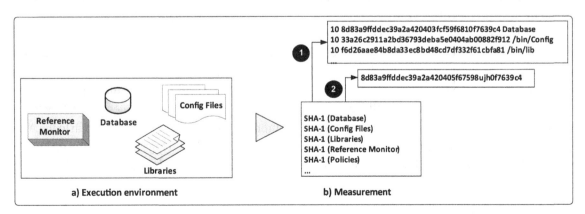

The Measurement Mechanism consists of agents that measure a file and save the measurement in an ordered list in the kernel. This file is known as the Stored Measurement Log (SML). The agent also extends the PCR10 of the TPM by the hash of the file.

The integrity challenge mechanism enables a remote challenger to send an attestation request to the target system that the challenger wants to attest. When the challenger sends an attestation request, it is requesting for the SML together with the TPM signed aggregate of the measurements recorded in the stored measurement log. When a system receives the attestation challenge from a challenger the SML and its TPM signed aggregate is sent in response to the challenger. The integrity challenge mechanism also verifies that the measurement list is fresh, complete and that the list has not been tampered with.

When the challenger gets the response of the attestation challenge request the Integrity Validation Mechanism validates the measurements received from the attested system and verifies that the entries in the list correspond to known good hashes i.e. validating that the attested system has no malicious or low integrity software or code running on it.

In our target architecture, IMA is used to measure the execution environment of a service in two steps (cf., Figure 1). In the first step, all the binaries, configurations and libraries, and so forth, are measured and their respective hashes are stored in the SML – we call it Execution environment Measurement List (EML).

In the second step, each respective measurement is aggregated with the 10th PCR contents through a special cryptographic mechanism by using the properties of SHA-1 hashes. This gives hardware assisted verification to a challenger that measurements were actually taken. Later on, the TPM signed aggregate can be used to verify the correctness of measurements (cf., Section 7.1)

6.2 Dynamic Measurements

The Behavior Manager is an internal service responsible for measuring the behavior of the reference monitor during the evaluation and enforcement of an activity policy. Each access decision call from the Policy Enforcement Point to the Policy Decision Point is intercepted by the behavior manager Service, which records the call and its parameters through the use of Trusted Platform Module (TPM) structures and capabilities. The TPM stores trust tokens in a shielded, tamper resistant memory locations referred to as Platform Configuration Registers (PCRs).

In this section, we describe how the behavior manager measures and stores the dynamic behavior of the reference monitor. In essence, the behavior monitor creates a log – called Attribute Behavior Log (ABL) for all the external attributes.

An external attribute might be an input parameter to a service or, it can be the output from another service. For example checking the validity of a credit card requires calling another service. The log contains the hash of the corresponding attribute. Whenever a service is called with some input parameters, the behavior manager creates a log entry in the ABL. Each entry in the ABL is 1) composed of the timestamp of the event, 2) the service identifier, 3) the id of the attribute and 4) the hash of the corresponding attribute. Logs and their corresponding PCRs are created and updated with the values of the individual service behaviors. They can then be sent out to appropriate authorities for their evaluation (Figure 6).

An ABL also contains the hash of the attributes, which a service may send as input to another service. For example, if the hospital service wants to send the corresponding medical record to a medical lab for further processing, the behavior monitor also log the medical record in to the ABL.

The hash of each log entry is stored in the TPM using the PCR extend operation. The PCR extend

Figure 6. Attribute behavior log

```
10 8d83a9ffddec39a2a420403fcf59f6810f7639c4 MedicalRecord LabTest
10 33a26c2911a2bd36793deba5e0404ab00882f9 PatientId       getMedicalRecord
10 f6d26aae84b8da33ec8bd48cd7df332f61cbfa8 CreditCard      CreditCardValidity
...
```

operation takes the hash of the new entry, concatenates it with the existing value of the PCR, computes the SHA-1 of the resulting structure and stores the value in the PCR. Each entry P_{e_x} is computed as follows:

$$P_{e_x} := SHA1\big(sha-1\big(e_{x-1}\big) \parallel SHA1\big(e_x\big)\big)$$

This re-use of the PCR allows for the storage of an infinite number of hashes in the limited number of PCRs available to the TPM.

The values of PCRs are secure SHA-1 hashes and can only be extended through a special operation PCR extend. These values can be reported to authorize challenger through public key signature of the TPM using Attestation Identity Keys (AIKs). The private part of AIKs is accessible only to the TPM and the reported values can therefore be verified to be signed by a genuine hardware TPM and unhampered. The Behavior Manager utilizes the PCRs for storing the information related to the intercepted events. The existing usage of PCRs is limited to hashes of files and executables. There has been no effort at utilizing the PCRs for storing run-time values of different data structures such as activity behavior and state transition behavior.

A business process can have these logs for each corresponding activity. In the following, we highlight the role of an attestation authority that can verify the trustworthiness of these logs generated in the measurement step.

7. BEHAVIORAL ATTESTATION

Behavioral attestation refers to a mechanism, which verifies that the behavior of individual services in a business process is trustworthy. An attestation authority collects the behavior logs such as execution environment log and attribute behavior log, of different services and their corresponding PCR values.

The EML is verified for following two properties 1) measurement correctness, 2) execution environment trustworthiness. The ABL is also verified for the measurement correctness and for the attributes trustworthiness and activities sequence. In the following, we first present a high-level description of verification of these logs against their corresponding PCRs. Afterwards; their combined effect of trust levels on the business process is presented.

7.1 EML Verification

The measurement correctness (cf., Figure 7) refers to a property that individual behaviors recorded for each activity are correct and trustworthy. For this, the following procedure is adopted: Let $E = \{e_1, e_2, ..., e_n\}$ be the set of dynamic entries in a log file representing an individual behavior. The measurement correctness procedure takes the hash of each individual entry and computes the final value according to the following procedure:

$$C_{e_x} := SHA1\big(SHA1\big(e_{x-1}\big) \parallel SHA1\big(e_x\big)\big)$$

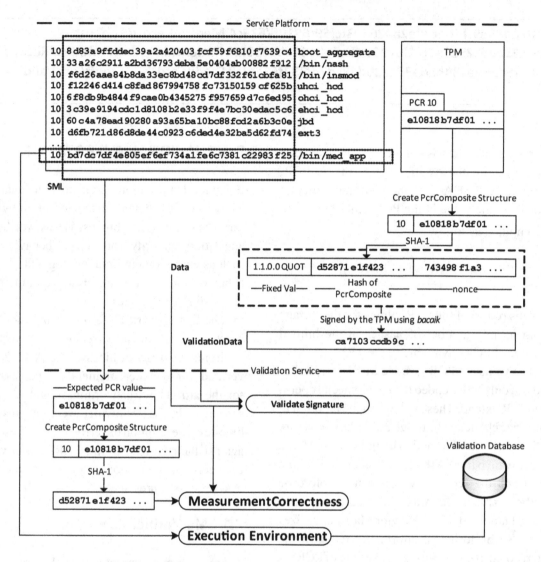

Figure 7. Measurement correctness and execution environment attestation

The resulting value for C_{e_n} must be equal to the TPM signed value of the PCR. If the value of the PCR matches with the computed value, the measurement can be considered trustworthy, i.e.,

$$C_{e_n} = P_{e_n}$$

where P_{e_n} is the PCR value returned by the TPM after the nth entry has been recorded.

The execution environment trustworthiness can be verified by inspecting each respective entry in the execution environment log of the service invokers and service provider. In a given activity, there are two log entries, one by the service invoker and one by the service provider. For example, it can be easily verified that if the services are running the correct version of medical applications (cf., Figure 7).

7.2 ABL Verification

For the attribute's log a verification procedure is adopted to see that if the log entries in the both the hashes of the both the log entries are correct and up to date. For example, it can be easily verified that whether a service s1 is called with attribute values a1, by inspecting the log of the invoker service and the log of the service provider.

These individual behaviors can be combined to draw useful conclusion about different activities taking place in a business process. For example, the activity sequence can be verified with the help of state transition behavior of an activity. Each individual activity has a log that includes the timestamp of the attribute change. It can be verified with the help of these timestamps, the sequence in which these actions were performed was trustworthy. The attestation authority can use these individual behaviors to compute a trust vector, which describes the trust level of the complete business process.

Definition 8 (Trust Levels) *Let* $L = \{l_1, l_2, ..., l_n\}$ *is a set of trust levels, where a partial order is defined on these trust levels, i.e.,* $l_1 \prec l_2 \prec ...... \prec l_n$

Based on the verification of the individual behaviors, each service can be associated with one of these trust levels. During service invocation, the subject service can choose from among multiple paths based on the trust levels of object services. Figure 5 describes selection from among different execution paths based on the trust level of different services. Moreover, the aggregate of these levels can be used to specify the trustworthiness of the complete business process.

8. IMPLEMENTATION

Eclipse (Foundation, 2001) is an open source project aiming to provide a universal toolset for development. Starting as an open Source IDE for Java only, but now it provides classical foundations for a plethora of languages, modeling tools, XML processing, and so forth. Eclipse also provides the

support for developing web services using the (WTP) project (des Rivieres, 2004) which extends the Eclipse platform with tools for developing web services. We have developed services using the WTP plug-in in order to simplify web services development, running and testing (Figure 8).

For measuring the integrity of a service platform, Integrity measurement architecture is used. The IMA patch is available for Linux 2.6.24 kernel. We have used Trusted Java (Winkler, 2006) libraries for the implementation of the daemon listening on the client for such requests. Trusted Java provides a Java software stack (jTSS) for the purpose of communicating with the TPM through the TPM driver. The service platform was a Dell Optiplex 745 Desktop equipped with a TPM. We created an Attestation Identity Key (labeled `bacaik') through the jTSS and registered it with a PrivacyCA provided by IAIK (Graz, 2008) using the Endorsement Key certificate created earlier. This bacaik was used for the purpose of signing the PCRs. The attestation service asks the service platform for attestation along with a nonce (for ensuring freshness of the values returned). Upon receiving an attestation request from the attestation service, our daemon running on the service platform reads the SML from /sys/kernel/security. It also asks the TPM to provide a quote over the value of its tenth PCR. The TPM attests the values of its PCRs through the quote. The TPM takes the index of the PCR to quote, a nonce for assuring the freshness of the quote and an AIK for signing the value with. It appends the current PCR value with the nonce and digitally signs the result. This resulting structure is called a TPM quote over a PCR value.

Upon receiving this quote from the service platform, the attestation authority first verifies the digital signature on the received quote to verify that it has indeed been signed by the TPM of the service platform. Afterwards, the expected value of the PCR is computed using the SML. If the expected values of the PCR and those returned by the SR match and if the nonce is returned in the

Figure 8. Alternative execution paths

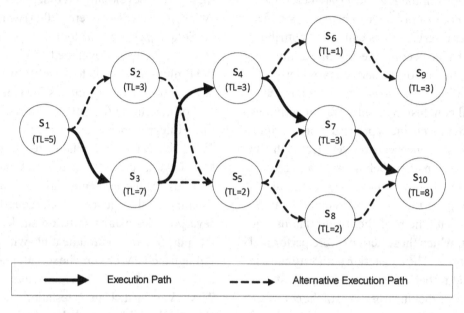

quote, the attestation authority can conclude that: 1) the SML or EML sent by the client is indeed correct as it is signed by a valid TPM and 2) the values of the EML are fresh as the TPM has also signed the nonce while performing the quote.

For providing assurance of the integrity of the execution environment of a service platform, the attestation service verifies the hash of different applications, libraries, and so forth that are needed by a service to run. For example, in a medical application, this will include binary of the medical application, its configuration files, its respective database, since the correctness and freshness of the EML is assured by the TPM signature, and the only requirement for establishing the integrity of the execution environment is that the hashes are to be of a known good value. For this purpose, we created a small database of known good hashes of two different versions of execution environments. If the hash provided by the service platform corresponds to a known good value already present in the database, the attestation authority can certify the integrity of the execution environment of a service platform.

In BA4BP, the behavioral manager interrupts the normal process of access request and response and performs attestation in the middle. We understand that this causes a time delay but we believe that for security-concerned web services, establishing the integrity of a service platform is essential and is worth the time delay. Moreover, the results of the attestation authorities can be cached to reduce this problem. Here, we describe the time taken during the actual validation process in our scenario. The time taken from the start of the validation request to the validation response was 4991 ms. This involves the web service invocation, integrity measurement and reporting. The time taken during the integrity measurement and signing on the service platform was 3925 ms. This time was expected because the TPM performs asymmetric encryption which is computationally expensive. The time taken for the re-computation and comparison of the SML with the PCR values was 416 ms. Overall, we believe that with caching support, this approach is very feasible, especially considering the added advantages of knowing in advance that the platform to which a resource is being released is in a healthy state.

9. RELATED WORK

A big community is working on the issues related to secure document exchange among the inter-organizational workflows. (Wei, 2008) presents web service architecture, in which current web services platforms split their processing in to two protection domains. The smaller part is responsible for executing security sensitive information such as credit card numbers. The larger domain is reserved for general processing. Also, the information flows taking place in the smaller part is analyzed. (Lufei, 2008) propose a secure access mechanism for remote services. In order to convey the web service security requirements such as specific encryption algorithms, an adaptive function module is introduced. (She, 2008) enhances the current web services security framework to facilitate the control of information flow through service chains. It extends the basic security models by introducing the concepts of delegation and pass-on.

Bertino, Castano, and Ferrari (2001) deal with workflow security in centralized and closed environments. (Bhatti, 2005) have extended the web services access control models to incorporate contextual information, such as time, location, or environmental state. Different security requirement specifications in XML have been detailed in Gudes (1999), Huang (1999), and Wainer (2003).

All these approaches are focused on the issues of authentication and authorization only. The only approach towards incorporating remote attestation on the web services level – WS-Attestation (Yoshihama, 2007) – only deals with the communication aspects of the problem. To the best of our knowledge dynamic behavioral attestation of business processes has not been investigated before.

10. CONCLUSION

In this paper, we have presented a novel framework BA4BP which enables finer-granular attestation at the web services level. Our framework incorporates XACML on top of business processes.

Our project, Dynamic Behavioral Attestation for Mobile Platforms (DBAMP) (DBAMP, 2008) is focusing on the attestation of business processes. BA4BP framework is part of the DBAMP project. We have not yet arrived at a perfect solution for measuring the trustworthiness of business processes. However, we believe that, as TPM is getting more and more sophisticated and powerful, this overhead is not going to hinder the process of attestation.

The BA4BP framework will open new avenues for bringing trust into business processes. This will significantly improve dynamic collaboration beyond non-technical measures such as social consent, legislation and contracts, and so forth. In order to improve the efficiency of behavior measurement and attestation, software TPM, which can emulate the hardware root-of-trust, is also under consideration. We are working on a stepwise implementation of the dynamic behavioral attestation of our approach.

REFERENCES

Alam, M., Seifert, J., & Zhang, X. (2007). *A model-driven framework for trusted computing based systems.*

Alam, M., Zhang, X., Nauman, M., & Ali, T. (2008). *Behavioral attestation for web services (BA4WS).*

Alam, M., Zhang, X., Nauman, M., Ali, T., & Seifert, J. (2008). *Model-based behavioral attestation.*

Anderson, S., Bohren, J., Boubez, T., Chanliau, M., Della-Libera, G., Dixon, B., et al. (2002). Web Services Trust Language (WS-Trust). *Public draft release, Actional Corporation, BEA Systems, Computer Associates International, International Business Machines Corporation, Layer, 7.*

Bertino, E., Castano, S., & Ferrari, E. (2001). Securing XML documents with Author-X. *IEEE Internet Computing, 5*(3), 21–31. doi:10.1109/4236.935172

Bhatti, R., Bertino, E., & Ghafoor, A. (2005). A trust-based context-aware access control model for web-services. *Distributed and Parallel Databases, 18*(1), 83–105. doi:10.1007/s10619-005-1075-7

Chen, L., Landfermann, R., Löhr, H., Rohe, M., Sadeghi, A., & Stüble, C. (2006). *A protocol for property-based attestation.*

DBAMP. *N. I. R. D. F. P.* (2008). Retrieved from http://serg.imsciences.edu.pk/projects/dbamp/

des Rivieres, J., & Wiegand, J. (2004). Eclipse: A platform for integrating development tools. *IBM Systems Journal, 43*(2), 371–383. doi:10.1147/sj.432.0371

Foundation, E. (2001). *Eclipse.* Retrieved August 2004, from http://www.eclipse.org

Grawrock, D. (2006). *The Intel safer computing initiative.*

Graz, T. U. O. (2008). *Privacy CA.* Retrieved from http://trustedjava.sourceforge.net/index.php?item=pca/about

Gudes, E., Olivier, M., & Van De Riet, R. (1999). Modelling, specifying and implementing workflow security in cyberspace. *Journal of Computer Security, 7*(4), 287–315.

Huang, W., & Atluri, V. (1999). *SecureFlow: a secure Web-enabled workflow management system.*

Jaeger, T., Sailer, R., & Shankar, U. (2006). *PRIMA: policy-reduced integrity measurement architecture.*

Kühn, U., Selhorst, M., & Stüble, C. (2007). *Realizing property-based attestation and sealing with commonly available hard-and software.*

Lorch, M., Proctor, S., Lepro, R., Kafura, D., & Shah, S. (2003). *First experiences using XACML for access control in distributed systems.*

Loscocco, P., & Smalley, S. (2001). *Meeting critical security objectives with security-enhanced linux.*

Lufei, H., Shi, W., & Chaudhary, V. (2008). Adaptive Secure Access to Remote Services in Mobile Environments. *IEEE Transactions on Services Computing, 1*(1), 49–61. doi:10.1109/TSC.2008.4

Mayer, F., MacMillan, K., & Caplan, D. (2006). *SELinux by example: using security enhanced Linux.* Upper Saddle River, NJ: Prentice Hall.

Mitchell, C. (2005). Trusted Computing. *Trusted computing,* 1.

Pearson, S., & Balacheff, B. (2002). *Trusted computing platforms: TCPA technology in context.* Upper Saddle River, NJ: Prentice Hall.

Poritz, J., Schunter, M., Van Herreweghen, E., & Waidner, M. (2004). *Property attestation—scalable and privacy-friendly security assessment of peer computers (Research Rep. No. RZ3548).* Philadelphia: IBM Corporation.

Sadeghi, A., & Stüble, C. (2004). *Property-based attestation for computing platforms: caring about properties, not mechanisms.*

Sailer, R., Zhang, X., Jaeger, T., & Van Doorn, L. (2003). *Design and implementation of a TCG-based integrity measurement architecture.*

She, W., Yen, I., & Thuraisingham, B. (2008). *Enhancing Security Modeling for Web Services Using Delegation and Pass-On.*

Shi, E., Perrig, A., & Van Doorn, L. (2005). *Bind: A fine-grained attestation service for secure distributed systems.*

Wainer, J., Barthelmess, P., & Kumar, A. (2003). W-RBAC-A workflow security model incorporating controlled overriding of constraints. *International Journal of Cooperative Information Systems*, *12*(4), 455–485. doi:10.1142/S0218843003000814

Weerawarana, S., Curbera, F., Leymann, F., Storey, T., & Ferguson, D. (2005). *Web Services Platform Architecture: SOAP, WSDL, WS-Policy, WS-Addressing, WS-BPEL, WS-Reliable Messaging and More.* Upper Saddle River, NJ: Prentice Hall.

Wei, J., Singaravelu, L., & Pu, C. (2008). A Secure Information Flow Architecture for Web Service Platforms. *IEEE Transactions on Services Computing*, *1*(2), 75–87. doi:10.1109/TSC.2008.10

Winkler, T. (2006). *Trusted Computing for the Java(tm) Platform.* Retrieved from http://trusted-java.sourceforge.net/index.php?item=pca/about

Yoshihama, S., Ebringer, T., Nakamura, M., Munetoh, S., Mishina, T., & Maruyama, H. (2007). WS-attestation: Enabling trusted computing on Web services. *Test and Analysis of Web Services*, 441-469.

This work was previously published in the International Journal of Web Services Research, Volume 7, Issue 1, edited by Liang-Jie (LJ) Zhang, pp. 51-71, copyright 2010 by IGI Publishing (an imprint of IGI Global).

Chapter 15
Analyzing Communities of Web Services Using Incentives

Babak Khosravifar
Concordia University, Canada

Jamal Bentahar
Concordia University, Canada

Ahmad Moazin
Concordia University, Canada

Philippe Thiran
University of Namur, Belgium

ABSTRACT

This paper proposes an effective mechanism dealing with reputation assessment of communities of web services (CWSs) known as societies composed of a number of functionally identical web services. The objective is to provide a general incentive for CWSs to act truthfully. The considered entities are designed as software autonomous agents equipped with advanced communication and reasoning capabilities. User agents request CWSs for services and accordingly rate their satisfactions about the received quality and community responsiveness. The strategies taken by different parties are private to individual agents, and the logging file that collects feedback is investigated by a controller agent. Furthermore, the accurate reputation assessment is achieved by maintaining a sound logging mechanism. To this end, the incentives for CWSs to act truthfully are investigated and analyzed, while the proposed framework defines the evaluation metrics involved in the reputation assessment of a community. In this paper, the proposed framework is described, a theoretical analysis of its assessment and its implementation along with discussion of empirical results are provided. Finally, the authors show how their model is efficient, particularly in very dynamic environments.

DOI: 10.4018/978-1-4666-1942-5.ch015

INTRODUCTION

As one of the recent technologies for developing loosely-coupled, cross-enterprise business processes (usually referred to as B2B applications), a plethora of web services exists on the web waiting to receive users' requests for processing. Such requests are usually competitive in a security and reputation-driven environment (Martino & Bertino, 2009; Zhang, 2008). To this end, the reputation assessment has been addressed in recent proposals (Jurca & Faltings, 2003; Jurca & Faltings, 2007; Liu et al., 2004). One general solution for such reputation assessment is collection of the after-interaction feedback that users provide with respect to the quality of the received service. However, in feedback-based reputation mechanisms, the precise reputation assessment needs to be verified. Selfish web services might manage to provide feedbacks that support them in the reputation mechanism. In general, online reputation mechanism is always subject to get violated with selfish web services. Another way to address the selection (and management) problem is to gather web services having similar functionalities to a community. Community of web services (CWSs) is a gathering of single and functionally similar web services that are aggregated to perform as one community while offering unique or variety services. The main property of a CWS is to facilitate and improve the process of web service discovery and selection and effectively regulate the process of user requests. There are underlying reasons for this. In general, the individual web services fail to accept all the requests for them, and thus refuse to accept a portion of their concurrent requests. This would decrease their overall reputation in the environment and would lead to lose some users. In CWSs, the community gathers a set of functionally homogeneous web services. Given that some communities offer the same functionality (hotels booking, weather forecasting, etc.), there is a competition between different communities. In this case, reputation is considered as a differentiation driver of the communities. Moreover, reputation helps users to select the most reputable community, which would provide the best QoS, and helps providers to join the best community, which would bring them the most value. Users assess the reputation of the community and upon that request for a service. Although the service selection process might be simplified, still communities might distract the reputation mechanism to support themselves. To this end, the reputation mechanism is needed to maintain a truthful service selection procedure.

Proposed Model

In this paper, we advance our previous work (Khosravifar et al., 2009) by providing more theoretical and practical results and discussions. Indeed in this paper, we extend the work done in (Elnaffar et al., 2008) by two contributions. In the first contribution, we propose a reputation model of a community of web services, which is based on involved metrics (responsiveness, inDemand, satisfaction that has been defined in (Elnaffar et al. 2008)). These factors are redefined here in a different way by considering the time factor we call time recency. This model is used by users and providers to estimate the reputation of a community. In the second contribution, we discuss more the feedback logging mechanism and give a reliable mechanism (capable of managing malicious acts of communities). We assume that CWSs may be encouraged to violate such run-time logging mechanism in support of themselves or against other communities. To this end, we try to discover feedback violations using the controller agent Cg (the agent that is assigned to monitor the logging data) that to some extent, makes sure that the violation is taken place. Then we propose a method to properly react for such violations. We provide a theoretical analysis based on backward induction to prove that there is an incentive for communities not to violate the logging system.

The idea is to prove that communities gain more if they do not violate the logging system compared to when they violate it. In this analysis, we derive the comparative values of reward and penalties for CWSs in order to obtain such an incentive. The simulation results reveal how, empirically, our trust model yields a system that autonomically adjusts the level of CWS's reputation.

What specifically distinguishes our model from other similar works in the literature (Weaver & Wu, 2006; Jurca & Faltings, 2003; Jurca & Faltings, 2007; Jurca et al., 2007) is: (1) its sound formation of the reputation assessment for the CWSs; and (2) its incentive-based reputation adjustment in the sense that although the communities are capable of distracting the logging system in support of themselves (or against their opponents), they will not take the risk to do that, given the fact that they are aware of possible consequent penalty that would decrease their current reputation level. In this paper, we prove that the best strategy for CWSs is to act truthfully. The advantages of using the incentive-based mechanism are: (1) we obtain an accurate information for deriving the involved metrics used for the reputation of a particular community; and (2) we obtain an overall higher reliability and efficiency in the sense that upon violation detection, CWSs are strictly encouraged to show an acceptable performance in their further user request processes. This factor is analytically proved and experimentally confirmed.

Organization

The remainder of this paper is organized as follows. First, we define the architecture of reputation-embedded CWSs, which is composed of extended UDDI, user and provider agents and reputation system. Then, we discuss the reputation model by its involved metrics and propose a methodology to combine them. Afterwards, we extend the discussion about maintaining a sound logging mechanism used as source of information for the metrics. We discuss the fake positive and negative corrections and provide the incentive to avoid fake attempts. In the next section, we present the simulation and outline the properties of our model in the experimental environment. The subsequent section discusses the related work and the last section concludes the paper.

ARCHITECTURE OF REPUTATION-EMBEDDED WEB SERVICE COMMUNITIES

In this section, we represent the CWSs architecture (Elnaffar et al., 2008), which is designed to maintain the reputation of the communities. Here we assume that each web service is associated with a community and do not function alone. If a web service is not registered in a community, it could not be invoked by a user. Indeed, a web service can be registered in one of many communities. In Figure 1, we represent different components of the architecture, with their reputation and interactions. These components together with their detailed performance are explained as follows:

- **User Agent:** It is a proxy between the user and other interacting parties such as the extended UDDI, CWS and the reputation system.
- **Master Agent:** This agent is considered as the representative of the community in the sense that it manages the community requests in selecting the proper web service. Meanwhile, the master agent hires (or fires) some web services to join (or leave) the community. In general, the master of the community always tends to increase the community's performance and consequently, its reputation level.
- **Provider Agent:** Like the user agent, it relates the provider with the extended UDDI, CWS and reputation system.
- **Extended UDDI:** The traditional UDDI XML schema is based on six types of infor-

Figure 1. Architecture of reputation-based CWSs

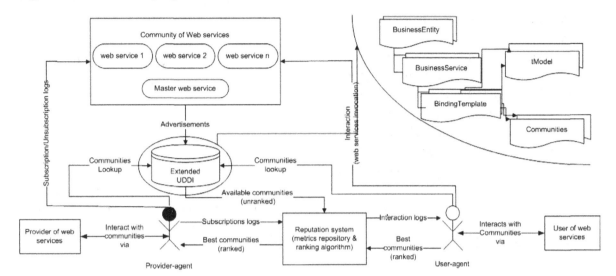

mation, allowing people to have information in order to invoke the web services [?]. In the UDDI registry, we restrict the access of the agents in the sense that user and provider agents only consult the list of masters, whereas the masters have access to the list of the web services in the UDDI registry. By adding this new information concerning the CWSs, we would clarify which CWS a web service belongs to.

- **Reputation System:** Considering the fact that the CWSs could offer the same service, they always compete in order to obtain more requests. Therefore, evaluating CWSs is unavoidable for the users and providers. To be able to compute the reputation of these communities, the user and provider agents must gather operational data, reflecting different performance metrics, about the interaction between the user, provider and CWS. The user agents should intercept some logs like *Submission log, Response Time log, Invocation log, Success log, Failure log, Recovery log* and so on. It is important that the user and provider agents are independent parties in order to intercept trusted run-time data about each web service interaction.

The reputation system is the core component in this architecture. Its first functionality is to register the run-time logs; and the second functionality is to rank the communities based on their reputation by using a ranking algorithm. The ranking algorithm would maintain a restrictive policy, avoiding the ranking violation, which could be done by some malicious CWSs. The violation, which has not been considered in (Elnaffar et al., 2008) could be done by providing some fake logging data (by some colluding users) that reflect positive feedback in support of the CWS, or by fake negative data that is registered against a particular community. To deal with this violation, we propose to assign a controller agent Cg. The task of this agent is to update the CWS reputation rankings in order to drop inaccurate registered data and thus enhance accuracy of the reputation system. The detailed discussion of this issue is provided.

- **Controller Agent:** Cg is the assigned agent that takes the logging file under surveillance and updates the assigned reputations to the communities. Cg is mainly responsible to remove the cheated feedbacks that support particular communities. Investigating the recent feedbacks, Cg recognizes the fake feedbacks and accordingly analyzes the further actions of the community. In general, Cg may fail to accurately detect the fake feedbacks or similarly may recognize normal feedbacks as fake. Therefore, malicious communities always consider this fake detection and analyze their chance of successful cheating.

REPUTATION MODEL

For simplification reasons, but without loss of generality, in the remainder of this paper, we only consider the users point of view (rather than users and providers) in reputation assessment. In order to assess the overall reputation of a CWS, the user needs to take some correlated factors into account. First, we present the involved metrics that a user may consider in this assessment. Consequently, we explain the methodology that the user uses to combine these metrics in order to assess the reputation of a CWS.

Metrics

- **Responsiveness Metric:** Let C_i be the community that is under consideration by user U_j. Responsiveness metric depicts the time to be served by a CWS. Let $Res_{C_i}^{U_j, R^t}$ be the time taken by the master of the community C_i to answer the request received at time t (R^t) by the user U_j. This time includes the time for selecting a web service from the community and the time taken by that web service to provide the service for the user U_j. When it is understood from the context, C_i will be removed from the notations. Equation 1 computes the response

time of the community C_i, computed with U_j during the period of time $[t_1, t_2]$ ($Res^{U_j, [t_1, t_2]}$), where n is the number of requests received by this community from U_j during this period of time.

$$Res^{U_j, [t_1, t_2]} = \frac{1}{n} \sum_{t=t_1}^{t_2} Res^{U_j, R^t} \times e^{-\lambda(t_2 - t)} \qquad (1)$$

Here the factor $e^{-\lambda(t_2 - t)}$, where $\lambda \in [0,1]$ is application-dependent and reflects the time recency of the received requests so that we can give more emphasize to the recent requests. If no request is received at a given time t, we suppose $Res^{U_j, R^t} = 0$.

- **InDemand Metric:** It depicts the users' interest for a community C_i in comparison with the other communities. This factor is computed in equation 2.

$$InD^{[t_1, t_2]} = \frac{Req^{[t_1, t_2]}}{\sum_{k=1}^{M} Req_{C_k}^{[t_1, t_2]}} \qquad (2)$$

In this equation, $Req^{[t_1, t_2]}$ is defined as the number of requests that C_i has received during $[t_1, t_2]$, and M represents the number of communities under consideration.

- **Satisfaction Metric:** Let Sat^{U_j, R^t} be a feedback rating value (which is supposed to be between 0 and 1) representing the satisfaction of U_j with the service regarding his request R^t sent at time t to C_i. Equation 3 shows the overall satisfaction of the user U_j to community C_i.

$$Sat^{U_j, [t_1, t_2]} = \frac{1}{n} \sum_{t=t_1}^{t_2} Sat^{U_j, R^t} \times e^{-\lambda(t_2 - t)} \qquad (3)$$

Metrics Combination

In order to compute the reputation value of a CWS (which is between 0 and 1), it is needed to combine these metrics in a particular way. Actually, the *Responsiveness* and *Satisfaction* metrics are the direct evaluations of the interactions between a user and a CWS whereas the *inDemand* metric is an assessment of a community in relation to other communities. In the first part, each user adds up his ratings of the *Responsiveness* and *Satisfaction* metrics for each interaction he has had with the CWS. Equation 4 computes the reputation of the community C_i during the interval $[t_1, t_2]$ from the user U_j's point of view. In this equation, ν represents the maximum possible response time, so that if a community does not respond, we would have $Res^{U_j,[t_1,t_2]} = \nu$. In the second part, the *inDemand* metric is added. Therefore, the overall reputation of C_i from the users' point of view is obtained in Equation 5.

$$Rep^{U_j,[t_1,t_2]} = \eta(1 - \frac{Res^{U_j,[t_1,t_2]}}{\nu}) + \kappa Sat^{U_j,[t_1,t_2]} \quad (4)$$

$$Rep^{[t_1,t_2]} = \chi \frac{1}{m} \sum_{j=1}^{m} \left(Rep^{U_j,[t_1,t_2]} \right) + \varphi \, InD^{[t_1,t_2]} \quad (5)$$

Where $\eta + \kappa = 1$ and $\chi + \varphi = 1$.

SOUND LOGGING MECHANISM

Without loss of generality, in a network composed of CWSs, master agents (as representatives of communities) are selfish and may alter their intentions in order to obtain more benefits (in terms of popularity). This could happen by improving one's reputation level or by degrading other's reputation level. We respectively refer to these cases as fake positive/negative alteration. Violating the logging feedbacks (distracting the reputation levels) could lead to system inconsistency in the sense that low quality CWSs may obtain more users or

high quality communities may lose some users. Therefore, it is important to avoid such attacks and keep the logging mechanism accurate. In the rest of this section, we explain how to perform fake positive/negative correction (recognition and adjustment) and thus effectively maintain a reputation adjustment.

In the proposed architecture for the CWS, the reputation is computed based on the information obtained from the logging system that over the elapsing time, users leave their feedbacks. Thus, it is essential to keep such logging file accurate and discourage malicious actions. It is the responsibility of the controller agent Cg to maintain an accurate attack-resilient logging file. As a part of the UDDI system, Cg has the authority to update information such as overall reputation level of any CWS. In this paper, we assume that this agent is highly secured in order to avoid being compromised. However, if Cg gets compromised with a given community, then inconsistent actions of Cg could be recognized by some other communities, given the fact that they are competing with one another. But this issue is out of the scope of this paper.

Fake Positive Correction

Fake Positive Recognition

One of the main responsibilities of the controller agent Cg is to perform fake positive correction. To this end, initially Cg should recognize a malicious behavior from one or a set of user agents (that could possibly collude with a particular community). This recognition is done based on the recent observable change in the reputation of a community. To this end, Cg would always check the recent feedbacks of the communities. So Cg would consider the reputation that is computed for a specific period of time $[t_1 - \varepsilon, t_1]$, where t_1 is the current time. The value ε is set by the controller agent regarding to the system inconsistency in the sense that if the network is inconsistent, so Cg would need to check most recent feedbacks (ε as relatively small amount). Otherwise, Cg would take even older feedbacks into account (ε as relatively large amount). Thus, $Rep^{[t_1-\varepsilon,t_1]}$ is the reputation of the community C_i obtained from data measured from $t_1 - \varepsilon$ to t_1. Different values of ε will be used in the simulation to observe the effect of the considered period on the overall recognition.

Let $U^{[t_1-\varepsilon,t_1]}$ be the set of users that during this time interval have provided a feedback for the community C_i, and t_b be the beginning time of collecting feedbacks. Cg would consider the positive feedbacks to be suspicious if the reputation improvement ($Rep^{[t_1-\varepsilon,t_1]} - Rep^{[t_b,t_1]}$) divided by the number of users that caused such improvement is greater than the predefined threshold ϑ, i.e:

$$\frac{Rep^{[t_1-\varepsilon,t_1]} - Rep^{[t_b,t_1]}}{|U^{[t_1-\varepsilon,t_1]}|} > \vartheta$$

The number of users ($|U^{[t_1-\varepsilon,t_1]}|$) is bounded by two factors: 1) communities cannot manage more than a maximum number of users by time unit considering their sizes (i.e. the number of web services populating the communities); and 2) in case of a malicious community, it is very unlikely that this community manages to collude with more than a certain number of users. This will prevent malicious communities from violating the feedbacks without being recognized by maximizing $|U^{[t_1-\varepsilon,t_1]}|$. In that case, it is assumed that community C_i had a drastic reputation increase in the recent ε time. The value ε is set with respect to the controller agent's success in fake feedback detection. Interacting in the environment, Cg would update this value in the sense that the most efficient value is figured out. The detail algorithms on how to learn this value is out of scope of this paper.

Fake Positive Adjustment

Exceeding the threshold ϑ, Cg would figure out that a particular community is receiving consequent positives. Then Cg, in order to reload the previous and actual reputation level, would freeze the recent positive logs and notifies the corresponding community of such suspending. So, Cg would observe the upcoming behavior (in terms of satisfaction and responsiveness) of the community in order to match the actual efficiency with the suspended enhanced reputation level. During this period, the community is encouraged to behave in such a way that reflects the suspended enhanced reputation level. As it is shown in Figure 2, the community's feedback is recognized as suspicious at time t_1. Feedbacks from time t_0 are freezed to investigate the further behavior of the suspicious community C_i. At time t_2 controller agent Cg would decide whether to penalyze community C_i or to redeem the freezed feedbacks. If the community shows the real improved performance, the suspended reputation trust level would be redeemed and considered for his reputation. But if the community fails to do so, the previous reputation level will be decreased by some applied penalties. In this case, the community would be in such a situation that either has to outperform its past in order to improve the enhanced reputation level, or would loose its current reputation, which is not wanted. Therefore, we form an incentive that communities would not risk their current reputation level and thus they do not by any means (colluding with users or providers) provide fake positives in support of themselves. Let $Evol^{[t_1,t_2]}$ be the evolutionary reputation value for the community C_i that is measured by the Cg during specified time interval $[t_1,t_2]$ (investigation period). This value is computed in Equation 6, where δ is a small value such that the reputation is measurable within $[t - \delta, t]$.

Figure 2. Fake positive correction cases

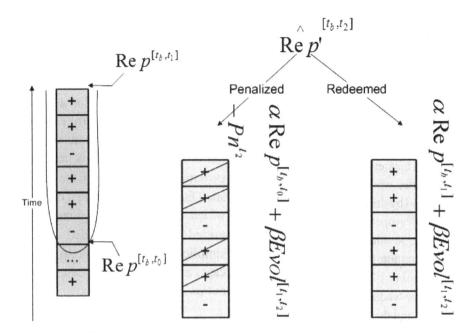

$$Evol^{[t_1,t_2]} = \frac{\sum_{t=t_1+\delta}^{t_2} Rep^{[t-\delta,t]}}{t_2 - t_1} \qquad (6)$$

Also, let Pn^t be the general penalty value that is assigned by Cg to C_i at a specific time t. Equation 7 computes the adjusted reputation level of C_i ($\mathrm{Re}\,p^{'[t_b,t_2]}$). This equation reflects the incentive we propose, so that CWSs in general would be able to analyze their further reputation adjustments upon fake action.

$$\mathrm{Re}\,p^{'[t_b,t_2]} = \begin{cases} \alpha Rep^{[t_b,t_1]} + \beta Evol^{[t_1,t_2]} & \text{if redeemed;} \\ \alpha Rep^{[t_b,t_0]} + \beta Evol^{[t_1,t_2]} - Pn^{t_2} & \text{if penalized.} \end{cases} \qquad (7)$$

where $\alpha + \beta = 1$.

As discussed before, Cg will decide to redeem the community C_i if the evolutionary value for the reputation is more than C_i's previous reputation value, i.e., $Evol_{C_i}^{[t_1,t_2]} \geq Rep_{C_i}^{[t_b,t_0]}$. If Cg decides to redeem the community C_i, then the previous reputation value (from time t_b to investigation time at t_1) would be considered together with the evolutionary reputation value as a result of investigation during $[t_1,t_2]$. If Cg decides to penalize the community C_i, then the previous reputation is considered regardless of the improved reputation obtained in the period of $[t_0,t_1]$. In addition to the evolutionary reputation, a penalty Pn^{t_2} would also be assigned at time t_2.

False Alarm Detection

It is worth to discuss more about alternatives of Cg's fake positives recognition. Consider the two cases that Cg falsely, and truly recognizes the fake positives. In the former case, the positives are real, therefore, they reflect the actual performance of the community. Then even being suspended, the community can easily prove the quality level as it continues as before and basically would not lose anything. In the later case, the positives are fake, so the community needs to improve its actual quality level to prove suspended enhanced reputation level. If the community failed to fulfill such reputation, Cg would decrease its previous reputation level.

Fake Negative Correction

Similar to the fake positive case, there might be some fake negatives in order to decrease the reputation level of a particular community (see Figure 3). This could happen when a community or a set of communities would like to weaken a particular community (by dropping its reputation level) hoping not to compete with them. However, one unique case should not be excluded in which, a particular community would mal-behave and after certain number of providing services and obtaining negative feedbacks, claims that the feedbacks were fake and do not reflect its actual reputation level. To avoid such a situation, each community is responsible to recognize a change in its reputation level and consequently report the case to Cg. Upon received report, Cg would decide whether the negative feedbacks were really as a result of the mal-behavior of the community or as a result of some other parties fake negatives. If Cg initiates the investigation at time t_1, after a period of evolutionary time, Cg would decide for the reputation adjustment at time t_2. In case of redeeming the community C_i that was suspected to have fake negative feedbacks, the negatives are discarded ($Rep^{[t_0, t_1]}$ is not considered), and a reward Rw^{t_2} is assigned at time t_2. The reason is to discourage the opponent communities not to cause a fake negative feedbacks for C_i and hope to degrade its reputation level. However, if after evolutionary investigation, Cg decides to penalize C_i, then the negative feedbacks are also considered (by considering $Rep^{[t_0, t_1]}$), and a penalty Pn^{t_2} is assigned to the community. Equation 8 computes the updated reputation value of the community C_i ($\operatorname{Re} p^{[t_0, t_2]}$).

$$Rep^{[t_0, t_2]} =$$
$$\begin{cases} \alpha Rep^{[t_0, t_1]} + \beta Evol^{[t_1, t_2]} + Rw^{t_2} & \text{if redeemed;} \\ \alpha Rep^{[t_0, t_0]} + \beta Evol^{[t_1, t_2]} - Pn^{t_2} & \text{if penalyzed.} \end{cases}$$
$$(8)$$

There is also a case that a malicious community tries to mislead controller agent Cg with the fake feedbacks that he managed to provide for himself and tries to act better than usual in the evolutionary time to get the reward Rw^{t_2}. All such false detections reflect diverse situations in which Cg needs to recognize the source of submitted feedbacks (colluded users). For sake of simplicity, in this paper we do not talk about these cases and consider such cases of false detection out os scope.

Theoretical Analysis

In this section, we will discuss in details the updates of reputation level when a particular community C_i causes fake feedbacks that is eventually beneficiary for itself. To this end, we follow the steps over this reputation updates and elaborate Cg's actions on them. For simplicity reasons, we only analyze the case of self-positive feedbacks and generalize our discussion to fake negative feedbacks. We objectively assume that penalizing a community is relative to the reputation improvement that community had obtained. In this section, we use backward induction reasoning technique to show that CWSs loose interest in doing malicious acts that cause extra (fake) positives for themselves or extra (fake) negatives for some others.

To better analyze the decisions the communities could take, we calculate the expected reputation value of a particular community in the case that the community acts maliciously to provide fake positive feedbacks for itself and the case that the community acts as normal and performs its actual capabilities. By comparing the two expected values, the typical community C_i will

Figure 3. Fake negative correction cases

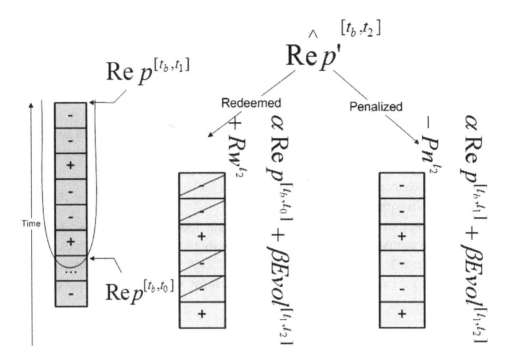

decide either to act maliciously or as normal. As discussed earlier, this decision is made based on the probability that C_i estimates to have a successful act. Being malicious, C_i always looks for the cases that could possibly cheat to increase its current reputation. Let q^t be the probability that the controller agent Cg notices the real intention of the community C_i and take actions with penalizing C_i at time t. We compute the expected reputation of C_i as a result of a malicious action in Equation 9 and as a result of normal action in Equation 10. In these equations, the expected value of the reputation for community C_i is measured under two assumptions.

In the case that C_i has faked the feedbacks ($E(Rep^{[t_b,t_2]} \mid C_i\ faked)$), the community decides to fake at time t_0 (therefore, the reputation till t_0 is considered as normal), the biased feedbacks are recognized by Cg at time t_1, and the investigation is finalized at time t_2. To this end, by penalizing C_i, its previous reputation till t_0 is considered together with the investigation period

$[t_1,t_2]$ with its penalty. If the controller agent Cg does not recognize C_i's malicious act, all the feedbacks are taken into account. In this analysis, we consider a very low possibility that Cg warns false negatives, which is the case that Cg falsely recognizes a malicious act. To this end, we assume that if the community C_i acts as normal, the reputation value would be measured as normal.

$$E(Rep^{[t_b,t_2]} \mid C_i\ faked) =$$
$$q^{t_2}(\alpha Rep^{[t_b,t_0]} + \beta Evol^{[t_1,t_2]} - Pn^{t_2}) \quad (9)$$
$$+ (1-q^{t_2})(\alpha Rep^{[t_b,t_1]} + \beta Evol^{[t_1,t_2]})$$

$$E(Rep_{C_i}^{[t_b,t_2]} \mid C_i\ notfaked) = Rep_{C_i}^{[t_b,t_2]} \quad (10)$$

Figure 4 is the tree representing the backward induction reasoning through actions of the community C_i and corresponding reactions made by the controller agent Cg in two steps. In this figure, *IMP* refers to the fact that the community's reputation is getting improved thanks to fake positives the community has provided. We also refer in this figure to PN as the state that the community's fake action is detected and thus penalized by Cg. As it is illustrated, the community that provides fake positives, obtains an improvement, which could be followed by a penalty. Here we state that the probability of Cg's detection given the fact that C_i has faked before is high. Therefore, if C_i has been already penalized, it is so hard to retaliate and improve again. There is a slight chance that C_i fakes and Cg ignores, which comes with a very small probability. Thus, we compute the expected reputation level of both cases and compare them.

Let $Imp^{[t_b,t_2]}$ be the difference between the adjusted reputation (in the case where the community is under investigation) and normal reputation (in the opposite case) within $[t_b, t_2]$, i.e:

$$Imp^{[t_b,t_2]} = \begin{cases} Rep'^{[t_b,t_2]} - Rep^{[t_b,t_0]}, & investigated\ by\ Cg; \\ Rep^{[t_b,t_2]} - Rep^{[t_b,t_0]}, & otherwise. \end{cases}$$

The following proposition gives the condition for the penalty to be used, so that the communities will not act maliciously. If

$$Pn^{t_2} > \frac{1}{q^{t_2}} Imp^{[t_b,t_2]} - \alpha Rep^{[t_0,t_1]},$$ then communities

obtain less reputation value if they act maliciously and provide fake feedbacks for themselves.

Proof. To prove the proposition, we should consider the condition true and prove that

Figure 4. The tree of backward induction reasoning

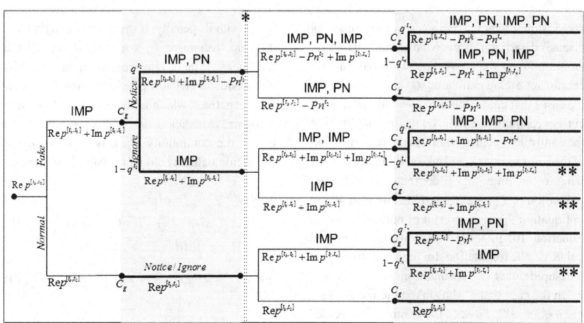

Properties:

1) White area C_i's turn, gray area Cg's turn.
2) Upper branch reflects fake action for C_i, and Notice for Cg.
3) * denotes start of a general time period of $[t_l, t_m, t_u]$.
4) IMP reflects improvement in one's reputation. PN reflects the assigned penalty via Cg.
5) ** highlights the cases that faked reputation is more than actual reputation.
6) For simplicity, at each step improvements and penalties are declared.

$E(Rep^{[t_b, t_2]} \mid C_i \ faked) < E(Rep^{[t_b, t_2]} \mid C_i \ Not \ faked)$. By simple calculation we get:

$$E(Rep^{[t_b, t_2]} \mid C_i \ Not \ faked) - E(Re \ p^{[t_b, t_2]} \mid C_i \ faked)$$
$$= Pn^{t_2} - \frac{1}{q^{t_2}} Imp^{[t_b, t_2]} + \alpha Rep^{[t_0, t_1]}$$

The obtained value is positive, so we are done.

In the previous proposition, we talked about the incentive that a rational community has to avoid fake feedbacks. Now we would like to discuss the general incentive of a malicious act in multiple times to generalize the ultimate reputation adjustment of bad communities that in general prefer to cheat on the logging system. To this end, we extend our analysis into more details by discussing about a particular community C_i that has previously made malicious act (for the first time action made at time t_{l1}, detection is made at time t_{m1}, and decision is made at time t_{n1}). In this analysis, we would like to investigate the community's further acts (made at general time t_l) in distracting the logging file and thus, its reputation treatment via the controller agent (detection at time t_m and decision at time t_n such that $t_n > t_m > t_l > t_{n1}$). Basically, as a result of the previous act, C_i could have been penalized (which means the community is less likely to act maliciously again) or have gained a reward (which means the community is very likely to act maliciously again). In the following we study the penalty Pn^{t_n} that should be assigned to these types of communities to avoid their multiple malicious acts.

Assume that C_i has made its malicious act at time t_{l1}. For the performed action, there is a chance ($q^{t_{n1}}$) that the controller agent Cg noticed the act at time t_{n1} and thus, penalized the community by $Pn^{t_{n1}}$. We also consider the chance ($1 - q^{t_{n1}}$) that the controller agent ignores the act and thus, the community has obtained the improvement $Imp^{[t_{l1}, t_{n1}]}$ through the feedbacks without any

penalty from the controller agent. Considering the probabilities of different strategies that the controller agent may take, as we discussed earlier, there is a small chance that Cg ignores the malicious act. This basically means the probability of notice (for the first time) ($q^{t_{n1}}$) is normally high and that is because the sensitivity of the controller agent in investigating the list of feedbacks for each particular community. However, once recognized, the controller agent becomes more sensitive to the recognized community's further actions. Therefore, the probability of missing the second fake action is less than the first one and so on (($q^{t_{n2}} > q^{t_{n1}}$)). Generally speaking, the community would be more interested to continue its malicious behavior when it has never been recognized via Cg and thus penalized. However, there is always a high possibility for this community to be recognized later (for the first time).

Considering the aforementioned cases, the expected reputation $E(Rep^{[t_b, t_n]})$ for a community that fakes the feedbacks again (for the second time or more) can be decomposed by the cases that Cg has previously (t_{nj}) noticed the community's malicious act ($Cg \ noticed \mid C_i \ faked$) with the probability $q^{t_{nj}}$ ($nj < n$) and Cg has previously ignored such action ($Cg \ ignored \mid C_i \ faked$) with the probability $1 - q^{t_{nj}}$. We study each case by analyzing the strategy that Cg has previously took in response to such fake action.

$$E(Rep^{[t_b, t_n]} \mid C_i \ fake \ again)$$
$$= (q^{t_{nj}})E(Rep^{[t_b, t_j]} \mid Cg \ noticed)$$
$$+ (1 - q^{t_{nj}})E(Rep^{[t_b, t_j]} \mid Cg \ ignored)$$

Consider the first case that Cg notices the current fake behavior of C_i. We expand this case to the cases that Cg noticed C_i's previous act and the case that Cg ignored C_i's previous malicious act. This basically influences the control of Cg

over the feedbacks of the community C_i since being recognized as malicious community.

$$E(Rep^{[t_b, t_n]} \mid Cg \ noticed) =$$
$$(q^{t_n})E(Rep^{[t_b, t_n]} \mid Cg \ noticed \ before) +$$
$$(1 - q^{t_n})E(Rep^{[t_b, t_n]} \mid Cg \ ignored \ before)$$

Basically the probability of notice for a community that has faked before is more than ordinary community without previous fake action. To this end, q^{t_n} is higher than $q^{t_{nj}}$ such that $q^{t_n} \times \alpha = q^{t_{nj}}$. The value α is a generic value ($0 < \alpha < 1$), but to be consistent we always use this value in order to apply the degradations.

Considering the case that Cg ignored the current fake behavior of the C_i, we expand this case to the case that Cg noticed C_i's previous malicious act and the case that Cg ignored C_i's previous malicious act. For simplicity, here we assume $q'^{t_n} = 1 - q^{t_n}$. This means that if the previous fake action is recognized, the current fake action would be recognized as well with the probability of q^{t_n}. Likewise, if the previous fake action is ignored, the current fake action is made with the probability of q^{t_n}.

$$E(Rep^{[t_b, t_n]} \mid Cg \ ignored) =$$
$$(q'^{t_n})E(Rep^{[t_b, t_n]} \mid Cg \ noticed \ before) +$$
$$(1 - q'^{t_n})E(Rep^{[t_b, t_n]} \mid Cg \ ignored \ before)$$

The value q'^{t_n} would be a very small value in the sense that if Cg noticed the previous act of C_i, now the possibility of ignore would be very small. In general, the controller agent would become very sensitive to the acts of malicious communities. Considering the updates made by Cg over the reputation values of communities, the following proposition holds.

If communities fake again, they make a drastic degradation in their reputation value.

Proof. *Given the fact that Cg noticed previous fake action of C_i, it would be more restrictive for C_i's further performance, therefore, the probability of noticing the new fake action is higher than before ($q^{t_n} > q^{t_{nj}}$). In this case Cg increases the checking accuracy for such community and we defined this improvement by the factor of $1 + \alpha$, which is multiplied to the previous notice probability value. Consequently, we rewrite the expected value as following. In Equation 11, the first line represents the case that fake action has been noticed before and now (so there is two penalties applied and no reward). Second line represents the case that fake action is noticed now but has been ignored before (so there is a current penalty but previous reward). Third line represents the case that fake action is ignored now but has been recognized before (so there is current rewards but previous penalty). Last line represents the case that fake action been ignored in both previous and current time (so there are just rewards and no penalties).*

$$E(Rep^{[t_b, t_n]} \mid C_i \ faked \ again) =$$
$$q^{t_n}(q^{t_{nj}})(Rep^{[t_b, t_{lj}]} - Pn^{t_{nj}} - Pn^{t_n})$$
$$+ q^{t_n}(1 - q^{t_{nj}})(Rep^{[t_b, t_{lj}]} - Pn^{t_{nj}} + Imp^{[t_l, t_n]})$$
$$+ (1 - q^{t_n})(q^{t_{nj}})(Rep^{[t_b, t_{lj}]} - Pn^{t_{nj}} + Imp^{[t_{lj}, t_{nj}]})$$
$$+ (1 - q^{t_n})(1 - q^{t_{nj}})(Rep^{[t_b, t_{lj}]} + Imp^{[t_{lj}, t_{nj}]} + Imp^{[t_l, t_n]})$$

(11)

Following the ideology that the expected value of faking again should be (strictly) less than not faking, we simplify the obtained value in Equation 11 to the following:

$$E(Rep^{[t_b,t_n]} \mid C_i \ fake \ again) <$$

$$E(Rep^{[t_b,t_n]} \mid C_i \ not \ fake \ again) \Rightarrow \frac{1-q^{t_n}}{q^{t_n}} Imp^{[t_l,t_n]} < Pn^{t_n}$$

$$(12)$$

Generalizing the case $\dfrac{1-q^{t_n}}{q^{t_n}} Imp^{[t_l,t_n]} < Pn^{t_n}$

to be valid in all t_n, it is shown that the required amount for the penalty for time t_n is less than the required amount for any previous time. This clarifies the incentive for faking again is less than the incentive for the first fake.

$$Pn^{t_n} < Pn^{t_{n'}}$$
$$n' < n \qquad\qquad (13)$$

Therefore, the probability of faking again is decreasing over time, so we are done.

EXPERIMENTAL RESULTS

In this section, we describe the implementation of a proof of concept prototype. In the implemented prototype, CWSs are composed of distributed web services ($Java^{\copyright TM}$ agents). The agent reasoning capabilities are implemented as Java modules. The testbed environment is populated with two agent types: (1) service provider agents that are known as web services and gathered in a community (we assume only one type of service is provided and therefore consumed); and (2) user agents that are seeking for the best service provided by a web service. In general, the simulation consists of a series of empirical experiments tailored to show the adjustment of the CWS's reputation level. Table 1 represents three types of CWSs we consider in our simulation: ordinary, faker and intermittent. Ordinary community acts normal and reveals what it has, the faker community is the one that provides fake feedbacks in support of itself, and the intermittent community

is the one that alternatively changes its strategies over the time. As it is shown in Table 1, the QoS value is divided into three ranges.

In each RUN, a number of users are selected to search for the best service. Strictly speaking, users are only directed to ask CWSs for a service and thus, user would not find out about the web service that is assigned by the master of the community. In order to find the best community, the requesting user would evaluate the CWSs regarding their reputation level. Some times, the users are in contact with some communities that are very good for the user, so the users re-select them. The selected community might be overloaded and consequently rejects the user requests. If the user is rejected from the best selected community, he would ask the second best community in terms of reputation level (and so on). After getting a response from a community, the user agent would provide a feedback relative to the quality of the obtained service and the community responsiveness. The feedbacks are logged in the logging mechanism that is supervised by Cg. The accumulated feedbacks would affect the reputation level of communities. In other words, the communities would lose their users if they receive negative feedbacks, by which their reputation level is dropped.

Considering the general incentive of CWSs to attract most possible users, communities in general, compete to increase their reputation level. Cheating on reputation level is done by colluding with a user (or a small group of users) to provide

Table 1. Simulation summarization over the obtained measurements

CWS Type	WS Density	WS Type	WS QoS
Ordinary	[25.0%, 35.0%]	Good	[0.5, 1.0]
Faker	[25.0%, 35.0%]	Bad	[0.0, 0.5]
Intermittent	[25.0%, 35.0%]	Fickle	[0.2, 0.8]

consecutive positive feedbacks in support of the malicious (faker) community. In the empirical experiment, we are interested observing the over-RUN reputation level of different types of communities and how fast and efficient the adjustment is performed by Cg. Figure 5 illustrates the plot of reputation level for a faker community $C8$. The upper plot represents the individual QoS for the community's assigned web services. In this plot the gray line defines the average QoS for the web services. The most prominent feature of the plot is the comparison of the reputation level with the average of the community web services QoS. The average value is assumed to be the actual QoS for the community and thus, community's reputation level. In general, there would be convergence to such value if the community is acting in an ordinary manner (for $C8$ is 0.173). The lower plot illustrates the reputation level of this community over the elapsing RUNs. Here we notify that the master of a community is responsible to assign the web services to the user requests. To this end, normally the high quality web services are assigned first until they become unavailable, which forces the master agent to assign other lower quality web services. Thus starting the RUNs, $C8$ gains reputation value (up to 0.313), which is better than its individual average quality of service. In Figure 4 the peek $P1$ defines the RUN in which the community $C8$ is out of high quality web services. After passing this point, the reputation level of this community is decreased.

Figure 6 illustrates community $C8$ reputation level in comparison with an ordinary community $C6$. $C8$ at point $P3$ decides to provide fake positive feedbacks for himself to increase self reputation level. For the interval of 30 RUNs, this community gains higher reputation level up to the point $P4$. The controller agent Cg, periodically verifies the feedback logs, in order to recognize the malicious actions. At $P4$ the controller agent Cg notices the malicious act of $C8$ and freezes the obtained feedbacks for investigation.

Peek $P2$ is the point in which the community $C8$ is penalized in his reputation level. After $P2$ a drastic decrease in reputation value is seen, which goes underneath $C8$'s average quality of service (up to 0.112). There is also a continuing but slower increase for the reputation of the faker community $C8$ that persists long after the first fake action recognition. Thus, there appear to be strong restriction effects, in which eventually the faker communities loose their users. However, there is also an ongoing effect of social influence, in which users doubt in communities that have drastic decrease in their reputation level.

We continue our discussion in more details by analyzing some parameters related to the controller agent's performance and accuracy. One of the main factors in such a system is the accuracy of the controller agent in fake detection. The controller agent is supposed to investigate the feedbacks and recognize the malicious acts while the requesting users provide their rates as feedbacks to obtained service quality. However, there are two possibilities for Cg to fail to accurately detect such actions. The false detections are detecting a non-fake action as fake, and ignoring a fake action as non-fake. The former case is called false positive (or α-error in statistics), which is rejecting of null-hypothesis when it is true. The latter case is called false negative (or β-error), which is accepting a null-hypothesis when it is actually false. The false positive is the case that controller agent would ignore a malicious act and thus, would not investigate it more closely. Since the controller agent is not re-acting to the initially detected action, there is a chance to recover the initial false alarm. Over the further investigation, the false negative (initially warned by Cg) is most likely corrected once the investigation is done, but the other cases, which have been ignored are not recognized as there is no further investigation over the detection.

To this end, one of the main objectives is to enhance the efficiency of the controller agent to

Figure 5. Communities overall quality of service vs. the number of simulation RUNs

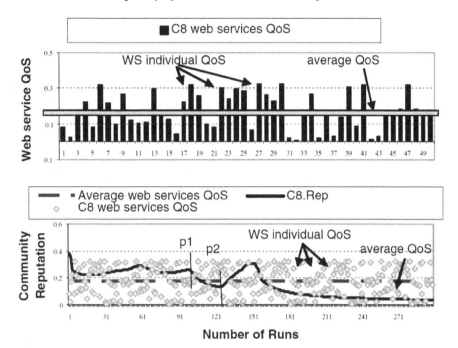

decrease the false alarm ratio and strengthen the logging feedback crawling algorithm. Figure 7 shows the controller agent's accuracy over the elapsing RUNs while the recognized communities are penalized and thus, discouraged to redo the fake actions. As shown in this figure, the controller agent is relatively less accurate in detection during the initial RUNs. Basically, detection weakness would highly encourage the faker and intermittent communities to do fake actions. Mostly as a result of the reward that they obtain without the penalty. Basically, the accuracy of Cg is increased while Cg acts successfully in detecting and thus, penalizing faker communities. Cg would act better over the Runs since previously detected communities are investigated more carefully and thus, the chance of failing to detect is decreasing.

In Figure 8 we discuss this issue as we observe the tendency of the communities to provide fake feedbacks in support of themselves. In this figure, the vertical axes plots the average percentage of the intermittent communities that might be encour-

aged to fake and the horizontal axes plots the RUNs, which reflects the elapse of time. In this figure, the average tendency to fake is decreasing as the number of intermittent agents that are penalized are increasing.

We take a narrower analysis on the characteristics of the controller agent Cg and their impact that eventually influence the incentive of different communities to act maliciously. To this end, we study the aforementioned issues towards the network condensity and the extent to which the controller agent is crawling the feedbacks. In the former study, the idea is to observe how dealing with different malicious communities make the controller agent sensitive to get suspicious while crawling the feedbacks. Basically, the controller agent sets the threshold ϑ by observing the number of malicious communities in the environment. This means that the controller agent tries to get more though when the number of malicious communities are increasing (see *Plot* (a) in Figure 9). However, this harsh manner could not be kept on since Cg cannot keep track of all communities at

Figure 6. Communities overall quality of service vs. the number of simulation RUNs

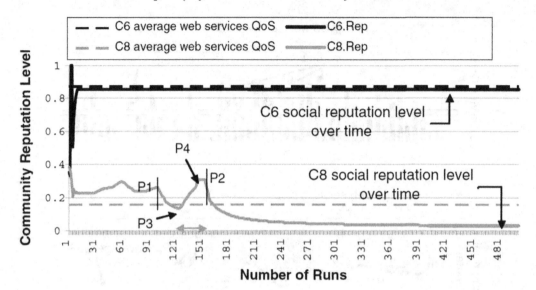

the same time. On the other hand, by getting suspicious for any community, the false positive ratio would be going up, which reflects the low efficiency of Cg in terms of detection performance. Following the idea that Cg tries to avoid the increase of the malicious communities, we observe that this agent increases the average penalty value assigned to malicious communities while their number is increasing. *Plot (b)* assigns a dot point to each community that gets penalized. The dot points are getting more condense, which shows their high number.

In the second part of the Figure 9, we study the efficiency of the controller agent versus its sensitivity. Since we analyzed the threshold that is set to declare Cg's sensitivity, here we study how well Cg can act with different thresholds. *Plot (c)* sketches a graph that shows a parabola for the effectiveness of Cg. In this graph there is a tradeoff between the false positive and false negative errors. At a low sensitivity period, there are high number of false negatives. This basically encourages the malicious communities to highly redo their malicious acts as they distract

in the logging file and increase their reputation and do not get penalized afterwards. To this end, the observed slope for the effectiveness is relatively small. There is a maximum point for the effectiveness, but this is not always true and may change depending on the environment and surrounded communities. Therefore, we cannot finalize the controller agent's efficiency to a specific value. *Plot (d)* is depicting the same problem from another point of view. Indeed, in this plot we study the false alarm in spite of effectiveness. The false alarm is computed as the sum of false positive and false negative ratios. In this plot, the total false detections is minimized once the controller agent reaches its maximum efficiency. Likewise the decreasing slope is so slow.

RELATED WORK

In the literature, the reputation of web services has been intensively stressed (Kalepu et al., 2003; Maximilien, 2002; Jurca & Faltings, 2003; Jurca & Faltings, 2007; Liu et al., 2004) aiming to facilitate and automate the good service selection.

Figure 7. Controller agent C_g's accuracy in detection vs. the number of simulation RUNs

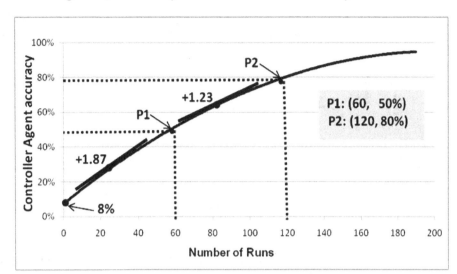

Figure 8. Communities' tendency to fake vs. the number of simulation RUNs

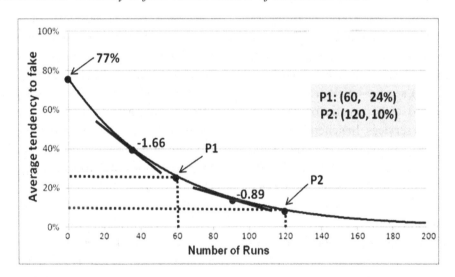

In (Ali et al., 2005), the authors have developed a framework aiming to select web services based on the trust policies expressed by the users. The framework allows the users to select a web service matching their needs and expectations. In Weaver and Wu (2006), the authors propose an indirect trust mechanism aimed at establishing trust relationships from extant trust relationships with privacy protection. In Malik and Bouguettaya (2007), the authors proposed to compute the repu-

tation of a web service according to the personal evaluation of the previous users. In general, the common characteristic of these methods is that the reputation of the web service is measured by a combination of data collected from users. To this end, the credibility of the user that provides this data should be taken into account. There should be a mechanism that recognizes the biased rates provided from the users and accordingly updates the credibility of the users. If the user tries to

Figure 9. Controller agent's characteristic analysis

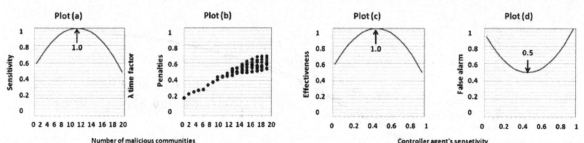

Plot (a). Sensitivity is computed for the ratio that Cg goes deep in the logging file. λ is the parameter to set the sensitivity.

Plot (b). Penalty is set with respect to the environment accuracy. The smooth slope for the penalty increases as +0.03.

Plot (c). Effectiveness is the extent to which detections are correct. False positive and false negative influence the total effectiveness.

Plot (d). False alarm is the sum of false positive and false negative.

provide a fake rating, then its credibility will be decreased and the rating of this user will have less importance in the reputation of the web service. In Maximilien (2005), the author designed a multi-agent framework based on an ontology for QoS. The users' ratings according to the different qualities are used to compute the reputation of the web service. In Jurca et al. (2007), and Jurca and Faltings (2007), service-level agreements are discussed in order to set the penalties over the lack of QoS for the web services. In general, in all the mentioned models, web services are considered to act individually and not in collaboration with other web services. In such systems, the service selection process is very complicated due to their relatively high number in the network. In addition, web services can easily rig the system by leaving and joining the network when they better off to do so (i.e. when a their reputation is fall off for some reason). This is a rational incentive for such web services that manage to start as new once they have shown a low efficiency. Meanwhile it is hard to manage the huge number of data in web services settings. Considering these inefficiencies, we focused more on the concept of gathering web services together so that we could address the problem of facing web services individually. Communities are in general aimed to get stronger and more publicized in the system, so they do not resign and register as new. In such methodology,

users interconnect with the community as the service provider and there would be a web service assigned through the community.

Regarding the aforementioned issue, there have been some proposals that try to gather web services and propose the concept of community-based multi-agent systems (Elnaffar et al., 2008; Kastidou et al., 2009; Fourguet et al., 2006). In Elnaffar et al. (2008), the authors propose a reputation-based architecture for CWSs and classify the involved metrics that affect the reputation of a community. They derive the involved metrics by processing some historical performance data recorded in a run-time logging system. The purpose is to be able to analyze the reputation in different points of view, such as users to CWSs, CWSs to web services, and web services to CWSs. The authors discuss the effect of different factors while diverse reputation directions are analyzed. However, they do not derive the overall reputation of a CWS from the proposed metrics. Failing to assess the general reputation for the community leads to failure in efficient service selection. Moreover, authors assume that the run-time logging mechanism is an accurate source of information. In general, in open reputation-feedback mechanisms, always the feedback file is subject to be the target by selfish entities. To this end, the feedback mechanism should be supervised and its precise assessment should be guaranteed. In Kastidou et al. (2009), the authors proposed a framework that explores the possibilities that the active communities act truthfully and provide their actual information upon request. This method is related to the ideas proposed in this paper in the sense that the communities are provided of the incentives that push them to act truthfully. However, in Kastidou et al. (2009), the concept of anonymity is not resolved and the registered communities are to be known in the system to manage a stable framework. In Fourguet et al. (2006), a layered reputation assessment system is proposed mainly addressing the issue of anonymity. In this work, the focus is on the layered policies that are applied to measure the reputation of different types of agents, specially the new comers. Although, the proposed work is nice in terms of anonymous reputation assessment, but the layered structure does not optimally organize a community-based environment that gathers web services and also the computational expenses seems to be relatively high.

To address the aforementioned problems, we elaborate in this paper on the reputation mechanism that is supervised by the controller agent and based on the incentives provided to encourage more truthful actions. What mainly distinguishes our proposed model from the related work in the literature is its detailed focus on the logging mechanism accuracy and reputation assessment. The reputation system is observed by the controller agent but still communities are allowed to take any policy that they get the most benefit from. The incentive-based system provides a mechanism that guarantees the least fake actions since communities that gain benefit from malicious acts are eventually penalized such that their further decisions are altered. In this work, the concept of anonymity is also barely observed since the infrastructure is based on communities. This means that the users face communities for their requested service and the concept of join or leave does not involve users. This mechanism maintains a better quality reputation management and control.

CONCLUSION

The contribution of this paper is the proposition of a new incentive-based reputation model for community of web services gathered to facilitate dynamic users requests. The reputation of the communities are independently accumulated in binary feedbacks reflecting the satisfaction of the users being serviced by the communities. The model represents a sound logging mechanism in order to maintain effective reputation assessment for the communities. The controller agent investigates the logging feedbacks released by the users to detect the fake feedbacks as a result of collusion between a community and a user (or a group of users), which are provided in support of the community. Upon detection, the controller agent maintains an adjustment in the logging system, so that the malicious community would be penalized in its reputation level.

Our model has the advantage of providing a suitable metrics used to assess the reputation of a community. Moreover, having a sound logging mechanism, the communities would obtain the incentive not to act maliciously. The proposed mechanism efficiency is analyzed through a defined testbed. Our objective for future work is to advance the assessment model to enhance the model efficiency using a comprehensive approach we developed in Khosravifar et al. (2009), which considers the trust issue as an optimization problem. In the logging system, we need to optimize detection process, trying to formulate it in order to be adaptable to diverse situations. Finally, we plan to extend the empirical analysis to capture more results reflecting the proposed model capabilities.

ACKNOWLEDGMENT

We would like to thank the anonymous reviewers for their valuable comments and suggestions. The second author is partially supported by Natural Sciences and Engineering Research Council of

Canada (NSERC), Fonds québécois de la recherche sur la nature et les technologies (NATEQ), and Fonds québécois de la recherche sur la société et la culture (FQRSC).

REFERENCES

Ali, A. S., Ludwig, S. A., & Rana, O. F. (2005, November 14-16). A Cognitive Trust-based Approach for Web Services Discovery and Selection. In *Proceedings of the 3rd European Conference on Web Services (ECOWS)*, Växjö, Sweden (pp. 38-40).

Elnaffar, S., Maamar, Z., Yahyaoui, H., Bentehar, J., & Thiran, P. (2008, March 25-28). Reputation of Communities of Web Services - Preliminary Investigations. In *Proceeding of the 22nd IEEE international Conference on Advanced information networking and application (AINA)*, Okinawa, Japan (pp. 1603-1608).

Fourguet, E., Larson, K., & Cowan, W. (2006). A Reputation Mechanism for Layered Communities. *SIGecom Exchanges*, 6(1), 11–22. doi:10.1145/1150735.1150738

Jurca, R., & Faltings, B. (2003, June 24-27). An Incentive Compatible Reputation Mechanism. In *Proceedings of the IEEE Conference on E-Commerce Technology (CEC)*, Newport Beach, CA (pp. 1026-1027).

Jurca, R., & Faltings, B. (2007). Obtaining Reliable Feedbacks for Sanctioning Reputation Mechanisms. *Journal of Artificial Intelligence Research*, 29(1), 391–419.

Jurca, R., Faltings, B., & Binder, W. (2007, May 8-12). Reliable QoS Monitoring Based on Client Feedback. In *Proceedings of the 16th International World Wide Web Conference (WWW)*, Banff, Canada (pp. 1003-1011).

Kalepu, S., Krishnaswamy, S., & Loke, S. W. (2003, December 10-12). Verity: A QoS Metric for Selecting Web Services and Providers. In *Proceedings of the 4th international Conference on Web Information Systems Engineering Workshops*, Rome, Italy (pp. 131-139).

Kastidou, G., Cohen, R., & Larson, K. (2009, July 11). A Graph-based Approach for Promoting Honesty in Community-based Multiagent Systems. In *Proceedings of the 8th International Workshop for Coordination, Organization, Institutions, and Norms in Agent Systems (COIN@ IJCAI)*, Pasadena, CA.

Khosravifar, B., Bentahar, J., Thiran, P., Moazin, A., & Guiot, A. (2009, July 6-10). An Approach to Incentive-based Reputation for Communities of Web Services. In *Proceedings of the 7th International Conference on Web Services (ICWS)*, Los Angeles (pp. 303-310).

Khosravifar, B., Gomrokchi, M., Bentahar, J., & Thiran, P. (2009, May 10-15). Maintenance-based Trust for Multi-Agent Systems. In *Proceedings of the 8th International joint Conference on Autonomous Agents and Multi-Agent Systems (AAMAS)*, Budapest, Hungary (pp. 1017-1024).

Liu, Y., Ngu, A. H., & Zeng, L. Z. (2004). QoS Computation and Policing in Dynamic Web Service Selection. In *Proceedings of the 13th International World Wise Conference on Alternate Track Papers and Posters* (pp. 66-73).

Malik, Z., & Bouguettaya, A. (2007, December 3-6). Evaluating Rater Credibility for Reputation Assessment of Web Services. In *Proceedings of the 8th International Conference on Web Information Systems Engineering (WISE)*, Nancy, France (pp. 38-49).

Martino, L. D., & Bertino, E. (2009). Security for Web Services: Standards and Research Issues. *International Journal of Web Services Research*, 6(4), 48–74.

Maximilien, E. (2005, July 25-29). Multiagent System for Dynamic Web Services Selection. In *Proceedings of the 1ˢᵗ Workshop on Service-Oriented Computing and agent-based Engineering (SOCABE)*, Utrecht, The Netherlands.

Maximilien, E. M., & Singh, M. (2002). Conceptual Model of Web Service Reputation. *SIGMOD Record, 31*(4), 36–41. doi:10.1145/637411.637417

Organization for the advanced of structured information standards. (2004). *Introduction to UDDI: Important Features and Functional Concepts.* Retrieved October 12, 2009, from http://www.oasis-open.org

Weaver, A., & Wu, Z. (2006). Using Web Service Enhancement to Establish Trust Relationships with Privacy Protection. *International Journal of Web Services Research, 6*(1), 49–68.

Zhang, L.-J. (2008). Web Services Security, Composition, and Discovery. *International Journal of Web Services Research, 5*(1), 1–23.

Chapter 16
DiALog:
A Distributed Model for Capturing Provenance and Auditing Information

Christoph Ringelstein
University of Koblenz-Landau, Germany

Steffen Staab
University of Koblenz-Landau, Germany

ABSTRACT

Service-oriented systems facilitate business workflows to span multiple organizations (e.g., by means of Web services). As a side effect, data may be more easily transferred over organizational boundaries. Thus, privacy issues arise. At the same time, there are personal, business and legal requirements for protecting privacy and IPR and allowing customers to request information about how and by whom their data was handled. Managing these requirements constitutes an unsolved technical and organizational problem. The authors propose to solve the information request problem by attaching meta-knowledge about how data was handled to the data itself. The authors present their solution, in form of an architecture, a formalization and an implemented prototype for logging and collecting logs in service-oriented and cross-organizational systems.

INTRODUCTION

Service-oriented systems facilitate organizations to offer business capabilities as independent services. As standardized interfaces are used for the communication a loose coupling is supported.

The loose coupling eases the integration of external services into internal workflows as well as the provisioning of services to consumers. The resulting flexibility facilitates the combination of services from different organizations into one comprehensive, integrated workflow leading to an agile virtual organization that is able to adapt more quickly to new organizational and business needs.

DOI: 10.4018/978-1-4666-1942-5.ch016

However, the new flexibility also shows disadvantages. An integrated workflow forwards and distributes data between organizations. The data may be confidential (e.g., personal data or intellectual property) and it may be involved in further processes (e.g., advertising). Thus, the distribution has the potential to violate concerns of privacy and IPR. Under such circumstances of flexible interworking between organizations, accounting for actions performed on data may be legally and/or contractually required.

To control the compliance with laws (e.g., Directive 95/46/EC in the EU), contracts, or policies, a data provider may request information about the processing and whereabouts of his data. The answer must contain details defined by the contract or law (e.g., *who* processed the data as well as *why* and *how* the data has been processed). The answer can be generated in different ways, e.g., by modeling and observing the distributed data processing. However, the answer can only be generated, if the model and the observation facilitate a detailed overview of the processing. Most frequently such an overview is lacking, even for internal workflows and data storage.

Hence, we require a model of the distributed processing of data in service-oriented systems in combination with a distributed mechanism for logging in service-oriented systems to collect the needed information and answer the request. Existing logging mechanisms, like the Extended Log File Format (Hallam-Baker et al., 1996) or *syslog* (Lonvick, 2001), are not sufficient to gain a full overview of a workflow that is distributed among multiple organizations, because they perform logging only in one execution environment. Because of the diversity of execution environments and because of a lack of standardized interfaces for exchanging logs, aggregating distributed logs remains a challenge.

In the following we present DIALOG (DIstributed Auditing LOGs) and sticky logging. DIALOG is a method for auditing the distributed processing of data in service-oriented systems.

Sticky logging monitors the processing of data items (independent of the actual business process) attaching the logs directly to the processed data as metadata. Furthermore, sticky logging allows for the reconstruction of how the data was processed by whom and why following the specification of DIALOG. Thus, sticky logging is a generic middleware for distributed logging. The paper is organized as follows: First, we present a scenario and analyze requirements for collecting information about the processing of private data in service-oriented systems. Following the requirements, we discuss various models for distributed processing of data. Then we introduce DIALOG and define notions of soundness and completeness relevant for the auditing in distributed systems. Based on DIALOG we present the architecture and a prototype[1] implementation of sticky logging. Before we eventually discuss our approach and conclude, we compare it with related work.

BUSINESS CASE

We now present a business case that we use as a running example throughout the paper. The business case comprises a system that includes several services and is distributed over different organizations. To prove the functionality of the sticky logging mechanism this business case has been realized using the sticky logging prototype (see below).

Small-Books Inc.

The Small-Books Inc. is a book-selling company. Main parts of the logistics like storing the books, packaging, and shipping are outsourced to a logistics company named Fast-Shipping Inc. Analogously, the payments are processed by a credit card company. Assume that a customer, Mr. Smith, orders books via the Web site of Small-Books. To place his order, he has to insert his address and credit card number. Having received the order

Small-Books possesses three instances of data related to the order: the list of ordered books, Mr. Smith's address and his credit card number. Small-Books uses the payment service of the credit card company. For this purpose, Small-Books passes the credit card number and the invoice value to the payment service. Then, Small-Books invokes the shipment service of Fast-Shipping. To this end, Small-Books passes the address and the list of books to Fast-Shipping. Figure 1 depicts an overview of the data flow. According to national laws realizing EU directives, Mr. Smith is now entitled to ask Small-Books about the processing of his data and Small-Books is legally required to fully answer his request, i.e. to explain to him which of his data items had been passed to which other organization and why. Likewise, contract might entitle the customers of Small-Books to answer to such requests.

REQUIREMENTS

In the Introduction, we have sketched different reasons leading to the obligation that data providers must be informed in hindsight about the distributed processing of their data, like contracts, laws, or organizational policies. Because contracts and policies depend on the issuing organizations, we focus here on the more general European privacy directive that is also elaborated in the business case. From the EU directive and the business case we derive requirements for an information service attending to the information rights of private customers.

An organization is responsible for its way of handling personal data and it must inform the person concerned about this handling. The legal requirements are defined in the EU Directive 95/46/EC. Especially Article 12 "Right of access" describes the information that must be given to the person concerned by the service provider, if requested:

- *Confirmation as to whether or not data relating to him* [the person concerned] *are being processed and information at least as to the purposes of the processing, the categories of data concerned, and the recipients or categories of recipients to whom the data are disclosed,*
- Communication to him in an intelligible form of the data undergoing processing and of any available information as to their source,

Figure 1. Data flow of the SBI-example

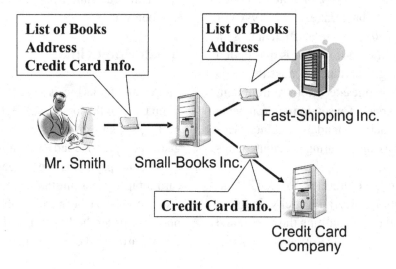

From the directive we derive the requirements for an information service to support organizations to be compliant with privacy laws:

Requirement 1: The information service must enable the person concerned to access information about the complete processing of his personal data at any time. The given answer must be exhaustive.

Requirement 2: The provided information must be sufficient to identify the service provider as well as the recipients and sources of personal data.

Requirement 3: The information service must inform about which personal data item is processed.

Requirement 4: The information service must ensure that beside the service provider only the person concerned has access to information about the processing of his data.

In order to respond to the requirements, we need to, *(i)*, model the processing of (private) data at a level able to respond to the question of *who*, *what* and *why*, we must be able to, *(ii)*, observe the processing of data in the model, and we must *(iii)* be able to reconstruct the data history based on our observations.

AUDITING THE DISTRIBUTED PROCESSING OF DATA

Fulfilling information requests according to privacy laws requires a global model of how private data has been processed. The overview spans the processing of the data by multiple organizations as well as during multiple business processes. The global model specifies all actions performed on the data during any execution of a workflow. We call the labeled transition system specifying the executions of the global workflows the *logical execution* (see Figure 2). Global models may exist in controlled environments (e.g. within one organization). If the global model is given, the actions performed on the data during the execution are monitored and audited by means of this model (cf., Aalst et al., 2008).

However, in a dynamic and distributed environment, it may not be possible to specify a global model. A lot of information about the processing of the data items may be lacking *a priori*. One reason is that workflows may be combined dynamically. Also, the processing of data items may continue after the actual execution of one workflow has ended (e.g., storing data in a database).

Figure 2. Logical execution

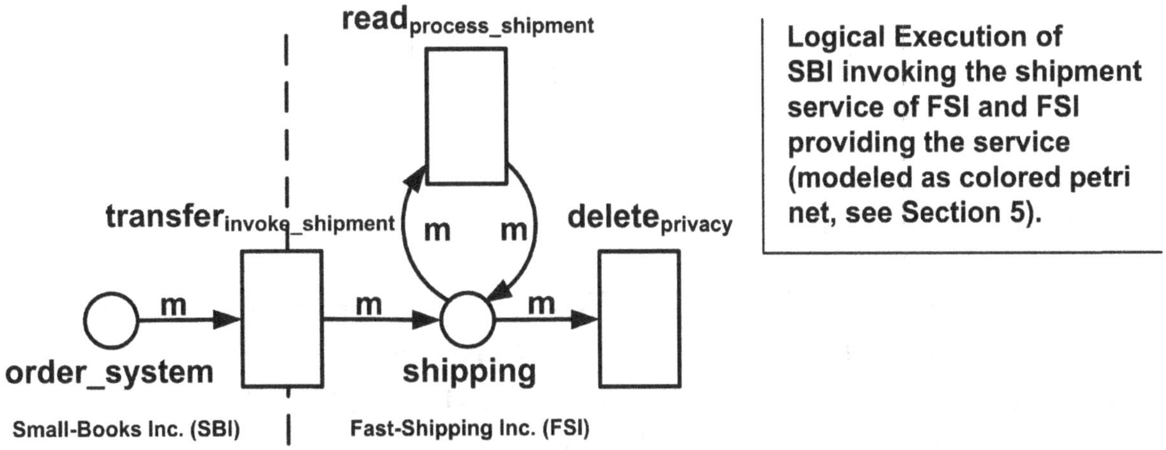

Logical Execution of SBI invoking the shipment service of FSI and FSI providing the service (modeled as colored petri net, see Section 5).

As part of the workflow execution, services call other services. We call this the *physical execution* of the workflow (see Figure 3). The physical execution implements the logical execution. Thereby, it will regularly happen that none of the participating organizations and individuals will know neither the complete logical nor the complete physical execution. When the workflow is enacted, only a subsystem of the logical execution may be involved in the actual execution. We call this subsystem the *executed subsystem* of the logical execution.

If the logical execution is unknown, its executed subsystem may still be reconstructed by observing the physical execution. Therefore the physical execution as well as the actions any services perform on the data have to be monitored leading to logs. We call these logs the *monitored execution* of the workflows (see Figure 4).

Below we introduce a logging mechanism capable to log the processing of data items in a distributed process. If the mechanism is capable to observe the relevant information, a transition system modeling the executed path of the logical execution can be derived from the logs (see below). We call this transition system the *reconstructed execution* (see Figure 5). The relationship between these different notions is depicted in Figure 6.

DIALOG

In this section we introduce DIALOG, a model of the distributed processing of data considering the requirements from above. We first define the structure of processing of data at the atomic level[2] of DIALOG. Then, we describe its dynamics. The reconstructed execution can be used for auditing purposes, if the reconstructed execution is *sound* and *complete* with respect to the executed subsystem of the logical execution. Thus, we define the soundness and completeness of reconstructed executions.

In the following we use the terms *category*, *item*, and *instance* to refer to different abstraction levels of data. We use "data category" to refer to the class of data (e.g., address data), the term "data item" to refer to a specific piece of information

Figure 3. Physical execution

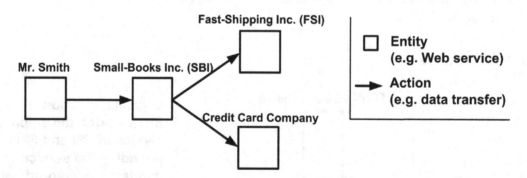

Figure 4. Monitored execution

n+0: (X, ('transfer', SBI_{order_system}, $FSI_{shipping}$, 'invoke shipment', t_0, t_{-1}))
n+1: (X, ('read', $FSI_{shipping}$, e, 'process shipment', t_1, t_0))
n+2: (X, ('read', $FSI_{shipping}$, e, 'process shipment', t_1, t_1))
n+3: (X, ('delete', $FSI_{shipping}$, e, 'privacy', t_2, t_1))

Figure 5. Reconstructed execution

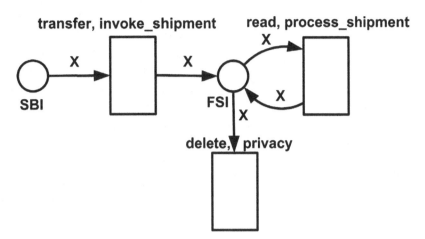

(e.g., specific person's address), and the term "data instance" as specific realization of a data item. See Table 1 for an overview about the three abstraction levels.

Modeling Distributed Data Processing

From the requirements we derive actions, actors, and data instances as properties of distributed service-oriented systems that should be modeled:

- **Actions:** To meet Requirement 1 the processing of data must be logged. We log all actions performed on the data. We distinguish the following six action types:
  ActionTypes = {create; read; update; copy; transfer; delete}
- **Actors:** Requirement 2 postulates to log information about the service provider as well as about recipients and sources of data. Thus, we model every actor that performs actions on the data, that receives data, or that hands data over (e.g., a Web service, a database, or a natural person).
- **Data Instance:** Requirement 3 demands to log which personal data is processed. During the execution of a process, copy

actions may occur that lead to multiple data instances of one data item. Thus, the formalization must model each data instance and all instances must be clearly identifiable.

We define DIALOG to model the distributed processing of data instances by means of colored petri nets $CPN = (\Sigma, P, T, A, N, C, G, E, I)^3$. Each net models the processing of one specific data item. The restriction allows for a clear identification of processed data instances. Additionally, the restriction allows for addressing data instances by one-dimensional indexes improving the readability. A model of multiple items can be reached

Figure 6. Relation between executions

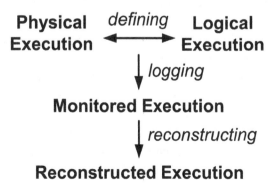

Table 1. Abstraction levels of data

Term	Example
data category	Customer address
data item	Mr. Smith's address ("Example Street 13, Some City")
data instance	"Example Street 13, Some City"@www.sbinc.com/database

by folding their colored petri nets into one and using two-dimensional indexes.

We represent data instances by *tokens*. The markings (without the token of the counter) represent the distribution of data instances of the observed data item in the process. The *color c* $\in$ Σ of these tokens is an integer used as identifier. Each data instance receives another, unique value allowing for unique identification of the data instance. We use *places p* $\in$ *P* to model actors. The value of the *color function C(p)* for the places is the integer type. The corresponding *initialization function* is $I(p) = \emptyset$. We model actions (or combinations of actions) as *transitions t* $\in$ *T* in combination with *arcs a1,a2,..* $\in$ *A*, and the *node function* of these arcs *N(a1),N(a2),...* Thereby the arcs connect the transitions with the places where the actions are performed. The *arc expressions* of these arcs *E(a1),E(a2),...* describe how data instances are moved. The *guard function* of all transitions *t* is $G(t) = true$. Finally, the label of a transition *t* consists of the category of an action and its purpose (written: *category$_{purpose}$*).

We do not define a specific granularity for modeling the data processing. Thus, DIALOG allows for modeling in any level of detail (e.g., a web shop may be modeled as one entity or as several entities (web service, DBMS, etc.)).

By using the integer value of a token as unique identifier of the represented data instance, we are able to clearly distinguish the single instances. Due to the statelessness of places, additional information is needed to create new unique identifiers. To this end we use a counter that is modeled as part

of the colored petri net. The counter is represented by the place p_c, whose initialization function is specified as: $I(pc) = \{1\}$

In the following, we present a list building blocks defining how actions are modeled by means of colored petri nets. The building blocks of all types of actions are also shown in Figure 7. An example model is depicted in Figure 8.

- **Create action:** The processing of a data item starts with the creation of its first data instance. Because we represent data instances by tokens, the create action generates a token. As depicted in Figure 7 we define the create action as a transition *t* with three arcs. One arc *a* leads from the transition to the place *p* representing the actor where the data is created. The arc c_o is connected with the place p_c (the place modeling the counter) and is used to control if the counter is set to *1*, which means that no data instance has been created before. The arc c_i is used to set the counter to *2*, which will be the identifier of the first copy.

- **Copy action:** During the execution of a workflow, additional data instances may be created through copying. Each copy action generates a new data instance and thus an additional token. As depicted in Figure 7 we define the copy action as a transition *t* with five arcs. Two arcs a_i and a_o lead to and from the place p_s that represents the actor performing the copy action. One arc a_d leads from the transition to the place p_d representing the actor where the new data instance is created. Analogous to the create action, the additional two arcs c_i and c_o are connected with the place p_c used to count the creations of data instances.

- **Read action:** Reading information from a data instance changes neither its content nor its location. As depicted in Figure 7 we define the read action as a transition *t* with

Figure 7. Modeling of actions

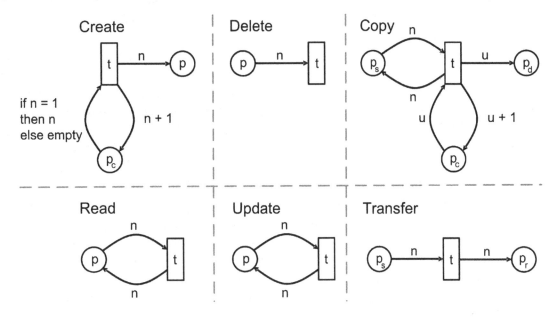

two arcs a_i and a_o leading to and from the place p that represents the actor performing the read action.

- **Update action:** Updating a data instance changes its content. However, performing an update action does not change the location of the data instance. The here presented formalization does not distinguish if a data instance has been changed or not. Analogously to the read action, we define the update action as a transition t with two

arcs a_i and a_o leading to and from the place p that represents the actor performing the update action (see Figure 7).

- **Transfer action:** If a data instance is transferred from one actor to another, the associated token must also be transferred. As depicted in Figure 7 we define the transfer action as a transition t with two arcs a_s and a_r. The arc a_s leads from the place p_s to the transition t. The place p_s represents the actor sending the data instance. The

Figure 8. Processing Mr. Smith's address data

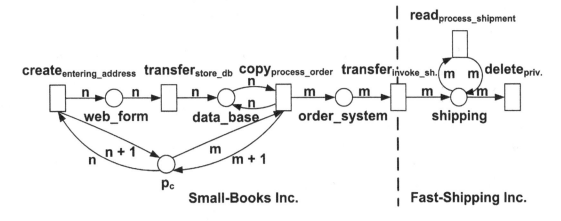

second arc a_r leads from the transition to the place p_r, which represents the receiving actor. During the transfer the data instance and thus the value of the token stays unchanged.

- **Delete action:** The processing of a data instance ends with its deletion. The token representing the data instance is removed, when the data instance is deleted. As depicted in Figure 7 we define the delete action as one arc a leading from the place p (the actor deleting the data instance) to a transition t that has no outgoing arc. Thus, the transition t 'consumes' the token.

To model a logical execution the above building blocks are combined. The combination adheres to the following rules:

- Only the above building blocks may be used. No additional elements (e.g., transitions) are allowed.
- The building blocks are connected by means of places that model entities (not the counter place).
- Each model contains only one counter for generating unique data instance. The counter is shared by the create action and all copy actions.

Each colored petri net models the processing of exactly one data item. However, the processing of a data item may interact with the processing of another data item. The interaction may result in a new data item based on the input data items (e.g., by merging these). The processing of the newly created data item is then modeled by means of a new colored petri net.

Example: *In the business case Mr. Smith orders a list of books. To this end, Mr. Smith enters his address data into a Web form of Small-Books Inc. In the following we model a snippet of the*

processing of the address data by means of the introduced formal model (see Figure 8).

The first actor *SBI:web_form* is the web form where Mr. Smith enters his address data. Entering the data creates the first instance of his address data and initializes the processing. We model this action as a create action by means of the transition $create_{entering\_address}$, an arc leading to actor *SBI:web_form*, and an arc connecting the transition with the place $p_{counter}$. From the Web form the data instance is transferred ($transfer_{store\_db}$) to the data base of Small-Books Inc. (*SBI:data_base*). To process the order, the data instance is copied ($copy_{process\_order}$) and the copy is transmitted ($transfer_{invoke\_shipment}$) to the Web service *FSI:shipping* offered by Fast-Shipping Inc. After the processing of the shipment ($read_{process\_shipment}$), the data instance is deleted by Fast-Shipping Inc. ($delete_{privacy}$).

Representation of Data Processing

In colored petri nets a marking is the distribution of tokens in the net. In DIALOG the markings represent the distribution of the instances of one data item representing one state of the workflow execution. The occurrence of a transition (also defined as step (Jensen, 1992)) leads from one state of the colored petri net to another. We define the processing of the workflow as the occurrence of steps Y^* in the colored petri net. The whole processing is a partially ordered set of steps due to parallel paths of the workflow. We define such a partial order of steps as a trace.

Definition 1 - Processing Trace: *Be W a (distributed) workflow modeled by means of a colored petri net, we define a trace t of the processing of a data item as a partial order of occurring steps Y^*.*

The monitored execution is a processing trace of the logical execution.

Qualities of Reconstructed Executions

A reconstructed execution can be used for auditing purposes if the reconstructed execution is complete and sound with respect to the actually executed subsystem of the logical execution (see above). The logical execution and the reconstructed execution are labeled transition systems. We define a labeled transition system as common:

Definition 2 - Labeled Transition Systems: *A labeled transition system is a triple (P, Δ, $\rightarrow$) where P is the set of places, Δ is the set of labels, and $\rightarrow \subseteq P \times \Delta \times P$ is the transition relation.*

We define a subsystem of a labeled transition system as follows:

Definition 3 - Subsystems of Labeled Transition Systems: *We define a subsystem (P_S, Δ_S, $\rightarrow_S$) of a labeled transition system (P_T, Δ_T, $\rightarrow_T$), where $P_S \subseteq P_T$, $\Delta_S \subseteq \Delta_T$ and $\rightarrow_S \subseteq \rightarrow_T$ with the following stability property: (x, δ, x') $\in \rightarrow_S$ with x, x' $\in P_T$ and $\delta \in \Delta_T$ implies x, x' $\in P_S$ and $\delta \in \Delta_S$.*

We define soundness of a reconstructed execution to express that the behavior of the reconstructed execution matches the behavior of the logical execution. The behavior of the reconstructed execution matches if a *simulation* relation between the reconstructed execution and the logical execution exists.

A *simulation* is a binary relation defining matching behavior of transition systems (cf., Kucera et al., 1999). A first transition system simulates a second transition system if the first system can match all of the state changes of the second system.

Definition 4 - Soundness of Reconstructed Executions: *Given a logical execution L and a monitored execution M, a reconstructed execu-*

tion E generated from M is sound with respect to L, if there exists a simulation R such that for all elements e $\in$ E there exists an element l $\in$ L so that (e, l) $\in$ R.

The reconstructed execution will model the complete behavior of an executed subsystem if a simulation relation between the executed subsystem of the logical execution and the reconstructed execution exists.

Definition 5 - Completeness of Reconstructed Executions: *Given a logical execution L and a monitored execution M, a reconstructed execution E generated from M is complete with respect to the executed subsystem S of L, if there exists a simulation R so that for all elements s $\in$ S there exists an element e $\in$ E so that (s, e) $\in$ R.*

STICKY LOGGING

Before we have discussed that the monitored execution serves as input for building the transition system of the reconstructed execution. Thus, a monitoring mechanism is required, which allows for observing the execution of the workflow. The sticky logging mechanism provides means to log the processing of data items and to reconstruct executions of the processing. We also prove that sticky logging can be used for the generation of sound and complete reconstructed executions. The basic idea of sticky logging is to attach the log directly to the data as metadata. Thereby, the log is transferred (with the data) along the processing path whenever the data is passed (e.g., as part of a service call). The log is returned to the service consumer after the processing. Thus, the log is made accessible to the person concerned. If data remains in the system of the service after a service call ends (e.g., in a data base), the log is not returned automatically. In such cases the log is only returned by request (see below).

The Data Structure of Sticky Logs

Fundamental for the sticky logging is that a log Λ is attached to the corresponding data instance d. A log is a partially ordered set of log entries λ that are used to record the performed actions on d and thus the occurrence of the transitions representing the actions. The data about an action consists of the category χ of the action, the performing actor α (i.e., the corresponding place), the receiving actor β of a transfer action ($\beta = \varepsilon$, if it is not a transfer action), and the purposes Ψ (see Ringelstein et al., 2007) of the action. To achieve the partial order of the actions, a unique identifier is assigned to each action id and the preceding action is linked by its identifier pid. Thus, we define a sticky log using the following data structure:

Definition 6 - Data Structure of Sticky Logs: *A sticky log m is a tuple (d, Λ) where:*

- *d is a data instance and*
- *Λ is the set of all log entries that are related to d, where a log entry λ is a n-tuple (χ, α, β, Ψ, id, pid) where:*
  - *χ is the category of the action,*
  - *α is the actor performing the action,*
  - *β is the actor receiving a transferred data instance, if the action is a transfer action, or the actor where a copy is created, if the action is a copy action,*
  - *Ψ is a set of purposes of performing the action,*
  - *id is the unique identifier of the action, and*
  - *pid is the unique identifier of the preceding action.*

Logging the Execution

To log the processing, the logging mechanism needs to perform certain operations whenever a transition occurs. If the transition represents a cre-ate or copy action, a new log needs to be created. If the transition models a transfer action, the log will also need to be transferred. As the token is transferred to another place, the log must also be transferred to the actor that is represented by the place. The processing of an instance ends with its deletion. The deletion does not cause the deletion of the sticky log. Instead the log is returned to the actor possessing the source data instance. The actor and the source data instance are identified by references specified during the copying of the data. The returned log is merged with the log of the source instance. After merging the logs, all references contained in logs of copies of the deleted data instance have to be updated to refer to the merged sticky log. If the deleted instance is the last instance of a specific data item, the log will be directly returned to the person or organization that initially created the first instance of the data. This person or organization is responsible for answering information requests by the person concerned.

Logging Operation

The occurrence of all actions requires the extension of the log by a log entry monitoring the action. In this section we present a mathematical operation defining the updates to the set of all sticky logs when an action occurs. The set of all sticky logs contains the logs associated with all actual existing instances of the observed data item. Listing 1 depicts the logging operation describing the capability of the sticky logging mechanism.

The input of the operation is the set of all sticky logs M associated with the observed data item, the occurred transition t, the arc expressions $E(a_i)$ of the input arc, and the places involved in the action p, p_s, p_d, and/or p_r (depending on the category of action). If the action is a copy action, the arc expression $E(a_d)$ of the output arc leading to p_d is also required. The output is set of all sticky logs, which is updated by the log entry λ

that is added to the sticky log *m* of the associated data instance *d*.

DIALOG does not define a specific level of detail for observing the processing. Thus, the sticky logging mechanism also does not define a specific level of detail. The specific level must be chosen whenever the sticky logging implementation is used by a service.

Listing 1: Logging Actions

The input is the set of sticky logs and the elements of the logical execution modeling the performed action.

```
01   INPUT: M: set of sticky_logs,
             t: transition,
             E(a_i): arc_expression,
             E(a_o): arc_expression,
             p: place,
             p_s: place,
             p_d: place,
             p_r: place;
```

The logical execution models data instances as tokens. When a transition occurs the value of the token is assigned to the variable n by the arc expression $E(a_i)$ of the input arc. The value of a token identifies the data instance uniquely. If the identifier in the monitored execution is based on this value, the data instance will also be uniquely identifiable in the monitored execution.

```
02   data_instance d =
         getDataInstance(E(a_i).evalu-
ateExpression());
```

The logical execution models the category as label (without index) of the transition.

```
03   category χ = t.getCategory();
```

The copy action is special, because two data instances are involved; the source instance and the newly created data instance. Thus, we need to identify the newly created data instance, too. Analogously to the arc expression $E(a_i)$, the arc expression $E(a_o)$ is used to identify the newly created instance.

```
04   if (χ == "copy")
05       data_instance created_d =
             getDataInstance(E(a_o).
evaluateExpression());
```

The logical execution models actors as labels of places p. Depending of the category of an action two actors may be involved. The transfer action involves two actors p_s (the sender) and p_r (the receiver). The copy action involves two actors p_s (the source) and p_d (the destination). All other actions involve only one actor.

```
06   if (χ == "transfer")
07       actor α = p_s.getActor();
08       actor β = p_r.getActor();

09   else
10       if (χ == "copy")
11           actor α = p_s.getActor();
12           actor β = p_d.getActor();

13       else
14           actor α = p.getActor();
15           actor β = ε;
```

The purpose is encoded as index of the label of the occurring transition t.

```
16   action_purpose Ψ = t.getLabel().
getIndex();
```

An identifier of the action as well as an identifier of the preceding action needs to be logged to achieve an order of actions. Actions are modeled by transitions t, which are clearly identifiable. Thus, a unique identifier can be created from t.

```
17  action_identifier id =
createId(t);
18  action_identifier pid =
getIdOfLastLogEntryOf(d);
```

After retrieving the information about the processing the log entry is created. If the action is a copy action, a second log entry for the newly created data instance will be created, too.

```
19  log_entry λ₁ = (χ, α, β, Ψ, id,
pid);
20  if (χ == "copy")
21      log_entry λ₂ = (χ, α, β, Ψ,
id, null);
```

Finally, the log entries are added to the associated sticky logs. Then the set of all sticky logs is updated and returned.

```
22  sticky_log m₁ =
M.getStickyLogOf(d);
23  set_of_log_entries Λ₁ =
m₁.getSetOfLogEntries();
24  M.updateStickyLog(d, Λ₁ ∪ {λ₁});
25  if (χ == "copy")
26      sticky_log m₂ =
M.getStickyLogOf(created_d);
27      set_of_log_entries λ₂ =
m₂.getSetOfLogEntries();
28
M.updateStickyLog(created_d,Λ₂ ∪
{λ₂});

29  OUPUT: M;
```

If the person concerned requests information before the processing ends or if data remains in the systems of some of the involved organizations, the current log needs to be received. The current log can be received by forwarding a request to all actors that received copies of the data item. The forwarding can be done following the same paths as the copied data instances. Then the logs are returned and merged.

Example: *In the snippet of our business case depicted in Figure 8, Small-Books Inc. (α = SBI) transfers the data d to Fast-Shipping Inc. (β = FSI). The data instance d has the identifier X. To log the action t_0 the Small-Books creates a log entry describing the action by its category χ = transfer, the involved actors α and β, as well as the purpose Ψ of invoking a shipment service. The log entry is then added to the log Λ. Finally, the Small-Books connects Λ with the data instance d, which contains Mr. Smith address data:*

$(X, \{('transfer', SBI, FSI, 'invoke shipment', t_0, t_{-1})\})$

Reconstructing the Execution

Based on the information logged by the sticky logging mechanism, a transition system modeling the processing of one data item can be reconstructed. The reconstruction of the transition system can be done by using the information contained in the above introduced data structure. Listing 2 depicts the reconstruction mechanism for a log entry as mathematical operation.

Reconstruct Operation

The reconstruction takes the set of all sticky logs M of one data item as input and creates a colored petri net, which models the actors involved in the processing and actions performed on the data. The reconstruction processes one sticky log at a time and log entry by log entry. To this end, each sticky log m of the set of all sticky logs M is selected and the corresponding places, transitions, arcs, and node functions are defined.

Listing 2 depicts an algorithm implementing the mathematical operation describing the reconstruction of one log entry. The input of the operation is the log entry in combination with the already reconstructed parts of the colored petri net modeling the reconstructed execution. However not the complete colored petri net, but only the required sets and function are passed. The required sets are the sets of places, transitions, and arcs and the required function is the node function. The output is the extended colored petri net, which now models also the actual processed log entry. Analogously only the extended parts of the colored petri net are returned.

Listing 2: Reconstructing Actions

The Input is the log entry and the sets of already reconstructed places P, transitions T, arcs A, and the node function N.

```
01   INPUT: λ: log_entry,
            P: set of places,
            T: set of transitions,
            A: set of arcs,
            N: node_function;
```

The first step of the reconstruction is the creation of the places p_i and p_o for the involved actors. The actors are specified by α and β of the log entry λ. For actors, which are mentioned multiple times, only one place is created. The actors are distinguished by the unique identifier of the actors, as defined by the monitored execution. The reconstructed places are added to the set of places.

```
02   get α from λ;
03   place p_α =
createPlaceModeling(α);
04   P ∪ {p_α};

05   get β from λ;
06   if (β != ε)
```

```
07       place p_β =
createPlaceModeling(β);
08       P ∪ {p_β};
09   else
10       place p_β = p_α;
```

Then a transition t modeling the logged action is reconstructed and added to the set of transitions T. For actions which occur multiple times only one transition is created. The action is identified in the log entry by the value of id, which uniquely identifies the transition.

```
11   get id from λ;
12   transition t =
createTransitionModeling(id);
13   T ∪ {id};
```

Then for the transition the input and output arcs a_i and a_o are created and added to the set of arcs A. In the same step, the node functions of these arcs $N(a_i)$ and $N(a_o)$ are defined as $N(a_i) = (p_i, t)$ and $N(a_o) = (t, p_o)$. If $\beta = \varepsilon$, α specifies p_i and p_o of the transition.

```
14   arc a_i = createArc();
15   arc a_o = createArc();
16   A ∪ {a_i, a_o}
17   N(a_i) = (p_α, t)
18   N(a_o) = (t, p_β)
```

Finally, the updated sets and node function are returned.

```
19   OUTPUT: P, T, A, N
```

PROOF OF SOUNDNESS AND COMPLETENESS

A sound and complete reconstructed execution can be used for auditing purposes. Thus, we prove that the sticky logging mechanism can create reconstructed executions with these qualities.

The following proof consists only of the first case proving soundness and completeness of create actions. The complete proof is presented in (Ringelstein et al., 2009).

- **Proposition:** A reconstructed execution created by means of the sticky logging mechanism is sound and complete (as defined above) regarding the executed subsystem of the logical execution. □
- **Proof by induction:** We prove the proposition by induction over the structural length of the colored petri net modeling the logical execution. The basis of the induction is a logical execution consisting only of a create action. We prove that the proposition holds for this minimal (not empty) logical execution. As induction step, we extend a given logical execution, which fulfills the proposition, by one action. Thereby, we prove the proposition by extending the workflow by each category of action.
- **Basis of Induction:** Each processing of a data item starts with the creation of the first data instance. Thus, the basis of the induction is a workflow consisting only of a create action creating the first data instance.

The logical execution L consists of the following elements: one transition t with the label *create*, one place p, and an arc a leading from t to p ($N(a)=(t,p)$) with the arc expression n (see Figure 9. In addition, the logical execution consists of two arcs and the place p_c modeling the counter for creating unique ids. The execution consists of the occurrence of the create transition. This step creates a new token with a new, unique value ($=x$) and adds this token to p. The monitoring of the logical execution leads to the following monitored execution M:

$$M = \{(X, (\text{'create'}, p, \varepsilon, \text{'none'}, t, \varepsilon))\}$$

The reconstruction based on the monitored execution leads to the following reconstructed execution E. The set of log entries consists of one log entry. Reconstructing a colored petri net leads to the following sets: the set of places $P = \{p'\}$, the set of transitions $T = \{t'\}$, and the set of arcs $A = \{a'\}$ with the node function $N(a') = (t', p')$.

Soundness: The following relation $R_1 = \{(t_0, t), (p_0, p), (a_0, a)\}$ is a simulation between L and E. Thus, the reconstructed execution is sound with respect to the logical execution.

Completeness: The parts of the colored petri net used to model the counter are not part of the actual executed subsystem S of the logical execution. Thus, the following relation $R_2 = \{(t, t'), (p, p'), (a, a')\}$ is a simulation between E and S. Because R_2 can be specified, the reconstructed execution is complete with respect to the executed subsystem of the logical execution.

- **Induction Step:** Given a sound and complete reconstructed execution E_n of a logical execution L_n. We show that a reconstructed execution E_{n+1} is also sound and complete with respect to associated logical execution L_{n+1}. Whereas, L_{n+1} extends the logical execution L_n by one additional action. In detail we have to prove the soundness and completeness for adding an action of each category.
- ***Read actions:*** We start with adding a read action. Before we add the action we choose one existing place p out of P as actor. Adding a read action to L_n adds one transition t_{n+1} with the label *read* and two arcs a_{m+1} and a_{m+2} leading from t_{n+1} to p. The node function for a_{m+1} and a_{m+2} is defined as $N(a_{m+1}) = (p, t_{n+1})$ and $N(a_{m+2}) = (t_{n+1}, p)$. The arc expression of both arcs is n. See Figure 10.

Monitoring the occurrence of t_{n+1}, which reads a data instance represented by a token with the value X at p, creates the log entry m_{n+1}:

Figure 9. Induction basis: Single create action

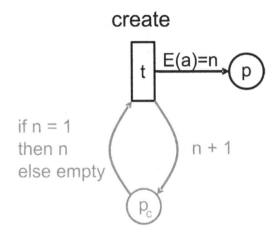

$$m_{n+1} = (X, (\text{'read'}, p', \varepsilon, \text{'none'}, t'_{n+1}, t'_n))$$

The log entry m_{n+1} is then added to the monitored execution M_n leading to M_{n+1}:

$$M_{n+1} = M_n \cup \{m_{n+1}\}$$

The reconstruction is an iterative process. E_{n+1} is reconstructed by processing M_n first. Afterwards, the last iteration step processes the newly added log entry m_{n+1}. Because E_n was reconstructed from M_n, it consists of the set of places P'_n, the set of transitions T'_n, and the set of arcs A'_n with the node function N'_n. E_{n+1} extends these sets. The set of places stays unchanged $P'_{n+1} = P'_n$, because the log entry contains only the actor modeled by p, which is already element of P'. However, the new transition t'_{n+1} is added to $T'n$ ($T'_{n+1} = T'_n \cup \{t_{n+1}\}$). Also the arcs are added to $A'n$ leading to $A'_{n+1} = A'_n \cup \{a_{m+1}, a_{m+2}\}$).

Soundness: Be $R_{1,n}$ the simulation between L_n and E_n. The following relation $R_{1,n+1} = R_{1,n} \cup \{(t'_{n+1}, t_{n+1}), (a'_{m+1}, a_{m+1}), (a'_{m+2}, a_{m+2})\}$ is a simulation between L_{n+1} and E_{n+1}. Thus, the reconstructed execution is sound with respect to the logical execution L_{n+1}.

Completeness: Be $R_{2,n}$ the simulation between E_n and executed subsystem S_n of the logical

execution. Because the action modeled by t_{n+1} is performed, the executed subsystem of L_{n+1} is S_{n+1}. The following relation $R_{2,n+1} = R_{2,n} \cup \{(t_{n+1}, t'_{n+1}), (a_{m+1}, a'_{m+1}), (a_{m+2}, a'_{m+2})\}$ is a simulation between E_{n+1} and S_{n+1}. Because $R_{2,n}$ can be specified, the reconstructed execution is complete with respect to the executed subsystem of the logical execution L_{n+1}.

- *Other actions:* The soundness and completeness proofs for copy, update, transfer, and delete actions are shown in (Ringelstein et al., 2009). ∎

Informing the Customer and Auditing a Service-Oriented System

Different organizations are involved in the distributed processing of the data. Each of these organizations monitors its parts of the processing by means of the sticky logging mechanism. If the processing ends or if information is requested[4], the log is transferred to the customer. The customer is able to generate the transition system of the reconstructed execution from the logs representing the monitored execution. The reconstructed execution represents the parts of the workflow involved in the processing of the customer's data. Finally, the customer is able to control if contractual or legal agreements have been violated.

Security and Privacy

To guarantee that an organization is not able to deny a made log entry, the sticky logging mechanism makes use of signatures. In addition, the signatures are used to assure that the log is not modified by another organization on its way. For both purposes each logging actor has to sign its log entries by means of a digital signature mechanism, e.g., the approach presented in (Carroll, 2003).

The sticky log is attached to the data instance and moved along the execution path. To restrict the access of third parties to the log, an access

Figure 10. Induction step: Read action

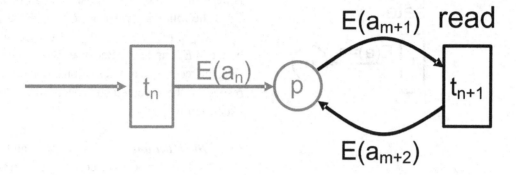

control mechanism is required (see Requirement 4). We propose that each actor encrypts the information it logs. If a public key infrastructure is utilized, the logging actors can use the public key of the person concerned to encrypt the logs. The person concerned can access the logs by means of its private key.

Prototype Implementation

To observe the data processing and to manage the passing of logs, the sticky logging mechanism is a layer between the execution environment (i.e., JBoss) and business software (i.e., Web services), as depicted in Figure 11. The prototype attaches the logs by including them into the SOAP messages (Gudgin et al., 2007) that are used to call services. After the execution of the service, the log is returned by the SOAP answer. Then the returned logs are merged with the log of the calling service. To handle and manage the logs, the prototype provides an API. The API can be integrated on server and client side and is designed to be used together with the message handler chain of the JBoss runtime environment.

The API of the prototype provides an interface to create log entries, to attach log entries to logs and to merge logs. The logs make use of the RDF formalism we presented in (Ringelstein et al., 2007). Jena[5] is used to handle the RDF statements.

To show the functionality of the sticky logging, the business case has been implemented by means of the prototype. The implementation provides a client application to order products of a Web shop. To this end, the client application uses operations of a Web service provided by the Web shop. The Web shop itself uses a parcel service for delivery. The pick-up of the order is requested by means of a Web service provided by the parcel service. At the end of the order processing the customer is informed about the complete processing of his private data (including the passing of his address to the parcel service).

RELATED WORK

Other work identifying the need for logging of data usage in distributed environments is presented by Weitzner et al. (2008). The authors analyze that access restrictions are not sufficient to achieve policy goals, because in many environments it can not be guaranteed that a specific agent has no access to a certain piece of information. Therefore, the authors demand transparency of information usage to enable accountability. Our contribution tackles the problem that they have analyzed, but for which they have not presented a solution.

Hallam-Baker introduced in (Hallam-Baker et al., 1996) the Extended Log File Format, which allows for logging the communication actions

Figure 11. Example architecture with JBoss

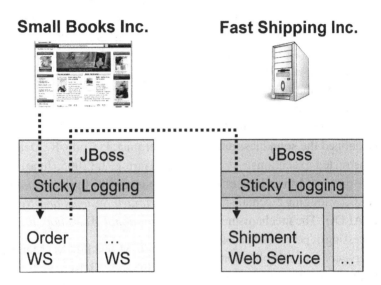

between Web applications. In addition, Barth et al. presented in (Barth et al., 2007) a logic to specify and verify privacy and utility goals of business processes in non-distributed environments. However both approaches do not observe the processing of specific data items in distributed environments.

Other models to represent workflows by Petri nets are analyzed in (Aalst, 1998) and (Aalst, 2004). The first approach models processes as activity flows. The second approach additionally models the control flow including data dependencies. However, both approaches do not allow for modeling the distributed processing of specific data items.

In (Aalst et al., 2004) the authors present an approach to use message logs and BPEL specifications for conformance checking of service behavior. In difference to our work they assume that a global model of the observed services is given by the BPEL specification. The authors of (Aldeco-Perez et al., 2008) present an architecture for auditing private data in IT-Systems by collecting provenance information. Their architecture is also based on requirements specified by privacy

laws. In difference to our paper, they do not present a formal model of the processing of private data.

The authors of (Cederquiest et al., 2005) propose to use an auditing mechanism to achieve accountability in distributed environments. The auditing is done based on policies and logged actions, conditions and obligations. The logs are located at the agents performing the actions. No mechanism is provided to make the logs accessible to the service customer. In addition, they do not provide a formal model of the data processing.

In the field of policy mechanisms various approaches for sticky policies exist (Karjoth et al., 2002; Wenningen et al., 2006). On the level of service calls they have a similar solution by attaching additional information to the transferred data. However, they aim to communicate polices and not to audit the data processing in distributed environments.

CONCLUSION

This paper introduces DIALOG and sticky logging and extends our previous work presented in (Ringelstein et al., 2007). In our previous paper we have introduced a semantic formalism and ontology to express sticky logs as well as a general description of the sticky logging mechanism. We now have extended this work by a formal model of distributed logging, i.e., DIALOG, the data structure of sticky logs, a method to reconstruct the model from a log, and a description how these can be used together. Based on the formal model of DIALOG we have defined the soundness and completeness of reconstructed executions.

In addition, we have presented an architecture and a prototype of the sticky logging mechanism, which implements DIALOG. The mechanism is designed to log the processing of personal data, but can also be used to observe contractual obligations or organization internal policies. The architecture consists of a data structure to store the information and of a set of operations describing how to log and how to manage the logs. Beside this, the architecture describes how to reconstruct a model from a log. The prototype provides an API to realize sticky logging as a generic extension of JBoss.

ACKNOWLEDGMENT

The prototype implementation is based on a student project of Martin Schnorr. This work has been supported by the European project Knowledge Sharing and Reuse across Media (X-Media, FP6-26978) funded by the Information Society Technologies (IST) 6th Framework Programme.

REFERENCES

Aldeco-Perez, R., & Moreau, L. (2008, September). Provenance-based Auditing of Private Data Use. In *Proceedings of the BCS International Academic Research Conference, Visions of Computer Science*.

Barth, A., Mitchell, J., Datta, A., & Sundaram, S. (2007). Privacy and Utility in Business Processes. In *Proceedings of the 2007 Computer Security Foundations Symposium*. Washington, DC: IEEE.

Carroll, J. J. (2003). Signing RDF Graphs. In *Proceedings of the SemanticWeb (ISWC 2003)* (pp. 369-384).

Cederquist, J., Conn, R., Dekker, M., Etalle, S., & den Hartog, J. (2005, June). An Audit Logic for Accountability. In *Proceedings of the Policies for Distributed Systems and Networks - Sixth IEEE International Workshop on* (pp. 34-43).

Gudgin, M., Hadley, M., Mendelsohn, N., Moreau, J. J., Frystyk Nielsen, H. F., Karmarkar, A., et al. (2007, April). *SOAP Version 1.2 Part 1: Messaging Framework* (2nd ed.). Retrieved from http://www.w3.org/TR/2007/REC-soap12-part1-20070427/

Hallam-Baker, P. M., & Behlendorf, B. (1996). *Extended Log File Format*. Retrieved from http://www.w3.org/TR/WD-logfile-960323.html

Jensen, K. (1992). *Coloured Petri Nets - Basic Concepts, Analysis Methods and Practical Use* (*Vol. 1*). New York: Springer.

Karjoth, G., Schunter, M., & Waidner, M. (2002). Platform for Enterprise Privacy Practices: Privacy-enabled Management of Customer Data. In *Proceedings of the 2nd Workshop on Privacy Enhancing Technologies (PET 2002)*.

Kucera, A., & Mayr, R. (1999). Simulation Preorder on Simple Process Algebras. In *Proceedings of the 26th International Colloquium on Automata, Languages and Programming* (pp. 503-512). London: Springer Verlag.

Lonvick, C. (2001). RFC 3164: The BSD syslog Protocol. *Internet Engineering Task Force*. Retrieved from http://www.ietf.org/rfc/rfc3164.txt

Narayanan, S., & McIlraith, S. A. (2002). Simulation, Verification and Automated Composition of Web Services. In *Proceedings of the WWW, 02*, 77–88.

Ringelstein, C., & Staab, S. (2007). Logging in Distributed Workflows. In *Proceedings of the Workshop on Privacy Enforcement and Accountability with Semantics*, Busan, South-Korea.

Ringelstein, C., & Staab, S. (2009). *Distributed Auditing Logs* (Tech. Rep.). Koblenz, Germany: University of Koblenz-Landau. Retrieved from http://userpages.uni-koblenz.de/~cringel/pub/TRDialog09.pdf van der Aalst, W. (1998). The Application of Petri Nets to Workflow Management. *The Journal of Circuits, Systems and Computers, 8*(1), 21-66.

van der Aalst, W., Weijters, T., & Maruster, L. (2004). Workflow Mining: Discovering Process Models from Event Logs. *IEEE Transactions on Knowledge and Data Engineering, 16*(9), 1128–1142. doi:10.1109/TKDE.2004.47

van der Aalst, W. M. P., Dumas, M., Ouyang, C., Rozinat, A., & Verbeek, E. (2008). Conformance Checking of Service Behavior. *ACM Transactions on Internet Technology, 8*(3), 1–30. doi:10.1145/1361186.1361189

Weitzner, D. J., Abelson, H., Berners-Lee, T., Feigenbaum, J., Hendler, J., & Sussman, G. J. (2008). Information Accountability. *Communications of the ACM, 51*(6). doi:10.1145/1349026.1349043

Wenning, R., Schunter, M., et al. (2006). *The Platform for Privacy Preferences 1.1 (P3P1.1) Specification.* Retrieved from http://www.w3.org/TR/2006/NOTE-P3P11-20061113/

ENDNOTES

[1] An actual version of the prototype can be downloaded at: http://isweb.unikoblenz.de/Research/StickyLogging

[2] The atomic level of our model may consist of many actions at the lower level of the implementation.

[3] To fully understand the implications of our model, we have to refer the reader to extensive descriptions of Petri Nets such as (Jensen, 1992). However, we expect that our examples are sufficiently self contained to explain the core ideas of our approach. The reader may also note that Petri nets have been used for quite a while already to model service behavior (Narayanan et al., 2002).

[4] The customer may request the information at any time as often as he wants during the processing.

[5] Jena – A Semantic Web Framework for Java: http://jena.sourceforge.net/

This work was previously published in the International Journal of Web Services Research, Volume 7, Issue 2, edited by Liang-Jie (LJ) Zhang, pp. 1-20, copyright 2010 by IGI Publishing (an imprint of IGI Global).

Chapter 17
Selective Service Provenance in the VRESCo Runtime

Anton Michlmayr
Vienna University of Technology, Austria

Florian Rosenberg
CSIRO ICT Centre, Australia

Philipp Leitner
Vienna University of Technology, Austria

Schahram Dustdar
Vienna University of Technology, Austria

ABSTRACT

In general, provenance describes the origin and well-documented history of a given object. This notion has been applied in information systems, mainly to provide data provenance of scientific workflows. Similar to this, provenance in Service-oriented Computing has also focused on data provenance. However, the authors argue that in service-centric systems the origin and history of services is equally important. This paper presents an approach that addresses service provenance. The authors show how service provenance information can be collected and retrieved, and how security mechanisms guarantee integrity and access to this information, while also providing user-specific views on provenance. Finally, the paper gives a performance evaluation of the authors' approach, which has been integrated into the VRESCo Web service runtime environment.

INTRODUCTION

The term 'provenance' is commonly used to describe the origin and well-documented history of some object and exists in various areas such as fine arts, archeology or wines. Provenance information can be used to prove the authenticity and estimate the value of objects. For instance, the price of wine depends on origin, vintage, and how the wine was stored. The notion of provenance was adopted in information systems to refer to the origin of some piece of electronic data (Moreau et al., 2008). Various research efforts have addressed

DOI: 10.4018/978-1-4666-1942-5.ch017

data provenance in different domains such as e-Science (Simmhan et al., 2005).

Service-oriented architecture (SOA) (Papazoglou et al., 2007) and Web services (Weerawarana et al., 2005) represent well-known paradigms for developing flexible and cross-organizational enterprise applications. Data provenance in such applications and the provenance of business processes as realized in Business Activity Monitoring (BAM) are important issues that have been addressed by several research projects (Curbera et al., 2008), (Rajbhandari & Walker, 2006), (Tsai et al., 2007). These approaches mainly focus on the provenance of the data produced, transformed or routed through an SOA system. In contrast to that, we argue that service provenance also plays a central role, for instance during service selection. If there are multiple alternative services available, service consumers might be interested in the history of the candidates. This includes creation date, ownership and modification information, as well as Quality of Service (QoS) attributes such as failure rate or response time. Additionally, service providers are also interested in service provenance, for instance, to identify services that do not perform as expected.

In this paper, we introduce a novel service provenance approach that has been integrated into the VRESCo runtime environment (Michlmayr et al., May 2009). In most current approaches, provenance information is captured at runtime and usually managed in a dedicated provenance store. In our approach, we have enhanced the existing VRESCo event processing mechanism (Michlmayr et al., 2008) in order to capture and maintain provenance information. Events are thereby published and correlated when certain situations occur (e.g., new service is created, service revision is added, QoS changes, service operation is invoked, etc.).

Security issues such as data integrity and access control represent a central problem, which is often neglected in provenance approaches (Tan et al., 2006). On the one hand, provenance information must be accurate while on the other hand, appropriate access control mechanisms should provide access to provenance information only to authorized parties. Moreover, service owners should define who is able to access which provenance information. For instance, while employees are able to access all information, sensitive in-house information might be hidden from business partners. Such security mechanisms are also discussed in this work.

The contribution of this paper is threefold: Firstly, we present a brief summary of related work in the field and position our work among these approaches. Secondly, we present the VRESCo service provenance approach including how provenance information is collected and retrieved at runtime. Furthermore, we give examples of its usage and applicability. Thirdly, we present access control mechanisms for Web service runtimes including authentication and authorization features. This also includes various types of visibility for events that are published in the runtime. It should be noted that the present paper represents an extended version of our work published in (Michlmayr et al., July 2009).

The remainder of this paper is organized as follows. Section 2 starts with the motivation of our work, while Section 3 presents related work regarding provenance. Section 4 then describes our provenance approach in detail, by showing how provenance information is collected, retrieved and visualized. Section 5 addresses the security mechanism of our provenance system, while Section 6 presents an evaluation of our work. Finally, Section 7 concludes the paper.

MOTIVATION

In this section, we want to present the motivation of our work. As already stated above, existing work on provenance mainly focuses on data provenance, meaning how and when data was created, transformed or accessed in processes (such as business processes or scientific workflows). This is important, for instance, to validate the results of scientific simulation runs. In contrast to that, however, we aim at addressing service provenance, which is the origin and well-documented history of services. Although conceptually similar at first glance, these two paradigms differ since our work introduces a different view on provenance in service-oriented systems.

The following motivating example highlights the motivation of our work. Furthermore, concrete examples are used throughout the paper to describe and evaluate our approach. As stated above, service selection represents an illustrative application for service provenance. If there are multiple alternative services, service consumers might want to take the origin and history of the alternatives into consideration. For instance, one service consumer may not trust specific service providers due to bad experience in the past. Other service consumers may pay special attention to QoS values of alternative services. If one service has performed well over the last months, it might be preferred over recently published services without documented QoS history. Once selected, the services may change, which also includes their behavior regarding QoS. In such cases, service consumers may want to automatically rebind to alternative services, which can be triggered based on existing provenance information. Besides service selection, another motivation for service provenance lies in the fact that service consumers and service providers may continuously query or subscribe to current provenance information (e.g., changing QoS attributes, new service revisions, etc.). For instance, service providers can use this information to verify if their services perform as expected. Otherwise, corrective actions can be triggered.

Current service registry standards, such as UDDI (OASIS, February 2005) and ebXML (OA-SIS, May 2005) provide only limited support for service provenance. In UDDI, the *businessEntity* construct can be used to store information about the owner of a service, but this construct is fixed and there is no further support for more complex structures regarding the history of a service. In ebXML, every *RegistryObject* can be associated to persons or organizations that have either sub-mitted this information or are responsible for it. In addition, ebXML provides full versioning of registry information. Therefore, the provenance model of ebXML is clearly advanced compared to UDDI, but there is still no support to further collect and process service provenance informa-tion. In addition, ebXML is rarely used in practice.

As a result, the motivation of our work is to provide rich support for service provenance. This includes how to collect, retrieve and visualize provenance information. Furthermore, we also aim at addressing security issues that typically occur in provenance systems. Finally, our approach is integrated into an existing service runtime envi-ronment, instead of introducing a dedicated and stand-alone provenance system.

RELATED WORK

Before going into the details of our approach, we want to give a brief overview of related work. The provenance of electronic data has already been addressed in various research efforts (Moreau et al., 2008). The focus of this research has often been on provenance in e-Science and scientific workflows (Simmhan et al., 2005), which led to different research prototypes such as Chimera (Foster et al., 2002). Over the years, research on data provenance resulted in the Open Provenance Model (Moreau et al., 2007) and reference ar-chitectures for provenance systems (Groth et al., 2006).

Additionally, there is some existing work in the area of data provenance in service-based systems (Tsai et al., 2007), (Rajbhandari & Walker, 2006), (Simmhan et al., 2008), (Chen et al., 2006), which is discussed in more detail below. In general, these approaches address data provenance, which aims at capturing the history of data generated by some processes. In contrast, our work focuses on service provenance by maintaining the origin and history of services and associated metadata.

There are several issues when designing provenance in service-centric systems. (Tsai et al., 2007) discuss the issues of data provenance in SOA systems compared to traditional data provenance techniques. Their main focus is on security, reliability and integrity of data routed through such a system. (Tan et al., 2006) also address security issues in SOA-based provenance systems. They use p-assertions (Moreau et al., 2008), which represent specific items that document parts of a process, as foundation for their considerations. Similar to our work, they argue that access control, trust and accountability of provenance information are crucial. In addition, we also address security mechanisms in service runtime environments, which have been implemented using a claim based authorization approach.

(Rajbhandari & Walker, 2006) present a system that incorporates provenance into scientific workflows to capture the history of produced data items. This history is captured by the workflow engine and recorded into a provenance database, which is structured using RDF schema. Furthermore, a provenance query service is used to query the provenance information stored in the database. (Heinis & Alonso, 2008) present another approach to provenance of scientific data. In their approach, they focus on how provenance data can be efficiently stored and queried in the provenance database.

Another interesting work in this area is described by (Simmhan et al., 2008), who introduce the Karma2 system. The goal of this work is to provide provenance in data-driven workflows. The authors describe their provenance model including different provenance activities (e.g., ServiceInvoked, DataProduced, Computation, etc.). The idea is to trace workflow executions for both process provenance (i.e., which services are invoked by a process) and data provenance (i.e.,

which data items are produced and consumed). The architecture of Karma uses a publish/subscribe infrastructure to publish provenance activities to interested subscribers. In addition, provenance queries are provided to display provenance information using graphs. Although our notion of provenance is different, there are some similarities to our work. Both approaches use provenance queries and provenance graphs for visualization. Additionally, provenance information is sent using a publish/subscribe infrastructure based on WS-Eventing (W3C, 2006). However, while our approach provides content-based subscriptions and complex event processing including event patterns, Karma2 supports only topic-based subscriptions (i.e., subscribers can only subscribe to receive either all or none events for one workflow). Furthermore, Karma2 uses a modified SOAP library for collecting provenance information while our work is integrated into the VRESCo runtime. Finally, our definition of service provenance also includes service metadata and QoS attributes.

(Chen et al., 2006) introduce what they call augmented provenance, which is based on the idea of semantic Web services (SWS). They address process provenance in scientific workflows with a special emphasis on Grid environments. Their approach applies ontologies to model metadata at various level of abstraction, while SWS are used for capturing execution-independent metadata. Similar to our work, the authors use metadata as source for provenance. However, they focus on SWS technology, while our work builds on the simplified VRESCo metadata model. Furthermore, they provide neither provenance graphs nor subscriptions.

(Curbera et al., 2008) present a slightly different view on provenance. They introduce the notion of business provenance in order to achieve compliance violation monitoring. The basic idea is to trace end-to-end business operations by capturing various business events, correlate these events into a provenance store, and monitor if some compliance goals are violated. The authors introduce a generic provenance data model, which can be represented in provenance graphs. These graphs are built based on the event information in the provenance store, and can be queried for root cause analysis. This work is complementary to ours since the authors address business provenance using business events, while we focus on service provenance based on events raised on the service management level.

SERVICE PROVENANCE APPROACH

The previous sections described the motivation and related work of our provenance approach, which is presented in detail in this section. We show how provenance information is collected, and how it can be queried, subscribed to, and visualized. First of all, however, we want to briefly introduce the VRESCo runtime environment which is used as foundation for our approach.

VRESCo Runtime Overview

The VRESCo project (Vienna Runtime Environment for Service-Oriented Computing) introduced in (Michlmayr et al., 2007) aims at addressing some of the current challenges in Service-oriented Computing, such as dynamic binding and invocation of services, service querying, service metadata, QoS-aware service composition, and complex event processing. The main objective of the project is to facilitate the engineering of SOA applications.

Figure 1 depicts an overview of the VRESCo runtime architecture. Services and associated service metadata (Rosenberg et al., 2008) are published into the Registry Database, which is accessed using an object-relational mapping (ORM) Layer. The Query Engine is used to query all information stored in this database, whereas the Event Notification Engine is responsible for publishing events when certain situations occur at runtime (e.g., new service is published, QoS

changes, etc.) (Michlmayr et al., 2008). The VRESCo core services are accessed either directly using SOAP or via the Client Library which provides a simple API. Furthermore, VRESCo offers mechanisms to dynamically bind and invoke services using the integrated DAIOS framework (Leitner et al., May/June 2009). Finally, the QoS Monitor presented in (Rosenberg et al., 2006) has been integrated to regularly measure the QoS attributes (e.g., response time, availability, etc.) of services. The security mechanisms realized by the Access Control Layer and the Certificate Store are discussed in more detail in Section 5.

The overall runtime environment is implemented in C#/.NET using Windows Communication Foundation (WCF) technology (Peiris et al., 2007), while the Client Library is currently provided for C# and Java. Furthermore, the open source framework NHibernate (Red Hat Inc., 2009) is used for the ORM Layer. Some of the VRESCo core services are described in more detail below; an extensive overview of the VRESCo runtime environment can be found in (Michlmayr et al., May 2009).

Collecting Provenance Information

In VRESCo, service provenance information is collected at runtime. This consists of various aspects, such as basic service information, service metadata and service runtime events. While the former two are mostly published by service providers, events are raised automatically by the runtime. These aspects are discussed in more detail next.

1. **Basic Service Information:** The first part of service provenance information is represented by what we call basic service information, which is kept in the Registry Database. This consists of required information to invoke services (e.g., service endpoint, binding, WSDL file, etc.). Furthermore, every service can be associated with service owner information. Another interesting feature of

Figure 1. VRESCo architectural overview

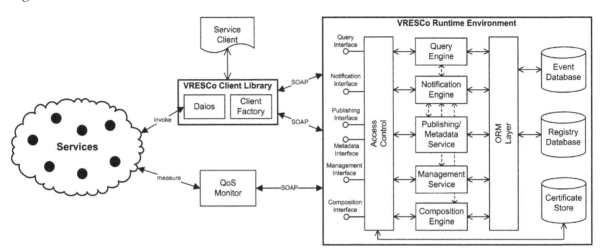

VRESCo is service versioning, which allows one service to have multiple service revisions. These service revisions are visualized in service revision graphs (Leitner et al., 2008). Service versioning information and revision tags (i.e., every revision can be tagged by the service provider) are part of service provenance information.

2. **Service Metadata:** Besides basic service information, another important source for provenance information is represented by service metadata as described in (Rosenberg et al., 2008). Briefly summarized, service metadata in VRESCo is used to describe the functionality and semantics of services that cannot be seen in the WSDL descriptions. To accomplish this, we have defined a mapping between our Service Model and Service Metadata Model shown in Figure 2, which is adapted from (Michlmayr et al., May 2009).

    In general, the VRESCo Metadata Model provides detailed descriptions of the service's purpose using service categories (i.e., services in the same domain), features (i.e., services performing the same task), as well as service operations including parameters, pre- and post-conditions. Thereby, data

concepts are used to model core entities in the domain that are used as service input and output. Since one of the main goals of VRESCo is dynamic invocation and service mediation, these data concepts can then be mapped using mapping functions. Among others, mapping functions include data type conversion, string manipulation, as well as mathematical and logical operators. Furthermore, CS-Script can be used to define custom C# mapping scripts. As a result, two services that perform the same task (i.e., implement the same feature) but have different interfaces can be invoked seamlessly. More information about service mediation can be found in (Leitner et al., August 2009). It should be noted that both basic service information and service metadata is published by the service provider using the Publishing and Metadata Service, respectively.

3. **Service Runtime Events:** The third and most important source of provenance information is provided by the VRESCo Event Notification Engine, which has been introduced in (Michlmayr et al., 2008). In general, the idea is to publish events when certain situations occur, such as new services

Figure 2. Service metadata and service model

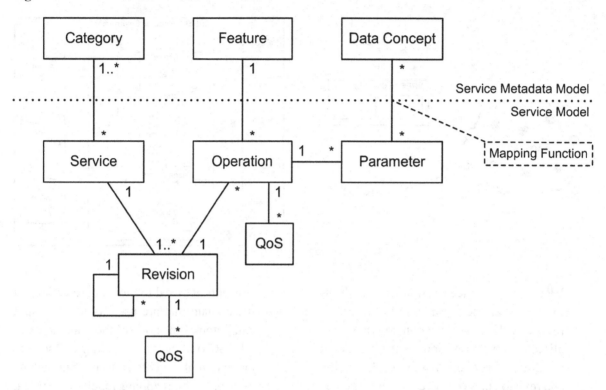

being published or existing services being modified. Subscribers are then enabled to receive notifications using different mechanisms (e.g., email, WS-Eventing, etc.).

This general idea has been followed by existing Web service registries such as UDDI and ebXML. However, both approaches focus on basic pre-defined events that enable users to track services and other metadata in the registry. In addition to that, the VRESCo Event Notification Engine provides several advanced concepts. Firstly, our approach provides events regarding changing QoS attributes, binding and invocation, as well as other runtime information. Secondly, VRESCo builds on content-based subscriptions and supports complex event processing mechanisms, such as event patterns and statistical functions on event streams. Thirdly, besides being able to subscribe to current events, users can search in historical

event information. Table 1 shows the main event groups provided by VRESCo, where we distinguish between internal events (i.e., published within the runtime) and external events (i.e., published outside the runtime).

Besides internal events that track the change history of users, services, revisions and metadata, most notable are QoS events, which are generated by the QoS Monitor (see Figure 1). These QoS events capture the current QoS values, such as response time or throughput. The aggregation of all QoS events then represents the history of a service. This information can be of great interest for service consumers during service selection. Moreover, for the same reason binding and invocation events are also important. These events show how often services have been accessed, including the identity of the service requester and her current IP address. Furthermore, they also record how many of these service invocations

Table 1. Events in VRESCo

Event Groups	Examples
Internal Events	
User Management	User is added/modified/deleted
Service Management	Service is added/modified/deleted
Versioning	Revisions are added/modified/deleted
Metadata	Feature/Concepts are added/modified/deleted
External Events	
Quality of Service	Response Time, Availability, Throughput
Binding/Invocation	Service invocation has failed/succeeded

have failed including the reasons for the failure (for instance, this can be retrieved from the exception returned by the service). Finally, the rebinding of service proxies from one service to another is also recorded by these events.

The architecture of the VRESCo Event Notification Engine is shown in Figure 3, which is adapted from (Michlmayr et al., 2008). The event processing functionality is based on the open source event processing engine Esper (EsperTech Inc., 2009). Therefore, subscriptions are defined using the Esper Event Processing Language (EPL), which is similar to SQL and provides various complex event processing mechanisms such as event patterns, sliding event windows and statistical functions on event streams.

The Subscription Manager is responsible for managing subscriptions in the Subscription Storage, and attaching corresponding listeners to Esper. These listeners are invoked when events match to subscriptions. Events are published using the Eventing Service: internal events are raised by the corresponding VRESCo core services (e.g., Publishing Service) while external events (e.g., QoS events) are raised by external components (e.g., QoS Monitor) and may need to be transformed using Event Adapters. The events are then fed into Esper, which performs the actual matching between subscriptions and events. Furthermore, events are persisted into the Event Database so that they can be accessed later. For performance

reasons, this operation is done periodically in batch mode using the Persist Queue.

When events match to subscriptions, Esper invokes the corresponding listener, which is then forwarded to the Notification Manager. The latter is finally responsible for notifying the interested subscriber depending on the given notification delivery mode. Currently, we provide email and Web service notifications (compliant with WS-Eventing (W3C, 2006)) for external subscribers, while internal subscribers within the runtime can register their own listeners. For performance reasons, the notifications are created and sent using a dedicated notification delivery thread pool. If notifications cannot be delivered they are persisted, and can later be retrieved by the subscribers.

To demonstrate the power of events, we briefly discuss how QoS events are realized. The QoS Monitor introduced in (Rosenberg et al., 2006) is used to regularly measure dependability attributes (e.g., response time, availability, etc.) of services within the runtime. The measured values are then published to the runtime using the Management Service (see Figure 1). Besides publishing QoS events, a dedicated QoS Scheduler is used to regularly aggregate the information inherent to these events. Subscribers can now take corrective actions if the QoS of some service is not as intended. To give a concrete example, the following subscription declares interest if the average

Figure 3. Eventing architecture

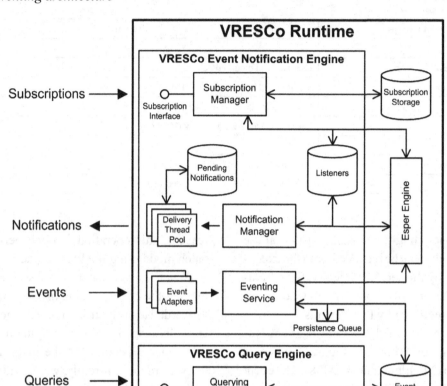

response time of service revision 17 within the last 6 hours was more than 500ms:

```
select * from
QoSRevisionEvent(Revision.Id=17
  and Property='ResponseTime').
win:time(6 hours).stat:uni('Value')
  where average > 500
```

The VRESCo Event Notification Engine opens new possibilities such as provenance subscriptions (described below) and notification-based rebinding (Michlmayr et al., May 2009). Furthermore, in our ongoing work we have integrated support for client- and server-side QoS monitoring and event-based SLA violation detection.

Provenance Queries

Once provenance information is collected at runtime, the next issue is how to access and query this information accordingly. This reaches from simple queries like "Who has created service X?" to more complex ones like "What is the average response time of service X?" or "How often has service X been invoked in the last 24 hours?".

The provenance query mechanism in VRESCo is based on the Query Engine, which uses the VRESCo Querying Language (VQL) (Michlmayr et al., May 2009). VQL provides a generic and type-safe querying language similar to the Hibernate Criteria API (Red Hat Inc., 2009), and can be used for querying all kinds of resources such as services, events or metadata. Therefore, from a client-side perspective the provenance queries are built just like "normal" service queries. Queries in VQL consist of multiple criteria where each criteria can have multiple expressions (e.g., =, >, !=, etc.). Furthermore, VQL provides different querying strategies that define if all criteria have to be fulfilled (QueryMode.EXACT) or not (Query-Mode.RELAXED), and if some criteria are more important than others (QueryMode.PRIORITY).

Listing 1 gives two examples for provenance queries. Initially, the *querier* (i.e., the proxy to the Query Engine) is created using the Client Library (line 1–2). The first query (line 5–9) returns all measuring points (*QoSRevisionEvents*) where the response time of service revision 815 was greater than 500 milliseconds. The second query (line 12–18) returns all service invocations (*ServiceInvokedEvents*) of service revision 4711 from user *telco1* that happened between 1.8.2009 and 31.8.2009. After the queries are built, they are executed using the *querier* in line 21–24, and the Query Engine returns all matching events.

Provenance Subscriptions

Besides using queries on the historic provenance information stored in the runtime, the Event Notification Engine enables users to subscribe to certain events of interest. Subscriptions for events or event patterns are specified in the Esper Event Processing Language (EPL) (EsperTech Inc., 2009). If such events or event patterns occur, notifications are sent to interested subscribers using email or WS-Eventing notifications. This mechanism is leveraged to receive notifications if provenance events of interest occur.

Listing 2 shows an example subscription in VRESCo, which is semantically equal to the first query shown in Listing 1. If the response time of revision 815 is greater than 500ms (line 5-7), a notification email should be sent to the given address. The date given in line 9 specifies how long the subscription is valid. Furthermore, the identifier returned in line 4 can be used to cancel or renew the subscription. The references provide

Listing 1. Provenance Queries

```
01 IVRESCoQuerier querier =
02 VRESCoClientFactory.CreateQuerier("joe", "pw");
03
04 // build provenance query regarding QoS
05 var query1 = new VQuery(typeof(QoSRevisionEvent));
06 query1.Add(Expression.Eq("Revision.Id", 815));
07 query1.Add(Expression.Eq("Property",
08 Constants.QOS_RESPONSE_TIME));
09 query1.Add(Expression.Gt("Value", 500));
10
11 // build provenance query regarding invocations
12 var query2 = new VQuery(typeof(ServiceInvokedEvent));
13 query2.Add(Expression.Eq("Revision.Id", 4711));
14 query2.Add(Expression.Eq("Publisher", "telco1"));
15 query2.Add(Expression.Gt("Timestamp",
16 new DateTime(2009, 8, 1)));
17 query2.Add(Expression.Lt("Timestamp",
18 new DateTime(2009, 8, 31)));
19
20 // execute provenance queries
21 var results1 = querier.FindByQuery(query1,
22 QueryMode.Exact) as IList<QoSRevisionEvent>;
23 var results2 = querier.FindByQuery(query2,
24 QueryMode.Exact) as IList<ServiceInvokedEvent>;
```

more details on VRESCo subscriptions (Michl-mayr et al., 2008) and EPL (EsperTech Inc., 2009).

Provenance Graphs

Besides querying provenance information, another useful feature is to illustrate this information using provenance graphs. The aim of these graphs is to give an overview of relevant provenance information, such as service versioning information, service ownership and service history regarding binding and invocation, as well as QoS attributes in a graphical way. The input of provenance graphs can either be services/revisions or provenance queries. In the first case, the graph is built with all provenance information that is available for the requested service or revision. In the second case, the result of a provenance query (which is a list of events as shown in Listing 1) is displayed in a graph. Therefore, pre-defined templates that control the graph generation are used. These templates are based on the event type returned by

Listing 2. Provenance Subscription

```
01 IVRESCoSubscriber subscriber =
02 VRESCoClientFactory.CreateSubscriber("joe", "pw");
03
04 int id = subscriber.SubscribePerEmail(
05 "select * from QoSRevisionEvent where " +
06 "Revision.Id = 815 and " +
07 "Property = 'ResponseTime' and Value > 500",
08 "joe@foo.bar",
09 new DateTime(2010, 1, 1));
```

the provenance query (i.e., only the relevant parts of the provenance graph are shown). Currently, we provide such templates for QoS events and service invocation events.

Due to the vast amount of information stored in the runtime, the provenance graphs tend to get overloaded quickly. Therefore, the information inherent to the events is divided into several groups such as core service details, versioning graph, invocations, QoS attributes, revision tags, and operations. Each group summarizes the information of the corresponding events.

Figure 4 gives an example of a provenance graph, which was generated using our approach. This graph shows provenance information of a specific service revision. First of all, parts of the versioning graph are shown on the top of the graph. This includes both predecessors (edge *previous*) and successors (edge *next*) of the current revision. The revision itself is positioned in the center and gives information about the corresponding service, owner, creation date, and the user that created this revision. While the first two elements are read from the metadata of this service, the last two elements are stored in the *RevisionPublishedEvent*. The bottom part illustrates the groups *Invocations* (i.e., number of successful/failed invocations, last successful/failed invocation), *QoS* (i.e., QoS events and aggregated QoS information), *Tags* (e.g., "v1"), and *Operations* (i.e., all operations of this revision including input and output parameters).

The service provenance graphs in VRESCo are built using the open source graph drawing libraries QuickGraph (Microsoft Cooperation, 2009) and GraphViz (Gansner & North, 2000). Before such a graph is built, all relevant provenance information (i.e., events and service metadata) is retrieved using the Query Engine. The corresponding graph is then generated using this information while the graph libraries are used to render the resulting graph according to the user's preferences (e.g., PDF or PNG). The graph image (or a graph representation as GraphViz' DOT file (Gansner & North, 2000)) is finally returned to the user. The overall approach of building provenance graphs is implemented as part of the VRESCo Querying Service.

Process Provenance

The main focus of our work is on service provenance, since this has received little attention by related approaches so far. However, additionally we have also implemented a first prototype for achieving process provenance, which is based on the VRESCo Composition Engine (Rosenberg et al., 2009). Compositions in VRESCo are defined in a domain-specific language called Vienna Composition Language (VCL). The overall idea is to define functional and QoS constraints which can make use of constraint hierarchies by leveraging hard (i.e., required) and soft (i.e., optional) constraints. The Composition Engine then tries to find an optimal solution for these constraints semi-automatically. Therefore, data flow analysis is applied to generate a structured composition model, while both constraint programming and integer programming can be used for solving the optimization problem. Finally, the optimized compositions are executed using Windows Workflow Foundation (WF) (Shukla & Schmidt, 2006).

The basic idea of process provenance is to trace the history of workflows (e.g., which services have been executed, workflow status,

Figure 4. Provenance graph

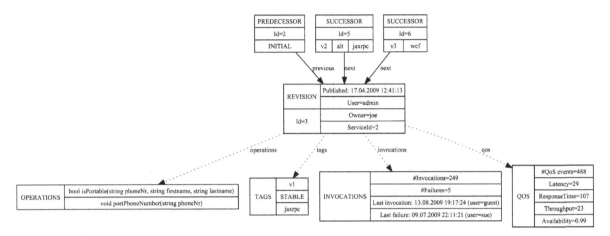

etc.). For this reason, WF provides a powerful tool called the WF Tracking Service (Jaganathan, 2007), which enables hooking into the workflow engine to receive certain events. In general, WF provides three types of such events. *Workflow events* capture the life-cycle of workflow instances (Created, Completed, Idle, Suspended, Resumed, Persisted, Unloaded, Loaded, Exception, Terminated, Aborted, Changed and Started). *Activity events* describe the status of individual activity instances (Executing, Closed, Compensating, Faulting and Canceling). Finally, *User events* can be used to track business- or workflow-specific data. In addition, tracking profiles are used to define event filters, while matching events are sent to the users using tracking channels.

To integrate these workflow events into VRESCo, we have implemented our own Tracking Service and Tracking Channel as shown in Figure 5. The Tracking Service reads the tracking profile from a configuration file (not shown in the figure) and listens to all events that match this profile (in our case, we listen to all WF events). When such events are published by the workflow engine, they are sent to the Tracking Channel and finally forwarded to the Eventing Service that feeds them into Esper. In addition to notifying interested subscribers, the events are persisted into the Event Database. As a result, users can subscribe to and search for workflow events in the same way as for all other events provided by the runtime.

Process provenance is provided since the workflow events are persisted in the Event Database. Therefore, it is easily possible to query the information inherent to these events (e.g., which workflow instances have been started, which services have been executed as part of the workflow activities, etc.). Furthermore, user events could be leveraged to implement data provenance (i.e., which data has been produced or consumed by the workflow activities). This is one potential extension to the presented provenance approach, which is left for future work.

PROVENANCE SECURITY CONSIDERATIONS

In the previous section, we have described our service provenance approach. One of the main issues in provenance systems is to build appropriate mechanisms for providing authentication and authorization. This is crucial since provenance information is often sensitive and access should be only granted to specific users. However, these security issues are often neglected in current provenance approaches (Tan et al., 2006). In this

Figure 5. Process provenance architecture

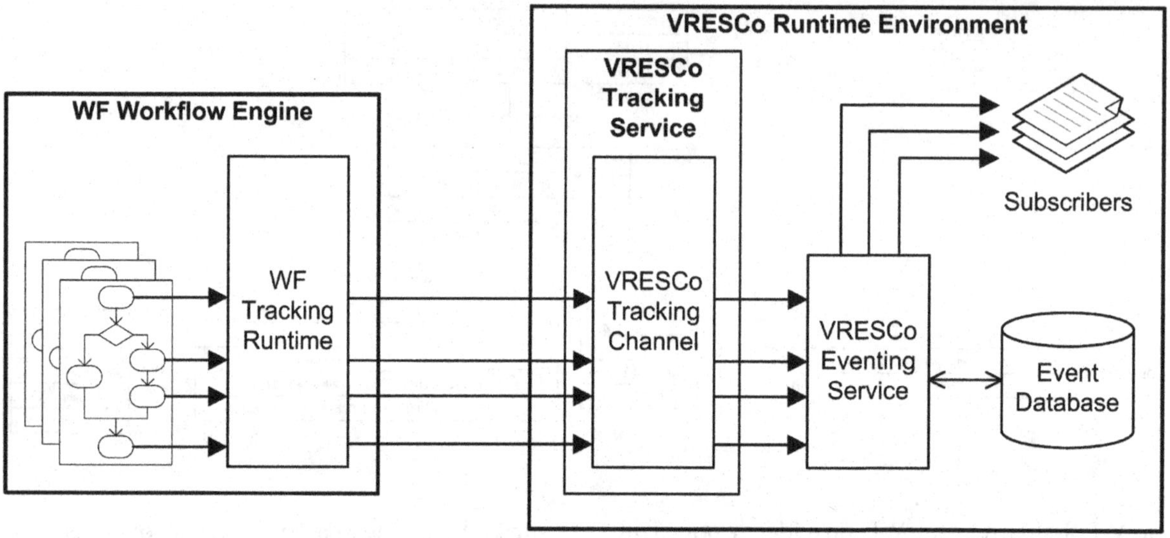

section, we describe the different access control mechanisms which have been integrated into the VRESCo runtime environment.

Client Authentication

Authentication mechanisms generally aim at confirming the identity of users or objects. The VRESCo runtime is not targeted at public Web services but focuses on enterprise scenarios. In these settings, security issues often play a crucial role since only specific clients should be able to access internal services and resources. Therefore, it is important to first authenticate these clients before authorization mechanisms can be applied successfully. Furthermore, this authentication mechanism must ensure the integrity of the service provenance information captured by the service runtime. If clients are not authenticated then bogus provenance information could be entered into the system.

For this reason, a dedicated User Management Service has been implemented, that is responsible for maintaining all users known to the runtime. In this service, users are assigned to specific user groups that allow fine-grained access control

policies. For every user, the runtime maintains several properties (e.g., first name, last name, company, etc.) and the needed user credentials such as username and password.

Figure 6 shows the VRESCo authentication mechanism by using a typical invocation of some core service (e.g., Publishing or Metadata Service). As shown in Figure 1, all client invocations of VRESCo core services pass the Access Control Layer (ACL). Basically, authentication is then done twofold: using certificates and username/password credentials. Before any VRESCo core service can be invoked, a secure communication channel between service requester and VRESCo host must be established. This is done using X.509 certificates and HTTPS (i.e., X.509 certificates are associated with every port where VRESCo core services are running). However, the channel can only be established if both communication parties trust each other's certificates. Therefore, in step 1 and 2, the certificates of client and service are verified by the other side (we assume that the certificates are exchanged before the first invocation). The client has to trust the service certificate, while the Certificate Validator verifies if the client's certificate is in the Certificate Store (step 3).

If this is not the case, an exception is returned to the requester and the requested core service is not executed. It should be noted that the use of certificates additionally enables to encrypt all messages which is provided as built-in functionality by the WCF platform (Peiris et al., 2007).

In addition to certificates, VRESCo provides authentication using username and password which follows the WS-Security specification (OASIS, 2006). For every invocation, these credentials are attached to the SOAP message by the Client Library (step 4). For instance, this can also be seen in the first two lines of Listing 1 and Listing 2, where username and password have to be specified when creating proxies for the VRESCo core services. The Username/Password Validator then verifies if these credentials match to the one's stored in the Registry Database (step 5). As before, if they do not match, an exception is returned to the requester and the requested core service is not executed. As a result, after executing steps 1 to 5 client and service are authenticated and both sides know the identity of the communicating party. In the next section, we show how authorization is provided in VRESCo.

Claim-Based Authorization

Authentication and authorization for Web services have been addressed by various research efforts (e.g., Bhargavan et al., 2004; Bhargavan et al., 2008; Felix & Ribeiro, 2007) and specifications such as WS-Security (OASIS, 2006). In general, authorization is often done role-based where different roles are assigned to users, while security privileges are directly granted to these roles. In our work, we follow the concept of claim-based authorization that goes one step further: Claims can be defined on different resources (for instance, following the well-known CRUD operations *Create*, *Read*, *Update* & *Delete*) for users and user groups. Users are allowed to access these resources if they provide the needed claim in their credentials. This

includes all user claims that belong to a specific user. Furthermore, users inherit the claims that are assigned to their user group.

Table 2 shows resources and their claims that have been implemented in VRESCo. We distinguish between resource- and instance-level claims: Resource-level claims apply to all instances of a resource (e.g., *Read* on all *services*), while instance-level claims refer only to a specific instance of a resource (e.g., *Update* on user *U1*).

Besides having claims for the core resources *Service*, *Category*, *User* and *User Group*, the resource *Claim* defines who is allowed to create, modify and delete custom claims. Therefore, users can dynamically add claims for other resources (e.g., regarding the service metadata model). Finally, claims on *QoS* can be used to restrict access to QoS information. In addition, the *PermissionManager* claim enables to assign service instance-level claims to other users or groups. This is of particular interest when service owners want to pass claims for their services to others. Besides assigning claims manually, some claims are generated automatically when users and resources are created.

Similar to users and user groups, claims are also managed by the User Management Service and stored in the Registry Database. The VRESCo core services use the ACL (as shown in Figure 6) to verify if the client has the required claims to invoke the current operation. After clients are authenticated, their identity is known and the Claim Checker can verify the claims stored in the database (step 6). If the claims are present the operation can finally be executed (step 7), otherwise an appropriate exception is returned to the requester. To give a concrete example for such claims, the Publishing Service requires the *Create* claim on resource *Service*, while the Query Engine requires the *Read* claim on the queried resources (i.e., either the resource-level *Read* claim on the queried resources or the instance-level *Read* claim on instances returned by the Query Engine).

Figure 6. Authentication and authorization in VRESCo

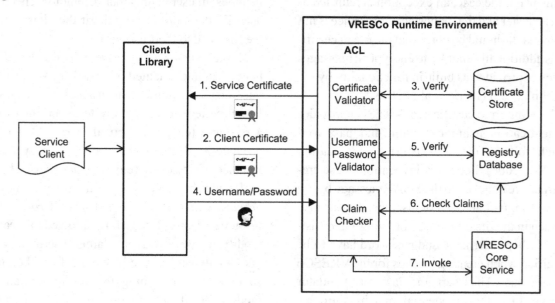

Event Visibility

In the first version of the VRESCo Event Engine, events were visible to all users. However, this can be problematic in business scenarios, especially regarding service provenance: For instance, a company might allow a partner company to see all events concerning service management and QoS, while events related to binding and invocation of services are only visible for employees.

(Mühl et al., 2006) discuss security issues in event-based systems and present access control techniques such as access control lists, capabilities, and role-based access control (RBAC). Access control lists represent a simple way to define the

Table 2. Resource claims

Resource	Resource-level	Instance-level
Category	●	
Service	●	●
User	●	●
User Group	●	
Claim	●	●
QoS	●	

permissions of different users for a specific security object. Capabilities define the permissions of a specific user for different security objects. Finally, RBAC extends capabilities by allowing users to have several roles which are abstractions between users and permissions, and grant permissions directly to these roles. (Fiege et al., 2002) use the notion of scopes to define visibility boundaries for events (i.e., only subscribers within specific scopes can access events).

In the VRESCo Event Notification Engine, we have integrated an access control mechanism following RBAC which is similar to the idea of scopes. As mentioned above, users are divided into different user groups. Access control can then be defined based on users and user groups according to the event visibilities shown in Table 3.

It should be noted that in our work the publisher defines the visibility of events. While one publisher may not want that other users can see events ("PUBLISHER"), another may not define any restrictions on events ("ALL"). Furthermore, it is possible to grant only specific users access to events (e.g., "joe"). RBAC is then introduced by either granting access to all users of a spe-

Table 3. Event visibility

Event Visibility	Description
ALL	Events are visible to all users
GROUP	Events are visible to users within the publisher's group
PUBLISHER	Events are visible to the publisher only
<:GroupName>	Events are visible to all users within a specific group
<Username>	Events are visible to a specific user only

cific group (e.g., ":admins"), or all users within the same group as the publisher ("GROUP").

Besides defining event visibilities for different users and groups, more fine-grained access control is provided by allowing users to specify event visibilities for different event types. In VRESCo events are classified in an event type hierarchy (e.g., *ServiceInvokedEvent* inherits from *ServiceManagementEvent*). If no event visibility is defined for a specific event type, the engine takes the visibility of the parent type, or the default visibility if none exists at all (i.e., "ALL" for the base type *VRESCoEvent*). Event visibility is then enforced by the Notification Manager.

Figure 7 gives an example of a *ServiceInvokedEvent*. As highlighted in this figure, the Notification Engine attaches event visibility and publisher to the event. When events match to subscriptions, the Notification Manager gets the name of the subscriber from the corresponding listener and extracts publisher name and event visibility from the notification payload. Based on this information, the Notification Manager can verify if the current event is visible to the corresponding subscriber, and either forwards or discards it.

Selective Service Provenance

The mechanisms introduced in this section provide fine-grained access control for service provenance information stored in the runtime. This guarantees that only authenticated and authorized users are able to access this information. It should be noted that this mechanism has an interesting side effect: different users can come to different conclusions regarding the provenance of services. In other words, two users (with different claims and event visibilities) may have different views on the same service.

To give a concrete example, we consider the provenance graph shown in Figure 4. This graph was generated for some user that had access to all provenance information (e.g., user *admin*). However, claims and event visibility may restrict the visible information for specific users. For instance, users without the resource-level *Read* claim on *Service* or without the instance-level *Read* claim on *Service 1* clearly would not receive any provenance information about this service. To give an example for event visibility, if the visibility of Binding/Invocation events is set to *telco1*, then other users might not see the *INVOCATIONS* node in the graph. This can be further refined, by granting user *telco1* access to *ServiceInvokedEvents* but restrict access to *ServiceInvocationFailedEvents* only to users within the user group *admins*. In that case, only information about successful invocations would be shown in the graph.

Another interesting feature enabled by event visibility was applied to QoS events. In our ongoing work, we have integrated an additional QoS Monitor into VRESCo. In contrast to the existing client-side monitor it represents a server-side approach using WCF Performance Counters (Peiris et al., 2007). By using two different event publishers for these two monitors, event visibility can be defined so that specific users see only events from one monitor, either monitors, or no QoS events at all. This is useful since client- and server-side monitoring results often differ for some QoS attributes (e.g., availability), while other attributes can only be measured by one approach (e.g., client-perceived response time of Web service requests).

Figure 7. Event visibility example

```
┌─────────────────────────────────────────┐
│         ServiceInvokedEvent               │
├─────────────────────────────────────────┤
│ -Id = 4711                                │
│ -RevisionId = 17                          │
│ -OperationId = 63                         │
│ -InvocationInfo = '128.131.172.242'       │
│ -Timestamp = '18.06.2009 13:01:47'        │
│ -Publisher = 'joe'                        │
│ -Visibility = ':admins'                   │
└─────────────────────────────────────────┘
```

EVALUATION

The evaluation in this section is twofold: Firstly, we discuss the usefulness and advantages of our work based on the motivating example. Then, we show some performance results of our approach.

Discussion

First of all, we want to highlight that there are several use cases for service provenance, which are of interest for both service consumers and service providers. On the one hand, service providers often want to know if their services perform as expected regarding various QoS attributes (e.g., response time, failure rate, throughput, etc.) or the expected number of service invocations. Otherwise, corrective actions may be taken in order to achieve the expected values. On the other hand, service provenance information is also of particular importance for service consumers, especially when it comes to service selection. As described in the motivation, if there are multiple candidate services, service consumers may want to take a look at the history of these alternatives. If a service had good performance during the last year it may be more trustworthy than services which have been recently published. Furthermore, our service mediation approach can be used to dynamically rebind to alternative services if the current service is removed from the runtime or does not fulfill the requirements any longer. As a result, provenance

information can be used for both service selection and dynamic rebinding.

Furthermore, security issues are often neglected in current provenance approaches. Therefore, one concern of our approach is the integrity of provenance information, as well as appropriate access control mechanisms. Firstly, we want to ensure that all provenance information is accurate which requires that all users within VRESCo are authenticated. Secondly, and this is even more important, only authorized users must be able to access services and metadata stored in the registry database. This has been implemented by the claim-based access control mechanism. Finally, considering provenance information we find it crucial that producers of provenance information are able to define who is authorized to see which piece of information (i.e., different clients may have different views of the same service). Therefore, we have introduced the notion of event visibility to provide fine-grained access control to events.

Performance Evaluation

In this section, we describe the performance of our system. The following experiments have been executed on an Intel Xeon Dual CPU X5450 with 3.0 GHz and 32GB RAM running on Windows Server 2007 SP1 and .NET v3.5, while MySQL v5.1 has been used as database. Furthermore, all test results represent the average of 10 repetitive runs.

The performance of our provenance approach is depicted in Figure 8. It illustrates how long it takes to generate the provenance graph shown in Figure 4 depending on the number of events that have to be considered. The red and black lines illustrate how long it takes to build the graph (i.e., generate the corresponding GraphViz DOT file) and render it (i.e., transform the DOT file into the desired format such as PNG) once all necessary information has been queried from the Registry Database. The lines are almost constant, which is due to the grouping of different events in the graph. The green and blue lines depict the query performance by distinguishing whether event visibility must be evaluated. This is done by using two query issuers with different event visibility: the first is user *admin* who can access all events, while only 25% of all events are visible to the second user (i.e., the remaining 75% have to be sorted out for this user). The graph shows that our approach scales linearly for several thousands of events and that the provenance queries perform well (e.g., about 1s for 20000 events). Furthermore, it can be seen that the overhead introduced when considering event visibility is acceptable (e.g., 13% for 20000 events, and 25% for 40000 events which is not shown in the figure). All results were measured on the server-side, since the client's SOAP request to the Query Engine heavily depends on the network latency. In general, the performance of the Query Engine is comparable to HQL and SQL, which has been shown in more detail in our previous work (Michlmayr et al., May 2009).

Next, we have evaluated the performance of the Event Notification Engine by using a simulation of QoS events to measure the throughput of the actual matching between events and subscriptions. These events were continuously published internally, while we increased the number of subscribers and varied the percentage of matching subscriptions (we have chosen values between 0% and 20% since higher values are unusual in typical settings). Finally, we measured how many events can be processed per second. It should be noted that we do not consider the time needed to actually notify external subscribers, since this is done by a dedicated delivery thread pool and varies significantly depending on the notification mechanism, such as email or Web services.

The results are depicted in Figure 9. It can be seen that the throughput clearly decreases with the number of matching subscriptions. The throughput starts about 2000 events per second without subscriptions and converges to about 200-300 events per second for 2000 subscriptions. Clearly, the percentage of matching subscriptions also slightly

Figure 8. Provenance performance

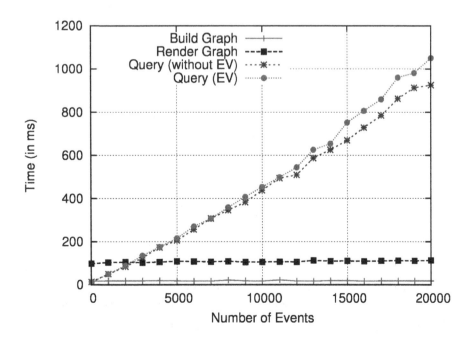

Figure 9. Eventing throughput

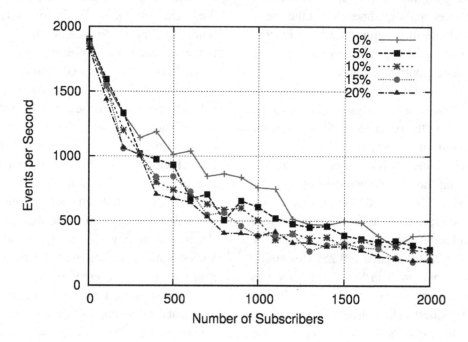

Figure 10. Eventing overhead

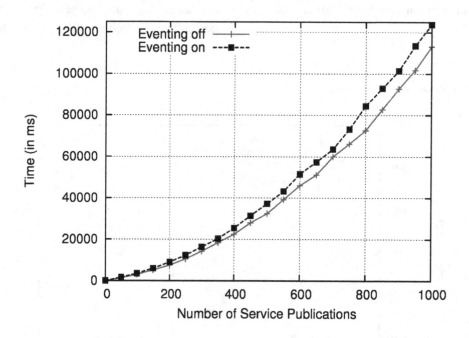

influences the throughput since more listeners have to be invoked. However, the measured throughput is still higher than the expected number of events in typical VRESCo environments.

Finally, the overhead of the Event Notification Engine is also of interest. To show this, we have measured the eventing overhead when services are published into the runtime. To be more concrete, we simulated a certain number of sequential Web service publications both with and without eventing support. The results depicted in Figure 10 show that the overhead is 10-15% in this setting, which seems acceptable when considering the possibilities opened up by the VRESCo eventing mechanism. It should be noted, however, that eventing support can be easily disabled in the configuration if not desired.

CONCLUSION AND FUTURE WORK

Provenance of electronic data has been an active research topic in the past years. In service-oriented systems, the main focus was on data provenance, meaning the origin and history of data produced by some processes. In this work, we have presented an approach for service provenance. Our approach is integrated into the VRESCo runtime where several security mechanisms have been implemented to guarantee access control and integrity of service provenance information. Since our work is based on runtime events, different event visibilities have been introduced to restrict access to these events. Provenance information can be obtained using provenance queries, or as notifications to provenance subscriptions. Furthermore, provenance graphs can be used to visualize the provenance information of a service. We have shown the performance and applicability of our approach for both service consumers and service providers based on some illustrative examples.

For future work, we consider to integrate data provenance produced by the VRESCo Composition Engine which is part of our ongoing research (Rosenberg et al., 2009). Furthermore, in addition to the current graph representation we envision to visualize provenance information regarding QoS and binding/invocation in dashboards, as often done in business activity monitoring.

ACKNOWLEDGMENT

The research leading to these results has received funding from the European Community's Seventh Framework Programme FP7/2007-2013 under grant agreement 215483 (S-Cube). Additionally, we would like to thank our students Andreas Huber, Thomas Laner and Christian Marek for their technical contributions to VRESCo.

REFERENCES

W3C. (2006, March). *Web Services Eventing (WS-Eventing)*. Retrieved November 10, 2009, from http://www.w3.org/Submission/WS-Eventing/

Bhargavan, K., Fournet, C., & Gordon, A. D. (2004, January 14-16). A Semantics for Web Services Authentication. In *Proceedings of the 31st ACM SIGPLAN-SIGACT Symposium on Principles of Programming Languages (POPL'04)*, Venice, Italy (pp. 198-209). New York: ACM.

Bhargavan, K., Fournet, C., & Gordon, A. D. (2008). Verifying Policy-Based Web Services Security. In *Proceedings of the ACM Transactions on Programming Languages and Systems (TOPLAS)*, *30*(6), 1-59.

Chen, L., Yang, X., & Tao, F. (2006, December 18-22). A Semantic Web Service Based Approach for Augmented Provenance. In *Proceedings of the 2006 IEEE/WIC/ACM International Conference on Web Intelligence (WI'06)*, Hong Kong, China (pp. 594-600). Washington, DC: IEEE Computer Society.

Curbera, F., Doganata, Y. N., Martens, A., Mukhi, N., & Slominski, A. (2008, November 12-14). Business Provenance - A Technology to Increase Traceability of End-to-End Operations. In *Proceedings of the 16th International Conference on Cooperative Information Systems (CoopIS'08)*, Monterrey, Mexico (pp. 100-119). New York: Springer.

EsperTech Inc. (2009). *Esper*. Retrieved November 10, 2009, from http://esper.codehaus.org/

Felix, P., & Ribeiro, C. (2007, November 2). A Scalable and Flexible Web Services Authentication Model. In *Proceedings of the 2007 ACM workshop on Secure web services (SWS'07)*, Fairfax, VA (pp. 66-72). New York: ACM.

Fiege, L., Mezini, M., Mühl, G., & Buchmann, A. P. (2002, June 10-14). Engineering Event-Based Systems with Scopes. In *Proceedings of the 16th European Conference on Object-Oriented Programming (ECOOP'02)*, Málaga, Spain (pp. 309-333). London, UK: Springer Verlag.

Foster, I., Vöckler, J., Wilde, M., & Zhao, Y. (2002, July 24-26). Chimera: A Virtual Data System for Representing, Querying, and Automating Data Derivation. In *Proceedings of the 14th International Conference on Scientific and Statistical Database Management (SSDBM'02)*, Edinburgh, Scotland, UK (pp. 37-46). Washington, DC: IEEE Computer Society.

Gansner, E. R., & North, S. C. (2000). An Open Graph Visualization System and its Applications to Software Engineering. *Software, Practice & Experience, 30*(11), 1203–1233. doi:10.1002/1097-024X(200009)30:11<1203::AID-SPE338>3.0.CO;2-N

Groth, P., Jiang, S., Miles, S., Munroe, S., Tan, V., Tsasakou, S., et al. (2006). *An Architecture for Provenance Systems* (Tech. Rep.). Southhampton, England: University of Southampton. Retrieved November 10, 2009, from http://eprints.ecs.soton.ac.uk/12023/1/provenanceArchitecture7.pdf

Heinis, T., & Alonso, G. (2008, June 10-12). Efficient Lineage Tracking for Scientific Workflows. In *Proceedings of the 2008 ACM SIGMOD International Conference on Management of Data (SIGMOD'08)*, Vancouver, Canada (pp. 1007-1018). New York: ACM.

Jaganathan, R. (2007, January). *Windows Workflow Foundation: Tracking Services Deep Dive*. Retrieved November 10, 2009, from http://msdn.microsoft.com/en-us/library/bb264458(VS.80).aspx

Leitner, P., Michlmayr, A., Rosenberg, F., & Dustdar, S. (2008, July 8-11). End-to-End Versioning Support for Web Services. In *Proceedings of the International Conference on Services Computing (SCC'08)*, Honolulu, HI (pp. 59-66). Washington, DC: IEEE Computer Society.

Leitner, P., Rosenberg, F., & Dustdar, S. (2009, May/June). DAIOS – Efficient Dynamic Web Service Invocation. *IEEE Internet Computing, 13*(3), 30–38. doi:10.1109/MIC.2009.57

Leitner, P., Rosenberg, F., Michlmayr, A., Huber, A., & Dustdar, S. (2009, August). A Mediator-Based Approach to Resolving Interface Heterogeneity of Web Services. In W. Binder & S. Dustdar (Eds.), Emerging Web Service Technologies (Vol. 3, pp. 55–74). Basel, Switzerland: Birkhäuser.

Michlmayr, A., Rosenberg, F., Leitner, P., & Dustdar, S. (2008, July 1-4). Advanced Event Processing and Notifications in Service Runtime Environments. In *Proceedings of the 2nd International Conference on Distributed Event-Based Systems (DEBS'08)*, Rome, Italy (pp. 115-125). New York: ACM.

Michlmayr, A., Rosenberg, F., Leitner, P., & Dustdar, S. (2009, May). *End-to-End Support for QoS-Aware Service Selection, Invocation and Mediation in VRESCo* (Tech. Rep. No. TUV-1841-2009-03). Vienna, Austria: Vienna University of Technology. Retrieved November 10, 2009, from http://www.infosys.tuwien.ac.at/Staff/michlmayr/papers/TUV-1841-2009-03.pdf

Michlmayr, A., Rosenberg, F., Leitner, P., & Dustdar, S. (2009, July 6-10). Service Provenance in QoS-Aware Web Service Runtimes. In *Proceedings of the 7th IEEE International Conference on Web Services (ICWS'09),* Los Angeles, CA (pp. 115-122). Washington, DC: IEEE Computer Society.

Michlmayr, A., Rosenberg, F., Platzer, C., Treiber, M., & Dustdar, S. (2007, September 3). Towards Recovering the Broken SOA Triangle – A Software Engineering Perspective. In *Proceedings of the 2nd International Workshop on Service Oriented Software Engineering (IW-SOSWE'07),* Dubrovnik, Croatia (pp. 22-28). New York: ACM.

Microsoft Cooperation. (2009). *Quickgraph.* Retrieved November 10, 2009, from http://www.codeplex.com/quickgraph

Moreau, L., Freire, J., Futrelle, J., McGrath, R., Mycrs, J., & Paulson, P. (2007). *The Open Provenance Model* (Tech. Rep.). Southampton, UK: University of Southampton. Retrieved November 11, 2009, from http://eprints.ecs.soton.ac.uk/14979/1/opm.pdf

Moreau, L., Groth, P., Miles, S., Vazquez-Salceda, J., Ibbotson, J., & Jiang, S. (2008). The Provenance of Electronic Data. *Communications of the ACM, 51*(4), 52–58. doi:10.1145/1330311.1330323

Mühl, G., Fiege, L., & Pietzuch, P. (2006). *Distributed Event-Based Systems.* New York: Springer Verlag.

OASIS. (2005, May). *ebXML Registry Services and Protocols.* Retrieved November 10, 2009, from http://oasis-open.org/committees/regrep/

OASIS. (2005, February). *Universal Description, Discovery and Integration (UDDI).* Retrieved November 10, 2009, from http://oasis-open.org/committees/uddi-spec/

OASIS. (2006, February). *WS-Security v1.1.* Retrieved November 10, 2009, from http://www.oasis-open.org/committees/wss/

Papazoglou, M. P., Traverso, P., Dustdar, S., & Leymann, F. (2007). Service-Oriented Computing: State of the Art and Research Challenges. *IEEE Computer, 40*(11), 38–45.

Peiris, C., Mulder, D., Cicoria, S., Bahree, A., & Pathak, N. (2007). *Pro WCF: Practical Microsoft SOA Implementation.* Berkeley, CA: Apress.

Rajbhandari, S., & Walker, D. W. (2006, September 25-28). Incorporating Provenance in Service Oriented Architecture. In *Proceedings of the International Conference on Next Generation Web Services Practices (NWeSP'06),* Seoul, Korea (pp. 33-40). Washington, DC: IEEE Computer Society.

Red Hat Inc. (2009). *Hibernate.* Retrieved November 10, 2009, from https://www.hibernate.org/

Rosenberg, F., Celikovic, P., Michlmayr, A., Leitner, P., & Dustdar, S. (2009, September 1-4). An End-to-End Approach for QoS-Aware Service Composition. In *Proceedings of the 13th IEEE International Enterprise Computing Conference (EDOC'09),* Auckland, New Zealand (pp. 151-160). Washington, DC: IEEE Computer Society.

Rosenberg, F., Leitner, P., Michlmayr, A., & Dustdar, S. (2008, September 16). Integrated Metadata Support for Web Service Runtimes. In *Proceedings of the Middleware for Web Services Workshop (MWS'08),* Munich, Germany (pp. 361-368). Washington, DC: IEEE Computer Society.

Rosenberg, F., Platzer, C., & Dustdar, S. (2006, September 18-22). Bootstrapping Performance and Dependability Attributes of Web Services. In *Proceedings of the International Conference on Web Services (ICWS'06),* Chicago, IL (pp. 205-212). Washington, DC: IEEE Computer Society.

Shukla, D., & Schmidt, B. (2006). *Essential Windows Workflow Foundation*. Reading, MA: Addison-Wesley.

Simmhan, Y. L., Plale, B., & Gannon, D. (2005). A Survey of Data Provenance in e-Science. *SIGMOD Record, 34*(3), 31–36. doi:10.1145/1084805.1084812

Simmhan, Y. L., Plale, B., & Gannon, D. (2008). Karma2: Provenance Management for Data Driven Workflows. *International Journal of Web Services Research, 5*(3), 1–22.

Tan, V., Groth, P. T., Miles, S., Jiang, S., Munroe, S., Tsasakou, S., et al. (2006, May 3-5). Security Issues in a SOA-Based Provenance System. In *Proceedings of the International Provenance and Annotation Workshop (IPAW'06)*, Chicago, IL (pp. 203-211). New York: Springer.

Tsai, W.-T., Wei, X., Zhang, D., Paul, R., Chen, Y., & Chung, J.-Y. (2007, March 21-23). A New SOA Data-Provenance Framework. In *Proceedings of the 8th International Symposium on Autonomous Decentralized Systems (ISADS'07)*, Sedona, AZ (pp. 105-112). Washington, DC: IEEE Computer Society.

Weerawarana, S., Curbera, F., Leymann, F., Storey, T., & Ferguson, D. F. (2005). *Web Services Platform Architecture: SOAP, WSDL, WS-Policy, WS-Addressing, WS-BPEL, WS-Reliable Messaging, and More*. Upper Saddle River, NJ: Prentice Hall.

This work was previously published in the International Journal of Web Services Research, Volume 7, Issue 2, edited by Liang-Jie (LJ) Zhang, pp. 65-86, copyright 2010 by IGI Publishing (an imprint of IGI Global).

Compilation of References

Aalst, W. M. P. (1998). The application of Petri Nets to workflow management. *The Journal of Circuits, Systems and Computers, 8*(1), 21–66.

Aalst, W. M. P., & Verbeek, H. (2008). Process Mining in Web Services: The WebSphere Case. *IEEE Data Eng. Bull., 31*(3), 45–48.

Abbes, S., & Benveniste, A. (2006). True-concurrency Probabilistic Models: Branching Cells and Distributed Probabilities for Event Structures. *Information and Computation, 204*(2), 231–274. doi:10.1016/j.ic.2005.10.001

Adhitya, A., Srinivasan, R., & Karimi, I. A. (2007). A Model-based Rescheduling Framework for Managing Abnormal Supply Chain Events. *Computers & Chemical Engineering, 31*(5/6), 496–518. doi:10.1016/j.compchemeng.2006.07.002

Aggarwal, R., Verma, K., Miller, J. A., & Milnor, W. (2004). Constraint Driven Web Service Composition in METEOR-S. IEEE International Conference on Services Computing, 23-30.

Aktas, M. S., et al. (2008b, December 3-5). Information federation in Grids. In *Proceedings of the 4th International Conference on Semantics, Knowledge and Grid (SKG 2008)*, Beijing, China. Aktas, M. S. (n.d.). *Fault Tolerant High Performance Information Service - FTHPIS - Hybrid WS-Context Service*. Retrieved July 2009 from http://www.opengrids.org/wscontext

Aktas, M. S. (2004). iSERVO: Implementing the International Solid Earth Research Virtual Observatory by Integrating Computational Grid and Geographical Information Web Services. *Pure and Applied Geophysics, 163*(11-12), 2281–2296. doi:10.1007/s00024-006-0137-8

Aktas, M. S. (2008a). XML Metadata Services. *Concurrency and Computation, 20*(7), 801–823. doi:10.1002/cpe.1276

Alam, M., Seifert, J., & Zhang, X. (2007). *A model-driven framework for trusted computing based systems*.

Alam, M., Zhang, X., Nauman, M., & Ali, T. (2008). *Behavioral attestation for web services (BA4WS)*.

Alam, M., Zhang, X., Nauman, M., Ali, T., & Seifert, I. (2008). *Model-based behavioral attestation*.

Aldeco-Perez, R., & Moreau, L. (2008, September). Provenance-based Auditing of Private Data Use. In *Proceedings of the BCS International Academic Research Conference, Visions of Computer Science*.

Ali, A. S., Ludwig, S. A., & Rana, O. F. (2005, November 14-16). A Cognitive Trust-based Approach for Web Services Discovery and Selection. In *Proceedings of the 3rd European Conference on Web Services (ECOWS)*, Växjö, Sweden (pp. 38-40).

Alves, A., et al. (2006). Web Services Business Process Execution Language, version 2.0. *OASIS Public Draft*. Retrieved November 16, 2006, from http://docs.oasis-open.org/wsbpel/2.0/

Anderson, A. H. (2004). An introduction to the Web Services Policy Language (WSPL). In *Proceedings of the Fifth IEEE International Workshop on Policies for Distributed Systems and Networks: POLICY 2004* (pp. 189-192).

Anderson, A., & Balasubramanian, D. (2005). *XACML-Based Web Services Policy Constraint Language (WS-PolicyConstraints)*. Santa Clara, CA: Sun Microsystems.

Anderson, S., Bohren, J., Boubez, T., Chanliau, M., Della-Libera, G., Dixon, B., et al. (2005). *Web Services Trust Language (WS-Trust).* IBM.

Andrews, T., Curbera, F., Dholakia, H., Goland, Y., Klein, J., & Leymann, F. (2003). *Business Process Execution Language for Web Services, Version 1.1. Standards proposal by BEA Systems.* International Business Machines Corporation, and Microsoft Corporation.

Ankolekar, A., Burstein, M., et al. (2002). DAML-S: Web Service Description for the Semantic Web. In *Proceedings of the 1st International Semantic Web Conference (ISWC), Sardinia, Italy.*

Ankolenkar, A., Paolucci, M., Srinivasan, N., & Sycara, K. (2004). *The OWL-S coalition* (Tech. Rep. OWL-S 1.1). OWL.

Aoyama, M., Weerawarana, S., Maruyama, H., Szyperski, C., Sullivan, K., & Lea, D. (2002). Web services engineering: promises and challenges. In *Proceedings of the International Conference on Software Engineering* (pp. 647-648).

Ardagna, D., & Pernici, B. (2007). Adaptive service composition in flexible processes. *IEEE Transactions on Software Engineering, 33*(6), 369–384. doi:10.1109/TSE.2007.1011

Arkin, A., Askary, S., Bloch, B., & Curbera, F. (2004, December). *Web services business process execution language version 2.0* (Tech. Rep. OASIS).

Arpinar, I. B., Zhang, R., Aleman-Meza, B., & Maduko, A. (2005). Ontology-driven web services composition platform. *Inf. Syst. E-Business Management, 3*(2), 175199.

Artail, H., & Al-Asadi, H. (2006). A Cooperative and Adaptive System for Caching Web Service Responses in MANETs. In *Proceedings of the International Conference on Web Services* (pp. 339-346).

Atkinson, B., Della-Libera, G., Hada, S., Hondo, M., Hallam-Baker, P., Klein, J., et al. (2002). *Web Services Security (WS-Security). Version, 1.* IBM.

Atluri, V., & Warner, J. (2005). Supporting conditional delegation in secure workflow management systems. In *Proceedings of the Tenth ACM Symposium on Access Control Models and Technologies* (pp. 49-58).

Aura, T. (2001). Distributed access-rights management with delegation certificates. In *secure internet programming* (LNCS 1603, pp. 211-235).

Avizienis, A., Laprie, J.-C., Randell, B., & Landwehr, C. (2004). Basic Concepts and Taxonomy of Dependable and Secure Computing. *IEEE Transactions on Dependable and Secure Computing, 1*(1), 11–33. doi:10.1109/TDSC.2004.2

Baader, F., & Nutt, W. (2003). In *the Description Logic Handbook: Theory, Implementation, and Applications.*

Baader, F., Sertkaya, B., & Turhan, A.-Y. (2004). Computing the least common subsumer w.r.t. a background terminology. In *Proceedings of the DL.*

Baeza-Yates, R., & Ribeiro-Neto, B. (1999). *Modern Information Retrieval.* New York: ACM Press.

Bajaj, S., Box, D., Chappell, D., Curbera, F., Daniels, G., Hallam-Baker, P., et al. (2004). *Web Services Policy Framework (WS-Policy).* Retrieved from http://www-106.ibm. com/developerworks/library/specification/ws-polfram

Bansal, S., & Vidal, J. M. (2003). Matchmaking of Web Services Based on the DAML-S Service Model. In *Proceedings of the International joint conference on Autonomous Agents and Multi-Agent Systems (AAMAS'03)* (pp. 926-927).

Barka, E. S., & Sandhu, R. S. (2000). *A role-based delegation model and some extensions.* Paper presented at the 23rd National Information Systems Security Conference.

Barr, J., & Kearney, B. (2001). *syndic8 feeds repository.* Retrieved from http://www.syndic8.com

Barros, A., Dumas, M., & Oaks, P. (2005, March). *Critical overview of the Web services choreography description language (ws-cdl).* Retrieved from http://www.bptrends.com

Barth, A., Mitchell, J., Datta, A., & Sundaram, S. (2007). Privacy and Utility in Business Processes. In *Proceedings of the 2007 Computer Security Foundations Symposium.* Washington, DC: IEEE.

Belhajjame, K., Embury, S. M., Paton, N. W., Stevens, R., & Globe, C. A. (2006). *Automatic Annotation of Web Services based on Workflow Definitions.*

Bellur, U., & Bondre, S. (2006, April 23-27). xSpace: a Tuple Space for XML and its Application in Orchestration of Web Services. In *Proceedings of the 21st ACM symposium on Applied computing (SAC '06)*, Dijon, France (pp. 766-772).

Bellwood, T., Clement, L., & von Riegen, C. (2003). *UDDI Version 3.0.1: UDDI Spec Technical Committee Specification*. Retrieved July 2009 from http://uddi.org/pubs/uddi-v3.0.1-20031014.htm

Ben-Abdallah, H., & Leue, S. (1997). Syntactic detection of process divergence and non-local choice in message sequence charts. In *Proceedings of the 2nd International Workshop on Tools and Algorithms for the Construction and Analysis of Systems*, Enschede, The Netherlands (pp. 259-274).

Benatallah, B., & Motahari-Nezhad, H. R. (2006). Servicemosaic project: modeling, analysis and management of web services interactions. In *Proceedings of the Asia-Pacific conference on Conceptual modeling* (pp. 53-79).

Benatallah, B., Casati, F., Grigori, D., Nezhad, H., & Toumani, F. (2005). Developing Adaptors for Web services Integration. In *Proceedings of the CAiSE*, Porto, Portugal (pp. 415-429).

Benatallah, B., Casati, F., & Toumani, F. (2006). Representing, analysing and managing web service protocols. *Data & Knowledge Engineering, 58*(3), 327–357. doi:10.1016/j.datak.2005.07.006

Benatallah, B., Sheng, Q. Z., & Dumas, M. (2003). The Self-Serve Environment for Web Services Composition. *IEEE Internet Computing, 7*(1). doi:10.1109/MIC.2003.1167338

Bener, A., Ozadali, V., & Ilhan, E. S. (2009). Semantic matchmaker with precondition and effect matching using SWRL. *International Journal of Expert Systems with Applications*, 9371-9377.

Berardi, D., Calvanese, D., Giacomo, G. D., Hull, R., & Mecella, M. (2005b). Automatic composition of Web services in colombo. In A. Cal, D. Calvanese, E. Franconi, M. Lenzerini, & L. Tanca (Eds.), *Proceedings of SEBD* (pp. 815).

Berardi, D., Calvanese, D., Giacomo, G. D., Hull, R., Lenzerini, M., & Mecella, M. (2005a). Modeling data processes for service specifications in colombo. In M. Missiko & A. D. Nicola (Eds.), *Proceedings of EMOI-INTEROP, volume 160 of CEUR Workshop*. Retrieved from CEUR-WS.org

Berardi, D., et al. (2003). Automatic Composition of E-Services That Export Their Behavior. *International Conference on Service Oriented Computing (ICSOC 2003)* (LNCS 2910, pp. 43-58).

Berardi, D., et al. (2005). Automatic Composition of Transition based Semantic Web Services with Messaging. In *Proceedings of the International Conference on Very Large DataBases (VLDB 2005)* (pp. 613-624).

Berbner, R., Spahn, M., Repp, N., Heckmann, O., & Steinmetz, R. (2006). Heuristics for QoS-aware Web Service Composition. In *Proceedings of the ICWS* (pp. 72-82).

Berners-Lee, T., Hendler, J., & Lassila, O. (2001). The semantic web. *Scientific American, 284*(5), 34–43. doi:10.1038/scientificamerican0501-34

Bernstein, A., & Klein, M. (2002). Discovering Services: Towards High-Precision Service Retrieval. In *Proceedings of the Web Services, E-Business, and the Semantic Web* (LNCS 2512, pp. 260-275).

Bernstein, P. (2003). Applying model management to classical meta data problems. In *Proceedings of CIDR* (pp. 209-220).

Bertino, E., Castano, S., & Ferrari, E. (2001). Securing XML documents with Author-X. *IEEE Internet Computing, 5*(3), 21–31. doi:10.1109/4236.935172

Bertino, E., Squicciarini, A. C., Paloscia, I., & Martino, L. (2006). Ws-AC: A fine grained access control system for web services. *World Wide Web (Bussum), 9*(2), 143–171. doi:10.1007/s11280-005-3045-4

Bessani, A. N., Alchieri, E. A. P., Correia, M., & Fraga, J. S. (2008, March 31-April 4). DepSpace: A Byzantine Fault-Tolerant Coordination Service. In *Proceedings of the 3rd ACM SIGOPS/EuroSys European Systems Conference (EuroSys '08)*, Glasgow, Scotland (pp. 163-176).

Bessani, A. N., Correia, M., Fraga, J. S., & Lung, L. C. (2009). Sharing Memory between Byzantine Processes using Policy-enforced Tuple Spaces. *IEEE Transactions on Parallel and Distributed Systems, 20*(3), 419–432. doi:10.1109/TPDS.2008.96

Bhargavan, K., Fournet, C., & Gordon, A. D. (2004, January 14-16). A Semantics for Web Services Authentication. In *Proceedings of the 31st ACM SIGPLAN-SIGACT Symposium on Principles of Programming Languages (POPL'04)*, Venice, Italy (pp. 198-209). New York: ACM.

Bhargavan, K., Fournet, C., & Gordon, A. D. (2008). Verifying Policy-Based Web Services Security. In *Proceedings of the ACM Transactions on Programming Languages and Systems (TOPLAS), 30*(6), 1-59.

Bhatti, R., Bertino, E., & Ghafoor, A. (2005). A trust-based context-aware access control model for web-services. *Distributed and Parallel Databases, 18*(1), 83–105. doi:10.1007/s10619-005-1075-7

Bhoj, P., Singhal, S., & Chutani, S. (2001). SLA Management in Federated Environments. *Computer Networks, 35*(1), 5–24. doi:10.1016/S1389-1286(00)00149-3

Bichier, M., & Lin, K.-J. (2006). Service-Oriented Computing. *IEEE Computer, 39*(3), 99–101.

Bilorusets, R., Bosworth, A., & Box, B. D. (2004). *Web Services Reliable Messaging Protocol (WS-ReliableMessaging)*. IBM.

Birkhok, G. (1993). *Lattice theory* (3rd ed.). Providence, RI: American Mathematical Society.

Bistarelli, S., & Santini, F. (2009). A Nonmonotonic Soft Concurrent Constraint Language for SLA Negotiation. *Electronic Notes in Theoretical Computer Science, 236*, 147–162. doi:10.1016/j.entcs.2009.03.020

Bonatti, P. A., & Festa, P. (2005). On optimal service selection. In Proceedings of the WWW (pp. 530-538).

Bouillard, A., Rosario, S., Benveniste, A., & Haar, S. (2009). *2009 (LNCS 5606* (pp. 263–282). Monotonicity in Service Orchestrations. In Proceedings of Petri Nets.

Bram, C. (2003). Incentives build robustness in bittorrent. In *Proceedings of the First Workshop on the Economics of Peer-to-Peer Systems.*

Brandt, S., Kusters, R., & Turhan, A. (2002). Approximation and difference in description logics. In *Proceedings of the KR* (pp. 203-214).

Bright, D., & Quirchmayr, G. (2004, August 30-September 3). Supporting Web-Based Collaboration between Virtual Enterprise Partners. In *Proceedings of the 15th International Workshop on Database and Expert Systems Applications*, Zaragoza, Spain (pp. 1029-1035).

Brogi, A., Canal, C., Pimentel, E., & Vallecillo, A. (2004). Formalizing Web service choreographies. *Electronic Notes in Theoretical Computer Science, 105*, 73–94. doi:10.1016/j.entcs.2004.05.007

Bultan, T., Fu, X., Hull, R., & Su, J. (2003). Conversation Specification: A New Approach to Design and Analysis of E-Service Composition. In *Proceedings of the International World Wide Web Conference (WWW 2003)* (pp. 403-410).

Bunting, B., Chapman, M., Hurley, O., Little, M., Mischinkinky, J., Newcomer, E., et al. (2003). *Web Services Context (WS-Context) version 1.0.* Retrieved from http://www.arjuna.com/library/specs/ws_caf_1-0/WS-CTX.pdf

Burdett, D., & Kavantzas, N. (2004). The WS-Choreography Model Overview. *W3C Working Draft.* Retrieved March 14, 2004, from http://www.w3.org/TR/ws-chor-model/

Cabrera, L. F., et al. (2005). *Web Services Coordination Specification - version 1.0.* Retrieved August 15, 2005, from http://www-128.ibm.com/developerworks/library/specification/ws-tx/

Cabri, G., Leonardi, L., & Zambonelli, F. (2000). Mobile Agents Coordination Models for Internet Applications. *IEEE Computer, 33*(2), 82–89.

Canfora, G., Di Penta, M., Esposito, R., & Villani, M.-L. (2005). An Approach for QoS-aware Service Composition based on Genetic Algorithms. Genetic and Evolutionary Computation Conference, 1069-1075.

Canfora, G., Penta, M. D., Esposito, R., & Villani, M. L. (2005). An approach for qos-aware service composition based on genetic algorithms. In *Proceedings of the GECCO* (pp. 10691075).

Cardoso, J., Sheth, A. P., Miller, J. A., Arnold, J., & Kochut, K. (2004). Quality of service for workflows and web service processes. *Journal of Web Semantics, 1*(3), 281–308. doi:10.1016/j.websem.2004.03.001

Carminati, B., Ferrari, E., & Hung, P. C. K. (2005). Web service composition: A security perspective. In *Proceedings of the 2005 International Workshop on Challenges in Web Information Retrieval and Integration* (pp. 248-253).

Carminati, B., Ferrari, E., & Hung, P. C. K. (2006). Security conscious web service composition. In *Proceedings of the IEEE International Conference on Web Services* (pp. 489-496)

Carriero, N., & Gelernter, D. (1989). How to Write Parallel Programs: a Guide to the Perplexed. *ACM Computing Surveys, 21*(3), 323–357. doi:10.1145/72551.72553

Carriero, N., & Gelernter, D. (1989). Linda in context. *Communications of the ACM, 32*(4), 444–458. doi:10.1145/63334.63337

Carroll, J. J. (2003). Signing RDF Graphs. In *Proceedings of the Semantic Web (ISWC 2003)* (pp. 369-384).

Castro, M., & Liskov, B. (2002). Practical Byzantine Fault-Tolerance and Proactive Recovery. *ACM Transactions on Computer Systems, 20*(4), 398–461. doi:10.1145/571637.571640

Cederquist, J., Conn, R., Dekker, M., Etalle, S., & den Hartog, J. (2005, June). An Audit Logic for Accountability. In *Proceedings of the Policies for Distributed Systems and Networks - Sixth IEEE International Workshop on* (pp. 34-43).

Ceri, S., Fraternali, P., & Bongio, A. (2000). Web modeling language (Webml): a modeling language for designing Web sites. *Computer Networks, 33*(1-6), 137-157.

Chan, P. P., Lyu, M. R., & Malek, M. (2007). Reliable web services: Methodology, experiment and modeling. In *Proceedings of the ICWS* (pp. 679-686).

Chandrasekaran, S., Silver, G. A., Miller, J. A., Cardoso, J., & Sheth, A. P. (2002). XML-based Modeling and Simulation: Web Service Technologies and their Synergy with Simulation. Winter Simulation Conference, 606-615.

Chandrasekaran, S., Miller, J. A., Silver, G., Arpinar, I. B., & Sheth, A. P. (2003). Performance Analysis and Simulation of Composite Web Services. *Electronic Markets: The International Journal, 13*(2), 120–132. doi:10.1080/1019678032000067217

Chen, L., Landfermann, R., Löhr, H., Rohe, M., Sadeghi, A., & Stüble, C. (2006). *A protocol for property-based attestation.*

Chen, L., Yang, X., & Tao, F. (2006, December 18-22). A Semantic Web Service Based Approach for Augmented Provenance. In *Proceedings of the 2006 IEEE/WIC/ACM International Conference on Web Intelligence (WI'06),* Hong Kong, China (pp. 594-600). Washington, DC: IEEE Computer Society.

Chinnici, R., Gudgin, M., Moreau, J. J., Schlimmer, J., & Weerawarana, S. (2004). Web Services Description Language (WSDL) Version 2.0 Part 1: Core Language. *W3C Working Draft, 3.*

Chu, F., & Xie, X. L. (1997). Deadlock analysis of Petri nets using siphons and mathematical programming. *IEEE Transactions on Robotics and Automation, 13*(6), 793–804. doi:10.1109/70.650158

Coalition, D. S. (2002). *DAML-S: Web Service description for Semantic Web.* Paper presented at the International Semantic Web Conference (ISWC), Sardinia, Italy.

Coleman, R., Bhardwaj, A., Dellucca, A., Finke, G., Sofia, A., Jutt, M., et al. (2004). *MicroSpaces software with version 1.5.2.* Retrieved July 2009 from http://microspaces.sourceforge.net

Colucci, S., Noia, T. D., Sciascio, E. D., Donini, F., & Mongiello, M. (2005). Concept abduction and contraction for semantic-based discovery of matches and negotiation spaces in an e-marketplace. In *Proceedings of the ECRA, 4,* 41–50.

Corp, I. B. M. (2007). *Damia.* Retrieved from http://services.alphaworks.ibm.com/damia/

Curbera, F., Doganata, Y. N., Martens, A., Mukhi, N., & Slominski, A. (2008, November 12-14). Business Provenance - A Technology to Increase Traceability of End-to-End Operations. In *Proceedings of the 16th International Conference on Cooperative Information Systems (CoopIS'08)*, Monterrey, Mexico (pp. 100-119). New York: Springer.

Curbera, F., Mukhi, N., Nagy, W., & Weerawarana, S. (2006). Implementing BPEL4WS: the Architecture of a BPEL4WS Implementation. *Concurrency and Computation, 18*(10), 1219–1228. doi:10.1002/cpe.1003

Czajkowski, K., et al. (2004). *The WS-Resource framework*. Retrieved October 2009 from http://www.globus.org/-wsrf/specs/ws-wsrf.pdf

Damodaran, S. (2004). B2B integration over the Internet with XML: RosettaNet successes and challenges. In *Proceedings of the 13th International World Wide Web Conference, Alternate Track Papers & Posters* (pp. 188-195).

DBAMP. *N. I. R. D. F. P.* (2008). Retrieved from http://serg.imsciences.edu.pk/projects/dbamp/

Dekeukelaere, F., Bhola, S., Steiner, M., Chari, S., & Yoshihama, S. (2008). SMash: secure component model for cross-domain mashups on unmodified browsers. In *Proceedings of the WWW* (pp. 535-544).

Deora, V., Shao, J., Gray, W. A., & Fiddian, N. J. (2003). A quality of service management framework based on user expectations. In *Proceedings of the ICSOC*.

des Rivieres, J., & Wiegand, J. (2004). Eclipse: A platform for integrating development tools. *IBM Systems Journal, 43*(2), 371–383. doi:10.1147/sj.432.0371

Dialani, V. (2002). *UDDI-M Version 1.0 API Specification*. Southampton, UK: University of Southampton.

Dobson, G., Lock, R., & Sommerville, I. (2005). QoSOnt: A QoS Ontology for Service-Centric Systems. In *Proceedings of the 31st EUROMICRO Conference on Software Engineering and Advanced Applications 2005* (pp. 80-87).

Domingue, J., Cabral, L., Galizia, S., Tanasescu, V., Gugliotta, A., Norton, B., & Pedrinaci, C. (2008). IRS-II: A broker-based approach to semantic Web services. *Journal of Web Semantics: Science, Services and Agents on the World Wide Web, 6*(1).

Dong, X., Halevy, A., Madhavan, J., Nemes, E., & Zhang, J. (2004). Similarity Search for Web Services. In *Proceedings of the 30th Intern. Conf. on Very Large Data Bases*, Toronto, Canada (pp. 372-383).

Dong, X., Halevy, A., Madhavan, J., Nemes, E., & Zhang, J. (2004, August 31-September 3). Similarity Search for Web Services. In *Proceedings of the 13th International Conference on Very Large Data Bases VLDB*, Toronto, ON, Canada (pp. 372-383).

Dorn, C., & Dustdar, S. (2006). Achieving Web Service Continuity in Ubiquitous Mobile Networks the SRR-WS Framework. In *Proceedings of the International Workshop on Ubiquitous Mobile Information and collaboration Systems (UMICS)*.

Duan, Z., Bernstein, A., et al. (2004). Semantics Based Verification and Synthesis of WSBPEL Abstract Processes. In *Proceedings of the 3rd IEEE International Conference on Web Services*, San Diego, CA.

Dwork, C., Lynch, N. A., & Stockmeyer, L. (1988). Consensus in the Presence of Partial Synchrony. *Journal of the ACM, 35*(2), 288–322. doi:10.1145/42282.42283

EGEE. (n.d.). *The Enabling Grids for E-science (EGEE) project*. Retrieved October 2009 from http://www.eu-egee.org

Elnaffar, S., Maamar, Z., Yahyaoui, H., Bentehar, J., & Thiran, P. (2008, March 25-28). Reputation of Communities of Web Services - Preliminary Investigations. In *Proceeding of the 22nd IEEE international Conference on Advanced information networking and application (AINA)*, Okinawa, Japan (pp. 1603-1608).

Ennals, R. J., & Garofalakis, M. N. (2007). MashMaker: mashups for the masses. In *Proceedings of the ACM SIGMOD international conference on Management of data* (pp. 1116-1118).

EsperTech Inc. (2009). *Esper*. Retrieved November 10, 2009, from http://esper.codehaus.org/

Ezpeleta, J., Colom, J., & Martinez, J. (1995). A Petri Net based Deadlock Prevention Policy for Flexible Manufacturing Systems. *IEEE Transactions on Robotics and Automation, 11*(2), 173–184. doi:10.1109/70.370500

Fahland, D., & Reisig, W. (2005). ASM-based semantics for BPEL: The negative control flow. In *Proceedings of the 12th International Workshop on Abstract State Machines*, Paris (pp. 131-151).

Fallside, D. C. (2000). *XML Schema Part 0: Primer (W3C Candidate Recommendation CR-xmlschema-0-20001024)* World Wide Web Consortium (W3C).

Fang, C. L., Liang, D., Lin, F., & Lin, C. C. (2007). Fault tolerant web services. *Journal of Systems Architecture*, *53*(1), 21–38. doi:10.1016/j.sysarc.2006.06.001

Fan, L., Cao, P., Almeida, J., & Broder, A. (1998). Summary Cache: A Scalable Wide-Area Web Cache Sharing Protocol. *ACM SIGCOMM*, *28*(4), 254–265. doi:10.1145/285243.285287

Fasbinder, M. (2008). *WebSphere Process Server business rules lifecycle*. IBM DeveloperWorks.

Favarim, F., Fraga, J. S., Lung, L. C., & Correia, M. (2007, July 12-14). GridTS: A New Approach for Fault Tolerant Scheduling in Grid Computing. In *Proceedings of the 6th IEEE International Symposium on Network Computing and Applications (NCA'07)*, Cambridge, MA (pp. 187-194). Washington, DC: IEEE Computer Press.

Felix, P., & Ribeiro, C. (2007, November 2). A Scalable and Flexible Web Services Authentication Model. In *Proceedings of the 2007 ACM workshop on Secure web services (SWS'07)*, Fairfax, VA (pp. 66-72). New York: ACM.

Fensel, D., Kifer, M., de Bruijn, J., & Domingue, J. (2005). Web Service Modeling Ontology. *W3C*.

Fensel, D., Polleres, A., & Bruijn, J. (2007). *Ontology-based Choreography of WSMO Services, WSMO Final Draft*. Retrieved from http://www.wsmo.org/TR/d14/v0.4/

Fenser, D., & Bussler, C. (2002). The Web Service Modeling Framework WSMF. *Electronic Commerce Research and Applications*, *1*(2), 113–137. doi:10.1016/S1567-4223(02)00015-7

Ferrara, A. (2004). Web services: A process algebra approach. In *Proceedings of the 2nd international conference on Service oriented computing* (pp. 242-251). New York: ACM Press.

Fiege, L., Mezini, M., Mühl, G., & Buchmann, A. P. (2002, June 10-14). Engineering Event-Based Systems with Scopes. In *Proceedings of the 16th European Conference on Object-Oriented Programming (ECOOP '02)*, Málaga, Spain (pp. 309-333). London, UK: Springer Verlag.

Filman, R. E., Elrad, T., Clarke, S., & Aksit, M. (2005). *Aspect-oriented software development*. Reading, MA: Addison-Wesley.

Fisteus, J., Fernández, L., & Kloos, C. (2004). Formal verification of BPEL4WS business collaborations. In *Proceedings of the 5th International Conference on Electronic Commerce and Web Technologies*, Zaragoza, Spain (pp. 76-85).

Florescu, D., Levy, A., & Mendelzon, A. (1998). Database techniques for the world-wide web: A survey. *SIGMOD Record*, *27*(3), 56–74. doi:10.1145/290593.290605

Foster, H., Sebastian, U., Jeff, M., & Jeff, K. (2003). Model-based Verification of Web Service Compositions. In *Proceedings of the 18th IEEE International Conference on Automated Software Engineering (ASE'03)* (p. 152).

Foster, H., Uchitel, S., et al. (2004a). Compatibility for Web Service Choreography. In *Proceedings of the 3rd IEEE International Conference on Web Services (ICWS)*, San Diego, CA. Washington, DC: IEEE.

Foster, H., Uchitel, S., et al. (2005a). Tool Support for Model-Based Engineering of Web Service Compositions. In *Proceedings of the 3rd IEEE International Conference on Web Services (ICWS2005)*, Orlando, FL. Washington, DC: IEEE.

Foster, H., Uchitel, S., et al. (2005b). Using a Rigorous Approach for Engineering Web Service Compositions: A Case Study. In *Proceedings of the 2nd IEEE International Conference on Services Computing (SCC2005)*, Orlando, FL. Washington, DC: IEEE.

Foster, H., Uchitel, S., Magee, J., & Kramer, J. (2003). Model-based verification of web service compositions. In *Proceedings of the ASE*.

Foster, H., Uchitel, S., Magee, J., & Kramer, J. (2005). Tool support for model-based engineering of Web service compositions. In *Proceedings of the 2005 IEEE International Conference on Web Services*, Orlando, FL (pp. 95-102).

Foster, I., Vöckler, J., Wilde, M., & Zhao, Y. (2002, July 24-26). Chimera: A Virtual Data System for Representing, Querying, and Automating Data Derivation. In *Proceedings of the 14th International Conference on Scientific and Statistical Database Management (SSDBM'02)*, Edinburgh, Scotland, UK (pp. 37-46). Washington, DC: IEEE Computer Society.

Foster, I., Czajkowski, K., Ferguson, D. E., Frey, J., Graham, S., & Maguire, T. (2005). Modeling and managing state in distributed systems: The role of OGSI and WSRF. *Proceedings of the IEEE*, *93*(3), 604–661. doi:10.1109/JPROC.2004.842766

Foundation, E. (2001). *Eclipse*. Retrieved August 2004, from http://www.eclipse.org

Fourguet, E., Larson, K., & Cowan, W. (2006). A Reputation Mechanism for Layered Communities. *SIGecom Exchanges*, *6*(1), 11–22. doi:10.1145/1150735.1150738

Fu, X. (2004). Formal Specification and Verification of Asynchronously Communicating Web Services. Unpublished doctoral thesis, University of California, Santa Barbara, CA.

Fu, X., Bultan, T., & Su, J. (2004). Analysis of Interacting BPEL Web Services. In *Proceedings of the 13th International World Wide Web Conference*, New York (pp. 621-630).

Gansner, E. R., & North, S. C. (2000). An Open Graph Visualization System and its Applications to Software Engineering. *Software, Practice & Experience*, *30*(11), 1203–1233. doi:10.1002/1097-024X(200009)30:11<1203::AID-SPE338>3.0.CO;2-N

Ganter, B., & Wille, R. (1999). *Formal concept analysis: Mathematical foundations*. Heidelberg, Germany: Springer Verlag.

Gao, L., Dahlin, M., Nayate, A., Zheng, J., & Iyengar, A. (2005). Improving Availability and Performance with Application-Specific Data Replication. *IEEE Transactions on Knowledge and Data Engineering*, *17*(1).

Gasser, M., & McDermott, E. (1990). An architecture for practical delegation in a distributed system. In *Proceedings of the IEEE Symposium on Security and Privacy* (pp. 20).

Gelernter, D. (1985). Generative Communication in Linda. *ACM Transactions on Programming Languages and Systems*, *7*(1), 80–112. doi:10.1145/2363.2433

Globus. (n.d.). *The Globus Toolkit*. Retrieved October 2009 from http://www.globus.org

GLUE. (n.d.). *The GLUE Schema*. Retrieved October 2009 from http://infnforge.cnaf.infn.it/glueinfomodel

Godik, S., & Moses, T. (2003). *eXtensible Access Control Markup Language (XACML) Version 1.0*. OASIS.

Godin, R., Missaoui, R., & Alaoui, H. (1991). Learning algorithms using a Galois lattice structure. In *Proceedings of the Third International Conference on Tools for Artificial Intelligence*, San Jose, CA (pp. 22-29). Washington, DC: IEEE Computer Society. Heß, A., & Kushmerick, N. (2003). *Learning to attach semantic metadata to web services*. Paper presented at the 2nd International Semantic Web Con-ference (ISWC), Sanibel Island, FL.

Google Inc. (2008). *Search-based keyword tool*. Retrieved from http://www.google.com/sktool/

Grawrock, D. (2006). *The Intel safer computing initiative*.

Graz, T. U. O. (2008). *Privacy CA*. Retrieved from http://trustedjava.sourceforge.net/index.php?item=pca/about

Grigori, D., & Bouzeghoub, M. (2005). Service retrieval based on behavioral specification. In *Proceedings of the IEEE International Conference on Services Computing (SCC'05)* (pp. 333-363).

GRIMOIRES. (n.d.). *GRIMOIRES UDDI compliant Web Service Registry with metadata annotation extension*. Retrieved from http://sourceforge.net/projects/grimoires

Groth, P., Jiang, S., Miles, S., Munroe, S., Tan, V., Tsasakou, S., et al. (2006). *An Architecture for Provenance Systems* (Tech. Rep.). Southhampton, England: University of Southampton. Retrieved November 10, 2009, from http://eprints.ecs.soton.ac.uk/12023/1/provenanceArchitecture7.pdf

Gudes, E., Olivier, M., & Van De Riet, R. (1999). Modelling, specifying and implementing workflow security in cyberspace. *Journal of Computer Security*, *7*(4), 287–315.

Gudgin, M., Hadley, M., Mendelsohn, N., Moreau, J. J., Frystyk Nielsen, H. F., Karmarkar, A., et al. (2007, April). *SOAP Version 1.2 Part 1: Messaging Framework* (2nd ed.). Retrieved from http://www.w3.org/TR/2007/REC-soap12-part1-20070427/

Hallam-Baker, P. M., & Behlendorf, B. (1996). *Extended Log File Format*. Retrieved from http://www.w3.org/TR/WD-logfile-960323.html

Hamadi, R., & Benatallah, B. (2003). A Petri Net-based Model for Web Service Composition. In *Proceedings of the Australasian Database Conference (ADC 2003)* (pp. 191-200).

Harel, D., & Naamad, A. (1996). The STATEMATE semantics of Statecharts. *ACM Transactions on Software Engineering and Methodology*, 5(4), 293–333. doi:10.1145/235321.235322

Harshavardhan Jegadeesan, S. B. (2008). A MOF 2-based Services Metamodel. *Journal of Object Technology*.

Hassine, A. B., Matsubara, S., & Ishida, T. (2006). A constraintbased approach to web service composition. In *Proceedings of the ISWC* (pp. 130-143).

Heb, A., & Kushmerick, N. (2003). Learning to Attach Semantic Metadata to Web Services. In *Proceedings of the International Semantic Web Conference* (pp. 258-273).

Heb, A., Johnston, E., & Kushmerick, N. (2004). ASSAM: A Tool for Semi-automatically Annotating Semantic Web Services. In *Proceedings of the International Semantic Web Conference* (pp. 320-334).

Heimdahl, M. P. E., & Leveson, N. G. (1996). Completeness and Consistency in Hierarchical State-Based Requirements. *IEEE Transactions on Software Engineering*, 22(6), 363–377. doi:10.1109/32.508311

Heinis, T., & Alonso, G. (2008, June 10-12). Efficient Lineage Tracking for Scientific Workflows. In *Proceedings of the 2008 ACM SIGMOD International Conference on Management of Data (SIGMOD '08)*, Vancouver, Canada (pp. 1007-1018). New York: ACM.

Herlihy, M., & Wing, J. M. (1990). Linearizability: A Correctness Condition for Concurrent Objects. *ACM Transactions on Programming Languages and Systems*, 12(3), 463–492. doi:10.1145/78969.78972

Hinz, S., Schmidt, K., & Stahl, C. (2005). Transforming BPEL to Petri Nets. In *Proceedings of the 3rd International Conference on Business Process Management*, Nancy, France (pp. 220-235).

Hofreiter, B., Huemer, C., & Naujok, K. D. (2004). UN/CEFACT's business collaboration framework-motivation and basic concepts. In *Proceedings of MKWI* (pp. 4).

Horrocks, I. (1998). Using an expressive description logic: Fact or fiction? In *Proceedings of the KR* (pp. 636-649).

Hou, L., Jin, Z., & Wu, B. (2006). Modeling and Verifying Web Services Driven by Requirements: An Ontology-based Approach. *Science in China Series F: Information Sciences*, 49(6), 792–820. doi:10.1007/s11432-006-2031-5

Huang, W., & Atluri, V. (1999). *SecureFlow: a secure Web-enabled workflow management system*.

Hu, H., Zhou, M. C., & Li, Z. W. (2009). Liveness Enforcing Supervision of Video Streaming Systems Using Nonsequential Petri Nets. *IEEE Transactions on Multimedia*, 11(8), 1446–1456. doi:10.1109/TMM.2009.2032678

Hull, R., & Su, J. (2005). Tools for composite web services: A short overview. *SIGMOD Record*, 34(2), 86–95. doi:10.1145/1083784.1083807

Hwang, S.-Y., Wang, H., Srivastava, J., & Paul, R. A. (2004). A Probabilistic QoS Model and Computation Framework for Web Services-Based Workflows. *Conceptual Modeling - ER*, 596-609.

Hwang, C.-L., & Yoon, K. (1981). *Multiple Criteria Decision Making*. LNEMS.

Hwang, S.-Y., Wang, H., Tang, J., & Srivastava, J. (2007). A Probabilistic Approach to Modeling and Estimating the QoS of Web-Services-based Workflows. *Information Science*, 177(23), 5484–5503. doi:10.1016/j.ins.2007.07.011

IBM. (2006). *Microsoft, RSA, and Verisign*. Retrieved from http://specs.xmlsoap.org

Index Service. (n.d.). *Index Service caGrid*. Retrieved October 2009 from http://cagrid.org/display/metadata13-/Index+Service

Intel Corp. (2007). *Mash Maker*. Retrieved from http://mashmaker.intel.com/web/

Iyengar, A., & Challenger, J. (1997). Improving web server performance by caching dynamic data. In *Proceedings of the USENIX Symposium on Internet Technologies and Systems* (pp. 49-60).

Jackson, C., & Wang, H. J. (2007). Subspace: secure cross-domain communication for web mashups. In Proceedings of the *WWW* (pp. 611-620).

Jaeger, M. C., Rojec-Goldmann, G., & Muhl, G. (2004). Qos aggregation for web service composition using work-flow patterns. In *Proceedings of the EDOC* (pp. 149-159).

Jaeger, T., Sailer, R., & Shankar, U. (2006). *PRIMA: policy-reduced integrity measurement architecture.*

Jaganathan, R. (2007, January). *Windows Workflow Foundation: Tracking Services Deep Dive.* Retrieved November 10, 2009, from http://msdn.microsoft.com/en-us/library/bb264458(VS.80).aspx

Jensen, K. (1992). *Coloured Petri Nets - Basic Concepts, Analysis Methods and Practical Use* (*Vol. 1*). New York: Springer.

Jeong, B., Cho, H., & Lee, C. (2008). On the functional quality of service (FQoS) to discover and compose interoperable Web services. *International Journal of Expert Systems with Applications*, 5411-5418.

Jurca, R., & Faltings, B. (2003, June 24-27). An Incentive Compatible Reputation Mechanism. In *Proceedings of the IEEE Conference on E-Commerce Technology (CEC)*, Newport Beach, CA (pp. 1026-1027).

Jurca, R., Faltings, B., & Binder, W. (2007, May 8-12). Reliable QoS Monitoring Based on Client Feedback. In *Proceedings of the 16th International World Wide Web Conference (WWW)*, Banff, Canada (pp. 1003-1011).

Jurca, R., & Faltings, B. (2007). Obtaining Reliable Feedbacks for Sanctioning Reputation Mechanisms. *Journal of Artificial Intelligence Research*, 29(1), 391–419.

Kalali, B., Alencar, P., & Cowan, D. (2003). *A service-oriented monitoring registry*. Paper presented at the Conference on the Centre for Advanced Studies on Collaborative Research.

Kalepu, S., Krishnaswamy, S., & Loke, S. W. (2003, December 10-12). Verity: A QoS Metric for Selecting Web Services and Providers. In *Proceedings of the 4th international Conference on Web Information Systems Engineering Workshops*, Rome, Italy (pp. 131-139).

Kamae, T., Krengel, U., & O'Brien, G. L. (1977). Stochastic Inequalities on Partially Ordered Spaces. *Annals of Probability*, 5(6), 899–912. doi:10.1214/aop/1176995659

Karjoth, G., Schunter, M., & Waidner, M. (2002). Platform for Enterprise Privacy Practices: Privacy-enabled Management of Customer Data. In *Proceedings of the 2nd Workshop on Privacy Enhancing Technologies (PET 2002)*.

Kastidou, G., Cohen, R., & Larson, K. (2009, July 11). A Graph-based Approach for Promoting Honesty in Community-based Multiagent Systems. In *Proceedings of the 8th International Workshop for Coordination, Organization, Institutions, and Norms in Agent Systems (COIN@IJCAI)*, Pasadena, CA.

Kavianpour, M. (2007). Soa and large scale and complex enterprise transformation. In *Proceedings of the ICSOC* (pp. 530-545).

Kazhamiakin, R., Pistore, M., & Santuari, L. (2006). Analysis of communication models in Web service compositions. In *Proceedings of the 15th international conference on World Wide Web (WWW '06)* (pp. 267-276). New York: ACM.

Keller, A., & Ludwig, H. (2003). The WSLA Framework: Specifying and Monitoring Service Level Agreements for Web Services. *Journal of Network and Systems Management*, 11(1). doi:10.1023/A:1022445108617

Khosravifar, B., Bentahar, J., Thiran, P., Moazin, A., & Guiot, A. (2009, July 6-10). An Approach to Incentive-based Reputation for Communities of Web Services. In *Proceedings of the 7th International Conference on Web Services (ICWS)*, Los Angeles (pp. 303-310).

Khosravifar, B., Gomrokchi, M., Bentahar, J., & Thiran, P. (2009, May 10-15). Maintenance-based Trust for Multi-Agent Systems. In *Proceedings of the 8th International joint Conference on Autonomous Agents and Multi-Agent Systems (AAMAS)*, Budapest, Hungary (pp. 1017-1024).

Khushraj, D., Lassila, O., & Finin, T. (2004). sTuples: Semantic Tuple Spaces. In *Proceedings of the First Annual IEEE International Conference on Mobile and Ubiquitous Systems: Networking and Services (MobiQuitous'04)* (pp. 268-277). Washington, DC: IEEE Computer Society.

Kim, J. W., & Candan, K. S. (2006). CP/CV: Concept Similarity Mining without Frequency Information from Domain Describing Taxonomies. In *Proceedings of the 15th ACM International Conference on Information and Knowledge Management* (pp. 483-492).

Kitchin, D., Quark, A., Cook, W., & Misra, J. (2009). The Orc Programming Language. In *Proceedings of FMOODS/FORTE* (LNCS 5522, pp. 1-25). New York: Springer Verlag.

Kleijnen, S., & Raju, S. (2003). *An open web services architecture*. New York: ACM Press.

Klusch, M., Benedik, F., Khalid, M., & Sykara, K. (2009). OWLS-MX: Hybrid OWL-S Service Matchmaker. *Journal of Web Semantics*, 7(2), 121–133. doi:10.1016/j.websem.2008.10.001

Klusch, M., & Kaufer, F. (2009). WSMO-MX: A Hybrid Semantic Web Service Matchmaker. *Web Intelligence and Agent Systems*, 7(1), 23–42.

König, D., Lohmann, N., Moser, S., Stahl, C., & Wolf, K. (2008). Extending the Compatibility Notion for Abstract WS-BPEL Processes. In *Proceedings of the 17th International World Wide Web Conference*, Beijing, China (pp. 785-794).

Kopecky, J., Vitvar, T., Bournez, C., & Farrell, J. (2007). SAWSDL: y Semantic annotations for WSDL and XML schema. *IEEE Internet Computing*, 11(6), 60–67. doi:10.1109/MIC.2007.134

Kortesniemi, Y., & Hasu, T. (2000). *A revocation, validation and authentication protocol for SPKI based delegation systems*. Paper presented at the Network and Distributed Systems Security Symposium.

Koshutanski, H., & Massacci, F. (2003). An access control framework for business processes for web services. In *Proceedings of the 2003 ACM Workshop on XML Security* (pp. 15-24).

Kotok, A. (2001). *Ebxml: The new global standard for doing business over the internet*. New York: New Riders Publishing.

Kowalski, R., & Sergot, M. J. (1986). A logic-based calculus of events. *New generation Computing*, 4(1), 67–95.

Krummenacher, R., Strang, T., & Fensel, D. (2005, March). *Triple spaces for and ubiquitous web of services*. Paper presented at the W3C Workshop on the Ubiquitous Web, Tokyo.

Kucera, A., & Mayr, R. (1999). Simulation Preorder on Simple Process Algebras. In *Proceedings of the 26th International Colloquium on Automata, Languages and Programming* (pp. 503-512). London: Springer Verlag.

Kühn, U., Selhorst, M., & Stüble, C. (2007). *Realizing property-based attestation and sealing with commonly available hard-and software*.

Kulathuramaiyer, N. (2007). Mashups: Emerging application development paradigm for a digital journal. *Journal of Universal Computer Science*, 13(4), 531–542.

Kusters, R. (2001). *Non-Standard Inferences in Description Logu ics (LNCS 2100)*. New York: Springer. doi:10.1007/3-540-44613-3

Lamport, L., Shostak, R., & Pease, M. (1982). The Byzantine Generals Problem. *ACM Transactions on Programming Languages and Systems*, 4(3), 382–401. doi:10.1145/357172.357176

Lassila, O., & Dixit, S. (2004, March). Interleaving discovery and composition for simple workflows. In *Semantic Web Services, AAAI Spring Symposium Series* (pp. 22-26).

Lecue, F., & Leger, A. (2006). A formal model for semantic web service composition. In *Proceedings of the ISWC* (pp. 385398).

Lecue, F., Boissier, O., Delteil, A., & Leger, A. (2009, March). Web service composition as a composition of valid and robust semantic links. *IJCIS*, 18(1).

Lecue, F., Delteil, A., & Leger, A. (2007). Applying abduction in semantic web service composition. In *Proceedings of the ICWS* (pp. 94 101).

Lecue, F., Delteil, A., & Leger, A. (2008). Optimizing causal link based web service composition. In *Proceedings of the ECAI* (pp. 45-49).

Le-Hung, V., Hauswirth, M., & Aberer, K. (2005). Towards P2P-based Semantic Web Service Discovery with QoS Support. In *Proceedings of the Business Process Management Workshops* (pp. 18-31).

Leitner, P., Michlmayr, A., Rosenberg, F., & Dustdar, S. (2008, July 8-11). End-to-End Versioning Support for Web Services. In *Proceedings of the International Conference on Services Computing (SCC'08),* Honolulu, HI (pp. 59-66). Washington, DC: IEEE Computer Society.

Leitner, P., Rosenberg, F., Michlmayr, A., Huber, A., & Dustdar, S. (2009, August). A Mediator-Based Approach to Resolving Interface Heterogeneity of Web Services. In W. Binder & S. Dustdar (Eds.), Emerging Web Service Technologies (Vol. 3, pp. 55–74). Basel, Switzerland: Birkhäuser.

Leitner, P., Rosenberg, F., & Dustdar, S. (2009, May/June). DAIOS – Efficient Dynamic Web Service Invocation. *IEEE Internet Computing, 13*(3), 30–38.doi:10.1109/MIC.2009.57

Lenzerini, M. (2002). Data integration: A theoretical perspective. *PODS,* 243-246. MyGrid. (n.d.). *UK e-Science project.* Retrieved October 2009 from http://www.mygrid.org.uk

Leu, D., Bastani, F., & Leiss, E. (1990). The effect of statically and dynamically replicated components on system reliability. *IEEE Transactions on Reliability, 39*(2), 209–216. doi:10.1109/24.55884

Li, H., Du, X., & Tian, X. (2007). Towards Semantic Web Services Discovery with QoS Support using Specific Ontologies. In *Proceedings of the Third International Conference on Semantics, Knowledge and Grid* (pp. 358-361).

Li, L., & Horrocks, I. (2003). A software framework for matchmaking based on semantic web technology. In Proceedings of the WWW (pp. 331-339).

Liu, W., Jia, W., & Pui, O. A. (2002). *Add exception notification mechanism to web services.* Paper presented at the Fifth International Conference on Algorithms and Architectures for Parallel Processing (ICA3PP).

Liu, X., & Deters, R. (2007). An efficient Dual Caching Strategy for Web Service-Enabled PDAs. In *Proceedings of the ACM Symposium on Applied Computing* (pp. 788-794).

Liu, X., Hui, Y., Sun, W., & Liang, H. (2007). Towards Service Composition Based on Mashup. In *Proceedings of the 2007 IEEE Congress on Services* (pp. 332-339).

Liu, Y., Ngu, A. H., & Zeng, L. Z. (2004). QoS Computation and Policing in Dynamic Web Service Selection. In *Proceedings of the 13th International World Wise Conference on Alternate Track Papers and Posters* (pp. 66-73).

Liu, Z., Squillante, M., & Wolf, J. (2001). On Maximizing Service-Level-Agreement profits. ACM Conference on Electronic Commerce, 213-223.

Li, Z. W., & Zhou, M. C. (2004). Elementary Siphons of Petri Nets and Their Applications to Deadlock Prevention in Flexible Manufacturing Systems. *IEEE Trans. on Sys., Man and Cybern. Part A, 34*(1), 38–51.

Li, Z. W., & Zhou, M. C. (2009). *Deadlock Resolution in Automated Manufacturing Systems: A Novel Petri Net Approach.* New York: Springer.

Lohmann, N. (2007). A feature-complete Petri net semantics for WS-BPEL 2.0. In *Proceedings of the 4th International Workshop on Web Services and Formal Methods,* Brisbane, Australia (pp. 77-91).

Lohmann, N., Massuthe, P., Stahl, C., & Weinberg, D. (2006). Analyzing Interacting BPEL Processes. In *Proceedings of the 4th International Conference on Business Process Management,* Vienna, Austria (pp. 17-32).

Lonvick, C. (2001). RFC 3164: The BSD syslog Protocol. *Internet Engineering Task Force.* Retrieved from http://www.ietf.org/rfc/rfc3164.txt

Lorch, M., Proctor, S., Lepro, R., Kafura, D., & Shah, S. (2003). *First experiences using XACML for access control in distributed systems.*

Loscocco, P., & Smalley, S. (2001). *Meeting critical security objectives with security-enhanced linux.*

Lucchi, R., & Zavattaro, G. (2004, March 14-17). WS-SecSpaces: a Secure Data-Driven Coordination Service for Web Services Applications. In *Proceedings of the 19th ACM Symposium on Applied Computing (SAC'04)*, Nicosia, Cyprus (pp. 487-491).

Lucchia, R., & Mazzara, M. (2007). A pi-calculus based semantics for WS-BPEL. *Journal of Logic and Algebraic Programming*, *70*(1), 96–118. doi:10.1016/j.jlap.2006.05.007

Ludwig, H., Keller, A., Dan, A., King, R. P., & Franck, R. (2002). *Web Service Level Agreement (WSLA) Language Specification*. IBM.

Ludwig, H., Keller, A., Dan, A., King, R., & Franck, R. (2003). A service level agreement language for dynamic electronic services. *Electronic Commerce Research*, *3*(1-2), 43–59. doi:10.1023/A:1021525310424

Lufei, H., Shi, W., & Chaudhary, V. (2008). Adaptive Secure Access to Remote Services in Mobile Environments. *IEEE Transactions on Services Computing*, *1*(1), 49–61. doi:10.1109/TSC.2008.4

Lyu, M. R. (1995). *Software Fault Tolerance. Trends in Software*. New York: Wiley.

Maamar, Z., Benslimane, D., Ghedira, C., Mahmoud, Q. H., & Yahyaoui, H. (2005, March 13-17). Tuple spaces for self-coordination of web services. In *Proceedings of the 20th ACM Symposium on Applied computing (SAC'05)*, Santa Fe, New Mexico (pp. 1656-1660).

Maedche, A. (2002). *Ontology learning for the semantic Web*. Dordrecht, The Netherlands: Kluwer.

Magee, J., & Kramer, J. (1999). *Concurrency: state models & Java programs*. New York: John Wiley & Sons, Inc.

Mahleko, B., & Wombacher, A. (2005). A grammar-based index for matching business processes. In *Proceedings of the International Conference on Web Services (ICWS'05)* (pp. 21-30).

Malik, Z., & Bouguettaya, A. (2007, December 3-6). Evaluating Rater Credibility for Reputation Assessment of Web Services. In *Proceedings of the 8th International Conference on Web Information Systems Engineering (WISE)*, Nancy, France (pp. 38-49).

Manolescu, I., Brambilla, M., Ceri, S., Comai, S., & Fraternali, P. (2005). Model-driven design and deployment of service-enabled Web applications. *ACM Transactions on Internet Technology*, *5*(3), 439–479. doi:10.1145/1084772.1084773

Marsan, M. A., Balbo, G., Bobio, A., Chiola, G., Conte, G., & Cumani, A. (1989). The Effect of Execution Policies on the Semantics and Analysis of Stochastic Petri Nets. *IEEE Transactions on Software Engineering*, *15*(7), 832–846. doi:10.1109/32.29483

Martens, A. (2003). Usability of Web services. In *Proceedings of the 4th Intern. Conf. on Web Info. Systems Eng. Workshops*, Rome, Italy (pp. 182-190).

Martens, A. (2005). Analyzing Web Service Based Business Processes. In M. Cerioli (Ed.), *Proceedings of the 8th International Conference on Fundamental Approaches to Software Engineering (FASE 2005)* (LNCS 3442, pp. 19-33). Berlin: Springer Verlag.

Martens, A., Hamadi, R., & Benatallah, B. (2003). A Petri Net based Model for Web Service Composition. In *Proceedings of the 14th Australian Database Conf.*, Adelaide, Australia (pp. 191-200).

Martino, L. D., & Bertino, E. (2009). Security for Web Services: Standards and Research Issues. *International Journal of Web Services Research*, *6*(4), 48–74.

Maximilien, E. (2005, July 25-29). Multiagent System for Dynamic Web Services Selection. In *Proceedings of the 1st Workshop on Service-Oriented Computing and agent-based Engineering (SOCABE)*, Utrecht, The Netherlands.

Maximilien, E. M., & Singh, M. (2002). Conceptual Model of Web Service Reputation. *SIGMOD Record*, *31*(4), 36–41. doi:10.1145/637411.637417

Maximilien, E., & Singh, M. (2002). Conceptual model of web service reputation. *SIGMOD Record*, *31*(4), 36–41. doi:10.1145/637411.637417

Mayer, F., MacMillan, K., & Caplan, D. (2006). *SELinux by example: using security enhanced Linux*. Upper Saddle River, NJ: Prentice Hall.

McIlraith, S., & Son, T. C. (2002). Adapting Golog-r Composition of Semantic Web Services. In *Proceedings of the International Conference on Principles of Knowledge Representation and Reasoning (KR 2002)* (pp. 482-496).

McIlraith, S. A., Son, T. C., & Zeng, H. (2001). Semantic web services. *IEEE Intelligent Systems, 16*(2), 46–53. doi:10.1109/5254.920599

Meadows, B., & Seaburg, L. (2004). *Universal Business Language 1.0*. OASIS.

Medina, A., Lakhina, A., Matta, I., & Byers, J. (2001). Brite: an approach to universal topology generation. In *Proceedings of the International Symposium on Modeling, Analysis and Simulation of Computer and Telecommunication Systems* (pp. 346-353).

Menascé, D. A. (2002). Qos issues in web services. *IEEE Internet Computing, 6*(6), 72–75. doi:10.1109/MIC.2002.1067740

Merideth, M. G., Iyengar, A., Mikalsen, T., Tai, S., Rouvellou, I., & Narasimhan, P. (2005). Thema: Byzantine-fault-tolerant middleware for web-service applications. In *Proceedings of the SRDS* (pp. 131-142).

Michel, S., Nguyen, K., Rosenstein, A., Zhang, L., Floyd, S., & Jacobson, V. (1998). Adaptive Web Caching: Towards a New Global Caching Architecture. *Computer Networks and ISDN Systems, 30*(22-23), 2169–2177. doi:10.1016/S0169-7552(98)00246-3

Michlmayr, A., Rosenberg, F., Leitner, P., & Dustdar, S. (2008, July 1-4). Advanced Event Processing and Notifications in Service Runtime Environments. In *Proceedings of the 2nd International Conference on Distributed Event-Based Systems (DEBS'08),* Rome, Italy (pp. 115-125). New York: ACM.

Michlmayr, A., Rosenberg, F., Leitner, P., & Dustdar, S. (2009, July 6-10). Service Provenance in QoS-Aware Web Service Runtimes. In *Proceedings of the 7th IEEE International Conference on Web Services (ICWS'09),* Los Angeles, CA (pp. 115-122). Washington, DC: IEEE Computer Society.

Michlmayr, A., Rosenberg, F., Leitner, P., & Dustdar, S. (2009, May). *End-to-End Support for QoS-Aware Service Selection, Invocation and Mediation in VRESCo* (Tech. Rep. No. TUV-1841-2009-03). Vienna, Austria: Vienna University of Technology. Retrieved November 10, 2009, from http://www.infosys.tuwien.ac.at/Staff/michlmayr/papers/TUV-1841-2009-03.pdf

Michlmayr, A., Rosenberg, F., Platzer, C., Treiber, M., & Dustdar, S. (2007, September 3). Towards Recovering the Broken SOA Triangle – A Software Engineering Perspective. In *Proceedings of the 2nd International Workshop on Service Oriented Software Engineering (IW-SOSWE'07),* Dubrovnik, Croatia (pp. 22-28). New York: ACM.

Microsoft Cooperation. (2009). *Quickgraph.* Retrieved November 10, 2009, from http://www.codeplex.com/quickgraph

Minsky, N. H., & Ungureanu, V. (2000). Law-Governed Interaction: a Coordination and Control Mechanism for Heterogeneous Distributed Systems. *ACM Transactions on Software Engineering and Methodology, 9*(3), 273–305. doi:10.1145/352591.352592

Misra, J., & Cook, W. (2007, March). Orchestration: A Basis for Wide-Area Computing. Journal of Software and Systems Modeling.

Mitchell, C. (2005). Trusted Computing. *Trusted computing, 1.*

Mitra, N. (2003). SOAP Version 1.2 Part 0: Primer. *W3C Recommendation, 24.*

Moreau, L., Freire, J., Futrelle, J., McGrath, R., Myers, J., & Paulson, P. (2007). *The Open Provenance Model* (Tech. Rep.). Southampton, UK: University of Southampton. Retrieved November 11, 2009, from http://eprints.ecs.soton.ac.uk/14979/1/opm.pdf

Moreau, L., Groth, P., Miles, S., Vazquez-Salceda, J., Ibbotson, J., & Jiang, S. (2008). The Provenance of Electronic Data. *Communications of the ACM, 51*(4), 52–58. doi:10.1145/1330311.1330323

Moritsu, T., Hiltunen, M. A., Schlichting, R. D., Toyouchi, J., & Namba, Y. (2006). Using web service transformations to implement cooperative fault tolerance. In *Proceedings of the ISAS* (pp. 76-91).

Mühl, G., Fiege, L., & Pietzuch, P. (2006). *Distributed Event-Based Systems.* New York: Springer Verlag.

Murata, T. (1989). Petri nets: Properties, analysis and applications. *Proceedings of the IEEE, 77*(4), 541–580. doi:10.1109/5.24143

Narayanan, R. (2009). Business rules change all the time, but your applications don't have to. *SAP Insider, 10*(2).

Narayanan, S., & McIlraith, S. (2002). Simulation, Verification and Automated Composition of Web Services. In *Proceedings of the International World Wide Web Conference (WWW 2002)* (pp. 77-88).

Nezhad, H., Benatallah, B., Martens, A., Curbera, F., & Casati, F. (2007). SemiAutomated Adaptation of Service Interactions. In *Proceedings of the 16th International World Wide Web Conference*, Banff, Alberta, Canada (pp. 993-1002).

NGS. (n.d.) *The National Grid Service (NGS)*. Retrieved October 2009 from http://www.grid-support.ac.uk

Nguyen, X. T., Kowalczyk, R., & Phan, M. T. (2006). Modelling and Solving QoS Composition Problem Using Fuzzy DisCSP. International Conference on Web Services, 55-62.

Ninan, A., Kulkarni, P., Shenoy, P., Ramamritham, K., & Tewari, R. (2003). Scalable Consistency Maintenance in Content Distribution Networks Using Cooperative Leases. *IEEE Transactions on Knowledge and Data Engineering, 15*(4), 813–828. doi:10.1109/TKDE.2003.1209001

Noy, N. F., & McGuinness, D. L. (2001). *Ontology development 101: A guide to creating your first ontology* (Tech. Rep. KSL-01-05 and SMI-2001, 880). Palo Alto, CA: Stanford Knowledge Systems Laboratory Stanford Medical Informatics.

O'Brien, L., Bass, L., & Merson, P. (2005). *Quality Attributes and Service-Oriented Architectures* (Tech. Rep. No. CMU/SEI-2005-TN-014). Pittsburgh, PA: Carnegie Mellon University.

O'Sullivan, J., Edmond, D., & ter Hofstede, A. H. M. (2005). *Formal description of non-functional service properties*. WSMO Working Group.

O'Sullivan, J., Edmond, D., & Ter Hofstede, A. (2002). What's in a service? Towards accurate description of non-functional service properties. *Distributed and Parallel Databases, 12*(2), 117–133. doi:10.1023/A:1016547000822

OASIS. (2005). Reference Model TC (OASIS Reference Model for Service Oriented Architectures Working Draft 10).

OASIS. (2005). *Web services reliable messaging*. Retrieved from http://specs.xmlsoap.org/ws/2005/02/rm/ws-reliablemessaging.pdf

OASIS. (2005, February). *Universal Description, Discovery and Integration (UDDI)*. Retrieved November 10, 2009, from http://oasis-open.org/committees/uddi-spec/

OASIS. (2005, May). *ebXML Registry Services and Protocols*. Retrieved November 10, 2009, from http://oasis-open.org/committees/regrep/

OASIS. (2006). *Index*. Retrieved from http://docs.oasis-open.org

OASIS. (2006, February). *WS-Security v1.1*. Retrieved November 10, 2009, from http://www.oasis-open.org/committees/wss/

Obelheiro, R. R., Bessani, A. N., Lung, L. C., & Correia, M. (2006, September). How Practical are Intrusion-Tolerant Distributed Systems? (Tech. Rep. No. DI-FCUL TR 06-15). Lisbon, Portugal: University of Lisbon, Dep. of Informatics.

Object Management Group. (2002, December 6). The Common Object Request Broker Architecture: Core Specification v3.0. *Standart formal.*

OGC. (n.d.). *The Open Geospatial Consortium (OGC)*. Retrieved July 2009 from http://www.opengis.org

OGF. (n.d.). *Open Grid Forum*. Retrieved October 2009 from http://www.ogf.org

OGF-GIN. (n.d.). *Grid Interoperation Now Community Group (GIN - CG)*. Retrieved from https://forge.gridforum.org/projects/gin

Oldevik, J., Neple, T., Grønmo, R., Aagedal, J., & Berre, A. J. (2005). Toward Standardised Model to Text Transformations. In *Proceedings of the Model Driven Architecture-Foundations and Applications, First European Conference (ECMDA-FA 2005)*, Nuremberg, Germany (LNCS 3748, pp. 239-253).

OMG. (2006). *Meta Object Facility (MOF) Core Specification Version 2.0*. Needham, MA: Author.

OMG. (2007). *UML 2.0 Infrastructure Specification*. Needham, MA: Author.

ORC Language Project. (2009). Retrieved from http://orc.csres.utexas.edu

Organization for the advanced of structured information standards. (2004). *Introduction to UDDI: Important Features and Functional Concepts*. Retrieved October 12, 2009, from http://www.oasis-open.org

Ortiz, G., & Hernandez, J. (2007, May 13-19). A case study on integrating extra-functional properties in web service model-driven development. In *Proceedings of the Second International Conference on Internet and Web Applications and Services, 2007 (ICIW '07)* (pp. 35-35).

O'Sullivan, J., Edmond, D., & ter Hofstede, A. H. M. (2002). What's in a service? *Distributed and Parallel Databases, 12*(2/3), 117–133. doi:10.1023/A:1016547000822

Ouyang, C., Aalst, W., Breutel, S., Dumas, M., & Verbeek, H. (2005). *Formal Semantics and Analysis of Control Flow in WS-BPEL* (BPM Center Report BPM-05-15). Retrieved from BPMcenter.org

Ouyang, C., Verbeek, E., Aalst, W. M. P., Breutel, S., Dumas, M., & Hofstede, A. (2005). WofBPEL: A Tool for Automated Analysis of BPEL Processes. In *Proceedings of the 3rd Intern. Conf. on Service Oriented Computing*, Amsterdam (pp. 484-489).

Ouzzani, M., & Bouguettaya, A. (2004). Efficient access to web services. *IEEE Internet Computing, 8*(2), 34–44. doi:10.1109/MIC.2004.1273484

OWL-S1. 2. (2008). *OWL-S: Semantic Markup for Web Services version 1.2*. Retrieved from http://www.daml.org/services/owl-s/1.2/overview/

OWS1. 2. (2003). *UDDI Experiment, OpenGIS Interoperability Program Report OGC 03-028*. Retrieved from http://www.opengeospatial.org/docs/03-028.pdf

Ozsu, T., & Valduriez, P. (1999). *Principles of distributed database* systems (2nd ed.). Upper Saddle River, NJ: Prentice Hall.

Paik, I. (2004). Intelligent Agent to Support Design in Supply Chain Based on Semantic Web Services. In *Proceedings of the Fourth International Conference on Hybrid Intelligent Systems*. Washington, DC: IEEE Computer Society.

Pallickara, S., & Fox, G. (2003). NaradaBrokering: A middleware framework and architecture for enabling durable peer-to-peer grids. In *Proceedings of Middleware 2003*.

Paolucci, M., Kawamura, T., Payne, T., & Sycara, K. (2002). Semantic matching of web services capabilities. In *Proceedings of the ISWC* (pp. 333347).

Papadimtriou, C. H., & Steiglitz, K. (1982). *Combinatorial Optimization: Algorithms and Complexity*. Upper Saddle River, NJ: Prentice-Hall.

Papadopolous, G., & Arbab, F. (1998). Coordination Models and Languages. *The Engineering of Large Systems, 46*.

Papazoglou, M. P., & Georgakopoulos, D. (2003). Service-oriented computing. *Communications of the ACM, 46*(10), 25–28. doi:10.1145/944217.944233

Papazoglou, M. P., Traverso, P., Dustdar, S., & Leymann, F. (2007). Service-Oriented Computing: State of the Art and Research Challenges. *IEEE Computer, 40*(11), 38–45.

Patil, A., Oundhakar, S., Seth, A., & Verma, K. (2004). METEOR-S Service Annotation Framework. In *Proceedings of the 13th international conference on World Wide Web* (pp. 553-562).

Pearson, S., & Balacheff, B. (2002). *Trusted computing platforms: TCPA technology in context*. Upper Saddle River, NJ: Prentice Hall.

Peiris, C., Mulder, D., Cicoria, S., Bahree, A., & Pathak, N. (2007). *Pro WCF: Practical Microsoft SOA Implementation*. Berkeley, CA: Apress.

Peltz, C. (2003). Web Services Orchestration and Choreography. *IEEE Computer, 36*(10), 46–52.

Peng, D., Huang, S., Wang, X., & Zhou, A. (2005). *Concept-based retrieval of alternate web services*. Paper presented at the 10th Conference on Database Systems for Advanced Applications (DASFAA), Beijing, China.

Perera, S., Herath, C., Ekanayake, J., Chinthaka, E., Ranabahu, A., & Jayasinghe, D. (2006). Axis2, middleware for next generation web services. In *Proceedings of ICWS, 2006*, 833–840.

Pistore, M., et al. (2005). Process-Level Composition of Executable Web Services: On the fly Versus Once-for-all Composition. In *Proceedings of the European Semantic Web Conference (ESWC 2005)* (LNCS 3532, pp. 62-77).

Pistore, M., Roveri, M., & Busetta, P. (2004). Requirements-driven verification of Web services. *Electronic Notes in Theoretical Computer Science, 105*, 95–108. doi:10.1016/j.entcs.2004.05.005

Poritz, J., Schunter, M., Van Herreweghen, E., & Waidner, M. (2004). *Property attestation—scalable and privacy-friendly security assessment of peer computers (Research Rep. No. RZ3548)*. Philadelphia: IBM Corporation.

Press, I. O. S. (2003). Electronic government-design, applications, and management, by å Grönlund. *Information Polity, 8*(3), 193–199.

Programmable Web. (2009). Retrieved from http://www.programmableweb.com

Rahm, E., & Bernstein, P. (2001). A survey of approaches to automatic schema matching. *The VLDB Journal*, 334–350. doi:10.1007/s007780100057

Rajbhandari, S., & Walker, D. W. (2006, September 25-28). Incorporating Provenance in Service Oriented Architecture. In *Proceedings of the International Conference on Next Generation Web Services Practices (NWeSP'06)*, Seoul, Korea (pp. 33-40). Washington, DC: IEEE Computer Society.

Ramasubramanian, V., & Terry, B. (2004). *Caching of XML Web Services for Disconnected Operation* (Tech. Rep. No. MSR-TR-2004-139). Microsoft Corp.

Ramaswamy, L., Iyengar, A., Liu, L., & Douglis, F. (2005). Automatic Fragment Detection in Dynamic Web Pages and Its Impact on Caching. *IEEE TKDE, 17*(6), 859–874.

Rao, J., Kungas, P., & Matskin, M. (2003, June). Application of linear logic to web service composition. In *Proceedings of the 1st International Conference on Web Services* (pp. 3-10).

Rao, Y., Feng, B., Han, J., & Li, Z. (2004). SX-RSRPM: A security integrated model for Web services. In *Proceedings of the 2004 International Conference on Machine Learning and Cybernetics* (Vol. 5, pp. 26-29).

Rao, J., Kungas, P., & Matskin, M. (2006). Composition of semantic web services using linear logic theorem proving. *Information Systems, 31*(4-5), 340–360. doi:10.1016/j.is.2005.02.005

Red Hat Inc. (2009). *Hibernate*. Retrieved November 10, 2009, from https://www.hibernate.org/

Riabov, A., Bouillet, E., Feblowitz, M., Liu, Z., & Ranganathan, A. (2008). Wishful search: interactive composition of data mashups. In *Proceedings of the WWW* (pp. 775-784).

Ricardo, B., & Berthier, R. (1999). *Modern information retrieval*. New York: ACM Press.

Ricci, A., Omicini, A., & Denti, E. (2001, June 20-22). The TuCSoN Coordination Infrastructure for Virtual Enterprises. In *Proceedings of the 10th IEEE International Workshops on Enabling Technologies: Infrastructure for Collaborative Enterprises*, Cambridge, MA (pp. 348-353).

Rich, K. K. (1991). *E. Artifice Intelligence*.

Rijsbergen, V. (1979). *Information Retrieval* (2nd ed.). Oxford, UK: Butterworth.

Ringelstein, C., & Staab, S. (2007). Logging in Distributed Workflows. In *Proceedings of the Workshop on Privacy Enforcement and Accountability with Semantics*, Busan, South-Korea.

Ringelstein, C., & Staab, S. (2009). *Distributed Auditing Logs* (Tech. Rep.). Koblenz, Germany: University of Koblenz-Landau. Retrieved from http://userpages.uni-koblenz.de/~cringel/pub/TRDialog09.pdf van der Aalst, W. (1998). The Application of Petri Nets to Workflow Management. *The Journal of Circuits, Systems and Computers, 8*(1), 21-66.

Rosario, S., Benveniste, A., & Jard, C. (2009). Flexible Probabilistic QoS Management of Transaction based Web Services Orchestrations. International Conference of Web Services, 107-114.

Rosario, S., Benveniste, A., & Jard, C. (2009-2). A Theory of QoS for Web Service Orchestrations (Inria Research Rep. No. 6951). Retrieved from http://hal.archives-ouvertes.fr/docs/00/39/15/92/PDF/RR-6951.pdf

Rosario, S., Kitchin, D., Benveniste, A., Cook, W. R., Haar, S., & Jard, C. (2007, September 28-29). Event Structure Semantics of Orc. In Proceedings of the Web Services and Formal Methods, 4th International Workshop (WS-FM 2007), Brisbane, Australia (pp. 154-168).

Rosario, S., Benveniste, A., Haar, S., & Jard, C. (2008). Probabilistic QoS and Soft Contracts for Transaction based Web Services Orchestrations. *IEEE Transactions on Service Computing, 1*(4), 187–200. doi:10.1109/TSC.2008.17

Rosenberg, F., Celikovic, P., Michlmayr, A., Leitner, P., & Dustdar, S. (2009, September 1-4). An End-to-End Approach for QoS-Aware Service Composition. In *Proceedings of the 13th IEEE International Enterprise Computing Conference (EDOC'09),* Auckland, New Zealand (pp. 151-160). Washington, DC: IEEE Computer Society.

Rosenberg, F., Leitner, P., Michlmayr, A., & Dustdar, S. (2008, September 16). Integrated Metadata Support for Web Service Runtimes. In *Proceedings of the Middleware for Web Services Workshop (MWS'08),* Munich, Germany (pp. 361-368). Washington, DC: IEEE Computer Society.

Rosenberg, F., Platzer, C., & Dustdar, S. (2006, September 18-22). Bootstrapping Performance and Dependability Attributes of Web Services. In *Proceedings of the International Conference on Web Services (ICWS'06),* Chicago, IL (pp. 205-212). Washington, DC: IEEE Computer Society.

Rouached, M., & Godart, C. (2007, July 9-13). Requirements-driven verification of wsbpel processes. In *Proceedings of the IEEE International Conference on Web Services (ICWS'07),* Salt Lake City, Utah.

Rouached, M., Gaaloul, G., van der Aalst, W., Bhiri, S., & Godart, C. (2006, November). Web service mining and verification of properties: An approach based on event calculus. In *Proceedings 14th International Conference on Cooperative Information Systems (CoopIS 2006).*

Russell, S., & Norvig, P. (1995). *Artificial Intelligence: a modern approach.* Upper Saddle River, NJ: Prentice-Hall.

Ryu, S., Casati, F., Skogsrud, H., Benatallah, B., & Saint-Paul, R. (2008). Supporting the dynamic evolution of Web service protocols in service-oriented architectures. *ACM Transactions on the Web, 2*(2).

Ryu, S., Saint-Paul, R., Benatallah, B., & Casati, F. (2007). A Framework for Managing the Evolution of Business Protocols in Web Services. In *Proceedings of the 4th Asia-Pacific Conference on Conceptual Modelling,* Ballarat, Victoria, Australia (pp. 49-59).

Sadeghi, A., & Stüble, C. (2004). *Property-based attestation for computing platforms: caring about properties, not mechanisms.*

Sahai, A., Durante, A., & Machiraju, V. (2001). *Towards automated SLA management for web services.* (Tech. Rep. HPL-2001-310 R. 1). Palo Alto, CA: Hewlett Packard.

Sailer, R., Zhang, X., Jaeger, T., & Van Doorn, L. (2003). *Design and implementation of a TCG-based integrity measurement architecture.*

Salas, J., Perez-Sorrosal, F., Marta Pati, M., & Jim'enez-Peris, R. (2006). Wsreplication: a framework for highly available web services. In *Proceedings of the WWW* (pp. 357-366).

Salatge, N., & Fabre, J. C. (2007). Fault tolerance connectors for unreliable web services. In *Proceedings of the DSN* (pp. 51-60). DOI http://dx.doi.org/10.1109/DSN.2007.48

Salaun, G., Bordeaux, L., & Schaerf, M. (2004). Describing and Reasoning on Web Services using Process Algebra. In *Proceedings of the International Conference on Web Services (ICWS'04)* (pp. 43-50).

Salton, G., & Buckley, C. (1998). Term weighting approaches in automatic retrieval. *Information Processing & Management, 24*(5), 513–523. doi:10.1016/0306-4573(88)90021-0

Saltzer, J., & Schroeder, M. (1975). The protection of information in computer systems. *Proceedings of the IEEE, 63*(9), 1278–1308. doi:10.1109/PROC.1975.9939

Sanchez, C., & Sheremetov, L. (2008a). A Model for Service Discovery with Incomplete Information. In *Proceedings of 5th International Conference on Electrical Engineering, Computing Science and Automatic Control* (pp. 340-345). Washington, DC: IEEE Computer Society Press.

Sanchez, C., & Sheremetov, L. (2008b). A Model for Semantic Service Matching with Leftover and Missing Information. In *Proceedings of 8th International Conference on Hybrid Intelligent Systems* (pp. 198-203). Washington, DC: IEEE Computer Society Press.

Santos, G. T., Lung, L. C., & Montez, C. (2005). Ftweb: A fault tolerant infrastructure for web services. In *Proceedings of the EDOC* (pp. 95-105).

Schneider, F. B. (1990). Implementing Fault-Tolerant Service Using the State Machine Approach: A Tutorial. *ACM Computing Surveys*, *22*(4), 299–319. doi:10.1145/98163.98167

Schoenmakers, B. (1999, August 15-19). A simple publicly verifiable secret sharing scheme and its application to electronic voting. In *Proceedings of the 19th International Cryptology Conference on Advances in Cryptology (CRYPTO 1999)*, Santa Barbara, CA (pp. 148-164).

Seeley, R. (2003). *Berners-Lee: Integrate Web services and Semantic Web*. Retrieved from http://www.adtmag.com/article.asp?id=7662

Segall, E. J. (1995, January 25-27). Resilient Distributed Objects: Basic Results and Applications to Shared Spaces. In *Proceedings of the 7th IEEE Symposium on Parallel and Distributed Processing (PDP'95)*, San Remo, Italy (pp. 320-327).

Shah, S., Ramamritham, K., & Shenoy, P. (2004). Resilient and Coherence Preserving Dissemination of Dynamic Data Using Cooperating Peers. *IEEE Transactions on Knowledge and Data Engineering*, *16*(7), 799–812. doi:10.1109/TKDE.2004.1318563

Shaikh Ali. A., Rana, O., Al-Ali, R., & Walker, D. (2003). UDDIe: An extended registry for web services. In Proceedings of the Service Oriented Computing: Models, Architectures and Applications, Orlando, FL. Washington, DC: IEEE Computer Society. Sun_Microsystems. (1999). *JavaSpaces specification revision 1.0*. Retrieved July 2009 from http://www.sun.com/jini/specs/js.ps

Shamir, A. (1979). How to Share a Secret. *Communications of the ACM*, *22*(11), 612–613. doi:10.1145/359168.359176

Shanahan, M. P. (1999). The Event Calculus Explained. In *Artificial Intelligence Today* (LNCS 1600, pp. 409-430). New York: Springer Verlag.

Shavitt, Y., & Shir, E. (2005). Dimes: let the internet measures itself. *ACM SIGCOMM*, *35*(5), 71–74. doi:10.1145/1096536.1096546

She, W., Thuraisingham, B. M., & Yen, I. (2007). Delegation-based security model for web services. In *Proceedings of the IEEE International Symposium on High Assurance Systems Engineering* (pp. 82-91).

She, W., Yen, I., & Thuraisingham, B. (2008). *Enhancing Security Modeling for Web Services Using Delegation and Pass-On*.

Shen, Z., & Su, J. (2005). Web Service Discovery Based on Behavior Signatures. In *Proceedings of the IEEE International Conference on Services Computing (SCC'05)* (pp. 279-286).

Sheng, Q. Z., Benatallah, B., Maamar, Z., & Ngu, A. H. (2009). Configurable composition and adaptive provisioning of web services. *IEEE Trans on Services Computing*, *2*(1), 34–49. doi:10.1109/TSC.2009.1

Sheu, G. W., Chang, Y. S., Liang, D., Yuan, S. M., & Lo, W. (1997). A fault-tolerant object service on corba. In *Proceedings of the ICDCS* (p. 393).

Shi, E., Perrig, A., & Van Doorn, L. (2005). *Bind: A fine-grained attestation service for secure distributed systems*.

Shukla, D., & Schmidt, B. (2006). *Essential Windows Workflow Foundation*. Reading, MA: Addison-Wesley

Shwentick, T. (2007). Automata for XML – A survey. *Journal of Computer and System Sciences*, *73*(3), 289–315.

Simmhan, Y. L., Plale, B., & Gannon, D. (2005). A Survey of Data Provenance in e-Science. *SIGMOD Record*, *34*(3), 31–36. doi:10.1145/1084805.1084812

Simmhan, Y. L., Plale, B., & Gannon, D. (2008). Karma2: Provenance Management for Data Driven Workflows. *International Journal of Web Services Research*, *5*(3), 1–22.

Sirin, E. (2004). HTN planning for Web Service Composition using SHOP2. *Journal of Web Semantics*, *1*(4), 377–396. doi:10.1016/j.websem.2004.06.005

Sivashanmugam, K., Verna, K., Seth, A., & Miller, J. (2003). Adding Semantics to Web Service Standards. In *Proceedings of the International Conference on Web Services* (pp. 395-401). CSREA Press, 395-401.

Skogsrud, H., Benatallah, B., & Casati, F. (2003). Model-driven trust negotiation for web services. *IEEE Internet Computing*, 45–51. doi:10.1109/MIC.2003.1250583

Smith, M. K., Welty, C., & McGuinness, D. L. (2004). OWL Web Ontology Language Guide. *W3C Recommendation, 10*.

Song, H. G., & Lee, K. (2005). sPAC (Web Services Performance Analysis Center): Performance Analysis and Estimation Tool of Web Services. *Business Process Management*, 109-119.

Spanoudakis, G., & Mahbub, K. (2006). Non Intrusive Monitoring of Service Based Systems. *International Journal of Cooperative Information Systems*, *15*(3), 325–358. doi:10.1142/S0218843006001384

Srivastava, B., & Koehler, J. (2003). Web Service Composition- Current Solutions and Open Problems. In *Proceedings of the Workshop on Planning for Web Services*.

Stahl, C. (2004). *Transformation von WSBPEL in Petrinetze*. Unpublished master's thesis, Humboldt University, Berlin.

Stoica, I., Adkins, D., Zhuang, S., Shenker, S., & Surana, S. (2004). Internet Indirection Infrastructure. *IEEE/ACM Transactions on Networking*, *12*(2), 205-218.

Stratulat, S. (2001). A general framework to build contextual cover set induction provers. *Journal of Symbolic Computation*, *32*(4), 403–445. doi:10.1006/jsco.2000.0469

Sycara, K., et al. (2002). LARKS: Dynamic Matchmaking Among Heterogeneous Software Agents in Cyberspace. In *Proceedings of the International Joint conference on Autonomous Agents and Multi-Agent Systems (AAMAS'02)* (pp. 173-203).

Sycara, K., Paolucci, M., Ankolekar, A., & Srinivasan, N. (2003). Automated Discovery, Interaction and Composition of Semantic Web Services. *Journal of Web Semantics*, *1*(1), 27–46. doi:10.1016/j.websem.2003.07.002

Sycline. (n.d.). *Home page*. Retrieved July 2009 from http://www.synclineinc.com

Tan, V., Groth, P. T., Miles, S., Jiang, S., Munroe, S., Tsasakou, S., et al. (2006, May 3-5). Security Issues in a SOA-Based Provenance System. In *Proceedings of the International Provenance and Annotation Workshop (IPAW'06)*, Chicago, IL (pp. 203-211). New York: Springer.

Tanenbaum, A., & Van Steen, M. (2002). *Distributed Systems Principles and Paradigms*. Upper Saddle River, NJ: Prentice Hall.

Tan, W., Foster, I., & Madduri, R. (2008). Scientific workflows that enable Web scale collaboration: Combining the power of Taverna and caGrid. *IEEE Internet Computing*, *12*(6), 30–37. doi:10.1109/MIC.2008.120

Tatemura, J., Po, O., Sawires, A., Agrawal, D., & Candan, K. S. (2005). Wrex: A scalable middleware architecture to enable xml caching for web-services. *Middleware*, 124-143.

Teege, G. (1994). In Doyle, J., Sandewall, E., & Torasso, P. (Eds.), *Making the difference: A subtraction operation for description logics* (pp. 540–550). San Francisco, CA: Morgan Kaufmann.

Terry, D. B., & Ramasubramanian, V. (2003). Caching xml web services for mobility. *ACM Queue; Tomorrow's Computing Today*, *1*(3), 70–78. doi:10.1145/846057.864024

Tewari, R., Dahlin, M., Vin, H., & Kay, J. (1999). Beyond Hierarchies: Design Considerations for Distributed Caching on the Internet. In *Proceedings of the International Conference on Distributed Computing Systems*.

Thaler, D., & Ravihsankar, C. (1998). Using Name-Based Mappings to Increase Hit Rates. *IEEE/ACM Transactions on Networking*, *6*(1), 1-14.

Thio, N., & Karunasekera, S. (2005). Automatic measurement of a qos metric for web service recommendation. In *Proceedings of the ASWEC* (pp. 202-211).

Tian, M. (2005). *QoS integration in Web services with the WS-QoS framework*. Berlin, Germany: Department of Mathematics and Computer Science, Freie Universität.

Toma, I., Roman, D., & Fensel, D. (2007). On describing and ranking services based on non-functional properties. *NWESP*, 61-66.

Tosic, V., Patel, K., & Pagurek, B. (2002, May 27-28). *WSOL-Web Service Offerings Language*. Paper presented at International Workshop on Web Services, E-Business, and the Semantic Web: CAiSE 2002, WES 2002, Toronto, Canada.

Tsai, W.-T., Wei, X., Zhang, D., Paul, R., Chen, Y., & Chung, J.-Y. (2007, March 21-23). A New SOA Data-Provenance Framework. In *Proceedings of the 8th International Symposium on Autonomous Decentralized Systems (ISADS'07)*, Sedona, AZ (pp. 105-112). Washington, DC: IEEE Computer Society.

Tsang, E. (1993). *Foundations of Constraint Satisfaction*.

Tuchinda, R., Szekely, P., & Knoblock, C. (2008). Building Mashups by Example. In *Proceedings of the International Conference on Intelligent User Interfaces* (pp. 139-148).

UDDI3. 0. (2004). *Universal Description Discovery Integration (UDDI) version 3.0*. Retrieved from http://uddi.org/pubs/uddi v3.htm

Valloppillil, V., & Ross, K. W. (1997). *Cache Array Routing Protocol v1.0*. Internet Draft.

Van Breugel, F., & Koshkina, M. (2006). *Models and verification of bpel*. Retrieved from http://www.cse.yorku.ca/ franck/research/drafts/tutorial.pdf

van der Aalst, W. M. P. (1997). Verification of Workflow Nets. International Conference on Application and Theory of Petri Nets, 407-426.

van der Aalst, W. M. P. (1998). The Application of Petri Nets to Workflow Management. The Journal of Circuits. *Systems and Computers, 8*(1), 21–66.

van der Aalst, W. M. P., Dumas, M., Ouyang, C., Rozinat, A., & Verbeek, E. (2008). Conformance Checking of Service Behavior. *ACM Transactions on Internet Technology, 8*(3), 1–30. doi:10.1145/1361186.1361189

van der Aalst, W. M. P., & van Hee, K. M. (2002). *Workflow Management: Models, Methods, and Systems*. Cambridge, MA: MIT Press.

van der Aalst, W., Weijters, T., & Maruster, L. (2004). Workflow Mining: Discovering Process Models from Event Logs. *IEEE Transactions on Knowledge and Data Engineering, 16*(9), 1128–1142. doi:10.1109/TKDE.2004.47

Verissimo, P., Neves, N. F., & Correia, M. (2003). Intrusion-Tolerant Architectures: Concepts and Design. *Architecting Dependable Systems, 2677*.

Verma, K., Sivashanmugam, K., Sheth, A., Patil, A., Oundhakar, S., & Miller, J. (2005). METEOR-S WSDI: A scalable P2P infrastructure of registries for semantic publication and discovery of web services. *Journal of Information Technology and Management*.

Vieira, M., Laranjeiro, N., & Madeira, H. (2007). Assessing robustness of web-services infrastructures. In *Proceedings of the DSN* (pp. 131-136). DOI http://dx.doi.org/10.1109/DSN.2007.16

W3C. (2004). *OWL-S: Semantic Markup for Web Services*. Retrieved from http://www.w3.org/Submission/OWL-S

W3C. (2006, March). *Web Services Eventing (WS-Eventing)*. Retrieved November 10, 2009, from http://www.w3.org/Submission/WS-Eventing/

Wahlisch, M., Schmidt, T. C., & Spat, W. (2008). What is happening from behind? - making the impact of internet topology visible. *Campus-Wide Information Systems, 25*(5), 392–406. doi:10.1108/10650740810921529

Wainer, J., Barthelmess, P., & Kumar, A. (2003). W-RBAC-A workflow security model incorporating controlled overriding of constraints. *International Journal of Cooperative Information Systems, 12*(4), 455–485. doi:10.1142/S0218843003000814

Wang, A. R., Li, Z. W., Jia, J. Y., & Zhou, M. C. (2009). An Effective Algorithm to Find Elementary Siphons in a Class of Petri Nets. *IEEE Trans. on Sys., Man and Cybern., Part A, 39*(4).

Wang, J., Vecchio, D. D., & Humphrey, M. (2005). Extending the security assertion markup language to support delegation for web services and grid services. In *Proceedings of the IEEE International Conference on Web Services* (pp. 67-74).

Wang, P., & Jin, Z. (2006). Web Service Composition: An Approach Using Effect-based Reasoning. In *Proceedings of the International Workshop on Engineering Service Oriented Applications: Design and Composition (WESOA 2006)* (LNCS 4652, pp. 62-73).

Wang, P., Jin, Z., & Liu, L. (2006). An Approach for Specifying Capability of Web Services based on Environment Ontology. In *Proceedings of the IEEE International Conference on Web Services (ICWS'06)* (pp. 365-372).

Wang, Y., & Stroulia, E. (2003). Flexible interface matching for web-service discovery. In *Proceedings of the 4th Intern. Conf. on Web Info. Sys. Eng.*, Rome, Italy (pp. 147-156).

Wang, J. (1999). A survey of web caching schemes for the internet. *ACM SIGCOMM, 29*(5), 36–46. doi:10.1145/505696.505701

Wang, P. (2008). Building Towards Capability Specifications of Web Services Based on an Environment Ontology. *IEEE Transactions on Knowledge and Data Engineering, 20*(4), 547–561. doi:10.1109/TKDE.2007.190719

Weaver, A., & Wu, Z. (2006). Using Web Service Enhancement to Establish Trust Relationships with Privacy Protection. *International Journal of Web Services Research, 6*(1), 49–68.

Weerawarana, S., Curbera, F., Leymann, F., Storey, T., & Ferguson, D. (2005). *Web Services Platform Architecture: SOAP, WSDL, WS-Policy, WS-Addressing, WS-BPEL, WS-Reliable Messaging and More*. Upper Saddle River, NJ: Prentice Hall.

Wei, J., Singaravelu, L., & Pu, C. (2008). A Secure Information Flow Architecture for Web Service Platforms. *IEEE Transactions on Services Computing, 1*(2), 75–87. doi:10.1109/TSC.2008.10

Weitzner, D. J., Abelson, H., Berners-Lee, T., Feigenbaum, J., Hendler, J., & Sussman, G. J. (2008). Information Accountability. *Communications of the ACM, 51*(6). doi:10.1145/1349026.1349043

Welch, V., Foster, I., Kesselman, C., Mulmo, O., Pearlman, L., Tuecke, S., et al. (2004). *X.509 proxy certificates for dynamic delegation*. Paper presented at the 3rd Annual PKI R&D Workshop.

Wenning, R., Schunter, M., et al. (2006). *The Platform for Privacy Preferences 1.1 (P3P1.1) Specification*. Retrieved from http://www.w3.org/TR/2006/NOTE-P3P11-20061113/

Winkler, T. (2006). *Trusted Computing for the Java(tm) Platform*. Retrieved from http://trustedjava.sourceforge.net/index.php?item=pca/about

Wohed, P., Aalst, W. M. P., Dumas, M., & Hofstede, A. (2003). Analysis of Web services composition languages: The case of BPEL4WS. In *Proceedings of the 22nd International Conference on Conceptual Modeling*, Chicago (pp. 200-215).

Wolsey, L. (1998). *Integer Programming*. New York: John Wiley and Sons.

Wombacher, A., Fankhuaser, P., & Neuhold, E. (2004). Transforming BPEL into annotated Deterministic Finite State Automata for Service Discovery. *International Conference on Web Services (ICWS'04)* (pp. 316-323).

Wombacher, A. (2004). Matchmaking for Business Processes Based on Choreographies. *International Journal of Web Services Research, 1*(4), 14–32.

Wong, J., & Hong, J. (2007). Making mashups with marmite: towards end-user programming for the web. In *Proceedings of the SIGCHI conference on Human factors in computing systems* (pp. 1435-1444).

Woodman, S., Palmer, D., et al. (2004). Notations for the Specification and Verification of Composite Web Services. In *Proceedings of the 8th IEEE International Enterprise Distributed Object Computing (EDOC) Conference*, Monterey, CA.

WSBPEL. (2007, April 11). Web Services Business Process Execution Language Version 2.0. OASIS Standard. Retrieved from http://docs.oasis-open.org/wsbpel/2.0/OS/wsbpel-v2.0-OS.html

WS-Context. (2007). *Web Services Context Specification (WS-Context) Version 1.0*. Retrieved from http://docs.oasis-open.org/ws-caf/ws-context/v1.0/wsctx.html

WSDL2. 0. (2007). *Web Services Description Language (WSDL) Version 2.0*. Retrieved from http://www.w3.org/TR/wsdl20

WSDL-S. (2005). *Web Service Semantics - WSDL-S*. Retrieved from http://www.w3.org/Submission/WSDL-S/

WS-Resource. (2006). *Web Services Resource 1.2*. Retrieved from http://docs.oasis-open.org/wsrf/wsrf-ws_resource-1.2-spec-os.pdf

Wu, D., Parsia, B., Sirin, E., Hendler, J. A., & Nau, D. S. (2003). Automating DAML-S web services composition using SHOP2. In *Proceedings of the International Semantic Web Conference* (pp. 95-210).

Wu, G., Wei, J., Qiao, X., & Li, L. (2007). A bayesian network based qos assessment model for web services. In *Proceedings of the SCC*.

Wu, W., et al. (2005). Grid Service Architecture for Videoconferencing. In M. P. Bekakos, G. A. Gravvanis, & H. R. Arabnia (Eds.), *Grid Computational Methods*.

Wu, N. Q., Zhou, M. C., & Li, Z. W. (2008). Resource-Oriented Petri Net for Deadlock Avoidance in Flexible Assembly Systems. *IEEE Trans. on Systems, Man, and Cybernetics. Part A, 38*(1), 56–69.

Xiong, P. C., Fan, Y. S., & Zhou, M. C. (2010). A Petri Net Approach to Analysis and Composition of Web Services. *IEEE Trans. on Sys., Man and Cybern. Part A, 40*(2), 376–387.

Xu, Q., & Qiu, R. G. (2004). Integration of Web Services and Agents for Supply Chain System Collaboration. In *Proceedings of the IEEE International Conference on Systems, Man and Cybernetics* (pp. 2079-2083).

Xu, W., Venkatakrishnan, V. N., Sekar, R., & Ramakrishnan, I. V. (2006). A framework for building privacy-conscious composite web services. In *Proceedings of the IEEE International Conference on Web Services* (pp. 655-662).

Yahoo Inc. (2007). *Yahoo pipes*. Retrieved from http://pipes.yahoo.com/

Yang, Y., Tan, Q., & Xiao, Y. (2005). Verifying Web services composition based on hierarchical colored petri nets. In *Proceedings of the first international workshop on Interoperability of heterogeneous information systems (IHIS '05)* (pp. 47-54). New York: ACM Press.

Ye, C. (2009). Atomicity Analysis of Service Composition across Organizations. *IEEE Transactions on Software Engineering, 35*(1), 2–28. doi:10.1109/TSE.2008.86

Yegneswaran, V., Barford, P., & Jha, S. (2004, February 4-6). Global Intrusion Detection in the DOMINO Overlay System. In *Proceedings of the 11th Network and Distributed Security Symposium (NDSS 2004)*, San Diego, CA.

Yellin, D., & Strom, R. (1997). Protocol specifications and component adaptors. *ACM Trans. on Prog. Lang. and Sys., 19*(2), 292–333.

Yendluri, P., & Yalçinalp, Ü. (2007). *Web Services Policy 1.5-Guidelines for Policy Assertion Authors*. W3C.

Yialelis, N., & Sloman, M. (1996). A security framework supporting domain-based access control in distributed systems. In *Proceedings of the Symposium on Network and Distributed System Security* (p. 26).

Yin, G., Wang, H., Shi, D., Jia, Y., & Teng, M. (2004). A rule-based framework for role-based constrained delegation. In *Proceedings of the 3rd International Conference on Information Security* (pp. 186-191).

Yin, J., Alvisi, L., Dahlin, M., & Iyengar, A. (2002). Engineering Web Cache Consistency. *ACM Transactions on Internet Technology, 2*(3), 224–259. doi:10.1145/572326.572329

Yoshihama, S., Ebringer, T., Nakamura, M., Munetoh, S., Mishina, T., & Maruyama, H. (2007). WS-attestation: Enabling trusted computing on Web services. *Test and Analysis of Web Services*, 441-469.

Yu, T., & Lin, K.-J. (2005). Service selection algorithms for composing complex services with multiple QoS constraints. In *Proceedings of the ICSOC* (pp. 130143).

Yu, T., Luon, C., & Kai-Tao, H. (2004). SRN: An Extended Petri-Net-Based Workflow Model for Web Service Composition. In *Proceedings of the IEEE International Conference on Web Services (ICWS'04)* (pp. 591-599).

Yu, T., Zhang, Y., & Lin, K. J. (2007). Efficient algorithms for web services selection with end-to-end qos constraints. *ACM Trans Web, 1*(1), 6. DOI http://doi.acm.org/10.1145/1232722.1232728

Yu, Q., Liu, X., Bouguettaya, A., & Medjahed, B. (2008). Deploying and managing Web services: issues, solutions, and directions. *The VLDB Journal, 17*(3), 537–572. doi:10.1007/s00778-006-0020-3

Zanikolas, S. (2005). A taxonomy of Grid Monitoring Systems. *Future Generation Computer Systems, 21*(1), 163–188. doi:10.1016/j.future.2004.07.002

Zaremski, A. M., & Wing, J. M. (1997). Specification matching of software components. *ACM Transactions on Software Engineering and Methodology, 6*(4), 333–369. doi:10.1145/261640.261641

Zeng, L., Benatallah, B., Ngu, A. H., Dumas, M., Kalagnanam, J., & Chang, H. (2004). Qos-aware middleware for web services composition. *IEEE Trans Softw Eng, 30*(5), 311-327. DOI http://dx.doi.org/10.1109/TSE.2004.11

Zeng, L., Lei, H., & Chang, H. (2007). Monitoring the QoS for Web Services. International Conference on Service Oriented Computing, 132-144.

Zeng, L., Benatallah, B., Ngu, A. H. H., Dumas, M., Kalagnanam, J., & Chang, H. (2004). QoS-Aware Middleware for Web Services Composition. *IEEE Transactions on Software Engineering*, *30*(5), 311–327. doi:10.1109/TSE.2004.11

Zhang, R., Arpinar, I. B., & Aleman-Meza, B. (2003). Automatic composition of semantic web services. In *Proceedings of the ICWS* (pp. 38-41).

Zhang, X., Oh, S., & Sandhu, R. S. (2003). PBDM: A flexible delegation model in RBAC. In *Proceedings of the 8th ACM symposium on Access Control Models and Technologies* (pp. 149-157).

Zhang, L. J., Zhang, J., & Cai, H. (2007). *Services Computing*. New York: Springer.

Zhang, L., Ahn, G.-J., & Chu, B.-T. (2003). A rule-based framework for role-based delegation and revocation. *ACM Transactions on Information and System Security*, *6*(3), 404–441. doi:10.1145/937527.937530

Zhang, L.-J. (2008). Web Services Security, Composition, and Discovery. *International Journal of Web Services Research*, *5*(1), 1–23.

Zheng, G., & Bouguettaya, A. (2007). A Web Service Mining Framework. In *Proceedings of the IEEE International Conference on Web Services* (pp. 1096-1103).

Zheng, Z., & Lyu, M. R. (2008a). A distributed replication strategy evaluation and selection framework for fault tolerant web services. In *Proceedings of the ICWS* (pp 145-152).

Zheng, Z., & Lyu, M. R. (2008b). Ws-dream: A distributed reliability assessment mechanism for web services. In *Proceedings of the DSN* (pp. 392-397).

Zhou, M., & Venkatesh, K. (1998). *Modeling, Simulation and Control of Flexible Manufacturing Systems: A Petri Net Approach*. Singapore, Singapore: World Scientific.

Zhuge, H., & Liu, J. (2004). Flexible retrieval of web service. *Journal of Systems and Software*, *70*(1-2), 107–116. doi:10.1016/S0164-1212(03)00003-7

Ziegler, P., et al. (2004). Three decades of data integration - all problems solved? *WCC*, 3-12

About the Contributors

Patrick Hung is an Associate Professor at Faculty of Business and Information Technology in University of Ontario Institute of Technology (UOIT) and an Adjunct Faculty Member at Department of Electrical and Computer Engineering in University of Waterloo, Canada. He is a founding member of the IEEE International Conference of Web Services (ICWS) and IEEE International Conference on Services Computing (SCC). He is an associate editor of the IEEE Transactions on Services Computing (TSC), International Journal of Web Services Research (JWSR), International journal of Business Process and Integration Management (IJBPIM), and the *International Journal on Systems and Service-Oriented Engineering* (IJSSOE).

* * *

Mehmet S. Aktas received his Ph.D. degree in Computer Science from Indiana University in 2007. During his graduate studies, he worked as a researcher in Community Grids Laboratory of Indiana University in various research projects for six years. During this time period, Aktas has worked for a number of prestigious research institutions ranging from NASA Jet Propulsion Laboratory to Los Alamos National Laboratory. Before joining the Indiana University, Aktas attended Syracuse University, where he received his M.S. degree in Computer Science and taught undergraduate-level computer science courses. He is currently working as a project manager in the Information Technologies Institute of Tubitak - Marmara Research Center. He is also part-time faculty member in the Computer Engineering Departments of Marmara University and Istanbul Technical University, where he teaches graduate-level computer science courses. His research interests span into systems, data and Web science.

Eduardo Adilio Pelinson Alchieri received a Master degree on Electrical Engineering from the Federal University of Santa Catarina (UFSC), Brazil, in 2007, with Prof. Joni da Silva Fraga as the adviser. He is presently working toward his Doctorate degree at UFSC. Alchieri's research interests span all areas of distributed computing, including both theory and practice. However, his current interests are reliable and secure algorithms to dynamic distributed computing systems.

Matias Alvarado is a research scientist at the Computing Department of Centre of Research and Advanced Studies, CINVESTAV of México. He obtained a PhD in Computer Science with major in Artificial Intelligence at Technical University of Catalonia, and is graduated in Mathematics from the National Autonomous University of Mexico (UNAM). His research interests include the formal modeling beside the computational simulation of supply chains, decision making, transactions' concurrency control, the web services design, as well as the signal processing and pattern recognition. He has published over 50 scientific papers. He has been a guess editor of Journal of Knowledge and Information Systems, Journal of Petroleum Science and Engineering, and Journal of Expert Systems with Applications. He has been invited professor at Oxford University, National University of Singapur, Benemérita Autonomous University of Puebla among others. His scientific experience includes research and technological deploy in the Mexican Petroleum Institute on applying Artificial Intelligence and Decision Making techniques to the optimal management of human knowledge and for engineering applications.

Sundar Balasubramaniam is an Associate Professor of Computer Science at BITS, Pilani. His current research interests include Service Oriented Architectures, Formal Methods and Real Time Systems. His past research and development experience includes design and development of Compilers, research and development on File System Synchronization, Mining and analysis of User Behavior on the web, research on Information Retrieval techniques for web portals, as well as research, design, and development of software for Automatic Management / Provisioning of large scale IT infrastructure.

Jamal Bentahar is an assistant professor of computer science and software engineering at the Concordia Institute for Information Systems Engineering at Concordia University, Montreal. His research interests include multi-agent systems, Web services, argumentation theory, logic and formal methods, and grid computing. He received his Ph.D. in computer science and software engineering from Laval University, Canada. He is a member of the IEEE, ACM and Professional Engineering Ontario.

Albert Benveniste was born in 1949. He graduated in 1971 from Ecole des Mines de Paris. He performed his These d'Etat in Mathematics, probability theory, in 1975, under the supervision of Paul-Andr\'e Meyer. From 1976 to 1979 he was associate professor in mathematics at Universit\'e de Rennes I. From 1979 to now he has been Directeur de Recherche at INRIA. His previous working areas include: system identification and change detection in signal processing and control (until 1995), vibration mechanics, reactive, real-time, and embedded systems design in computer science, and network and service management in telecommunications with emphasis on distributed systems. His current interests also include: component and contract based design of embedded systems, real-time architectures, Quality of Service management of Web services, and distributed active XML documents. In 1980 Albert Benveniste was co-winner of the IEEE Trans. on Automatic Control Best Transaction Paper Award for his paper on blind deconvolution in data communications. In 1990 he received the CNRS silver medal and in 1991 he has been elected IEEE fellow.

Alysson Neves Bessani is a Visiting Assistant Professor of the Department of Informatics of the University of Lisboa Faculty of Sciences, Portugal, and a member of LASIGE research unit and the Navigators research team. He received his B.S. degree in Computer Science from Maring´a State University, Brazil in 2001, the MSE in Electrical Engineering from Santa Catarina Federal University (UFSC), Brazil in 2002 and the PhD in Electrical Engineering from the same university in 2006. His main interests are distributed algorithms, Byzantine fault tolerance, coordination, middleware and systems architecture.

Maricela Bravo is a posdoctoral research fellow at the Computing Department of CINVESTAV-IPN, México D.F. In 2006 she obtained a PhD in Computing Science, specialized in Distributed Systems, at the National Centre of Research and Technological Development (CENIDET), Mexico. In 2003 she obtained a MSc in Computer Science at CENIDET. In 1996 she obtained a BSc in Information Systems at Zacatepec Institute of Technology, Mexico. Her research interests include Web service architecture design, development and integration. Web service specialized tasks, such as classification, composition, substitution and QoS optimization. Ontology design and integration for electronic commerce applications that use Ontologies for interoperability issues. She was a full-time professor of the Informatics Engineering program at Morelos State Polytechnic University, México (from 2007 to 2008). A part-time professor of the Computer Science program at Pablo Guardado Chávez University, Chiapas, México (from 2005 to 2008). A part-time professor of the Computer Engineering program at UniSol University, Morelos, México (from 2006 to 2007). A part-time professor of the Telecommunications and Computer Science Engineering program at Baja California Institute of Technology, Baja California, México (from 1998 to 2000). She has published over 15 scientific papers in journals and proceedings of international conferences.

Schahram Dustdar is Full Professor of Computer Science with a focus on Internet Technologies heading the Distributed Systems Group, Institute of Information Systems, Vienna University of Technology (TU Wien). He is also Honorary Professor of Information Systems at the Department of Computing Science at the University of Groningen (RuG), The Netherlands. He is Chair of the IFIP Working Group 6.4 on Internet Applications Engineering and a founding member of the Scientific Academy of Service Technology. More information can be found at http://www.infosys.tuwien.ac.at/Staff/sd.

Walid Fdhila is a Ph.D. student at Nancy University, France. He is a member of the ECOO team of the LORIA-INRIA research laboratory and teaching assistant at National Polytechnic Institute of Lorraine. His research interests are in the area of Decentralized Workflows, Service Oriented Computing and Business Process Management.

Geoffrey C. Fox received a Ph.D. in Theoretical Physics from Cambridge University and is now professor of Computer Science, Informatics, and Physics at Indiana University. He is director of the Community Grids Laboratory of the Pervasive Technology Laboratories at Indiana University. He previously held positions at Caltech, Syracuse University and Florida State University. He has published over 550 papers in physics and computer science and been a major author on four books. Fox has worked in a variety of applied computer science fields with his work on computational physics evolving into contributions to parallel computing and now to Grid systems. He has worked on the computing issues in several application areas – currently focusing on Earthquake Science.

Joni da Silva Fraga is a Professor in the Department of Automation and Systems at Federal University of Santa Catarina, in Brazil. His research interests include distributed computing systems, algorithms, security and fault tolerance in distributed systems. He served as reviewer and as member of the PC in the main dependability related international conferences and as program chair. He is a member of the IEEE and the Brazilian Computer Society.

Claude Godart (Ph.D.) is full time Professor at Nancy University, France and scientific director of the INRIA ECOO project. His centre of interest concentrates on the consistency maintenance of the data mediating the cooperation between several partners. This encompasses advanced transaction models, user centric workflow and Web services composition models. He has been implicated in several transfer projects with industries (France, Europe, and Japan) for a wide range of applications including e-commerce, software processes and e-learning.

Osama Al-Haj Hassan received the BS degree in Computer Science from Princess Sumayya University for Technology (PSUT) and the MS degree in Computer Science from New York Institute of Technology (NYIT). Currently a PhD student in the Computer Science department at the University of Georgia (UGA). His research interests are in distributed systems, Web 2.0, caching and replication techniques, Peer-to-Peer networks and event based systems.

Claude Jard graduated as an engineer in telecommunications in 1981. He obtained his Ph.D. in Computer Science from the University of Rennes in 1984. He was the head of the protocol validation group at the French National Research Centre in Telecommunications (CNET) from1981 to 1986. He has been a Research supervisor, and then a Research director at the French National Centre for Scientific Research (CNRS) since 1987. Currently, he is a professor in Computer Science at the Ecole Normale Supérieure de Cachan. He is the Director of the research of the Brittany branch of this school. Prof. Jard's research works relate to the formal analysis of asynchronous parallel systems. His current interests are the non-functional aspects like time and QoS in large scale systems. He is the author or co-author of more than 140 publications, carried out primarily within three research communities: theoretical computer science, protocol engineering, and distributed systems.

Harshavardhan Jegadeesan works in the Research & Breakthrough Innovation group of SAP Labs, India. His areas of interest include enterprise service-oriented architectures, enterprise systems and business process platforms.

Zhi Jin received the MS degree in computer science and the PhD degree from the Changsha Institute of Technology, China, in 1987 and 1992, respectively. She is now a professor of computer science in the Key Laboratory of High Confidence Software Technologies of the Ministry of Education, Peking University. Her current research is on service-oriented computing, software requirements engineering and knowledge engineering. She is the co-author of a book published by Kluwer Academic Publishers and has published more than 90 referred papers in the area of requirements engineering and knowledge-based software engineering. She is a senior member of the IEEE.

Babak Khosravifar is a Ph.D. candidate in the Department of Electrical and Computer Engineering, Concordia University in Montreal, Canada. He is a research assistant in Multi-Agent and Web Services Laboratory at Concordia University under the direction of Dr. Jamal Bentahar. His research interests include multi-agent systems, trust frameworks, reputation mechanism, Web services, and game theory. He received his master of Computer Engineering from Eastern Mediterranean University, Cyprus.

Freddy Lecue is a researcher in the Centre for Service Research at the University of Manchester. He is working on European Union projects SOA4ALL, COMMIUS and SUDDEN funded by the European Commission 7th Framework Programme. He holds a PhD in Computer Science (Ecole des Mines de Saint-Etienne, France) awarded by the French Association in Artificial Intelligence, a MSc in Computer Science Web Intelligence (Ecole des Mines de Saint Etienne, France) and a BSc in Computer Science (University Jean Monnet of Saint-Etienne, France). Prior to joining the University of Manchester, He was a Research engineer in France Telecom R&D, Rennes, France, from 2005 to 2008. During his research position in France Telecom R&D, Dr Freddy Lecue worked not only on internal projects funded by France Telecom R&D, but also on projects associated with the Network of Excellence KNOWLEDGE WEB and the European Union project SPICE funded by the European Commission 6th Framework Programme.

Philipp Leitner has a BSc and MSc in business informatics from Vienna University of Technology. He is currently a PhD candidate and university assistant at the Distributed Systems Group at the same university. Philipp's research is focused on middleware for distributed systems, especially for SOAP-based and RESTful Web services. More information can be found at http://www.infosys.tuwien.ac.at/Staff/leitner.

Lin Liu is an Associate Professor at the School of Software, Tsinghua University. Her research interests are in the areas of software requirements engineering, information systems and knowledge engineering. Her past and current researches are centered on agent-oriented requirements engineering methodologies. Dr. Liu has published 20 papers including journal papers with Information Systems Journal and Requirements Engineering Journal, and conference papers in the Proceedings of RE, CAiSE, ER, etc. She has also participated more than 10 research projects, and is currently leading investigation of two research projects in the area of requirements engineering.

Michael R. Lyu received the B.S. degree in electrical engineering from National Taiwan University, Taipei, Taiwan, R.O.C., in 1981; the M.S. degree in computer engineering from University of California, Santa Barbara, in 1985; and the Ph.D. degree in computer science from the University of California, Los Angeles, in 1988. He is currently a Professor in the Department of Computer Science and Engineering, Chinese University of Hong Kong, Hong Kong, China. He is also Director of the Video over Internet and Wireless (VIEW) Technologies Laboratory. He was with the Jet Propulsion Laboratory as a Technical Staff Member from 1988 to 1990. From 1990 to 1992, he was with the Department of Electrical and Computer Engineering, University of Iowa, Iowa City, as an Assistant Professor. From 1992 to 1995, he was a Member of Technical Staff in the applied research area of Bell Communications Research (Bellcore), Morristown, NJ. From 1995 to 1997, he was a Research Member of Technical Staff at Bell Laboratories, Murray Hill, NJ. His research interests include software reliability engineering, distributed systems, fault-tolerant computing, mobile networks, Web technologies, multimedia information processing, and E-commerce systems. He has published over 270 refereed journal and conference papers in these areas. He has participated in more than 30 industrial projects and helped to develop many commercial systems and software tools. He was the editor of two book volumes: Software Fault Tolerance (New York: Wiley, 1995) and The Handbook of Software Reliability Engineering (New York: IEEE and New McGraw-Hill, 1996). Dr. Lyu received Best Paper Awards at ISSRE'98 and ISSRE'2003. Dr. Lyu initiated the First International Symposium on Software Reliability Engineering (ISSRE) in 1990. He was the Program Chair for ISSRE'96 and General Chair for ISSRE'2001. He was also PRDC'99 Program Co-Chair, WWW10 Program Co-Chair, SRDS'2005 Program Co-Chair, PRDC'2005 General Co-Chair, and ICEBE'2007 Program Co-Chair, and served in program committees for many other conferences including HASE, ICECCS, ISIT, FTCS, DSN, ICDSN, EUROMICRO, APSEC, PRDC, PSAM, ICCCN, ISESE, and WI. He has been frequently invited as a keynote or tutorial speaker to conferences and workshops in the U.S., Europe, and Asia. He has been on the Editorial Board of the IEEE TRANSACTIONS ON KNOWLEDGE AND DATA ENGINEERING, the IEEE TRANSACTIONS ON RELIABILITY, the Journal of Information Science and Engineering, and Software Testing, Veriðcation & Reliability Journal. Dr. Lyu is an IEEE Fellow and AAAS Fellow for his contributions to software reliability engineering and software fault tolerance. He was also named Croucher Senior Research Fellow in 2008.

Nikolay Mehandjiev is Senior Lecturer with the Centre for Service Research at the University of Manchester. He received his Ph.D. in 1997 from the University of Hull, where he also held academic position. He has held visiting positions with BT Research Labs, the University of New South Wales, Atos Origin, SAP Research and the University of Sussex. He researches the design of flexible service systems, using software agents and collaborative service composition models. He has co-authored two books and has guest-edited three special issues of international journals, including the Communications of ACM.

Anton Michlmayr received the MSc degree in computer science from Vienna University of Technology. He is currently a PhD candidate and university assistant in the Distributed Systems Group at Vienna University of Technology. His research interests include software architectures and middleware for distributed systems with an emphasis on service-oriented architectures and distributed event-based systems. More information can be found at http://www.infosys.tuwien.ac.at/Staff/michlmayr.

John A. Miller is a Professor of Computer Science at the University of Georgia and has also been the Graduate Coordinator for the department for 9 years. His research interests include database systems, simulation, Web services and bioinformatics. Dr. Miller received a B.S. in Applied Mathematics from Northwestern University in 1980 and an M.S. and Ph.D. in Information and Computer Science from the Georgia Institute of Technology in 1982 and 1986, respectively. During his undergraduate education, he worked as a programmer at the Princeton Plasma Physics Laboratory. Dr. Miller is the author of over 140 publications covering all areas of his research interests. He is an Associate Editor for the ACM Transactions on Modeling and Computer Simulation, IEEE Transactions on Systems, Man and Cybernetics and SIMULATION: Transactions of the Society for Modeling and Simulation International as well as an Editorial Board Member for the Journal of Simulation and International Journal of Simulation and Process Modeling.

Ahmad Moazin is a research assistant in Multi-Agent and Web Services Laboratory at Concordia University under the direction of Dr. Jamal Bentahar. His research interests include multi-agent systems, trust and reputation, Web services, and argumentation theory. He received his master of Information Systems Security from Concordia University.

Dunlu Peng is an associate professor of University of Shanghai for Science and Technology, Shanghai, China. He received his Ph.D degree from Fudan University, Shanghai, China in June 2006. His research interests include Web Applications and Service-Oriented Computing.

Marlon Pierce has focused his postdoctoral research on computational sciences with an emphasis on Grid computing and computational Web portals, since earning his Ph.D. in computational condensed matter physics. Prior to joining the Community Grids Laboratory (CGL), Pierce served as Information and Communication/Enabling Technologies On-Site Lead at the Aeronautical Systems Major Shared Resource Center for the U.S. Department o f Defense. In his role as Assistant Director of the Community Grids Lab Pierce supervises the research activities of numerous Ph.D. students and acts as principal investigator on multiple federally-funded research projects. Pierce leads research efforts in the following areas: the application of service-oriented architectures and real-time streaming techniques to geographical information systems and sensor networks; the development of open source science Web portal software for accessing Grid computing and data resources; and Grid-based distributed computing applications in computational chemistry and material science, chemical informatics, and geophysics.

Lakshmish Ramaswamy received the PhD degree in Computer Science from Georgia Tech in 2005. He is currently an assistant professor in the computer science department at the University of Georgia. His research interests are broadly in the area of distributed systems, and more specifically in performance, scalability, security and privacy of Web services, overlay networks, events-based middleware, and mobile systems. He is the recipient of best paper award of the 13th World Wide Web conference (WWW-2004) and the 2005 Pat Goldberg best paper award. He has served on the program committees of several international conferences and workshops. He was the program co-chair of DEPSA-2007 and SENS-2006 workshops. He is a member of IEEE and the IEEE computer society.

Christoph Ringelstein is a senior researcher and doctoral student in the institute Web Science and Technologies (WeST) at the Department of Computer Science at the University of Koblenz-Landau since 2005. His research focuses on distributed data processing, provenance, SOA and Web services.

Sidney Rosario is a Ph.d candidate in the DISTRIBCOM team at INRIA Rennes, under the supervision of Albert Benveniste and Claude Jard. He got his bachelors' degree in Computer Science in the year 2004 and his masters' degree in 2006. His research interests include the formal modelling of distributed systems and their performance evaluations.

Florian Rosenberg is currently a research scientist at the CSIRO ICT Centre in Australia. He received his PhD in June 2009 with a thesis on "QoS-Aware Composition of Adaptive Service-Oriented Systems" while working as a research assistant at the Distributed Systems Group, Vienna University of Technology. His general research interests include service-oriented computing and software engineering. He is particularly interested in all aspects related to QoS-aware service composition and adaptation. More information can be found at http://www.florianrosenberg.com.

Mohsen Rouached (Ph.D.) is a postdoctoral researcher at Claude Bernard University of Lyon. He is a member of the BD team of the LIRIS research laboratory, France, where he is involved in the S-Cube European Network of excellence. Before joining LIRIS, he was a researcher in the ECOO team of the LORIA-INRIA research laboratory and teaching assistant at Nancy University. His research interests lie in the area of Service Oriented Computing, Business Process Management, Semantic Web and ontologies, Formal verification and validation techniques, and Process Intelligence.

Steffen Staab (Ph.D.) is a full professor for databases and information systems in the Department of Computer Science at the University of Koblenz-Landau and heads the institute Web Science and Technologies (WeST). His research interests range from ontology management and ontology learning to the application of Semantic Web technologies in areas such as multimedia, personal information management, peer-to-peer - and web services. Before his current position Prof. Staab held positions as researcher, project leader and lecturer at the University of Freiburg, the University of Stuttgart/Fraunhofer Institute IAO, the University of Karlsruhe, and at Ontoprise GmbH. His research led to over 200 refereed publications and 7 books, including the Handbook on Ontologies (now in its 2nd edition). He is Editor-in-Chief of the Journal of Web semantics and on the editorial board of several other journals.

Philippe Thiran is an associate professor in Web and Science Engineering at the Faculty of Computer Science of the University of Namur (Belgium). His research interests include Web services, databases, and distributed information systems. He received his Ph.D. in computer science from the University of Namur. He is a member of the PReCISE Research Center.

Puwei Wang received the PhD degree in computer science from the Institute of Computing Technology, Chinese Academy of Sciences in 2008. He is now a faculty in the Key Laboratory of Data Engineering and Knowledge Engineering of the Ministry of Education, Renmin University of China. His current research interests include semantic Web Services and knowledge grid.

Xiaoling Wang received the Ph.D. degree in computer application from Southeast University, China, in 2003. She is an associate professor in East China Normal University, China. Her research interests include XML data management and Web Services.

Budan Wu received the PhD degree in computer science from the Academy of Mathematics and Systems Science, Chinese Academy of Sciences in 2009. She is now a faculty in the State Key Laboratory of Networking and Switching Technology, Beijing University of Posts and Telecommunications. Her current research interests include service-oriented computing.

Zibin Zheng received his B.Eng. degree and M.Phil. degree in Computer Science from the Sun Yat-sen University, Guangzhou, China, in 2005 and 2007, respectively. He is currently a Ph.D. candidate in the department of Computer Science and Engineering, The Chinese University of Hong Kong. He received SIGSOFT Distringuish Paper Award at ICSE'2010, Best Student Paper Award at ICWS'2010, and IBM Ph.D. Fellowship Award 2010-2011. He served as program committee member of IEEE CLOUD'2009 and CLOUDCOMPUTING'2010. He also served as reviewer for international journal and conferences, including TSE, TPDS, TSC, JSS, DSN, ICEBE, ISSRE, KDD, SCC, WSDM, WWW, etc. His research interests include service computing, software reliability engineering, and cloud computing.

Aoying Zhou is currently a professor of computer science at East China Normal University, Shanghai, China. He received his Bachelor and Master degree in computer science from Sichuan University in Chengdu,China in 1985 and 1988, respectively, and his Ph.D. degree from Fudan University in 1993. He severed as the program co-chair of WAIM'2000, the conference co-chair of ER'2004, and PC member of SIGMOD'2008, WWW'2007, SIGIR'2007, SIGMOD'2007, EDBT'2006, VLDB'2005, ICDCS'2005, DASFAA, PAKDD, etc. His research interests include Web Data Management, Web Search and Web Mining, Web Services, Data Streams, and Peer-to-Peer Computing.

Index